Software Architecture with C# 9 and .NET 5

Second Edition

Architecting software solutions using microservices, DevOps, and design patterns for Azure

Gabriel Baptista

Francesco Abbruzzese

BIRMINGHAM - MUMBAI

Software Architecture with C# 9 and .NET 5

Second Edition

Producer: Caitlin Meadows

Acquisition Editor – Peer Reviews: Saby Dsilva

Content Development Editor: Alex Patterson

Technical Editor: Aniket Shetty

Project Editor: Parvathy Nair

Copy Editor: Safis Editing

Proofreader: Safis Editing

Indexer: Rekha Nair

Presentation Designer: Ganesh Bhadwalkar

First published: November 2019

Second edition: December 2020

Production reference: 2231220

Published by Packt Publishing Ltd.
Livery Place
35 Livery Street
Birmingham B3 2PB, UK.

ISBN 978-1-80056-604-0

www.packt.com

Packt>

Subscribe to our online digital library for full access to over 7,000 books and videos, as well as industry leading tools to help you plan your personal development and advance your career. For more information, please visit our website.

Why subscribe?

- Spend less time learning and more time coding with practical eBooks and Videos from over 4,000 industry professionals
- Learn better with Skill Plans built especially for you
- Get a free eBook or video every month
- Fully searchable for easy access to vital information
- Copy and paste, print, and bookmark content

Did you know that Packt offers eBook versions of every book published, with PDF and ePub files available? You can upgrade to the eBook version at www.Packt.com and as a print book customer, you are entitled to a discount on the eBook copy. Get in touch with us at customercare@packtpub.com for more details.

At www.Packt.com, you can also read a collection of free technical articles, sign up for a range of free newsletters, and receive exclusive discounts and offers on Packt books and eBooks.

Contributors

About the authors

Gabriel Baptista is a software architect who leads technical teams across a diverse range of projects using Microsoft platform for retail and industry. He is a specialist in Azure solutions and a published computing professor, teaching software engineering, development, and architecture. He speaks on Channel 9, one of the most prestigious community sites for the .NET stack, and co-founded SMIT, a start-up for developing solutions, for which DevOps philosophy is the key to delivering user needs.

To my dear family, Murilo, Heitor, and Denise, who always encourage me to move forward. To my parents, Elisabeth and Virgílio, and my grandmothers, Maria and Lygia, who have always motivated and inspired me. A special thank to the Packt team, who made all the effort to produce an incredible new edition of the book.

Francesco Abbruzzese is the author of the *MVC Controls Toolkit* and of the *Blazor Controls Toolkit* libraries. He has contributed to the diffusion and evangelization of the Microsoft web stack since the first version of ASP.NET MVC. His company, Mvcct Team, offers web applications, tools, and services for web technologies. He moved from AI systems, where he implemented one of the first decision support systems for financial institutions, to top-10 video game titles such as Puma Street Soccer.

To my beloved parents, to whom I owe everything. A special thanks to the whole Packt staff and to the reviewers that contributed to improve the overall book's code.

About the reviewers

Mike Goatly has been coding since an early age, when he got his first ZX Spectrum 48k. His professional career has been a journey through many industries, including video on-demand, fintech, and retail. He has always been focused on the Microsoft stack, learning C#/.NET back in the early v1 beta days, and since 2014 he has been building cloud-based software in Azure. Mike currently holds the Azure Developer Associate and DevOps Engineer Expert certifications.

I would like to thank my beautiful wife and children for their patience and allowing me the time needed to help with this book.

Kirk Larkin is an expert in C#, .NET, and ASP.NET Core with a Bachelor's degree in Computer Science. With over 15 years' professional experience, he is a lead software engineer and a Microsoft MVP. He is a top answerer on Stack Overflow for ASP.NET Core, a Pluralsight Guides author, and a primary author for numerous ASP.NET Core documentation topics. He lives in the UK with his wife and two daughters.

Table of Contents

Preface

This book covers the most common design patterns and frameworks involved in modern cloud-based and distributed software architectures. It discusses when and how to use each pattern, by providing you with practical real-world scenarios. This book also presents techniques and processes such as DevOps, microservices, Kubernetes, continuous integration, and cloud computing, so that you can have a best-in-class software solution developed and delivered for your customers.

This book will help you to understand the product that your customer wants from you. It will guide you to deliver and solve the biggest problems you can face during development. It also covers the do's and don'ts that you need to follow when you manage your application in a cloud-based environment. You will learn about different architectural approaches, such as layered architectures, service-oriented architecture, microservices, Single Page Applications, and cloud architecture, and understand how to apply them to specific business requirements.

Finally, you will deploy code in remote environments or on the cloud using Azure. All the concepts in this book will be explained with the help of real-world practical use cases where design principles make the difference when creating safe and robust applications. By the end of the book, you will be able to develop and deliver highly scalable and secure enterprise-ready applications that meet the end customers' business needs.

It is worth mentioning that this book will not only cover the best practices that a software architect should follow for developing C# and .NET Core solutions, but it will also discuss all the environments that we need to master in order to develop a software product according to the latest trends.

This second edition was improved in code, and explanations, and was adapted to the new opportunities offered by C# 9 and .Net 5. We added all new frameworks and technologies that emerged in the last year such as gRPC, and Blazor, and described Kubernetes in more detail in a dedicated chapter.

Who this book is for

This book is for any software architect who wishes to improve their knowledge related to Azure Solutions with C#. It is also for engineers and senior developers who are aspiring to become architects or wish to build enterprise applications with the .NET stack. Experience with C# and .NET is required.

What this book covers

Chapter 1, Understanding the Importance of Software Architecture, explains the basics of software architecture. This chapter will give you the right mindset to face customer requirements, and then select the right tools, patterns, and frameworks.

Chapter 2, Non-Functional Requirements, guides you in an important stage of application development, that is, collecting and accounting for all constraints and goals that the application must fulfill, such as scalability, availability, resiliency, performance, multithreading, interoperability, and security.

Chapter 3, Documenting Requirements with Azure DevOps, describes techniques for documenting requirements, bugs, and other information about your applications. While most of the concepts are general, the chapter focuses on the usage of Azure DevOps and GitHub.

Chapter 4, Deciding the Best Cloud-Based Solution, gives you a wide overview of the tools and resources available in the cloud, and on Microsoft Azure. Here, you will learn how to search for the right tools and resources and how to configure them to fulfill your needs.

Chapter 5, Applying a Microservice Architecture to Your Enterprise Application, offers a broad overview of microservices and Docker containers. Here, you will learn how the microservices-based architecture takes advantage of all the opportunities offered by the cloud and you will see how to use microservices to achieve flexibility, high throughput, and reliability in the cloud. You will learn how to use containers and Docker to mix different technologies in your architecture as well as make your software platform independent.

Chapter 6, Azure Service Fabric, describes Azure Service Fabric that is Microsoft-specific microservices orchestrator. Here, you will implement a simple microservices based application.

Chapter 7, Azure Kubernetes Service, describes the Azure implementation of Kubernetes that is a de-facto standard for microservices orchestration. Here you will package and deploy microservices applications on Kubernetes.

Chapter 8, Interacting with Data in C# – Entity Framework Core, explains in detail how your application can interact with various storage engines with the help of **Object-Relational Mappings (ORMs)** and in particular with Entity Framework Core 5.0.

Chapter 9, How to Choose Your Data Storage in the Cloud, describes the main storage engines available in the cloud and in Microsoft Azure. Here, you will learn how to choose the best storage engines to achieve the read/write parallelism you need and how to configure them.

Chapter 10, Working with Azure Functions, describes the serverless model of computation and how to use it in the Azure cloud. Here, you will learn how to allocate cloud resources just when they are needed to run some computation, thus paying only for the actual computation time.

Chapter 11, Design Patterns and .NET 5 Implementation, describes common software patterns with .NET 5 examples. Here, you will learn the importance of patterns and best practices for using them.

Chapter 12, Understanding the Different Domains in Software Solutions, describes the modern Domain-Driven Design software production methodology, how to use it to face complex applications that require several knowledge domains, and how to use it to take advantage of cloud- and microservices-based architectures.

Chapter 13, Implementing Code Reusability in C# 9, describes patterns and best practices to maximize code reusability in your .NET 5 applications with C# 9. It also discusses the importance of code refactoring.

Chapter 14, Applying Service-Oriented Architectures with .NET Core, describes service oriented architecture, which enables you to expose the functionalities of your applications as endpoints on the web or on a private network so that users can interact with them through various types of clients. Here, you will learn how to implement service-oriented architecture endpoints with ASP.NET Core, and gRPC, and how-to self-document them with existing OpenAPI packages.

Chapter 15, Presenting ASP.NET Core MVC, describes in detail the ASP.NET Core framework. Here, you will learn how to implement web applications based on the **Model-View-Controller (MVC)** pattern and how to organize them according to the prescriptions of Domain-Driven Design, described in *Chapter 12, Understanding the Different Domains in Software Solutions*.

Chapter 16, Blazor WebAssembly, describes the new Blazor framework that leverages the power of WebAssembly to run .Net in the user browser. Here you will learn how to implement Single Page Applications in C#.

Chapter 17, Best Practices in Coding C# 9, describes best practices to be followed when developing .NET 5 applications with C# 9.

Chapter 18, Testing Your Code with Unit Test Cases and TDD, describes how to test your applications. Here, you will learn how to test .NET Core applications with xUnit and see how easily you can develop and maintain code that satisfies your specifications with the help of test-driven design.

Chapter 19, Using Tools to Write Better Code, describe metrics that evaluate the quality of your software and how to measure them with the help of all the tools included in Visual Studio.

Chapter 20, Understanding DevOps Principles, describes the basics of the DevOps software development and maintenance methodology. Here, you will learn how to organize your application's continuous integration/continuous delivery cycle. It also describes how to automate the whole deployment process, from the creation of a new release in your source repository, through various testing and approval steps, to the final deployment of the application in the actual production environment. Here, you will learn how to use Azure Pipelines and GitHub Actions to automate the whole deployment process.

Chapter 21, Challenges of Applying CI Scenarios, complements the description of DevOps with continuous integration scenarios.

Chapter 22, Automation for Functional Tests , is dedicated to automatic functional tests – that is, tests that verify automatically whether a version of a whole application conforms to the agreed functional specifications. Here, you will learn how to simulate user operations with automation tools and how to use these tools together with xUnit to write your functional tests.

To get the most out of this book

- The book covers many subjects. Understand it as a guidance that you may want to revisit many times for different circumstances.
- Do not forget to have Visual Studio Community 2019 or higher installed.
- Be sure that you understand C# .NET principles.

Download the example code files

The code bundle for the book is hosted on GitHub at `https://github.com/PacktPublishing/Software-Architecture-with-C-9-and-.NET-5`. We also have other code bundles from our rich catalog of books and videos available at `https://github.com/PacktPublishing/`. Check them out!

Download the color images

We also provide a PDF file that has color images of the screenshots/diagrams used in this book. You can download it here: https://static.packt-cdn.com/downloads/9781800566040_ColorImages.pdf.

Conventions used

There are a number of text conventions used throughout this book.

CodeInText: Indicates code words in text, database table names, folder names, filenames, file extensions, pathnames, dummy URLs, user input, and Twitter handles. For example; "They are copied in the final string just once, when you call sb.ToString() to get the final result."

A block of code is set as follows:

```
[Fact]
public void Test1()
{
    var myInstanceToTest = new ClassToTest();
    Assert.Equal(5, myInstanceToTest.MethodToTest(1));
}
```

Any command-line input or output is written as follows:

```
kubectl create -f myClusterConfiguration.yaml
```

Bold: Indicates a new term, an important word, or words that you see on the screen, for example, in menus or dialog boxes, also appear in the text like this. For example: "In the **Solution Explorer**, you have the option to **Publish...** by right-clicking."

 Warnings or important notes appear like this.

 Tips and tricks appear like this.

Get in touch

Feedback from our readers is always welcome.

General feedback: Email feedback@packtpub.com, and mention the book's title in the subject of your message. If you have questions about any aspect of this book, please email us at questions@packtpub.com.

Errata: Although we have taken every care to ensure the accuracy of our content, mistakes do happen. If you have found a mistake in this book we would be grateful if you would report this to us. Please visit, http://www.packtpub.com/submit-errata, selecting your book, clicking on the Errata Submission Form link, and entering the details.

Piracy: If you come across any illegal copies of our works in any form on the Internet, we would be grateful if you would provide us with the location address or website name. Please contact us at copyright@packtpub.com with a link to the material.

If you are interested in becoming an author: If there is a topic that you have expertise in and you are interested in either writing or contributing to a book, please visit http://authors.packtpub.com.

Reviews

Please leave a review. Once you have read and used this book, why not leave a review on the site that you purchased it from? Potential readers can then see and use your unbiased opinion to make purchase decisions, we at Packt can understand what you think about our products, and our authors can see your feedback on their book. Thank you!

For more information about Packt, please visit packtpub.com.

1
Understanding the Importance of Software Architecture

Software architecture is one of the most discussed topics in the software industry today, and its importance will certainly grow more in the future. The more we build complex and fantastic solutions, the more we need great software architectures to maintain them. But the speed at which new features are added to these software solutions keeps increasing, and new architectural opportunities keep emerging. That is the reason why you decided to read this book; it's the reason why we decided to write its second edition.

It's not a simple task to write about this important topic, which offers so many alternative techniques and solutions. The main objective of this book is not to build an exhaustive and never-ending list of available techniques and solutions, but to show how various families of techniques are related, and how they impact, in practice, the construction of a maintainable and sustainable solution.

The need to keep our focus on creating actual, effective enterprise solutions keeps increasing; users always need more new features in their applications. Moreover, the need to deliver frequent application versions (due to a quickly changing market) increases our obligation to have sophisticated software architecture and development techniques.

The following topics will be covered in this chapter:

- The understanding of what software architecture is
- Some software development process models that may help you as a software architect
- The process for gathering the right information to design high-quality software
- Design techniques for helping in the process of development
- Cases where the requirements impact the system results
- An introduction to the case study of the book

The case study of this book will take you through the process of creating the software architecture for a travel agency called **World Wild Travel Club (WWTravelClub)**. The purpose of this case study is to help you understand the theory explained in each chapter, and to provide an example of how to develop an enterprise application with Azure, Azure DevOps, C# 9, .NET 5, ASP.NET, and other technologies that will be introduced in this book.

By the end of this chapter, you will be able to understand exactly what the mission of software architecture is. You will also learn what Azure is, and how to create your account on the platform. You'll also get an overview of software processes, models, and other techniques that will enable you to conduct your team.

What is software architecture?

If you are reading this book today, you should thank the computer scientists who decided to consider software development as an engineering area. This happened in the last century, more specifically, at the end of the sixties, when they proposed that the way we develop software is quite like the way we construct buildings. That is why we have the name **software architecture**. Like an architect designs a building and oversees its construction based on that design, the main goal of a software architect is to ensure that the software application is implemented well; and good implementation requires the design of a great solution.

In a professional development project, you must do the following things:

- Define the customer requirements for the solution
- Design a great solution to meet those requirements
- Implement the designed solution
- Validate the solution with your customer
- Deliver the solution in the working environment

Software engineering defines these activities as the software development life cycle. All the theoretical software development process models (waterfall, spiral, incremental, agile, and so on) are somehow related to this cycle. No matter which model you use, if you do not work with the essential tasks presented earlier during your project, you will not deliver acceptable software as a solution.

The main point about designing great solutions is foundational to the purpose of this book. You must understand that great real-world solutions bring with them a few fundamental constraints:

- The solution needs to meet user requirements
- The solution needs to be delivered on time
- The solution needs to adhere to the project budget
- The solution needs to deliver good quality
- The solution needs to guarantee safe and effective future evolution

Great solutions need to be sustainable, and you must understand that there is no sustainable software without great software architecture. Nowadays, great software architectures depend on both modern tools and modern environments to perfectly fit users' requirements.

For this reason, this book will use some great tools provided by Microsoft. The company has announced .NET 5 as a unified platform for software development, which gives us a great opportunity to create fantastic solutions.

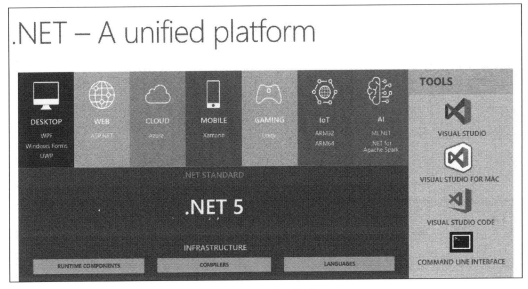

Figure 1.1: .NET 5 platform

NET 5 is delivered together with C# 9. Considering the .NET approach of targeting so many platforms and devices, C# is now one of the most used programming languages in the world and runs on small devices up to huge servers in different operating systems and environments.

The book will also use **Azure**, which is Microsoft's cloud platform, where you will find all the components the company provides to build advanced software architecture solutions. One of them is **Azure DevOps**, an application life cycle management environment where you can build solutions using the latest approach for developing software.

Being a software architect means understanding the aforementioned technologies, and a lot of others, too. This book will guide you on a journey where, as a software architect working in a team, you will provide optimal solutions with the tools listed. Let us start this journey by creating your Azure account.

Creating an Azure account

Microsoft Azure is one of the best cloud solutions currently available on the market. It is important to know that, inside Azure, we will find a selection of components that can help us define the architecture of twenty-first-century solutions.

 If you want to check the variety of components Microsoft Azure has, just check this incredible website developed by Alexey Polkovnikov: https://azurecharts.com/.

This subsection will guide you in creating an Azure account. If you already have one, you can skip this part.

Start your access into Azure using the website address https://azure.microsoft.com. There, you will find the information you need to start your subscription. Translation to your native language is usually set automatically.

1. Once you have accessed this portal, it is possible to sign up. If you have never done this before, it is possible to **Start free**, so you will be able to use some Azure features without spending any money. Please check the options for free plans at https://azure.microsoft.com/en-us/free/.

2. The process for creating a free account is quite simple, and you will be guided by a form that requires you to have a **Microsoft Account** or **GitHub Account**.

3. During the process you will also be asked for a credit card number, to verify your identity and to keep out spam and bots. However, you will not be charged unless you upgrade the account.

4. To finish the assignment, you will need to accept the subscription agreement, offer details, and privacy statement.

Once you finish the form, you will be able to access the Azure portal. As you can see in the following screenshot, the panel shows a dashboard that you can customize, and a menu on the left, where you can set up the Azure components you are going to use in your solution. Throughout this book, we will come back to this screenshot to set up the components to help us create modern software architecture. To find the next page, just select the left-menu icon (hamburger menu) and click on **All services**.

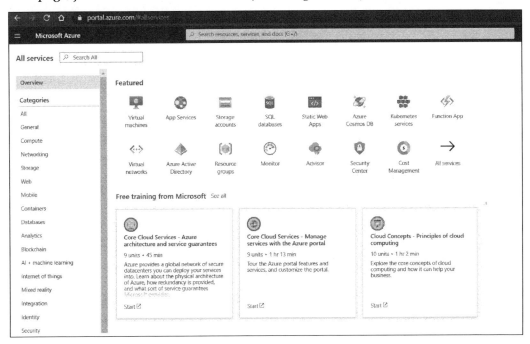

Figure 1.2: The Azure portal

Once you have your Azure account created, you are ready to understand how a software architect can conduct a team to develop software, taking advantage of all the opportunities offered by Azure. However, it is important to keep in mind that a software architect needs to go beyond technologies because this role is played by people who are expected to define how the software will be delivered.

Today, a software architect not only architects the basis of a software, but also determines how the whole software development and deployment process is conducted. The next topic will cover some of the most widely used software development paradigms the world over. We'll start by describing what the community refers to as traditional software engineering. After that, we'll cover the agile models that have changed the way we build software nowadays.

Software development process models

As a software architect, it's important for you to understand some of the common development processes that are currently used in most enterprises. A software development process defines how people in a team produce and deliver software. In general, this process relates to a software engineering theory, called a **software development process model**. From the time software development was defined as an engineering process, many process models for developing software have been proposed. Let us review the traditional software models, and then look at the agile ones that are currently common.

Reviewing traditional software development process models

Some of the models introduced in the software engineering theory are already considered traditional and quite obsolete. This book does not aim to cover all of them, but here, we will give a brief explanation of the ones that are still used in some companies – waterfall and incremental models.

Understanding the waterfall model principles

This topic may appear strange in a software architecture book from 2020, but yes, you may still find companies where the most traditional software process model remains the guideline for software development. This process executes all fundamental tasks in sequence. Any software development project consists of the following steps:

- Requirements, where a product requirement document is created, and it is the basis for the software development

- Design, where the software architecture is developed according to requirements

- Implementation, where the software is programmed

- Verification, where tests are taken in the application
- Maintenance, where the cycle starts again, after a delivery

Let us look at a diagrammatic representation of this:

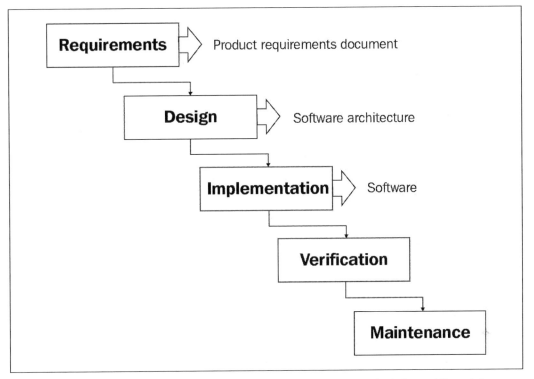

Figure 1.3: The waterfall development cycle (https://en.wikipedia.org/wiki/Waterfall_model)

Often, the use of waterfall models causes problems related to delays in the delivery of a functional version of the software, and user dissatisfaction due to the distance between expectations and the final product delivered. Besides, in my experience, having application tests start only after the completion of development always feels terribly stressful.

Analyzing the incremental model

Incremental development is an approach that tries to overcome the biggest problem of the waterfall model: the user can test the solution only at the end of the project. The idea of this model is to give the users opportunities to interact with the solution as early as possible so that they can give useful feedback, which will help during the development of the software.

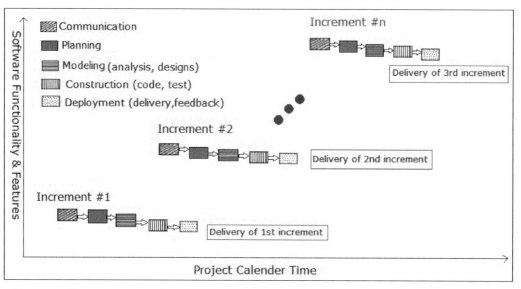

Figure 1.4: The incremental development cycle (https://en.wikipedia.org/wiki/Incremental_build_model)

The incremental model presented in the preceding picture was introduced as an alternative to the waterfall approach. The idea of the model is to run for each increment a set of practices related to software development (**Communication, Planning, Modeling, Construction,** and **Deployment**). Although it mitigated the problems related to the lack of communication with the customer, for big projects, fewer increments were still a problem because the increments remained too long.

When the incremental approach was used on a large scale—mainly at the end of the last century—many problems related to project bureaucracy were reported, due to the large amount of documentation required. This clunky scenario caused the rise of a very important movement in the software development industry – **agile**.

Understanding agile software development process models

At the beginning of this century, developing software was considered one of the most chaotic activities in engineering. The percentage of software projects that failed was incredibly high, and this fact proved the need for a different approach to deal with the flexibility required by software development projects.

In 2001, the Agile Manifesto was introduced to the world, and from that time forward various agile process models were proposed. Some of them have survived up until now and are still very common.

The Agile Manifesto is translated into more than 60 languages. Please check out its link at https://agilemanifesto.org/.

One of the biggest differences between agile models and traditional models is the way developers interact with the customer. The message that all agile models transmit is that the faster you deliver software to the user, the better. This idea is sometimes confusing for software developers who understand this as – *let's try coding, and that's all, folks!*

However, there is an important observation of the Agile Manifesto that many people do not read when they start working with agile:

Manifesto for Agile Software Development

We are uncovering better ways of developing software by doing it and helping others do it. Through this work we have come to value:

Individuals and interactions over processes and tools

Working software over comprehensive documentation

Customer collaboration over contract negotiation

Responding to change over following a plan

That is, while there is value in the items on the right, we value the items on the left more.

Figure 1.5: Manifesto for Agile software development

A software architect always needs to remember this. Agile processes do not mean a lack of discipline. Moreover, when you use the agile process, you'll quickly understand that there is no way to develop good software without discipline. On the other hand, as a software architect, you need to understand that *soft* means flexibility. A software project that refuses to be flexible tends to ruin itself over time.

The 12 principles behind agile are foundational to this flexible approach:

1. Continuously delivering valuable software to satisfy the customer must be the highest priority of any developer.

2. Changing requirements needs to be understood as an opportunity to make the customer more competitive.

3. Do use a weekly timescale to deliver software.

4. A software team must be composed of business people and developers.

5. A software team needs to be trusted and should have the correct environment to get the project done.

6. The best way to communicate with a software team is face to face.

7. You can understand the greatest software team achievement as when the software is really working on production.

8. Agile is working properly when it delivers sustainable development.

9. The more you invest in techniques and good design, the more agile you are.

10. Simplicity is essential.

11. The more self-organized the teams are, the better-quality delivery you will have.

12. Software teams tend to improve their behavior from time to time, analyzing and adjusting their process.

Even 20 years after the launch of the Agile Manifesto, its importance and connection to the current needs of software teams remain intact. Certainly, there are many companies where this approach is not well accepted, but as a software architect you should understand this as an opportunity to transform practices and evolve the team with you are working.

There are many techniques and models that were presented to the software community with the agile approach. The next subtopics will discuss Lean software development, Extreme Programming, and Scrum, so that you can decide, as a software architect, which ones you might use to improve your software delivery.

Lean software development

After the Agile Manifesto, the approach of Lean software development was introduced to the community as an adaptation of a well-known movement in automobile engineering; Toyota's model for building cars. The worldwide Lean manufacturing method delivers a high level of quality even with few resources.

Mary and Tom Poppendieck listed seven Lean principles for software development, really connected to agile and to the approach of many companies of this century. I've listed them here:

1. **Eliminate waste**: You may consider waste to be anything that will interfere with the delivery of the real need of a customer.

2. **Build quality in**: An organization that wants to guarantee quality needs to promote it in processes that build code from the beginning, instead of only consider it after code is being tested.

3. **Create knowledge**: Companies that achieved excellence have a common pattern of generating new knowledge by disciplined experimentation, documenting it, and guaranteeing that this knowledge is spread all over the organization.

4. **Defer commitment**: Plan decisions to its last chance before causing damage to the project.

5. **Deliver fast**: The faster you deliver software, the more elimination of waste you have. Companies that compete using time frequency have significant advantages over their competitors.

6. **Respect people**: Giving reasonable objectives to the team, together with plans that will guide them to self-organize their routine, is a matter of respecting people that you work with.

7. **Optimize the whole**: A Lean company improves all the cycle of value; from the moment it receives a new requirement up to the one it delivers when the software is done.

The Lean principles cause a team or company approach to improve the quality of the features that the customer really needs. It also creates a reduction in time spent on features that will not be used by the time the software is delivered to the customer. In Lean, deciding the features that are important to the customer guides the team in delivering software that matters, and this is exactly what the Agile Manifesto intends to promote in software teams.

Extreme Programming

Just before the release of the Agile Manifesto, some of the participants who designed the document, especially Kent Beck, presented to the world the **Extreme Programming (XP) methodology** for developing software.

XP is based on values of simplicity, communication, feedback, respect, and courage. It was considered later as a social change in programming, according to Beck in his second book about the topic. It certainly promotes a huge change in the flow of development.

XP indicates that every team should have the simplicity to do only what it was asked for, communicating face to face daily, demonstrating the software early to get feedback, respecting the expertise of each member of the team, and having the courage to tell the truth about progress and estimates, considering the team's work as a whole.

XP also delivers a set of rules. These rules may be changed by the team if they detect something is not working properly, but it's important to always maintain the values of the methodology.

These rules are divided into planning, managing, designing, coding, and testing. Don Wells has mapped XP at the site http://www.extremeprogramming.org/. Although some of the ideas of the methodology were criticized strongly by many companies and specialists, there are many good practices that are used today:

- **Writing software requirements using user stories**: User stories are considered an agile approach to describe user needs, together with the acceptance tests that will be used to guarantee the correct implementation.

- **Divide software into iterations and deliver small releases**: The practice of iterating in software development is defended by all methodologies after waterfall. The fact of delivering faster versions decreases the risks of not achieving the customer's expectations.

- **Avoid working overtime and guarantee a sustainable velocity**: Although this must be one of the hardest tasks a software architect may deal with, overtime working indicates something is not working properly in the process.

- **Keep things simple**: While developing solutions, it is quite common to try to anticipate features that the customer would like to have. This approach increases the complexity of the development and the time to market the solution. A different approach will cause high costs, and probably a low level of features that are actually used, in the system you are developing.

- **Refactoring**: The approach of refactoring the code continuously is good because it enables the evolution of your software and guarantees the design improvement that will truly be necessary due to the normal technical changes of the platforms you use to develop.

- **Keep the customer always available**: If you follow the rule from XP, you should have an expert customer inside your team. This is certainly something that is hard to get and deal with, but the main idea of this approach is guaranteeing that the customer is involved in all parts of development. As another bonus, having the customer close to your team means they understand the difficulties and expertise the team has, enabling an increase of the trust between the parties.

- **Continuous integration**: This practice is one of the bases of the current DevOps approach. The less difference you have between your personal code repository and the main code repository, the better.

- **Code the unit test first**: A unit test is an approach where you program specific code for testing a single unit (class/method) of your project. This is discussed in a current development methodology called **Test-Driven Development (TDD)**. The main goal here is to guarantee that every business rule has its own unit test case.

- **Code must be written to agreed standards**: The need of determining standards for coding is connected to the idea that no matter which developer you have working on a specific part of the project, the code must be written so that any of them will understand it.

- **Pair programming**: Pair programming is another difficult approach to achieve in every single minute of a software project, but the technique itself—one programmer coding and the other actively observing and offering comments, criticism, and advice—is useful in critical scenarios.

- **Acceptance tests**: The adoption of acceptance tests to meet user stories is a good way to guarantee that new released versions of the software do not cause damage to its current needs. An even better option is to have these acceptance tests automated.

It is worth mentioning that many of these rules are today considered vital practices in different software development methodologies, including DevOps and Scrum. We will discuss DevOps later in this book, in *Chapter 20, Understanding DevOps Principles*. Let's get into the Scrum model right now.

Getting into the Scrum model

Scrum is an agile model for the management of software development projects. The model comes from Lean principles and is one of the widely used approaches for developing software nowadays.

 Please check this link for more information about the Scrum framework: https://www.scrum.org/.

As you can see in the following figure, the basis of Scrum is that you have a flexible backlog of user requirements (**Product Backlog**) that needs to be discussed in each agile cycle, called a **Sprint**. The Sprint goal (**Sprint Backlog**) is determined by the Scrum Team, composed of the Product Owner, the Scrum Master, and the Development Team. The **Product Owner** is responsible for prioritizing what will be delivered in that Sprint. During the Sprint, this person will help the team to develop the required features. The person who leads the team in the Scrum process is called the **Scrum Master**. All the meetings and processes are conducted by this person.

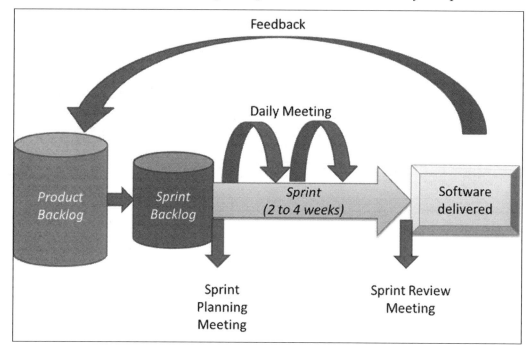

Figure 1.6: The Scrum process

It is important to notice that the Scrum process does not discuss how the software needs to be implemented, nor which activities will be done. Again, you must remember the basis of software development, discussed at the beginning of this chapter; that means Scrum needs to be implemented together with a process model. DevOps is one of the approaches that may help you use a software development process model together with Scrum. Check *Chapter 20, Understanding DevOps Principles*, to understand it better.

Gathering the right information to design high-quality software

Fantastic! You just started a software development project. Now, it's time to use all your knowledge to deliver the best software you can. Your first question is probably – *How do I start?* Well, as a software architect, you're going to be the one to answer it. And you can be sure your answer is going to evolve with each software project you lead.

Defining a software development process is the first task. This is generally done during the project planning process, or might happen before it starts.

Another very important task is to gather the software requirements. No matter which software development process you decide to use, collecting real user needs is part of a difficult and continuous job. Of course, there are techniques to help you with this, and you can be sure that gathering requirements will help you to define important aspects of your software architecture.

These two tasks are considered by most experts in software development as the keys to success at the end of the development project journey. As a software architect, you need to enable them so that you can avoid as many problems as possible while guiding your team.

Understanding the requirements gathering process

There are many different ways to represent the requirements. The most traditional approach consists of you having to write a perfect specification before the beginning of the analysis. Agile methods suggest instead that you need to write user stories, as soon as you are ready to start a development cycle.

 Remember: You do not write requirements just for the user; you write them for you and your team too.

The truth is, that no matter the approach you decide to adopt in your projects, you will have to follow some steps to gather requirements. This is what we call **requirements engineering**.

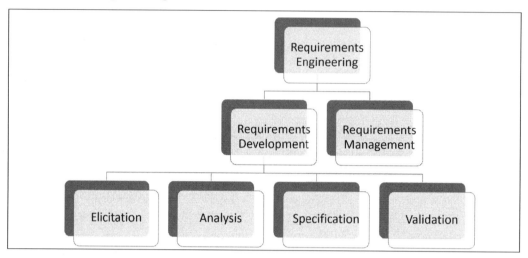

Figure 1.7: Requirements engineering process

During this process, you need to be sure that the solution is feasible. In some cases, the feasibility analysis is part of the project planning process too, and by the time you start the requirements elicitation, you will have the feasibility report already done. So, let us check the other parts of this process, which will give you a lot of important information for the software architecture.

Detecting exact user needs

There are a lot of ways to detect what exactly the user needs for a specific scenario. This process is known as elicitation. In general, this can be done using techniques that will help you to understand what we call user requirements. Here, you have a list of common techniques:

- **The power of imagination**: If you are an expert in the area where you are providing solutions, you may use your own imagination to find new user requirements. Brainstorming can be conducted together so that a group of experts can define user needs.

- **Questionnaires**: This tool is useful for detecting common and important requirements such as the number and kind of users, peak system usage, and the commonly used **operating system (OS)** and web browser.

- **Interviews**: Interviewing the users helps you as an architect to detect user requirements that perhaps questionnaires and your imagination will not cover.

- **Observation**: There is no better way to understand the daily routine of a user than being with them for a day.

As soon as you apply one or more of these techniques, you will have great and valuable information about the user's needs.

 Remember: You can use these techniques in any situation where the real need is to gather requirements, no matter if it is for the whole system or for a single story.

At that moment, you will be able to start analyzing these user needs, and detecting the user and system requirements. Let's see how to do so in the next section.

Analyzing requirements

When you've detected the user needs, it's time to begin analyzing the requirements. To do so, you can use techniques such as the following:

- **Prototyping**: Prototypes are fantastic to clarify and to materialize the system requirements. Today, we have many tools that can help you to mock interfaces. A nice open source tool is the **Pencil Project**. You will find further information about it at `https://pencil.evolus.vn/`.

- **Use cases**: The **Unified Modeling Language (UML)** use case model is an option if you need detailed documentation. The model is composed of a detailed specification and a diagram. **ArgoUML** is another open source tool that can help you out with this. You can see the model created in *Figure 1.8*:

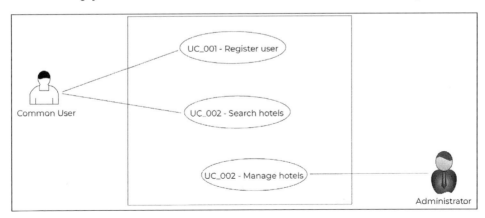

Figure 1.8: Use case diagram example

While you are analyzing the requirements of the system, you will be able to clarify exactly what the users' needs are. This is helpful when you're not sure about the real problem you need to solve, and is much better than just starting to program the system and hoping for the best. Time invested in requirements analysis is time invested in better code later.

Writing the specifications

After you finish the analysis, it's important to register it as a specification. The specification document can be written using traditional requirements, or user stories, which are commonly used in agile projects.

A requirements specification represents the technical contract between the user and the team. There are some basic rules that this document needs to follow:

- All stakeholders need to understand exactly what is written in the technical contract, even if they are not technicians.
- The document needs to be clear.
- You need to classify each requirement.
- Use simple future tense to represent each requirement:
    - Bad example: A common user registers himself.
    - Good example: A common user shall register himself.
- Ambiguity and controversy need to be avoided.

Some additional information can help the team to understand the context of the project they are going to work on. Here are some tips about how to add useful information:

- Write an introductory chapter to give a full idea of the solution.
- Create a glossary to make understanding easier.
- Describe the kind of user the solution will cover.
- Write functional and non-functional requirements:
    - Functional requirements are quite simple to understand because they describe exactly what the software will do. On the other hand, non-functional requirements determine the restrictions related to the software, which means scalability, robustness, security, and performance. We will cover these aspects in the next section.
- Attach documents that can help the user to understand rules.

If you decide to write user stories, a good tip to follow is to write short sentences representing each moment in the system with each user, as follows:

```
As <user>, I want <feature>, so that <reason>
```

This approach will explain exactly the reason why that feature will be implemented. It's also a good tool to help you analyze the stories that are most critical, and prioritize the success of the project. They can also be great for informing the automated acceptance tests that should be built.

Understanding the principles of scalability, robustness, security, and performance

Detecting requirements is a task that will let you understand the software you are going to develop. However, as a software architect, you have to pay attention to more than just the functional requirements for that system. Understanding the non-functional requirements is important, and one of the earliest activities for a software architect.

We are going to look at this in more detail in *Chapter 2, Non-Functional Requirements,* but at this point, it's important to know that the principles of scalability, robustness, security, and performance need to be applied for the requirements gathering process. Let us look at each concept:

- **Scalability**: As a software developer, globalization gives you the opportunity to have your solution running all over the world. This is fantastic, but you, as a software architect, need to design a solution that provides that possibility. Scalability is the possibility for an application to increase its processing power as soon as it is necessary, due to the number of resources that are being consumed.

- **Robustness**: No matter how scalable your application is, if it is not able to guarantee a stable and always-on solution, you are not going to get any peace. Robustness is important for critical solutions, where you do not have the opportunity for maintenance at any time due to the kind of problem that the application solves. In many industries, the software cannot stop, and lots of routines run when nobody is available (overnight, holidays, and so on). Designing a robust solution will give you the freedom to live while your software is running well.

- **Security**: This is another really important area that needs to be discussed after the requirements stage. Everybody worries about security, and different laws dealing with it are in place and being proposed in different parts of the world. You, as a software architect, must understand that security needs to be provided by design. This is the only way to cope with all the needs that the security community is discussing right now.

- **Performance**: The process of understanding the system you are going to develop will probably give you a good idea of what you'll need to do to get the desired performance from the system. This topic needs to be discussed with the user, to identify most of the bottlenecks you will face during the development stage.

It is worth mentioning that all these concepts are requirements for the new generation of solutions that the world needs. What differentiates good software from incredible software is the amount of work done to meet the project requirements.

Reviewing the specification

Once you have the specification written, it is time to confirm with the stakeholders whether they agree with it. This can be done in a review meeting, or can be done online using collaboration tools.

This is when you present all the prototypes, documents, and information you have gathered. As soon as everybody agrees with the specification, you are ready to start studying the best way to implement this part of your project.

It is worth mentioning that you might use the process described here for both the complete software or for a small part of it.

Using design techniques as a helpful tool

Defining a solution is not easy. Determining its technology increases the difficulty of doing so. It is true that, during your career as a software architect, you will find many projects where your customer will bring you a solution *ready for development*. This can get quite complicated if you consider that solution as the correct solution; most of the time, there will be architectural and functional mistakes that will cause problems in the solution in the future.

There are some cases where the problem is worse—when the customer does not know the best solution for the problem. Some design techniques can help us with this, and we will introduce two of them here: **Design Thinking** and **Design Sprint**.

What you must understand is that these techniques can be a fantastic option to discover real requirements. As a software architect, you are committed to helping your team to use the correct tools at the correct time, and these tools may be the right options to ensure the project's success.

Design Thinking

Design Thinking is a process that allows you to collect data directly from the users, focusing on achieving the best results to solve a problem. During this process, the team will have the opportunity to discover all *personas* that will interact with the system. This will have a wonderful impact on the solution since you can develop the software by focusing on the user experience, which can have a fantastic impact on the results.

The process is based on the following steps:

- **Empathize**: In this step, you must execute field research to discover the users' concerns. This is where you find out about the users of the system. The process is good for making you understand why and for whom you are developing this software.
- **Define**: Once you have the users' concerns, it is time to define their needs to solve them.
- **Ideate**: The needs will provide an opportunity to brainstorm some possible solutions.
- **Prototype**: These solutions can be developed as mock-ups to confirm whether they are good ones.
- **Test**: Testing the prototypes will help you to understand the prototype that is most connected to the real needs of the users.

The focus of a technique like this one is to accelerate the process of detecting the right product, considering the **minimum viable product** (**MVP**). For sure, the prototype process will help stakeholders to understand the final product and, at the same time, engage the team to deliver the best solution.

Design Sprint

Design Sprint is a process focused on solving critical business questions through design in a five-day sprint. This technique was presented by Google, and it is an alternative that allows you to quickly test and learn from an idea, needing to build and launch a solution to market.

The process is based on a week dedicated by experts to solve the problem mentioned, in a war room prepared for that purpose. The week is separated like this:

- **Monday**: The focus of this day is to identify the target of the sprint and map the challenge to achieve it.

- **Tuesday**: After understanding the goal of the sprint, participants start sketching solutions that may solve it. It is time to find customers to test the new solution that will be provided.

- **Wednesday**: This is when the team needs to decide the solutions that have the greatest chance to solve the problem. Besides, on Wednesday the team must draw these solutions into a storyboard, preparing a plan for the prototype.

- **Thursday**: It is time to prototype the idea planned on the storyboard.

- **Friday**: Having completed the prototype, the team presents it to customers, learning by getting information from their reaction to the solution designed.

As you can see in both techniques, the acceleration of collecting reactions from customers comes from prototypes that will materialize your team's ideas into something more tangible for the end-user.

Common cases where the requirements gathering process impacted system results

All the information discussed up to this point in the chapter is useful if you want to design software following the principles of good engineering. This discussion is not related to developing by using traditional or agile methods, but focuses on building software professionally or as an amateur.

It's also a good idea to know about some cases where failing to perform the activities you read about caused some trouble for the software project. The following cases intend to describe what could go wrong, and how the preceding techniques could have helped the development team to solve the problems.

In most cases, simple action could have guaranteed better communication between the team and the customer, and this easy communication flow would have transformed a big problem into a real solution. Let's examine three common cases where the requirements gathering impacted the results of performance, functionality, and usability.

Case 1 – my website is too slow to open that page!

Performance is one of the biggest problems that you as a software architect will deal with during your career. The reason why this aspect of any software is so problematic is that we do not have infinite computational resources to solve problems. Besides, the cost of computation is still high, especially if you are talking about software with a high number of simultaneous users.

You cannot solve performance problems by writing requirements. However, you will not end up in trouble if you write them correctly. The idea here is that requirements must present the desired performance of a system. A simple sentence, describing this, can help the entire team that works on the project:

 Non-functional requirement: Performance – any web page of this software shall respond in at least 2 seconds, even when 1,000 users are accessing it concurrently.

The preceding sentence just makes everybody (users, testers, developers, architects, managers, and so on) sure that any web page has a target to achieve. This is a good start, but it's not enough. A great environment to both develop and deploy your application is also important. This is where .NET 5 can help you a lot; especially if you are talking about web apps, ASP.NET Core is considered one of the fastest options to deliver solutions today.

If you talk about performance, you, as a software architect, should consider the use of the techniques listed in the following sections together with specific tests to guarantee this non-functional requirement. It's also important to mention that ASP. NET Core will help you to use them easily, together with some **Platform as a Service (PaaS)** solutions delivered by Microsoft Azure.

Understanding caching

Caching is a great technique to avoid queries that can consume time and, in general, give the same result. For instance, if you are fetching the available car models in a database, the number of cars in the database can increase, but they will not change. Once you have an application that constantly accesses car models, a good practice is to cache that information.

It is important to understand that a cache is stored in the backend and that cache is shared by the whole application (*in-memory caching*). A point to focus on is that when you are working on a scalable solution, you can configure a *distributed cache* to solve it using the Azure platform. In fact, ASP.NET provides both, so you can decide on the one that bests fits your needs. *Chapter 2, Non-Functional Requirements*, covers scalability aspects in the Azure platform.

Applying asynchronous programming

When you develop ASP.NET applications, you need to keep in mind that your app needs to be designed for simultaneous access by many users. Asynchronous programming lets you do this simply, giving you the keywords async and await.

The basic concept behind these keywords is that async enables any method to run asynchronously. On the other hand, await lets you synchronize the call of an asynchronous method without blocking the thread that is calling it. This easy-to-develop pattern will make your application run without performance bottlenecks and better responsiveness. This book will cover more about this subject in *Chapter 2, Non-Functional Requirements*.

Dealing with object allocation

One very good tip to avoid a lack of performance is to understand how the **Garbage Collector (GC)** works. The GC is the engine that will free memory automatically when you finish using it. There are some very important aspects of this topic, due to the complexity that the GC has.

Some types of objects are not collected by the GC if you do not dispose of them. The list includes any object that interacts with I/O, such as files and streaming. If you do not correctly use the C# syntax to create and destroy this kind of object, you will have memory leaks, which will deteriorate your application performance.

The incorrect way of working with I/O objects is:

```
System.IO.StreamWriter file = new System.IO.StreamWriter(@"C:\sample.
txt");
file.WriteLine("Just writing a simple line");
```

The correct way of working with I/O objects is:

```
using (System.IO.StreamWriter file = new System.IO.StreamWriter(@"C:\
sample.txt"))
{
file.WriteLine("Just writing a simple line");
}
```

It might be worth noting that this correct approach also ensures the file gets written (it calls Flush). In the incorrect example, the contents might not even be written to the file. Even though the preceding practice is mandatory for I/O objects, it is totally recommended that you keep doing this in all disposable objects. Indeed, using code analyzers in your solutions with warnings as errors will prevent you from accidentally making these mistakes! This will help the GC and will keep your application running with the right amount of memory. Depending on the type of object, mistakes here can snowball, and you could end up with other bad things at scale, for instance, port/connection exhaustion.

Another important aspect that you need to know about is that the time spent by the GC to collect objects will interfere with the performance of your app. Because of this, avoid allocating large objects; otherwise, it can cause you trouble waiting for the GC to finish its task.

Getting better database access

One of the most common performance Achilles' heels is database access. The reason why this is still a big problem is the lack of attention while writing queries or lambda expressions to get information from the database. This book will cover Entity Framework Core in *Chapter 8, Interacting with Data in C# – Entity Framework Core*, but it is important to know what to choose and the correct data information to read from a database. Filtering columns and lines is imperative for an application that wants to deliver on performance.

The good thing is that best practices related to caching, asynchronous programming, and object allocation fit completely into the environment of databases. It's only a matter of choosing the correct pattern to get better-performance software.

Case 2 – the user's needs are not properly implemented

The more that technology is used in a wide variety of areas, the more difficult it is to deliver exactly what the user needs. Maybe this sentence sounds weird to you, but you must understand that developers, in general, study how to develop software, but they rarely study to deliver the needs of a specific area. Of course, it is not easy to learn how to develop software, but it is even more difficult to understand a specific need in a specific area. Software development nowadays delivers software to all possible types of industries. The question here is *how can a developer, whether a software architect or not, evolve enough to deliver software in the area they are responsible for?*

Gathering software requirements will help you in this tough task; writing them will make you understand and organize the architecture of the system. There are several ways to minimize the risks of implementing something different from what the user really needs:

- Prototyping the interface to achieve an understanding of the user interface faster
- Designing the data flow to detect gaps between the system and the user operation
- Frequent meetings to be updated on the user's current needs and aligned to incremental deliveries

Again, as a software architect, you will have to define how the software will be implemented. Most of the time, you are not going to be the one who programs it, but you will always be the one responsible for this. For this reason, some techniques can be useful to avoid the wrong implementation:

- Requirements are reviewed with the developers to guarantee that they understand what they need to develop.
- Code inspection to validate a predefined code standard. We will cover this in *Chapter 19, Using Tools to Write Better Code*.
- Meetings to eliminate impediments.

Remember, the implementation matching the user needs is your responsibility. Use every tool you can to meet it.

Case 3 – the usability of the system does not meet user needs

Usability is a key point for the success of a software project. The way the software is presented and how it solves a problem can help the user to decide whether they want to use it or not. As a software architect, you must keep in mind that delivering software with good usability is mandatory nowadays.

There are basic concepts of usability that this book does not intend to cover, but a good way to meet the correct user needs when it comes to usability is by understanding who is going to use the software. Design Thinking can help you a lot with that, as was discussed earlier in this chapter.

Understanding the user will help you to decide whether the software is going to run on a web page, or a cell phone, or even in the background. This understanding is very important to a software architect because the elements of a system will be better presented if you correctly map who will use them.

On the other hand, if you do not care about that, you will just deliver software that works. This can be good for a short time, but it will not exactly meet the real needs that made a person ask you to architect the software. You must keep in mind the options and understand that good software is designed to run on many platforms and devices.

You will be happy to know that .NET 5 is an incredible cross-platform option for that. So, you can develop solutions to run your apps in Linux, Windows, Android, and iOS. You can run your applications on big screens, tablets, cell phones, and even drones! You can embed apps on boards for automation or in HoloLens for mixed reality. Software architects must be open-minded to design exactly what their users need.

Case study – introducing World Wild Travel Club

As we mentioned at the beginning of this chapter, the case study of this book will take you on a journey of creating the software architecture for a travel agency called **World Wild Travel Club (WWTravelClub)**.

WWTravelClub is a travel agency that was created to change the way people make decisions about their vacations and other trips around the world. To do so, they are developing an online service where every detail of a trip experience will be assisted by a club of experts specifically selected for each destination.

The concept of this platform is that you can be both a visitor and a destination expert at the same time. The more you participate as an expert in a destination, the higher the points you will score. These points can be exchanged for tickets that people buy online using the platform.

The customer came with the following requirements for the platform. It is important to know that, in general, customers do not bring the requirements ready for development. That is why the requirements gathering process is so important:

- Common user view:
    - Promotional packages on the home page
    - Search for packages
    - Details for each package:
        - Buy a package
        - Buy a package with a club of experts included:
            - Comment on your experience

- Ask an expert
- Evaluate an expert
- Register as a common user
- Destination expert view:
    - The same view as the common user view
    - Answer the questions asking for your destination expertise
    - Manage the points you scored answering questions:
    - Exchange points for tickets
- Administrator view:
    - Manage packages
    - Manage common users
    - Manage destination experts

To finish this, it is important to note that WWTravelClub intends to have more than 100 destination experts per package and will offer around 1,000 different packages all over the world.

Understanding user needs and system requirements

To summarize the user needs of WWTravelClub, you can read the following user stories:

- US_001: As a common user, I want to view promotional packages on the home page, so that I can easily find my next vacation
- US_002: As a common user, I want to search for packages I cannot find on the home page so that I can explore other trip opportunities
- US_003: As a common user, I want to see the details of a package, so that I can decide which package to buy
- US_004: As a common user, I want to register myself, so that I can start buying the package
- US_005: As a registered user, I want to process the payment, so that I can buy a package

- US_006: As a registered user, I want to buy a package with an expert recommendation included, so that I can have an exclusive trip experience
- US_007: As a registered user, I want to ask for an expert, so that I find out the best things I can do on my trip
- US_008: As a registered user, I want to comment on my experience, so that I can give feedback from my trip
- US_009: As a registered user, I want to evaluate an expert who helps me, so that I can share with others how fantastic they were
- US_010: As a registered user, I want to register as a destination expert view, so that I can help people who travel to my city
- US_011: As an expert user, I want to answer questions about my city, so that I can score points to be exchanged in the future
- US_012: As an expert user, I want to exchange points for tickets, so that I can travel around the world more
- US_013: As an administrator user, I want to manage packages, so that users can have fantastic opportunities to travel
- US_014: As an administrator user, I want to manage registered users, so that WWTravelClub can guarantee good service quality
- US_015: As an administrator user, I want to manage expert users, so that all of the questions regarding our destinations are answered
- US_016: As an administrator user, I want to offer more than 1,000 packages around the world, so that different countries can experience the WWTravelClub service
- US_017: As the CEO, I want to have more than 1,000 users simultaneously accessing the website, so that the business can scale effectively
- US_018: As a user, I want to access WWTravelClub in my native language, so that I can easily understand the package offered
- US_019: As a user, I want to access WWTravelClub in the Chrome, Firefox, and Edge web browsers, so that I can use the web browser of my preference
- US_020: As a user, I want to know my credit card information is stored securely, so I can buy packages safely

Notice that while you start writing the stories, information related to non-functional requirements such as security, environment, performance, and scalability can be included.

However, some system requirements may be omitted when you write user stories and need to be included in the software specification. These requirements can be related to legal aspects, hardware, and software prerequisites, or even points of attention for the correct system delivery. They need to be mapped and listed as well as user stories. The WWTravelClub system requirements are presented in the following list. Notice that requirements are written in the future because the system does not exist yet:

- SR_001: The system shall use Microsoft Azure components to deliver the scalability required

- SR_002: The system shall respect **General Data Protection Regulation (GDPR)** requirements

- SR_003: The system shall run on the Windows, Linux, iOS, and Android platforms

- SR_004: Any web page of this system shall respond in at least 2 seconds with a 1,000-user concurrently access

The idea of having this list of user stories and system requirements is to help you understand how complex the development of a platform might be if you think about it from an architectural perspective.

Summary

In this chapter, you learned the purpose of a software architect in a software development team. Also, this chapter covered the basics of software development process models and the requirements gathering process. You also had the opportunity to learn about how to create your Azure account, which will be used during the case study of this book, which was presented to you in the previous section. Moreover, you even learned about functional and non-functional requirements and how to create them using user stories. These techniques will help you deliver a better software project.

In the next chapter, you will have the opportunity to understand how important functional and non-functional requirements are for software architecture.

Questions

1. What is the expertise that a software architect needs to have?
2. How can Azure help a software architect?

3. How does a software architect decide the best software development process model to use in a project?

4. How does a software architect contribute to gathering requirements?

5. What kind of requirements does a software architect need to check in a requirement specification?

6. How do Design Thinking and Design Sprint help a software architect in the process of gathering requirements?

7. How do user stories help a software architect in the process of writing requirements?

8. What are good techniques to develop very good performance software?

9. How does a software architect check whether a user requirement is correctly implemented?

Further reading

Here, you have some books and links you may consider reading to gather more information about this chapter.

For Azure information, check these out:

- https://www.packtpub.com/virtualization-and-cloud/hands-azure-developers
- https://azure.microsoft.com/en-us/overview/what-is-azure/
- https://azure.microsoft.com/en-us/services/devops/
- https://www.microsoft.com/en-us/hololens
- https://azurecharts.com/

.NET 5 information can be found here:

- https://docs.microsoft.com/en-us/dotnet/
- https://docs.microsoft.com/en-us/aspnet/
- https://www.packtpub.com/web-development/hands-full-stack-web-development-aspnet-core
- https://docs.microsoft.com/en-us/aspnet/core/performance/performance-best-practices

Software development process model links:

- https://agilemanifesto.org/
- https://www.amazon.com/Software-Engineering-10th-Ian-Sommerville/dp/0133943038
- https://www.amazon.com/Software-Engineering-Practitioners-Roger-Pressman/dp/0078022126/
- https://scrumguides.org/
- https://www.packtpub.com/application-development/professional-scrummasters-handbook
- https://en.wikipedia.org/wiki/Incremental_build_model
- https://en.wikipedia.org/wiki/Waterfall_model
- http://www.extremeprogramming.org/
- https://www.gv.com/sprint/

2

Non-Functional Requirements

Once you have gathered the system requirements, it is time to think about the impact they have on the architectural design. Scalability, availability, resiliency, performance, multithreading, interoperability, security, and other subjects need to be analyzed so that we can meet user needs. We refer to these aspects as non-functional requirements.

The following topics will be covered in this chapter:

- How do .NET 5 and Azure enable scalability, availability, and resiliency?
- Performance issues that need to be considered when programming in C#
- Software usability, that is, how to design effective user interfaces
- .NET 5 and interoperability
- Achieving security by design
- Book use case – understanding the main types of .NET Core projects

Technical requirements

The samples provided in this chapter will require Visual Studio 2019 Community Edition with .NET 5 SDK installed.

You can find the sample code for this chapter at https://github.com/PacktPublishing/Software-Architecture-with-C-9-and-.NET-5.

Enabling scalability, availability, and resiliency with Azure and .NET 5

A short search on scalability returns a definition such as *the ability of a system to keep working well when there is an increase in demand.* Once developers read this, many of them incorrectly conclude *that scalability only means adding more hardware to keep things working without stopping the app.*

Scalability relies on technologies involving hardware solutions. However, as a software architect, you must be aware that good software will keep scalability in a sustainable model, which means that a well-architected software can save a lot of money. Hence, it is not just a matter of hardware but also a matter of overall software design. The point here is that the running cost of a system should also be a factor in the architectural decisions.

In *Chapter 1, Understanding the Importance of Software Architecture,* while discussing software performance, we proposed some good tips to overcome bad performance issues. The same tips will help you with scalability too. The fewer resources we spend on each process, the more users the application can handle.

Although scalability is important, cloud computing applications must be designed to work with system failures. Every time you guarantee that your application recovers from a failure without exposing this failure to the end user, you are creating a resilient application.

 You may find cloud architecture resiliency patterns at https://docs.microsoft.com/en-us/azure/architecture/patterns/category/resiliency.

The reason why resiliency is especially important in cloud scenarios is because the infrastructure provided to you may need a small amount of time to manage updates, resets, and even hardware upgrades. You are also more likely to be working with multiple systems, and transient errors are likely to occur in communicating with them. That is why this non-functional requirement started to be spread in recent years.

The possibility of having scalable and resilient solutions gets more exciting when you can enable high availability in the system. All the approaches presented in this book will guide you to design solutions with good availability, but in some cases, you will need to design specific alternatives to achieve the goal you have.

 You may find cloud architecture availability patterns at `https://docs.microsoft.com/en-us/azure/architecture/patterns/category/availability`.

It is worth knowing that Azure and .NET 5 web apps can be configured to achieve these non-functional requirements. Let us check this out in the following subsections.

Creating a scalable web app in Azure

It is simple to create a web app in Azure, ready for scaling. The reason why you must do so is to be able to maintain different numbers of users during different seasons. The more users you have, the more hardware you will need. Let us show you how to create a scalable web application in Azure.

As soon as you log in to your Azure account, you will be able to create a new resource (web app, database, virtual machine, and so on), as you can see in the following screenshot:

Figure 2.1: Microsoft Azure – Create a resource

After that, you can select **Web App** in the **Popular Options,** or even type it into the **Search the Marketplace** textbox. This action will take you to the following screen:

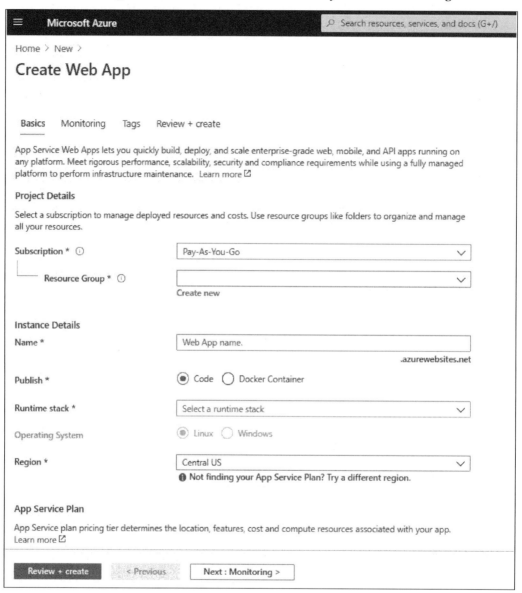

Figure 2.2: Microsoft Azure – Creating a web app

The required **Project Details** are as follows:

- **Subscription**: This is the account that will be charged for all application costs.
- **Resource Group**: This is the collection of resources you can define to organize policies and permissions. You may specify a new resource group name or add the web app to a group specified during the definition of other resources.

Besides these, the **Instance Details** are as follows:

- **Name**: As you can see, the web app name is the URL that your solution will assume after its creation. The name is checked to ensure it is available.
- **Publish**: This parameter indicates whether the web app will be delivered directly or whether it is going to use Docker technology to publish content. Docker will be discussed in more detail in *Chapter 5, Applying a Microservice Architecture to Your Enterprise Application*. If you opt for the Docker Container publication, you will be able to configure the **Image Source**, **Access Type**, and **Image** and tag information to have it deployed to the web app.
- **Runtime stack**: This option is obviously only available when you decide to deliver code directly. At the time this chapter was written, you could define stacks for .NET Core, ASP.NET, Java 11, Java 8, Node, PHP, Python, and Ruby.
- **Operating System**: This is the option for defining the OS that will host the web app. Both Windows and Linux may be used for ASP.NET Core projects.
- **Region**: You may consider where you want to deploy your application, considering Azure has many different data centers all over the world.
- **App Service Plan**: This is where you define the hardware plan that is used to handle the web app and the region of the servers. This choice defines application scalability, performance, and costs.
- **Monitoring**: This is a useful Azure toolset for monitoring and troubleshooting web apps. In this section, you will be able to enable Application Insights. It is always recommended that you keep the same regions for different components of your solution, since this will save costs in terms of traffic exchange from one data center to another.

Once you have created your web app, this application may be scaled in two conceptually different ways: Vertically (**Scale up**) and Horizontally (**Scale out**). Both are available in the web app settings, as you can see in the following screenshot:

Figure 2.3: Scaling options of web apps

Let us check out the two types of scaling.

Vertical scaling (Scaling up)

Scaling up means changing the specification of hardware that will host your application. In Azure, you have the opportunity of starting with free, shared hardware and moving to an isolated machine in a few clicks. The following screenshot shows the user interface for scaling up a web app:

Figure 2.4: Vertical scaling options

By choosing one of the options provided, you can select more powerful hardware (machines with more CPUs, storage, and RAM). Monitoring your application and its App Service plan will guide you on how to decide the best infrastructure for running the solution you are proving. It will also offer key insights, such as possible CPU, memory, and I/O bottlenecks.

Horizontal scaling (Scaling out)

Scaling out means splitting all requests among more servers with the same capacity instead of using more powerful machines. The load on all the servers is automatically balanced by the Azure infrastructure. This solution is advised when the overall load may change considerably in the future since horizontal scaling can be automatically adapted to the current load. The following screenshot shows an automatic **Scale out** strategy defined by two simple rules, which is triggered by CPU usage:

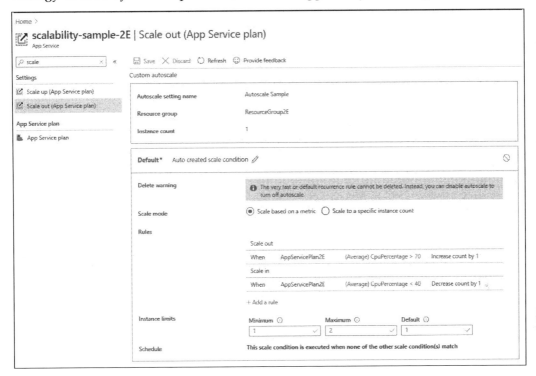

Figure 2.5: Horizontal scaling sample

It is worth highlighting that you can choose to have a hardcoded instance count or implement rules for automatic scale in/out.

A complete description of all the available auto-scale rules is beyond the purpose of this book. However, they are quite self-explanatory, and the *Further reading* section contains links to the full documentation.

The *Scale out* feature is only available in paid service plans.

In general, horizontal scaling is a way to guarantee availability in the application even with a number of simultaneous accesses. For sure, its use is not the only way to keep a system available, but it will definitely help.

Creating a scalable web app with .NET 5

Among all the available frameworks for implementing web apps, running it with ASP.NET Core 5 ensures good performance, together with low production and maintenance costs. The union of C#, a strongly typed and advanced general-purpose language, and continuous performance improvements achieved in the framework, mark this option out in recent years as one of the best for enterprise development.

The steps that follow will guide you through the creation of an ASP.NET Core Runtime 5-based web app. All the steps are quite simple, but some details require attention.

It is worth mentioning that .NET 5 brings the opportunity to develop to any platform – Desktops (WPF, Windows Forms, and UWP), Web (ASP.NET), Cloud (Azure), Mobile (Xamarin), Gaming (Unity), IoT (ARM32 and ARM64), and AI (ML.NET and .NET for Apache Spark). So, the recommendation from now on is to only use .NET 5. In this scenario, you can run your web app on both Windows and cheaper Linux servers.

Nowadays, Microsoft recommends classic .NET, just in case the features you need are not available in .NET Core, or even when you deploy your web app in an environment that does not support .NET Core. In any other case, you should prefer .NET Core Framework because it allows you to do the following:

- Run your web app in Windows, Linux, macOS, or Docker containers
- Design your solution with microservices
- Have high performance and scalable systems

Containers and microservices will be covered in *Chapter 5, Applying a Microservice Architecture to Your Enterprise Application*. There, you will get a better understanding of the advantages of these technologies. For now, it is enough to say that .NET 5 and microservices were designed for performance and scalability, which is why you should prefer .NET 5 in all your new projects.

The following procedure will show you how to create an ASP.NET Core web app in Visual Studio 2019 with .NET 5:

- As soon as you start VS 2019, you will be able to click on **Create a new project**.
- Once you select **ASP.NET Core Web Application**, you will be directed to a screen where you will be asked to set up the **Project name**, **Location**, and **Solution name**:

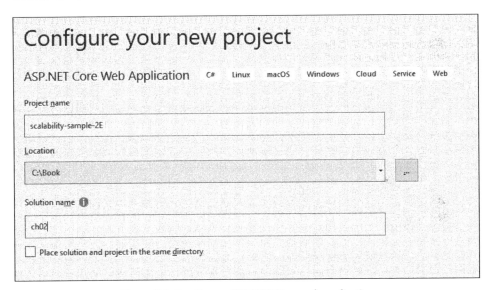

Figure 2.6: Creating an ASP.NET Core web application

- After that, you will be able to select the .NET version to use. Select **ASP.NET Core 5.0** to get the most advanced and brand-new platform. For this demo, you can select the **Web Application** template.
- Now that we are done with adding the basic details, you can connect your web app project to your Azure account and have it published.

- If you right-click the project you created, in **Solution Explorer**, you have the option to **Publish**:

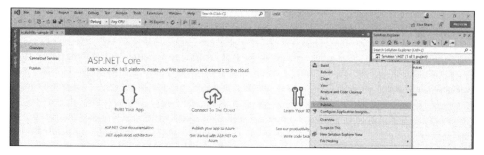

Figure 2.7: Publishing the ASP.NET Core web application

- You will find different targets to publish your web app. Select **Azure** as the target.

- Then, you will be able to decide the **Specific target** to publish. Select **Azure App Service (Windows)** for this demo.

- You may be required to define your Microsoft Account credentials at this time. This is because there is full integration between Visual Studio and Azure. This gives you the opportunity to view all the resources you created in the Azure portal in your development environment:

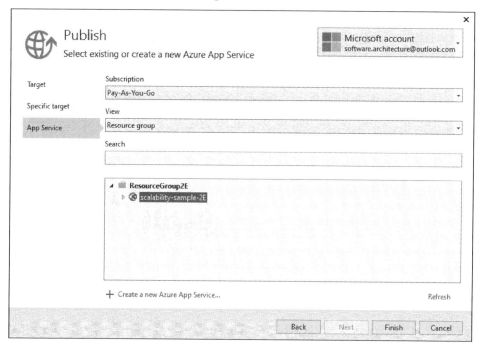

Figure 2.8: Integration between Visual Studio and Azure

- Once you have decided on your **Publish** settings, that is, the publish profile, the web app will be automatically published when you click **Publish**. Pay attention here to select the F1 tier of pricing so that this process does not incur any costs:

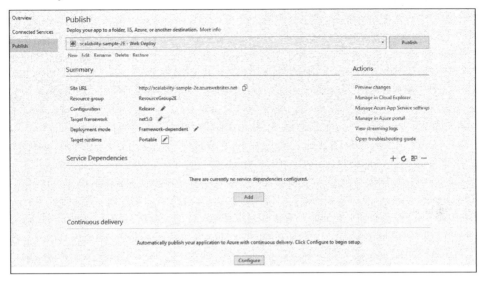

Figure 2.9: Publish profile options

- You have currently two modes for deployment. The first, Framework-dependent, will require a web app configured with the target framework. The second, self-contained, will no longer need this feature since the binaries of the framework will be published together with the application.

- It is worth mentioning that in order to publish ASP.NET Preview versions in Framework-dependent mode, you must add an extension in the web app setup panel in Azure Portal, as shown in the following screenshot. However, consider using the self-contained mode, especially when you are under preview versions:

Figure 2.10: Adding extensions in Azure Web App Service

For more information on deploying ASP.NET Core 5.0 to Azure App Service, please refer to the following link: `https://docs.` `microsoft.com/en-us/aspnet/core/host-and-deploy/azure-` `apps/?view=aspnetcore-5.0&tabs=visual-studio`.

Here, we described the simplest way to deploy a web app. In *Chapter 20, Understanding DevOps Principles* and *Chapter 21, Challenges of Applying CI Scenarios,* we will introduce you to the Azure DevOps **Continuous Integration/Continuous Delivery (CI/CD)** pipeline. This pipeline is a further Azure toolset that automates all the required steps to get the application in production, that is, building, testing, deployment in staging, and deployment in production.

Performance issues that need to be considered when programming in C#

Nowadays, C# is one of the most commonly used programming languages all over the world, so good tips about C# programming are fundamental for the design of good architectures that satisfy the most common non-functional requirements.

The following sections mention a few simple but effective tips – the associated code samples are available in the GitHub repository of this book.

String concatenation

This is a classic one! A naive concatenation of strings with the + string operator may cause serious performance issues since each time two strings are concatenated, their contents are copied into a new string.

So, if we concatenate, for instance, 10 strings that have an average length of 100, the first operation has a cost of 200, the second one has a cost of *200+100=300*, the third one has a cost of *300+100=400*, and so on. It is not difficult to convince yourself that the overall cost grows like $m*n^2$, where n is the number of strings and m is their average length. n^2 is not too big for small n (say, $n < 10$), but it becomes quite big when n reaches the magnitude of 100-1,000, and unacceptable for magnitudes of 10,000-100,000.

Let us look at this with some test code, which compares naive concatenation with the same operation that is performed with the help of the StringBuilder class (the code is available in this book's GitHub repository):

```
Hello Readers!
Here you have some samples regarding to performance issues.
Please select the option you want to check:
0 - Bye bye!
1 - String Concatenation
This is a classic one! But you should remember about this, anyway!
Start running method: ExecuteStringConcatenationWithNoComponent
Concatenating 100000 strings....
The method ExecuteStringConcatenationWithNoComponent took 22,8933254 second(s).
Start running method: ExecuteStringConcatenationWithStringBuilder
Concatenating 100000 strings....
The method ExecuteStringConcatenationWithStringBuilder took 0,0181133 second(s).
The results are the same! You can compare the numbers.
Press any key to continue...
```

Figure 2.11: Concatenation test code result

If you create a StringBuilder class with something like var sb =new System.Text. StringBuilder(), and then you add each string to it with sb.Append(currString), the strings are not copied; instead, their pointers are queued in a list. They are copied in the final string just once, when you call sb.ToString() to get the final result. Accordingly, the cost of StringBuilder-based concatenation grows simply as *m*n*.

Of course, you will probably never find a piece of software with a function like the preceding one that concatenates 100,000 strings. However, you need to recognize pieces of code similar to these ones where the concatenation of some 20-100 strings, say, in a web server that handles several requests simultaneously, might cause bottlenecks that damage your non-functional requirements for performance.

Exceptions

Always remember that exceptions are much slower than normal code flow! So, the usage of try-catch needs to be concise and essential, otherwise, you will create big performance issues.

The following two samples compare the usage of try-catch and Int32.TryParse to check whether a string can be converted into an integer, as follows:

```csharp
private static string ParseIntWithTryParse()
{
    string result = string.Empty;
    if (int.TryParse(result, out var value))
        result = value.ToString();
    else
        result = "There is no int value";
    return $"Final result: {result}";
}


private static string ParseIntWithException()
{
    string result = string.Empty;
    try
    {
        result = Convert.ToInt32(result).ToString();
    }
    catch (Exception)
    {
        result = "There is no int value";
    }
    return $"Final result: {result}";
}
```

The second function does not look dangerous, but it is thousands of times slower than the first one:

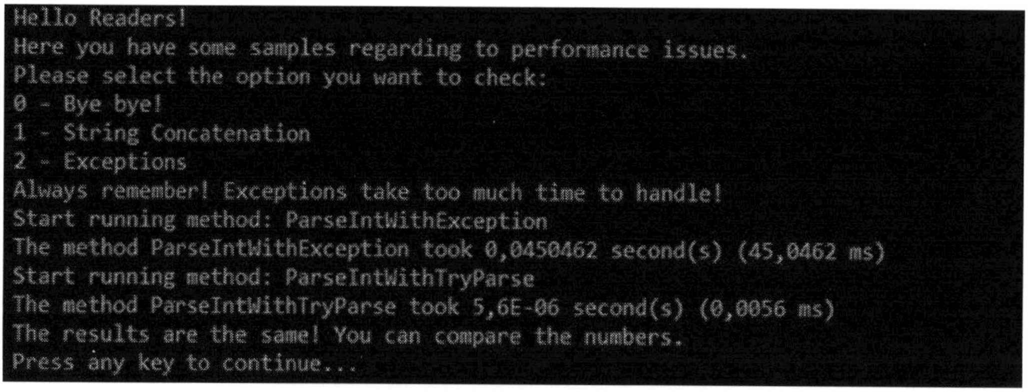

```
Hello Readers!
Here you have some samples regarding to performance issues.
Please select the option you want to check:
0 - Bye bye!
1 - String Concatenation
2 - Exceptions
Always remember! Exceptions take too much time to handle!
Start running method: ParseIntWithException
The method ParseIntWithException took 0,0450462 second(s) (45,0462 ms)
Start running method: ParseIntWithTryParse
The method ParseIntWithTryParse took 5,6E-06 second(s) (0,0056 ms)
The results are the same! You can compare the numbers.
Press any key to continue...
```

Figure 2.12: Exception test code result

To sum this up, exceptions must be used to deal with exceptional cases that break the normal flow of control, for instance, situations when operations must be aborted for some unexpected reasons, and control must be returned several levels up in the call stack.

Multithreading environments for better results – dos and don'ts

If you want to take advantage of all the hardware that the system you are building provides, you must use multithreading. This way, when a thread is waiting for an operation to complete, the application can leave the CPU to other threads, instead of wasting CPU time.

On the other hand, no matter how hard Microsoft is working to help with this, parallel code is not as simple as eating a piece of cake: it is error-prone and difficult to test and debug. The most important thing to remember as a software architect when you start considering using threads is *does your system require them?* Non-functional and some functional requirements will answer this question for you.

As soon as you are sure that you need a multithreading system, you should decide on which technology is more adequate. There are a few options here, as follows:

- **Creating an instance of** System.Threading.Thread: This is a classic way of creating threads in C#. The entire thread life cycle will be in your hands. This is good when you are sure about what you are going to do, but you need to worry about every single detail of the implementation. The resulting code is hard to conceive and debug/test/maintain. So, to keep development costs acceptable, this approach should be confined to a few fundamental, performance critical modules.

- **Programming using** System.Threading.Tasks.Parallel **classes**: Since .NET Framework 4.0, you can use parallel classes to enable threads in a simpler way. This is good because you do not need to worry about the life cycle of the threads you create, but it will give you less control about what is happening in each thread.

- **Develop using asynchronous programming**: This is, for sure, the easiest way to develop multithreaded applications since the compiler takes on most of the work. Depending on the way you call an asynchronous method, you may have the Task created running in parallel with the Thread that was used to call it or even have this Thread waiting without suspending for the task created to conclude. This way, asynchronous code mimics the behavior of classical synchronous code while keeping most of the performance advantages of general parallel programming:

- The overall behavior is deterministic and does not depend on the time taken by each task to complete, so non-reproducible bugs are more difficult to happen, and the resulting code is easy to test/debug/maintain. Defining a method as an asynchronous task or not is the only choice left to the programmer; everything else is automatically handled by the runtime. The only thing you should be concerned about is which methods should have asynchronous behavior. It is worth mentioning that defining a method as `async` does not mean it will execute on a separate thread. You may find useful information in a great sample at `https://docs.microsoft.com/en-us/dotnet/csharp/programming-guide/concepts/async/`.

- Later in this book, we will provide some simple examples of asynchronous programming. For more information about asynchronous programming and its related patterns, please check *Task-Based Asynchronous Patterns* in the Microsoft documentation (`https://docs.microsoft.com/en-us/dotnet/standard/asynchronous-programming-patterns/task-based-asynchronous-pattern-tap`).

No matter the option you choose, there are some dos and don'ts that, as a software architect, you must pay attention to. These are as follows:

- **Do use concurrent collections** (`System.Collections.Concurrent`): As soon as you start a multithreading application, you have to use these collections. The reason for this is that your program will probably manage the same list, dictionary, and so on from different threads. The use of concurrent collections is the most convenient option for developing thread-safe programs.

- **Do worry about static variables**: It is not possible to say that static variables are prohibited in multithreading development, but you should pay attention to them. Again, multiple threads taking care of the same variable can cause a lot of trouble. If you decorate a static variable with the `[ThreadStatic]` attribute, each thread will see a different copy of that variable, hence solving the problem of several threads competing on the same value. However, `ThreadStatic` variables cannot be used for extra-thread communications since values written by a thread cannot be read by other threads. In asynchronous programming, `AsyncLocal<T>` is the option for doing something like that.

- **Do test system performance after multithreading implementations**: Threads give you the ability to take full advantage of your hardware, but in some cases, badly written threads can waste CPU time just doing nothing! Similar situations may result in almost 100% CPU usage and unacceptable system slowdowns. In some cases, the problem can be mitigated or solved by adding a simple `Thread.Sleep(1)` call in the main loop of some threads to prevent them from wasting too much CPU time, but you need to test this. A use case for this implementation is a Windows Service with many threads running in its background.

- **Do not consider multithreading easy**: Multithreading is not as simple as it seems in some syntax implementations. While writing a multithreading application, you should consider things such as the synchronization of the user interface, threading termination, and coordination. In many cases, programs just stop working well due to a bad implementation of multithreading.

- **Do not forget to plan the number of threads your system should have**: This is important especially for 32-bit programs. There is a limitation regarding how many threads you can have in any environment. You should consider this when you are designing your system.

- **Do not forget to end your threads**: If you do not have the correct termination procedure for each thread, you will probably have trouble with memory and handling leaks.

Usability – why inserting data takes too much time

Scalability, performance tips, and multithreading are the main tools we can use to tune machine performance. However, the effectiveness of the system you design depends on the overall performance of the whole processing pipeline, which includes both humans and machines.

As a software architect, you cannot improve the performance of humans, but you can improve the performance of man-machine interaction by designing an effective **user interface (UI)**, that is, a user interface that ensures fast interaction with humans, which, in turn, means the following:

- The UI must be easy to learn in order to reduce the time that is needed for learning and time wasting before the target users learn to operate it quickly. This constraint is fundamental if UI changes are frequent, and for public websites that need to attract the greatest possible number of users.

- The UI must not cause any kind of slowdown in data insertion; data entry speed must be limited only by the user's ability to type, not by system delays or by additional gestures that could be avoided.

It is worth mentioning that we have UX experts in the market. As a software architect, you must decide when they are essential to the success of the project. The following are a few simple tips when it comes to designing *easy to learn* user interfaces:

- Each input screen must state its purpose clearly.
- Use the language of the user, not the language of developers.
- Avoid complications. Design the UI with the average case in mind; more complicated cases can be handled with extra inputs that appear only when needed. Split complex screens into more input steps.
- Use past inputs to understand user intentions and to put users on the right paths with messages and automatic UI changes; for instance, cascading drop-down menus.
- Error messages are not bad notes the system gives to the user, but they must explain how to insert correct input.

Fast user interfaces result from efficacious solutions to the following three requirements:

- Input fields must be placed in the order they are usually filled, and it should be possible to move to the next input with the *Tab* or *Enter* key. Moreover, fields that often remain empty should be placed at the bottom of the form. Simply put, the usage of the mouse while filling a form should be minimized. This way, the number of user gestures is kept to a minimum. In a web application, once the optimal placement of input fields has been decided, it is enough to use the tabindex attribute to define the right way users move from one input field to the next with the *Tab* key.
- System reactions to user inputs must be as fast as possible. Error messages (or information ones) must appear as soon as the user leaves the input field. The simplest way to achieve this is to move most of the help and input validation logic to the client side so that system reactions do not need to pass through both communication lines and servers.
- Efficacious selection logic. Selecting an existing item should be as easy as possible; for example, selecting one out of some thousands of products in an offer must be possible with a few gestures and with no need to remember the exact product name or its barcode. The next subsection analyzes techniques we can use to decrease complexity to achieve fast selection.

In *Chapter 16, Blazor WebAssembly*, we will discuss how this Microsoft technology can help us with the challenges of building web-based applications with C# code in the front-end.

Designing fast selection logic

When all the possible choices are in the order of magnitude of 1-50, the usual drop-down menu is enough. For instance, this currency selection drop-down menu:

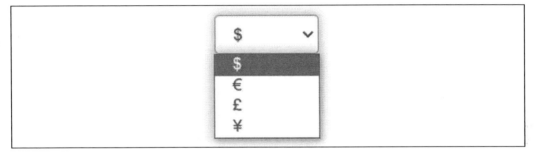

Figure 2.13: Simple drop-down menu

When the order of magnitude is higher but less than a few thousand, an autocomplete that shows the names of all the items that start with the characters typed by the user is usually a good choice:

Figure 2.14: Complex drop-down menu

A similar solution can be implemented with a low computational cost since all the main databases can efficiently select strings that start with a given substring.

When names are quite complex, when searching for the characters that were typed in by the user, they should be extended inside each item string. This operation cannot be performed efficiently with usual databases and requires ad hoc data structures.

Finally, when we are searching inside descriptions composed of several words, more complex search patterns are needed. This is the case, for instance, with product descriptions. If the chosen database supports full-text search, the system can search for the occurrence of several words that have been typed by the user inside all the descriptions efficiently.

However, when descriptions are made up of names instead of common words, it might be difficult for the user to remember a few exact names contained in the target description. This happens, for instance, with multi-country company names. In these cases, we need algorithms that find the best match for the character that was typed by the user. Substrings of the string that was typed by the user must be searched in different places of each description. In general, similar algorithms can't be implemented efficiently with databases based on indexes, but require all the descriptions to be loaded in memory and ranked somehow against the string that was typed by the user.

The most famous algorithm in this class is probably the **Levenshtein** algorithm, which is used by most spell checkers to find a word that best fits the mistyped one by the user. This algorithm minimizes the Levenshtein distance between the description and the string typed by the user, that is, the minimum number of character removals and additions needed to transform one string into another.

The Levenshtein algorithm works great, but has a very high computational cost. Here, we give a faster algorithm that works well for searching character occurrences in descriptions. Characters typed by the user don't need to occur consecutively in the description but must occur in the same order. Some characters may miss. Each description is given a penalty that depends on the missing characters and on how far the occurrences of the characters typed by the user are from the others. More specifically, the algorithm ranks each description with two numbers:

- The number of characters typed by the user that occurs in the description: the more characters contained in the description, the higher its rank.
- Each description is given a penalty equal to the total distance among the occurrences of the characters typed by the user in the description.

The following screenshot shows how the word **Ireland** is ranked against the string **ilad**, which was typed by the user:

Figure 2.15: Sample of Levenshtein usage

The number of occurrences is four (4), while the total distance between character occurrences is three (3).

Once all the descriptions have been rated, they are sorted according to the number of occurrences. Descriptions with the same number of occurrences are sorted according to the lowest penalties. The following is an autocomplete that implements the preceding algorithm:

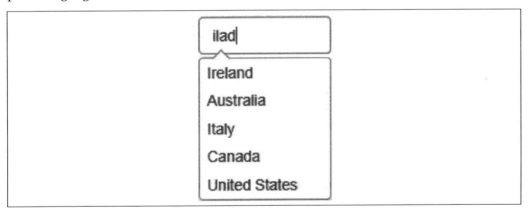

Figure 2.16: Levenshtein algorithm user interface experience

The full class code, along with a test console project, is available in this book's GitHub repository.

Selecting from a huge number of items

Here, *huge* does not refer to the amount of space needed to store the data, but to the difficulty the user has in remembering the features of each item. When an item must be selected from among more than 10,000-100,000 items, there is no hope of finding it by searching for character occurrences inside a description. Here, the user must be driven toward the right item through a hierarchy of categories.

In this case, several user gestures are needed to perform a single selection. In other words, each selection requires interaction with several input fields. Once it's decided that the selection can't be done with a single input field, the simplest option is cascading drop-down menus, that is, a chain of drop-down menus whose selection list depends on the values that were selected in the previous drop-down menus.

For example, if the user needs to select a town located anywhere in the world, we may use the first drop-down menu to select the country, and once the country has been chosen, we may use this choice to populate a second one with all the towns in the selected country. A simple example is as follows:

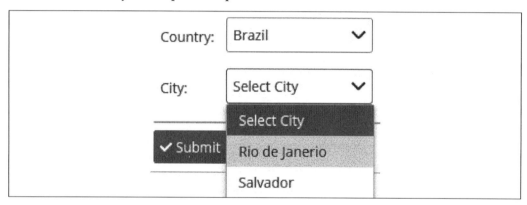

Figure 2.17: Cascading drop-down menu example

Clearly, each drop-down menu can be replaced by an autocomplete when required due to having a high number of options.

If making the right selection can be done by intersecting several different hierarchies, cascading drop-down menus become inefficient too, and we need a filter form, as follows:

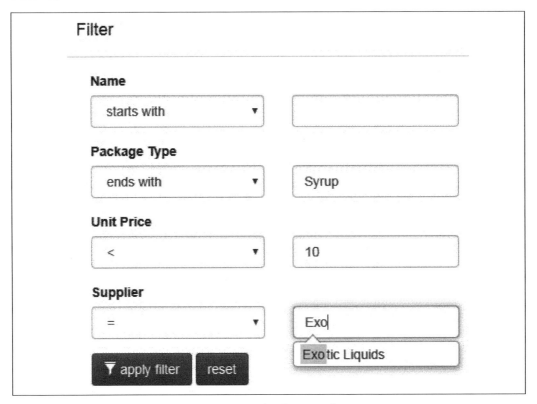

Figure 2.18: Filter form sample

Now, let us understand interoperability with .NET Core.

The fantastic world of interoperability with .NET Core

.NET Core brought Windows developers the ability to deliver their software into various platforms. And you, as a software architect, need to pay attention to this. Linux and macOS are no longer a problem for a C# lover – it is much better than that – they are great opportunities to deliver to new customers. Therefore, we need to ensure performance and multi-platform support, two common non-functional requirements in several systems.

Both console applications and web apps designed with .NET Core in Windows are almost completely compatible with Linux and macOS, too. This means you do not have to build the app again to run it on these platforms. Also, very platform-specific behaviors now have multi-platform support, as shown, for instance, by the `System.IO.Ports.SerialPort` class, which, starting from .NET Core 3.0, is on Linux.

Microsoft offers scripts to help you install .NET Core on Linux and macOS. You can find them at `https://docs.microsoft.com/dotnet/core/tools/dotnet-install-script`. Once you have the SDK installed, you just need to call **dotnet** the same way you do in Windows.

However, you must be aware of some features that are not fully compatible with Linux and macOS systems. For instance, no equivalent to the Windows Registry exists in these OSes and you must develop an alternative yourself. If needed, an encrypted JSON config file can be a good option.

Another important point is that Linux is case-sensitive, while Windows is not. Please, remember this when you work with files. Another important thing is that the Linux path separator is different from the Windows separator. You can use the `Path.PathSeparator` field and all the other `Path` class members to ensure your code is multi-platform.

Besides, you can also adapt your code to the underlying OS by using the runtime checks provided by .NET Core, as follows:

```
using System;
using System.Runtime.InteropServices;

namespace CheckOS
{
    class Program
    {
        static void Main()
        {
            if (RuntimeInformation.IsOSPlatform(OSPlatform.Windows))
                Console.WriteLine("Here you have Windows World!");
            else if(RuntimeInformation.IsOSPlatform(OSPlatform.Linux))
                Console.WriteLine("Here you have Linux World!");
            else if (RuntimeInformation.IsOSPlatform(OSPlatform.OSX))
                Console.WriteLine("Here you have macOS World!");
        }
    }
}
```

Creating a service in Linux

The following script can be used to encapsulate a command-line .NET Core app in Linux. The idea is that this service works like a Windows service. This can be useful, considering that most Linux installations are command-line only and run without a user logged in:

- The first step is to create a file that will run the command-line app. The name of the app is app.dll and it is installed in appfolder. The application will be checked every 5,000 milliseconds. This service was created on a CentOS 7 system. Using a Linux terminal, you can type this:

```
cat >sample.service<<EOF
[Unit]
Description=Your Linux Service
After=network.target
[Service]
ExecStart=/usr/bin/dotnet $(pwd)/appfolder/app.dll 5000
Restart=on-failure
[Install]
WantedBy=multi-user.target
EOF
```

- Once the file has been created, you must copy the service file to a system location. After that, you must reload system and enable the service so that it will restart on reboots:

```
sudo cp sample.service /lib/systemd/system
sudosystemctl daemon-reload
sudosystemctl enable sample
```

- Done! Now, you can start, stop, and check the service using the following commands. The whole input that you need to provide in your command-line app is as follows:

```
# Start the service
sudosystemctl start sample

# View service status
sudosystemctl status sample

# Stop the service
sudosystemctl stop sample
```

Now that we have learned about a few concepts, let us learn how to implement them in our use case.

Achieving security by design

As we have seen up to here in the book, the opportunities and techniques we have for developing software are incredible. If you add all the information you will read about in relation to cloud computing in the next chapters, you will see that the opportunities just increase, as does the complexity to maintain all of this computing environment.

As a software architect, you must understand that these opportunities come with many responsibilities. The world has changed a lot in the last years. The second decade of the 21st century has required lots of technology. Apps, social media, Industry 4.0, Big Data, and artificial intelligence are no longer future objectives, but mainly current projects that you will lead and deal with in your routine.

Considering this scenario, security must have a different approach. The world has moved to regulate companies that manage personal data. For instance, GDPR – the General Data Protection Regulation – is not only mandatory for European territory, since it has changed the way software is developed not only in Europe but all over the globe. There are many initiatives comparable to GDPR that must be enlisted to our belt of techniques and regulations, considering the software you design will be impacted by them.

Security by design must be one of your areas of focus for designing new applications. This subject is huge, and it is not going to be completely covered in this book, but as a software architect, you have to understand the necessity of having a specialist in the information security area in your team to guarantee the policies and the practices needed to avoid cyber attacks and maintain confidentiality, privacy, integrity, authenticity, and availability of the services you architect.

When it comes to protecting your ASP.NET Core application, it is worth mentioning that the framework has many features to help us out with that. For instance, it includes authentication and authorization patterns. In the OWASP Cheat Sheet Series, you'll be able to read about many other .NET practices.

 The Open Web Application Security Project® (OWASP) is a nonprofit foundation that works to improve the security of software. Check out its information at `https://owasp.org/`.

ASP.NET also provides features to help us out with GDPR. Basically, there are APIs and templates to guide you in the implementation of policy declaration and cookie usage consent.

List of practices for achieving a safe architecture

The following list of practices related to security certainly does not cover the entirety of the subject. However, these practices will certainly help you, as a software architect, to explore some solutions related to this topic.

Authentication

Define an authentication method for your web app. There are many authentication options available nowadays, from ASP.NET Core Identity to external provider authentication methods, such as Facebook or Google. As a software architect, you must consider who the target audience of the application is. It would also be worth considering using Azure Active Directory as a starting point if you choose to go down this route.

You may find it useful to design authentication associated with Azure AD, a component for managing the Active Directory of the company you are working for. This alternative is pretty good in some scenarios, especially for internal usage. Azure currently offers Active Directory for usage as **B2B – Business to Business**, or **B2C – Business to Consumer**.

Depending on the scenario of the solution you are building, you will need to implement **MFA – Multi Factor Authentication**. The idea of this pattern is to ask for at least two forms of proof of identity before allowing the solution usage. It is worth mentioning that Azure AD facilitates this for you.

Do not forget that you must determine an authentication method for the APIs you provide. JSON Web Token is a pretty good pattern, and its usage is totally cross-platform.

You must determine the authorization model you will use in your web app. There are four model options:

1. **Simple**, where you just use the [Authorize] attribute in the class or method;
2. **Role-based**, in which you may declare Roles for accessing the Controller you are developing;

3. **Claims-based**, where you can define values that must be received during the authentication to indicate that the user is authorized;

4. **Policy-based**, in which there is a policy established to define the access in that Controller.

You may also define a controller or method in a class as being fully accessible to any user, by defining the attribute [AllowAnonymous]. Be sure this kind of implementation will not cause any vulnerabilities in the system you are designing.

The model you decide to use will define exactly what each user will be able to do in the application.

Sensitive data

While designing, you, as a software architect, will have to decide which part of the data you store is sensitive, and it will need to be protected. By connecting to Azure, your web app will be able to store protected data in components such as Azure Storage and Azure Key Vault. Storage in Azure will be discussed in *Chapter 9, How to Choose Your Data Storage in the Cloud*.

It is worth mentioning that Azure Key Vault is used to protect secrets your app may have. Consider using this solution when you have this kind of requirement.

Web security

It is totally unacceptable to have a production solution deployed without the HTTPS protocol enabled. Azure Web Apps and ASP.NET Core solutions have various possibilities to not only use but enforce the usage of this security protocol.

Thera are many known attacks and malicious patterns, such as cross-site request forgery, Open Redirect, and cross-site scripting. ASP.NET Core guarantees and presents APIs to solve them. You need to detect the ones that are useful for your solution.

Good programming practices, such as avoiding SQL injections by using parameters in your queries, is another important goal to achieve.

 You may find cloud architecture security patterns at https://docs.microsoft.com/en-us/azure/architecture/patterns/category/security.

To finish, it is worth mentioning that security needs to be treated using the onion approach, which means that there are many layers of security to be implemented. You must have a policy determined to guarantee a process to access the data, including physical access to people who use the system you are developing. In addition, you will also have to develop a disaster recovery solution in case the system is attacked. The disaster recovery solution will depend on your cloud solution. We will discuss this later in *Chapter 4, Deciding the Best Cloud-Based Solution.*

Book use case – understanding the main types of .NET Core projects

The development of this book's use case will be based on various kinds of .NET Core Visual Studio projects. This section describes all of them. Let us select **New project** in the Visual Studio **File** menu.

You can filter **.NET Core** project types by typing in the search engine, as follows:

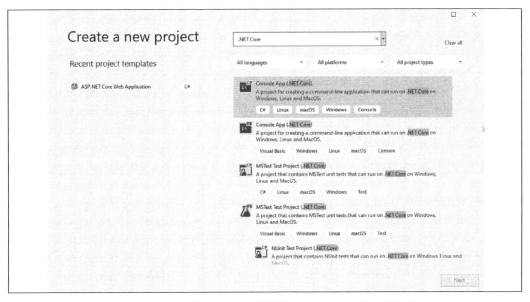

Figure 2.19: Searching types of .NET Core projects in Visual Studio

There, you will find common C# projects (console, a class library, Windows Form, WPF), and various types of test projects, each based on a different test framework: xUnit, NUnit, and MSTest. Choosing among the various testing frameworks is just a matter of preference since all of them offer comparable features. Adding tests to each piece of software that composes a solution is a common practice and allows software to be modified frequently without jeopardizing its reliability.

You may also want to define your class library projects under the **.NET Standard, which will be** discussed in *Chapter 13, Implementing Code Reusability in C# 9*. These class libraries are based on standards that make them compatible with several .NET versions. For instance, libraries based on 2.0 standards are compatible with all .NET Core versions greater than or equal to 2.0, and with all .NET Framework versions greater than 4.6. This compatibility advantage comes at the price of having fewer available features.

Besides filtering **Project Types** to **Cloud**, we have several more project types. Some of them will enable us to define microservices. Microservice-based architectures allow an application to be split into several independent microservices. Several instances of the same microservice can be created and distributed across several machines to fine-tune the performance of each application part. Microservices will be described in:

- *Chapter 5, Applying a Microservice Architecture to Your Enterprise Application*
- *Chapter 6, Azure Service Fabric*
- *Chapter 7, Azure Kubernetes Service*

Finally, testing will be discussed in detail in *Chapter 18, Testing Your Code with Unit Test Cases and TDD*, and *Chapter 22, Automation for Functional Tests*. Finally, we have the ASP.NET Core application we already described in the *Creating a scalable web app with .NET 5* subsection. There, we defined an ASP.NET Core application, but Visual Studio also contains project templates for projects based on RESTful APIs and the most important single-page application frameworks, such as Angular, React, Vue.js, and the Blazor framework based on WebAssembly, which will be discussed in *Chapter 16, Blazor WebAssembly*. Some of them are available with the standard Visual Studio installation, while others require the installation of an SPA package.

Summary

Functional requirements that describe system behavior must be completed with non-functional requirements that constrain system performance, scalability, availability, resilience, interoperability, usability, and security.

Performance requirements come from response time and system load requirements. As a software architect, you should ensure you have the required performance at the minimum cost, building efficient algorithms and taking full advantage of the available hardware resources with multithreading.

Scalability is the ability of a system to be adapted to an increasing load. Systems can be scaled vertically by providing more powerful hardware, or horizontally by replicating and load balancing the same hardware, which increases the availability. The cloud, in general, and Azure can help us implement strategies dynamically, with no need to stop your application.

Tools such as .NET Core that run on several platforms can ensure interoperability, that is, the capability of your software to run on different target machines and with different operating systems (Windows, Linux, macOS, Android, and so on).

Usability is ensured by taking care of the input field's order, the effectiveness of the item selection logic, and how easy your system is to learn.

Besides, the more complex your solution is, the better resilience it should have. The idea of resilience is not to guarantee that the solution does not fail. Instead, the idea is to guarantee that the solution has an action defined when each part of the software fails.

As a software architect, you must consider security from the very beginning of the design. Following the guidelines to determine the correct patterns and having a security specialist in your team would be a great option to achieve all the current regulations we have.

In the next chapter, you will learn how Azure DevOps tools can help us when it comes to collecting, defining, and documenting our requirements.

Questions

1. Which are the two conceptual ways to scale a system?
2. Can you deploy your web app automatically from Visual Studio to Azure?
3. What is multithreading useful for?
4. What are the main advantages of the asynchronous pattern over other multithreading techniques?
5. Why is the order of input fields so important?
6. Why is the .NET Core Path class so important for interoperability?
7. What is the advantage of a .NET standard class library over a .NET Core class library?
8. List the various types of .NET Core Visual Studio projects.

Further reading

The following are some books and links you may consider reading in order to gather more information in relation to this chapter:

- `https://www.packtpub.com/virtualization-and-cloud/hands-azure-developers`
- `https://docs.microsoft.com/en-us/azure/architecture/best-practices/auto-scaling`
- `https://docs.microsoft.com/en-us/aspnet/core/host-and-deploy/azure-apps/`
- `https://docs.microsoft.com/en-us/dotnet/standard/parallel-processing-and-concurrency`
- `https://docs.microsoft.com/en-us/dotnet/standard/parallel-programming/`
- `https://devblogs.microsoft.com/dotnet/performance-improvements-in-net-5/`
- `https://docs.microsoft.com/en-us/dotnet/standard/security/`
- `https://docs.microsoft.com/en-us/aspnet/core/security/`
- `https://owasp.org/`
- `https://cheatsheetseries.owasp.org/cheatsheets/DotNet_Security_Cheat_Sheet.html`
- `https://docs.microsoft.com/en-us/aspnet/core/security/gdpr`
- `https://docs.microsoft.com/en-us/azure/architecture/patterns/category/resiliency`
- `https://docs.microsoft.com/en-us/azure/architecture/patterns/category/availability`

3
Documenting Requirements with Azure DevOps

Azure DevOps is an evolution of Visual Studio Team Services, and it offers a variety of new features that can help developers to document and organize their software. The purpose of this chapter is to present an overview of this tool provided by Microsoft.

The following topics will be covered in this chapter:

- Creating an Azure DevOps project using your Azure account
- Understanding the functionalities offered by Azure DevOps
- Organizing and managing requirements using Azure DevOps
- Presenting use cases in Azure DevOps

The first two sections of this chapter summarize all the functionalities offered by Azure DevOps, while the remaining sections focus specifically on the tools for documenting requirements and supporting the overall development process. Most of the functionality introduced in the first two sections will be analyzed in more detail in other chapters.

Technical requirements

This chapter requires you to create a new free Azure account or use an existing one. The *Creating an Azure account* section of *Chapter 1, Understanding the Importance of Software Architecture*, explains how to create one. The *Azure DevOps repository* subsection also requires Visual Studio 2019 Community Edition (free) or better.

Introducing Azure DevOps

Azure DevOps is a Microsoft **Software-as-a-Service (SaaS)** platform that enables you to deliver continuous value to your customers. By creating an account there, you will be able to easily plan your project, store your code safely, test it, publish the solution to a staging environment, and then publish the solution to the actual production infrastructure.

Of course, Azure DevOps is a complete framework and the ecosystem that it provides for software development is currently available. The automation of all the steps involved in software production ensures the continuous enhancement and improvement of an existing solution in order to adapt it to market needs.

You can start the process moving in your Azure portal. If you don't know how to create an Azure portal account, then please check *Chapter 1, Understanding the Importance of Software Architecture*. The steps to create an Azure DevOps account are quite simple:

1. Select **Create a resource** and then **DevOps Starter**:

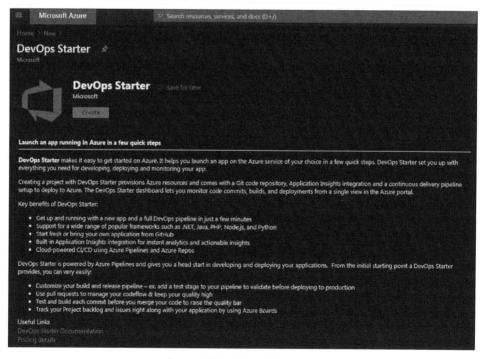

Figure 3.1: DevOps starter page

2. As soon as you start the wizard for creating the project, you can choose from several different platforms how you want to deliver your system. This is one of the greatest advantages of Azure DevOps, as you are not limited to Microsoft tools and products, but can rather choose from all common platforms, tools, and products available on the market:

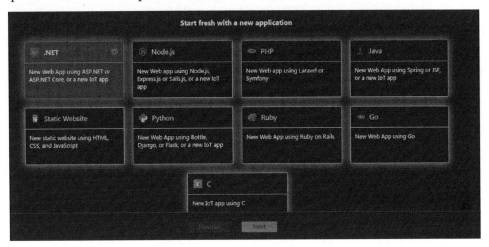

Figure 3.2: DevOps technology selection

3. The options available will depend on the platform chosen in the first step. In some cases, you can choose from several deployment options, as you can see in the following screenshot, which appears if you select the .NET platform:

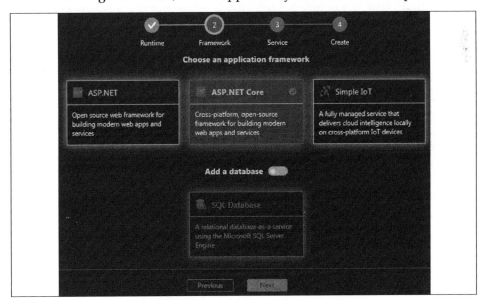

Figure 3.3: DevOps technology selection, more details

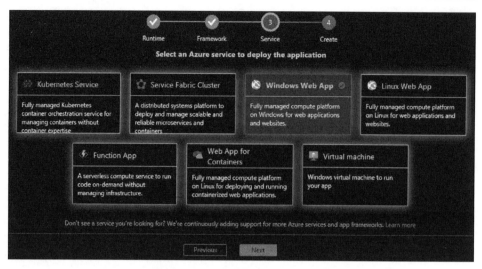

Figure 3.4: DevOps deployment options

4. Once the setup is complete, you will be able to manage the project using the project portal according to the information you provided. It is worth mentioning that this wizard will create an Azure DevOps Service if you do not have one. Moreover, the resource selected for deployment is also automatically created, so for instance if you select **Windows Web App**, a web app will be created, and if you select **Virtual Machine**, a virtual machine will be created. The Azure DevOps organization is where you can organize all of your Azure DevOps projects. The whole process takes less than 20 minutes:

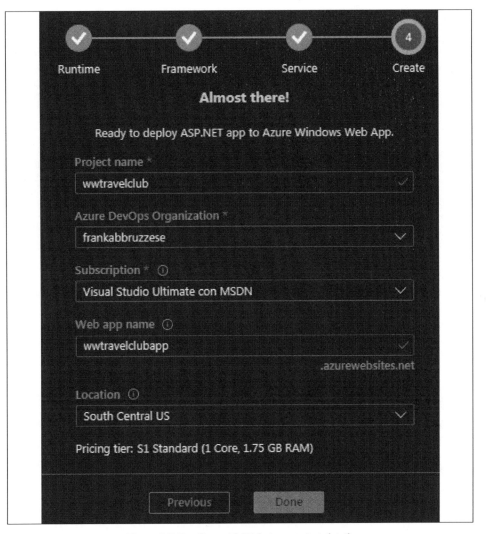

Figure 3.5: DevOps with Web App project details

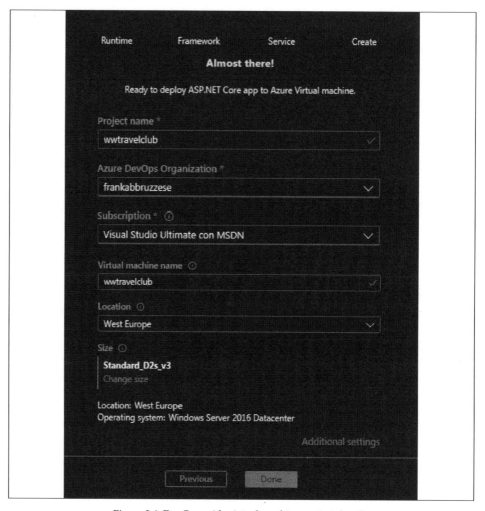

Figure 3.6: DevOps with virtual machine project details

5. After that, you will be able to start planning your project. The following
    screenshot shows the page that appears once the Azure DevOps project
    creation is complete. In the remainder of this book, we will come back to this
    page several times to introduce and describe various useful features that
    ensure a faster and more efficacious deployment:

Figure 3.7: DevOps project page

As you can see from the preceding screenshot, the process for creating an Azure DevOps account and starting to develop the best-in-class DevOps tool is quite simple. It is worth mentioning that you can start using this fantastic tool at no cost, as long as you have no more than five developers on your team, plus any number of stakeholders.

It is worth mentioning that there is no limit on the number of stakeholders because the functionalities available to them are very limited. Essentially, they have read-only privileges on boards and work items, and very limited possibilities to modify them. More specifically, they can add new work items and existing tags to work items, and they can provide feedback. Concerning builds and releases, they can just approve releases (some other limited functionalities are in preview at the time of writing this book).

Organizing your work using Azure DevOps

DevOps will be discussed in detail in *Chapter 20, Understanding DevOps Principles,* but you need to understand it as a philosophy that is focused in delivering value to customers. It is the union of people, process, and products, where **Continuous Integration and Continuous Deployment (CI/CD)** methodology is used to apply continuous improvements to a software application delivered to the production environment. Azure DevOps is a powerful tool whose range of applications encompasses all the steps involved in both the initial development of an application and in its subsequent CI/CD process.

Azure DevOps contains tools for collecting requirements and for organizing the whole development process. They can be accessed by clicking the **Boards** menu on the Azure DevOps page and will be described in more detail in the next two sections:

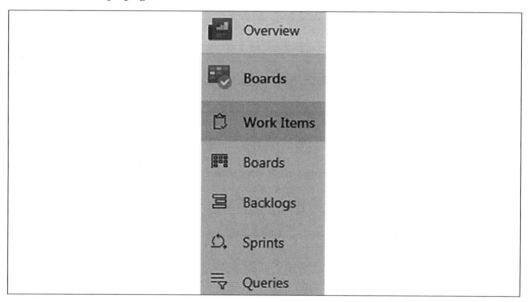

Figure 3.8: Boards menu

All other functionalities available in Azure DevOps are briefly reviewed in the following subsections. They will be discussed in detail in other chapters. More specifically, CI and build/test pipelines are discussed in *Chapter 18, Testing Your Code with Unit Test Cases and TDD,* and *Chapter 21, Challenges of Applying CI Scenarios,* while DevOps principles and release pipelines are discussed in *Chapter 20, Understanding DevOps Principles.*

Azure DevOps repository

The **Repos** menu item gives you access to a default Git repository where you can place your project's code:

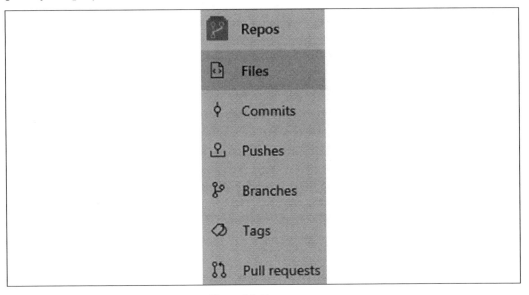

Figure 3.9: Repos menu

Clicking the **Files** item, you enter the default repository initial page. It is empty and contains instructions on how to connect to this default repository.

You can add further repositories through the drop-down menu at the top of the page:

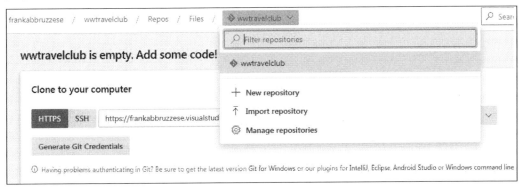

Figure 3.10: Adding a new repository

All created repositories are accessible through the same drop-down menu.

As shown in the preceding screenshot, each repository's initial page contains the repository address and a button to generate repository-specific credentials, so you can connect to your DevOps repositories with your favorite Git tools. However, you can also connect from inside Visual Studio in a very simple way:

1. Start Visual Studio and ensure you are logged in to it with the same Microsoft account used to define your DevOps project (or that was used to add you as a team member).

2. Select the **Team Explorer** tab and then click the connection button:

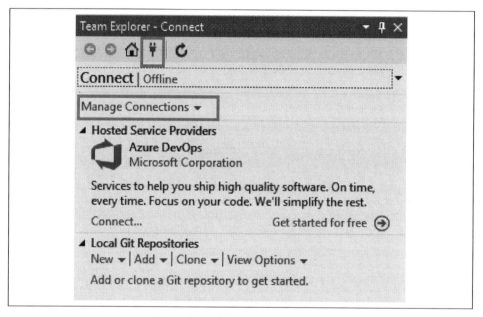

Figure 3.11: Adding a new repository

3. Clicking the **Connect...** link for Azure DevOps, you will be walked through setting up a connection with one of your Azure DevOps projects.

Once connected to your DevOps remote repository, you can use Visual Studio Git tools, and can interact also with other DevOps functionalities from within Visual Studio. At the time of writing this book, the kind of interaction depends on the **New Git user experience** checkbox setting in the Visual Studio options:

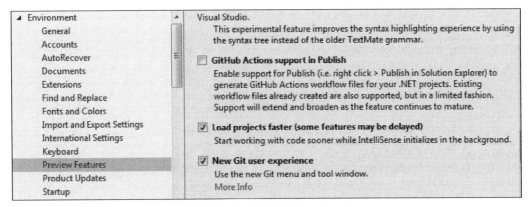

Figure 3.12: New Git user experience checkbox

If it is not checked, you will have the "classic" Visual Studio experience where you use Team Explorer for accessing both Git and other DevOps functionalities:

1. Click the Team Explorer **Home** button. Now, you will see commands for performing Git operations and for interaction with other Azure DevOps areas:

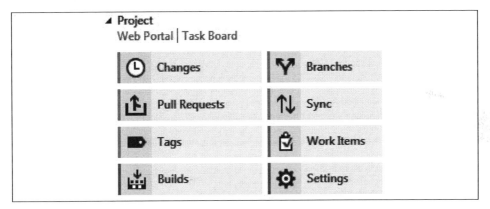

Figure 3.13: Team Explorer options

2. If you are the one designated to initialize the DevOps repository, create a start solution and commit your code by clicking the **Changes** button and then following the subsequent instructions.

3. Click the **Sync** button to synchronize your local repository with the remote Azure DevOps repository.

4. Once all team members have initialized both their local machine repositories and the Azure DevOps repository with the preceding steps, you can now open Visual Studio. The solution created in your local repository will appear in the bottom area of the **Team Explorer** window.

5. Click the window to open the solution on your local machine. Then, synchronize with the remote repository to ensure the code you are modifying is up to date.

If, instead, the **New Git user experience** checkbox is checked, the **Team Explorer** window has commands just for non-Git DevOps operations and an **Open Git Changes** link for opening a new window dedicated to Git operations:

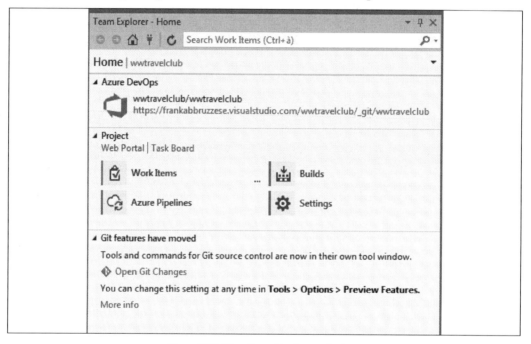

Figure 3.14: New Team Explorer window

As soon as you go to this window, you are asked to clone or create a new repository. In both cases, you will be prompted to provide the address of the remote DevOps repository. Once you have created a local repository connected to the remote DevOps repository, you can start using the new Git window that offers more options than the ones offered by the classic Team Explorer window, and, in general, a more complete user experience:

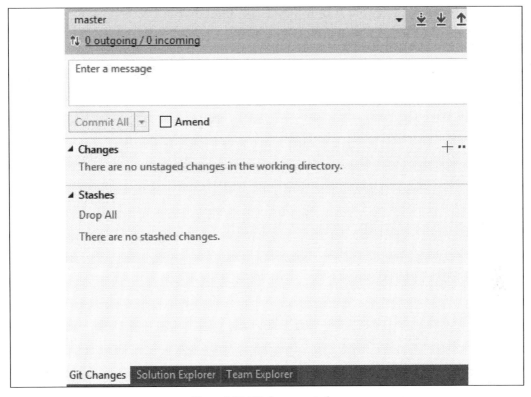

Figure 3.15: Git changes window

When you have changes to commit, you can insert a message in the textbox at the top of the window and commit them locally by clicking the **Commit All** button, or you can click the dropdown next to this button to access more options:

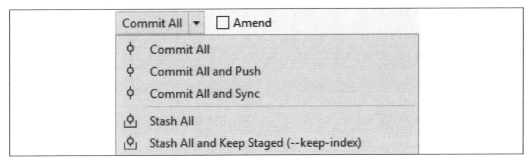

Figure 3.16: Commit options

You can commit and push or commit and sync, but you can also stage your changes. The three arrows in the top right of the Git Changes window trigger a fetch, pull, and push, respectively. Meanwhile, the dropdown at the top of the window takes care of operations on branches:

Figure 3.17: Branches operations

Package feeds

The **Artifacts** menu handles the software packages used or created by the project. There, you can define feeds for basically all types of packages including NuGet, Node.js, and Python. Private feeds are needed since commercial projects use also private packages, so you need a place to put them. Moreover, packages produced during builds are placed in these feeds, so other modules having them as dependencies can immediately use them.

Once in the **Artifacts** area, you can create several feeds by clicking the **+ Create Feed** button, where each feed can handle several kinds of packages, as shown in *Figure 3.18*:

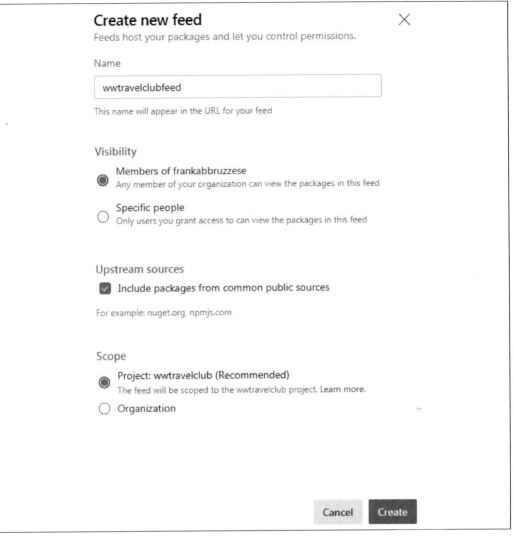

Figure 3.18: Feed creation

If you select the option to connect to packages from public sources, by default, the feed connects to npmjs, nuget.org, and pypi.org. However, you can go to the upstream sources tab in the **Feed** settings page and remove/add package sources. The settings page can be reached by clicking the settings icon in the upper-right corner of the feed page. A screenshot of the page of the newly created feed follows:

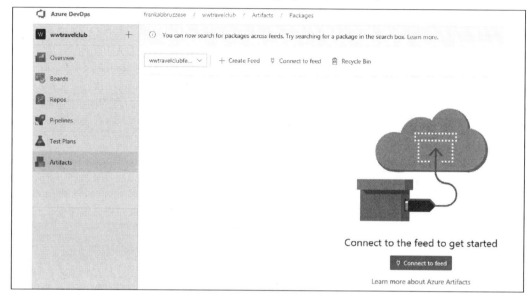

Figure 3.19: Feed page

The **Connect to feed** button for each feed shows a window that explains, for each package type, how to connect to the feed. In particular, for NuGet packages you should add all project feeds to your Visual Studio projects'/solutions' nuget.config file so that local machines can also use them, otherwise, your local build would fail:

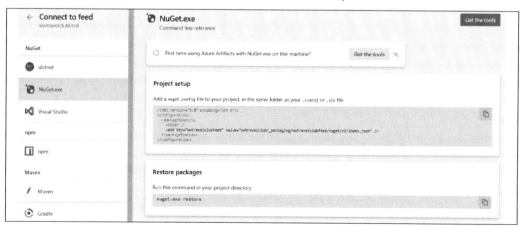

Figure 3.20: Feed connection information

Test plans

The **Test Plans** section allows you to define the test plans you want to use and their settings. Tests are discussed in detail in *Chapter 18, Testing Your Code with Unit Test Cases and TDD*, and *Chapter 22, Automation for Functional Tests*, but here we would like to summarize the opportunities offered by Azure DevOps. Test-related operations and settings can be accessed through the **Test Plans** menu item:

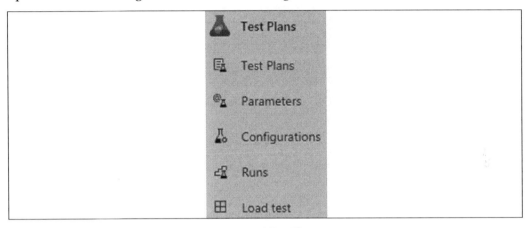

Figure 3.21: Feed Test Plans menu

Here, you may define, execute, and track test plans made up of the following:

- Manual acceptance tests
- Automatic unit tests
- Load tests

Automatic unit tests must be defined in test projects contained in the Visual Studio solution and based on a framework such as NUnit, xUnit, and MSTest (Visual Studio has project templates for all of them). Test Plans gives you the opportunity to execute these tests on Azure and to define the following:

- A number of configuration settings
- When to execute them
- How to track them and where to report their results in the overall project documentation

For manual tests, you may define complete instructions for the operator in the project documentation, covering the environment in which to execute them (for example, an operating system), and where to report their results. You can also define how to execute load tests and how to measure results.

Pipelines

Pipelines are automatic action plans that specify all steps from the code build until the software deployment is in production. They can be defined in the **Pipelines** area, which is accessible through the **Pipelines** menu item:

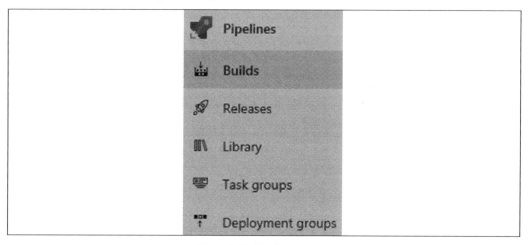

Figure 3.22: Pipelines menu

There, you can define a complete pipeline of tasks to be executed alongside their triggering events, which encompass steps such as code building, launching test plans, and what to do after the tests are passed.

Typically, after the tests are passed, the application is automatically deployed in a staging area where it can be beta-tested. You can also define the criteria for automatic deployment to production. Such criteria include, but are not limited to, the following:

- The number of days the application was beta-tested
- The number of bugs found during beta-testing and/or removed by the last code change
- Manual approval by one or more managers/team members

The criteria decision will depend on the way the company wants to manage the product that is being developed. You, as a software architect, have to understand that when it comes to moving code to production, the safer, the better.

Managing system requirements in Azure DevOps

Azure DevOps enables you to document system requirements using work items. Work items are stored in your project as chunks of information that can be assigned to a person. They are classified into various types and may contain a measure of the development effort required, a status, and the development stage (iteration) they belong to.

DevOps is usually combined with agile methodologies, so Azure DevOps uses iterations, and the whole development process is organized as a set of sprints. The work items available depends on the *Work Item Process* you select while creating the Azure DevOps project. The following subsections contain a description of the most common work item types that appears when an **Agile** or **Scrum** *Work Item Process* is selected (the default is **Agile**).

Epic work items

Imagine you are developing a system made of various subsystems. You are probably not going to conclude the whole system in a single iteration. Therefore, we need an umbrella spanning several iterations to encapsulate all features of each subsystem. Each Epic work item represents one of these umbrellas that can contain several features to be implemented in various development iterations.

In the Epic work item, you can define the state and acceptance criteria as well as the start date and target date. Besides this, you can also provide a priority and an effort estimate. All of this detailed information helps the stakeholders to follow the development process. This is really useful as a macro view of the project.

Feature work items

All of the information that you provide in an Epic work item can also be placed in a Feature work item. So, the difference between these two types of work items is not related to the kind of information they contain, but to their roles and the goals that your team will reach to conclude them. Epics may span several iterations and are hierarchically above Features, that is, each Epic work item is linked to several children Features, while each Feature work item is usually implemented in a few sprints and is part of a single Epic work item.

It is worth mentioning that all work items have sections for team discussions. There, you will be able to find a team member in the discussion area by typing the @ character (like in many forums/social media applications). Inside each work item, you can link and attach various information. You may also check the history of the current work item in a specific section.

Feature work items are the places to start recording user requirements. For instance, you can write a Feature work item called **Access Control** to define the complete functionally needed to implement the system access control.

Product Backlog items/User Story work items

Which of these work items is available depends on the selected *Working Item Process*. There are minor differences between them, but their purpose is substantially the same. They contain detailed requirements for the Features, described by the Features work items they are connected to. More specifically, each Product Backlog/ User Story work item specifies the requirements of a single functionality that is a part of the behavior described in its father Features work item. For instance, in a Features work item for system access control, the maintenance of the users and the login interface should be two different User Stories/Product Backlog items. These requirements will guide the creation of other children work items:

- **Tasks**: These are important work items that describe the job that needs to be done to meet the requirements stated in the father Product Backlog items/ User Story work item. Task work items can contain time estimates that help team capacity management and overall scheduling.

- **Test cases**: These items describe how to test the functionality described by the requirements.

The number of tasks and test cases you will create for each Product Backlog/User Story work item will vary according to the development and testing scenario you use.

Use case – presenting use cases in Azure DevOps

This section clarifies the concepts outlined in the previous section with the practical example of WWTravelClub. Considering the scenario described in *Chapter 1, Understanding the Importance of Software Architecture*, we decided to define three Epic work items, as follows:

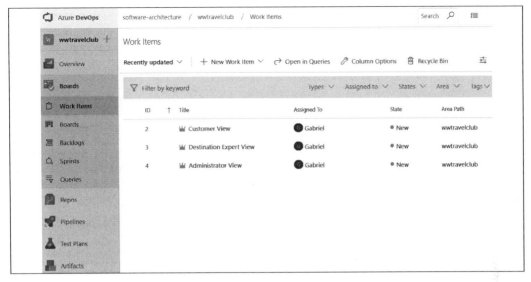

Figure 3.23: User case Epics

The creation of these work items is quite simple:

1. Inside each work item, we link the different types of work items, as you can see in *Figure 3.24*.

2. It is really important to know that the connections between work items are really useful during software development. Hence, as a software architect, you have to provide this knowledge to your team and, more than that, you have to incentivize them to make these connections:

Figure 3.24: Defining a link

3. As soon as you create a Feature work item, you will be able to connect it to several Product Backlog work items that detail its specifications. The following screenshot shows the details of a Product Backlog work item:

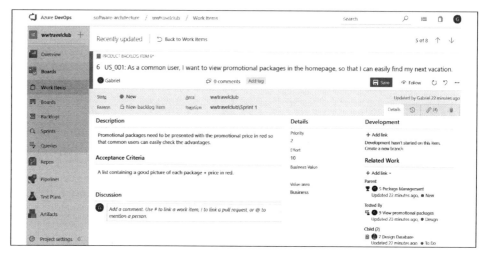

Figure 3.25: Product Backlog work item

4. After that, Task and Test Case work items can be created for each Product Backlog work item. The user interface provided by Azure DevOps is really efficacious because it enables you to track the chain of functionalities and the relationships between them:

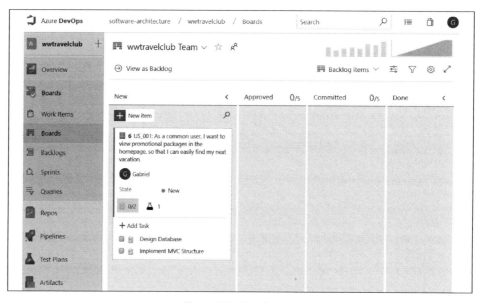

Figure 3.26: Board view

5. As soon as you complete the input for the Product Backlog and Tasks work items, you will be able to plan the project sprints together with your team. The plan view enables you to drag and drop Product Backlog work items to each planned sprint:

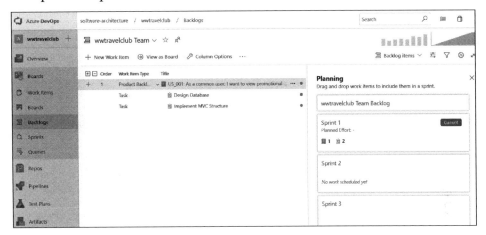

Figure 3.27: Backlog view

By clicking a specific sprint on the right, you will see just the work items assigned to that sprint. Each sprint page is quite similar to the backlog page, but contains more tabs:

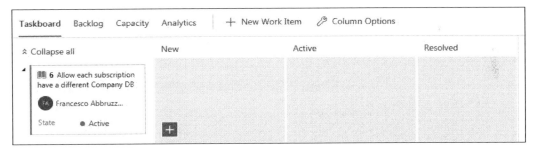

Figure 3.28: User case Epics

Also useful is the sprints menu on the left that enables each user to jump immediately to the current sprints of all projects they are engaged in.

This is how these work items are created. Once you understand this mechanism, you will be able to create and plan any software project. It is worth mentioning that the tool itself will not solve problems related to team management. However, the tool is a great way to incentivize the team to update the project status, so you can maintain a clear perspective of how the project is evolving.

Summary

This chapter covered how you can create an Azure DevOps account for a software development project, and how to start managing your projects with Azure DevOps. It also gave a short review of all Azure DevOps functionalities, explaining how to access them through the Azure DevOps main menu. This chapter described in more detail how to manage system requirements and how to organize the necessary work with various kinds of work items, along with how to plan and organize sprints that will deliver epic solutions with many features.

The next chapter discusses the different models of software architecture. We will also learn about the fundamental hints and criteria for choosing from among the options offered by a sophisticated cloud platform such as Azure while developing the infrastructure of your solution.

Questions

1. Is Azure DevOps available only for .NET projects?
2. What kind of test plans are available in Azure DevOps?
3. Can DevOps projects use private NuGet packages?
4. Why do we use work items?
5. What is the difference between Epics and Features work items?
6. What kind of relationship exists between Tasks and Product Backlog items/ User Story work items?

Further reading

Here are some books and links you may consider reading with a view to gathering more information about this chapter:

- https://go.microsoft.com/fwlink/?LinkID=825688
- https://www.packtpub.com/virtualization-and-cloud/hands-devops-azure-video
- https://www.packtpub.com/application-development/mastering-non-functional-requirements

4

Deciding the Best Cloud-Based Solution

When designing your application to make it cloud-based, you must understand different architectural designs – from the simplest to the most sophisticated. This chapter discusses different software architecture models and teaches you how to take advantage of the opportunities offered by the cloud in your solutions. This chapter will also discuss the different types of cloud service that we can consider while developing our infrastructure, what the ideal scenarios are, and where we can use each of them.

The following topics will be covered in this chapter:

- Infrastructure as a Service solutions
- Platform as a Service solutions
- Software as a Service solutions
- Serverless solutions
- How to use hybrid solutions and why they are so useful

It is worth mentioning that the choice to be made between these options depends on different aspects of the project scenario. This will be also discussed in the chapter.

Technical requirements

For the practical content in this chapter, you must create or use an Azure account. We explained the account creation process in *Chapter 1, Understanding the Importance of Software Architecture*, in the *Creating an Azure account* section.

Different software deployment models

Cloud solutions can be deployed with different models. The way you decide to deploy your applications depends on the kind of team you work with. In companies where you have infrastructure engineers, you will probably find more people working with **Infrastructure as a Service (IaaS)**. On the other hand, in companies where IT is not the core business, you will find a bunch of **Software as a Service (SaaS)** systems. It is common for developers to decide to use the **Platform as a Service (PaaS)** option, or to go serverless, as they have no need to deliver infrastructures in this scenario.

As a software architect, you must cope with this environment and be sure that you are optimizing the cost and work factors, not only during the initial development of the solution but also during its maintenance. Also, as an architect, you must understand the needs of your system and work hard to connect those needs to best-in-class peripheral solutions to speed up delivery and keep the solution as close as possible to the customer's specifications.

IaaS and Azure opportunities

Infrastructure as a Service was the first generation of cloud services provided by many different cloud players. Its definition is easily found in many places, but we can summarize it as "your computing infrastructure delivered on the Internet". In the same way that we have virtualization of services in a local data center, IaaS will also give you virtualized components, such as servers, storage, and firewalls, in the cloud.

In Azure, several services are provided with an IaaS model. Most of them are paid for and you should pay attention to this when it comes to testing. It is worth mentioning that this book does not set out to describe all IaaS services that Azure provides in detail. However, as a software architect, you just need to understand that you will find services such as the following:

- **Virtual machines**: Windows Server, Linux, Oracle, Data Science, and Machine Learning
- **Network**: Virtual networks, load balancers, and DNS zones
- **Storage**: Files, tables, databases, and Redis

To create any service in Azure, you must find the service that best fits your needs and then create a resource. The following screenshot shows a Windows Server virtual machine being configured.

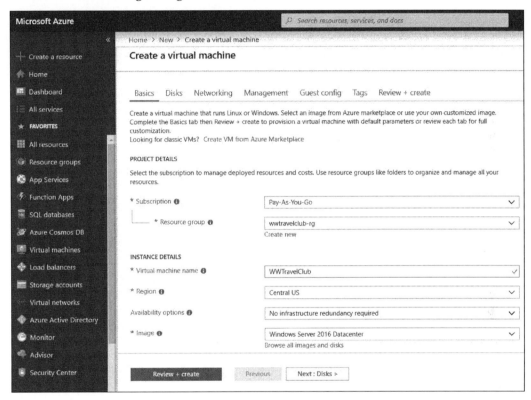

Figure 4.1: Creating a virtual machine in Azure

Following the wizard provided by Azure to set up your virtual machine, you will be able to connect to it by using **Remote Desktop Protocol** (**RDP**). The next screenshot presents some of the hardware options you have for deploying a virtual machine. It is curious to think about it, considering the different capacities we have available just by clicking on the **Select** button.

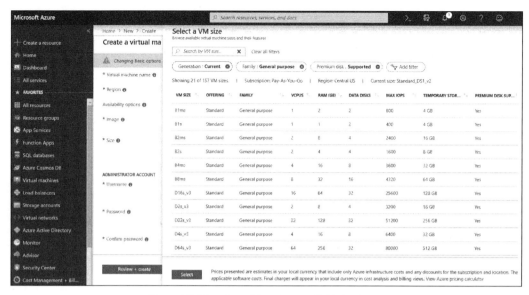

Figure 4.2: Virtual machine sizes available in Azure

If you compare the on-premises velocity to deliver hardware with the cloud velocity, you will realize that there is nothing better than the cloud when it comes to time-to-market. For instance, the **D64s_v3** machine presented at the bottom of the screenshot with 64 CPUs, 256 GB of RAM, and temporary storage of 512 GB is something you probably will not find in an on-premises data center. Besides, in some use cases, this machine will just be used for some hours during the month, so it would be impossible to justify its purchase in an on-premises scenario. That is the reason why cloud computing is so amazing!

Security responsibility in IaaS

Security responsibility is another important thing to know about an IaaS platform. Many people think that once you decide to go on the cloud, all the security is done by the provider. However, this is not true, as you can see in the following screenshot:

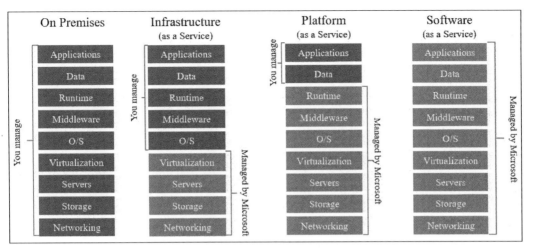

Figure 4.3: Managing security in cloud computing

IaaS will force you to take care of security from the operating system to the application. In some cases, this is inevitable, but you must understand that this will increase your system cost.

IaaS can be a good option if you just want to move an already existing on-premises structure to the cloud. This enables scalability, due to the tools that Azure gives you along with all the other services. However, if you are planning to develop an application from scratch, you should also consider other options available on Azure.

Let us look at one of the fastest systems in the next section, that is, PaaS.

PaaS – a world of opportunities for developers

If you are studying or have studied software architectures, you will probably perfectly understand the meaning of the next sentence: The world demands high speed when it comes to software development! If you agree with this, you will love PaaS.

As you can see in the preceding screenshot, PaaS allows you to worry about security only in terms of aspects that are closer to your business: your data and applications. For developers, this represents freedom from having to implement a bunch of configurations that make your solution work safely.

Security handling is not the only advantage of PaaS. As a software architect, you can introduce these services as an opportunity to deliver richer solutions faster. Time-to-market can surely justify the cost of many applications that run on a PaaS basis.

There are lots of services delivered as PaaS nowadays in Azure and, again, it is not the purpose of this book to list all of them. However, some do need to be mentioned. The list keeps growing and the recommendation here is: use and test these services as much as you can! Make sure that you will deliver better-designed solutions with this thought in mind.

On the other hand, it is worth mentioning that, with PaaS solutions, you will not have full control of the operating system. In fact, in many situations, you do not even have a way to connect to it. This is good most of the time, but in some debugging situations, you may miss this feature. The good thing is that PaaS components are evolving every single day and one of the biggest concerns from Microsoft is making them widely visible.

The following sections present the most common PaaS components delivered by Microsoft for .NET web apps, such as Azure Web Apps and Azure SQL Server. We also describe Azure Cognitive Services, a very powerful PaaS platform that demonstrates how wonderful development is in the PaaS world. We will explore some of them in greater depth in the remainder of this book.

Web apps

A Web App is a PaaS option you can use to deploy your web app. You can deploy different types of application, such as .NET, .NET Core, Java, PHP, Node.js, and Python. A sample of this was presented in *Chapter 1, Understanding the Importance of Software Architecture*.

The good thing is that creating a web app does not require any structure and/or IIS web server setup. In some cases, where you are using Linux to host your .NET application, you do not have IIS at all.

Moreover, web apps have a plan option where you do not need to pay for usage. Of course, there are limitations, such as only running 32-bit apps and failing to enable scalability, but this can be a wonderful scenario for prototyping.

SQL Databases

Imagine how fast you can deploy a solution if you have the complete power of an SQL server without needing to pay for a big server to deploy this database. This applies to SQL databases. With them, you can use Microsoft SQL Server to perform what you need the most – storage and data processing. In this scenario, Azure assumes responsibility for backing up the database.

The SQL database even gives you the option to manage performance by itself. This is called automatic tuning. Again, with PaaS components, you will be able to focus on what is important to your business: a very fast time-to-market.

The steps for creating a SQL database are quite simple, like what we've seen before for other components. However, there are two things you need to pay attention to: the creation of the server itself and how you will be charged.

When you **Create a resource**, you can search for SQL Database and you will find this wizard to help you:

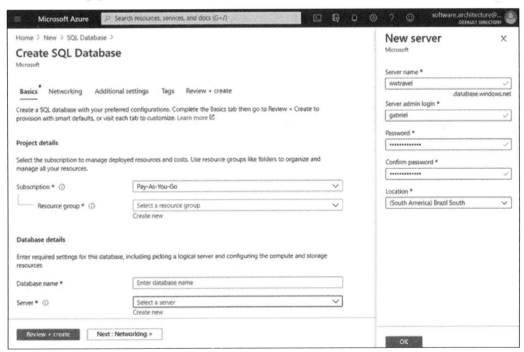

Figure 4.4: Creating a SQL database in Azure

The SQL database depends on a SQL server to host it. For this reason, as you can see, you must create (at least for the first database) a `database.windows.net` server, where your databases will be hosted. This server will provide all the parameters you need to access the SQL server database using current tools, such as Visual Studio, SQL Server Management Studio, and Azure Data Studio. It is worth mentioning that you have a bunch of features regarding security, such as Transparent Data Encryption and IP firewalls.

As soon as you decide on the name of your database server, you will be able to choose the pricing tier on which your system will be charged. Especially in SQL databases, there are several different pricing options, as you can see in the following screenshot. You should study each of them carefully because, depending on your scenario, you may save money by optimizing a pricing tier:

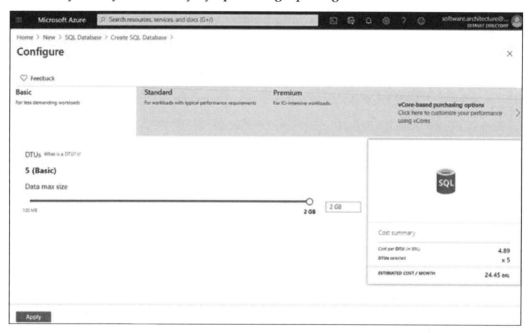

Figure 4.5: Configuring the Azure SQL Database pricing tier

For more information about SQL configuration, you can use this link: `https://azure.microsoft.com/en-us/services/sql-database/`.

Once you have the configuration done, you will be able to connect to this server database in the same way you do when your SQL server is installed on-premises. The only detail that you must pay attention to is the configuration of the Azure SQL Server firewall, but this is quite simple to set up and a good demonstration of how safe the PaaS service is.

Azure Cognitive Services

Artificial Intelligence (AI) is one of the most frequently discussed topics in software architecture. We are a step away from a really great world where AI will be everywhere. To make this come true, as a software architect you cannot think about AI as software you need to reinvent from scratch all the time.

Azure Cognitive Services can help you with this. In this set of APIs, you will find various ways to develop vision, knowledge, speech, search, and language solutions. Some of them need to be trained to make things happen, but these services provide APIs for that too.

The great thing about PaaS is evident from this scenario. The number of jobs you will have to perform to prepare your application in an on-premises or IaaS environment is enormous. In PaaS, you just do not need to worry about this. You are totally focused on what really matters to you as a software architect: the solution to your business problem.

Setting up Azure Cognitive Services in your Azure account is also quite simple. First, you will need to add Cognitive Services like any other Azure component, as you can see in the following screenshot:

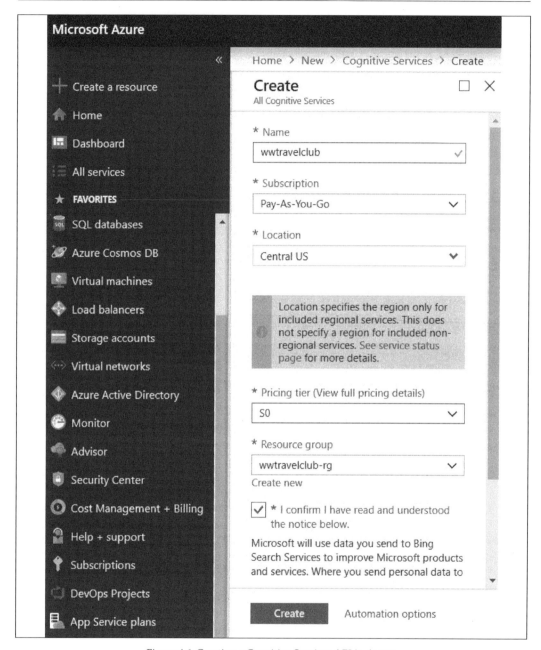

Figure 4.6: Creating a Cognitive Services API in Azure

As soon as you have done this, you will be able to use the APIs provided by the server. You will find two important features in the service that you have created: endpoints and access keys. They are going to be used in your code to access APIs.

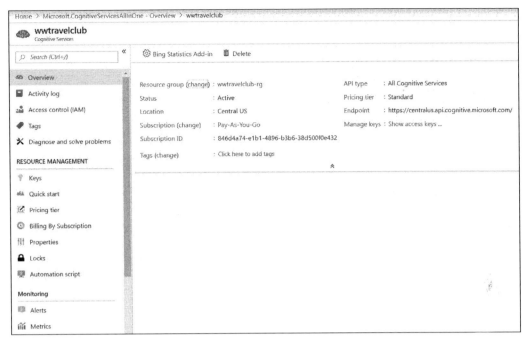

Figure 4.7: Cognitive Services endpoint created

The following code sample shows how you can use Cognitive Services to translate sentences. The main concept underlying this translation service is that you can post the sentence you want to translate, according to the key and region where the service was set. The following code enables you to post a request to the service API:

```
private static async Task<string> PostAPI(string api, string key,
string region, string textToTranslate)
{
    using var client = new HttpClient();
    using var request = new HttpRequestMessage(HttpMethod.Post, api);
    request.Headers.Add("Ocp-Apim-Subscription-Key", key);
    request.Headers.Add("Ocp-Apim-Subscription-Region", region);
    client.Timeout = TimeSpan.FromSeconds(5);

    var body = new[] { new { Text = textToTranslate } };
    var requestBody = JsonConvert.SerializeObject(body);
    request.Content = new StringContent(requestBody, Encoding.UTF8,
"application/json");
    var response = await client.SendAsync(request);
        response.EnsureSuccessStatusCode();
```

```
        return await response.Content.ReadAsStringAsync();
}
```

It is worth mentioning that the preceding code will allow you to post requests to translate any text into any language provided you define it in the parameters. The following is the main program that calls the previous method:

```
static async Task Main()
{

    var host = "https://api.cognitive.microsofttranslator.com";
    var route = "/translate?api-version=3.0&to=es";
    var subscriptionKey = "[YOUR KEY HERE]";
    var region = "[YOUR REGION HERE]";

    var translatedSentence = await PostAPI(host + route,
    subscriptionKey,region, "Hello World!");

    Console.WriteLine(translatedSentence);

}
```

 For further information, visit https://docs.microsoft.com/
en-us/azure/cognitive-services/translator/reference/
v3-0-languages.

This is a perfect example of how easily and quickly you can use services such as this to architect your projects. Also, this kind of approach to development is wonderful, since you are using a piece of code already tested and used by other solutions.

SaaS – just sign in and get started!

SaaS is probably the easiest way to use cloud-based services. Cloud players provide many good options that solve common problems in a company for their end users.

A good example of this type of service is Office 365. The key point with these platforms is that you do not need to worry about application maintenance. This is particularly convenient in scenarios where your team is totally focused on developing the core business of the application. For example, if your solution needs to deliver good reports, maybe you can design them using Power BI (which is included in Office 365).

Another pretty good example of a SaaS platform is Azure DevOps. As a software architect, before Azure DevOps, you needed to install and configure **Team Foundation Server (TFS)** (or even older tools like Microsoft Visual SourceSafe) to have your team work with a common repository and an application life cycle management tool.

We used to spend a lot of time just working either on preparing the server for TFS installation or on upgrading and continuously maintaining the TFS already installed. This is no longer needed due to the simplicity of SaaS Azure DevOps.

Understanding what serverless means

A serverless solution is a solution where the focus is not on where the code runs. Even in a "serverless" solution, there is always a server. The thing is that you just do not know or care which one your code executes on.

You may now be thinking that serverless is just another option – of course, this is true, as this architecture does not deliver a complete solution. But the key point here is that, in a serverless solution, you have a very fast, simple, and agile application life cycle since almost all serverless code is stateless and loosely coupled with the remainder of the system. Some authors refer to this as **Function as a Service (FaaS)**.

Of course, the server runs somewhere. The key point here is that you do not need to worry about this or even scalability. This will enable you to focus completely on your app business logic. Again, the world needs fast development and good customer experiences at the same time. The more you focus on customer needs, the better!

In *Chapter 10*, *Working with Azure Functions*, you will explore one of the best serverless implementations that Microsoft provides in Azure – Azure Functions. There, we will focus on how you can develop serverless solutions and learn about their advantages and disadvantages.

Why are hybrid applications so useful in many cases?

Hybrid solutions are solutions whose parts do not share a uniform architectural choice; each part makes a different architectural choice. In the cloud, the word hybrid refers mainly to solutions that mix cloud subsystems with on-premises subsystems. However, it can refer also to mixing web subsystems with device-specific subsystems, such as mobiles or any other device that runs code.

Due to the number of services Azure can provide and the number of design architectures that can be implemented, hybrid applications are probably the best answer to the main question addressed in this chapter, that is, how to use the opportunities offered by the cloud in your projects. Nowadays, many current projects are moving from an on-premises solution to a cloud architecture and, depending on where you are going to deliver these projects, you will still find many bad preconceptions regarding moving to the cloud. Most of them are related to cost, security, and service availability.

You need to understand that there is some truth in these preconceptions, but not in the way people think. For sure, you as a software architect cannot ignore them. Especially when you develop a critical system, you must decide whether everything can go on the cloud or whether it is better to deliver part of the system on the edge.

 The edge computing paradigm is an approach used to have part of the system deployed on machines or devices closer to the location they are needed. This helps with reducing response times and the amount of bandwidth spent.

Mobile solutions can be considered a classic example of hybrid applications, since they mix a web-based architecture with a device-based architecture to offer a better user experience. There are lots of scenarios where you can replace a mobile application with a responsive website. However, when it comes to interface quality and performance, maybe a responsive web site will not give the end user what they really need.

In the next section, we will discuss the practical example of the book use case.

Book use case – which is the best cloud solution?

If you go back to *Chapter 1, Understanding the Importance of Software Architecture*, you will find a system requirement that describes the system environments where our WWTravelClub example application is supposed to run.

 SR_003: The system shall run on Windows, Linux, iOS, and Android platforms.

At first sight, any developer would respond by saying: web apps. However, the iOS and Android platforms will also need your attention as a software architect. In this scenario, as in several situations, user experience is the key to the success of the project. The decision needs to be driven not only by development speed but again by the benefits gained by delivering a great user experience.

Another decision that the software architect must make in this project is related to the technology for the mobile application if they decide to develop one. Again, this is going to be a choice between hybrid and native apps since, in this case, a cross-platform solution such as Xamarin can be used. So, with mobile applications, you also have the option to keep writing the code in C#.

The following screenshot represents our first choice for the WWTravelClub architecture. The decision to rely on Azure components is related to cost and maintenance considerations. Each of the following items will be discussed later on in this book, in *Chapter 8, Interacting with Data in C# – Entity Framework Core, Chapter 9, How to Choose Your Data Storage in the Cloud*, and *Chapter 10, Working with Azure Functions*, together with the reasons for the choice. For now, it is enough to know that WWTravelClub is a hybrid application, running Xamarin Apps on mobiles and an ASP.NET Core web app on the server side.

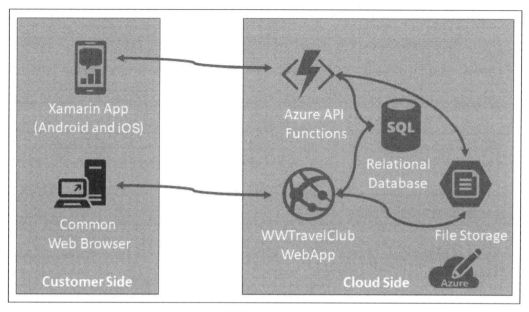

Figure 4.8: WWTravelClub architecture

As you can verify in the picture, the WWTravelClub architecture was designed mainly with PaaS and serverless components provided by Azure. All the development will be conducted on the Azure DevOps SaaS Microsoft platform.

In the imaginary scenario we have with WWTravelClub, the sponsors have indicated that no one in the WWTravelClub team specializes in infrastructure. Therefore, the software architecture uses PaaS services. Considering this scenario and the required development speed, these components will surely perform well.

While we fly through the chapters and technologies discussed in this book, this architecture will change and evolve without being constrained by any earlier choices. This is a great opportunity offered by Azure and by modern architecture design. You can easily change components and structures as your solution evolves.

Summary

In this chapter, you learned how to take advantage of the services offered by the cloud in your solutions, and the various options you can choose from.

This chapter covered different ways to deliver the same application in a cloud-based structure. We also noted how rapidly Microsoft is delivering all of these options to its customers, because you can experience all of these options in actual applications and choose the one that best fits your needs since there is no *silver bullet* that works in all situations. As a software architect, you need to analyze your environment and your team, and then decide on the best cloud architecture to implement in your solution.

The next chapter is dedicated to how to build a flexible architecture made up of small scalable software modules called microservices.

Questions

1. Why should you use IaaS in your solution?
2. Why should you use PaaS in your solution?
3. Why should you use SaaS in your solution?
4. Why should you use serverless in your solution?
5. What is the advantage of using an Azure SQL Server database?
6. How can you accelerate AI in your application with Azure?
7. How can hybrid architectures help you to design a better solution?

Further reading

You can check out these web links to decide which topics covered in this chapter you should study in greater depth:

- https://visualstudio.microsoft.com/xamarin/
- https://www.packtpub.com/application-development/xamarin-cross-platform-application-development
- https://www.packtpub.com/virtualization-and-cloud/learning-azure-functions
- https://azure.microsoft.com/overview/what-is-iaas/
- https://docs.microsoft.com/en-us/azure/security/azure-security-iaas
- https://azure.microsoft.com/services/app-service/web/

- https://azure.microsoft.com/services/sql-database/
- https://azure.microsoft.com/en-us/services/virtual-machines/data-science-virtual-machines/
- https://docs.microsoft.com/azure/sql-database/sql-database-automatic-tuning
- https://azure.microsoft.com/en-us/services/cognitive-services/
- https://docs.microsoft.com/en-us/azure/architecture/
- https://powerbi.microsoft.com/
- https://office.com
- https://azure.microsoft.com/en-us/overview/what-is-serverless-computing/
- https://azure.microsoft.com/en-us/pricing/details/sql-database/
- https://www.packtpub.com/virtualization-and-cloud/professional-azure-sql-database-administration

5

Applying a Microservice Architecture to Your Enterprise Application

This chapter is dedicated to describing highly scalable architectures based on small modules called microservices. The microservices architecture allows for fine-grained scaling operations where every single module can be scaled as required without it affecting the remainder of the system. Moreover, they allow for better **Continuous Integration/Continuous Deployment (CI/CD)** by permitting every system subpart to evolve and be deployed independently of the others.

In this chapter, we will cover the following topics:

- What are microservices?
- When do microservices help?
- How does .NET deal with microservices?
- Which tools are needed to manage microservices?

By the end of this chapter, you will have learned how to implement a single microservice in .NET. *Chapter 6, Azure Service Fabric*, and *Chapter 7, Azure Kubernetes Service*, also explain how to deploy, debug, and manage a whole microservices-based application.

Technical requirements

In this chapter, you will require the following:

- Visual Studio 2019 free Community edition or better with all the database tools installed.

- A free Azure account. The *Creating an Azure account* section in *Chapter 1, Understanding the Importance of Software Architecture*, explains how to create one.

- Docker Desktop for Windows if you want to debug Docker containerized microservices in Visual Studio (`https://www.docker.com/products/docker-desktop`).

What are microservices?

Microservice architectures allow each module that makes up a solution to be scaled independently from the others to achieve the maximum throughput with minimal cost. In fact, scaling whole systems instead of their current bottlenecks inevitably results in a remarkable waste of resources, so fine-grained control of subsystem scaling has a considerable impact on the system's overall cost.

However, microservices are more than scalable components – they are software building blocks that can be developed, maintained, and deployed independently of each other. Splitting development and maintenance among modules that can be independently developed, maintained, and deployed improves the overall system's CI/CD cycle (the CI/CD concept was explained in more detail in the *Organizing your work using Azure DevOps* section in *Chapter 3, Documenting Requirements with Azure DevOps*).

The CI/CD improvement is due to microservice *independence* because it enables the following:

- Scaling and distributing microservices on different types of hardware.

- Since each microservice is deployed independently from the others, there can't be binary compatibility or database structure compatibility constraints. Therefore, there is no need to align the versions of the different microservices that compose the system. This means that each of them can evolve, as needed, without being constrained by the others.

- Assigning their development to completely separate smaller teams, thus simplifying job organization and reducing all the inevitable coordination inefficiencies that arise when handling large teams.

- Implementing each microservice with more adequate technologies and in a more adequate environment, since each microservice is an independent deployment unit. This means choosing tools that best fit your requirements and an environment that minimizes development efforts and/or maximizes performance.

- Since each microservice can be implemented with different technologies, programming languages, tools, and operating systems, enterprises can use all available human resources by matching environments with developers' competencies. For instance, underused Java developers can also be involved in .NET projects if they implement microservices in Java with the same required behavior.

- Legacy subsystems can be embedded in independent microservices, thus enabling them to cooperate with newer subsystems. This way, companies may reduce the time to market of new system versions. Moreover, this way, legacy systems can evolve slowly toward more modern systems with an acceptable impact on costs and the organization.

The next subsection explains how the concept of microservices was conceived. Then, we will continue this introductory section by exploring basic microservice design principles and analyzing why microservices are often designed as Docker containers.

Microservices and the evolution of the concept of modules

For a better understanding of the advantages of microservices, as well as their design techniques, we must keep the two-folded nature of software modularity, and of software modules, in mind:

- Code modularity refers to code organization that makes it easy for us to modify a chunk of code without affecting the remainder of the application. It is usually enforced with object-oriented design, where modules can be identified with classes.

- **Deployment modularity** depends on what your deployment units are and which properties they have. The simplest deployment units are executable files and libraries. Thus, for instance, **dynamic link libraries (DLLs)** are, for sure, more modular than static libraries since they must not be linked with the main executable before being deployed.

While the fundamental concepts of code modularity have reached stasis, the concept of deployment modularity is still evolving and microservices are currently state of the art along this evolution path.

As a short review of the main milestones on the path that led to microservices, we can say that, first, monolithic executables were broken into static libraries. Later on, DLLs replaced static libraries.

A great change took place when .NET (and other analogous frameworks, such as Java) improved the modularity of executables and libraries. In fact, with .NET, they can be deployed on different hardware and on different operating systems since they are deployed in an intermediary language that's compiled when the library is executed for the first time. Moreover, they overcome some versioning issues of previous DLLs since any executable brings with it a DLL with a version that differs from the version of the same DLL that is installed in the operating system.

However, .NET can't accept two referenced DLLs – let's say, *A* and *B* – using two different versions of a common dependency – let's say, *C*. For instance, suppose there is a newer version of *A* with a lot of new features we would like to use that, in turn, rely on a newer version of *C* that's not supported by *B*. In this situation, we should renounce the newer version of *A* because of the incompatibility of *C* with *B*. This difficulty has led to two important changes:

- The development world moved from DLLs and/or single files to package management systems such as NuGet and npm, which automatically check version compatibility with the help of semantic versioning.

- **Service-Oriented Architecture (SOA)**. Deployment units started being implemented as SOAP and then as REST web services. This solves the version compatibility problem since each web service runs in a different process and can use the most adequate version of each library with no risk of causing incompatibilities with other web services. Moreover, the interface that's exposed by each web service is platform-agnostic, that is, web services can connect with applications using any framework and run on any operating system since web service protocols are based on universally accepted standards. SOAs and protocols will be discussed in more detail in *Chapter 14, Applying Service-Oriented Architectures with .NET Core*.

Microservices are an evolution of SOA and add more features and more constraints that improve the scalability and the modularity of services to improve the overall CI/CD cycle. It's sometimes said that *microservices are SOA done well*.

Microservices design principles

To sums things up, the microservice architecture is an SOA that maximizes independence and fine-grained scaling. Now that we've clarified all the advantages of microservice independence and fine-grained scaling, as well as the very nature of independence, we are in a position to look at microservice design principles.

Let's start with principles that arise from the independence constraint. We will discuss them each in a separate subsection.

The independence of design choices

The design of each microservice must not depend on the design choices that were made in the implementation of other microservices. This principle enables the full independence of each microservice CI/CD cycle and leaves us with more technological choices on how to implement each microservice. This way, we can choose the best available technology to implement each microservice.

Another consequence of this principle is that different microservices can't connect to the same shared storage (database or filesystem) since sharing the same storage also means sharing all the design choices that determined the structure of the storage subsystem (database table design, database engine, and so on). Thus, either a microservice has its own data storage or it has no storage at all and communicates with other microservices that take care of handling storage.

Here, having dedicated data storage doesn't mean that the physical database is distributed within the process boundary of the microservice itself, but that the microservice has exclusive access to a database or set of database tables that are handled by an external database engine. In fact, for performance reasons, database engines must run on dedicated hardware and with OS and hardware features that are optimized for their storage functionalities.

Usually, *independence of design choices* is interpreted in a lighter form by distinguishing between logical and physical microservices. More specifically, a logical microservice is implemented with several physical microservices that use the same data storage but that are load-balanced independently. That is, the logical microservice is designed as a logical unit and then split into more physical microservices to achieve better load balance.

Independence from the deployment environment

Microservices are scaled out on different hardware nodes and different microservices can be hosted on the same node. Therefore, the less a microservice relies on the services offered by the operating system and on other installed software, the more available hardware nodes it can be deployed on. More node optimization can also be performed.

This is the reason why microservices are usually containerized and use Docker. Containers will be discussed in more detail in the *Containers and Docker* subsection of this chapter, but basically, containerization is a technique that allows each microservice to bring its dependencies with it so that it can run anywhere.

Loose coupling

Each microservice must be loosely coupled with all the other microservices. This principle has a two-fold nature. On the one hand, this means that, according to object-oriented programming principles, the interface that's exposed by each microservice must not be too specific, but as general as possible. However, it also means that communications among microservices must be minimized in order to reduce communication costs since microservices don't share the same address space and run on different hardware nodes.

No chained requests/responses

When a request reaches a microservice, it must not cause a recursive chain of nested requests/responses to other microservices since a similar chain would result in an unacceptable response time. Chained requests/responses can be avoided if the private data models of all the microservices synchronize with push notifications each time they change. In other words, as soon as the data that's handled by a microservice changes, those changes are sent to all the microservices that may need them to serve their requests. This way, each microservice has all the data it needs to serve all its incoming requests in its private data storage, with no need to ask other microservices for the data that it lacks.

In conclusion, every microservice must contain all the data it needs to serve incoming requests and ensure fast responses. To keep their data models up to date and ready for incoming requests, microservices must communicate their data changes as soon as they take place. These data changes should be communicated through asynchronous messages since synchronous nested messages cause unacceptable performance because they block all the threads involved in the call tree until a result is returned.

It is worth pointing out that the *Independence of design choices* principle is substantially the bounded context principle of domain-driven design, which we will talk about in detail in *Chapter 12, Understanding the Different Domains in Software Solutions*. In this chapter, we will see that, often, a full domain-driven design approach is useful for the *update* subsystem of each microservice.

 It's not trivial that, in general, all systems that have been developed according to the bounded context principle are better implemented with a microservice architecture. In fact, once a system has been decomposed into several completely independent and loosely coupled parts, it is very likely that these different parts will need to be scaled independently because of different traffic and different resource requirements.

At the preceding constraints, we must also add some best practices for building a reusable SOA. More details on these best practices will be given in *Chapter 14, Applying Service-Oriented Architectures with .NET Core*, but nowadays, most SOA best practices are automatically enforced by tools and frameworks that are used to implement web services.

Fine-grained scaling requires that microservices are small enough to isolate well-defined functionalities, but this also requires a complex infrastructure that takes care of automatically instantiating microservices, allocating instances on various hardware computational resources, commonly called **nodes**, and scaling them as needed. These kinds of structures will be introduced in the *Which tools are needed to manage microservices?* section of this chapter, and discussed in detail in *Chapter 6, Azure Service Fabric*, and *Chapter 7, Azure Kubernetes Service*.

Moreover, fine-grained scaling of distributed microservices that communicate through asynchronous communication requires each microservice to be resilient. In fact, communication that's directed to a specific microservice instance may fail due to a hardware fault or for the simple reason that the target instance was killed or moved to another node during a load balancing operation.

Temporary failures can be overcome with exponential retries. This is where we retry the same operation after each failure with a delay that increases exponentially until a maximum number of attempts is reached. For instance, first, we would retry after 10 milliseconds, and if this retry operation results in a failure, a new attempt is made after 20 milliseconds, then after 40 milliseconds, and so on.

On the other hand, long-term failures often cause an explosion of retry operations that may saturate all system resources in a way that is similar to a denial-of-service attack. Therefore, usually, exponential retries are used together with a *circuit break strategy*: after a given number of failures, a long-term failure is assumed and access to the resource is prevented for a given time by returning an immediate failure without attempting the communication operation.

It is also fundamental that the congestion of some subsystems, due to either failure or to a requests peak, does not propagate to other system parts, in order to prevent overall system congestion. **Bulkhead isolation** avoids congestion propagation in the following ways:

- Only a maximum number of similar simultaneous outbound requests are allowed; let's say, 10. This is similar to putting an upper bound on thread creation.
- Requests exceeding the previous bound are queued.
- If the maximum queue length is reached, any further requests result in exceptions being thrown to abort them.

Retry policies may make it so that the same message is received and processed several times because the sender has received no confirmation that the message has been received or simply because it has timed-out the operation, while the receiver actually received the message. The only possible solution to this problem is designing all messages so that they're idempotent, that is, designing messages in such a way that processing the same message several times has the same effect as processing it once.

Updating a database table field to a value, for instance, is an idempotent operation since repeating it once or twice has exactly the same effect. However, incrementing a decimal field is not an idempotent operation. Microservice designers should make an effort to design the overall application with as many idempotent messages as possible. The remaining non-idempotent messages must be transformed into idempotent ones in the following way, or with some other similar techniques:

- Attach both a time and some identifier that uniquely identify each message.
- Store all the messages that have been received in a dictionary that's been indexed by the unique identifier attached to the message mentioned in the previous point.
- Reject old messages.
- When a message that may be a duplicate is received, verify whether it's contained in the dictionary. If it is, then it has already been processed, so reject it.
- Since old messages are rejected, they can be periodically removed from the dictionary to avoid it growing exponentially.

We will use this technique in the example at the end of *Chapter 6, Azure Service Fabric*.

It is worth pointing out that some message brokers, such as Azure Service Bus, offer facilities for implementing the technique described previously. Azure Service Bus is discussed in the *.NET communication facilities* subsection.

In the next subsection, we will talk about microservice containerization based on Docker.

Containers and Docker

We've already discussed the advantages of having microservices that don't depend on the environment where they run: better hardware usage, the ability to mix legacy software with newer modules, the ability to mix several development stacks in order to use the best stack for each module implementation, and so on. Independence from the hosting environment can be easily achieved by deploying each microservice with all its dependencies on a private virtual machine.

However, starting a virtual machine with its private copy of the operating system takes a lot of time, and microservices must be started and stopped quickly to reduce load balancing and fault recovery costs. In fact, new microservices may be started either to replace faulty ones or because they were moved from one hardware node to another to perform load balancing. Moreover, adding a whole copy of the operating system to each microservice instance would be an excessive overhead.

Luckily, microservices can rely on a lighter form of technology: containers. Containers are a kind of light virtual machine. They do not virtualize a full machine – they just virtualize the OS filesystem level that sits on top of the OS kernel. They use the OS of the hosting machine (kernel, DLLs, and drivers) and rely on the OS's native features to isolate processes and resources to ensure an isolated environment for the images they run.

As a consequence, containers are tied to a specific operating system, but they don't suffer the overhead of copying and starting a whole OS in each container instance.

On each host machine, containers are handled by a runtime that takes care of creating them from *images* and creating an isolated environment for each of them. The most famous container runtime is Docker, which is a *de facto* standard for containerization.

Images are files that specify what is put in each container and which container resources, such as communication ports, to expose outside the container. Images need not to explicitly specify their full content, but they can be layered. This way, images are built by adding new software and configuration information on top of existing images.

For instance, if you want to deploy a .NET application as a Docker image, it is enough to just add your software and files to your Docker image and then reference an already existing .NET Docker image.

To allow for easy image referencing, images are grouped into registries that may be either public or private. They are similar to NuGet or npm registries. Docker offers a public registry (`https://hub.docker.com/_/registry`) where you can find most of the public images you may need to reference in your own images. However, each company can define private registries. For instance, Azure offers Microsoft Container Registry, where you can define your private container registry service: `https://azure.microsoft.com/en-us/services/container-registry/`. There, you can also find most of the .NET related images you might need to reference in your code.

Before instantiating each container, the Docker runtime must solve all the recursive references. This cumbersome job is not performed each time a new container is created since the Docker runtime has a cache where it stores the fully assembled images that correspond to each input image and that it's already processed.

Since each application is usually composed of several modules to be run in different containers, Docker also allows .yml files, also known as composition files, that specify the following information:

- Which images to deploy.

- How the internal resources that are exposed by each image must be mapped to the physical resources of the host machine. For instance, how communication ports that are exposed by Docker images must be mapped to the ports of the physical machine.

We will analyze Docker images and .yml files in the *How does .NET deal with microservices?* section of this chapter.

The Docker runtime handles images and containers on a single machine but, usually, containerized microservices are deployed and load-balanced on clusters that are composed of several machines. Clusters are handled by pieces of software called **orchestrators**. Orchestrators will be introduced in the *Which tools are needed to manage microservices?* section of this chapter, and described in detail in *Chapter 6, Azure Service Fabric*, and *Chapter 7, Azure Kubernetes Service*.

Now that we have understood what microservices are, what problems they can solve, and their basic design principles, we are ready to analyze when and how to use them in our system architecture. The next section analyzes when we should use them.

When do microservices help?

The answer to this question requires us to understand the roles microservices play in modern software architectures. We will look at this in the following two subsections:

- Layered architectures and microservices
- When is it worth considering microservice architectures?

Let's start with a detailed look at layered architectures and microservices.

Layered architectures and microservices

Enterprise systems are usually organized in logical independent layers. The first layer is the one that interacts with the user and is called the presentation layer, while the last layer takes care of storing/retrieving data and is called the data layer. Requests originate in the presentation layer and pass through all the layers until they reach the data layer, and then come back, traversing all the layers in reverse until they reach the presentation layer, which takes care of presenting the results to the user/client. Layers can't be *jumped*.

Each layer takes data from the previous layer, processes it, and passes it to the next layer. Then, it receives the results from its next layer and sends them back to its previous layer. Also, thrown exceptions can't jump layers – each layer must take care of intercepting all the exceptions and either *solving them* somehow or transforming them into other exceptions that are expressed in the language of its previous layer. The layer architecture ensures the complete independence of the functionalities of each layer from the functionalities of all the other layers.

For instance, we can change the database engine without affecting all the layers that are above the data layer. In the same way, we can completely change the user interface, that is, the presentation layer, without affecting the remainder of the system.

Moreover, each layer implements a different kind of system specification. The data layer takes care of what the system *must remember*, the presentation layer takes care of the system-user interaction protocol, and all the layers that are in the middle implement the domain rules, which specify how data must be processed (for instance, how an employee paycheck must be computed). Typically, the data and presentation layers are separated by just one domain rule layer, called the business or application layer.

Each layer *speaks* a different language: the data layer *speaks* the language of the chosen storage engine, the business layer speaks the language of domain experts, and the presentation layer speaks the language of users. So, when data and exceptions pass from one layer to another, they must be translated into the language of the destination layer.

A detailed example of how to build a layered architecture will be given in the *Use case – understanding the domains of the use case* section in *Chapter 12, Understanding the Different Domains in Software Solutions*, which is dedicated to domain-driven design.

That being said, how do microservices fit into a layered architecture? Are they adequate for the functionalities of all the layers or just some layers? Can a single microservice span several layers?

The last question is the easiest to answer: yes! In fact, we've already stated that microservices should store the data they need within their logical boundaries. Therefore, there are microservices that span the business and data layers. Some others take care of encapsulating shared data and remain confined in the data layer. Thus, we may have business layer microservices, data layer microservices, and microservices that span both layers. So, what about the presentation layer?

The presentation layer

The presentation layer can also fit into a microservice architecture if it is implemented on the server side. Single-page applications and mobile applications run the presentation layer on the client machine, so they either connect directly to the business microservices layer or, more often, to an *API gateway* that exposes the public interface and takes care of routing requests to the right microservices.

In a microservices architecture, when the presentation layer is a website, it can be implemented with a set of microservices. However, if it requires heavy web servers and/or heavy frameworks, containerizing them may not be convenient. This decision must also consider the loss of performance that happens when containerizing the web server and the possible need for hardware firewalls between the web server and the remainder of the system.

ASP.NET is a lightweight framework that runs on the light Kestrel web server, so it can be containerized efficiently and used in a microservice for intranet applications. However, public high-traffic websites require dedicated hardware/ software components that prevent them from being deployed together with other microservices. In fact, while Kestrel is an acceptable solution for an intranet website, public websites need a more complete web server such as IIS, Apache, or NGINX. In this case, security and load balancing requirements are more compelling and require dedicated hardware/software nodes and components. Accordingly, architectures based on microservices usually offer specialized components that take care of interfacing with the outside world. For instance, in *Chapter 7, Azure Kubernetes Service*, we will see that in **Kubernetes** clusters, this role is played by the so-called **ingresses**.

Monolithic websites can be easily broken into load-balanced smaller subsites without microservice-specific technologies, but a microservice architecture can bring all the advantages of microservices into the construction of a single HTML page. More specifically, different microservices may take care of different areas of each HTML page. Unfortunately, at the time of writing, a similar scenario is not easy to implement with the available .NET technology.

A proof of concept that implements a website with ASP.NET-based microservices that cooperate in the construction of each HTML page can be found here: `https://github.com/Particular/Workshop/tree/master/demos/asp-net-core`. The main limit of this approach is that microservices cooperate just to generate the data that's needed to generate the HTML page and not to generate the actual HTML page. Instead, this is handled by a monolithic gateway. In fact, at the time of writing, frameworks such as ASP.NET MVC don't provide any facilities for the distribution of HTML generation. We will return to this example in *Chapter 15, Presenting ASP.NET Core MVC*.

Now that we've clarified which parts of a system can benefit from the adoption of microservices, we are ready to state the rules when it comes to deciding how they're adopted.

When is it worth considering microservice architectures?

Microservices can improve the implementation of both the business and data layer, but their adoption has some costs:

- Allocating instances to nodes and scaling them has a cost in terms of cloud fees or internal infrastructures and licenses.

- Splitting a unique process into smaller communicating processes increases communication costs and hardware needs, especially if the microservices are containerized.

- Designing and testing software for a microservice requires more time and increases engineering costs, both in time and complexity. In particular, making microservices resilient and ensuring that they adequately handle all possible failures, as well as verifying these features with integration tests, can increase the development time by more than one order of magnitude.

So, when are microservices worth the cost of using them? Are there functionalities that must be implemented as microservices?

A rough answer to the second question is: yes, when the application is big enough in terms of traffic and/or software complexity. In fact, as an application grows in complexity and its traffic increases, it's recommended that we pay the costs connected to scaling it since this allows for more scaling optimization and better handling when it comes to the development team. The costs we pay for these would soon exceed the cost of microservice adoption.

Thus, if fine-grained scaling makes sense for our application, and if we are able to estimate the savings that fine-grained scaling and development give us, we can easily compute an overall application throughput limit that makes the adoption of microservices convenient.

Microservice costs can also be justified by the increase in the market value of our products/services. Since the microservice architecture allows us to implement each microservice with a technology that has been optimized for its use, the quality that's added to our software may justify all or part of the microservice costs.

However, scaling and technology optimizations are not the only parameters to consider. Sometimes, we are forced to adopt a microservice architecture without being able to perform a detailed cost analysis.

If the size of the team that takes care of the CI/CD of the overall system grows too much, the organization and coordination of this big team cause difficulties and inefficiencies. In this type of situation, it is desirable to move to an architecture that breaks the whole CI/CD cycle into independent parts that can be taken care of by smaller teams.

Moreover, since these development costs are only justified by a high volume of requests, we probably have high traffic being processed by independent modules that have been developed by different teams. Therefore, scaling optimizations and the need to reduce interaction between development teams make the adoption of a microservice architecture very convenient.

From this, we may conclude that, if the system and the development team grows too much, it is necessary to split the development team into smaller teams, each working on an efficient bounded context subsystem. It is very likely that, in a similar situation, a microservices architecture is the only possible option.

Another situation that forces the adoption of a microservice architecture is the integration of newer subparts with legacy subsystems based on different technologies since containerized microservices are the only way to implement an efficient interaction between the legacy system and the new subparts in order to gradually replace the legacy subparts with newer ones. Similarly, if our team is composed of developers with experience in different development stacks, an architecture based on containerized microservices may become a *must*.

In the next section, we will analyze building blocks and tools that are available so that we can implement .NET-based microservices.

How does .NET deal with microservices?

.NET was conceived as a multi-platform framework that was light and fast enough to implement efficient microservices. In particular, ASP.NET is the ideal tool for implementing text-REST and binary gRPC APIs to communicate with a microservice, since it can run efficiently with light web servers such as Kestrel and is itself light and modular.

The whole .NET framework evolved with microservices as a strategic deployment platform in mind and has facilities and packages for building efficient and light HTTP and gRPC communication to ensure service resiliency and to handle long-running tasks. The following subsections describe some of the different tools or solutions that we can use to implement a .NET-based microservice architecture.

.NET communication facilities

Microservices need two kinds of communication channels.

- The first is a communication channel to receive external requests, either directly or through an API gateway. HTTP is the usual protocol for external communication due to available web service standards and tools. .NET's main HTTP/gRPC communication facility is ASP.NET since it's a lightweight HTTP/gRPC framework, which makes it ideal for implementing Web APIs in small microservices. We will describe ASP.NET apps in detail in *Chapter 14, Applying Service-Oriented Architectures with .NET Core*, which is dedicated to HTTP and gRPC services. .NET also offers an efficient and modular HTTP client solution that is able to pool and reuse heavy connection objects. Also, the HttpClient class will be described in more detail in *Chapter 14, Applying Service-Oriented Architectures with .NET Core*.

- The second is a different type of communication channel to push updates to other microservices. In fact, we have already mentioned that intra-microservice communication cannot be triggered by an on-going request since a complex tree of blocking calls to other microservices would increase request latency to an unacceptable level. As a consequence, updates must not be requested immediately before they're used and should be pushed whenever state changes take place. Ideally, this kind of communication should be asynchronous to achieve acceptable performance. In fact, synchronous calls would block the sender while they are waiting for the result, thus increasing the idle time of each microservice. However, synchronous communication that just puts the request in a processing queue and then returns confirmation of the successful communication instead of the final result is acceptable if communication is fast enough (low communication latency and high bandwidth). A publisher/subscriber communication would be preferable since, in this case, the sender and receiver don't need to know each other, thus increasing the microservices' independence. In fact, all the receivers that are interested in a certain type of communication merely need to register to receive a specific *event*, while senders just need to publish those events. All the wiring is performed by a service that takes care of queuing events and dispatching them to all the subscribers. The publisher/subscriber pattern will be described in more detail in *Chapter 11, Design Patterns and .NET 5 Implementation*, along with other useful patterns.

While .NET doesn't directly offer tools that may help in asynchronous communication or client/server tools that implement publisher/subscriber communication, Azure offers a similar service with *Azure Service Bus*. Azure Service Bus handles both queued asynchronous communication through Azure Service Bus *queues* and publisher/subscriber communication through Azure Service Bus *topics*.

Once you've configured Azure Service Bus on the Azure portal, you can connect to it in order to send messages/events and to receive messages/events through a client contained in the `Microsoft.Azure.ServiceBus` NuGet package.

Azure Service Bus has two types of communication: queue-based and topic-based. In queue-based communication, each message that's placed in the queue by a sender is removed from the queue by the first receiver that pulls it from the queue. Topic-based communication, on the other hand, is an implementation of the publisher/subscriber pattern. Each topic has several subscriptions and a different copy of each message sent to a topic can be pulled from each topic subscription.

The design flow is as follows:

1. Define an Azure Service Bus private namespace.
2. Get the root connection strings that were created by the Azure portal and/or define new connection strings with fewer privileges.
3. Define queues and/or topics where the sender will send their messages in binary format.
4. For each topic, define names for all the required subscriptions.
5. In the case of queue-based communication, the sender sends messages to a queue and the receivers pull messages from the same queue. Each message is delivered to one receiver. That is, once a receiver gains access to the queue, it reads and removes one or more messages.
6. In the case of topic-based communication, each sender sends messages to a topic, while each receiver pulls messages from the private subscription associated with that topic.

There are also other commercial alternatives to Azure Service Bus, such as NServiceBus, MassTransit, Brighter, and ActiveMQ. There is also a free open source option: RabbitMQ. RabbitMQ can be installed locally, on a virtual machine, or in a Docker container. Then, you can connect with it through the client contained in the `RabbitMQ.Client` NuGet package.

The functionalities of RabbitMQ are similar to the ones offered by Azure Service Bus but you have to take care of all the implementation details, confirmations of performed operations, and so on, while Azure Service Bus takes care of all the low-level operations and offers you a simpler interface. Azure Service Bus and RabbitMQ will be described alongside publisher/subscriber-based communication in *Chapter 11, Design Patterns and .NET 5 Implementation*.

If microservices are published to Azure Service Fabric, which will be described in the next chapter (*Chapter 6, Azure Service Fabric*), we can use built-in reliable binary communication.

Communication is resilient since communication primitives automatically use a retry policy. This communication is synchronous, but this is not a big limitation since microservices in Azure Service Fabric have built-in queues; thus, once the receiver has received a message, they can just put it in a queue and return it immediately, without blocking the sender.

The messages in the queue are then processed by a separate thread. The main limitation of this built-in communication is that it is not based on the publisher/subscriber pattern; the senders and receivers must know each other. When this is not acceptable, you should use Azure Service Bus. We will learn how to use Service Fabric's built-in communication in *Chapter 6, Azure Service Fabric*.

Resilient task execution

Resilient communication and, in general, resilient task execution can be implemented easily with the help of a .NET library called Polly, whose project is a member of the .NET Foundation. Polly is available through the Polly NuGet package.

In Polly, you define policies, and then execute tasks in the context of those policies, as follows:

```
var myPolicy = Policy
  .Handle<HttpRequestException>()
  .Or<OperationCanceledException>()
  .Retry(3);
....

....
myPolicy.Execute(()=>{
    //your code here
});
```

The first part of each policy specifies the exceptions that must be handled. Then, you specify what to do when one of those exceptions is captured. In the preceding code, the `Execute` method is retried up to three times if a failure is reported either by an `HttpRequestException` exception or by an `OperationCanceledException` exception.

The following is the implementation of an exponential retry policy:

```
var erPolicy= Policy
    ...
    //Exceptions to handle here
    .WaitAndRetry(6,
        retryAttempt => TimeSpan.FromSeconds(Math.Pow(2,
            retryAttempt)));
```

The first argument of WaitAndRetry specifies that a maximum of six retries is performed in the event of failure. The lambda function passed as the second argument specifies how much time to wait before the next attempt. In this specific example, this time grows exponentially with the number of the attempt by a power of 2 (2 seconds for the first retry, 4 seconds for the second retry, and so on).

The following is a simple circuit breaker policy:

```
var cbPolicy=Policy
    .Handle<SomeExceptionType>()
    .CircuitBreaker(6, TimeSpan.FromMinutes(1));
```

After six failures, the task can't be executed for 1 minute since an exception is returned.

The following is the implementation of the Bulkhead Isolation policy (see the *Microservices design principles* section for more information):

```
Policy
    .Bulkhead(10, 15)
```

A maximum of 10 parallel executions is allowed in the Execute method. Further tasks are inserted in an execution queue. This has a limit of 15 tasks. If the queue limit is exceeded, an exception is thrown.

> For the Bulkhead Isolation policy to work properly and, in general, for every strategy to work properly, task executions must be triggered through the same policy instance; otherwise, Polly is unable to count how many executions of a specific task are active.

Policies can be combined with the Wrap method:

```
var combinedPolicy = Policy
    .Wrap(erPolicy, cbPolicy);
```

Polly offers several more options, such as generic methods for tasks that return a specific type, timeout policies, task result caching, the ability to define custom policies, and so on. It is also possible to configure Polly as part of an HttPClient definition in the dependency injection section of any ASP.NET and .NET application. This way, it is quite immediate to define resilient clients.

The link to the official Polly documentation is in the *Further reading* section.

Using generic hosts

Each microservice may need to run several independent threads, each performing a different operation on requests received. Such threads need several resources, such as database connections, communication channels, specialized modules that perform complex operations, and so on. Moreover, all processing threads must be adequately initialized when the microservice is started and gracefully stopped when the microservice is stopped as a consequence of either load balancing or errors.

All of these needs led the .NET team to conceive and implement *hosted services* and *hosts*. A host creates an adequate environment for running several tasks, known as **hosted services**, and provides them with resources, common settings, and graceful start/stop.

The concept of a web host was mainly conceived to implement the ASP.NET Core web framework, but, with effect from .NET Core 2.1, the host concept was extended to all .NET applications.

At the time of writing this book, a Host is automatically created for you in any ASP.NET Core or Blazor project, so you have to add it manually only in other project types.

All features related to the concept of a Host are contained in the Microsoft.Extensions.Hosting NuGet package.

First, you need to configure the host with a fluent interface, starting with a HostBuilder instance. The final step of this configuration is calling the Build method, which assembles the actual host with all the configuration information we provided:

```
var myHost=new HostBuilder()
    //Several chained calls
    //defining Host configuration
    .Build();
```

Host configuration includes defining the common resources, defining the default folder for files, loading the configuration parameters from several sources (JSON files, environment variables, and any arguments that are passed to the application), and declaring all the hosted services.

It is worth pointing out that ASP.NET Core and Blazor projects use methods that perform a pre-configuration of the Host that include several of the tasks listed previously.

Then, the host can be started, which causes all the hosted services to be started:

```
host.Start();
```

The program remains blocked on the preceding instruction until the host is shut down. The host can be shut down either by one of the hosted services or externally by calling await host.StopAsync(timeout). Here, timeout is a time span defining the maximum time to wait for the hosted services to stop gracefully. After this time, all the hosted services are aborted if they haven't been terminated.

Often, the fact that a microservice is being shut down is signaled by a cancellationToken being passed when the microservice is started by the orchestrator. This happens when microservices are hosted in Azure Service Fabric.

Therefore in most cases, instead of using host.Start(), we can use the RunAsync or Run method, possibly passing it a cancellationToken that we received from the orchestrator or from the operating system:

```
await host.RunAsync(cancellationToken)
```

This way of shutting down is triggered as soon as the cancellationToken enters a canceled state. By default, the host has a 5-second timeout for shutting down; that is, it waits 5 seconds before exiting once a shutdown has been requested. This time can be changed within the ConfigureServices method, which is used to declare *hosted services* and other resources:

```
var myHost = new HostBuilder()
    .ConfigureServices((hostContext, services) =>
    {
        services.Configure<HostOptions>(option =>
        {
            option.ShutdownTimeout = System.TimeSpan.FromSeconds(10);
        });
        ....
        ....
        //further configuration
    })
    .Build();
```

However, increasing the host timeout doesn't increase the orchestrator timeout, so if the host waits too long, the whole microservice is killed by the orchestrator.

If no cancellation token is explicitly passed to Run or RunAsync, a cancellation token is automatically generated and is automatically signaled when the operating system informs the application it is going to kill it. This cancellation token is passed to all hosted services to give them the opportunity to stop gracefully.

Hosted services are implementations of the IHostedService interface, whose only methods are StartAsync(cancellationToken) and StopAsync(cancellationToken).

Both methods are passed a cancellationToken. The cancellationToken in the StartAsync method signals that a shutdown was requested. The StartAsync method periodically checks this cancellationToken while performing all operations needed to start the host, and if it is signaled, the host start process is aborted. On the other hand, the cancellationToken in the StopAsync method signals that the shutdown timeout expired.

Hosted services can be declared in the same ConfigureServices method that's used to define host options, as follows:

```
services.AddHostedService<MyHostedService>();
```

However, some project templates, like the ASP.NET Core project template, define a ConfigureServices method in a different class. This works fine if this method receives the same services parameter that is available in the HostBuilder.ConfigureServices method.

Most declarations inside ConfigureServices require the addition of the following namespace:

```
using Microsoft.Extensions.DependencyInjection;
```

Usually, the IHostedService interface isn't implemented directly but can be inherited from the BackgroundService abstract class, which exposes the easier-to-implement ExecuteAsync(CancellationToken) method, which is where we can place the whole logic of the service. A shutdown is signaled by passing cancellationToken as an argument, which is easier to handle. We will look at an implementation of IHostedService in the example at the end of *Chapter 6, Azure Service Fabric.*

To allow a hosted service to shut down the host, we need to declare an IApplicationLifetime interface as its constructor parameter:

```
public class MyHostedService: BackgroundService
{
    private readonly IHostApplicationLifetime applicationLifetime;
    public MyHostedService(IHostApplicationLifetime
applicationLifetime)
    {
        this.applicationLifetime=applicationLifetime;
    }
    protected Task ExecuteAsync(CancellationToken token)
    {
        ...
        applicationLifetime.StopApplication();
        ...
    }
}
```

When the hosted service is created, it is automatically passed an implementation of IHostApplicationLifetime, whose StopApplication method will trigger the host shutdown. This implementation is handled automatically, but we can also declare custom resources whose instances will be automatically passed to all the host service constructors that declare them as parameters. Therefore, say we define a constructor like this one:

```
Public MyClass(MyResource x, IResourceInterface1 y)
{
    ...
}
```

There are several ways to define the resources needed by the preceding constructor:

```
services.AddTransient<MyResource>();
services.AddTransient<IResourceInterface1, MyResource1>();
services.AddSingleton<MyResource>();
services.AddSingleton<IResourceInterface1, MyResource1>();
```

When we use AddTransient, a different instance is created and passed to all the constructors that require an instance of that type. On the other hand, with AddSingleton, a unique instance is created and passed to all the constructors that require the declared type. The overload with two generic types allows you to pass an interface and a type that implements that interface. This way, a constructor requires the interface and is decoupled from the specific implementation of that interface.

If resource constructors contain parameters, they will be automatically instantiated with the types declared in ConfigureServices in a recursive fashion. This pattern of interaction with resources is called **dependency injection** (DI) and will be discussed in detail in *Chapter 11, Design Patterns and .NET 5 Implementation*.

HostBuilder also has a method we can use to define the default folder, that is, the folder used to resolve all relative paths mentioned in all .NET methods:

```
.UseContentRoot("c:\\<deault path>")
```

It also has methods that we can use to add logging targets:

```
.ConfigureLogging((hostContext, configLogging) =>
    {
        configLogging.AddConsole();
        configLogging.AddDebug();
    })
```

The previous example shows a console-based logging source, but we can also log into Azure targets with adequate providers. The *Further reading* section contains links to some Azure logging providers that can work with microservices that have been deployed in Azure Service Fabric. Once you've configured logging, you can enable your hosted services and log custom messages by adding an `ILoggerFactory` or an `ILogger<T>` parameter in their constructors.

Finally, `HostBuilder` has methods we can use to read configuration parameters from various sources:

```
.ConfigureHostConfiguration(configHost =>
    {
        configHost.AddJsonFile("settings.json", optional: true);
        configHost.AddEnvironmentVariables(prefix: "PREFIX_");
        configHost.AddCommandLine(args);
    })
```

The way parameters can be used from inside the application will be explained in more detail in *Chapter 15*, *Presenting ASP.NET Core MVC*, which is dedicated to ASP.NET.

Visual Studio support for Docker

Visual Studio offers support for creating, debugging, and deploying Docker images. Docker deployment requires us to install *Docker Desktop for Windows* on our development machine so that we can run Docker images. The download link can be found in the *Technical requirements* section at the beginning of this chapter. Before we start any development activity, we must ensure it is installed and running (you should see a Docker icon in the window notification bar when the Docker runtime is running).

Docker support will be described with a simple ASP.NET MVC project. Let's create one. To do so, follow these steps:

1. Name the project `MvcDockerTest`.
2. For simplicity, disable authentication, if not already disabled.
3. You are given the option to add Docker support when you create the project, but please don't check the Docker support checkbox. You can test how Docker support can be added to any project after it has been created.

Once you have your ASP.NET MVC application scaffolded and running, right-click on its project icon in **Solution Explorer** and select **Add** and then **Container Orchestrator Support | Docker Compose**.

You'll get a dialog asking you to pick what operating system your container should use; pick the same one you chose when installing *Docker Desktop for Windows*. This will enable not only the creation of a Docker image but also the creation of a Docker Compose project, which helps you configure Docker Compose files so that they run and deploy several Docker images simultaneously. In fact, if you add another MVC project to the solution and enable container orchestrator support for it, the new Docker image will be added to the same Docker Compose file.

The advantage of enabling Docker Compose instead of just `Docker` is that you can manually `configure` how the image is run on the development machine, as well as how Docker image ports are mapped to external ports by editing the Docker Compose files that are added to the solution.

If your Docker runtime has been installed properly and is running, you should be able to run the Docker image from Visual Studio.

Analyzing the Docker file

Let's analyze the Docker file that was created by Visual Studio. It is a sequence of image creation steps. Each step enriches an existing image with something else with the help of the `From` instruction, which is a reference to an already existing image. The following is the first step:

```
FROM mcr.microsoft.com/dotnet/aspnet:x.x AS base
WORKDIR /app
EXPOSE 80
EXPOSE 443
```

The first step uses the `mcr.microsoft.com/dotnet/aspnet:x.x` ASP.NET (Core) runtime that was published by Microsoft in the Docker public repository (where `x.x` is the ASP.NET (Core) version that was selected in your project).

The `WORKDIR` command creates the directory that follows the command within the image that is going to be created. If the directory doesn't exist yet, it is created in the image. The two `EXPOSE` commands declare which ports of the image ports will be exposed outside the image and mapped to the actual hosting machine. Mapped ports are decided in the deployment stage either as command-line arguments of a Docker command or within a Docker Compose file. In our case, there are two ports: one for HTTP (80) and another for HTTPS (443).

This intermediate image is cached by Docker, which doesn't need to recompute it since it doesn't depend on the code we write but only on the selected version of the ASP.NET (Core) runtime.

The second step produces a different image that will not be used to deploy. Instead, it will be used to create application-specific files that will be deployed:

```
FROM mcr.microsoft.com/dotnet/core/sdk:x  AS build
WORKDIR /src
COPY ["MvcDockerTest/MvcDockerTest.csproj", "MvcDockerTest/"]
RUN dotnet restore MvcDockerTest/MvcDockerTest.csproj
COPY . .
WORKDIR /src/MvcDockerTest
RUN dotnet build MvcDockerTest.csproj -c Release -o /app/build

FROM build AS publish
RUN dotnet publish MvcDockerTest.csproj -c Release -o /app/publish
```

This step starts from the ASP.NET SDK image, which contains parts we don't need to add for deployment; these are needed to process the project code. The new `src` directory is created in the `build` image and makes the current image directory. Then, the project file is copied into `/src/MvcDockerTest`.

The `RUN` command executes an operating system command on the image. In this case, it calls the `dotnet` runtime, asking it to restore the NuGet packages that were referenced by the previously copied project file.

Then, the `COPY..` command copies the whole project file tree into the `src` image directory. Finally, the project directory is made the current directory and the `dotnet` runtime is asked to build the project in release mode and copy all the output files into the new `/app/build` directory. Finally, the `dotnet publish` task is executed in a new image called `publish`, outputting the published binaries into `/app/publish`.

The final step starts from the image that we created in the first step, which contains the ASP.NET (Core) runtime, and adds all the files that were published in the previous step:

```
FROM base AS final
WORKDIR /app
COPY --from=publish /app/publish .
ENTRYPOINT ["dotnet", "MvcDockerTest.dll"]
```

The `ENTRYPOINT` command specifies the operating system command that's needed to execute the image. It accepts an array of strings. In our case, it accepts the `dotnet` command and its first command-line argument, that is, the DLL we need to execute.

Publishing the project

If we right-click on our project and click **Publish**, we are presented with several options:

- Publish the image to an existing or new web app (automatically created by Visual Studio)
- Publish to one of several Docker registries, including a private Azure Container Registry that, if it doesn't already exist, can be created from within Visual Studio

Docker Compose support allows you to run and publish a multi-container application and add further images, such as a containerized database that is available everywhere.

The following Docker Compose file adds two ASP.NET applications to the same Docker image:

```
version: '3.4'

services:
  mvcdockertest:
    image: ${DOCKER_REGISTRY-}mvcdockertest
    build:
      context: .
      dockerfile: MvcDockerTest/Dockerfile

  mvcdockertest1:
    image: ${DOCKER_REGISTRY-}mvcdockertest1
    build:
      context: .
      dockerfile: MvcDockerTest1/Dockerfile
```

The preceding code references existing Docker files. Any environment-dependent information is placed in the `docker-compose.override.yml` file, which is merged with the `docker-compose.yml` file when the application is launched from Visual Studio:

```
version: '3.4'

services:
  mvcdockertest:
    environment:
      - ASPNETCORE_ENVIRONMENT=Development
      - ASPNETCORE_URLS=https://+:443;http://+:8
```

```
    ports:
      - "3150:80"
      - "44355:443"
    volumes:
      - ${APPDATA}/Asp.NET/Https:/root/.aspnet/https:ro
  mvcdockertest1:
    environment:
      - ASPNETCORE_ENVIRONMENT=Development
      - ASPNETCORE_URLS=https://+:443;http://+:80
      - ASPNETCORE_HTTPS_PORT=44317
    ports:
      - "3172:80"
      - "44317:443"
    volumes:
      - ${APPDATA}/Asp.NET/Https:/root/.aspnet/https:ro
```

For each image, the file defines some environment variables, which will be defined in the image when the application is launched, the port mappings, and some host files.

The files in the host are directly mapped into the images. Each declaration contains the path in the host, how the path is mapped in the image, and the desired access rights. In our case, `volumes` are used to map the self-signed HTTPS certificate that's used by Visual Studio.

Now, suppose we want to add a containerized SQL Server instance. We would need something like the following instructions split between `docker-compose.yml` and `docker-compose.override.yml`:

```
sql.data:
  image: mssql-server-linux:latest
  environment:
  - SA_PASSWORD=Pass@word
  - ACCEPT_EULA=Y
  ports:
  - "5433:1433"
```

Here, the preceding code specifies the properties of the SQL Server container, as well as the SQL server's configuration and installation parameters. More specifically, the preceding code contains the following information:

- `sql.data` is the name that's given to the container.
- `image` specifies where to take the image from. In our case, the image is contained in a public Docker registry.

- `environment` specifies the environment variables that are needed by SQL Server, that is, the administrator password and the acceptance of a SQL Server license.

- As usual, `ports` specifies the port mappings.

- `docker-compose.override.yml` is used to run the images from within Visual Studio.

If you need to specify parameters for either the production environment or the testing environment, you can add further `docker-compose-xxx.override.yml` files, such as `docker-compose-staging.override.yml` and `docker-compose-production.override.yml`, and then launch them manually in the target environment with something like the following code:

```
docker-compose -f docker-compose.yml -f docker-compose-staging.
override.yml
```

Then, you can destroy all the containers with the following code:

```
docker-compose -f docker-compose.yml -f docker-compose.test.staging.yml
down
```

While `docker-compose` has a limited capability when it comes to handling node clusters, it is mainly used in testing and development environments. For production environments, more sophisticated tools are needed, as we will see later in this chapter (in the *Which tools are needed to manage microservices?* section).

Azure and Visual Studio support for microservice orchestration

Visual Studio has specific project templates for microservice applications based on the Service Fabric platform, where you can define various microservices, configure them, and deploy them to Azure Service Fabric, which is a microservice orchestrator. Azure Service Fabric will be described in more detail in *Chapter 6, Azure Service Fabric*.

Visual Studio also has specific project templates for defining microservices to be deployed in Azure Kubernetes, and has extensions for debugging a single microservice while it communicates with other microservices deployed in Azure Kubernetes.

Also available are tools for testing and debugging several communicating microservices in the development machine with no need to install any Kubernetes software, and for deploying them automatically on Azure Kubernetes with just minimal configuration information.

All Visual Studio tools for Azure Kubernetes will be described in *Chapter 7, Azure Kubernetes Service.*

Which tools are needed to manage microservices?

Effectively handling microservices in your CI/CD cycles requires both a private Docker image registry and a state-of-the-art microservice orchestrator that's capable of doing the following:

- Allocating and load-balancing microservices on available hardware nodes
- Monitoring the health state of services and replacing faulty services if hardware/software failures occur
- Logging and presenting analytics
- Allowing the designer to dynamically change requirements such as hardware nodes allocated to a cluster, the number of service instances, and so on

The following subsection describes the Azure facilities we can use to store Docker images. The microservices orchestrators available in Azure are each described in a dedicated chapter, namely, *Chapter 6, Azure Service Fabric*, and *Chapter 7, Azure Kubernetes Service.*

Defining your private Docker registry in Azure

Defining your private Docker registry in Azure is easy. Just type `Container registries` into the Azure search bar and select **Container registries**. On the page that appears, click on the **Add** button.

The following form will appear:

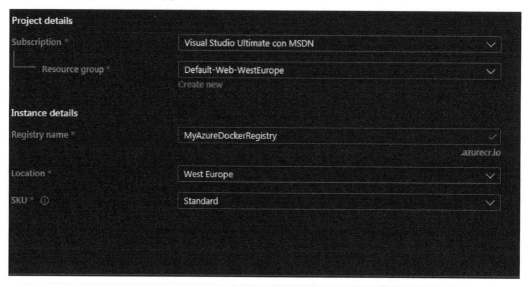

Figure 5.1: Creating an Azure private Docker registry

The name you select is used to compose the overall registry URI: `<name>.azurecr.io`. As usual, you can specify the subscription, resource group, and location. The **SKU** dropdown lets you choose from various levels of offerings that differ in terms of performance, available memory, and a few other auxiliary features.

Whenever you mention image names in Docker commands or in a Visual Studio publish form, you must prefix them with the registry URI: `<name>.azurecr.io/<my imagename>`.

If images are created with Visual Studio, then they can be published by following the instructions that appear once you've published the project. Otherwise, you must use `docker` commands to push them into your registry.

The easiest way to use Docker commands that interact with the Azure registry is by installing the Azure CLI on your computer. Download the installer from `https://aka.ms/installazurecliwindows` and execute it. Once the Azure CLI has been installed, you can use the `az` command from Windows Command Prompt or PowerShell. In order to connect with your Azure account, you must execute the following login command:

```
az login
```

This command should start your default browser and should drive you through the manual login procedure.

Once logged into your Azure account, you can log in to your private registry by typing the following command:

```
az acr login --name {registryname}
```

Now, let's say you have a Docker image in another registry. As a first step, let's pull the image on your local computer:

```
docker pull other.registry.io/samples/myimage
```

If there are several versions of the preceding image, the latest will be pulled since no version was specified. The version of the image can be specified as follows:

```
docker pull other.registry.io/samples/myimage:version1.0
```

Using the following command, you should see myimage within the list of local images:

```
docker images
```

Then, tag the image with the path you want to assign in the Azure registry:

```
docker tag myimage myregistry.azurecr.io/testpath/myimage
```

Both the name and destination tag may have versions (:<version name>).

Finally, push it to your registry with the following command:

```
docker push myregistry.azurecr.io/testpath/myimage
```

In this case, you can specify a version; otherwise, the latest version is pushed.

By doing this, you can remove the image from your local computer using the following command:

```
docker rmi myregistry.azurecr.io/testpath/myimage
```

Summary

In this chapter, we described what microservices are and how they have evolved from the concept of a module. Then, we talked about the advantages of microservices and when it is worth using them, as well as general criteria for their design. We also explained what Docker containers are and analyzed the strong connection between containers and microservice architectures.

Then, we took on a more practical implementation by describing all the tools that are available in .NET so that we can implement microservice-based architectures. We also described infrastructures that are needed by microservices and how the Azure cluster offers Azure Kubernetes Service and Azure Service Fabric.

The next chapter discusses the Azure Service Fabric orchestrator in detail.

Questions

1. What is the two-fold nature of the module concept?
2. Is scaling optimization the only advantage of microservices? If not, list some further advantages.
3. What is Polly?
4. What Docker support is offered by Visual Studio?
5. What is an orchestrator and what orchestrators are available on Azure?
6. Why is publisher/subscriber-based communication so important in microservices?
7. What is RabbitMQ?
8. Why are idempotent messages so important?

Further reading

The following are links to the official documentation for Azure Service Bus and RabbitMQ, two event bus technologies:

*   **Azure Service Bus**: https://docs.microsoft.com/en-us/azure/service-bus-messaging/
*   **RabbitMQ**: https://www.rabbitmq.com/getstarted.html
*   The documentation for Polly, a tool for reliable communication/tasks, can be found here: https://github.com/App-vNext/Polly.

- More information on Docker can be found on Docker's official website: `https://docs.docker.com/`.

- The official documentation for Kubernetes and `.yaml` files can be found here: `https://kubernetes.io/docs/home/`.

- The official documentation for Azure Kubernetes can be found here: `https://docs.microsoft.com/en-US/azure/aks/`.

- The official documentation for Azure Service Fabric can be found here: `https://docs.microsoft.com/en-US/azure/service-fabric/`.

- The official documentation for Azure Service Fabric's reliable services can be found here: `https://docs.microsoft.com/en-us/azure/service-fabric/service-fabric-reliable-services-introduction`.

6

Azure Service Fabric

This chapter is dedicated to describing Azure Service Fabric, which is a Microsoft opinionated microservices orchestrator. It is available on Azure, but Service Fabric software is also available for download, meaning users can use it to define their own on-premises microservices clusters.

While Service Fabric is not as diffused as Kubernetes, it has a better learning curve and enables you to experiment with the fundamental concepts of microservices, and to build sophisticated solutions in a very short space of time. Moreover, it offers an integrated deployment environment, which includes everything you need to implement a complete application. More specifically, it also offers its integrated communication protocol, and an easy and reliable way to store state information.

In this chapter, we will cover the following topics:

- Visual Studio support for Azure Service Fabric applications
- How to define and configure an Azure Service Fabric cluster
- How to code reliable services, and their communication in practice, through the "logging microservices" use case

By the end of this chapter, you will have learned how to implement a complete solution based on Azure Service Fabric.

Technical requirements

In this chapter, you will require the following:

- Visual Studio 2019 free Community Edition or better, with all the database tools and the Azure development workload installed.

- A free Azure account. The *Creating an Azure account* section in *Chapter 1, Understanding the Importance of Software Architecture*, explains how to create one.

- A local emulator for Azure Service Fabric to debug your microservices in Visual Studio. It is free and can be downloaded from `https://docs.microsoft.com/en-us/azure/service-fabric/service-fabric-get-started#install-the-sdk-and-tools`.

  To avoid installation issues, ensure that your version of Windows is up to date. Moreover, the emulator uses PowerShell high-privilege-level commands that, by default, are blocked by PowerShell. To enable them, you need to execute the following command in the Visual Studio Package Manager Console or in any PowerShell console. Visual Studio or an external PowerShell console must be started as an *administrator* for the following command to be successful:

```
Set-ExecutionPolicy -ExecutionPolicy Unrestricted -Force -Scope
CurrentUser
```

Visual Studio support for Azure Service Fabric

Visual Studio has a specific project template for microservice applications, based on the Service Fabric platform, where you can define various microservices, configure them, and deploy them to Azure Service Fabric, which is a microservice orchestrator. Azure Service Fabric will be described in more detail in the next section.

In this section, we will describe the various types of microservice you can define within a Service Fabric Application. A complete code example will be provided in the last section of this chapter. If you want to debug microservices on your development machine, you need to install the Service Fabric emulator listed in this chapter's technical requirements.

Service Fabric Applications can be found by selecting **Cloud** in the *Visual Studio project type drop-down filter*:

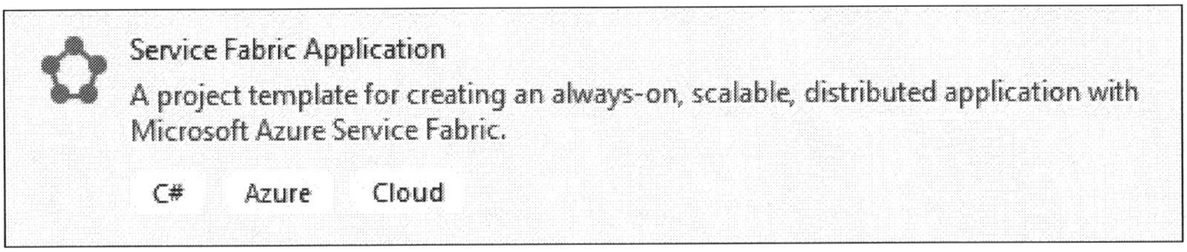

Service Fabric Application

A project template for creating an always-on, scalable, distributed application with
Microsoft Azure Service Fabric.

C#   Azure   Cloud

Figure 6.1: Selecting a Service Fabric Application

Once you have selected the project and chosen the project and solution names, you
can choose from a variety of services:

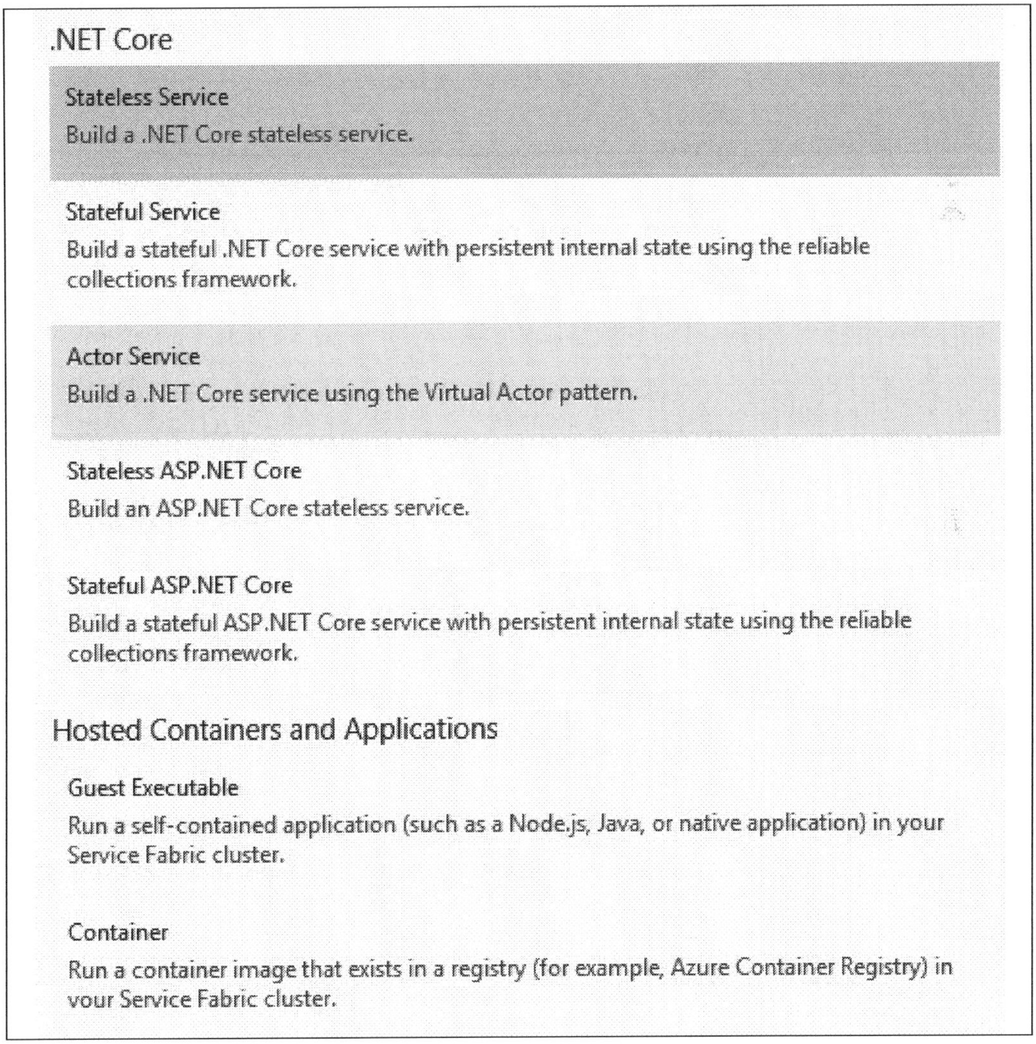

.NET Core

Stateless Service
Build a .NET Core stateless service.

Stateful Service
Build a stateful .NET Core service with persistent internal state using the reliable
collections framework.

Actor Service
Build a .NET Core service using the Virtual Actor pattern.

Stateless ASP.NET Core
Build an ASP.NET Core stateless service.

Stateful ASP.NET Core
Build a stateful ASP.NET Core service with persistent internal state using the reliable
collections framework.

Hosted Containers and Applications

Guest Executable
Run a self-contained application (such as a Node.js, Java, or native application) in your
Service Fabric cluster.

Container
Run a container image that exists in a registry (for example, Azure Container Registry) in
your Service Fabric cluster.

Figure 6.2: Choice of services

All projects under .NET Core use a microservice model that is specific to Azure Service Fabric. The Guest Executable adds a wrapper around an existing Windows application to turn it into a microservice that can run in Azure Service Fabric. The Container application enables the addition of any Docker image in the Service Fabric application. All the other choices scaffold a template that allows you to code a microservice with a Service Fabric-specific pattern.

If you select **Stateless Service** and fill in all the request information, Visual Studio creates two projects: an application project that contains configuration information for the overall application, and a project for the specific service you have chosen that contains both the service code and a service-specific configuration. If you want to add more microservices to your application, right-click on the application project and select **Add | New Service Fabric Service**.

 If you right-click on the solution and select **Add | New project**, a new Service Fabric application will be created instead of a new service being added to the already existing application.

If you select **Guest Executable**, you need to provide the following:

- The service name.
- A folder containing the main executable file, along with all the files it needs in order to work properly. You need this if you want to create a copy of this folder in your project or simply to link to the existing folder.
- Whether to add a link to this folder, or to copy the selected folder into the Service Fabric project.
- The main executable file.
- Arguments to pass on the command line to that executable.
- Which folder to use as a working folder on Azure. You want to use the folder containing the main executable (`CodeBase`), the folder where Azure Service Fabric will package the entire microservice (`CodePackage`), or a new subfolder named `Work`.

If you select **Container**, you need to provide the following:

- The service name.
- The complete name of a Docker image in your private Azure Container Registry.

- The username that will be used to connect to Azure Container Registry. The password will be specified manually in the same `RepositoryCredentials` XML element of the application configuration file that was automatically created for the username.

- The port where you can access your service (host port) and the port inside the container that the host port must be mapped to (container port). The container port must be the same port that was exposed in the Dockerfile and used to define the Docker image.

Afterward, you may need to add further manual configuration to ensure that your Docker application works properly. The *Further reading* section contains links to the official documentation where you can find more details.

There are five types of .NET Core native Service Fabric services. The Actor service pattern is an opinionated pattern that was conceived several years ago by Carl Hewitt. We will not discuss it here, but the *Further reading* section contains some links that provide more information on this.

The remaining four patterns refer to the usage (or not) of ASP.NET (Core) as the main interaction protocol and to the fact that the service has or hasn't got an internal state. In fact, Service Fabric allows microservices to use distributed queues and dictionaries that are globally accessible to all instances of the microservice that declares them, independent of the hardware node where they are running (they are serialized and distributed to all available instances when they're needed).

Stateful and stateless templates differ mainly in terms of their configuration. All native services are classes that specify just two methods. Stateful services specify:

```
protected override IEnumerable<ServiceReplicaListener>
CreateServiceReplicaListeners()


protected override async Task RunAsync(CancellationToken
cancellationToken)
```

While stateless services specify:

```
protected override IEnumerable< ServiceInstanceListener >
CreateServiceInstanceListeners()


protected override async Task RunAsync(CancellationToken
cancellationToken)
```

The CreateServiceReplicaListeners and CreateServiceInstanceListeners methods specify a list of listeners that are used by the microservice to receive messages and the code that handles those messages. Listeners may use any protocol, but they are required to specify an implementation of the relative socket.

RunAsync contains the code for background threads that asynchronously run tasks that are triggered by received messages. Here, you can build a host that runs several hosted services.

ASP.NET Core templates follow the same pattern; however, they use a unique ASP.NET Core-based listener and no RunAsync implementation, since background tasks can be launched from inside ASP.NET Core, whose listener defines a complete WebHost. However, you may add further listeners to the array of listeners returned by the CreateServiceReplicaListeners implementation created by Visual Studio, and also a custom RunAsync override.

It is worth pointing out that as RunAsync is optional, and since the ASP.NET Core template doesn't implement it, CreateServiceReplicaListeners and CreateServiceInstanceListeners are also optional, and, for instance, a background worker operating on a timer doesn't need to implement any of them.

More details on Service Fabric's native services pattern will be provided in the following section, while a complete code example will be provided in the *Use case – Logging microservices* section of this chapter, which is dedicated to this book's use case.

Defining and configuring your Azure Service Fabric cluster

Azure Service Fabric is the main Microsoft orchestrator that can host Docker containers, native .NET applications, and a distributed computing model called **reliable services**. We have already explained how we can create applications that contain these three types of services in the *Visual Studio support for Azure Service Fabric* section. In this section, we will explain how to create an Azure Service Fabric cluster in the Azure portal and provide some more details on reliable services. More practical details regarding *reliable services* will be provided in the example described in the *Use case – Logging microservices* section.

You can enter the Service Fabric section of Azure by typing Service Fabric into the Azure search bar and selecting **Service Fabric Cluster**.

A summary page of all of your Service Fabric clusters appears which, in your case, should be empty. When you click the **Add** button to create your first cluster, a multi-step wizard is shown. The following subsections describe the available steps.

Step 1 – Basic information

The following screenshot shows the creation of Azure Service Fabric:

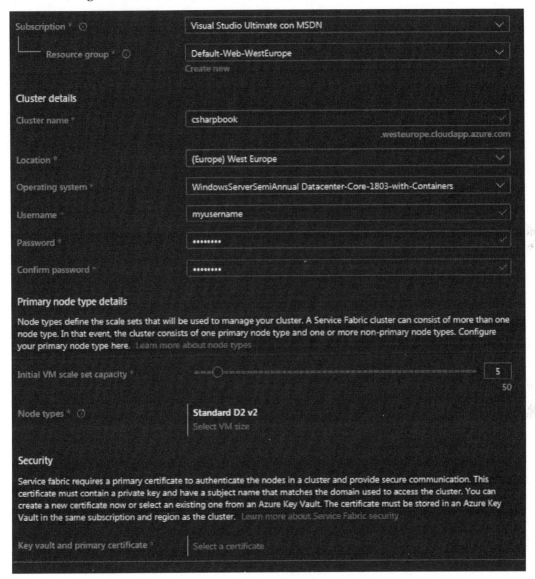

Figure 6.3: Azure Service Fabric creation

Here, you can choose the operating system, resource group, subscription, location, and username and password that you want to use to connect the remote desktop to all the cluster nodes.

You are required to choose a cluster name, which will be used to compose the cluster URI as `<cluster name>.<location>.cloudapp.azure.com`, where `location` is a name associated with the data center location you have chosen. Let's select Windows, since Service Fabric was primarily conceived for Windows. A better choice for Linux machines is Kubernetes, which will be described in the next chapter.

Then you are required to select your node type, that is, the kind of virtual machine you would like to use for your primary nodes, and the initial scale set, that is, the maximum number of virtual machines to use. Please choose a cheap node type and no more than three nodes, otherwise you might quickly waste all your free Azure credit.

More details on node configurations will be given in the next subsection.

Finally, you have the option to select a certificate to secure your node-to-node communications. Let's click the **Select a certificate** link, and in the window that opens, select the automatic creation of a new key vault and of a new certificate. More information on security will be provided in the *Step 3 – Security configuration* section.

Step 2 – Cluster configuration

In the second step, you can fine-tune the cluster node type and number:

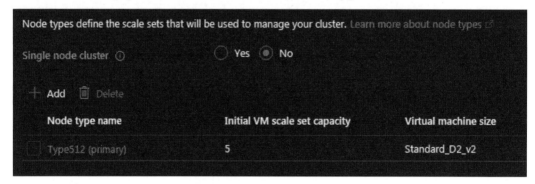

Figure 6.4: Cluster configuration

More specifically, in the previous step, we selected the cluster primary node. Here, we can choose whether to add various kinds of secondary nodes with their scale capacities. Once you have created different node types, you can configure services to run only on specific node types whose capabilities are adequate to their needs.

Let's click the **Add** button to add a new node type:

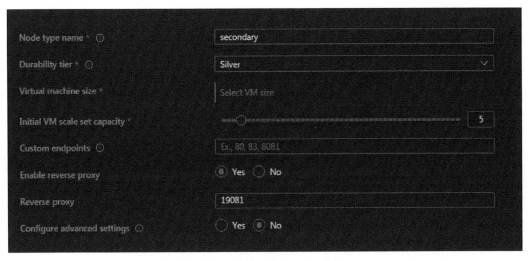

Figure 6.5: Adding a new node type

Nodes of a different node type can be scaled independently, and the **primary node** type is where Azure Service Fabric runtime services will be hosted. For each node type, you can specify the type of machine (**Durability tier**), machine dimensions (CPU and RAM), and the initial number of nodes.

You can also specify all the ports that will be visible from outside the cluster (**Custom endpoints**).

The services that are hosted on the different nodes of a cluster can communicate through any port since they are part of the same local network. Therefore, **Custom endpoints** must declare the ports that need to accept traffic from outside the cluster. The port that are exposed in **Custom endpoints** are the cluster's public interface, which can be reached through the cluster URI, that is, <cluster name>.<location>.cloudapp.azure.com. Their traffic is automatically redirected to all the microservices that have had the same ports opened by the cluster load balancer.

To understand the **Enable reverse proxy** option, we must explain how communications are sent to several instances of services whose physical addresses change during their lifetimes. From within the cluster, services are identified with a URI such as fabric://<application name>/<service name>. That is, this name allows us to access one of the several load-balanced instances of <service name>. However, these URIs can't be used directly by communication protocols. Instead, they are used to get the physical URI of the required resource, along with all its available ports and protocols from the Service Fabric naming service.

Later, we will learn how to perform this operation with *reliable services*. However, this model is not adequate for Dockerized services that weren't conceived to run specifically on Azure Service Fabric, since they are not aware of Service Fabric-specific naming services and APIs.

Therefore, Service Fabric provides two more options that we can use to standardize URLs instead of interacting directly with its naming service:

- **DNS**: Each service can specify its `hostname` (also known as its **DNS name**). The DNS service takes care of translating it into the actual service URL. For example, if a service specifies an `order.processing` DNS name and it has an HTTP endpoint on port `80` and a `/purchase` path, we can reach this endpoint with `http://order.processing:80/purchase`. By default, the DNS service is active, but you can deactivate it either by showing the advanced settings selection in the secondary node screen by clicking **Configure advanced settings**, or by going to the **Advanced** tab.

- **Reverse proxy**: Service Fabric's reverse proxy intercepts all the calls that have been directed to the cluster address and uses the name service to send them to the right application and service within that application. Addresses that are resolved by the reverse proxy service have the following structure: `<cluster name>.<location>.cloudapp.azure.com: <port>//<app name>/<service name>/<endpoint path>?PartitionKey=<value>& PartitionKind=value`. Here, partition keys are used to optimize stateful reliable services and will be explained at the end of this subsection. This means that stateless services lack the query string part of the previous address. Thus, a typical address that's solved by reverse proxy may be something similar to `myCluster.eastus.cloudapp.azure.com: 80//myapp/ myservice/<endpoint path>?PartitionKey=A & PartitionKind=Named`. If the preceding endpoint is called from a service hosted on the same cluster, we can specify `localhost` instead of the complete cluster name (that is, from the same cluster, not from the same node): `localhost: 80//myapp/ myservice/<endpoint path>?PartitionKey=A & PartitionKind=Named`. By default, reverse proxy is not enabled.

Since we are going to use Service Fabric reliable services with Service Fabric built-in communication facilities, and since these built-in communication facilities don't need either reverse proxy or DNS, please avoid changing these settings.

Moreover, if you are creating the Service Fabric cluster with the sole purpose of experimenting with the simple example at the end of the chapter, please stick with just the primary nodes and avoid wasting your free Azure credit by creating secondary nodes as well.

Step 3 – Security configuration

Once the second step is complete, we come to a security page:

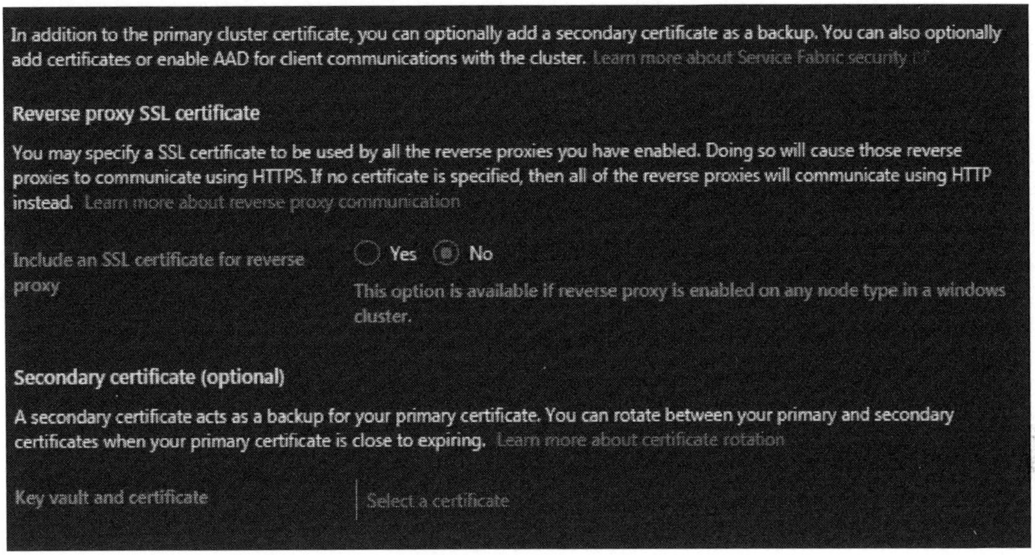

In addition to the primary cluster certificate, you can optionally add a secondary certificate as a backup. You can also optionally add certificates or enable AAD for client communications with the cluster. Learn more about Service Fabric security

Reverse proxy SSL certificate

You may specify a SSL certificate to be used by all the reverse proxies you have enabled. Doing so will cause those reverse proxies to communicate using HTTPS. If no certificate is specified, then all of the reverse proxies will communicate using HTTP instead. Learn more about reverse proxy communication

Include an SSL certificate for reverse proxy — ○ Yes ⦿ No

This option is available if reverse proxy is enabled on any node type in a windows cluster.

Secondary certificate (optional)

A secondary certificate acts as a backup for your primary certificate. You can rotate between your primary and secondary certificates when your primary certificate is close to expiring. Learn more about certificate rotation

Key vault and certificate | Select a certificate

Figure 6.6: Security page

We already defined the main certificate in the first step. Here, you have the option to select a secondary certificate to be used when the primary certificate is near to its expiration. You can add also a certificate that will be used to enable HTTPS communication on reverse proxies. Since, in our example, we will not use Dockerized services (so we will not require reverse proxies), we don't need this option.

At this point, we can click the review and create button to create the cluster. Submitting your approval will create the cluster. Pay attention to this: a cluster may spend your free Azure credit in a short time, so just keep your cluster on when you are testing. Afterward, you should delete it.

We need to download our primary certificate to our development machine, since we need it to deploy our application. Once the certificate has been downloaded, it is enough to double-click on it to install it on our machine. Before deploying the application, you are required to insert the following information into the **Cloud Publish Profile** of your Visual Studio Service Fabric applications (see this chapter's *Use case – Logging microservices* section for more details):

```
<ClusterConnectionParameters
    ConnectionEndpoint="<cluster name>.<location
    code>.cloudapp.azure.com:19000"
    X509Credential="true"
```

```
ServerCertThumbprint="<server certificate thumbprint>"
FindType="FindByThumbprint"
FindValue="<client certificate thumbprint>"
StoreLocation="CurrentUser"
StoreName="My" />
```

Since both the client (Visual Studio) and the server use the same certificate for authentication, the server and client thumbprint are the same. The certificate thumbprint can be copied from your Azure Key Vault. It is worth mentioning that you can also add client-specific certificates to the main server certificate by selecting the corresponding option in *step 3*.

As we mentioned in the *Visual Studio support for Azure Service Fabric* subsection, Azure Service Fabric supports two kinds of *reliable service*: stateless and stateful. Stateless services either don't store permanent data or they store it in external supports such as the Redis cache or databases (see *Chapter 9, How to Choose Your Data Storage in the Cloud*, for the main storage options offered by Azure).

Stateful services, on the other hand, use Service Fabric-specific distributed dictionaries and queues. Each distributed data structure is accessible from all the *identical* replicas of a service, but only one replica, called the primary replica, is allowed to write on them to avoid synchronized access to those distributed resources, which may cause bottlenecks.

All the other replicas, known as secondary replicas, can only read from these distributed data structures.

You can check if a replica is primary by looking at the context object your code receives from the Azure Service Fabric runtime, but usually, you don't need to do this. In fact, when you declare your service endpoints, you are required to declare those that are read-only. A read-only endpoint is supposed to receive requests so that it can read data from the shared data structures. Therefore, since only read-only endpoints are activated for secondary replicas, if you implement them correctly, write/update operations should automatically be prevented on stateful secondary replicas with no need to perform further checks.

In stateful services, secondary replicas enable parallelism on read operations, so in order to get parallelism on write/update operations, stateful services are assigned different data partitions. More specifically, for each stateful service, Service Fabric creates a primary instance for each partition. Then, each partition may have several secondary replicas.

Distributed data structures are shared between the primary instance of each partition and its secondary replicas. The whole extent of data that can be stored in a stateful service is split among the chosen number of partitions, according to a partition key that is generated by a hashing algorithm on the data to be stored.

Typically, partition keys are integers that belong to a given interval that is split among all the available partitions. For instance, a partition key can be generated by calling a well-known hashing algorithm on one or more string fields to get integers that are then processed to get a unique integer (using, for instance, an exclusive OR operation on the integer bits). Then, this integer can be constrained to the integer interval that was chosen for the partition key by taking the remainder of an integer division (for instance, the remainder of a division for 1,000 will be an integer in the 0-999 interval). It is important to be sure that all services use exactly the same hashing algorithm, so the better solution is to provide a common hashing library to all of them.

Let's say we want four partitions, which will be selected with an integer key in the 0-999 interval. Here, Service Fabric will automatically create four primary instances of our stateful service and assign them the following four partition key subintervals: 0-249, 250-499, 500-749, and 750-999.

From within your code, you are required to compute the partition key of the data you send to a stateful service. Then, Service Fabric's runtime will select the right primary instance for you. The following section provides more practical details on this and how to use reliable services in practice.

Use case – Logging microservices

In this section, we will look at a microservice-based system that logs data about purchases relating to various destinations in our WWTravelClub use case. In particular, we will design microservices that take care of computing daily revenues per location. Here, we're assuming that these microservices receive data from other subsystems hosted in the same Azure Service Fabric application. More specifically, each purchase log message is composed of the location name, the overall package cost, and the date and time of the purchase.

As a first step, let's ensure that the Service Fabric emulator that we mentioned in the *Technical requirements* section of this chapter has been installed and is running on your development machine. Now, we need to switch it so that it runs **5 nodes**: right-click on the small Service Fabric cluster icon you have in your Windows notification area, and, in the context menu that opens, select **Switch Cluster Mode -> 5 nodes**.

Now, we can follow the steps set out in the *Visual Studio support for Azure Service Fabric* section to create a Service Fabric project named `PurchaseLogging`. Select a .NET Core stateful reliable service and name it `LogStore`.

The solution that's created by Visual Studio is composed of a `PurchaseLogging` project, which represents the overall application, and a `LogStore` project, which will contain the implementation of the first microservice that's included in the `PurchaseLogging` application.

Under the `PackageRoot` folder, the `LogStore` service and each reliable service contain the `ServiceManifest.xml` configuration file and a `Settings.xml` folder (under the `Config` subfolder). The `Settings.xml` folder contains some settings that will be read from the service code. The initial file contains predefined settings that are needed by the Service Fabric runtime. Let's add a new `Settings` section, as shown in the following code:

```xml
<?xml version="1.0" encoding="utf-8" ?>
<Settings xmlns:xsd="http://www.w3.org/2001/XMLSchema"
          xmlns:xsi="http://www.w3.org/2001/XMLSchema-instance"
          xmlns="http://schemas.microsoft.com/2011/01/fabric">
<!-- This is used by the StateManager's replicator. -->
<Section Name="ReplicatorConfig">
<Parameter Name="ReplicatorEndpoint" Value="ReplicatorEndpoint" />
</Section>
<!-- This is used for securing StateManager's replication traffic. -->
<Section Name="ReplicatorSecurityConfig" />

<!-- Below the new Section to add -->

<Section Name="Timing">
<Parameter Name="MessageMaxDelaySeconds" Value="" />
</Section>
</Settings>
```

We will use the value of `MessageMaxDelaySeconds` to configure the system component and ensure message idempotency. The setting value is empty because most of the settings are overridden when the services are deployed by the overall application settings contained in the `PurchaseLogging` project.

The `ServiceManifest.xml` file contains a number of configuration tags that are automatically handled by Visual Studio, as well as a list of endpoints. Two endpoints are preconfigured since they are used by the Service Fabric runtime. Here, we must add the configuration details of all the endpoints our microservice will listen to. Each endpoint definition has the following format:

```
<Endpoint Name="<endpoint name>" PathSuffix="<the path of the endpoint
URI>" Protocol="<a protcol like Tcp, http, https, etc.>" Port="the
exposed port" Type="<Internal or Input>"/>
```

If `Type` is `Internal`, the port will be opened just inside the cluster's local network; otherwise, the port will be available from outside the cluster as well. In the preceding case, we must declare that port in the configuration of the Azure Service Fabric cluster as well, otherwise the cluster load balancer/firewall will not forward messages to it.

 Public ports can be reached directly from the cluster URI (`<cluster name>.<location code>.cloudapp.azure.com`) since the load balancer that interfaces each cluster will forward the input traffic it receives to them.

In this example, we won't define endpoints since we are going to use the predefined remoting-based communication, but we will show you how to use them later on in this section.

The `PurchaseLogging` project contains a reference to the `LogStore` project under the *services* Solution Explorer node and contains various folders with various XML configuration files. More specifically, we have the following folders:

- `ApplicationPackageRoot`, which contains the overall application manifest named `ApplicationManifest.xml`. This file contains some initial parameter definitions and then further configurations. Parameters have the following format:

  ```
  <Parameter Name="<parameter name>" DefaultValue="<parameter
  definition>" />
  ```

- Once defined, parameters can replace any value in the remainder of the file. Parameter values are referenced by enclosing the parameter name between square brackets, as shown in the following code:

  ```
  <UniformInt64Partition PartitionCount="[LogStore_
  PartitionCount]" LowKey="0" HighKey="1000" />
  ```

Some parameters define the number of replicas and partitions for each service and are automatically created by Visual Studio. Let's replace these initial values suggested by Visual Studio with those in the following code snippet:

```
<Parameter Name="LogStore_MinReplicaSetSize" DefaultValue="1" />
<Parameter Name="LogStore_PartitionCount" DefaultValue="2" />
<Parameter Name="LogStore_TargetReplicaSetSize" DefaultValue="1" />
```

We will use just two partitions to show you how partitions work, but you can increase this value to improve write/update parallelism. Each partition of the LogStore service doesn't need several replicas, since replicas improve performance on read operations and this service is not designed to offer read services. In similar situations, you may choose two to three replicas to make the system redundant and more robust to failures. However, we've left one since, as this is just an example, we are not concerned with failures.

The preceding parameters are used to define the role of the LogStore service inside the overall application. This definition is generated automatically by Visual Studio in the same file, below the initial definition created by Visual Studio, with just the partition interval changed to 0-1,000:

```
<Service Name="LogStore" ServicePackageActivationMode="ExclusiveProcess">
<StatefulService ServiceTypeName="LogStoreType"
    TargetReplicaSetSize=
    "[LogStore_TargetReplicaSetSize]"
    MinReplicaSetSize="[LogStore_MinReplicaSetSize]">
<UniformInt64Partition PartitionCount="
        [LogStore_PartitionCount]"
        LowKey="0" HighKey="1000" />
</StatefulService>
</Service>
```

- ApplicationParameters contains possible overrides for parameters defined in ApplicationManifest.xml for various deployment environments: the cloud (that is, the actual Azure Service Fabric cluster) and local emulators with one or five nodes.

- PublishProfiles contains the settings that are needed to publish the application in the same environments handled by the ApplicationParameters folder. You just need to customize the cloud publish profile with the actual name of your Azure Service Fabric URI and with the authentication certificate you downloaded during the Azure cluster configuration process:

```
<ClusterConnectionParameters
    ConnectionEndpoint="<cluster name>.<location
    code>.cloudapp.azure.com:19000"
    X509Credential="true"
    ServerCertThumbprint="<server certificate thumbprint>"
    FindType="FindByThumbprint"
    FindValue="<client certificate thumbprint>"
    StoreLocation="CurrentUser"
    StoreName="My" />
```

The remaining steps that need to be followed in order to complete the application have been organized into several subsections. Let's start by looking at ensuring message idempotency.

Ensuring message idempotency

Messages can become lost because of failures or small timeouts caused by load balancing. Here, we will use a predefined remoting-based communication that performs automatic message retries in the event of failures. However, this may cause the same messages to be received twice. Since we are summing up the revenues of purchase orders, we must protect ourselves from summing up the same purchase several times.

To do this, we will implement a library containing the necessary tools to ensure that message replicas are discarded.

Let's add a new .NET Standard 2.0 library project called **IdempotencyTools** to our solution. Now, we can remove the initial class scaffolded by Visual Studio. This library needs a reference to the same version of the `Microsoft.ServiceFabric.Services` NuGet package referenced by `LogStore`, so let's verify the version number and add the same NuGet package reference to the `IdempotencyTools` project.

The main tool that ensures message idempotency is the `IdempotentMessage` class:

```
using System;
using System.Runtime.Serialization;

namespace IdempotencyTools
{
    [DataContract]
    public class IdempotentMessage<T>
    {
        [DataMember]
        public T Value { get; protected set; }
        [DataMember]
        public DateTimeOffset Time { get; protected set; }
        [DataMember]
        public Guid Id { get; protected set; }

        public IdempotentMessage(T originalMessage)
        {
            Value = originalMessage;
            Time = DateTimeOffset.Now;
```

```
                        Id = Guid.NewGuid();
                }
        }
    }
```

We added the `DataContract` and `DataMember` attributes since they are needed by the remoting communication serializer we are going to use for all internal messages. Basically, the preceding class is a wrapper that adds a `Guid` and a time mark to the message class instance that's passed to its constructor.

The `IdempotencyFilter` class uses a distributed dictionary to keep track of the messages it has already received. To avoid the indefinite growth of this dictionary, older entries are periodically deleted. Messages that are too old to be found in the dictionary are automatically discarded.

The time interval entries are kept in the dictionary and are passed in the `IdempotencyFilter` static factory method, which creates new filter instances, along with the dictionary name and the `IReliableStateManager` instance, which are needed to create the distributed dictionary:

```
public class IdempotencyFilter
{
    protected IReliableDictionary<Guid, DateTimeOffset> dictionary;
    protected int maxDelaySeconds;
    protected DateTimeOffset lastClear;
    protected IReliableStateManager sm;
    protected IdempotencyFilter() { }
    public static async Task<IdempotencyFilter> NewIdempotencyFilter(
        string name,
        int maxDelaySeconds,
        IReliableStateManager sm)
    {
        return new IdempotencyFilter()
            {
                dictionary = await
                sm.GetOrAddAsync<IReliableDictionary<Guid,
                DateTimeOffset>>(name),
                maxDelaySeconds = maxDelaySeconds,
                lastClear = DateTimeOffset.UtcNow,
                sm = sm,
            };
    }
    ...
    ...
```

The dictionary contains each message time mark indexed by the message `Guid` and is created by invoking the `GetOrAddAsync` method of the `IReliableStateManager` instance with the dictionary type and name. `lastClear` contains the time of the removal of all old messages.

When a new message arrives, the `NewMessage` method checks whether it must be discarded. If the message must be discarded, it returns `null`; otherwise, it adds the new message to the dictionary and returns the message without the `IdempotentMessage` wrapper:

```
public async Task<T> NewMessage<T>(IdempotentMessage<T> message)
{
    DateTimeOffset now = DateTimeOffset.Now;
    if ((now - lastClear).TotalSeconds > 1.5 * maxDelaySeconds)
    {
        await Clear();
    }
    if ((now - message.Time).TotalSeconds > maxDelaySeconds)
        return default(T);
    using (var tx = this.sm.CreateTransaction())
    {
        ...
        ...
    }
}
```

As a first step, the method verifies whether it's time to clear the dictionary and whether the message is too old. Then, it starts a transaction to access the dictionary. All distributed dictionary operations must be enclosed in a transaction, as shown in the following code:

```
using (ITransaction tx = this.sm.CreateTransaction())
{
    if (await dictionary.TryAddAsync(tx, message.Id, message.Time))
    {
        await tx.CommitAsync();
        return message.Value;
    }
    else
    {
        return default;
    }
}
```

If the message Guid is found in the dictionary, the transaction is aborted since the dictionary doesn't need to be updated and the method returns default(T), which is actually null since the message must not be processed. Otherwise, the message entry is added to the dictionary and the unwrapped message is returned.

The code of the Clear method can be found in the GitHub repository associated with this book.

The Interaction library

There are some types that must be shared among all microservices. If the internal communication is implemented with either remoting or WCF, each microservice must expose an interface with all the methods other microservices call. Such interfaces must be shared among all microservices. Moreover, with all communication interfaces, the classes that implement the messages must also be shared among all microservices (or among some subsets of them). Therefore, all of these structures are declared in external libraries that are referenced by the microservices.

Now, let's add a new .NET Standard 2.0 library project called Interactions to our solution. Since this library must use the IdempotentMessage generic class, we must add it as a reference to the IdempotencyTools project. We must also add a reference to the remoting communication library contained in the Microsoft.ServiceFabric. Services.Remoting NuGet package, since all interfaces that are used to expose the microservice's remote methods must inherit from the IService interface defined in this package.

IService is an empty interface that declares the communication role of the inheriting interface. The Microsoft.ServiceFabric.Services.Remoting NuGet package version must match the version of the Microsoft.ServiceFabric.Services package declared in the other projects.

The following code shows the declarations of the interface that need to be implemented by the LogStore class:

```
using System;
using System.Collections.Generic;
using System.Text;
using System.Threading.Tasks;
using IdempotencyTools;
using Microsoft.ServiceFabric.Services.Remoting;
```

```
namespace Interactions
{
    public interface ILogStore: IService
    {
        Task<bool> LogPurchase(IdempotentMessage<PurchaseInfo>
        idempotentMessage);
    }
}
```

The following is the code of the PurchaseInfo message class, which is referenced in the ILogStore interface:

```
using System;
using System.Collections.Generic;
using System.Runtime.Serialization;
using System.Text;

namespace Interactions
{
    [DataContract]
    public class PurchaseInfo
    {
        [DataMember]
        public string Location { get; set; }
        [DataMember]
        public decimal Cost { get; set; }
        [DataMember]
        public DateTimeOffset Time { get; set; }
    }
}
```

Now, we are ready to implement our main LogStore microservice.

Implementing the receiving side of communications

To implement the LogStore microservice, we must add a reference to the Interaction library, which will automatically create references to the remoting library and to the IdempotencyTools project.

Then, the `LogStore` class must implement the `ILogStore` interface:

```
internal sealed class LogStore : StatefulService, ILogStore
...
...
private IReliableQueue<IdempotentMessage<PurchaseInfo>> LogQueue;
public async Task<bool>
    LogPurchase(IdempotentMessage<PurchaseInfo> idempotentMessage)
{
    if (LogQueue == null) return false;
    using (ITransaction tx = this.StateManager.CreateTransaction())
    {
        await LogQueue.EnqueueAsync(tx, idempotentMessage);
        await tx.CommitAsync();
        return true;
    }
}
```

Once the service receives a `LogPurchase` call from the remoting runtime, it puts the message in the `LogQueue` to avoid the caller remaining blocked, waiting for message processing completion. This way, we achieve both the reliability of a synchronous message passing protocol (the caller knows that the message has been received) and the performance advantages of asynchronous message processing that are typical of asynchronous communication.

`LoqQueue`, as a best practice for all distributed collections, is created in the `RunAsync` method, so `LogQueue` may be null if the first call arrives before the Azure Service Fabric runtime has called `RunAsync`. In this event, the method returns `false` to signal that the service isn't ready yet, in which case the sender will wait a little and will then resend the message. Otherwise, a transaction is created to enqueue the new message.

However, our service will not receive any communication if we don't furnish an implementation of `CreateServiceReplicaListeners()` that returns all the listeners that the service would like to activate. In the case of remoting communications, there is a predefined method that performs the whole job, so we just need to call it:

```
protected override IEnumerable<ServiceReplicaListener>
    CreateServiceReplicaListeners()
{
    return this.CreateServiceRemotingReplicaListeners<LogStore>();
}
```

Here, `CreateServiceRemotingReplicaListeners` is an extension method defined in the remoting communication library. It creates listeners for both primary replicas and secondary replicas (for read-only operations). When creating the client, we can specify whether its communications are addressed just to primary replicas or to secondary replicas as well.

If you would like to use different listeners, you must create an `IEnumerable` of `ServiceReplicaListener` instances. For each listener, you must invoke the `ServiceReplicaListener` constructor with three arguments:

- A function that receives the reliable service context object as its input and returns an implementation of the `ICommunicationListener` interface.

- The name of the listener. This second argument becomes obligatory when the service has more than one listener.

- A Boolean that is true if the listener must be activated on secondary replicas.

For instance, if we would like to add both custom and HTTP listeners, the code becomes something like the following:

```
return new ServiceReplicaListener[]
{
    new ServiceReplicaListener(context =>
    new MyCustomHttpListener(context, "<endpoint name>"),
    "CustomWriteUpdateListener", true),

    new ServiceReplicaListener(serviceContext =>
    new KestrelCommunicationListener(serviceContext, "<endpoint name>",
    (url, listener) =>
        {
            ...
        })
        "HttpReadOnlyListener",
    true)
};
```

`MyCustomHttpListener` is a custom implementation of `ICommunicationListener`, while `KestrelCommunicationListener` is a predefined HTTP listener based on Kestrel and ASP.NET Core. The following is the full code that defines the `KestrelCommunicationListener` listener:

```
new ServiceReplicaListener(serviceContext =>
new KestrelCommunicationListener(serviceContext, "<endpoint name>",
(url, listener) =>
```

```
    {
        return new WebHostBuilder()
        .UseKestrel()
        .ConfigureServices(
            services => services
            .AddSingleton<StatefulServiceContext>(serviceContext)
            .AddSingleton<IReliableStateManager>(this.StateManager))

        .UseContentRoot(Directory.GetCurrentDirectory())
        .UseStartup<Startup>()
        .UseServiceFabricIntegration(listener,

        ServiceFabricIntegrationOptions.UseUniqueServiceUrl)
        .UseUrls(url)
        .Build();
    })
    "HttpReadOnlyListener",
    true)
```

`ICommunicationListener` implementations must also have a `Close` method, which must close the opened communication channel, and an `Abort` method, which must **immediately** close the communication channel (ungracefully, that is, without informing connected clients and so on).

Now that we have turned communications on, we can implement the service logic.

Implementing service logic

Service logic is executed by the tasks that are launched as independent threads when `RunAsync` is invoked by the Service Fabric runtime. It's good practice to create an `IHost` and design all the tasks as `IHostedService` implementations also when you only need to implement one task. In fact, `IHostedService` implementations are independent chunks of software that are easier to unit test. `IHost` and `IHostedService` were discussed in detail in the *Using generic hosts* subsection of *Chapter 5, Applying a Microservice Architecture to Your Enterprise Application*.

In this section, we will implement the logic that computes daily revenues for each location in an `IHostedservice` named `ComputeStatistics`, which uses a distributed dictionary whose keys are the location names and whose values are instances of a class called `RunningTotal`. This class stores the current running total and the day that is being computed:

```
namespace LogStore
{
    public class RunningTotal
    {
        public DateTime Day { get; set; }
        public decimal Count { get; set; }

        public RunningTotal
                Update(DateTimeOffset time, decimal value)
        {
            ...
        }
    }
}
```

This class has an `Update` method that updates the instance when a new purchase message is received. First of all, the incoming message time is normalized to universal time. Then, the day part of this time is extracted and compared with the current `Day` of the running total, as shown in the following code:

```
public RunningTotal Update(DateTimeOffset time, decimal value)
{
    var normalizedTime = time.ToUniversalTime();
    var newDay = normalizedTime.Date;
    ...
    ...
}
```

If it's a new day, we assume that the running total computation of the previous day has finished, so the `Update` method returns it in a new `RunningTotal` instance and resets `Day` and `Count` so that it can compute the running total for the new day. Otherwise, the new value is added to the running `Count` and the method returns `null`, meaning that the day total isn't ready yet. This implementation can be seen in the following code:

```
public RunningTotal Update(DateTimeOffset time, decimal value)
{
    ...
    ...
    var result = newDay > Day && Day != DateTime.MinValue ?
    new RunningTotal
    {
```

```
            Day=Day,
            Count=Count
        }
        : null;
    if(newDay > Day) Day = newDay;
    if (result != null) Count = value;
    else Count += value;
    return result;
}
```

The `IHostedService` implementation of `ComputeStatistics` requires some parameters in order to work properly, as follows:

- The queue containing all the incoming messages
- The `IReliableStateManager` service, so that it can create the distributed dictionary where it stores data
- The `ConfigurationPackage` service, so that it can read the settings defined in the `Settings.xml` service file and possibly those overridden in the application manifest

The preceding parameters must be passed in the `ComputeStatistics` constructor when a `ComputeStatistics` instance is created by `IHost` through dependency injection. We will return to the `IHost` definition in the next subsection. For now, let's concentrate on the `ComputeStatistics` constructor and its fields:

```
namespace LogStore
{
    public class ComputeStatistics : BackgroundService
    {
        IReliableQueue<IdempotentMessage<PurchaseInfo>> queue;
        IReliableStateManager stateManager;
        ConfigurationPackage configurationPackage;
        public ComputeStatistics(
            IReliableQueue<IdempotentMessage<PurchaseInfo>> queue,
            IReliableStateManager stateManager,
            ConfigurationPackage configurationPackage)
        {
            this.queue = queue;
            this.stateManager = stateManager;
            this.configurationPackage = configurationPackage;
        }
```

All the constructor parameters are stored in private fields so that they can be used when ExecuteAsync is called:

```
protected async override Task ExecuteAsync(CancellationToken
stoppingToken)
{
    bool queueEmpty = false;
    var delayString=configurationPackage.Settings.Sections["Timing"]
        .Parameters["MessageMaxDelaySeconds"].Value;
    var delay = int.Parse(delayString);
    var filter = await IdempotencyFilter.NewIdempotencyFilterAsync(
        "logMessages", delay, stateManager);
    var store = await
        stateManager.GetOrAddAsync<IReliableDictionary<string,
RunningTotal>>("partialCount");
....
...
```

Before entering its loop, the ComputeStatistics service prepares some structures and parameters. It declares that the queue isn't empty, meaning it can start dequeuing messages. Then, it extracts MessageMaxDelaySeconds from the service settings and turns it into an integer. The value of this parameter was left empty in the Settings.xml file. Now, it's time to override it and define its actual value in ApplicationManifest.xml:

```
<ServiceManifestImport>
<ServiceManifestRef ServiceManifestName="LogStorePkg"
ServiceManifestVersion="1.0.0" />
<!--code to add start -->
<ConfigOverrides>
<ConfigOverride Name="Config">
<Settings>
<Section Name="Timing">
<Parameter Name="MessageMaxDelaySeconds" Value="[MessageMaxDelaySecon
ds]" />
</Section>
</Settings>
</ConfigOverride>
</ConfigOverrides>
<!--code to add end-->
</ServiceManifestImport>
```

`ServiceManifestImport` imports the service manifest in the application and overrides some configuration. Its version number must be changed every time its content and/or the service definition is changed and the application is redeployed in Azure because version number changes tell the Service Fabric runtime what to change in the cluster. Version numbers also appear in other configuration settings. They must be changed every time the entities they refer to change.

`MessageMaxDelaySeconds` is passed to the instance of the idempotency filter, along with a name for the dictionary of the already received messages, and with the instance of the `IReliableStateManager` service. Finally, the main distributed dictionary that's used to store running totals is created.

After this, the service enters its loop and finishes when `stoppingToken` is signaled, that is, when the Service Fabric runtime signals that the service is going to be stopped:

```
while (!stoppingToken.IsCancellationRequested)
    {
        while (!queueEmpty && !stoppingToken.IsCancellationRequested)
        {
            RunningTotal total = null;
            using (ITransaction tx = stateManager.CreateTransaction())
            {
                ...
                ...
                ...
            }
        }
        await Task.Delay(100, stoppingToken);
        queueEmpty = false;
    }
}
```

The inner loop runs until the queue becomes empty and then exits and waits 100 milliseconds before verifying whether new messages have been enqueued.

The following is the code for the inner loop, which is enclosed in a transaction:

```
RunningTotal finalDayTotal = null;
using (ITransaction tx = stateManager.CreateTransaction())
{
```

```
        var result = await queue.TryDequeueAsync(tx);
        if (!result.HasValue) queueEmpty = true;
        else
        {
            var item = await filter.NewMessage<PurchaseInfo>(result.Value);
            if(item != null)
            {
                var counter = await store.TryGetValueAsync(tx,
                item.Location);
                //counter update
                ...
            }
            ...
            ...
        }
    }
}
```

Here, the service is trying to dequeue a message. If the queue is empty, it sets queueEmpty to true to exit the loop; otherwise, it passes the message through the idempotency filter. If the message survives this step, it uses it to update the running total of the location referenced in the message. However, correct operation of the distributed dictionary requires that the old counter is replaced with a new counter each time an entry is updated. Accordingly, the old counter is copied into a new RunningTotal object. This new object can be updated with the new data if we call the Update method:

```
//counter update
var newCounter = counter.HasValue ?
new RunningTotal
{
    Count=counter.Value.Count,
    Day= counter.Value.Day
}
: new RunningTotal();
finalDayTotal = newCounter.Update(item.Time, item.Cost);
if (counter.HasValue)
    await store.TryUpdateAsync(tx, item.Location,
    newCounter, counter.Value);
else
    await store.TryAddAsync(tx, item.Location, newCounter);
```

Then, the transaction is committed, as shown in the following code:

```
if(item != null)
{
    ...
    ...
}
await tx.CommitAsync();
if(finalDayTotal != null)
{
    await SendTotal(finalDayTotal, item.Location);
}
```

When the Update method returns a complete computation result, that is, when total != null, the following method is called:

```
protected async Task SendTotal(RunningTotal total, string location)
{
    //Empty, actual application would send data to a service
    //that exposes daily statistics through a public Http endpoint
}
```

The SendTotal method sends the total to a service that publicly exposes all the statistics through an HTTP endpoint. After reading *Chapter 14, Applying Service-Oriented Architectures with .NET Core*, which is dedicated to the Web API, you may want to implement a similar service with a stateless ASP.NET Core microservice connected to a database. The stateless ASP.NET Core service template automatically creates an ASP.NET Core-based HTTP endpoint for you.

However, since this service must receive data from the SendTotal method, it also needs remote-based endpoints. Therefore, we must create them, just as we did for the LogStore microservice, and concatenate the remote-based endpoint array with the pre-existing array containing the HTTP endpoint.

Defining the microservice's host

Now we have everything in place to define the microservice's RunAsync method:

```
protected override async Task RunAsync(CancellationToken
cancellationToken)
{
    LogQueue = await
```

```
        this.StateManager
        .GetOrAddAsync<IReliableQueue
<IdempotentMessage<PurchaseInfo>>>("logQueue");
    var configurationPackage = Context
        .CodePackageActivationContext
        .GetConfigurationPackageObject("Config");
    ...
    ...
```

Here, the service queue is created, and the service settings are saved in
configurationPackage.

After that, we can create the IHost service, as we explained in the *Using generic
hosts* subsection of *Chapter 5, Applying a Microservice Architecture to Your Enterprise
Application*:

```
var host = new HostBuilder()
    .ConfigureServices((hostContext, services) =>
    {
        services.AddSingleton(this.StateManager);
        services.AddSingleton(this.LogQueue);
        services.AddSingleton(configurationPackage);
        services.AddHostedService<ComputeStatistics>();
    })
    .Build();
await host.RunAsync(cancellationToken);
```

ConfigureServices defines all singleton instances that are needed by IHostedService
implementations, so they are injected into the constructor of all the implementations
that reference their types. Then, AddHostedService declares the unique
IHostedService of the microservice. Once the IHost is built, we run it until the
RunAsync cancellation token is signaled. When the cancellation token is signaled, the
request to shut down is passed to all IHostedService implementations.

Communicating with the service

Since we haven't implemented the whole purchase logic yet, we will implement a
stateless microservice that sends random data to the LogStore service. Right-click
on the PurchaseLogging project in the **Solution Explorer** and select **Add | Service
Fabric Service**. Then, select the .NET Core stateless template and name the new
microservice project FakeSource.

Now, let's add a reference to the `Interaction` project. Before moving on to the service code, we need to update the replica count of the newly created service in `ApplicationManifest.xml` as well as in all the other environment-specific parameter overrides (the cloud, one local cluster node, five local cluster nodes):

```
<Parameter Name="FakeSource_InstanceCount" DefaultValue="2" />
```

This fake service needs no listeners and its `RunAsync` method is straightforward:

```
string[] locations = new string[] { "Florence", "London", "New York",
"Paris" };

protected override async Task RunAsync(CancellationToken
cancellationToken)
{
    Random random = new Random();
    while (true)
    {
        cancellationToken.ThrowIfCancellationRequested();

        PurchaseInfo message = new PurchaseInfo
        {
            Time = DateTimeOffset.UtcNow,
            Location= locations[random.Next(0, locations.Length)],
            Cost= 200m*random.Next(1, 4)
        };
        //Send message to counting microservices
        ...
        ...

        await Task.Delay(TimeSpan.FromSeconds(1), cancellationToken);
    }
}
```

In each loop, a random message is created and sent to the counting microservices. Then, the thread sleeps for a second and starts a new loop. The code that sends the created messages is as follows:

```
//Send message to counting microservices
var partition = new ServicePartitionKey(Math.Abs(message.Location.
GetHashCode()) % 1000);
var client = ServiceProxy.Create<ILogStore>(
    new Uri("fabric:/PurchaseLogging/LogStore"), partition);
try
```

```
{
    while (!await client.LogPurchase(new
    IdempotentMessage<PurchaseInfo>(message)))
    {
        await Task.Delay(TimeSpan.FromMilliseconds(100),
        cancellationToken);
    }
}
catch
{

}
```

Here, a key in the 0-9,999 interval is computed from the location string. We used GetHashCode since we are sure that all involved services use the same .NET Core version and accordingly we are sure they use the same GetHashCode implementation that computes the hash in exactly the same way. However, in general, it is better to provide a library with a standard hash code implementation.

This integer is passed to the ServicePartitionKey constructor. Then, a service proxy is created, and the URI of the service to call and the partition key are passed. The proxy uses this data to ask the naming service for a physical URI for a primary instance for the given partition value.

ServiceProxy.Create also accepts a third optional argument that specifies whether messages that are sent by the proxy can also be routed to secondary replicas. The default is that messages are routed just to primary instances. If the message target returns false, meaning that it's not ready (remember that LogPurchase returns false when the LogStore message queue hasn't been created yet), the same transmission is attempted after 100 milliseconds.

Sending messages to a remoting target is quite easy. However, other communication listeners require that the sender interacts manually with the naming service to get a physical service URI. This can be done with the following code:

```
ServicePartitionResolver resolver = ServicePartitionResolver.
GetDefault();

ResolvedServicePartition partition =
await resolver.ResolveAsync(new Uri("fabric:/MyApp/MyService"),
    new ServicePartitionKey(.....), cancellationToken);
//Look for a primary service only endpoint
var finalURI= partition.Endpoints.First(p =>
    p.Role == ServiceEndpointRole.StatefulPrimary).Address;
```

Moreover, in the case of generic communication protocols, we must manually handle failures and retries with a library such as Polly (see the *Resilient task execution* subsection of *Chapter 5, Applying a Microservice Architecture to Your Enterprise Application*, for more information).

Testing the application

To test the application, you need to start Visual Studio with administrator permissions. Therefore, close Visual studio, then right-click on the Visual Studio icon and select the option to launch it as an administrator. Once you are again in Visual Studio, load the PurchaseLogging solution, and place a breakpoint in the ComputeStatistics.cs file:

```
total = newCounter.Update(item.Time, item.Cost);
if (counter.HasValue)...//put breakpoint on this line
```

Each time the breakpoint is hit, look at the content of newCounter to verify how the running totals of all the locations change. Before launching the application in debug mode, ensure the local cluster is running with five nodes. If you change from one to five nodes, the local cluster menu grays out until the operation is completed, so wait until the menu normalizes.

Once you launch the application and the application is built, a console appears and you start receiving notifications of the operation completed in Visual Studio. The application takes some minutes to load on all nodes; after that, your breakpoint should start being hit.

Summary

In this chapter, we described how to define a Service Fabric solution in Visual Studio, and how to set up and configure a Service Fabric cluster in Azure.

We described Service Fabric building blocks, reliable services, the various types of reliable services, and their roles within a Service Fabric application.

Finally, we put these concepts into practice by implementing a Service Fabric application. Here, we provided more practical details on the architecture of each reliable service and how to organize and code their communications.

The next chapter describes another famous microservices orchestrator, Kubernetes, and its implementation in the Azure Cloud.

Questions

1. What is a reliable service?

2. Can you list the different types of reliable services and their roles in a Service Fabric application?

3. What is `ConfigureServices`?

4. What kinds of port must be declared during the definition of an Azure Service Fabric cluster?

5. Why are partitions of reliable stateful services needed?

6. How can we declare that a remoting communication must be addressed by secondary replicas? What about other types of communication?

Further reading

- The official documentation for Azure Service Fabric can be found here: `https://docs.microsoft.com/en-US/azure/service-fabric/`.

- The official documentation for Azure Service Fabric's reliable services can be found here: `https://docs.microsoft.com/en-us/azure/service-fabric/service-fabric-reliable-services-introduction`.

- More information about the Actor model can be found here: `https://www.researchgate.NET/publication/234816174_Actors_A_conceptual_foundation_for_concurrent_object-oriented_programming`.

- The official documentation for Actor models that can be implemented in Azure Service Fabric can be found here: `https://docs.microsoft.com/en-US/azure/service-fabric/service-fabric-reliable-actors-introduction`.

Microsoft has also implemented an advanced Actor model that is independent of Service Fabric. This is known as the Orleans framework. More information about Orleans can be found at the following links:

- **Orleans – Virtual Actors**: `https://www.microsoft.com/en-us/research/project/orleans-virtual-actors/?from=https%3A%2F%2Fresearch.microsoft.com%2Fen-us%2Fprojects%2Forleans%2F`.

- **Orleans Documentation**: `https://dotnet.github.io/orleans/docs/index.html`

7

Azure Kubernetes Service

This chapter is dedicated to describing the Kubernetes microservices orchestrator and, in particular, its implementation in Azure named Azure Kubernetes Service. The chapter explains the fundamental Kubernetes concepts, and then focuses on how to interact with a Kubernetes cluster, and how to deploy an Azure Kubernetes application. All concepts are put into practice with simple examples. We recommend reading *Chapter 5*, *Applying a Microservice Architecture to Your Enterprise Application*, and *Chapter 6*, *Azure Service Fabric*, before dealing with this chapter, since it relies on the concepts explained in these previous chapters.

More specifically, in this chapter you will learn about the following topics:

- Kubernetes basics
- Interacting with Azure Kubernetes clusters
- Advanced Kubernetes concepts

By the end of this chapter, you will have learned how to implement and deploy a complete solution based on Azure Kubernetes.

Technical requirements

- Visual Studio 2019 free Community Edition or better, with all the database tools installed or any other `.yaml` file editor such as Visual Studio Code.
- A free Azure account. The *Creating an Azure account* section in *Chapter 1*, *Understanding the Importance of Software Architecture*, explains how to create one.

The code for this chapter is available at `https://github.com/PacktPublishing/`
`Software-Architecture-with-C-9-and-.NET-5`.

Kubernetes basics

Kubernetes is an advanced, open source orchestrator that you can install locally
on your private machine's cluster. At the time of writing, it is the most widespread
orchestrator, so Microsoft also offers it as a better alternative to Azure Service Fabric,
since it is currently the *de facto* standard, and can rely on a wide ecosystem of tools
and applications. This section introduces basic Kubernetes concepts and entities.

A Kubernetes cluster is a cluster of virtual machines running the Kubernetes
orchestrator. As for Azure Service Fabric, the virtual machines composing the
cluster are called nodes. The smallest software unit we can deploy on Kubernetes is
not a single application, as in the case of Azure Service Fabric, but an aggregate of
containerized applications called pods. While Kubernetes supports various types of
containers, the most commonly used container type is Docker, which we analyzed in
Chapter 5, Applying a Microservice Architecture to Your Enterprise Application, so we will
confine our discussion to Docker.

pods are important since applications belonging to the same pod are ensured to run
on the same node. This means that they can easily communicate through localhost
ports. Communication between different pods, however, is more complex since
the IP addresses of pods are ephemeral resources because pods have no fixed
node where they run, but are moved from one node to another by the orchestrator.
Moreover, pods may be replicated to increase performance, so, in general, it makes
no sense addressing a message to a specific pod, but just to any of the identical
replicas of the same pod.

While, in Azure Service Fabric, the infrastructure gives automatically virtual net
addresses to groups of identical replicas, in Kubernetes we need to define explicit
resources called Services that are assigned virtual addresses by the Kubernetes
infrastructure and forward their communications to sets of identical pods. In short,
Services are Kubernetes way to assign constant virtual addresses to sets of pod
replicas.

All Kubernetes entities may be assigned name value pairs called labels that are
used to reference them through a pattern matching mechanism. More specifically,
Selectors select Kubernetes entities by listing labels they must have.

Thus, for instance, all pods that receive traffic from the same Service are selected by
specifying labels they must have in the Service definition.

The way a Service routes its traffic to all connected pods depends on the way pods are organized. Stateless pods are organized in so called ReplicaSets, which are similar to stateless replicas of Azure Service Fabric services. As Azure Service Fabric stateless services, ReplicaSets have a unique virtual address assigned to the whole group and traffic is split equally among all pods of the group.

Stateful Kubernetes pod replicas are organized into so called StatefulSets. Similar to Azure Service Fabric stateful services, StatefulSets use sharding to split the traffic among all their pods. For this reason, Kubernetes Services assign a different name to each pod of the StatefulSet they are connected to. These names look like the following: basename-0.<base URL>, basename-1.<base URL>, ..., basename-n.<base URL>. This way, message sharding is easily accomplished as follows:

1. Each time a message must be sent to a StatefulSet composed of *N* replicas, you compute a hash between 0 and *N*-1, say x.

2. Add the postfix x to a base name to get a cluster address, such as basename-x.<base URL>.

3. Send the message to the basename-x.<base URL> cluster address.

Kubernetes has no predefined storing facilities, and you can't use node disk storage since pods are moved among available nodes, so long-term storage must be provided with sharded cloud databases or with other kinds of cloud storage. While each pod of a StatefulSet can access a sharded cloud database with the usual connection string technique, Kubernetes offers a technique to abstract disk-like cloud storage offered by the external Kubernetes cluster environment. We will describe these in the *Advanced Kubernetes concepts* section.

All Kubernetes entities mentioned in this short introduction can be defined in a .yaml file, which, once deployed to a Kubernetes cluster, causes the actual creation of all entities defined in the file. The subsection that follows describes .yaml files, while the other subsections thereafter describe in detail all the basic Kubernetes objects mentioned so far, and explain how to define them in a .yaml file. Further Kubernetes objects will be described throughout the whole chapter.

.yaml files

.yaml files, like JSON files, are a way to describe nested objects and collections in a human-readable way, but they do it with a different syntax. You have objects and lists, but object properties are not surrounded by {}, and lists are not surrounded by []. Instead, nested objects are declared by simply indenting their content with spaces. The number of spaces can be freely chosen, but once they've been chosen, they must be used consistently.

List items can be distinguished from object properties by preceding them with a hyphen (-).

Here is an example involving nested objects and collections:

```
Name: Jhon
Surname: Smith
Spouse:
   Name: Mary
   Surname: Smith
Addresses:
- Type: home
   Country: England
   Town: London
   Street: My home street
- Type: office
   Country: England
   Town: London
   Street: My home street
```

The preceding `Person` object has a `Spouse` nested object, and a nested collection of addresses.

`.yaml` files can contain several sections, each defining a different entity, that are separated by a line containing the `---` string. Comments are preceded by a # symbol, which must be repeated on each comment line.

Each section starts with the declaration of the Kubernetes API group and version. In fact, not all objects belong to the same API group. For objects that belong to the core API group, we can specify just the API version, as in the following example:

```
apiVersion: v1
```

While objects belonging to different API groups must also specify the API name, as in the following example:

```
apiVersion: apps/v1
```

In the next subsection, we analyze in detail `ReplicaSets` and `Deployments` that are built on top of them.

ReplicaSets and Deployments

The most important building block of Kubernetes applications is the ReplicaSet, that is, a pod replicated *n* times. Usually, however, you adopt a more complex object that is built on top of the ReplicaSet – the Deployment. Deployments not only create a ReplicaSet, but also monitor them to ensure that the number of replicas is kept constant, independent of hardware faults and other events that might involve the ReplicaSets. In other words, they are a declarative way of defining ReplicaSets and pods.

Each Deployment has a name (metadata->name), an attribute that specifies the desired number of replicas (spec->replicas), a key-value pair (spec -> selector-> matchLabels) that selects the pods to monitor, and a template (spec->template) that specifies how to build the pod replicas:

```
apiVersion: apps/v1
kind: Deployment
metadata:
  name: my-deployment-name
  namespace: my-namespace #this is optional
spec:
    replicas: 3
    selector:
      matchLabels:
        my-pod-label-name: my-pod-label-value
        ...
    template:
      ...
```

namespace is optional and, if not provided, a namespace called default is assumed. Namespaces are a way of keeping separate the objects of a Kubernetes cluster. For instance, a cluster can host the objects of two completely independent applications each placed in a separate namespace.

Indented inside the template is the definition of the pod to replicate. Complex objects such as Deployments can also contain other kinds of templates, for instance, a template of disk-like memory required by the external environment. We will discuss this further, in the *Advanced Kubernetes concepts* section.

In turn, the pod template contains a metadata section with labels used to select the pods, and a spec section with a list of all of the containers:

```
metadata:
  labels:
```

```
        my-pod-label-name: my-pod-label-value
        ...
    spec:
      containers:
        ...
      - name: my-container-name
        image: <Docker imagename>
        resources:
          requests:
            cpu: 100m
            memory: 128Mi
          limits:
            cpu: 250m
            memory: 256Mi
        ports:
        - containerPort: 6379
        env:
        - name: env-name
          value: env-value
          ...
```

Each container has a name and must specify the name of the Docker image to use for creating the containers. In case the Docker image is not contained in the public Docker registry, the name must be a URI that also includes the repository location.

Then, containers must specify the memory and CPU resources that they need to be created in the resources->requests object. A pod replica is created only if these resources are currently available. The resources->limits object, instead, specifies the maximum resources a container replica can actually use. If, during the container execution, these limits are exceeded, actions are taken to limit them. More specifically, if the CPU limit is exceeded, the container is throttled (its execution is stopped to restore its CPU consumption), while, if the memory limits are exceeded, the container is restarted. containerPort must be the port exposed by the container. Here, we can also specify further information, such as the protocol used.

CPU time is expressed in millicores, where 1,000 millicores means 100% of the CPU time, while memory is expressed in Mebibytes (*1Mi = 1024*1024 bytes*), or other units. env lists all the environment variables to pass to the containers with their values.

Both containers and pod templates can contain further fields, such as properties that define virtual files, and properties that define commands that returns the readiness and the health state of the container. We will analyze these in the *Advanced Kubernetes concepts* section.

The following subsection describes pod sets conceived to store state information.

StatefulSets

StatefulSets are very similar to a ReplicaSet, but while pods of a ReplicaSet are indistinguishable processors that contribute in parallel to the same workload through load balancing strategies, pods in a StatefulSet have a unique identity, and can contribute to the same workload only through sharding. This is because StatefulSets were conceived to store information, and information cannot be stored in parallel, merely split among several stores by means of sharding.

For the same reason, each pod instance is always kept tied to any virtual disk space it requires (see the *Advanced Kubernetes concepts* section), so that each pod instance is responsible for writing to a specific store.

Moreover, StatefulSets pods instances have ordinal numbers attached to them. They are started in sequence according to these numbers, and they are stopped in reverse order. If the StatefulSet contains N replicas, these numbers go from zero to N-1. Moreover, a unique name for each instance is obtained by chaining the pod name specified in the template, with the instance ordinal, in the following way – <pod name>-<instance ordinal>. Thus, instance names will be something like mypodname-0, mypodname-1, and so on. As we will see in the *Services* subsection, instance names are used to build unique cluster network URIs for all instances, so that other pods can communicate with a specific instance of a StatefulSets pods.

Here is a typical StatefulSet definition:

```
apiVersion: apps/v1
kind: StatefulSet
metadata:
  name: my-stateful-set-name
spec:
  selector:
    matchLabels:
      my-pod-label-name: my-pod-label-value
...
  serviceName: "my-service-name"
  replicas: 3
  template:
    ...
```

The template part is the same as that of Deployments. The main conceptual difference with Deployments is the serviceName field. It specifies the name of a service that must be connected with StatefulSets to provide unique network addresses for all pod instances. We will discuss this subject in more detail in the *Services* subsection. Moreover, usually, StatefulSets use some form of storage. We will discuss this in detail in the *Advanced Kubernetes concepts* section.

It is worth pointing out also that the default ordered creation and stop strategy of StatefulSets can be changed by specifying an explicit Parallel value for the spec->podManagementPolicy property (the default value is OrderedReady).

The following subsection describes how to provide stable network addresses to both ReplicaSets and StatefulSets.

Services

Since pod instances can be moved between nodes, they have no stable IP address attached to them. Services take care of assigning a unique and stable virtual address to a whole ReplicaSet and of load balancing the traffic to all its instances. Services are not software objects created in the cluster, just an abstraction for the various settings and activities needed to put in place their functionalities.

Services work at level 4 of the protocol stack, so they understand protocols such as TCP, but they aren't able to perform, for instance, HTTP-specific actions/ transformations, such as for instance, ensuring a secure HTTPS connection. Therefore, if you need to install HTTPS certificates on the Kubernetes cluster, you need a more complex object that is capable of interacting at level 7 of the protocol stack. The Ingress object was conceived for this. We will discuss this in the next subsection.

Services also handle assigning a unique virtual address to each instance of a StatefulSet. In fact, there are various kinds of Services; some were conceived for ReplicaSet and others for StatefulSet.

A ClusterIP service type is assigned a unique cluster internal IP address. It specifies the ReplicaSets or Deployments it is connected to through label pattern matching. It uses tables maintained by the Kubernetes infrastructure to load balance the traffic it receives among all pod instances to which it is connected.

Therefore, other pods can communicate with the pods connected to a Service by interacting with this Service that is assigned the stable network name `<service name>.<service namespace>.svc.cluster.local`. Since they are just assigned local IP addresses, a `ClusterIP` service can't be accessed from outside the Kubernetes cluster. Here is the definition of a typical `ClusterIP` service:

```
apiVersion: v1
kind: Service
metadata:
  name: my-service
  namespace: my-namespace
spec:
  selector:
    my-selector-label: my-selector-value
    ...
  ports:
    - name: http
      protocol: TCP
      port: 80
      targetPort: 9376
    - name: https
      protocol: TCP
      port: 443
      targetPort: 9377
```

Each Service can work on several ports, and can route any port (`port`) to the ports exposed by the containers (`targetPort`). However, it is very often the case that `port = targetPort`. Ports can be given names, but these names are optional. Also, the specification of the protocol is optional, in which case all supported level 4 protocols are allowed. The `spec->selector` property specifies all the name/value pairs that select the pods for the Service to route the communications it receives to.

Since a `ClusterIP` service can't be accessed from outside the Kubernetes cluster, we need other Service types to expose a Kubernetes application on a public IP address.

`NodePort`-type Services are the simplest way to expose pods to the outside word. In order to implement a `NodePort` service, the same port x is opened on all nodes of the Kubernetes cluster and each node routes the traffic it receives on this port to a newly created `ClusterIP` service.

In turn, the ClusterIP service routes its traffic to all pods selected by the service:

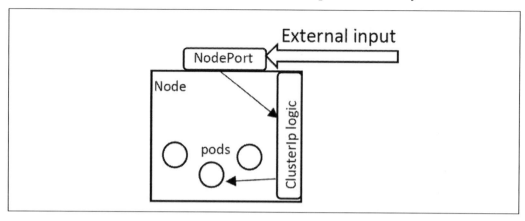

Figure 7.1: NodePort service

Therefore, it is enough to communicate with port x through a public IP of any cluster node in order to access the pods connected to the NodePort service. Of course, the whole process is completely automatic and hidden to the developer, whose only preoccupation is getting the port number x in terms of where to forward the external traffic.

The definition of a NodePort service is identical to the definition of a ClusterIP service, the only difference being that they specify a value of NodePort for the spec->type property:

```
...
spec:
  type: NodePort
  selector:
  ...
```

As a default, a node port x in the range 30000-327673 is automatically chosen for each targetPort specified by the Service. The port property associated with each targetPort is meaningless for NodePortServices since all traffic passes through the selected node port x, and, for convention, is set to the same value of the targetPort. The developer can also set the node port x directly through a nodePort property:

```
...
ports:
    - name: http
      protocol: TCP
      port: 80
      targetPort: 80
```

```
        nodePort: 30007
      - name: https
        protocol: TCP
        port: 443
        targetPort: 443
        nodePort: 30020
  ...
```

When the Kubernetes cluster is hosted in a cloud, the more convenient way to expose some pods to the outside world is through a `LoadBalancer` service, in which case the Kubernetes cluster is exposed to the outside world through a level 4 load balancer of the selected cloud provider.

The definition of a `LoadBalancer` service is identical to that of a `ClusterIp` service, the only difference being that the `spec->type` property must be set to `LoadBalancer`:

```
  ...
  spec:
    type: LoadBalancer
    selector:
    ...
```

If no further specification is added, a dynamic public IP is randomly assigned. However, if a specific public IP address to the cloud provider is required, it can be used as a public IP address for the cluster load balancer by specifying it in the `spec->loadBalancerIP` property:

```
  ...
  spec:
    type: LoadBalancer
    loadBalancerIP: <your public ip>
    selector:
    ...
```

In Azure Kubernetes, you must also specify the resource group where the IP address was allocated, in an annotation:

```
apiVersion: v1
kind: Service
metadata:
  annotations:
    service.beta.kubernetes.io/azure-load-balancer-resource-group: <IP
resource group name>
  name: my-service name
  ...
```

In Azure Kubernetes, you can remain with a dynamic IP address, but you can get a public static domain name of the type `<my-service-label>.<location>.cloudapp. azure.com`, where `<location>` is the geographic label you have chosen for your resources. `<my-service-label>` is a label that you verified makes the previous domain name unique. The chosen label must be declared in an annotation of your service, as shown here:

```
apiVersion: v1
kind: Service
metadata:
  annotations:
service.beta.kubernetes.io/azure-dns-label-name: <my-service-label>
  name: my-service-name
...
```

`StatefulSets` don't need any load balancing since each pod instance has its own identity, but just require a unique URL address for each pod instance. This unique URL is provided by the so called headless Services. Headless Services are defined like `ClusterIP` services, the only difference being that they have a `spec->clusterIP` property set to none:

```
...
spec:
clusterIP: none
  selector:
...
```

All `StatefulSets` handled by a headless Service must place the Service name in their `spec-> serviceName` property, as already stated in the *StatefulSets* subsection.

The unique name provided by a headless Service to all `StatefulSets` pod instances it handles is `<unique pod name>.<service name>.<namespace>.svc.cluster.local`.

Services only understand low-level protocols, such as TCP/IP, but most web applications are situated on the more sophisticated HTTP protocol. That's why Kubernetes offers higher-level entities called `Ingresses` that are built on top of services. The following subsection describes these and explains how to expose a set of `pods` through a level 7 protocol load balancer, which could offer you typical HTTP services, instead of through a `LoadBalancer` service.

Ingresses

Ingresses are mainly conceived to work with HTTP(S). They provide the following services:

- HTTPS termination. They accept HTTPS connections and route them in HTTP format to any service in the cloud.

- Name-based virtual hosting. They associate several domain names with the same IP address and route each domain, or <domain>/<path prefix>, to a different cluster Service.

- Load balancing.

Ingresses rely on web servers to offer the above services. In fact, Ingresses can be used only after having installed an Ingress Controller. Ingress Controllers are custom Kubernetes objects that must be installed in the cluster. They handle the interface between Kubernetes and a web server, which can be either an external web server or a web server that is part of the Ingress Controller installation.

We will describe the installation of an Ingress Controller based on the NGINX web server in the *Advanced Kubernetes concepts* section, as an example of the use of Helm. The *Further reading* section contains information on how to install also an Ingress Controller that interfaces an external Azure application gateway.

HTTPS termination and name-based virtual hosting can be configured in the Ingress definition in a way that is independent of the chosen Ingress Controller, while the way load balancing is achieved depends on the specific Ingress Controller chosen and on its configuration. Some Ingress Controller configuration data can be passed in the metadata-> annotations field of the Ingress definition.

Name-based virtual hosting is defined in a spec>rules section of the Ingress definition:

```
...
spec:
...
  rules:
  - host: *.mydomain.com
    http:
      paths:
      - path: /
        pathType: Prefix
        backend:
          service:
            name: my-service-name
```

```
            port:
              number: 80
      - host: my-subdomain.anotherdomain.com
  ...
```

Each rule specifies an optional hostname that can contain the * wildcard. If no hostname is provided, the rule matches all hostnames. For each rule, we can specify several paths, each redirected to a different service/port pair, where the service is referenced through its name. The way the match with each `path` is carried out depends on the value of `pathType`; if this value is `Prefix`, the specified `path` must be a prefix of any matching path. Otherwise, if this value is `Exact`, the match must be exact. Matches are case-sensitive.

HTTPS termination on a specific hostname is specified by associating it a certificate encoded in a Kubernetes secret:

```
  ...
  spec:
  ...
    tls:
    - hosts:
        - www.mydomain.com
      secretName: my-certificate1
        - my-subdomain.anotherdomain.com
      secretName: my-certificate2
  ...
```

HTTPS certificates can be obtained free of charge at `https://letsencrypt.org/`. The procedure is explained on the website, but basically, as with all certificate authorities, you provide a key and they return the certificate based on that key. It is also possible to install a **certificate manger** that takes care of automatically installing and renewing the certificate. The way a key/certificate pair is encoded in a Kubernetes secret string is detailed in the *Advanced Kubernetes concepts* section.

The whole `Ingress` definition looks like the following code:

```
apiVersion: networking.k8s.io/v1
kind: Ingress
metadata:
  name: my-example-ingress
  namespace: my-namespace
spec:
  tls:
  ...
```

```
    rules:
    ...
```

Here, the `namespace` is optional, and if not specified, is assumed to be `default`.

In the next section, we will put in practice some of the concepts explained here by defining an Azure Kubernetes cluster and deploying a simple application.

Interacting with Azure Kubernetes clusters

To create an **Azure Kubernetes Service** (**AKS**) cluster, type `AKS` into the Azure search box, select **Kubernetes services**, and then click the **Add** button. The following form will appear:

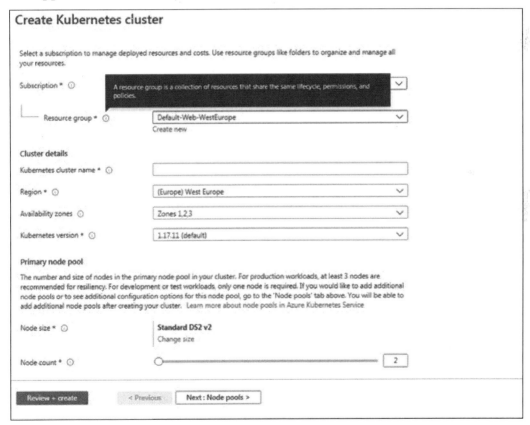

Figure 7.2: Creating a Kubernetes cluster

It is worth mentioning that you can get help by just hovering any circled **i** with the mouse, as shown in the preceding screenshot.

As usual, you are required to specify a subscription, resource group, and region. Then, you can choose a unique name (**Kubernetes cluster name**), and the version of Kubernetes you would like to use. For computational power, you are asked to select a machine template for each node (node size) and the number of nodes. The initial screen shows a default of three nodes. We decreased it to two, because three nodes are too much for the Azure free credit. Moreover, the default virtual machine should also be replaced by a cheaper one, so click **Change size** and select **DS1 v2**.

The **Availability zones** setting allows you to spread your nodes across several geographic zones for a better fault tolerance. The default is three zones. Please change it to two zones since we have just two nodes.

Following the preceding changes, you should see the following settings:

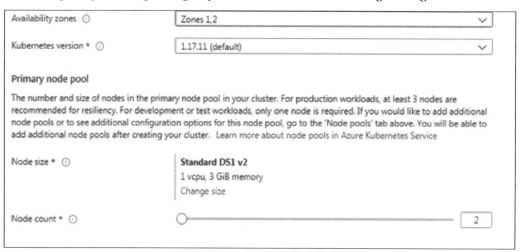

Figure 7.3: Chosen settings

Now you can create your cluster by clicking the **Review + create** button. A review page should appear, confirm, and create the cluster.

If you click **Next**, instead of **Review + create**, you can also define other node types, and then you can provide security information, namely, a *service principal*, and specify whether you wish to enable role-based access control. In Azure, service principals are accounts that are associated with services you may use to define resource access policies. You may also change the default network settings and other settings.

Deployment may take a little while (10-20 minutes). After that time, you will have your first Kubernetes cluster! At the end of the chapter, when the cluster is no longer required, please don't forget to delete it in order to avoid wasting your Azure free credit.

In the next subsection, you will learn how to interact with your cluster through Kubernetes' official client, Kubectl.

Using Kubectl

Once you have created your cluster, you can interact with it with Azure Cloud Shell. Click on the console icon on the top right of your Azure portal page. The following screenshot shows the Azure Shell icon:

Figure 7.4: Azure Shell icon

When prompted, select the **Bash Shell**. Then you will be prompted to create a storage account, so confirm and create it.

We will use this shell to interact with our cluster. On the top of the shell there is a file icon that we will use to upload our .yaml files:

Figure 7.5: How to upload files in Azure Cloud Shell

It is also possible to download a client called Azure CLI and to install it on your local machine (see https://docs.microsoft.com/en-US/cli/azure/install-azure-cli), but, in this case, you also need to install all tools needed to interact with the Kubernetes cluster (Kubectl and Helm) that are pre-installed in the Azure Cloud Shell.

Once you've created a Kubernetes cluster, you can interact with it through the kubectl command-line tool. kubectl is integrated in the Azure Shell, so you just need to activate your cluster credentials to use it. You can do this with the following Cloud Shell command:

```
az aks get-credentials --resource-group <resource group> --name
<cluster name>
```

The preceding command stores the credentials that were automatically created to enable your interaction with the cluster in a /.kube/config configuration file. From now on, you can issue your kubectl commands with no further authentication.

If you issue the kubectl get nodes command, you get a list of all your Kubernetes nodes. In general, kubectl get <object type> lists all objects of a given type. You can use it with nodes, pods, statefulset, and so on. kubectl get all shows a list of all the objects created in your cluster. If you also add the name of a specific object, you will get information on just that specific object, as shown here:

```
kubectl get <object type><object name>
```

If you add the --watch option, the object list will be continuously updated, so you can see the state of all the selected objects changing over time. You can leave this watch state by hitting *Ctrl* + *c*.

The following command shows a detailed report on a specific object:

```
kubectl describe <object name>
```

All objects described in a .yaml file, say myClusterConfiguration.yaml, can be created with the following command:

```
kubectl create -f myClusterConfiguration.yaml
```

Then, if you modify the .yaml file, you can reflect all modifications on your cluster with the apply command, as shown here:

```
kubectl apply -f myClusterConfiguration.yaml
```

apply does the same job of create but, if the resource already exists, apply overrides it, while create exits with an error message.

You can destroy all objects that were created with a .yaml file by passing the same file to the delete command, as shown here:

```
kubectl delete -f myClusterConfiguration.yaml
```

The delete command can also be passed an object type and a list of names of objects of that type to destroy, as shown in the following example:

```
kubectl delete deployment deployment1 deployment2...
```

The preceding kubectl command shown should suffice for most of your practical needs. For more details, the *Further reading* section contains a link to the official documentation.

In the next subsection, we will use kubectl `create` to install a simple demo application.

Deploying the demo Guestbook application

The Guestbook application is a demo application used in the examples of the official Kubernetes documentation. We will use it as an example of a Kubernetes application since its Docker images are already available in the public Docker repository, so we don't need to write software.

The Guestbook application stores the opinions of customers who visit a hotel or a restaurant. It is composed of an UI tier implemented with a `Deployment`, and of a database layer implemented with an in-memory store based on Redis. In turn, the Redis store is implemented with a unique master storage used for write/update and several read-only replicas, always based on Redis, that achieve a read parallelism. Write/update parallelism could be implemented with several sharded Redis masters, but for the very nature of the applications, write operations should not be predominant, so a single master database should suffice in the practical case of a single restaurant/hotel. The whole application is composed of three `.yaml` files that you can find in the GitHub repository associated with this book.

Here is the code for the master storage based on Redis that is contained in the `redis-master.yaml` file:

```yaml
apiVersion: apps/v1
kind: Deployment
metadata:
  name: redis-master
  labels:
    app: redis
spec:
  selector:
    matchLabels:
      app: redis
      role: master
      tier: backend
  replicas: 1
  template:
    metadata:
      labels:
        app: redis
        role: master
        tier: backend
```

```
    spec:
      containers:
      - name: master
        image: k8s.gcr.io/redis:e2e
        resources:
          requests:
            cpu: 100m
            memory: 100Mi
        ports:
        - containerPort: 6379
---
apiVersion: v1
kind: Service
metadata:
  name: redis-master
  labels:
    app: redis
    role: master
    tier: backend
spec:
  ports:
  - port: 6379
    targetPort: 6379
  selector:
    app: redis
    role: master
    tier: backend
```

The file is composed of two object definitions separated by a line containing just `---`, that is, the object definition separator of `.yaml` files. The first object is a `Deployment` with a single replica, and the second object is a `ClusterIPService` that exposes the `Deployment` on the 6379 port at the internal `redis-master.default.svc.cluster.local` network address. The `Deployment pod template` defines the three app, role, and tier labels with their values that are used in the `selector` definition of the Service to connect the Service with the unique pod defined in the `Deployment`.

Let's upload the `redis-master.yaml` file on Cloud Shell, and then deploy it in the cluster with the following command:

```
kubectl create -f redis-master.yaml
```

Once the operation is complete, you can inspect the content of the cluster with `kubectl get all`.

The slave storage is defined in the `redis-slave.yaml` file and is completely analogous, the only difference being that this time we have two replicas, and a different Docker image.

Let's upload this file as well and deploy it with the following command:

```
kubectl create -f redis-slave.yaml
```

The code for the UI tier is contained in the `frontend.yaml` file. `Deployment` has three replicas and a different Service type. Let's upload and deploy this file with the following command:

```
kubectl create -f frontend.yaml
```

It is worthwhile analyzing the Service code in the `frontend.yaml` file:

```yaml
apiVersion: v1
kind: Service
metadata:
  name: frontend
  labels:
    app: guestbook
    tier: frontend
spec:
  type: LoadBalancer
  ports:
  - port: 80
  selector:
    app: guestbook
    tier: frontend
```

This type of Service is of the `LoadBalancer` type, since it must expose the application on a public IP address. In order to get the public IP address assigned to the service, and then to the application, use the following command:

```
kubectl get service
```

The preceding command should display information on all the installed services. You should find the public IP under the `EXTERNAL-IP` column of the list. If you see only <none> values, please repeat the command until the public IP address is assigned to the load balancer.

Once you get the IP address, navigate with the browser to this address. The application home page should now appear!

Once you have finished experimenting with the application, remove the application from the cluster to avoid wasting your Azure free credit (public IP addresses cost money) with the following commands:

```
kubectl delete deployment frontend redis-master redis-slave
kubectl delete service frontend redis-master redis-slave
```

In the next section, we will analyze other important Kubernetes features.

Advanced Kubernetes concepts

In this section, we will discuss other important Kubernetes features, including how to assign permanent storage to StatefulSets, how to store secrets such as passwords, connection strings, or certificates, how a container can inform Kubernetes about its health state, and how to handle complex Kubernetes packages with Helm. All subjects are organized in dedicated subsections. We will start with the problem of permanent storage.

Requiring permanent storage

Since pods are moved among nodes, they can't rely on the permanent storage offered by the current node where they are running. This leaves us with two options:

1. **Using external databases**: With the help of databases, ReplicaSets can also store information. However, if we need a better performance in terms of write/update operations, we should use distributed sharded databases based on non-SQL engines such as Cosmos DB or MongoDB (see *Chapter 9, How to Choose Your Data Storage in the Cloud*). In this case, in order to take maximum advantage of table sharding, we need StatefulSets, where each pod instance takes care of a different table shard.

2. **Using cloud storage**: Not being tied to a physical cluster node, cloud storage can be associated permanently with specific pod instances of StatefulSets.

Since access to external databases doesn't require any Kubernetes-specific technique, but can be done with the usual connection strings, we will concentrate on cloud storage.

Kubernetes offers an abstraction of storage called **PersistentVolumeClaim** (PVC) that is independent of the underlying storage provider. More specifically, PVCs are allocation requests that are either matched to predefined resources or allocated dynamically. When the Kubernetes cluster is in the cloud, typically, you use dynamic allocation carried out by dynamic providers installed by the cloud provider.

Cloud providers such as Azure offer different storage classes with different performance and different costs. Moreover, the PVC can also specify the accessMode, which can be:

- ReadWriteOnce – The volume can be mounted as read-write by a single pod.
- ReadOnlyMany – The volume can be mounted as read-only by many pods.
- ReadWriteMany – The volume can be mounted as read-write by many pods.

Volume claims can be added to StatefulSets in a specific spec->volumeClaimTemplates object:

```
volumeClaimTemplates:
-  metadata:
     name: my-claim-template-name
spec:
   resources:
     request:
       storage: 5Gi
   volumeMode: Filesystem
   accessModes:
     - ReadWriteOnce
   storageClassName: my-optional-storage-class
```

The storage property contains the storage requirements. volumeMode set to Filesystem is a standard setting that means the storage will be available as a file path. The other possible value is Block, which allocates the memory as unformatted. storageClassName must be set to an existing storage class offered by the cloud provider. If omitted, the default storage class will be assumed.

All available storage classes can be listed with the following command:

```
kubectl get storageclass
```

Once volumeClaimTemplates has defined how to create permanent storage, then each container must specify which file path to attach that permanent storage to in the spec->containers->volumeMounts property:

```
...
volumeMounts
- name: my-claim-template-name
  mountPath: /my/requested/storage
  readOnly: false
...
```

Here, `name` must correspond to the name given to the PVC.

The following subsection shows how to use Kubernetes secrets.

Kubernetes secrets

Secrets are sets of key-value pairs that are encrypted to protect them. They can be created by putting each value in a file, and then invoking the following `kubectl` command:

```
kubectl create secret generic my-secret-name \
    --from-file=./secret1.bin \
    --from-file=./secret2.bin
```

In this case, the filenames become the keys and the file contents are the values.

When the values are strings, they can be specified directly in the `kubectl` command, as shown here:

```
kubectl create secret generic dev-db-secret \
    --from-literal=username=devuser \
    --from-literal=password=sdsd_weew1'
```

In this case, keys and values are listed one after the other, separated by the = character.

Once defined, secrets can be referred to in the `spec->volume` property of a pod (`Deployment` or `StatefulSettemplate`), as shown here:

```
...
volumes:
  - name: my-volume-with-secrets
    secret:
      secretName: my-secret-name
...
```

After that, each container can specify in which path to mount them in the `spec->containers->volumeMounts` property:

```
...
volumeMounts:
    - name: my-volume-with-secrets
      mountPath: "/my/secrets"
      readOnly: true
...
```

In the preceding example, each key is seen as a file with the same name of the key. The content of the file is the secret value, base64-encoded. Therefore, the code that reads each file must decode its content (in .NET, `Convert.FromBase64` will do the job).

When secrets contain strings, they can also be passed as environment variables in the `spec->containers->env` object:

```yaml
env:
    - name: SECRET_USERNAME
      valueFrom:
        secretKeyRef:
          name: dev-db-secret
          key: username
    - name: SECRET_PASSWORD
      valueFrom:
        secretKeyRef:
          name: dev-db-secret
          key: password
```

Here, the `name` property must match the secret name. Passing secrets as environment variables is very convenient when containers host ASP.NET Core applications, since, in this case, environment variables are all immediately available in the configuration object (see the *Loading configuration data and using it with the options framework* section of *Chapter 15, Presenting ASP.NET Core MVC*).

Secrets can also encode the key/certificate pair of an HTTPS certificate, with the following `kubectl` command:

```
kubectl create secret tls test-tls --key="tls.key" --cert="tls.crt"
```

Secrets defined in this way can be used to enable HTTPS termination in `Ingresses`. It is enough to place the secret names in the `spec->tls->hosts->secretName` properties of an `Ingress`.

Liveness and readiness checks

Kubernetes automatically monitors all containers to ensure they are still alive and that they keep their resource consumption within the limits declared in the `spec->containers->resources->limits` object. When some conditions are violated, the container is either throttled, or restarted, or the whole pod instance is restarted on a different node. How does Kubernetes know that a container is in a healthy state? While it can use the operating system to check the healthy state of nodes, it has no universal check that works with all containers.

Therefore, the containers themselves must inform Kubernetes of their healthy state, otherwise Kubernetes must renounce verifying them. Containers can inform Kubernetes of their healthy state in two ways, either by declaring a console command that returns the healthy state, or by declaring an endpoint that provides the same information.

Both declarations are provided in the `spec->containers->livenessProb` object. The console command check is declared as shown here:

```
...
  livenessProbe:
    exec:
      command:
      - cat
      - /tmp/healthy
    initialDelaySeconds: 10
    periodSeconds: 5
...
```

If `command` returns 0, the container is considered healthy. In the preceding example, we suppose that the software running in the container records its state of health in the `/tmp/healthy` file, so that the `cat/tmp/healthy` command returns it. PeriodSeconds is the time between checks, while `initialDelaySeconds` is the initial delay before performing the first check. An initial delay is always necessary so as to give the container time to start.

The endpoint check is quite similar:

```
...
  livenessProbe:
    exec:
      httpGet:
        path: /healthz
        port: 8080
        httpHeaders:
          - name: Custom-Health-Header
            value: container-is-ok
    initialDelaySeconds: 10
    periodSeconds: 5
...
```

The test is successful if the HTTP response contains the declared header with the declared value. You may also use a pure TCP check, as shown here:

```
...
   livenessProbe:
     exec:
       tcpSocket:
         port: 8080
     initialDelaySeconds: 10
     periodSeconds: 5
...
```

In this case, the check succeeds if Kubernetes is able to open a TCP socket to the container on the declared port.

In a similar way, the readiness of containers once they are installed is monitored with a readiness check. The readiness check is defined in exactly the same way as the liveness check, the only difference being that livenessProbe is replaced with readinessProbe.

The following subsection explains how to autoscale Deployments.

Autoscaling

Instead of modifying manually the number of replicas in a Deployment, in order to adapt it to a decrease or increase in load, we can let Kubernetes decide for itself the number of replicas trying to keep constant a declared resource consumption. Thus, for instance, if we declare a target 10% CPU consumption, when the average resource consumption of each replica exceeds this limit, a new replica is created, while if the average CPU falls below this limit, a replica is destroyed. The typical resource used to monitor replicas is CPU consumption, but we can also use memory consumption.

Autoscaling is achieved by defining a HorizontalPodAutoscaler object. Here is an example of the HorizontalPodAutoscaler definition:

```
apiVersion: autoscaling/v2beta1
kind: HorizontalPodAutoscaler
metadata:
  name: my-autoscaler
spec:
  scaleTargetRef:
    apiVersion: extensions/v1beta1
    kind: Deployment
    name: my-deployment-name
```

```
minReplicas: 1
maxReplicas: 10
metrics:
- type: Resource
  resource:
    name: cpu
    targetAverageUtilization: 25
```

spec-> scaleTargetRef->name specifies the name of the Deployment to autoscale, while targetAverageUtilization specifies the target resource (in our case, CPU) percentage usage (in our case, 25%).

The following subsection gives a short introduction to the Helm package manager and Helm charts, and explains how to install Helm charts on a Kubernetes cluster. An example of how to install an Ingress Controller is given.

Helm – Installing an Ingress Controller

Helm charts are a way to organize the installation of complex Kubernetes applications that contain several .yaml files. A Helm chart is a set of .yaml files, organized into folders and subfolders. Here is a typical folder structure of a Helm chart taken from the official documentation:

```
Chart.yaml          # A YAML file containing information about the chart
LICENSE             # OPTIONAL: A plain text file containing the license for the chart
README.md           # OPTIONAL: A human-readable README file
values.yaml         # The default configuration values for this chart
values.schema.json  # OPTIONAL: A JSON Schema for imposing a structure on the values.yaml file
charts/             # A directory containing any charts upon which this chart depends.
crds/               # Custom Resource Definitions
templates/          # A directory of templates that, when combined with values,
                    # will generate valid Kubernetes manifest files.
templates/NOTES.txt # OPTIONAL: A plain text file containing short usage notes
```

Figure 7.6: Folder structure of a Helm chart

The .yaml files specific to the application are placed in the top templates directory, while the charts directory may contain other Helm charts used as helper libraries. The top-level Chart.yaml file contains general information on the package (name and description), together with both the application version and the Helm chart version. The following is a typical example:

```
apiVersion: v2
name: myhelmdemo
```

```
description: My Helm chart
type: application
version: 1.3.0
appVersion: 1.2.0
```

Here, `type` can be either `application` or `library`. Only `application` charts can be deployed, while `library` charts are utilities for developing other charts. `library` charts are placed in the `charts` folder of other Helm charts.

In order to configure each specific application installation, Helm chart `.yaml` files contain variables that are specified when Helm charts are installed. Moreover, Helm charts also provide a simple templating language that allows some declarations to be included only if some conditions depending on the input variables are satisfied. The top-level `values.yaml` file declares default values for the input variables, meaning that the developer needs to specify just the few variables for which they require values different from the defaults. We will not describe the Helm chart templates language, but you can find it in the official Helm documentation referred to in the *Further reading* section.

Helm charts are usually organized in public or private repositories in a way that is similar to Docker images. There is a Helm client that you can use for downloading packages from a remote repository and for installing charts in Kubernetes clusters. The Helm client is immediately available in the Azure Cloud Shell, so you can start using Helm for your Azure Kubernetes cluster with no need to install it.

A remote repository must be added before using its packages, as shown in the following example:

```
helm repo add <my-repo-local-name> https://kubernetes-charts.storage.
googleapis.com/
```

The preceding command makes available the packages of a remote repository and gives a local name to it. After that, any package of the remote repository can be installed with a command such as the following:

```
helm install <instance name><my-repo-local-name>/<package name> -n
<namespace>
```

Here, `<namespace>` is the namespace where to install the application. As usual, if not provided, the `default` namespace is assumed. `<instance name>` is the name that you give to the installed application. You need this name to get information about the installed application with the following command:

```
helm status <instance name>
```

You can get also information about all applications installed with Helm with the help of the following command:

```
helm ls
```

The application name is also needed to delete the application from the cluster, by means of the following command:

```
helm delete <instance name>
```

When we install an application, we may also provide a `.yaml` file with all the variable values we want to override. We can also specify a specific version of the Helm chart, otherwise the more recent version is assumed. Here is an example with both the version and values overridden:

```
helm install <instance name><my-repo-local-name>/<package name> -f
values.yaml –version <version>
```

Finally, value overrides can also be provided in-line with the `--set` option, as shown here:

```
...--set <variable1>=<value1>,<variable2>=<value2>...
```

We can also upgrade an existing installation with the `upgrade` command, as shown here:

```
helm upgrade <instance name><my-repo-local-name>/<package name>...
```

The `upgrade` command may specify new value overrides with the `-f` option or with the `--set` option, and it can specify a new version with `--version`.

Let's use Helm to provide an `Ingress` for the guestbook demo application. More specifically, we will use Helm to install an `Ingress-Controller` based on Nginx. The detailed procedure to be observed is as follows:

1. Add the remote repository:
    ```
    helm repo add gcharts https://kubernetes-charts.storage.
    googleapis.com/
    ```

2. Install the `Ingress-Controller`:
    ```
    helm install ingress gcharts/nginx-ingress
    ```

3. When the installation is complete, you should see an entry for the installed `Ingress-Controller` among the installed services if you type `kubectl get service`. The entry should contain a public IP. Please make a note of this IP since it will be the public IP of the application.

4. Open the `frontend.yaml` file and remove the `type: LoadBalancer` line. Save and upload this to Azure Cloud Shell. We changed the service type of the frontend application from `LoadBalancer` to `ClusterIP` (the default). This service will be connected to the new Ingress you are going to define.

5. Deploy `redis-master.yaml`, `redis-slave.yaml`, and `frontend.yaml` with `kubectl`, as detailed in the *Deploying the demo Guestbook application* subsection. Create a `frontend-ingress.yaml` file and place the following code in it:

```
apiVersion: extensions/v1beta1
kind: Ingress
metadata:
  name: simple-frontend-ingress
spec:
  rules:
  - http:
      paths:
      - path:/
        backend:
          serviceName: frontend
          servicePort: 80
```

6. Upload `frontend-ingress.yaml` to Cloud Shell and deploy it with the following command:

```
kubectl apply -f frontend-ingress.yaml
```

7. Open the browser and navigate to the public IP you annotated in *step 3*. There, you should see the application running.

Since the public IP allocated to `Ingress-Controller` is available in the Azure *Public IP Addresses* section of Azure (use the Azure search box to find it), you can retrieve it there and assign it a hostname of the type `<chosen name>.<your Azure region>.cloudeapp.com`.

You are encouraged to assign a hostname to the application public IP, and then to use this hostname to get a free HTTPS certificate from `https://letsencrypt.org/`. Once you get a certificate, you can generate a secret from it with the following command:

```
kubectl create secret tls guestbook-tls --key="tls.key" --cert="tls.crt"
```

Then you can add the preceding secret to your `frontend-ingress.yamlIngress` by adding the following `spec->tls` section to it:

```
...
spec:
...
  tls:
  - hosts:
      - <chosen name>.<your Azure region>.cloudeapp.com
secretName: guestbook-tls
```

Following the correction, upload the file to your Azure Cloud Shell, and update the previous `Ingress` definition with the following:

```
kubectl apply frontend-ingress.yaml
```

At this point, you should be able to access the Guestbook application with HTTPS.

When you are done experimenting, please don't forget to delete everything from your cluster to avoid wasting your free Azure credit. You can do this by means of the following commands:

```
kubectl delete frontend-ingress.yaml
kubectl delete frontend.yaml
kubectl delete redis-slave.yaml
kubectl delete redis-master.yaml
helm delete ingress
```

Summary

In this chapter, we described Kubernetes basic concepts and objects, and then we explained how to create an Azure Kubernetes cluster. We also showed how to deploy applications, and how to monitor and inspect the state of your cluster with a simple demo application.

The chapter also described more advanced Kubernetes features that cover a fundamental role in practical applications, including how to provide persistent storage to the containers running on Kubernetes, how to inform Kubernetes of the health state of your containers, and how to offer advanced HTTP services, such as HTTPS and name-based virtual hosting.

Finally, we reviewed how to install complex applications with Helm, and gave a short description of Helm and Helm commands.

In the next chapter, you will learn how to connect your .NET application with databases with Entity Framework.

Questions

1. Why are Services needed?
2. Why is an `Ingress` needed?
3. Why is Helm needed?
4. Is it possible to define several Kubernetes objects in the same `.yaml` file? If yes, how?
5. How does Kubernetes detect container faults?
6. Why are persistent volume claims needed?
7. What is the difference between a `ReplicaSet` and a `StatefulSet`?

Further reading

-   A good book for extending the knowledge acquired in this chapter is the following: `https://www.packtpub.com/product/hands-on-kubernetes-on-azure-second-edition/9781800209671`.

-   The official documentation for Kubernetes and `.yaml` files can be found here: `https://kubernetes.io/docs/home/`.

-   More information on Helm and Helm charts can be found in the official documentation. This is extremely well written and contains some good tutorials: `https://helm.sh/`.

-   The official documentation for Azure Kubernetes can be found here: `https://docs.microsoft.com/en-US/azure/aks/`.

-   The official documentation on the Azure Application Gateway-based `Ingress Controller` is available here: `https://github.com/Azure/application-gateway-kubernetes-ingress`.

-   `Ingress` certificate release and renewal can be automated as explained here: `https://docs.microsoft.com/en-us/azure/application-gateway/ingress-controller-letsencrypt-certificate-application-gateway`. While the procedure specifies an Azure Application Gateway-based ingress controller, it is adequate for any `Ingress Controller`.

8

Interacting with Data in C# – Entity Framework Core

As we mentioned in *Chapter 5, Applying a Microservice Architecture to Your Enterprise Application*, software systems are organized into layers, and each layer communicates with the previous and next layers through interfaces that don't depend on how the layer is implemented. When the software is a business/enterprise system, it usually contains at least three layers: the data layer, the business layer, and the presentation layer. In general, the interface that's offered by each layer and the way the layer is implemented depends on the application.

However, it turns out that the functionalities offered by data layers are quite standard, since they just map data from a data storage subsystem into objects and vice versa. This led to the conception of general-purpose frameworks for implementing data layers in a substantially declarative way. These tools are called **Object-Relational Mapping (ORM)** tools since they are data storage subsystems based on relational databases. However, they also work well with the modern non-relational storage classified as NoSQL databases (such as MongoDB and Azure Cosmos DB) since their data model is closer to the target object model than a purely relational model.

In this chapter, we will cover the following topics:

- Understanding ORM basics
- Configuring Entity Framework Core
- Entity Framework Core migrations

- Querying and updating data with Entity Framework Core
- Deploying your data layer
- Understanding Entity Framework Core advanced features – global filters

This chapter describes ORMs and how to configure them, and then focuses on Entity Framework Core, the ORM included in .NET 5.

Technical requirements

This chapter requires the free Visual Studio 2019 Community edition or better with all the database tools installed.

All the concepts in this chapter will be clarified with practical examples based on the WWTravelClub book use case. You will find the code for this chapter at `https://github.com/PacktPublishing/Software-Architecture-with-C-9-and-.NET-5`.

Understanding ORM basics

ORMs map relational DB tables into in-memory collections of objects where object properties correspond to DB table fields. Types from C#, such as Booleans, numeric types, and strings, have corresponding DB types. If GUIDs are not available in the mapped database, then types such as GUIDs are mapped to their equivalent string representations. All date and time types are mapped either to C# `DateTime` when date/time contains no time zone information or to `DateTimeOffset` when date/time also contains explicit time zone information. Any DB time duration is mapped to a `TimeSpan`. Finally, single characters should not be mapped at all to DB fields.

Since the string properties of most object-oriented languages have no length limits associated with them (while DB string fields usually have length limits), the DB limits are taken into account in the DB mapping configuration. In general, when the mapping between DB types and object-oriented language types needs options to be specified, these options are declared in the mapping configuration.

The way the whole configuration is defined depends on the specific ORM. Entity Framework Core offers three options:

- Data annotations (property attributes)
- Name conventions
- A fluent configuration interface based on configuration objects and methods

While the fluent interface can be used to specify any configuration option, the data annotations and name conventions can be used for a smaller subset of them.

Personally, I prefer using the fluent interface for most settings. I use name conventions only for specifying the principal key with an ID property name, since I find that relying on name conventions also for more complex settings is very dangerous. In fact, there are no compilation-time checks on name conventions so a reengineering operation might erroneously change or destroy some ORM settings.

I use data annotations mainly for specifying constraints on the possible values of properties, such as the maximum length of a value, or the fact that a property is obligatory and can't be null. In fact, these constraints restrict the type specified in each property, so placing them next to the properties they are applied to increases the code's readability.

All other settings are better grouped and organized by using the fluent interface in order to increase code readability and maintainability.

Each ORM adapts to a specific DB type (Oracle, MySQL, SQL Server, and so on) with DB-specific adapters called **providers** or **connectors**. Entity Framework Core has providers for most of the available DB engines.

 A complete list of providers can be found at `https://docs.microsoft.com/en-US/ef/core/providers/`.

Adapters are necessary for the differences in DB types, for the way transactions are handled, and for all the other features that are not standardized by the SQL language.

Relations among tables are represented with object pointers. For instance, in a one-to-many relationship, the class that's mapped to the *one* side of the relationship contains a collection that is populated with the related objects on the *many* side of the relationship. On the other hand, the class mapped to the *many* side of the relationship has a simple property that is populated with a uniquely related object on the *one* side of the relationship.

The whole database (or just a part of it) is represented by an in-memory cache class that contains a property for each collection that's mapped to a DB table. First, the query and update operations are performed on an instance of an in-memory cache class, and then this instance is synchronized with the database.

The in-memory cache class that's used by Entity Framework Core is called `DbContext` and it also contains the mapping configuration. More specifically, the application-specific in-memory cache class is obtained by inheriting `DbContext` and adding it to all the mapped collections and all the necessary configuration information.

Summing up, `DbContext` subclass instances contain partial snapshots of the DB that are synchronized with the database to get/update the actual data.

DB queries are performed with a query language made of method calls on the collections of the in-memory cache class. The actual SQL is created and executed during the synchronization stage. For instance, Entity Framework Core performs **Language Integrated Queries (LINQ)** on the collections mapped to the DB tables.

In general, LINQ queries produce `IEnumerable` instances, that is, collections whose elements are not computed when `IEnumerable` is created at the end of the query, but when you actually attempt to retrieve the collection elements from `IEnumerable`. This is called lazy evaluation or deferred execution. It works as follows:

- LINQ queries that start from a mapped collection of a `DbContext` create a specific subtype of `IEnumerable` called `IQueryable`.

- An `IQueryable` contains all the information that's needed to issue a query to the database, but the actual SQL is produced and executed when the first element of the `IQueryable` is retrieved.

- Typically, each Entity Framework query ends with a `ToList` or `ToArray` operation that transforms the `IQueryable` into a list or array, thereby causing the actual execution of the query on the database.

- If the query is expected to return just a single element or no element at all, we typically execute a `SingleOrDefault` operation that returns a single element, if any, or `null`.

Also, updates, deletions, and the addition of new entities to a DB table are performed by mimicking these operations on a `DbContext` collection property that represents the database table. However, entities may only be updated or deleted this way after they have been loaded in that memory collection by means of a query. An update query requires the in-memory representation of the entity to be modified as needed, while a delete query requires the in-memory representation of the entity to be removed from its in-memory mapped collection. In Entity Framework Core, the removal operation is performed by calling the `Remove(entity)` method of the collection.

The addition of a new entity has no further requirements. It is enough to add the new entity to the in-memory collection. Updates, deletions, and additions that are performed on various in-memory collections are actually passed to the database with an explicit call to a DB synchronization method.

For instance, Entity Framework Core passes all the changes that are performed on a DbContext instance to the database when you call the DbContext.SaveChanges() method.

Changes that are passed to the database during a synchronization operation are executed in a single transaction. Moreover, for ORMs, such as Entity Framework Core, that have an explicit representation of transactions, a synchronization operation is executed in the scope of a transaction, since it uses that transaction instead of creating a new one.

The remaining sections in this chapter explain how to use Entity Framework Core, along with some example code based on this book's WWTravelClub use case.

Configuring Entity Framework Core

Since database handling is confined within a dedicated application layer, it is good practice to define your Entity Framework Core (DbContext) in a separate library. Accordingly, we need to define a .NET Core class library project. As we discussed in the *Book use case – understanding the main types of .NET Core projects* sections of *Chapter 2, Non-Functional Requirements*, we have two different kinds of library projects: **.NET Standard** and **.NET (Core)**.

While .NET Core libraries are tied to a specific .NET Core version, .NET Standard 2.0 libraries have a wide range of applications since they work with any .NET version greater than 2.0 and also with the classical .NET Framework 4.7.2 and above.

However, version 5 of the Microsoft.EntityFrameworkCore package, which is the version that comes with .NET 5, depends just on .NET Standard 2.1. This means that it is not designed to work with a specific .NET (Core) version but that it just requires a .NET Core version that supports .NET Standard 2.1. Therefore, Entity Framework 5 works properly with .NET 5 and with any .NET Core version higher than or equal to 2.1.

Since our library is not a general-purpose library (it's just a component of a specific .NET 5 application), instead of choosing a .NET Standard library project, we can simply choose a .NET 5 library. Our .NET 5 library project can be created and prepared as follows:

1. Open Visual Studio and define a new solution named WWTravelClubDB and then select **Class Library (.NET Core)** for the latest .NET Core version available.

2. We must install all Entity Framework Core-related dependencies. The simplest way to have all the necessary dependencies installed is to add the NuGet package for the provider of the database engine we are going to use – in our case, SQL Server – as we mentioned in *Chapter 4, Deciding the Best Cloud-Based Solution*. In fact, any provider will install all the required packages since it has all of them as dependencies. So, let's add the latest stable version of `Microsoft.EntityFrameworkCore.SqlServer`. If you plan to use several database engines, you can also add other providers since they can work side by side. Later in this chapter, we will install other NuGet packages that contain tools that we need to process our Entity Framework Core. Then, we will explain how to install further tools that are needed to process Entity Framework Core's configuration.

3. Let's rename the default `Class1` class to `MainDbContext`. This was automatically added to the class library.

4. Now, let's replace its content with the following code:

```
using System;
using Microsoft.EntityFrameworkCore;

namespace WWTravelClubDB
{
    public class MainDbContext: DbContext
    {
        public MainDbContext(DbContextOptions options)
            : base(options)
        {
        }
        protected override void OnModelCreating(ModelBuilder
        builder)
        {
        }
    }
}
```

5. We inherit from `DbContext` and we are required to pass `DbContextOptions` to the `DbContext` constructor. `DbContextOptions` contains creation options such as the database connection string, which depends on the target DB engine.

6. All the collections that have been mapped to database tables will be added as properties of `MainDbContext`. The mapping configuration will be defined inside of the overridden `OnModelCreating` method with the help of the `ModelBuilder` object passed as a parameter.

The next step is the creation of all the classes that represent all the DB table rows. These are called **entities**. We need an entity class for each DB table we want to map. Let's create a `Models` folder in the project root for all of them. The next subsection explains how to define all the required entities.

Defining DB entities

DB design, like the whole application design, is organized in iterations. Let's suppose that, in the first iteration, we need a prototype with two database tables: one for all the travel packages and another one for all the locations referenced by the packages. Each package covers just one location, while a single location may be covered by several packages, so the two tables are connected by a one-to-many relationship.

So, let's start with the location database table. As we mentioned at the end of the previous section, we need an entity class to represent the rows of this table. Let's call `Destination` the entity class:

```
namespace WWTravelClubDB.Models
{
    public class Destination
    {
        public int Id { get; set; }
        public string Name { get; set; }
        public string Country { get; set; }
        public string Description { get; set; }
    }
}
```

All the DB fields must be represented by read/write C# properties. Suppose that each destination is something like a town or a region that can be defined by just its name and the country it is in, and that all the relevant information is contained in its `Description`. In future iterations, we will probably add several more fields. `Id` is an auto-generated key.

However, now, we need to add information about how all the fields are mapped to DB fields. In Entity Framework Core, all the primitive types are mapped automatically to DB types by the DB engine-specific provider that's used (in our case, the SQL Server provider).

Our only preoccupations are as follows:

- **Length limits on the string**: They can be taken into account by applying adequate MaxLength and MinLength attributes to each string property. All the attributes that are useful for the entity's configuration are contained in the System.ComponentModel.DataAnnotations and System.ComponentModel.DataAnnotations.Schema namespaces. Therefore, it's good practice to add both of them to all the entity definitions.

- **Specifying which fields are obligatory and which ones are optional**: If the project is not using the new Nullable Reference Type feature, by default, all the reference types (such as all the strings) are assumed to be optional, while all the value types (numbers and GUIDs, for instance) are assumed to be obligatory. If we want a reference type to be obligatory, then we must decorate it with the Required attribute. On the other side, if we want a T type property to be optional, and T is a value type or the Nullable Reference Type feature is on, then we must replace T with T?.

- **Specifying which property represents the primary key**: The key may be specified by decorating a property with the Key attribute. However, if no Key attribute is found, a property named Id (if there is one) is taken as the primary key. In our case, there is no need for the Key attribute.

Since each destination is on the *one* side of a one-to-many relationship, it must contain a collection for the related package entities; otherwise, we will not be able to refer to the related entities in the clauses of our LINQ queries.

Putting everything together, the final version of the Destination class is as follows:

```csharp
using System.Collections.Generic;
using System.ComponentModel.DataAnnotations;
using System.ComponentModel.DataAnnotations.Schema;

namespace WWTravelClubDB.Models
{
    public class Destination
    {
        public int Id { get; set; }
        [MaxLength(128), Required]
        public string Name { get; set; }
        [MaxLength(128), Required]
        public string Country { get; set; }
        public string Description { get; set; }
        public ICollection<Package> Packages { get; set; }
    }
}
```

Since the `Description` property has no length limits, it will be implemented with a SQL Server nvarchar(`MAX`) field of indefinite length. We can write the code for the `Package` class in a similar way:

```
using System;
using System.ComponentModel.DataAnnotations;
using System.ComponentModel.DataAnnotations.Schema;
namespace WWTravelClubDB.Models
{
    public class Package
    {
        public int Id { get; set; }
        [MaxLength(128), Required]
        public string Name { get; set; }
        [MaxLength(128)]
        public string Description { get; set; }
        public decimal Price { get; set; }
        public int DurationInDays { get; set; }
        public DateTime? StartValidityDate { get; set; }
        public DateTime? EndValidityDate { get; set; }
        public Destination MyDestination { get; set; }
        public int DestinationId { get; set; }
    }
}
```

Each package has a duration in days, as well as optional start and stop dates in which the package offer is valid. `MyDestination` connects packages with their destinations in the many-to-one relationship that they have with the `Destination` entity, while `DestinationId` is the external key of the same relation.

While it is not obligatory to specify the external key, it is good practice to do so since this is the only way to specify some properties of the relationship. For instance, in our case, since `DestinationId` is an int (value type), it is obligatory. Therefore, the relationship here is one-to-many and not (0, 1)-to-many. Defining `DestinationId` as int?, instead of int, would turn the one-to-many relationship into a (0, 1)-to-many relationship. Moreover, as we will see later on in this chapter, having an explicit representation of the foreign key simplifies the update operations a lot, and some queries.

In the next section, we will explain how to define the in-memory collection that represents the database tables.

Defining the mapped collections

Once we have defined all the entities that are object-oriented representations of the database rows, we need to define the in-memory collections that represent the database tables themselves. As we mentioned in the *Understanding ORM basics* section, all the database operations are mapped to the operations on these collections (the *Querying and updating data with Entity Framework Core* section of this chapter explains how). It is enough to add a DbSet<T> collection property to our DbContext for each entity, T. Usually, the name of each of these properties is obtained by pluralizing the entity name. Thus, we need to add the following two properties to our MainDbContext:

```
public DbSet<Package> Packages { get; set; }
public DbSet<Destination> Destinations { get; set; }
```

Up until now, we've translated database stuff into properties, classes, and data annotations. However, Entity Framework needs further information to interact with a database. The next subsection explains how to provide it.

Completing the mapping configuration

The mapping configuration information that we couldn't specify in the entity definitions must be added in the OnModelCreating DbContext method. Each configuration information relative to an entity, T, starts with builder.Entity<T>() and continues with a call to a method that specifies that kind of constraint. Further nested calls specify further properties of the constraint. For instance, our one-to-many relationship may be configured as follows:

```
builder.Entity<Destination>()
    .HasMany(m => m.Packages)
    .WithOne(m => m.MyDestination)
    .HasForeignKey(m => m.DestinationId)
    .OnDelete(DeleteBehavior.Cascade);
```

The two sides of the relationship are specified through the navigation properties that we added to our entities. HasForeignKey specifies the external key. Finally, OnDelete specifies what to do with packages when a destination is deleted. In our case, it performs a cascade delete of all the packages related to that destination.

The same configuration can be defined by starting from the other side of the relationship, that is, starting with builder.Entity<Package>():

```
builder.Entity<Package>()
    .HasOne(m => m.MyDestination)
```

```
        .WithMany(m => m.Packages)
        .HasForeignKey(m => m.DestinationId)
        .OnDelete(DeleteBehavior.Cascade);
```

The only difference is that the previous statement's `HasMany-WithOne` methods are replaced by the `HasOne-WithMany` methods since we started from the other side of the relationship. Here we can also choose the precision with which each decimal property is represented in its mapped database field. As a default, decimals are represented by 18 digits and 2 decimals. You can change this setting for each property with something like:

```
...
.Property(m => m.Price)
        .HasPrecision(10, 3);
```

The `ModelBuilder` builder object allows us to specify database indexes with something such as the following:

```
builder.Entity<T>()
    .HasIndex(m => m.PropertyName);
```

Multi-property indexes are defined as follows:

```
builder.Entity<T>()
    .HasIndex("propertyName1", "propertyName2", ...);
```

Starting from version 5 indexes can also be defined with attributes applied to the class. Following is the case of a single property index:

```
[Index(nameof(Property), IsUnique = true)]
public class MyClass
{
    public int Id { get; set; }

    [MaxLength(128)]
    public string Property { get; set; }
}
```

Following is the case of a multi-property index:

```
[Index(nameof(Property1), nameof(Property2), IsUnique = false)]
public class MyComplexIndexClass
{
```

```
    public int Id { get; set; }

    [MaxLength(64)]
    public string Property1 { get; set; }

    [MaxLength(64)]
    public string Property2 { get; set; }
}
```

If we add all the necessary configuration information, then our `OnModelCreating` method will look as follows:

```
protected override void OnModelCreating(ModelBuilder builder)
{
    builder.Entity<Destination>()
        .HasMany(m => m.Packages)
        .WithOne(m => m.MyDestination)
        .HasForeignKey(m => m.DestinationId)
        .OnDelete(DeleteBehavior.Cascade);

    builder.Entity<Destination>()
        .HasIndex(m => m.Country);

    builder.Entity<Destination>()
        .HasIndex(m => m.Name);

    builder.Entity<Package>()
        .HasIndex(m => m.Name);

    builder.Entity<Package>()
        .HasIndex(nameof(Package.StartValidityDate),
                  nameof(Package.EndValidityDate));
}
```

The previous example show a one-to-many relation, but Entity Framework Core 5 also supports many-to-many relations:

```
modelBuilder
    .Entity<Teacher>()
    .HasMany(e => e.Classrooms)
    .WithMany(e => e.Teachers)
```

In the preceding case, the join entity and the database join table are created automatically, but you can also specify an existing entity as the join entity. In the previous example, the join entity might be the course that the teacher teaches in each classroom:

```
modelBuilder
  Entity<Teacher>()
  .HasMany(e => e.Classrooms)
  .WithMany(e => e.Teachers)
     .UsingEntity<Course>(
          b => b.HasOne(e => e.Teacher).WithMany()
          .HasForeignKey(e => e.TeacherId),
          b => b.HasOne(e => e.Classroom).WithMany()
          .HasForeignKey(e => e.ClassroomId));
```

Once you've configured Entity Framework Core, we can use all the configuration information we have to create the actual database and put all the tools we need in place in order to update the database's structure as the application evolves. The next section explains how.

Entity Framework Core migrations

Now that we've configured Entity Framework and defined our application-specific DbContext subclass, we can use the Entity Framework Core design tools to generate the physical database and create the database structure snapshot that's needed by Entity Framework Core to interact with the database.

Entity Framework Core design tools must be installed in each project that needs them as NuGet packages. There are two equivalent options:

- **Tools that work in any Windows console**: These are available through the Microsoft.EntityFrameworkCore.Design NuGet package. All Entity Framework Core commands are in dotnet ef ..... format since they are contained in the ef command line's .NET Core application.

- **Tools that are specific to the Visual Studio Package Manager Console**: These are contained in the Microsoft.EntityFrameworkCore.Tools NuGet package. They don't need the dotnet ef prefix since they can only be launched from the **Package Manager Console** inside of Visual Studio.

Entity Framework Core's design tools are used within the design/update procedure. This procedure is as follows:

1. We modify DbContext and entities' definitions as needed.
2. We launch the design tools to ask Entity Framework Core to detect and process all the changes we made.
3. Once launched, the design tools update the database structure snapshot and generate a new *migration*, that is, a file containing all the instructions we need in order to modify the physical database to reflect all the changes we made.
4. We launch another tool to update the database with the newly created migration.
5. We test the newly configured DB layer and, if new changes are necessary, we go back to *step 1*.
6. When the data layer is ready, it is deployed in staging or production, where all the migrations are applied once more to the actual staging/production database.

This is repeated several times in the various software project iterations and during the lifetime of the application.

If we operate on an already existing database, we need to configure DbContext and its models to reflect the existing structure of all the tables we want to map. Then, if we want to start using migration instead of continuing with direct database changes, we can call the design tools with the IgnoreChanges option so that they generate an empty migration. Also, this empty migration must be passed to the physical database so that it can synchronize a database structure version associated with the physical database with the version that's been recorded in the database snapshot. This version is important because it determines which migrations must be applied to a database and which ones have already been applied.

The whole design process needs a test/design database and, if we operate on an existing database, the structure of this test/design database must reflect the actual database – at least in terms of the tables we want to map. To enable design tools so that we can interact with the database, we must define the DbContextOptions options that they pass to the DbContext constructor. These options are important at design time since they contain the connection string of the test/design database. The design tools can be informed about our DbContextOptions options if we create a class that implements the IDesignTimeDbContextFactory<T> interface, where T is our DbContext subclass:

```
using Microsoft.EntityFrameworkCore;
using Microsoft.EntityFrameworkCore.Design;
```

```
namespace WWTravelClubDB
{
    public class LibraryDesignTimeDbContextFactory
        : IDesignTimeDbContextFactory<MainDbContext>
    {
        private const string connectionString =
            @"Server=(localdb)\mssqllocaldb;Database=wwtravelclub;
                Trusted_Connection=True;MultipleActiveResultSets=true";
        public MainDbContext CreateDbContext(params string[] args)
        {
            var builder = new DbContextOptionsBuilder<MainDbContext>();

            builder.UseSqlServer(connectionString);
            return new MainDbContext(builder.Options);
        }
    }
}
```

connectionString will be used by Entity Framework to create a new database in the local SQL Server instance that's been installed in the development machine and connects with Windows credentials. You are free to change it to reflect your needs.

Now, we are ready to create our first migration! Let's get started:

1. Let's go to the **Package Manager Console** and ensure that **WWTravelClubDB** is selected as our default project.

2. Now, type Add-Migration initial and press *Enter* to issue this command. Verify that you added the Microsoft.EntityFrameworkCore.Tools NuGet package before issuing this command, otherwise you might get an "unrecognized command" error:

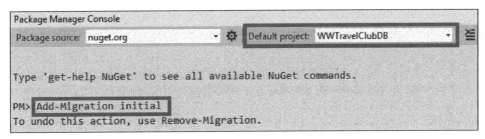

Figure 8.1: Adding the first migration

initial is the name we gave our first migration. So, in general, the command is Add-Migration <migration name>. When we operate on an existing database, we must add the -IgnoreChanges option to the first migration (and just to that) so that an empty migration is created. References to the whole set of commands can be found in the *Further reading* section.

3. If, after having created the migration, but before having applied the migration to the database, we realize we made some errors, we can undo our action with the Remove-Migration command. If the migration has already been applied to the database, the simplest way to correct our error is to make all the necessary changes to the code and then apply another migration.

4. As soon as the Add-Migration command is executed, a new folder appears in our project:

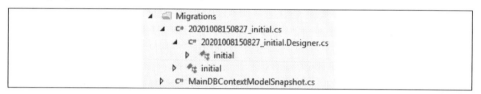

Figure 8.2: Files created by the Add-Migration command

 20201008150827_initial.cs is our migration expressed in an easy to understand language.

You may review the code to verify that everything is okay, and you may also modify the migration content (only if you are enough of an expert to do it reliably). Each migration contains an Up method and a Down method. The Up method implies the migration, while the Down method undoes its changes. Accordingly, the Down method contains the reverse actions of all the actions included in the Up method in reverse order.

20201008150827_initial.Designer.cs is the Visual Studio designer code you *must not* modify, while MainDBContextModelSnapshot.cs is the overall database structure snapshot. If you add further migrations, new migration files and their designer counterparts will appear and the unique MainDBContextModelSnapshot.cs database structure snapshot will be updated to reflect the database's overall structure.

The same command can be issued in a Windows console by typing dotnet ef migrations add initial. However, this command must be issued from within the project's root folder (not from within the solution's root folder).

Migrations can be applied to the database by typing Update-Database in the Package Manager Console. The equivalent Windows console command is dotnet ef database update. Let's try using this command to create the physical database!

The next subsection explains how to create database stuff that Entity Framework is unable to create automatically. After that, in the next section, we will use Entity Framework's configuration and the database we generated with dotnet ef database update to create, query, and update data.

Understanding stored procedures and direct SQL commands

Some database structures, like, for instance, stored procedures, can't be generated automatically by the Entity Framework Core commands and declarations we described previously. Stored procedures such as generic SQL strings can be included manually in the Up and Down methods through the migrationBuilder.Sql("<sql scommand>") method.

The safest way to do this is by adding a migration without performing any configuration changes so that the migration is empty when it's created. Then, we can add the necessary SQL commands to the empty Up method of this migration and their converse commands in the empty Down method. It is good practice to put all the SQL strings in the properties of resource files (.resx files).

Now, you are ready to interact with the database through Entity Framework Core.

Querying and updating data with Entity Framework Core

To test our DB layer, we need to add a console project based on the same .NET Core version as our library to the solution. Let's get started:

1. Let's call the new console project WWTravelClubDBTest.

2. Now, we need to add our data layer as a dependency of the console project by right-clicking on the **References** node of the console project and selecting **Add reference**.

3. Remove the content of the Main static method in the program.cs file and start by writing the following:

```
Console.WriteLine("program start: populate database, press a key
to continue");
Console.ReadKey();
```

4. Then, add the following namespaces at the top of the file:

```
using WWTravelClubDB;
using WWTravelClubDB.Models;
using Microsoft.EntityFrameworkCore;
using System.Linq;
```

Now that we have finished preparing our test project, we can experiment with queries and data updates. Let's start by creating some database objects, that is, some destinations and packages. Follow these steps to do so:

1. First, we must create an instance of our `DbContext` subclass with an appropriate connection string. We can use the same `LibraryDesignTimeDbContextFactory` class that's used by the design tools to get it:

```
var context = new LibraryDesignTimeDbContextFactory()
    .CreateDbContext();
```

2. New rows can be created by simply adding class instances to the mapped collections of our `DbContext` subclass. If a `Destination` instance has packages associated with it, we can simply add them to its `Packages` property:

```
var firstDestination= new Destination
{
    Name = "Florence",
    Country = "Italy",
    Packages = new List<Package>()
    {
        new Package
        {
            Name = "Summer in Florence",
            StartValidityDate = new DateTime(2019, 6, 1),
            EndValidityDate = new DateTime(2019, 10, 1),
            DurationInDays=7,
            Price=1000
        },
        new Package
        {
            Name = "Winter in Florence",
            StartValidityDate = new DateTime(2019, 12, 1),
            EndValidityDate = new DateTime(2020, 2, 1),
            DurationInDays=7,
            Price=500
```

```
            }
        }
    };
    context.Destinations.Add(firstDestination);
    context.SaveChanges();
    Console.WriteLine(
        "DB populated: first destination id is "+
        firstDestination.Id);
    Console.ReadKey();
```

There is no need to specify primary keys since they are auto-generated and will be filled in by the database. In fact, after the SaveChanges() operation synchronizes our context with the actual DB, the firstDestination.Id property has a non-zero value. The same is true for the primary keys of Package.

When we declare that an entity (in our case, Package) is a child of another entity (in our case, Destination) by inserting it in a parent entity collection (in our case, the Packages collection), there is no need to explicitly set its external key (in our case, DestinationId) since it is inferred automatically by Entity Framework Core. Once created and synchronized with the firstDestination database, we can add further packages in two different ways:

- Create a Package class instance, set its DestinationId external key to firstDestinatination.Id and add it to context.Packages
- Create a Package class instance, with no need to set its external key, and then add it to the Packages collection of its parent Destination instance.

The latter option is the only possibility when a child entity (Package) is added with its parent entity (Destination) and the parent entity has an auto-generated principal key since, in this case, the external key isn't available at the time we perform the additions. In most of the other circumstances, the former option is simpler since the second option requires the parent Destination entity to be loaded in memory, along with its Packages collection, that is, together with all the packages associated with the Destination object (by default, connected entities aren't loaded by queries).

Now, let's say we want to modify the *Florence* destination and give a 10% increment to all Florence package prices. How do we proceed? Follow these steps to find out how:

1. First, comment out all previous instructions for populating the database while keeping the DbContext creation instruction.
2. Then, we need to load the entity into memory with a query, modify it, and call SaveChanges() to synchronize our changes with the database.

If we want to modify, say, just its description, a query such as the following is enough:

```
var toModify = context.Destinations
    .Where(m => m.Name == "Florence").FirstOrDefault();
```

3. We need to load all the related destination packages that are not loaded by default. This can be done with the `Include` clause, as follows:

```
var toModify = context.Destinations
    .Where(m => m.Name == "Florence")
    .Include(m => m.Packages)
    .FirstOrDefault();
```

4. After that, we can modify the description and package prices, as follows:

```
toModify.Description =
    "Florence is a famous historical Italian town";
foreach (var package in toModify.Packages)
    package.Price = package.Price * 1.1m;
context.SaveChanges();

var verifyChanges= context.Destinations
    .Where(m => m.Name == "Florence")
    .FirstOrDefault();

Console.WriteLine(
    "New Florence description: " +
    verifyChanges.Description);
Console.ReadKey();
```

If entities included with the `Include` method themselves contain a nested collection we would like to include, we can use `ThenInclude` as shown here:

```
.Include(m => m.NestedCollection)
.ThenInclude(m => m.NestedNestedCollection)
```

Since Entity Framework always tries to translate each LINQ in a single SQL query, sometimes the resulting query might be too complex and slow. In such cases, starting from version 5, we can give Entity Framework the permission to split the LinQ query into several SQL queries, as shown here:

```
.AsSplitQuery().Include(m => m.NestedCollection)
.ThenInclude(m => m.NestedNestedCollection)
```

Performance issues can be addressed by inspecting the SQL generated by a LinQ query with the help of the `ToQueryString` method:

```
var mySQL = myLinQQuery.ToQueryString ();
```

Starting from version 5, included nested collection can also be filtered with `Where` as shown here:

```
.Include(m => m.Packages.Where(l-> l.Price < x))
```

So far, we've performed queries whose unique purpose is to update the retrieved entities. Next, we will explain how to retrieve information that will be shown to the user and/or be used by complex business operations.

Returning data to the presentation layer

To keep the layers separated and to adapt queries to the data that's actually needed by each *use case*, DB entities aren't sent as they are to the presentation layer. Instead, the data is projected into smaller classes that contain the information that's needed by the *use case*. These are implemented by the presentation layer's caller method. Objects that move data from one layer to another are called **Data Transfer Objects** (**DTOs**). As an example, let's create a DTO containing the summary information that is worth showing when returning a list of packages to the user (we suppose that, if needed, the user can get more details by clicking the package they are interested in):

1. Let's add a DTO to our WWTravelClubDBTest project that contains all the information that needs to be shown in a list of packages:

```
namespace WWTravelClubDBTest
{
    public class PackagesListDTO
    {
        public int Id { get; set; }
        public string Name { get; set; }
        public decimal Price { get; set; }
        public int DurationInDays { get; set; }
        public DateTime? StartValidityDate { get; set; }
        public DateTime? EndValidityDate { get; set; }
        public string DestinationName { get; set; }
        public int DestinationId { get; set; }
        public override string ToString()
        {
            return string.Format("{0}. {1} days in {2}, price:
            {3}", Name, DurationInDays, DestinationName, Price);
```

```
        }
    }
}
```

 We don't need to load entities in memory and then copy their data into the DTO, but database data can be projected directly into the DTO, thanks to the LINQ `Select` clause. This minimizes how much data is exchanged with the database.

2. As an example, we can populate our DTOs with a query that checks all the packages that are available around August 10:

```
var period = new DateTime(2019, 8, 10);
var list = context.Packages
    .Where(m => period >= m.StartValidityDate
    && period <= m.EndValidityDate)
    .Select(m => new PackagesListDTO
    {
        StartValidityDate=m.StartValidityDate,
        EndValidityDate=m.EndValidityDate,
        Name=m.Name,
        DurationInDays=m.DurationInDays,
        Id=m.Id,
        Price=m.Price,
        DestinationName=m.MyDestination.Name,
        DestinationId = m.DestinationId
    })
    .ToList();
foreach (var result in list)
    Console.WriteLine(result.ToString());
Console.ReadKey();
```

3. In the `Select` clause, we can also navigate to any related entities to get the data we need. For instance, the preceding query navigates to the related `Destination` entity to get the `Package` destination name.

4. The programs stop at each `Console.ReadKey()` method, waiting for you to hit any key. This way, you have time to analyze the output that's produced by all the code snippets that we added to the `Main` method.

5. Now, right-click on the WWTravelClubDBTest project in Solution Explorer and set it as the start project. Then, run the solution.

Now, we will learn how to handle operations that can't be efficaciously mapped to the immediate operations in the in-memory collections that represent the database tables.

Issuing direct SQL commands

Not all database operations can be executed efficiently by querying the database with LINQ and updating in-memory entities. For instance, counter increments can be performed more efficiently with a single SQL instruction. Moreover, some operations can be executed with acceptable performance if we define adequate stored procedures/SQL commands. In these cases, we are forced to either issue direct SQL commands to the database or call database stored procedures from our Entity Framework code. There are two possibilities: SQL statements that perform database operations but do not return entities, and SQL statements that do return entities.

SQL commands that don't return entities can be executed with the DbContext method, as follows:

```
int DbContext.Database.ExecuteSqlRaw(string sql, params object[]
parameters)
```

Parameters can be referenced in the string as {0}, {1}, ..., {n}. Each {m} is filled with the object contained at the m index of the parameters array, which is converted from a .NET type into the corresponding SQL type. The method returns the number of affected rows.

SQL commands that return collections of entities must be issued through the FromSqlRaw method of the mapped collection associated with those entities:

```
context.<mapped collection>.FromSqlRaw(string sql, params object[]
parameters)
```

Thus, for instance, a command that returns Package instances would look something like this:

```
var results = context.Packages.FromSqlRaw("<some sql>", par1, par2,
...).ToList();
```

SQL strings and parameters work like this in the ExecuteSqlRaw method. The following is a simple example:

```
var allPackages =context.Packages.FromSqlRaw(
    "SELECT * FROM Products WHERE Name = {0}",
    myPackageName)
```

It is good practice to put all the SQL strings in resource files and encapsulate all the ExecuteSqlRaw and FromSqlRaw calls inside the public methods that you defined in your DbContext subclasses, in order to keep the dependence from a specific database inside of your Entity Framework Core-based data layer.

Handling transactions

All the changes that are made to a DbContext instance are passed in a single transaction at the first SaveChanges call. However, sometimes, it is necessary to include queries and updates in the same transaction. In these cases, we must handle the transaction explicitly. Several Entity Framework Core commands can be included in a transaction if we put them inside a using block associated with a transaction object:

```
using (var dbContextTransaction = context.Database.BeginTransaction())
try{
   ...
   ...
   dbContextTransaction.Commit();
}
catch
{
   dbContextTransaction.Rollback();
}
```

In the preceding code, context is an instance of our DbContext subclass. Inside of the using block, the transaction can be aborted and committed by calling its Rollback and Commit methods. Any SaveChanges calls that are included in the transaction block use the transaction they are already in, instead of creating new ones.

Deploying your data layer

When your database layer is deployed in production or in staging, usually, an empty database already exists, so you must apply all the migrations in order to create all the database objects. This can be done by calling context.Database.Migrate(). The Migrate method applies the migrations that haven't been applied to the databases yet, so it may be called safely several times during the application's lifetime. context is an instance of our DbContext class that must be passed through a connection string with enough privileges to create tables and to perform all the operations included in our migrations. Thus, typically, this connection string is different from the string we will use during normal application operations.

During the deployment of a web application on Azure, we are given the opportunity to check migrations with a connection string we provide. We can also check migrations manually by calling the context.Database.Migrate() method when the application starts. This will be discussed in detail in *Chapter 15, Presenting ASP.NET Core MVC*, which is dedicated to ASP.NET MVC web applications.

For desktop applications, we can apply migrations during the installation of the application and of its subsequent updates.

At the first application installation and/or in subsequent application updates, we may need to populate some tables with initial data. For web applications, this operation can be performed at application start, while for desktop applications, this operation can be included in the installation.

Database tables can be populated with Entity Framework Core commands. First, though, we need to verify whether the table is empty in order to avoid adding the same table rows several times. This can be done with the `Any()` LINQ method, as shown in the following code:

```
if(!context.Destinations.Any())
{
    //populate here the Destinations table
}
```

Let's take a look at a few advanced features that Entity Framework Core has to share.

Understanding Entity Framework Core advanced features

An interesting Entity Framework advanced feature that is worth mentioning is global filters, which were introduced at the end of 2017. They enable techniques such as soft delete and multi-tenant tables that are shared by several users, where each user just *sees* its records.

Global filters are defined with the `modelBuilder` object, which is available in the `DbContext` `OnModelCreating` method. The syntax for this method is as follows:

```
modelBuilder.Entity<MyEntity>().HasQueryFilter(m => <define filter
condition here>);
```

For instance, if we add an `IsDeleted` property to our `Package` class, we may soft delete a `Package` without removing it from the database by defining the following filter:

```
modelBuilder.Entity<Package>().HasQueryFilter(m => !m.IsDeleted);
```

However, filters contain DbContext properties. Thus, for instance, if we add a CurrentUserID property to our DbContext subclass (whose value is set as soon as a DbContext instance is created), then we can add a filter like the following one to all the entities that refer to a user ID:

```
modelBuilder.Entity<Document>().HasQueryFilter(m => m.UserId ==
CurrentUserId);
```

With the preceding filter in place, the currently logged-in user can only access the documents they own (the ones that have their UserId). Similar techniques are very useful in the implementation of multi-tenant applications.

Another interesting feature that is worth mentioning is mapping entities to un-updatable database queries, which was introduced in version 5.

When you define an entity, you can define explicitly either the name of the mapped database table or the name of a mapped updatable view:

```
modelBuilder.Entity<MyEntity1>().ToTable("MyTable");
modelBuilder.Entity<MyEntity2>().ToView("MyView");
```

When an entity is mapped to a view, no table is generated by database migration, so the database view must be defined manually by the developer.

If the view we would like to map out entity is not updatable, LinQ cannot use it to pass updates to the database. In this case, we can map the same entity simultaneously to a view and a table:

```
modelBuilder.Entity<MyEntity>().ToTable("MyTable").ToView("MyView");
```

Entity Framework will use the view for the queries and the table for the updates. This is useful when we create a newer version of a database table but we want to also take data from the old version of the table in all queries. In this case, we may define a view that takes data from both the old and the new tables, but pass all updates only on the new table.

Summary

In this chapter, we looked at the essentials of ORM basics and why they are so useful. Then, we described Entity Framework Core. In particular, we discussed how to configure database mappings with class annotations and other declarations and commands that are included in DbContext subclasses.

Then, we discussed how to automatically create and update the physical database structure with the help of migrations, as well as how to query and pass updates to the database through Entity Framework Core. Finally, we learned how to pass direct SQL commands and transactions through Entity Framework Core, as well as how to deploy a data layer based on Entity Framework Core.

This chapter also reviewed a couple of advanced features that were introduced in the latest Entity Framework Core releases.

In the next chapter, we will discuss how Entity Framework Core can be used with NoSQL data models and the various types of storage options that are available in the cloud and, in particular, in Azure.

Questions

1. How does Entity Framework Core adapt to several different database engines?

2. How are primary keys declared in Entity Framework Core?

3. How is a string field's length declared in Entity Framework Core?

4. How are indexes declared in Entity Framework Core?

5. How are relations declared in Entity Framework Core?

6. What are the two important migration commands?

7. By default, are related entities loaded by LINQ queries?

8. Is it possible to return database data in a class instance that isn't a database entity? If yes, how?

9. How are migrations applied in production and staging?

Further reading

- More details about migration commands can be found at `https://docs.microsoft.com/en-US/ef/core/miscellaneous/cli/index` and at the other links contained there.

- More details about Entity Framework Core can be found in the official Microsoft documentation: `https://docs.microsoft.com/en-us/ef/core/`.

- An exhaustive set of examples of complex LINQ queries can be found here: `https://code.msdn.microsoft.com/101-LINQ-Samples-3fb9811b`.

9

How to Choose Your Data Storage in the Cloud

Azure, like other clouds, offers a wide range of storage devices. The simplest approach is to define a scalable set of virtual machines hosted in the cloud where we can implement our custom solutions. For instance, we can create a SQL Server cluster on our cloud-hosted virtual machines to increase reliability and computational power. However, usually, custom architectures are not the optimal solution and do not take full advantage of the opportunities offered by the cloud infrastructure.

Therefore, this chapter will not discuss such custom architectures but will focus mainly on the various **Platform as a Service (PaaS)** storage offerings that are available in the cloud and on Azure. These offerings include scalable solutions based on plain disk space, relational databases, NoSQL databases, and in-memory data stores such as Redis.

Choosing a more adequate storage type is based not only on the application's functional requirements but also on performance and scaling-out requirements. In fact, while scaling out when processing resources causes a linear increase in performance, scaling out storage resources does not necessarily imply an acceptable increase in performance. In a few words, no matter how much you duplicate your data storage devices, if several requests affect the same chunk of data, they will always queue for the same amount of time to access it!

Scaling out data causes linear increases in read operation throughput since each copy can serve a different request, but it doesn't imply the same increase in throughput for write operations since all copies of the same chunk of data must be updated! Accordingly, more sophisticated techniques are required to scale out storage devices, and not all storage engines scale equally well.

Relational databases do not scale well in all scenarios. Therefore, scaling needs and the need to distribute data geographically play a fundamental role in the choice of a storage engine, as well as in the choice of a SaaS offering.

In this chapter, we will cover the following topics:

- Understanding the different repositories for different purposes
- Choosing between relational or NoSQL storage
- Azure Cosmos DB – an opportunity to manage a multi-continental database
- Use case – storing data

Let's get started!

Technical requirements

This chapter requires that you have the following:

- Visual Studio 2019 free Community edition or better, with all the database tools components installed.
- A free Azure account. The *Creating an Azure account* subsection in *Chapter 1, Understanding the Importance of Software Architecture*, explains how to create one.
- For a better development experience, we advise that you also install the local emulator of Cosmos DB, which can be found at `https://aka.ms/cosmosdb-emulator`.

Understanding the different repositories for different purposes

This section describes the functionalities that are offered by the most popular data storage techniques. Mainly, we will focus on the functional requirements they are able to satisfy. Performance and scaling-out features will be analyzed in the next section, which is dedicated to comparing relational and NoSQL databases.

In Azure, the various offerings can be found by typing product names into the search bar at the top of all Azure portal pages.

The following subsections describe the various kinds of databases that we can use in our C# projects.

Relational databases

Relational databases are the most common and studied type of storage. With them, society evolves, guaranteeing a high level of service and an uncountable amount of stored data. Dozens of applications have been designed to store data in this kind of database, and we can find them in banks, stores, industries, and so on. When you store data in a relational database, the basic principle is to define the entities and properties you will save in each of them, defining the correct relationship between these entities.

For decades, relational databases were the only option imagined for designing great projects. Many big companies in the world have built their own database management system. Oracle, MySQL, and MS SQL Server would be listed by many as the ones you can trust to store your data.

Usually, clouds offer several database engines. Azure offers a variety of popular database engines, such as Oracle, MySQL, and SQL Server (Azure SQL).

Regarding the Oracle database engine, Azure offers configurable virtual machines with various Oracle editions installed on them, which you can easily verify by the suggestions you get after typing `Oracle` into the Azure portal search bar. Azure fees do not include Oracle licenses; they just include computation time, so you must bring your own license to Azure.

With MySQL on Azure, you pay to use a private server instance. The fees you incur depend on the number of cores you have, how much memory must be allocated, and on backup retention time.

MySQL instances are redundant, and you can choose between local or geographically distributed redundancy:

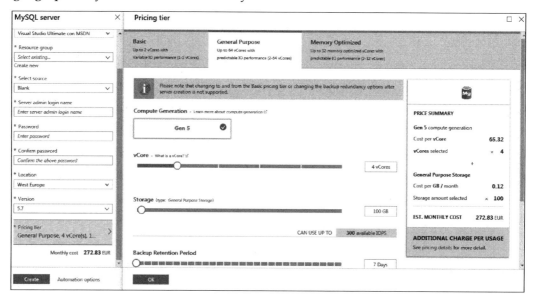

Figure 9.1: Creating a MySQL server on Azure

Azure SQL is the most flexible offer. Here, you can configure resources that are used by every single database. When you create a database, you have the option to place it on an existing server instance or create a new instance. There are several pricing options that you may choose while defining your solution and Azure keeps incrementing them to make sure you will be able to handle your data in the cloud. Basically, they vary due to the computing capacity you need.

For instance, in the **Database Transaction Units (DTUs)** model, fees are based on the database storage capacity that has been reserved and a linear combination of I/O operations, CPU usage, and memory usage that is determined by a reference workload. Roughly, maximal database performance increases linearly when you increase DTUs.

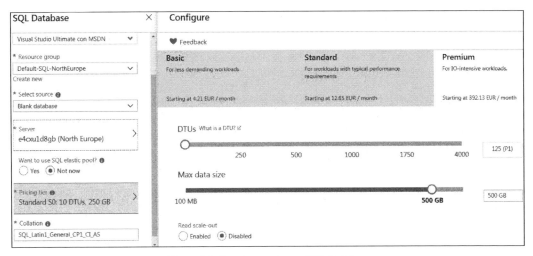

Figure 9.2: Creating an Azure SQL Database

You can also configure data replication by enabling read scale-out. This way, you can improve the performance of read operations. Backup retention is fixed for each offering level (basic, standard, and premium).

If you select **Yes** for **Want to use SQL elastic pool?**, the database will be added to an elastic pool. Databases that are added to the same elastic pool will share their resources, so resources that are not used by a database can be used during the usage CPU peaks of other databases. It is worth mentioning that elastic pools can only contain databases hosted on the same server instance. Elastic pools are an efficient way to optimize resource usage to reduce costs.

NoSQL databases

One of the biggest challenges that relational databases have caused software architects is related to how we deal with database structural schema changes. The agility of changes needed at the beginning of this century brought the opportunity of using a new database style, called NoSQL. There are several types of NoSQL database, as we can see here:

- **Document-Oriented Database**: The most common one, where you have the key and complex data called a document.
- **Graph Database**: Social media tend to use this kind of database since the data is stored as graphs.

- **Key-Value Database**: A useful database for implementing caches since you have the opportunity of storing key-value pairs.

- **Wide-Column Store Database**: A database where the same column in each row can store different data.

In NoSQL databases, relational tables are replaced with more general collections that can contain heterogeneous JSON objects. That is, collections have no predefined structure and no predefined fields with length constraints (in the case of strings) but can contain any type of object. The only structural constraint associated with each collection is the name of the property that acts as a primary key.

More specifically, each collection entry can contain nested objects and object collections nested in object properties, that is, related entities that, in relational databases, are contained in different tables and connected through external keys. In NoSQL, databases can be nested in their father entities. Since collection entries contain complex nested objects instead of simple property/value pairs, as is the case with relational databases, entries are not called tuples or rows, but *documents*.

No relations and/or external key constraints can be defined between documents that belong to the same collection or to different collections. If a document contains the primary key of another document in one of its properties, it does so at its own risk. The developer has the responsibility of maintaining and keeping these coherent references.

Finally, since NoSQL storage is quite cheap, whole binary files can be stored as the values of document properties as Base64 strings. The developer can define rules to decide what properties to index in a collection. Since documents are nested objects, properties are tree paths. Usually, by default, all the paths are indexed, but you can specify which collection of paths and sub-paths to index.

NoSQL databases are queried either with a subset of SQL or with a JSON-based language where queries are JSON objects whose paths represent the properties to query, and whose values represent the query constraints that have been applied to them.

The possibility of nesting children objects inside documents can be simulated in relational databases with the help of one-to-many relationships. However, with relational databases, we are forced to redefine the exact structure of all the related tables, while NoSQL collections do not impose any predefined structure on the objects they contain. The only constraint is that each document must provide a unique value for the primary key property. Therefore, NoSQL databases are the only option when the structure of our objects is extremely variable.

However, often they are chosen for the way they scale out read and write operations and, more generally, for their performance advantages in distributed environments. Their performance features will be discussed in the next section, which compares them to relational databases.

The graph data model is an extreme case of a completely unstructured document. The whole database is a graph where queries can add, change, and delete graph documents.

In this case, we have two kinds of document: nodes and relationships. While relationships have a well-defined structure (the primary key of the nodes connected by the relationship, plus the relationship's name), nodes have no structure at all since properties and their values are added together during node update operations. Graph data models were conceived to represent the features of people and the objects they manipulate (media, posts, and so on), along with their relationships in *social applications*. The Gremlin language was conceived specifically to query graph data models. We will not discuss this in this chapter, but references are available in the *Further reading* section.

NoSQL databases will be analyzed in detail in the remaining sections of this chapter, which are dedicated to describing Azure Cosmos DB and comparing it with relational databases.

Redis

Redis is a distributed concurrent in-memory storage based on key-value pairs and supports distributed queuing. It can be used as permanent in-memory storage and as a web application cache for database data. Alternatively, it can be used as a cache for pre-rendered content.

Redis can also be used to store a web application's user session data. In fact, ASP.NET Core supports session data to overcome the fact that the HTTP protocol is stateless. More specifically, user data that is kept between page changes is maintained in server-side stores such as Redis and indexed by a session key stored in cookies.

Interaction with the Redis server in the cloud is typically based on a client implementation that offers an easy-to-use interface. The client for .NET and .NET Core is available through the `StackExchange.Redis` NuGet package. The basic operations of the `StackExchange.Redis` client have been documented at `https://stackexchange.github.io/StackExchange.Redis/Basics`, while the full documentation can be found at `https://stackexchange.github.io/StackExchange.Redis`.

The user interface for defining a Redis server on Azure is quite simple:

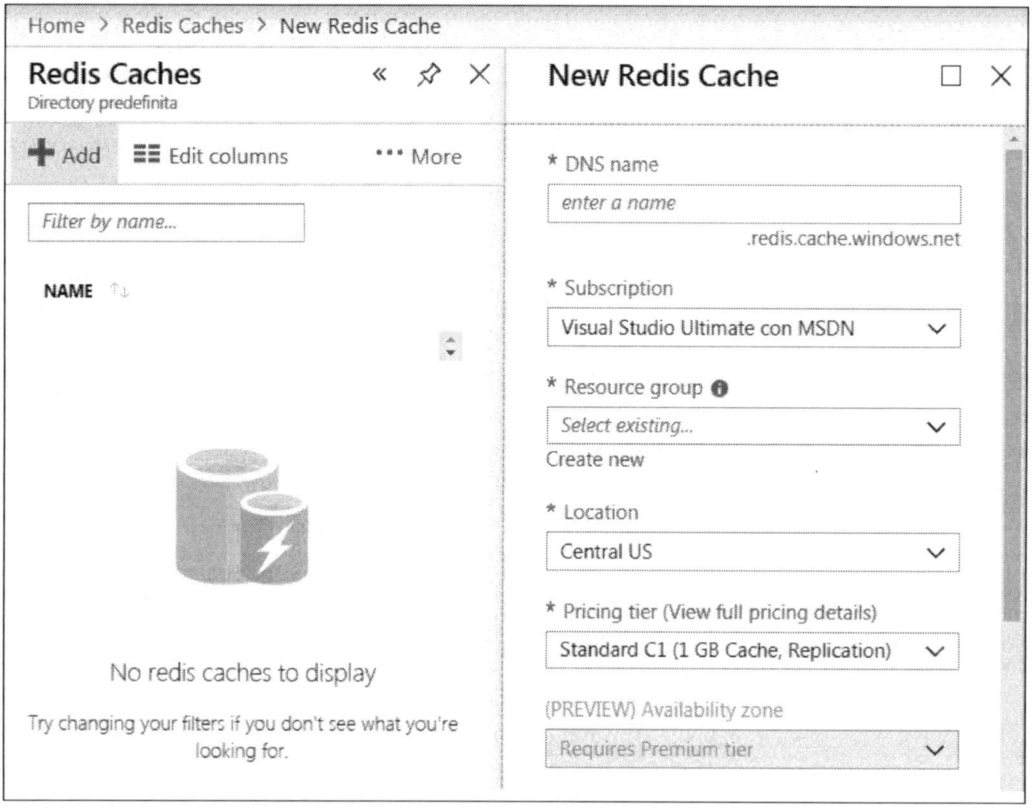

Figure 9.3: Creating a Redis cache

The **Pricing tier** dropdown allows us to select one of the available memory/replication options. A quick-start guide that explains how to use Azure Redis credentials and the URI with the StackExchange.Redis .NET Core client can be found at https://docs.microsoft.com/en-us/azure/azure-cache-for-redis/cache-dotnet-core-quickstart.

Azure storage accounts

All clouds offer scalable and redundant general-purpose disk memory that you can use as virtual disks in virtual machines and/or as external file storage. Azure *storage account* disk space can also be structured in **Tables** and **Queues**. Consider using this option if you need cheap blob storage. However, there are more sophisticated options, as we have mentioned before. Depending on the scenario you have, Azure NoSQL databases are a better option than tables and Azure Redis is a better option than Azure storage queues.

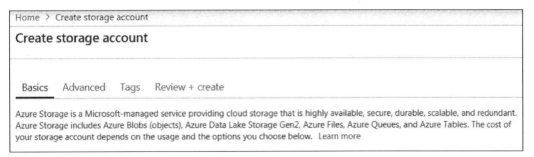

Figure 9.4: Creating a storage account

In the rest of this chapter, we will focus on NoSQL databases and how they differ from relational databases. Next, we will look at how to choose one over the other.

Choosing between structured or NoSQL storage

As a software architect, you may consider some aspects of structured and NoSQL storage to decide the best storage option for you. In many cases, both will be needed. The key point here will surely be how organized your data is and how big the database will become.

In the previous section, we stated that NoSQL databases should be preferred when data has almost no predefined structure. NoSQL databases not only keep variable attributes close to their owners, but they also keep some related objects close since they allow related objects to be nested inside properties and collections.

Unstructured data can be represented in relational databases since variable properties of a tuple, t, can be placed in a connected table containing the property name, property value, and the external key of t. However, the problem in this scenario is performance. In fact, property values that belong to a single object would be spread all over the available memory space. In a small database, *all over the available memory space* means far away but on the same disk; in a bigger database, it means far away but in different disk units; in a distributed cloud environment, it means far away but in different – and possibly geographically distributed – servers.

In NoSQL database design, we always try to put all related objects that are likely to be processed together into a single entry. Related objects that are accessed less frequently are placed in different entries. Since external key constraints are not enforced automatically and NoSQL transactions are very flexible, the developer can choose the best compromise between performance and coherence.

Therefore, we can conclude that relational databases perform well when tables that are usually accessed together can be stored close together. NoSQL databases, on the other hand, automatically ensure that related data is kept close together since each entry keeps most of the data it is related to inside it as nested objects. Therefore, NoSQL databases perform better when they are distributed to a different memory and to different geographically distributed servers.

Unfortunately, the only way to scale out storage write operations is to split collection entries across several servers according to the values of *shard keys*. For instance, we can place all the records containing usernames that start with **A** on a server, the records containing usernames that start with **B** on another server, and so on. This way, write operations for usernames with different start letters may be executed in parallel, ensuring that the write throughput increases linearly with the number of servers.

However, if a *shard* collection is related to several other collections, there is no guarantee that related records will be placed on the same server. Also, putting different collections on different servers without using collection sharding increases write throughput linearly until we reach the limit of a single collection per server, but it doesn't solve the issue of being forced to perform several operations on different servers to retrieve or update data that's usually processed together.

This issue becomes catastrophic for performance in relational databases if access to related distributed objects must be transactional and/or must ensure structural constraints (such as external key constraints) are not violated. In this case, all related objects must be blocked during the transaction, preventing other requests from accessing them during the whole lifetime of a time-consuming distributed operation.

NoSQL databases do not suffer from this problem and perform better with sharding and consequently with write-scaled output. This is because they do not distribute related data to different storage units and instead store them as nested objects of the same database entry. On the other hand, they suffer from different problems, like not supporting transactions by default.

It is worth mentioning that there are situations where relational databases perform well with sharding. A typical instance is a multi-tenant application. In a multi-tenant application, all entries collections can be partitioned into non-overlapping sets called **tenants**. Only entries belonging to the same tenant can refer to each other, so if all the collections are sharded in the same way according to their object tenants, all related records end up in the same shard, that is, in the same server, and can be navigated efficiently.

Multi-tenant applications are not rare in the cloud since all applications that offer the same services to several different users are often implemented as multi-tenant applications, where each tenant corresponds to a user subscription. Accordingly, relational databases are conceived to work in the cloud, such as Azure SQL Server, and usually offer sharding options for multi-tenant applications. Typically, sharding is not a cloud service and must be defined with database engine commands. Here, we will not describe how to define shards with Azure SQL Server, but the *Further reading* section contains a link to the official Microsoft documentation.

In conclusion, relational databases offer a pure, logical view of data that is independent of the way they are actually stored and use a declarative language to query and update them. This simplifies development and system maintenance, but it may cause performance issues in a distributed environment that requires write scale-out. In NoSQL databases, you must handle more details about how to store data, as well as some procedural details for all the update and query operations, manually, but this allows you to optimize performance in distributed environments that require both read and write scale-out.

In the next section, we will look at Azure Cosmos DB, the main Azure NoSQL offering.

Azure Cosmos DB – an opportunity to manage a multi-continental database

Azure Cosmos DB is Azure's main NoSQL offering. Azure Cosmos DB has its own interface that is a subset of SQL, but it can be configured with a MongoDB interface. It can also be configured as a graph data model that can be queried with Gremlin. Cosmos DB allows replication for fault tolerance and read scale-out, and replicas can be distributed geographically to optimize communication performance. Moreover, you can specify which data center all the replicas are placed in. The user also has the option to write-enable all the replicas so that writes are immediately available in the geographical area where they are done. Write scale-up is achieved with sharding, which the user can configure by defining which properties to use as shard keys.

Creating an Azure Cosmos DB account

You can define a Cosmos DB account by typing `Cosmos DB` into the Azure portal search bar and clicking **Add**. The following page will appear:

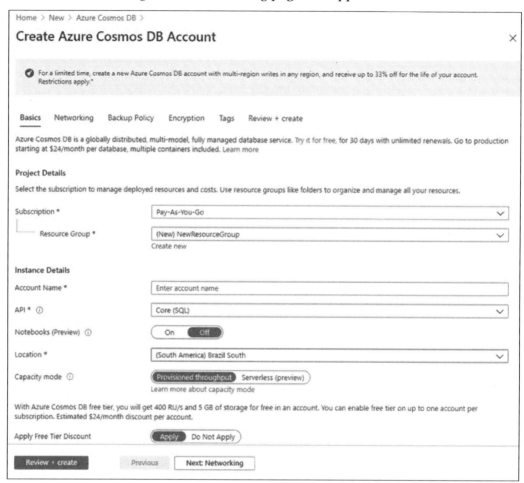

Figure 9.5: Creating an Azure Cosmos DB account

The account name you choose is used in the resource URI as {account_name}.documents.azure.com. The **API** dropdown lets you choose the kind of interface you prefer (for example, SQL, MongoDB, or Gremlin). Then, you can decide which data center the main database will be placed in and whether you want to enable geographically distributed replication. Once you have enabled geographically distributed replication, you can choose the number of replicas you want to use and where to place them.

Microsoft has been improving many of its Azure services. By the time this book was written, the Serverless option for capacity mode and Notebooks were in Preview. The best way to keep updated about new features of any Azure Component is by checking its documentation from time to time.

The **Multi-region Writes** toggle lets you enable writes on geographically distributed replicas. If you do not do this, all write operations will be routed to the main data center. Finally, you may also define backup policies and encryption during the creation process.

Creating an Azure Cosmos container

Once you have created your account, select **Data Explorer** to create your databases and containers inside of them. A container is the unit of scalability both for provisioned throughput and storage.

Since databases just have a name and no configuration, you can directly add a container and then the database where you wish to place it:

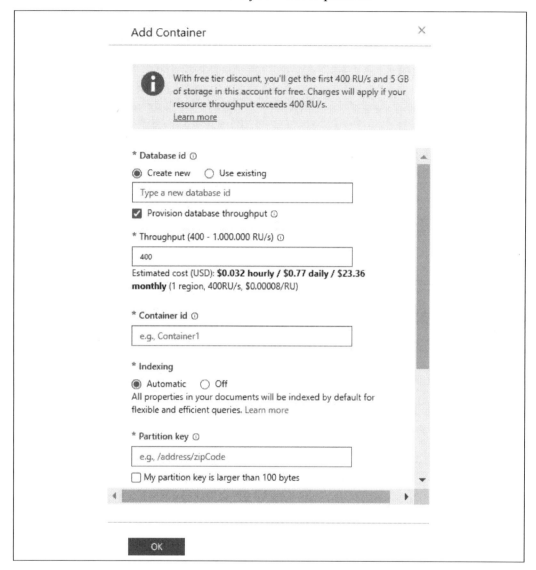

Figure 9.6: Adding a container in Azure Cosmos DB

Here, you can decide on database and container names and the property to use for sharding (the partition key). Since NoSQL entries are object trees, property names are specified as paths. You can also add properties whose values are required to be unique.

However, uniqueness IDs are checked inside each shard, so this option is only useful in certain situations, such as multi-tenant applications (where each tenant is included in a single shard). The fees depend on the collection throughput that you choose.

This is where you need to target all resource parameters to your needs. Throughput is expressed in request units per second, where request units per second is defined as the throughput we have when performing a read of 1 KB per second. Hence, if you check the *Provision database throughput* option, the chosen throughput is shared with the whole database, instead of being reserved as a single collection.

Accessing Azure Cosmos data

After creating the Azure Cosmos container, you will be able to access data. To get connection information, you can select the **Keys** menu. There, you will see all the information you need to connect with your Cosmos DB account from your application. **The connection information page** will provide you with the account URI and two connection keys, which can be used interchangeably to connect with the account.

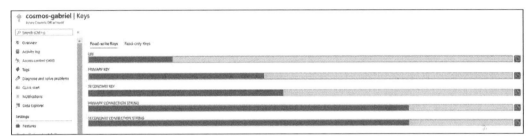

Figure 9.7: Connection information page

There are also keys with read-only privileges. Every key can be regenerated, and each account has two equivalent keys, like many other Azure Components. This approach enables operations to be handled efficiently; that is, when a key is changed, the other one is kept. Therefore, existing applications can continue using the other key before upgrading to the new key.

Defining database consistency

Considering that you are in the context of a distributed database, Azure Cosmos DB enables you to define the default read consistency level you will have. By selecting **Default consistency** in the main menu of your Cosmos DB account, you can choose the default replication consistency that you wish to apply to all your containers.

This default can be overridden in each container, either from Data Explorer or programmatically. Consistency problems in read/write operations are a consequence of data replication. More specifically, the results of various read operations may be incoherent if the read operations are executed on different replicas that have received different partial updates.

The following are the available consistency levels. These have been ordered from the weakest to the strongest:

- **Eventual**: After enough time has passed, if no further write operations are done, all the reads converge and apply all the writes. The order of writes is also not guaranteed, so while writes are being processed, you could also end up reading an earlier version than the one you have previously read.

- **Consistent Prefix**: All the writes are executed in the same order on all the replicas. So, if there are n write operations, each read is consistent with the result of applying the first m writes for some m less or equal to n.

- **Session**: This is the same as the consistency prefix but also guarantees that each writer sees the result of its own writes in all subsequent read operations and that subsequent reads of each reader are coherent (either the same database or a more updated version of it).

- **Bounded Staleness**: This is associated either with a delay time, Delta, or with several operations, N. Each read sees the results of all the write operations that were performed before a time Delta (or before the last N operations). That is, its reads converge with the result of all the writes with a maximum time delay of Delta (or a maximum operations delay of N).

- **Strong**: This is bounded staleness combined with Delta = 0. Here, each read reflects the result of all previous write operations.

The strongest consistency can be obtained to the detriment of performance. By default, the consistency is set to **Session**, which is a good compromise between coherence and performance. A lower level of consistency is difficult to handle in applications and is only usually acceptable if sessions are either read-only or write-only.

If you select the **Settings** option in the **Data Explorer** menu of the container of your database, you can configure which paths to index and which kind of indexing to apply to each data type of each path. The configuration consists of a JSON object. Let us analyze its various properties:

```
{
    "indexingMode": "consistent",
    "automatic": true,
    ...
```

If you set `indexingMode` to `none` instead of `consistent`, no index is generated, and the collection can be used as a key-value dictionary that is indexed by the collection primary key. In this scenario, no **secondary** indexes are generated, so the primary key could not efficiently be searched on. When `automatic` is set to `true`, all document properties are automatically indexed:

```
{
    ...
    "includedPaths": [
        {
            "path": "/*",
            "indexes": [
                {
                    "kind": "Range",
                    "dataType": "Number",
                    "precision": -1
                },
                {
                    "kind": "Range",
                    "dataType": "String",
                    "precision": -1
                },
                {
                    "kind": "Spatial",
                    "dataType": "Point"
                }
            ]
        }
    ]
},
...
```

Each entry in the `IncludedPaths` specifies a path pattern such as `/subpath1/subpath2/?` (settings apply just to the `/subpath1/subpath2/property`) or `/subpath1/subpath2/*` (settings apply to all the paths starting with `/subpath1/subpath2/`).

Patterns contain the `[]` symbol when settings must be applied to child objects contained in collection properties; for example, `/subpath1/subpath2/[]/?`, `/subpath1/subpath2/[]/childpath1/?`, and so on. Settings specify the index type to apply to each data type (string, number, geographic point, and so on). Range indexes are needed for comparison operations, while hash indices are more efficient if we need equality comparisons.

It is possible to specify a precision, that is, the maximum number of characters or digits to use in all the index keys. -1 means the maximum precision and is always recommended:

```
...
"excludedPaths": [
  {
        "path": "/\"_etag\"/?"
    }
  ]
```

Paths contained in excludedPaths are not indexed at all. Index settings can also be specified programmatically.

Here, you have two options to connect to Cosmos DB: use a version of its official client for your preferred programming language or use Cosmos DB's Entity Framework Core provider. In the following subsections, we will have a look at both options. Then, we will describe how to use Cosmos DB's Entity Framework Core provider with a practical example.

The Cosmos DB client

The Cosmos DB client for .NET 5 is available through the Microsoft.Azure. Cosmos NuGet package. It offers full control of all Cosmos DB features, while the Cosmos DB Entity Framework provider is easier to use but hides some Cosmos DB peculiarities. Follow these steps to interact with Cosmos DB through the official Cosmos DB client for .NET 5.

The following code sample shows the creation of a database and a container using the client component. Any operation requires the creation of a client object. Do not forget that the client must be disposed of by calling its Dispose method (or by enclosing the code that references it in a using statement) when you do not need it anymore:

```
public static async Task CreateCosmosDB()
{
    using var cosmosClient = new CosmosClient(endpoint, key);
    Database database = await
        cosmosClient.CreateDatabaseIfNotExistsAsync(databaseId);
    ContainerProperties cp = new ContainerProperties(containerId,
        "/DestinationName");
    Container container = await database.CreateContainerIfNotExistsAsyn
c(cp);
```

```
    await AddItemsToContainerAsync(container);
}
```

During collection creation, you can pass a `ContainerProperties` object, where you can specify the consistency level, how to index properties, and all the other collection features.

Then, you must define the .NET classes that correspond to the structure of the JSON document you need to manipulate in your collections. You can also use the `JsonProperty` attribute to map class property names to JSON names if they are not equal:

```
public class Destination
{
    [JsonProperty(PropertyName = "id")]
    public string Id { get; set; }
    public string DestinationName { get; set; }
    public string Country { get; set; }
    public string Description { get; set; }
    public Package[] Packages { get; set; }
}
```

Once you have all the necessary classes, you can use client methods to `ReadItemAsync`, `CreateItemAsync`, and `DeleteItemAsync`. You can also query data using a `QueryDefinition` object that accepts SQL commands. You can find a complete introduction to this library at `https://docs.microsoft.com/en-us/azure/cosmos-db/sql-api-get-started`.

The Cosmos DB Entity Framework Core provider

The Cosmos DB provider for Entity Framework Core is contained in the `Microsoft.EntityFrameworkCore.Cosmos` NuGet package. Once you've added this to your project, you can proceed in a similar way to when you used the SQL Server provider in *Chapter 8, Interacting with Data in C# – Entity Framework Core*, but with a few differences. Let us look:

- There are no migrations since Cosmos DB databases have no structure to update. Instead, they have a method that ensures that the database, along with all the necessary collections, is created:

  ```
  context.Database.EnsureCreated();
  ```

- By default, the DbSet<T> properties from DBContext are mapped to a unique container since this is the cheapest option. You can override this default by explicitly specifying which container you want to map some entities to by using the following configuration instruction:

```
builder.Entity<MyEntity>()
    .ToContainer("collection-name");
```

- The only useful annotation on entity classes is the Key attribute, which becomes obligatory when the principal keys are not called Id.

- Principal keys must be strings and cannot be auto-incremented to avoid synchronization issues in a distributed environment. The uniqueness of primary keys can be ensured by generating GUIDs and transforming them into strings.

- When defining relationships between entities, you can specify that an entity or a collection of entities is owned by another entity, in which case it is stored together with the father entity.

We will look at the usage of Cosmos DB's Entity Framework provider in the next section.

Use case – storing data

Now that we have learned how to use NoSQL, we must decide whether NoSQL databases are adequate for our book use case WWTravelClub application. We need to store the following families of data:

- **Information about available destinations and packages**: Relevant operations for this data are reads since packages and destinations do not change very often. However, they must be accessed as fast as possible from all over the world to ensure a pleasant user experience when users browse the available options. Therefore, a distributed relational database with geographically distributed replicas is possible, but not necessary since packages can be stored inside their destinations in a cheaper NoSQL database.

- **Destination reviews**: In this case, distributed write operations have a non-negligible impact. Moreover, most writes are additions since reviews are not usually updated. Additions benefit a lot from sharding and do not cause consistency issues like updates do. Accordingly, the best option for this data is a NoSQL collection.

- **Reservations**: In this case, consistency errors are not acceptable because they may cause overbooking. Reads and writes have a comparable impact, but we need reliable transactions and good consistency checks. Luckily, data can be organized in a multi-tenant database where tenants are destinations since reservation information belonging to different destinations is completely unrelated. Accordingly, we may use sharded SQL Azure database instances.

In conclusion, the best option for data in the first and second bullet points is Cosmos DB, while the best option for the third point is Azure SQL Server. Actual applications may require a more detailed analysis of all data operations and their frequencies. In some cases, it is worth implementing prototypes for various possible options and executing performance tests with typical workloads on all of them.

In the remainder of this section, we will migrate the destinations/packages data layer we looked at in *Chapter 8, Interacting with Data in C# – Entity Framework Core*, to Cosmos DB.

Implementing the destinations/packages database with Cosmos DB

Let's move on to the database example we built in *Chapter 8, Interacting with Data in C# – Entity Framework Core*, to Cosmos DB by following these steps:

1. First, we need to make a copy of the WWTravelClubDB project and make WWTravelClubDBCosmo the new root folder.

2. Open the project and delete the migrations folder since migrations are not required anymore.

3. We need to replace the SQL Server Entity Framework provider with the Cosmos DB provider. To do this, go to **Manage NuGet Packages** and uninstall the Microsoft.EntityFrameworkCore.SqlServer NuGet package. Then, install the Microsoft.EntityFrameworkCore.Cosmos NuGet package.

4. Then, do the following on the Destination and Package entities:

   - Remove all data annotations.
   - Add the [Key] attribute to their Id properties since this is obligatory for Cosmos DB providers.

- Transform the type of the Id properties of both Package and Destination, and the PackagesListDTO classes from int to string. We also need to turn the DestinationId external references in Package and in the PackagesListDTO classes into string. In fact, the best option for keys in distributed databases is a string generated from a GUID, because it is hard to maintain an identity counter when table data is distributed among several servers.

5. In the MainDBContext file, we need to specify that packages related to a destination must be stored inside the destination document itself. This can be achieved by replacing the Destination-Package relation configuration in the OnModelCreatingmethod method with the following code:

```
builder.Entity<Destination>()
    .OwnsMany(m =>m.Packages);
```

6. Here, we must replace HasMany with OwnsMany. There is no equivalent to WithOne since once an entity is owned, it must have just one owner, and the fact that the MyDestination property contains a pointer to the father entity is evident from its type. Cosmos DB also allows the use of HasMany, but in this case, the two entities are not nested one in the other. There is also an OwnOne configuration method for nesting single entities inside other entities.

7. Actually, both OwnsMany and OwnsOne are available for relational databases, but in this case, the difference between HasMany and HasOne is that children entities are automatically included in all queries that return their father entities, with no need to specify an Include LINQ clause. However, child entities are still stored in separate tables.

8. LibraryDesignTimeDbContextFactory must be modified to use Cosmos DB connection data, as shown in the following code:

```
using Microsoft.EntityFrameworkCore;
using Microsoft.EntityFrameworkCore.Design;

namespace WWTravelClubDB
{
    public class LibraryDesignTimeDbContextFactory
        : IDesignTimeDbContextFactory<MainDBContext>
    {
        private const string endpoint = "<your account
endpoint>";
        private const string key = "<your account key>";
        private const string databaseName = "packagesdb";
        public "MainDBContext CreateDbContext"(params string[]
    args)
```

```
            {
                var builder = new DbContextOptionsBuilder<Main
DBContext>();

builder.UseCosmos(endpoint, key, databaseName);
                return new MainDBContext(builder.Options);
            }
        }
}
```

9. Finally, in our test console, we must explicitly create all entity principal keys using GUIDs:

```
var context = new LibraryDesignTimeDbContextFactory()
    .CreateDbContext();
context.Database.EnsureCreated();
var firstDestination = new Destination
{
    Id = Guid.NewGuid().ToString(),
    Name = "Florence",
    Country = "Italy",
    Packages = new List<Package>()
    {
    new Package
    {
        Id=Guid.NewGuid().ToString(),
        Name = "Summer in Florence",
        StartValidityDate = new DateTime(2019, 6, 1),
        EndValidityDate = new DateTime(2019, 10, 1),
        DuratioInDays=7,
        Price=1000
    },
    new Package
    {
        Id=Guid.NewGuid().ToString(),
        Name = "Winter in Florence",
        StartValidityDate = new DateTime(2019, 12, 1),
        EndValidityDate = new DateTime(2020, 2, 1),
        DuratioInDays=7,
        Price=500
    }
    }
};
```

10. Here, we call `context.Database.EnsureCreated()` instead of applying migrations since we only need to create the database. Once the database and collections have been created, we can fine-tune their settings from the Azure portal. Hopefully, future versions of the Cosmos DB Entity Framework Core provider will allow us to specify all collection options.

11. Finally, the final query, which starts with `context.Packages.Where...` must be modified since queries can't start with entities that are nested in other documents (in our case, `Packages` entities). Therefore, we must start our query from the unique root `DbSet<T>` property we have in our `DBContext`, that is, `Destinations`. We can move from listing the external collection to listing all the internal collections with the help of the `SelectMany` method, which performs a logical merge of all nested `Packages` collections. However, since `CosmosDB` SQL doesn't support `SelectMany`, we must force `SelectMany` to be simulated on the client with `AsEnumerable()`, as shown in the following code:

```
var list = context.Destinations
    .AsEnumerable() // move computation on the client side
    .SelectMany(m =>m.Packages)
    .Where(m => period >= m.StartValidityDate....)
    ...
```

12. The remainder of the query remains unchanged. If you run the project now, you should see the same outputs that were received in the case of SQL Server (except for the primary key values).

13. After executing the program, go to your Cosmos DB account. You should see something like the following:

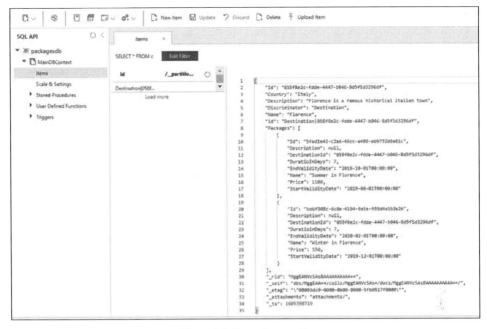

Figure 9.8: Execution results

The packages have been nested inside their destinations as required and Entity Framework Core creates a unique collection that has the same name as the `DBContext` class.

If you would like to continue experimenting with Cosmos DB development without wasting all your free Azure portal credit, you can install the Cosmos DB emulator available at this link: `https://aka.ms/cosmosdb-emulator`.

Summary

In this chapter, we looked at the main storage options available in Azure and learned when to use them. Then, we compared relational and NoSQL databases. We pointed out that relational databases offer automatic consistency checking and transaction isolation, but NoSQL databases are cheaper and offer better performance, especially when distributed writes form a high percentage of the average workload.

Then, we described Azure's main NoSQL option, Cosmos DB, and explained how to configure it and how to connect with a client.

Finally, we learned how to interact with Cosmos DB with Entity Framework Core and looked at a practical example based on the WWTravelClubDB use case. Here, we learned how to decide between relational and NoSQL databases for all families of data involved in an application. This way, you can choose the kind of data storage that ensures the best compromise between data coherence, speed, and parallel access to data in each of your applications.

In the next chapter, we will learn all about Serverless and Azure Functions.

Questions

1. Is Redis a valid alternative to relational databases?
2. Are NoSQL databases a valid alternative to relational databases?
3. What operation is more difficult to scale out in relational databases?
4. What is the main weakness of NoSQL databases? What is their main advantage?
5. Can you list all Cosmos DB consistency levels?
6. Can we use auto-increment integer keys with Cosmos DB?
7. Which Entity Framework configuration method is used to store an entity inside its related father document?
8. Can nested collections be searched efficiently with Cosmos DB?

Further reading

- In this chapter, we did not talk about how to define sharding with Azure SQL. Here is the link to the official documentation if you want to find out more: https://docs.microsoft.com/en-us/azure/sql-database/sql-database-elastic-scale-introduction.

- Cosmos DB was described in detail in this chapter, but further details can be found in the official documentation: https://docs.microsoft.com/en-us/azure/cosmos-db/.

- The following is a reference to the Gremlin language, which is supported by Cosmos DB: http://tinkerpop.apache.org/docs/current/reference/#graph-traversal-steps.

- The following is a general description of the Cosmos DB Graph Data Model: https://docs.microsoft.com/en-us/azure/cosmos-db/graph-introduction.

- Details on how to use Cosmos DB's official .NET client can be found at https://docs.microsoft.com/en-us/azure/cosmos-db/sql-api-dotnetcore-get-started. A good introduction to the MvcControlsToolkit.Business.DocumentDB NuGet package we mentioned in this chapter is the *Fast Azure Cosmos DB Development with the DocumentDB Package* article contained in Issue 34 of DNCMagazine. This can be downloaded from https://www.dotnetcurry.com/microsoft-azure/aspnet-core-cosmos-db-documentdb.

10
Working with Azure Functions

As we mentioned in *Chapter 4, Deciding the Best Cloud-Based Solution*, the serverless architecture is one of the newest ways to provide flexible software solutions. To do so, Microsoft Azure provides Azure Functions, an event-driven, serverless, and scalable technology that accelerates your project development. The main goal of this chapter is to get you familiar with Azure Functions and the best practices you can implement while using it. It is worth mentioning that the use of Azure Functions is a great alternative for having a serverless implementation that can accelerate your development. With them, you can deploy APIs faster, enable services triggered by timers, and even trigger processes by receiving events from storage.

In this chapter, we will cover the following topics:

- Understanding the Azure Functions app
- Programming Azure Functions using C#
- Maintaining Azure Functions
- Use case – implementing Azure Functions to send emails

By the end of this chapter, you will understand how to use Azure Functions in C# to speed up your development cycle.

Technical requirements

This chapter requires that you have the following:

- Visual Studio 2019 free Community Edition or better with all the Azure tools installed.

- A free Azure account. The *Creating an Azure account* section of *Chapter 1, Understanding the Importance of Software Architecture*, explains how to create one.

You can find the sample code for this chapter at `https://github.com/ PacktPublishing/Software-Architecture-with-C-9-and-.NET-5/tree/master/ch10`.

Understanding the Azure Functions app

The Azure Functions app is an Azure PaaS where you can build pieces of code (functions) and connect them to your application and use triggers to start them. The concept is quite simple – you build a function in the language you prefer and decide on the trigger that will start it. You can write as many functions as you want in your system. There are cases where the system is written entirely with functions.

The steps for creating the necessary environment are as simple as the ones we need to follow to create the function itself. The following screenshot shows the parameters that you must decide on when you create the environment. After you select **Create a resource** in Azure and filter by **Function App**, clicking the **Create** button, you will see the following screen:

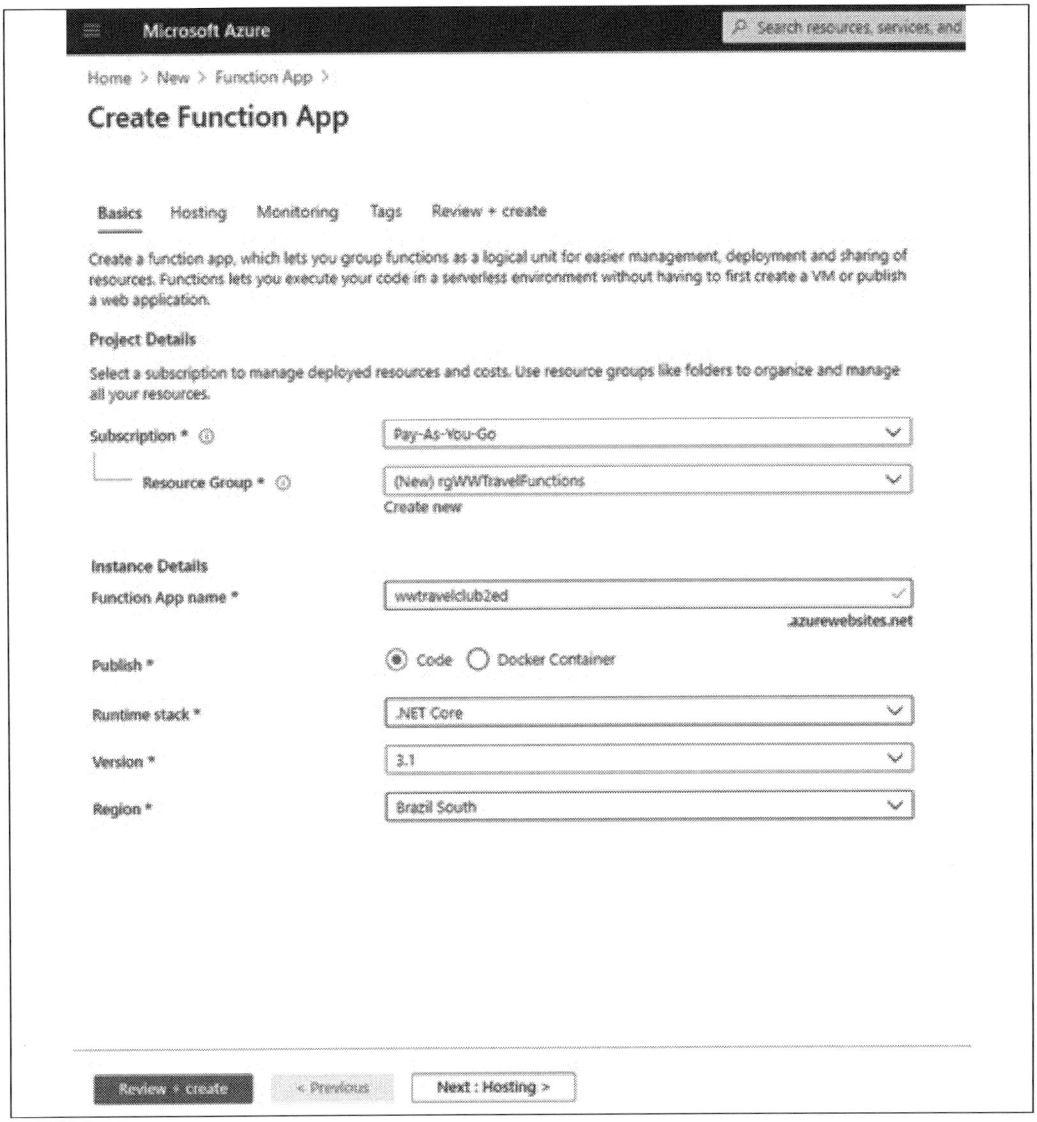

Figure 10.1: Creating an Azure function

There are a couple of key points that you should consider while creating your Azure Functions environment. The possibilities given for running functions increase from time to time, as do the programming language options and publishing styles. One of the most important configurations we have is the hosting plan, which is where you will run your functions. There are three options for the hosting plan: a Consumption (Serverless), Premium, and App Service plan. Let's talk about these now.

Consumption plan

If you choose a Consumption plan, your functions will only consume resources when they are executed. This means that you will only be charged while your functions are running. Scalability and memory resources will be automatically managed by Azure. This is truly what we call serverless.

Something we need to take note of while writing functions in this plan is the timeout. By default, after 5 minutes, the function will timeout. You can change the timeout value using the functionTimeout parameter in the host.json file. The maximum value is 10 minutes.

When you choose the Consumption plan, the way in which you will be charged will depend on what you are executing, execution time, and memory usage. More information on this can be found at https://azure.microsoft.com/en-us/pricing/details/functions/.

Note that this can be a good option when you do not have App Services in your environment, and you are running functions with low periodicity. On the other hand, if you need continuous processing, you may want to consider the App Service plan.

Premium plan

Depending on what you use your functions for, especially if they need to run continuously or almost continuously, or if some function executions take longer than 10 minutes, you may want to consider a Premium plan. Besides, you may need to connect your function to a VNET/VPN environment, and in this case, you will be forced to run in this plan.

You may also need more CPU or memory options than what is provided with the Consumption plan. The Premium plan gives you one core, two core, and four core instance options.

It is worth mentioning that even with unlimited time to run your function, if you decide to use an HTTP trigger function, 230 seconds is the maximum allowed for responding to a request. The reason why this is a limit is related to Azure Load Balancer. You may have to redesign your solution in such situations to adhere to the best practices set by Microsoft (`https://docs.microsoft.com/en-us/azure/azure-functions/functions-best-practices`).

App Service plan

The App Service plan is one of the options you can choose when you want to create an Azure Functions app. The following is a list of reasons (suggested by Microsoft) as to why you should use the App Service plan instead of the Consumption plan to maintain your functions:

- You can use underutilized existing App Service instances.
- You want to run your function app on a custom image.

In the App Service plan scenario, the `functionTimeout` value varies according to the Azure Function runtime version. However, the value is at least 30 minutes. You may find a tabled comparison between the timeouts in each consumption plan at `https://docs.microsoft.com/en-us/azure/azure-functions/functions-scale#timeout`.

Programming Azure functions using C#

In this section, you will learn how to create Azure functions. It is worth mentioning that there are several ways to create them using C#. The first one is by creating the functions and developing them in the Azure portal itself. To do this, let us consider that you have created an Azure Functions app with similar configurations to the ones from the screenshot at the beginning of the chapter.

By selecting the resource created and navigating to the **Functions** menu, you will be able to **Add** new functions to this environment, as you can see in the following screenshot:

Figure 10.2: Adding a function

Here, you will need to decide the kind of trigger that you want to use to start the execution. The most frequently used ones are **HTTP trigger** and **Timer trigger**. The first enables the creation of an HTTP API that will trigger the function. The second means functions will be triggered by a timer set according to your decision.

When you decide on the trigger you want to use, you must name the function. Depending on the trigger you decide on, you will have to set up some parameters. For instance, HTTP trigger requires that you set up an authorization level. Three options are available, that is, **Function, Anonymous,** and **Admin**:

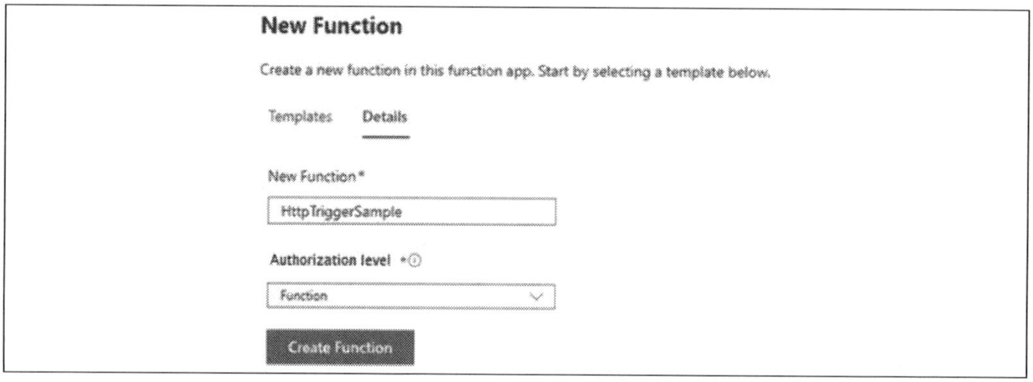

New Function

Create a new function in this function app. Start by selecting a template below.

Templates   Details

New Function *

HttpTriggerSample

Authorization level *ⓘ

Function

Create Function

Figure 10.3: Configuring an HTTP function

It is worth mentioning that this book does not cover all the options that are available when it comes to building functions. As a software architect, you should understand that Azure provides a good service for serverless architectures in terms of functions. This can be useful in several situations. This was discussed in more detail in *Chapter 4, Deciding the Best Cloud-Based Solution*.

The result of this is as follows. Notice that Azure provides an editor that allows us to run the code, check logs, and test the function that we have created. This is a good interface for testing and coding basic functions:

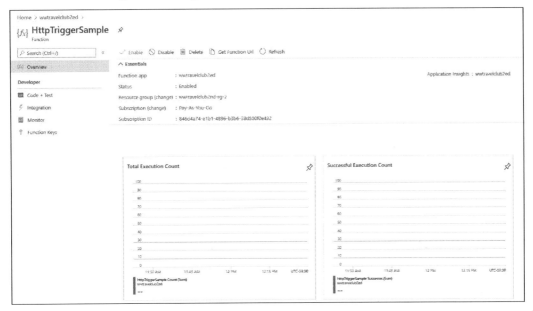

Figure 10.4: HTTP function environment

However, if you want to create more sophisticated functions, you may need a more sophisticated environment so that you can code and debug them more efficaciously. This is where the Visual Studio Azure Functions project can help you. Besides, using Visual Studio to execute the development of the function moves you in the direction of using source control and CI/CD for your functions.

In Visual Studio, you can create a project dedicated to Azure Functions by going to **Create a new project**:

Figure 10.5: Creating an Azure Functions project in Visual Studio 2019

Once you have submitted your project, Visual Studio will ask you for the type of trigger you are using and for the Azure version that your function will run on:

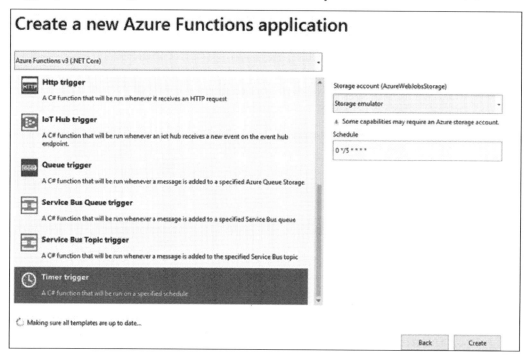

Figure 10.6: Creating a new Azure Functions application

It is worth mentioning that Azure Functions supports different platforms and programming languages. At the time of writing, there are three runtime versions of Azure Functions, and C# can run in all of them. The first version is compatible with .NET Framework 4.7. In the second one, you can create functions that run on .NET Core 2.2. In the third one, you will be able to run .NET Core 3.1 and .NET 5.

As a software architect, you must keep code reusability in mind. In this case, you should pay attention to which version of Azure Functions Project you will decide to build your functions in. However, it is always recommended that you use the latest version of the runtime, as soon as it acquires general availability status.

By default, the code that is generated is like that generated when you create Azure functions in the Azure portal:

```
using System;
using Microsoft.Azure.WebJobs;
using Microsoft.Extensions.Logging;

namespace FunctionAppSample
{
    public static class FunctionTrigger
    {
        [FunctionName("FunctionTrigger")]
        public static void Run([TimerTrigger("0 */5 * * * *")]
            TimerInfo myTimer, ILogger log)
        {
            log.LogInformation($"C# Timer trigger function " +
                $"executed at: {DateTime.Now}");
        }
    }
}
```

The publish method follows the same steps as the publish procedure for web apps that we described in *Chapter 1, Understanding the Importance of Software Architecture.* However, it is always recommended to use a CI/CD pipeline, as we are going to describe in *Chapter 20, Understanding DevOps Principles.*

Listing Azure Functions templates

There are several templates in the Azure portal that you can use in order to create Azure functions. The number of templates that you can choose from is updated continuously. The following are just a few of them:

- **Blob Trigger**: You may want to process something for a file as soon as this file is uploaded to your blob storage. This can be a good use case for Azure Functions.

- **Cosmos DB Trigger**: You may want to synchronize data that arrives in a Cosmos DB database with a processing method. Cosmos DB was discussed in detail in *Chapter 9, How to Choose Your Data Storage in the Cloud.*

- **Event Grid Trigger**: This is a good way to manage Azure events. Functions can be triggered so that they manage each event.

- **Event Hub Trigger**: With this trigger, you can build functions that are linked to any system that sends data to Azure Event Hub.

- **HTTP Trigger**: This trigger is useful for building serverless APIs and web app events.

- **IoT Hub Trigger**: When your application is connected to devices through the use of IoT Hub, you can use this trigger whenever a new event is received by one of the devices.

- **Queue Trigger**: You can handle queue processing using a function as a service solution.

- **Service Bus Queue Trigger**: This is another messaging service that can be a trigger for functions. Azure Service Bus will be covered in more detail in *Chapter 11, Design Patterns and .NET 5 Implementation.*

- **Timer Trigger**: This is commonly used with functions and is where you specify time triggers so that you can continuously process data from your system.

Maintaining Azure functions

Once you have created and programmed your function, you need to monitor and maintain it. To do this, you can use a variety of tools, all of which you can find in the Azure portal. These tools will help you solve problems due to the amount of information you will be able to collect with them.

The first option when it comes to monitoring your function is using the **Monitor** menu inside the Azure Functions interface in the Azure portal. There, you will be able to check all your function executions, including successful results and failures:

Figure 10.7: Monitoring a function

It will take about 5 minutes for any results to be available. The date shown in the grid is in UTC time.

By clicking on **Run query in Application Insights**, the same interface allows you to connect to this tool. This will take you to a world of almost infinite options that you can use to analyze your function data. Application Insights is one of the best **Application Performance Management (APM)** systems available nowadays:

Figure 10.8: Monitoring using Application Insights

Beyond the query interface, you can also check all the performance issues of your function using the Insights interface in the Azure portal. There, you can analyze and filter all the requests that have been received by your solution and check their performance and dependencies. You can also trigger alerts when something abnormal happens to one of your endpoints:

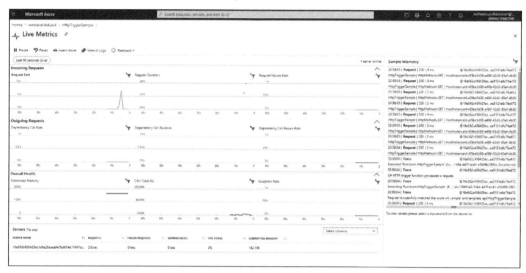

Figure 10.9: Monitoring using Application Insights Live Metrics

As a software architect, you will find a good daily helper for your projects in this tool. It is worth mentioning that Application Insights works on several other Azure services, such as web apps and virtual machines. This means that you can monitor the health of your system and maintain it using the wonderful features provided by Azure.

Use case – Implementing Azure Functions to send emails

Here, we will use a subset of the Azure components we described previously. The use case from WWTravelClub proposes a worldwide implementation of the service, and there is a chance that this service will need different architecture designs to face all the performance key points that we described in *Chapter 1, Understanding the Importance of Software Architecture*.

If you go back to the user stories that were described in *Chapter 1, Understanding the Importance of Software Architecture*, you will find that many needs are related to communication. Because of this, it is common to have some alerts be provided by emails in the solution. The use case of this chapter will focus on how to send emails. The architecture will be totally serverless.

The following diagram shows the basic structure of the architecture. To give users a great experience, all the emails that are sent by the application will be queued asynchronously, thereby preventing significant delays in the system's responses:

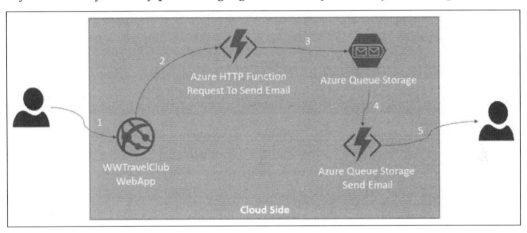

Figure 10.10: Architectural design for sending emails

Note that there are no servers that manage Azure functions for enqueuing or dequeuing messages from Azure Queue Storage. This is exactly what we call serverless. It is worth mentioning that this architecture is not restricted to only sending emails – it can also be used to process any HTTP POST request.

Now, we will learn how to set up security in the API so that only authorized applications can use the given solution.

First step – Creating Azure Queue storage

It is quite simple to create storage in the Azure portal. Let us learn how. First, you will need to create a storage account by clicking on **Create a resource** in the main page of the Azure portal and searching for **Storage account**. Then, you will be able to set up its basic information, such as **Storage account name** and **Location**. Information about **Networking**, and **Data protection**, as shown in the following screenshot, can be checked in this wizard too. There are default values for these settings that will cover the demo:

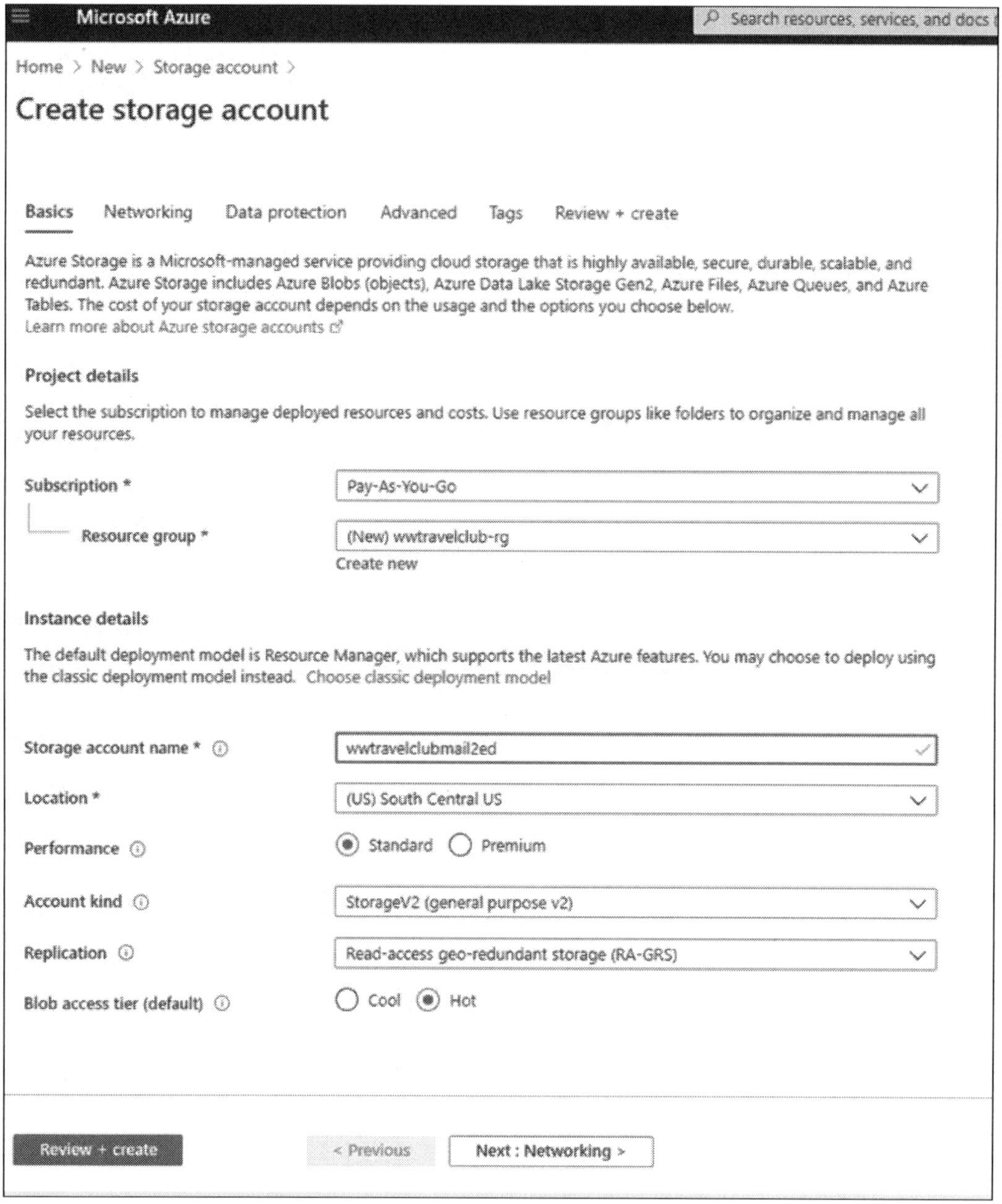

Figure 10.11: Creating an Azure storage account

Once you have the storage account in place, you will be able to set up a queue. You will find this option by clicking on the **Overview** link in the storage account and selecting the **Queues** option, or by selecting **Queues** via the storage account menu. Then, you will find an option to add the queue (**+ Queue**), where you just need to provide its name:

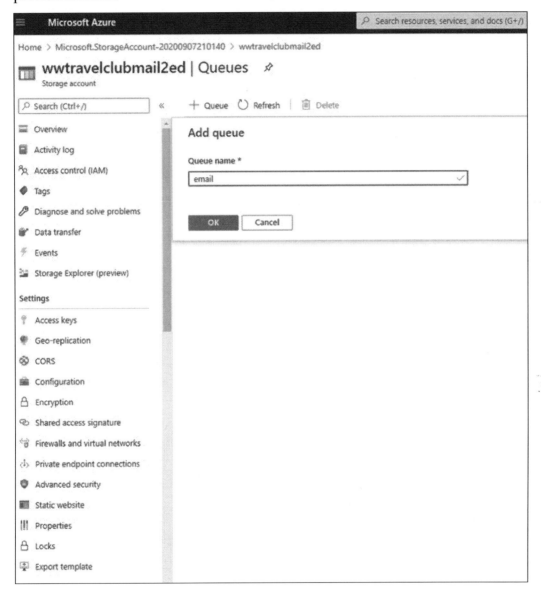

Figure 10.12: Defining a queue to monitor emails

The created queue will give you an overview of the Azure portal. There, you will find your queue's URL and use Storage Explorer:

Figure 10.13: Queue created

Note that you will also be able to connect to this storage using Microsoft Azure Storage Explorer (`https://azure.microsoft.com/en-us/features/storage-explorer/`):

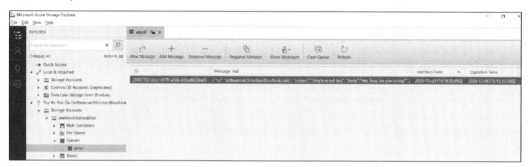

Figure 10.14: Monitoring the queue using Microsoft Azure Storage Explorer

This tool is especially useful if you are not connected to the Azure portal.

Second step – Creating the function to send emails

Now, you can start programming in earnest, informing the queue that an email is waiting to be sent. Here, we need to use an HTTP trigger. Note that the function is a static class that runs asynchronously. The following code is gathering the request data coming from the HTTP trigger and inserting the data into a queue that will be treated later:

```
public static class SendEmail
{
    [FunctionName(nameof(SendEmail))]
    public static async Task<HttpResponseMessage>RunAsync(
[HttpTrigger(AuthorizationLevel.Function, "post")] HttpRequestMessage
req, ILogger log)
    {
        var requestData = await req.Content.ReadAsStringAsync();
        var connectionString = Environment.GetEnvironmentVariable("Azur
eQueueStorage");
        var storageAccount = CloudStorageAccount.
Parse(connectionString);
        var queueClient = storageAccount.CreateCloudQueueClient();
        var messageQueue = queueClient.GetQueueReference("email");
        var message = new CloudQueueMessage(requestData);
        await messageQueue.AddMessageAsync(message);
        log.LogInformation("HTTP trigger from SendEmail function
processed a request.");
        var responseObj = new { success = true };
        return new HttpResponseMessage(HttpStatusCode.OK)
        {
            Content = new StringContent(JsonConvert.
SerializeObject(responseObj), Encoding.UTF8, "application/json"),
        };
    }
}
```

In some scenarios, you may try to avoid the queue setup indicated in the preceding code by using a queue output binding. Check the details at https://docs.microsoft.com/en-us/azure/ azure-functions/functions-bindings-storage-queue- output?tabs=csharp.

You can use a tool such as Postman to test your function by running the Azure
Functions Emulator:

Figure 10.15: Postman function test

The result will appear in Microsoft Azure Storage Explorer and the Azure portal. In
the Azure portal, you can manage each message and dequeue each of them or even
clear the queue storage:

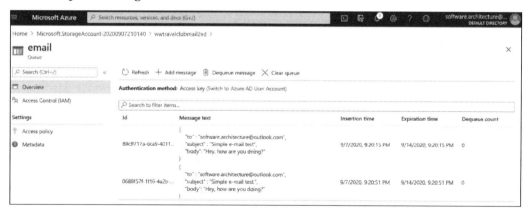

Figure 10.16: HTTP trigger and queue storage test

Third step – Creating the queue trigger function

After this, you can create a second function. This one will be triggered by data entering your queue. It is worth mentioning that, for Azure Functions v3, you will have the `Microsoft.Azure.WebJobs.Extensions.Storage` library added as a NuGet reference automatically:

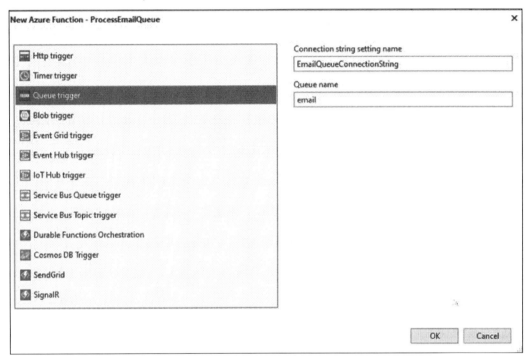

Figure 10.17: Creating a queue trigger

Once you have set the connection string inside `local.settings.json`, you will be able to run both functions and test them with Postman. The difference is that, with the second function running, if you set a breakpoint at the start of it, you will check whether the message has been sent:

Figure 10.18: Queue triggered in Visual Studio 2019

From this point, the way to send emails will depend on the mail options you have. You may decide to use a proxy or connect directly to your email server.

There are several advantages to creating an email service this way:

- Once your service has been coded and tested, you can use it to send emails from any of your applications. This means that your code can always be reused.

- Apps that use this service will not be stopped from sending emails due to the asynchronous advantages of posting in an HTTP service.

- You do not need to pool the queue to check whether data is ready for processing.

Finally, the queue process runs concurrently, which delivers a better experience in most cases. It is possible to turn it off by setting some properties in `host.json`. All the options for this can be found in the *Further reading* section at the end of this chapter.

Summary

In this chapter, we looked at some of the advantages of developing functionality with serverless Azure functions. You can use it as a guideline for checking the different types of triggers that are available in Azure Functions and for planning how to monitor them. We also saw how to program and maintain Azure functions. Finally, we looked at an example of an architecture where you connect multiple functions to avoid pooling data and to enable concurrent processing.

In the next chapter, we will analyze the concept of design patterns, learn why they are so useful, and learn about some of the common patterns.

Questions

1.   What are Azure functions?
2.   What are the programming options for Azure functions?
3.   What are the plans that can be used with Azure functions?
4.   How can you deploy Azure functions with Visual Studio?
5.   What triggers can you use to develop Azure functions?
6.   What is the difference between Azure Functions v1, v2, and v3?
7.   How does Application Insights help us to maintain and monitor Azure functions?

Further reading

If you want to learn more when it comes to creating Azure functions, check out the following links:

- Azure Functions scale and hosting: `https://docs.microsoft.com/en-us/azure/azure-functions/functions-scale`
- *Azure Functions – Essentials [Video]*, by Praveen Kumar Sreeram: `https://www.packtpub.com/virtualization-and-cloud/azure-functions-essentials-video`
- Azure Functions runtime overview: `https://docs.microsoft.com/en-us/azure/azure-functions/functions-versions`

- An overview of Azure Event Grid: `https://azure.microsoft.com/en-us/resources/videos/an-overview-of-azure-event-grid/`

- Timer trigger for Azure Functions: `https://docs.microsoft.com/en-us/azure/azure-functions/functions-bindings-timer`

- The Application Insights section from the book, *Azure for Architects,* by Ritesh Modi: `https://subscription.packtpub.com/book/virtualization_and_cloud/9781788397391/12/ch12lvl1sec95/application-insights`

- Monitoring Azure Functions using the Application Insights section from the book, *Azure Serverless Computing Cookbook,* by Praveen Kumar Sreeram: `https://subscription.packtpub.com/book/virtualization_and_cloud/9781788390828/6/06lvl1sec34/monitoring-azure-functions-using-application-insights`

- Get started with Azure Queue storage using .NET: `https://docs.microsoft.com/en-us/azure/storage/queues/storage-dotnet-how-to-use-queues`

- Azure Functions triggers and bindings concepts: `https://docs.microsoft.com/en-us/azure/azure-functions/functions-triggers-bindings`

- Azure Queue storage bindings for Azure Functions: `https://docs.microsoft.com/en-us/azure/azure-functions/functions-bindings-storage-queue`

11

Design Patterns and .NET 5 Implementation

Design patterns can be defined as ready-to-use architectural solutions for common problems you encounter during software development. They are essential for understanding the .NET Core architecture and useful for solving ordinary problems that we face when designing any piece of software. In this chapter, we will look at the implementation of some design patterns. It is worth mentioning that this book does not explain all the known patterns we can use. The focus here is to explain the importance of studying and applying them.

In this chapter, we will cover the following topics:

- Understanding design patterns and their purpose
- Understanding the available design patterns in .NET 5

By the end of this chapter, you will have learned about some of the use cases from **WWTravelClub** that you can implement with design patterns.

Technical requirements

For completing this chapter, you will need the free Visual Studio 2019 Community Edition or better, with all the database tools installed, and a free Azure account. The *Creating an Azure account* subsection of *Chapter 1, Understanding the Importance of Software Architecture*, explains how to create one.

You can find the sample code for this chapter at `https://github.com/`
`PacktPublishing/Software-Architecture-with-C-9-and-.NET-5`.

Understanding design patterns and their purpose

Deciding the design of a system is challenging, and the responsibility associated with this task is enormous. As software architects, we must always keep in mind that features such as great reusability, good performance, and good maintainability are important to deliver a good solution. This is where design patterns help and accelerate the design process.

As we mentioned previously, design patterns are solutions that have already been discussed and defined so that they can solve common software architectural problems. This approach grew in popularity after the release of the book *Design Patterns – Elements of Reusable Object-Oriented Software*, where the **Gang of Four (GoF)** divided these patterns into three types: creational, structural, and behavioral.

A little bit later, Uncle Bob introduced the SOLID principles to the developer community, giving us the opportunity to efficaciously organize the functions and data structures of each system. The SOLID design principles indicate how the components of software should be designed and connected. It is worth mentioning that, compared to the design patterns presented by GoF, the SOLID principles do not deliver code recipes. Instead, they give you the basic principles to follow when you design your solutions, keeping the software's structure strong and reliable. They can be defined as follows:

- **Single Responsibility**: A module or function should be responsible for a single purpose
- **Open-Closed**: A software artifact should be open for extension but closed for modification
- **Liskov Substitution**: The behavior of a program needs to remain unchanged when you substitute one of its components for another component that has been defined by a supertype of the primer object

- **Interface Segregation**: Creating huge interfaces will cause dependencies to occur while you are building concrete objects, but these are harmful to the system architecture

- **Dependency Inversion**: The most flexible systems are the ones where object dependencies only refer to abstractions

As technologies and software problems change, more patterns are conceived. The advance of cloud computing has brought a bunch of them, all of which can be found at https://docs.microsoft.com/en-us/azure/architecture/patterns/. The reason why new patterns emerge is related to the challenges we face when new solutions are developed. Today, availability, data management, messaging, monitoring, performance, scalability, resiliency, and security are aspects we must deal with when delivering cloud solutions.

The reason why you should always consider developing using design patterns is quite simple—as a software architect, you cannot spend time reinventing the wheel. However, there is another great reason for using and understanding them: you will find many of these patterns already implemented in .NET 5.

In the next few subsections, we will cover some of the most well-known patterns. However, the idea of this chapter is to let you know that they exist and need to be studied so that you can accelerate and simplify your project. Moreover, each pattern will be presented with a C# code snippet so that you can easily implement them in your projects.

Builder pattern

There are cases where you will have a complex object with different behaviors due to its configuration. Instead of setting this object up while using it, you may want to decouple its configuration from its usage, using a customized configuration that is already built. This way, you have different representations of the instances you are building. This is where you should use the Builder pattern.

The following class diagram shows the pattern that has been implemented for a scenario from this book's use case. The idea behind this design choice is to simplify the way rooms from WWTravelClub are described:

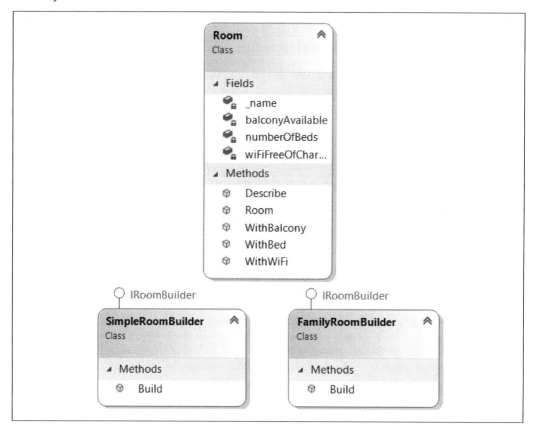

Figure 11.1: Builder pattern

As shown in the following code, the code for this is implemented in a way where the configurations of the instances are not set in the main program. Instead, you just build the objects using the Build() method. This example is simulating the creation of different room styles (a single room and a family room) in WWTravelClub:

```
using DesignPatternsSample.BuilderSample;
using System;

namespace DesignPatternsSample
{
    class Program
    {
        static void Main()
```

```
        {
            #region Builder Sample
            Console.WriteLine("Builder Sample");
            var simpleRoom = new SimpleRoomBuilder().Build();
            simpleRoom.Describe();

            var familyRoom = new FamilyRoomBuilder().Build();
            familyRoom.Describe();
            #endregion
            Console.ReadKey();
        }
    }
}
```

The result of this implementation is quite simple but clarifies the reason why you need to implement a pattern:

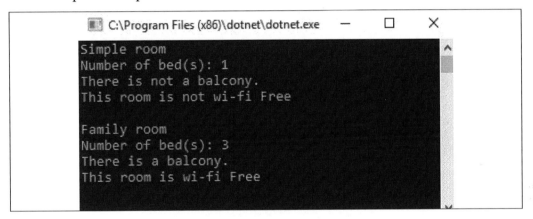

Figure 11.2: Builder pattern sample result

As soon as you have the implementation, evolving this code becomes simpler and easier. For example, if you need to build a different style of room, you must just create a new builder for that type of room, and you will be able to use it.

The reason why this implementation becomes quite simple is related to the usage of chaining methods, as we can see in the Room class:

```
public class Room
{
    private readonly string _name;
    private bool wiFiFreeOfCharge;

    private int numberOfBeds;
```

```
        private bool balconyAvailable;

        public Room(string name)
        {
            _name = name;
        }
        public Room WithBalcony()
        {
            balconyAvailable = true;
            return this;
        }

        public Room WithBed(int numberOfBeds)
        {
            this.numberOfBeds = numberOfBeds;
            return this;
        }

        public Room WithWiFi()
        {
            wiFiFreeOfCharge = true;
            return this;
        }
        ...
    }
```

Fortunately, if you need to increase the configuration settings for the product, all the concrete classes you used previously will be defined in the Builder interface and stored there so that you can update them with ease.

We will also see a great implementation of the Builder pattern in .NET 5 in the *Understanding the available design patterns in .NET 5* section. There, you will be able to understand how Generic Host was implemented using HostBuilder.

Factory pattern

The Factory pattern is useful in situations where you have multiple objects from the same abstraction, and you do not know which needs to be created by the time you start coding. This means you will have to create the instance according to a certain configuration or according to where the software is living now.

For instance, let us check out the WWTravelClub sample. Here, there is a user story that describes that this application will have customers from all over the world paying for their trips. However, in the real world, there are different payment services available for each country. The process of paying is similar for each country, but this system will have more than one payment service available. A good way to simplify this payment implementation is by using the Factory pattern. The following diagram shows the basic idea of its architectural implementation:

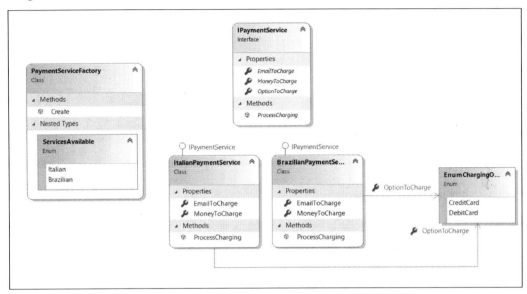

Figure 11.3: Factory pattern

Notice that, since you have an interface that describes what the payment service for the application is, you can use the Factory pattern to change the concrete class according to the services that are available:

```
static void Main()
{
    #region Factory Sample
    ProcessCharging(PaymentServiceFactory.ServicesAvailable.Brazilian,
        "gabriel@sample.com", 178.90f, EnumChargingOptions.CreditCard);

    ProcessCharging(PaymentServiceFactory.ServicesAvailable.Italian,
        "francesco@sample.com", 188.70f, EnumChargingOptions.
DebitCard);
    #endregion
    Console.ReadKey();
}
private static void ProcessCharging
```

```
        (PaymentServiceFactory.ServicesAvailable serviceToCharge,
        string emailToCharge, float moneyToCharge,
        EnumChargingOptions optionToCharge)
    {
        PaymentServiceFactory factory = new PaymentServiceFactory();
        var service = factory.Create(serviceToCharge);
        service.EmailToCharge = emailToCharge;
        service.MoneyToCharge = moneyToCharge;
        service.OptionToCharge = optionToCharge;
        service.ProcessCharging();
    }
```

Once again, the service's usage has been simplified due to the implemented pattern. If you had to use this code in a real-world application, you would change the instance's behavior by defining the service you need in the Factory pattern.

Singleton pattern

When you implement Singleton in your application, you will have a single instance of the object implemented in the entire solution. This can be considered as one of the most used patterns in every application. The reason is simple—there are many use cases where you need some classes to have just one instance. Singletons solve this by providing a better solution than a global variable does.

In the Singleton pattern, the class is responsible for creating and delivering a single object that will be used by the application. In other words, the Singleton class creates a single instance:

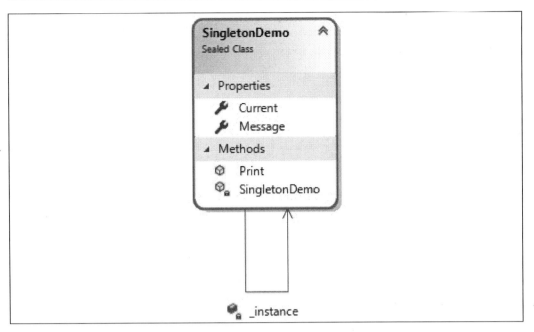

Figure 11.4: Singleton pattern

To do so, the object that is created is static and is delivered in a static property or method. The following code implements the Singleton pattern, which has a Message property and a Print() method:

```
public sealed class SingletonDemo
{
    #region This is the Singleton definition
    private static SingletonDemo _instance;
    public static SingletonDemo Current => _instance ??= new
        SingletonDemo();
    #endregion
    public string Message { get; set; }
    public void Print()
    {
        Console.WriteLine(Message);
    }
}
```

Its usage is simple—you just need to call the static property every time you need to use the Singleton object:

```
SingletonDemo.Current.Message = "This text will be printed by " +
    "the singleton.";
SingletonDemo.Current.Print();
```

One of the places where you may use this pattern is when you need to deliver the app configuration in a way that can be easily accessed from anywhere in the solution. For instance, let us say you have some configuration parameters that are stored in a table that your app needs to query at several decision points. Instead of querying the configuration table directly, you can create a Singleton class to help you:

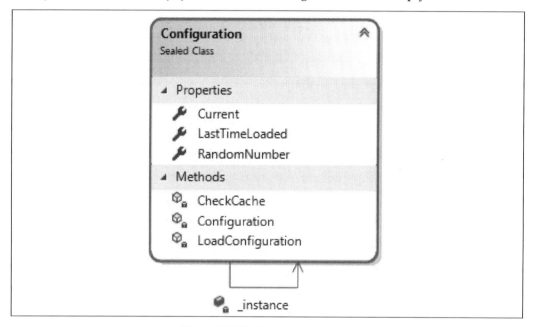

Figure 11.5: Singleton pattern usage

Moreover, you will need to implement a cache in this Singleton, thus improving the performance of the system, since you will be able to decide whether the system will check each configuration in the database every time it needs it or if the cache will be used. The following screenshot shows the implementation of the cache where the configuration is loaded every 5 seconds. The parameter that is being read in this case is just a random number:

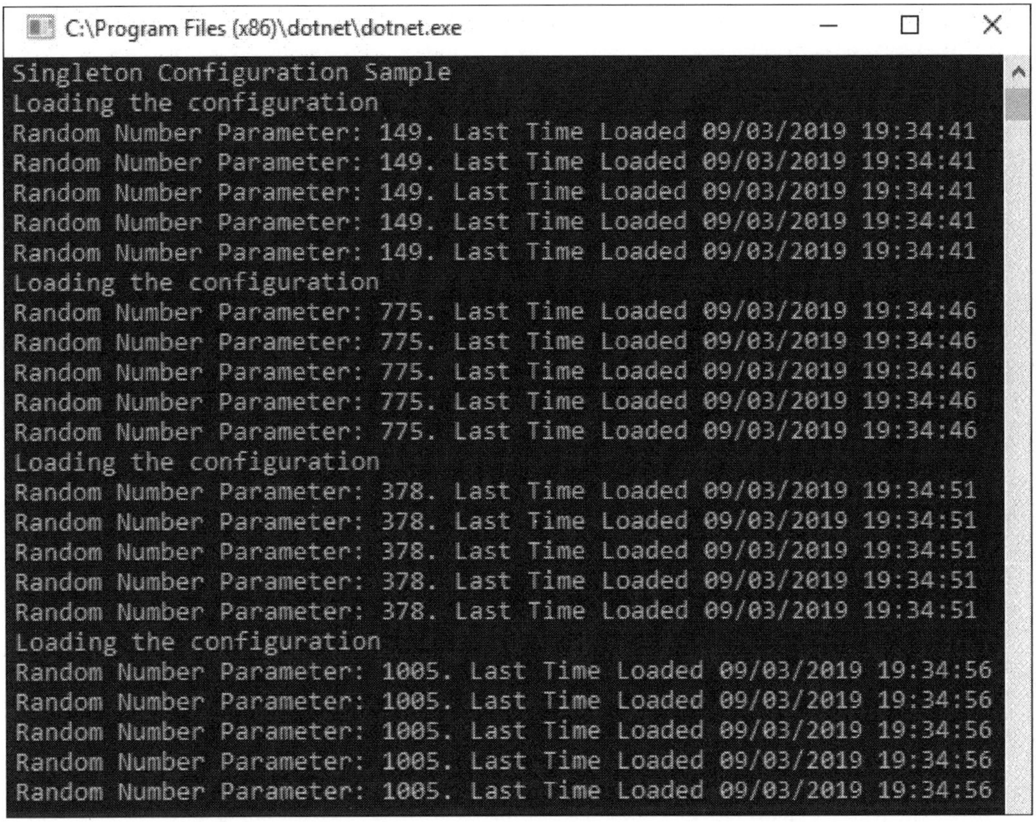

Figure 11.6: Cache implementation inside the Singleton pattern

This is great for the application's performance. Besides, using parameters in several places in your code is simpler since you do not have to create configuration instances everywhere in the code.

It is worth mentioning that due to the dependency injection implementation in .NET 5, Singleton pattern usage became less common, since you can set dependency injection to handle your Singleton objects. We will cover dependency injection in .NET 5 in later sections of this chapter.

Proxy pattern

The Proxy pattern is used when you need to provide an object that controls access to another object. One of the biggest reasons why you should do this is related to the cost of creating the object that is being controlled. For instance, if the controlled object takes too long to be created or consumes too much memory, a proxy can be used to guarantee that the largest part of the object will only be created when it is required.

The following class diagram is of a **Proxy** pattern implementation for loading pictures from **Room**, but only when requested:

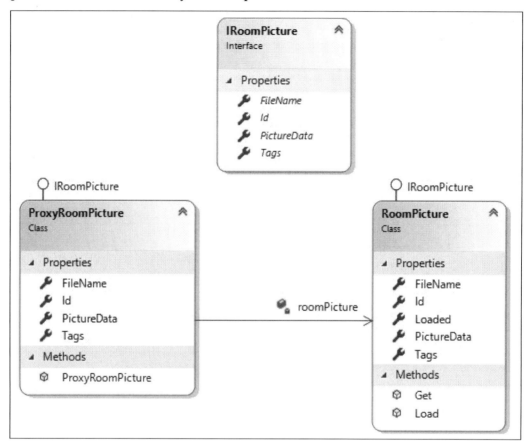

Figure 11.7: Proxy pattern implementation

The client of this proxy will request its creation. Here, the proxy will only gather basic information (`Id`, `FileName`, and `Tags`) from the real object and will not query `PictureData`. When `PictureData` is requested, the proxy will load it:

```
static void Main()
{
    Console.WriteLine("Proxy Sample");
    ExecuteProxySample(new ProxyRoomPicture());
}
private static void ExecuteProxySample(IRoomPicture roomPicture)
{
    Console.WriteLine($"Picture Id: {roomPicture.Id}");
    Console.WriteLine($"Picture FileName: {roomPicture.FileName}");
```

```
    Console.WriteLine($"Tags: {string.Join(";", roomPicture.Tags)}");
    Console.WriteLine($"1st call: Picture Data");
    Console.WriteLine($"Image: {roomPicture.PictureData}");
    Console.WriteLine($"2nd call: Picture Data");
    Console.WriteLine($"Image: {roomPicture.PictureData}");
}
```

If `PictureData` is requested again, since image data is already in place, the proxy will guarantee that image reloading will not be repeated. The following screenshot shows the result of running the preceding code:

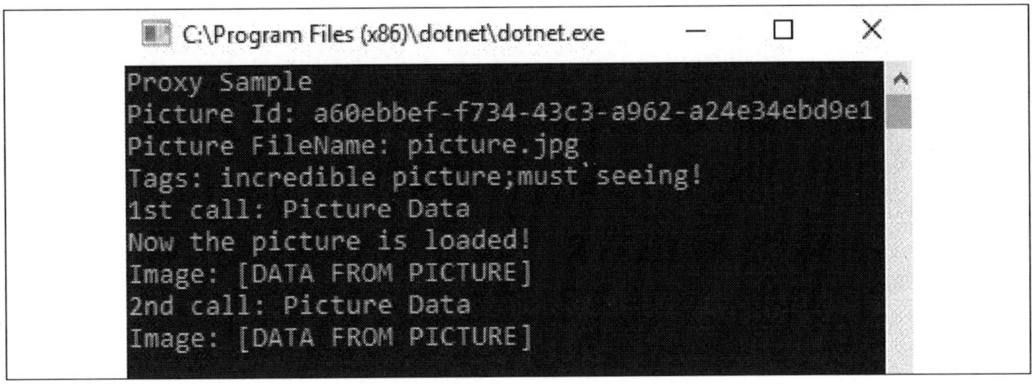

Figure 11.8: Proxy pattern result

This technique can be referred to as another well-known pattern: **lazy loading**. In fact, the Proxy pattern is a way of implementing lazy loading. Another approach for implementing lazy loading is the usage of the `Lazy<T>` type. For instance, in Entity Framework Core 5, as discussed in *Chapter 8, Interacting with Data in C# – Entity Framework Core*, you can turn on lazy loading using proxies. You can find out more about this at `https://docs.microsoft.com/en-us/ef/core/querying/related-data#lazy-loading`.

Command pattern

There are many cases where you need to execute a **command** that will affect the behavior of an object. The Command pattern can help you with this by encapsulating this kind of request in an object. The pattern also describes how to handle undo/redo support for the request.

For instance, let us imagine that, on the WWTravelClub website, users might have the ability to evaluate the packages by specifying whether they like, dislike, or even love their experience.

The following class diagram is an example of what can be implemented to create this rating system with the Command pattern:

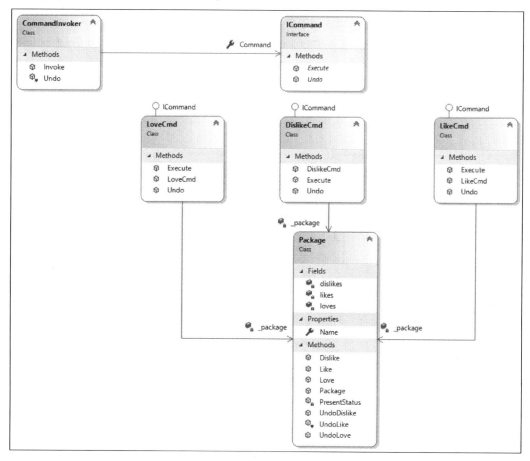

Figure 11.9: Command pattern

Notice the way this pattern works—if you need a different command, such as Hate, you do not need to change the code and classes that use the command. The Undo method can be added in a similar way to the Redo method. The full code sample for this is available in this book's GitHub repository.

It might also help to mention that ASP.NET Core MVC uses the command pattern for its IActionResult hierarchy. Besides, the business operation described in *Chapter 12, Understanding the Different Domains in Software Solutions*, will make use of this pattern to execute business rules.

Publisher/Subscriber pattern

Providing information from an object to a group of other objects is common in all applications. The Publisher/Subscriber pattern is almost mandatory when there is a large volume of components (subscribers) that will receive a message containing the information that was sent by the object (publisher).

The concept here is quite simple to understand and is shown in the following diagram:

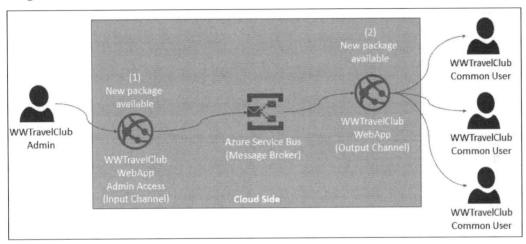

Figure 11.10: Publisher/Subscriber sample case

When you have an indefinite number of different possible subscribers, it is essential to decouple the component that broadcasts information from the components that consume it. The Publisher/Subscriber pattern does this for us.

Implementing this pattern is complex, since distributing environments is not a trivial task. Therefore, it is recommended that you consider already existing technologies for implementing the message broker that connects the input channel to the output channels, instead of building it from scratch. Azure Service Bus is a reliable implementation of this pattern, so all you need to do is connect to it.

RabbitMQ, which we have mentioned in *Chapter 5, Applying a Microservice Architecture to Your Enterprise Application*, is another service that can be used to implement a message broker, but it is a lower-level implementation of the pattern and requires several related tasks, such as retries, in case errors have to be coded manually.

Dependency Injection pattern

The Dependency Injection pattern is considered a good way to implement the Dependency Inversion principle. One useful side effect is that it forces any implementation to follow all the other SOLID principles.

The concept is quite simple. Instead of creating instances of the objects that the component depends on, you just need to define their dependencies, declare their interfaces, and enable the reception of the objects by **injection**.

There are three ways to perform dependency injection:

- Use the constructor of the class to receive the objects
- Tag some class properties to receive the objects
- Define an interface with a method to inject all the necessary components

The following diagram shows the implementation of the Dependency Injection pattern:

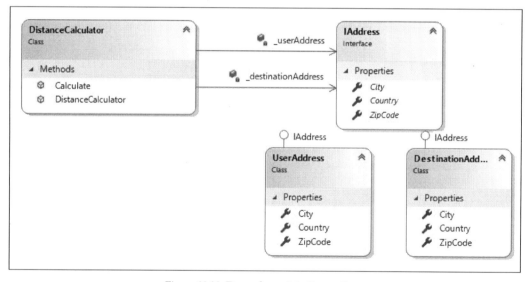

Figure 11.11: Dependency Injection pattern

Apart from this, Dependency Injection can be used with an **Inversion of Control (IoC)** container. This container enables the automatic injection of dependencies whenever they are asked for. There are several IoC container frameworks available on the market, but with .NET Core, there is no need to use third-party software since it contains a set of libraries to solve this in the `Microsoft.Extensions. DependencyInjection` namespace.

This IoC container is responsible for creating and disposing of the objects that are requested. The implementation of Dependency Injection is based on constructor types. There are three options for the injected component's lifetime:

- **Transient**: The objects are created each time they are requested.

- **Scoped**: The objects are created for each scope defined in the application. In a web app, a **scope** is identified with a web request.

- **Singleton**: Each object has the same application lifetime, so a single object is reused to serve all the requests for a given type. If your object contains state, you should not use this one, unless it is thread-safe.

The way you are going to use these options depends on the business rules of the project you are developing. It is also a matter of how you are going to register the services of the application. You need to be careful in deciding the correct one, since the behavior of the application will change according to the type of object you are injecting.

Understanding the available design patterns in .NET 5

As we discovered in the previous sections, C# allows us to implement any of the patterns. .NET 5 provides many implementations in its SDK that follow all the patterns we have discussed, such as Entity Framework Core proxy lazy loading. Another good example that has been available since .NET Core 2.1 is .NET Generic Host.

In *Chapter 15*, *Presenting ASP.NET Core MVC*, we will detail the hosting that's available for web apps in .NET 5. This web host helps us since the startup of the app and lifetime management is set up alongside it. The idea of .NET Generic Host is to enable this pattern for applications that do not need HTTP implementation. With this Generic Host, any .NET Core program can have a startup class where we can configure the dependency injection engine. This can be useful for creating multi-service apps.

You can find out more about .NET Generic Host at `https://docs.microsoft.com/en-us/aspnet/core/fundamentals/host/generic-host`, which contains some sample code and is the current recommendation from Microsoft. The code provided in the GitHub repository is simpler, but it focuses on the creation of a console app that can run a service for monitoring. The great thing about this is the way the console app is set up to run, where the builder configures the services that will be provided by the application, and the way logging will be managed.

This is shown in the following code:

```
public static void Main()
{

    var host = new HostBuilder()
        .ConfigureServices((hostContext, services) =>

        {
            services.AddHostedService<HostedService>();
            services.AddHostedService<MonitoringService>();
        })

        .ConfigureLogging((hostContext, configLogging) =>

        {
            configLogging.AddConsole();
        })
        .Build();
    host.Run();

    Console.WriteLine("Host has terminated. Press any key to finish the
App.");

    Console.ReadKey();

}
```

The preceding code gives us an idea of how .NET Core uses design patterns. Using the Builder pattern, .NET Generic Host allows you to set the classes that will be injected as services. Apart from this, the Builder pattern helps you configure some other features, such as the way logs will be shown/stored. This configuration allows the services to inject `ILogger<out TCategoryName>` objects into any instance.

Summary

In this chapter, we understood why design patterns help with the maintainability and reusability of the parts of the system you are building. We also looked at some typical use cases and code snippets that you can use in your projects. Finally, we presented .NET Generic Host, which is a good example of how .NET uses design patterns to enable code reusability and enforce best practices.

All this content will help you while architecting new software or even maintaining an existing one, since design patterns are already-known solutions for some real-life problems in software development.

In the next chapter, we will cover the domain-driven design approach. We will also learn how to use the SOLID design principles so that we can map different domains to our software solutions.

Questions

1. What are design patterns?
2. What is the difference between design patterns and design principles?
3. When is it a good idea to implement the Builder pattern?
4. When is it a good idea to implement the Factory pattern?
5. When is it a good idea to implement the Singleton pattern?
6. When is it a good idea to implement the Proxy pattern?
7. When is it a good idea to implement the Command pattern?
8. When is it a good idea to implement the Publisher/Subscriber pattern?
9. When is it a good idea to implement the Dependency Injection pattern?

Further reading

The following are some books and websites where you can find out more regarding what was covered in this chapter:

- *Clean Architecture: A Craftsman's Guide to Software Structure and Design,* Martin, Robert C., Pearson Education, 2018.
- *Design Patterns: Elements of Reusable Object-Oriented Software*, Erica Gamma et al., Addison-Wesley, 1994.
- *Design Principles and Design Patterns*, Martin, Robert C., 2000.
- If you need to get more info about design patterns and architectural principles, please check these links:
    - https://www.packtpub.com/application-development/design-patterns-using-c-and-net-core-video
    - https://docs.microsoft.com/en-us/dotnet/standard/modern-web-apps-azure-architecture/architectural-principles

- If you want to check specific cloud design patterns, you can find them at:
  - `https://docs.microsoft.com/en-us/azure/architecture/patterns/`

- If you want to better understand the idea of Generic Host, follow this link:
  - `https://docs.microsoft.com/en-us/aspnet/core/fundamentals/host/generic-host`

- There is a very good explanation about service bus messaging at this link:
  - `https://docs.microsoft.com/en-us/azure/service-bus-messaging/service-bus-dotnet-how-to-use-topics-subscriptions`

- You can learn more about dependency injection by checking these links:
  - `https://docs.microsoft.com/en-us/aspnet/core/fundamentals/dependency-injection`
  - `https://www.martinfowler.com/articles/injection.html`

12
Understanding the Different Domains in Software Solutions

This chapter is dedicated to a modern software development technique called **domain-driven design (DDD)**, which was first proposed by Eric Evans. While DDD has existed for more than 15 years, it has achieved great success in the last few years because of its ability to cope with two important problems.

The first problem is modeling complex systems. No single expert has in-depth knowledge of the whole domain; this knowledge is instead split among several people. As we will see, DDD copes with this problem by splitting the whole CI/CD cycle into independent parts, assigned to different teams. This way each team can focus on a specific domain of knowledge by interacting only with the experts of that domain.

The second problem DDD copes with well is big projects with several development teams. There are many reasons why a project is split among several teams, the most common being the team's size and all of its members having different skills and/or different locations. In fact, experience has proven that teams of more than 6-8 people are not efficacious and, clearly, different skills and locations prevent tight interaction from occurring. Team splitting prevents tight interaction from happening for all the people involved in the project.

In turn, the importance of the two aforementioned problems has grown in the last few years. Software systems have always taken up a lot of space inside every organization, and they became more and more complex and geographically distributed. At the same time, the need for frequent updates increased so that these complex software systems could be adapted to the needs of a quickly changing market.

These problems led to the conception of more sophisticated CI/CD cycles and the adoption of complex distributed architectures that may leverage reliability, high throughput, quick updates, and the capability to evolve legacy subsystems gradually. Yes—we are speaking of the microservices and container-based architectures we analyzed in *Chapter 5, Applying a Microservice Architecture to Your Enterprise Application.*

In this scenario, it's common to implement complex software systems with associated fast CI/CD cycles that always require more people to evolve and maintain them. In turn, this created a need for technologies that were adequate for high-complexity domains and for the cooperation of several loosely coupled development teams.

In this chapter, we will analyze the basic principles, advantages, and common patterns related to DDD, as well as how to use them in our solutions. More specifically, we will cover the following topics:

- What are software domains?
- Understanding domain-driven design
- Using SOLID principles to map your domains
- Use case—understanding the domains of the use case

Let's get started.

Technical requirements

This chapter requires Visual Studio 2019 free Community Edition or better with all the database tools installed.

All the code snippets in this chapter can be found in the GitHub repository associated with this book, `https://github.com/PacktPublishing/Software-Architecture-with-C-9-and-.NET-5`.

What are software domains?

As we discussed in *Chapter 2, Non-Functional Requirements,* and *Chapter 3, Documenting Requirements with Azure DevOps,* the transfer of knowledge from domain experts to the development team plays a fundamental role in software design. Developers try to communicate with experts and describe their solutions in a language that domain experts and stakeholders can understand. However, often, the same word has a different meaning in various parts of an organization, and what appear to be the same conceptual entities have completely different shapes in different contexts.

For instance, in our WWTravelClub use case, the order-payment and packages-handling subsystems use completely different models for customers. Order-payment characterizes a customer by their payment methods and currency, bank accounts, and credit cards, while packages-handling is more concerned with the locations and packages that have been visited and/or purchased in the past, the user's preferences, and their geographical location. Moreover, while order-payment refers to various concepts with a language that we may roughly define as a **bank language**, packages-handling uses a language that is typical of travel agencies/operators.

The classical way to cope with these discrepancies is to use a unique abstract entity called **customer**, which projects into two different views—the order-payment view and the package-handling view. Each projection operation takes some operations and some properties from the **customer** abstract entity and changes their names. Since domain experts only give us the projected views, our main task as system designers is to create a conceptual model that can explain all the views. The following diagram shows how different views are handled:

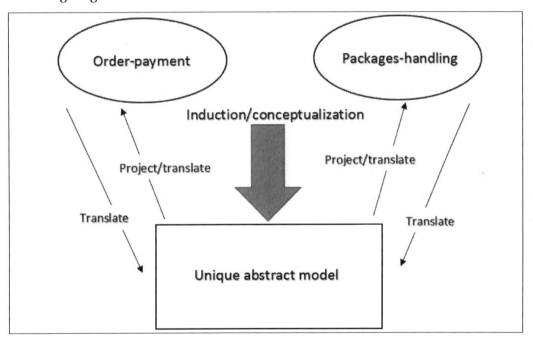

Figure 12.1: Creating a unique model

The main advantage of the classic approach is that we have a unique and coherent representation of the data of the domain. If this conceptual model is built successfully, all the operations will have a formal definition and purpose and the whole abstraction will be a rationalization of the way the whole organization should work, possibly highlighting and correcting errors and simplifying some procedures.

However, what are the downsides of this approach?

The sharp adoption of a new monolithic data model may cause an acceptable impact in a small organization, when the software is destined for a small part of the overall organization, or when the software automatizes a small enough percentage of the data flow. However, if the software becomes the backbone of a complex geographically distributed organization, sharp changes become unacceptable and unfeasible. Complex structured companies require a gradual transition from the old organization to the new organization. In turn, a gradual transition is possible only if old data models can coexist with new data models, and if each of the various components of the organization is allowed to change at its own speed, that is, if each component of the organization can evolve independently of the others.

Moreover, as the complexity of the software system grows, several other issues appear, as follows:

- **Coherency issues**: Arriving at a uniquely coherent view of data becomes more difficult since we can't retain the complexity when we break these tasks into smaller, loosely coupled tasks.

- **Difficulties updating**: As complexity grows, there is a need for frequent system changes, but it is quite difficult to update and maintain a unique global model. Moreover, bugs/errors that are introduced by changes in small subparts of the system may propagate to the whole organization through the uniquely shared model.

- **Team organization issues**: System modeling must be split among several teams, and only loosely-coupled tasks can be given to separate teams; if two tasks are strongly coupled, they need to be given to the same team.

- **Parallelism issues**: The need to move to a microservice-based architecture makes the bottleneck of a unique database more unacceptable.

- **Language issues**: As the system grows, we need to communicate with more domain experts, each speaking a different language and each with a different view of that data model. Thus, we need to translate our unique model's properties and operations to/from more languages to be able to communicate with them.

As the system grows, it becomes more inefficient to deal with records with hundreds/thousands of fields. Such inefficiencies originate in database engines that inefficiently handle big records with several fields (memory fragmentation, problems with too many related indices, and so on). However, the main inefficiencies take place in **object-relational mappings** (ORMs) and business layers that are forced to handle these big records in their update operations. In fact, while query operations usually require just a few fields that have been retrieved from the storage engine, updates and business processing involve the whole entity.

As the traffic in the data storage subsystem grows, we need read and update/write parallelism in all the data operations. As we discussed in *Chapter 9, How to Choose Your Data Storage in the Cloud*, while read parallelism is easily achieved with data replication, write parallelism requires sharding, and it is difficult to shard a uniquely monolithic and tightly connected data model.

These issues are the reason for DDD's success in the last few years because they were characterized by more complex software systems that became the backbones of entire organizations. DDD's basic principles will be discussed in detail in the next section.

Understanding domain-driven design

DDD is about the construction of a unique domain model that keeps all the views as separate models. Thus, the whole application domain is split into smaller domains, each with a separate model. These separate domains are called **Bounded Contexts**. Each domain is characterized by the language spoken by the experts and used to name all the domain concepts and operations. Thus, each domain defines a common language used by both the expert and the development team called a **Ubiquitous Language**. Translations are not needed anymore, and if the development team uses interfaces as bases for its code, the domain expert is able to understand and validate them since all the operations and properties are expressed in the same language that's used by the expert.

Here, we're getting rid of a cumbersome unique abstract model, but now we have several separated models that we need to relate somehow. DDD proposes that it will handle all of these separated models, that is, all the Bounded Contexts, as follows:

- We need to add Bounded Context boundaries whenever the meanings of the language terms change. For instance, in the WWTravelClub use case, order-payment and packages-handling belong to different Bounded Contexts because they give a different meaning to the word **customer**.

- We need to explicitly represent relations among bounded contexts. Different development teams may work on different Bounded Contexts, but each team must have a clear picture of the relationship between the Bounded Context it is working on and all the other models. For this reason, such relationships are represented in a unique document that's shared with every team.

- We need to keep all the Bounded Contexts aligned with CI. Meetings are organized and simplified system prototypes are built in order to verify that all the Bounded Contexts are evolving coherently, that is, that all the Bounded Contexts can be integrated into the desired application behavior.

The following diagram shows how the WWTravelClub example that we discussed in the previous section changes with the adoption of DDD:

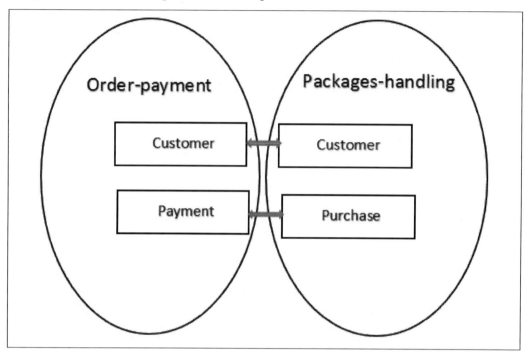

Figure 12.2: Relations among DDD Bounded Contexts

There is a relationship between the customer entities of each Bounded Context, while the Purchase entity of the packages-handling Bounded Context is related to the payments. Identifying entities that map to each other in the various Bounded Contexts is the first step of formally defining the interfaces that represent all the possible communications among the contexts.

For instance, from the preceding diagram, we know that payments are done after purchases, and so we can deduce that the order-payment Bounded Context must have an operation to create a payment for a specific customer. In this domain, new customers are created if they don't already exist. The payment creation operation is triggered immediately after purchase. Since several more operations are triggered after an item is purchased, we can implement all the communication related to a purchase event with the Publisher/Subscriber pattern we explained in *Chapter 11, Design Patterns and .NET 5 Implementation*. These are known as **domain events** in DDD. Using events to implement communications between Bounded Contexts is very common since it helps keep Bounded Contexts loosely coupled.

Once an instance of either an event or an operation that's been defined in the Bounded Context's interface crosses the context boundary, it is immediately translated into the Ubiquitous Language of the receiving context. It is important that this translation is performed before the input data starts interacting with the other domain entities to avoid the Ubiquitous Language of the other domain becoming contaminated by extra context terms.

Each Bounded Context implementation must contain a Data Model Layer completely expressed in terms of the Bounded Context Ubiquitous Language (class and interface names and property and method names), with no contamination from other Bounded Contexts' Ubiquitous Languages, and without contamination from programming technical stuff. This is necessary to ensure good communication with domain experts and to ensure that domain rules are translated correctly into code so that they can be easily validated by domain experts.

When there is a strong mismatch between the communication language and the target Ubiquitous Language, an anti-corruption layer is added to the receiving Bounded Context boundary. The only purpose of this anti-corruption layer is to perform a language translation.

The document that contains a representation of all the Bounded Contexts, along with the Bounded Contexts' mutual relationships and interface definitions, is called a **Context Mapping**. The relationships among contexts contain organizational constraints that specify the kind of cooperation that's required among the team that works on the different Bounded Contexts. Such relationships don't constrain the Bounded Context interfaces but do affect the way they may evolve during the software CI/CD cycle. They represent patterns of team cooperation. The most common patterns are as follows:

- **Partner**: This is the original pattern suggested by Eric Evans. The idea is that the two teams have a mutual dependency on each other for delivery. In other terms, they decide together and, if needed, change the Bounded Context's mutual communication specifications during the software CI/CD cycle.

- **Customer/supplier development teams**: In this case, one team acts as a customer and another acts as a supplier. Both teams define the interface of the customer side of the Bounded Context and some automated acceptance tests to validate it. After that, the supplier can work independently. This pattern works when the customer's Bounded Context is the only active part that invokes the interface methods that are exposed by the other Bounded Context. This is adequate for the interaction between the order-payment and the packages-handling contexts, where order-payment acts as a supplier since its functions are subordinate to the needs of packages-handling. When this pattern can be applied, it decouples the two Bounded Contexts completely.

- **Conformist**: This is similar to the customer/supplier, but in this case, the customer side accepts an interface that's been imposed by the supplier side with no negotiation stage. This pattern offers no advantages to the other patterns, but sometimes we are forced into the situation depicted by the pattern since either the supplier's Bounded Context is implemented in a preexisting product that can't be configured/modified too much, or because it is a legacy subsystem that we don't want to modify.

It is worth pointing out that the separation in Bounded Contexts is only efficacious if the resulting Bounded Contexts are loosely coupled; otherwise, the reduction of complexity that's obtained by breaking a whole system into subparts would be overwhelmed by the complexity of the coordination and communication processes.

However, if Bounded Contexts are defined with the language criterion, that is, Bounded Context boundaries are added whenever the **Ubiquitous Language** changes, this should actually be the case. In fact, different languages may arise as a result of a loose interaction between organization subparts since the more each subpart has tight interactions inside of it and loose interactions with other subparts, the more each subpart ends up defining and using its own internal language, which differs from the language used by the other subparts.

Moreover, all human organizations can grow by evolving into loosely coupled subparts for the same reason complex software systems may be implemented as the cooperation of loosely coupled submodules: this is the only way humans are able to cope with complexity. From this, we can conclude that complex organizations/artificial systems can always be decomposed into loosely coupled subparts. We just need to understand *how*.

Beyond the basic principles we've mentioned so far, DDD provides a few basic primitives to describe each Bounded Context, as well as some implementation patterns. While Bounded Context primitives are an integral part of DDD, these patterns are useful heuristics we can use in our implementation, so their usage in some or all Bounded Contexts is not obligatory once we opt for DDD adoption.

In the next section, we will describe primitives and patterns.

Entities and value objects

DDD entities represent domain objects that have a well-defined identity, as well as all the operations that are defined on them. They don't differ too much from the entities of other, more classical approaches. Also, DDD entities are the starting point of the storage layer design.

The main difference is that DDD stresses their object-oriented nature, while other approaches use them mainly as **records** whose properties can be written/updated without too many constraints. DDD, on the other hand, forces strong SOLID principles on them to ensure that only certain information is encapsulated inside of them and that only certain information is accessible from outside of them, to stipulate which operations are allowed on them, and to set which business-level validation criteria apply to them.

In other words, DDD entities are richer than the entities of record-based approaches. In other approaches, operations that manipulate entities are defined outside of them in classes that represent business and/or domain operations. In DDD, these operations are moved to the entity definitions as their class methods. The reason for this is that they offer better modularity and keep related chunks of software in the same place so that they can be maintained and tested easily.

For the same reason, business validation rules are moved inside of DDD entities. DDD entity validation rules are business-level rules, so they must not be confused with database integrity rules or with user-input validation rules. They contribute to the way entities represent domain objects by encoding the constraints the represented objects must obey. In .NET (Core), business validation can be carried out with one of the following techniques:

- Calling the validation methods in all the class methods that modify the entity

- Hooking the validation methods to all the property setters

- Decorating the class and/or its properties with custom validation attributes and then invoking the `TryValidateObject` static method of the `System.ComponentModel.DataAnnotations.Validator` class on the entity each time it is modified

Once detected, validation errors must be handled somehow; that is, the current operation must be aborted and the error must be reported to an appropriate error handler. The simplest way to handle validation errors is by throwing an exception. This way, both purposes are easily achieved and we can choose where to intercept and handle them. Unfortunately, as we discussed in the *Performance issues that need to be considered while programming in C# section of Chapter 2, Non-Functional Requirements*, exceptions imply big performance penalties, so, often, different options are considered. Handling errors in the normal flow of control would break modularity by spreading the code that's needed to handle the error all over the stack of methods that caused the error, with a never-ending set of conditions all over that code. Therefore, more sophisticated options are needed.

A good alternative to exceptions is to notify errors to an error handler that is defined in the dependency injection engine. Being scoped, the same service instance is returned while each request is being processed so that the handler that controls the execution of the whole call stack can inspect possible errors when the flow of control returns to it and can handle them appropriately. Unfortunately, this sophisticated technique can't abort the operation's execution immediately or return it to the controlling handler. This is why exceptions are recommended for this scenario, notwithstanding their performance issues.

Business-level validation must not be confused with input validation, which will be discussed in more detail in *Chapter 15, Presenting ASP.NET Core MVC*, since the two types of validation have different and complementary purposes. While business-level validation rules encode domain rules, input validation enforces the format of every single input (string length, correct email and URL formats, and so on), ensures that all the necessary input has been provided, enforces the execution of the chosen user-machine interaction protocols, and provides fast and immediate feedback that drives the user to interact with the system.

Since DDD entities must have a well-defined identity, they must have properties that act as primary keys. It is common to override the `Object.Equals` method of all the DDD entities in such a way that two objects are considered equal whenever they have the same primary keys. This is easily achieved by letting all the entities inherit from an abstract `Entity` class, as shown in the following code:

```
public abstract class Entity<K>: IEntity<K>
    where K: IEquatable<K>
{

    public virtual K Id { get; protected set; }
    public bool IsTransient()
    {
        return Object.Equals(Id, default(K));
    }
    public override bool Equals(object obj)
    {
        return obj is Entity<K> entity &&
            Equals(entity);
    }
    public bool Equals(IEntity<K> other)
    {
```

```
        if (other == null ||
            other.IsTransient() || this.IsTransient())
            return false;

        return Object.Equals(Id, other.Id);
    }
    int? _requestedHashCode;
    public override int GetHashCode()
    {
        if (!IsTransient())
        {
            if (!_requestedHashCode.HasValue)
                _requestedHashCode = HashCode.Combine(Id);
            return _requestedHashCode.Value;
        }
        else
            return base.GetHashCode();
    }
    public static bool operator ==(Entity<K> left, Entity<K> right)
    {
        if (Object.Equals(left, null))
            return (Object.Equals(right, null));
        else
            return left.Equals(right);
    }
    public static bool operator !=(Entity<K> left, Entity<K> right)
    {
        return !(left == right);
    }
}
```

It is worth pointing out that, once we've redefined the Object.Equals method in the Entity class, we can also override the == and != operators.

The IsTransient predicate returns true whenever the entity has been recently created and hasn't been recorded in the permanent storage, so its primary key is still undefined.

> In .NET, it is good practice that, whenever you override the Object.Equals method of a class, you also override its Object.GetHashCode method so that class instances can be efficiently stored in data structures such as dictionaries and sets. That's why the Entity class overrides it.

It is also worth implementing an `IEntity<K>` interface that defines all the properties/methods of `Entity<K>`. This interface is useful whenever we need to hide data classes behind interfaces.

Value objects, on the other hand, represent complex types that can't be encoded with numbers or strings. Therefore, they have no identity and no principal keys. They have no operations defined on them and are immutable; that is, once they've been created, all their fields can be read but cannot be modified. For this reason, they are usually encoded with classes whose properties have protected/private setters. Two value objects are considered equal when all their independent properties are equal (some properties are not independent since they just show data that's been encoded by other properties in a different way, as is the case for the ticks of `DateTime` and its representation of the date and time fields).

Value types are easily implemented with C# 9 record types, since all `record` types automatically override the `Equals` method so that it performs a property by property comparison. Moreover, `record` types behave like `structs`, in that a new instance is created at each assignment. However, record types are also immutable; that is, once initialized, the only way to change their values is to create a new instance. Here is an example of how to modify a `record`:

```
var modifiedAddress = myAddress with {Street = "new street"}
```

Here is an example of how to define a `record`:

```
public record Address
{
    public string Country {get; init;}
    public string Town {get; init;}
    public string Street {get; init;}
}
```

The `init` keyword is what makes `record` types properties immutable, since it means they can be only initialized.

Typical value objects include costs represented as a number and a currency symbol, locations represented as longitude and latitude, addresses, and contact information. When the interface of the storage engine is Entity Framework, which we analyzed in *Chapter 8, Interacting with Data in C# – Entity Framework Core*, and *Chapter 9, How to Choose Your Data Storage in the Cloud*, value objects are connected with the entity that uses them through the `OwnsMany` and `OwnsOne` relationships. In fact, such relationships also accept classes with no principal keys defined on them.

When the storage engine is a NoSQL database, value objects are stored inside the record of the entities that use them. On the other hand, in the case of relational databases, they can either be implemented with separated tables whose principal keys are handled automatically by Entity Framework and are hidden from the developer (no property is declared as a principal key) or, in the case of OwnsOne, they are flattened and added to the table associated with the entity that uses them.

Using SOLID principles to map your domains

In the following subsections, we will describe some of the patterns that are commonly used with DDD. Some of them can be adopted in all projects, while others can only be used for certain Bounded Contexts. The general idea is that the business layer is split into two layers:

- Application layer
- Domain layer

Here, the domain layer is an abstraction of the data layer based on the Ubiquitous Language. It is where DDD entities and value objects are defined together with abstractions of the operations to retrieve and save them. These operations are defined in interfaces that are implemented in the underlying data layer (Entity Framework in our case).

The application layer, instead, defines operations that use the domain layer interfaces, to get DDD entities and value objects, and that manipulate them to implement the application business logic.

As we will see later on in this chapter, it is common to implement the domain layer with just interfaces that are implemented in the data layer. Thus, the data layer must have a reference to the domain layer since it must implement its interfaces, while the application layer is where each domain layer interface is connected with its implementation through a record of the application layer dependency injection engine. More specifically, the only data layer objects referenced by the application layer are these interface implementations that are referenced only in the dependency injection engine.

Each application layer operation requires the interfaces it needs from the dependency engine, uses them to get DDD entities and value objects, manipulates them, and possibly saves them through the same interfaces. Here is a diagram that shows the relations among the three layers discussed in this section:

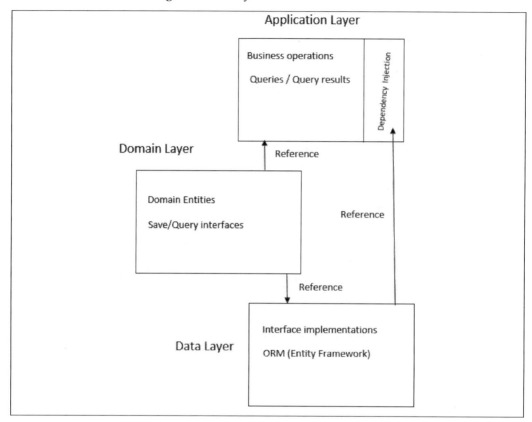

Figure 12.3: Relations among layers

Thus, the domain layer contains the representation of the domain objects, the methods to use on them, validation constraints, and its relationship with various entities. To increase modularity and decoupling, communication among entities is usually encoded with events, that is, with a Publisher/Subscriber pattern. This means entity updates can trigger events that have been hooked to business operations, and these events act on other entities.

This layered architecture allows us to change the whole data layer without affecting the domain layer, which only depends on the domain specifications and language and doesn't depend on the technical details of how the data is handled.

The application layer contains the definitions of all the operations that may potentially affect several entities and the definitions of all the queries that are needed by the applications. Both business operations and queries use the interfaces defined in the domain layer to interact with the data layer.

However, while business operations manipulate and exchange entities with these interfaces, queries send query specifications and receive generic **Data Transfer Objects (DTOs)** from them. In fact, the purpose of queries is just to show data to the user, not to act on them; accordingly, query operations don't need whole entities with all their methods, properties, and validation rules, but just property tuples.

Business operations are invoked either by other layers (typically the presentation layer) or by communication operations. Business operations may also be hooked to events that are triggered when some entities are modified by other operations.

Summing up, the application layer operates on the interfaces defined in the domain layer instead of interacting directly with their data layer implementations, which means that the application layer is decoupled from the data layer. More specifically, data layer objects are only mentioned in the dependency injection engine definitions. All the other application layer components refer to the interfaces that are defined in the domain layers, and the dependency injection engine injects the appropriate implementations.

The application layer communicates with other application components through one or more of the following patterns:

- It exposes business operations and queries on a communication endpoint, such as an HTTP Web API (see *Chapter 14, Applying Service-Oriented Architectures with .NET Core*). In this case, the presentation layer may connect to this endpoint or to other endpoints that, in turn, take information from this and other endpoints. Application components that collect information from several endpoints and expose them in a unique endpoint are called gateways. They may be either custom or general purpose, such as Ocelot.

- It is referenced as a library by an application that directly implements the presentation layer, such as an ASP.NET Core MVC Web application.

- It doesn't expose all the information through endpoints and communicates some of the data it processes/creates to other application components that, in turn, expose endpoints. Such communication is often implemented with the Publisher/Subscriber pattern to increase modularity.

Before we describe these patterns, we need to understand the concept of aggregates.

Aggregates

So far, we have talked about entities as the **units** that are processed by a DDD-based business layer. However, several entities can be manipulated and made into single entities. An example of this is a purchase order and all of its items. In fact, it makes absolutely no sense to process a single order-item independently of the order it belongs to. This happens because order-items are actually subparts of an order, not independent entities.

There is no transaction that may affect a single order-item without it affecting the order that the item is in. Imagine that two different people in the same company are trying to increase the total quantity of cement, but one increases the quantity of type-1 cement (item 1) while the other increases the quantity of type-2 cement (item 2). If each item is processed as an independent entity, both quantities will be increased, which could cause an incoherent purchase order since the total quantity of cement would be increased twice.

On the other hand, if the whole order, along with all its order-items, is loaded and saved with every single transaction by both people, one of the two will overwrite the changes of the other one, so whoever makes the final change will have their requirements set. In a web application, it isn't possible to lock the purchase order for the whole time the user sees and modifies it, so an optimistic concurrency policy is used. If the data layer is based on **Entity Framework (EF)** Core we can use the EF concurrency check attribute. If we decorate a property with the [ConcurrencyCheck] attribute, when EF saves changes, the transaction is aborted and a concurrency exception is generated whenever the value in the database of the property decorated with [ConcurrencyCheck] differs from the one retrieved when the entity was read.

For instance, it is enough to add a version number decorated with [ConcurrencyCheck] to each purchase order and to do the following:

1. Read the order without opening any transaction, and update it.
2. Before saving the updated purchase order, we increment the counter.
3. When we save all changes, if someone else incremented this counter before we were able to save our changes, a concurrency exception is generated and the operation is aborted.
4. Repeat from *step 1* until no concurrency exception occurs.

It is also possible to use an automatically generated TimeStamp instead of a counter. However, as we will see shortly, we need counters to implement the **Command Query Responsibility Segregation (CQRS)** pattern.

A purchase order, along with all its subparts (its order-items), is called an **aggregate**, while the order entity is called the root of the aggregate. Aggregates always have roots since they are hierarchies of entities connected by **subpart** relations.

Since each aggregate represents a single complex entity, all the operations on it must be exposed by a unique interface. Therefore, the aggregate root usually represents the whole aggregate, and all the operations on the aggregate are defined as methods of the root entity.

When the aggregate pattern is used, the units of information that are transferred between the business layer and the data layer are called aggregates, queries, and query results. Thus, aggregates replace single entities.

What about the WWTravelClub location and packages entities we looked at in *Chapter 8, Interacting with Data in C# – Entity Framework Core*, and *Chapter 9, How to Choose Your Data Storage in the Cloud*? Are packages part of the unique aggregates that are rooted in their associated locations? No! In fact, locations are rarely updated, and changes that are made to a package have no influence on its location or on the other packages associated with the same location.

The repository and Unit of Work patterns

The repository pattern is an entity-centric approach to the definition of the domain layer interfaces: each aggregate has its own repository interface that defines how to retrieve and save it, and that defines all queries that involve entities in the aggregate. The data layer implementation of each repository interface is called a repository.

With the repository pattern, each operation has an easy-to-find place where it must be defined: the interface of the aggregate the operation works on, or, in case of a query, the aggregate that contains the root entity of the query.

Often, application layer operations that span several aggregates and that, accordingly, use several different repository interfaces must be executed in a unique transaction. The **Unit of Work** pattern is a solution that maintains the independence of the domain layer from the underlying data layer. It states that each repository interface must also contain a reference to a Unit of Work interface that represents the identity of the current transaction. This means that several repositories with the same Unit of Work reference belong to the same transaction.

Both the repository and the unit of work patterns can be implemented by defining some seed interfaces:

```
public interface IUnitOfWork
{
    Task<bool> SaveEntitiesAsync();
    Task StartAsync();
    Task CommitAsync();
    Task RollbackAsync();
}


public interface IRepository<T>: IRepository
{
    IUnitOfWork UnitOfWork { get; }
}
```

All repository interfaces inherit from `IRepository<T>` and bind `T` to the aggregate root they are associated with, while Unit of Work simply implements `IUnitOfWork`. When using Entity Framework, `IUnitOfWork` is usually implemented with `DBContext`, which means that `SaveEntitiesAsync()` can perform other operations and then call the `DBContext SaveChangeAsync` method so that all the pending changes are saved in a single transaction. If a wider transaction that starts when some data is retrieved from the storage engine is needed, it must be started and committed/aborted by the application layer handler, which takes care of the whole operation with the help of the `IUnitOfWork StartAsync`, `CommitAsync`, and `RollbackAsync` methods. `IRepository<T>` inherits from an empty `IRepository` interface to help automatic repository discovery. The GitHub repository associated with this book contains a `RepositoryExtensions` class whose `AddAllRepositories IServiceCollection` extension method automatically discovers all the repository implementations contained in an assembly and adds them to the dependency injection engine.

Here's a diagram of the application layer/domain layer/data layer architecture based on the repository and Unit of Work patterns:

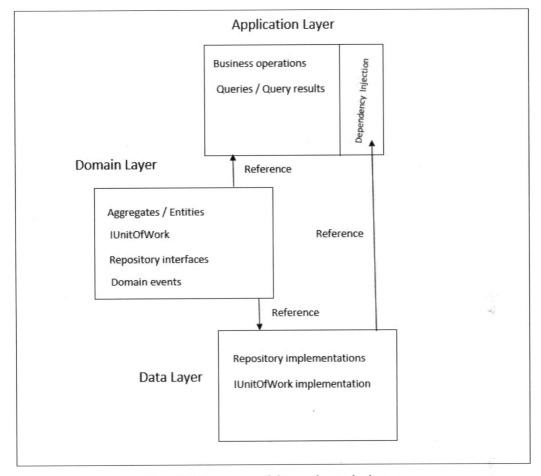

Figure 12.4: Layer responsibilities and mutual references

The main advantage of avoiding direct references to repository implementations is that the various modules can be tested easily if we mock these interfaces. The domain events mentioned in the domain layer are the events that implement the communication between different Bounded Contexts mentioned in the *Understanding domain-driven design* section.

DDD entities and Entity Framework Core

DDD requires entities to be defined in a way that is different from the way we defined entities in *Chapter 8, Interacting with Data in C# – Entity Framework Core*. In fact, Entity Framework entities are record-like lists of public properties with almost no methods, while DDD entities should have methods that encode domain logic, more sophisticated validation logic, and read-only properties. While further validation logic and methods can be added without breaking Entity Framework's operations, adding read-only properties that must not be mapped to database properties can create problems that must be handled adequately. Preventing properties from being mapped to the database is quite easy — all we need to do is decorate them with the NotMapped attribute.

The issues that read-only properties have are a little bit more complex and can be solved in three fundamental ways:

- **Map EF entities to different classes**. Define the DDD entities as different classes and copy data to/from them when entities are returned/passed to repository methods. This is the easiest solution, but it requires that you write some code so that you can convert the entities between the two formats. DDD entities are defined in the domain layer, while the EF entities continue being defined in the data layer. This is the cleaner solution, but it causes a non-trivial overhead in both code writing and maintenance. I recommend it when you have complex aggregates with several complex methods.

- **Map table fields to private properties**. Let Entity Framework Core map fields to private class fields so that you can decide how to expose them to properties by writing custom getters and/or setters. It is sufficient to give either the _<property name> name or the _<property name in camel case> name to these private fields, and Entity Framework will use them instead of their associated properties. In this case, DDD entities defined in the domain layer are used also as data layer entities. The main disadvantage of this approach is that we can't use data annotations to configure each property because DDD entities can't depend on how the underlying data layer is implemented. Therefore, we must configure all database mapping in the OnModelCreating DbContext method. This is the simpler solution but it generates code that is not readable and is difficult to maintain, so I don't advise adopting it at all.

- **Define DDD as interfaces**. Hide each Entity Framework class with all its public properties behind an interface that, when needed, only exposes property getters. The interface is defined in the domain layer, while the entity continues being defined in the data layer. In this case, the repository must expose a Create method that returns an implementation of the interface; otherwise, the higher layers won't be able to create new instances that can be added to the storage engine since interfaces can't be created with new. This is the solution I prefer when there are several simple entities.

For instance, suppose that we would like to define a DDD interface called IDestination for the Destination class defined in the *Defining DB entities* subsection of *Chapter 8, Interacting with Data in C# – Entity Framework Core*, and suppose we would like to expose the Id, Name, and Country properties as read-only since once a destination is created it can't be modified anymore. Here, it is sufficient to let Destination implement IDestination and to define Id, Name, and Country as read-only in IDestination:

```
public interface IDestination
{
    int Id { get; }
    string Name { get; }
    string Country { get; }
    string Description { get; set; }
    ...
}
```

Now that we've discussed the basic patterns of DDD and how to adapt Entity Framework for the needs of DDD, we can discuss more advanced DDD patterns. In the next section, we will introduce the CQRS pattern.

Command Query Responsibility Segregation (CQRS) pattern

In its general form, the usage of this pattern is quite easy: use different structures to store and query data. Here, the requirements regarding how to store and update data differ from the requirements of queries. In the case of DDD, the unit of storage is the **aggregate**, so additions, deletions, and updates involve aggregates, while queries usually involve more or less complicated transformations of properties that have been taken from several aggregates.

Moreover, usually, we don't perform business operations on query results. We just use them to compute other data (averages, sums, and so on). Therefore, while updates require entities with full object-oriented semantics (methods, validation rules, encapsulated information, and so on), query results just need sets of property/ value pairs, so **Data Transfer Objects (DTOs)** with only public properties and no methods work well.

In its common form, the pattern can be depicted as follows:

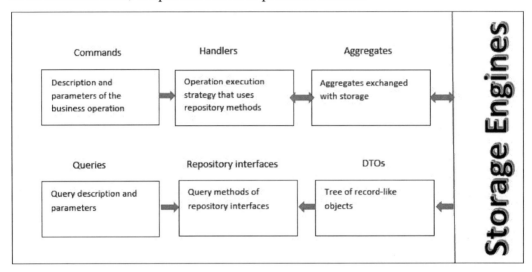

Figure 12.5: Commands and queries processing

The main takeaway from this is that the extraction of query results don't need to pass through the construction of entities and aggregates, but the fields shown in the query must be extracted from the storage engine and projected into ad hoc DTOs. If queries are implemented with LINQ, we need to use the Select clause to project the necessary properties into DTOs:

```
ctx.MyTable.Where(...)....Select(new MyDto{...}).ToList();
```

However, in more complex situations, CQRS may be implemented in a stronger form. Namely, we can use different Bounded Contexts to store preprocessed query results. This approach is common when queries involve data stored in different Bounded Contexts that are handled by different distributed microservices.

In fact, the other option would be an aggregator microservice that queries all the necessary microservices in order to assemble each query result. However, recursive calls to other microservices to build an answer may result in unacceptable response times. Moreover, factoring out some preprocessing ensures better usage of the available resources. This pattern is implemented as follows:

1. Query handling is delegated to specialized microservices.

2. Each query-handling microservice uses a database table for each query it must handle. There, it stores all fields to be returned by the query. This means that queries are not computed at each request, but pre-computed and stored in specific database tables. Clearly, queries with child collections need additional tables, one for each child collection.

3. All microservices that process updates forward all changes to the interested query-handling microservices. Records are versioned so the query-handling microservices that receive the changes can apply them in the right order to their query-handling tables. In fact, since communication is asynchronous to improve performance, changes are not ensured to be received in the same order they were sent.

4. Changes received by each query-handling microservice are cached while they wait for the changes to be applied. Whenever a change has a version number that immediately follows the last change applied, it is applied to the right query-handling table.

The usage of this stronger form of the CQRS pattern transforms usual local database transactions into complex time-consuming distributed transactions since a failure in a single query preprocessor microservice should invalidate the whole transaction. As we explained in *Chapter 5, Applying a Microservice Architecture to Your Enterprise Application*, implementing distributed transactions is usually unacceptable for performance reasons, and sometimes is not supported at all, so the common solution is to renounce the idea of a database that is immediately consistent overall, and to accept that the overall database will eventually be consistent after each update. Transient failures can be solved with the retry policies that we analyzed in *Chapter 5, Applying a Microservice Architecture to Your Enterprise Application*, while permanent failures are handled by performing corrective actions on the already committed local transactions instead of pretending to implement an overall globally distributed transaction.

As we discussed in *Chapter 5, Applying a Microservice Architecture to Your Enterprise Application*, communication between microservices is often implemented with the Publisher/Subscriber pattern to improve microservice separation.

At this point, you may be asking the following question:

"Why do we need to keep the original data once we have all the preprocessed query results? We will never use it to answer queries!"

Some of the answers to this question are as follows:

- They are the source of truth that we may need to recover from failures.
- We need them to compute new preprocessed results when we add new queries.
- We need them to process new updates. In fact, processing updates usually requires that some of the data is retrieved from the database, possibly shown to the user, and then modified. For instance, to modify an item in an existing purchase order, we need the whole order so that we can show it to the user and compute the changes so that we can forward it to other microservices. Moreover, whenever we modify or add data to the storage engine, we must verify the coherence of the overall database (unique key constraints, foreign key constraints, and so on).

In the next section, we will describe a common pattern that's used for handling operations that span several aggregates and several Bounded Contexts.

Command handlers and domain events

To keep aggregates separated, usually, interactions with other aggregates and other Bounded Contexts are done through events. It is good practice to store all the events when they are created during the processing of each aggregate, instead of executing them immediately, in order to prevent event execution from interfering with the ongoing aggregate processing. This is easily achieved by adding the following code to the abstract Entity class defined in the *Entities and value objects* subsection of this chapter, as follows:

```
public List<IEventNotification> DomainEvents { get; private set; }
public void AddDomainEvent(IEventNotification evt)
{
    DomainEvents ??= new List<IEventNotification>();
    DomainEvents.Add(evt);
}
public void RemoveDomainEvent(IEventNotification evt)
{
    DomainEvents?.Remove(evt);
}
```

Here, IEventNotification is an empty interface that's used to mark classes as events.

Event processing is usually performed immediately before changes are stored in the storage engine. Accordingly, a good place to perform event processing is immediately before the command handler calls the SaveEntitiesAsync() method of each IUnitOfWork implementation (see the *The repository and Unit of Work patterns* subsection). Similarly, if event handlers can create other events, they must process them after they finish processing all their aggregates.

Subscriptions to an event, T, can be provided as an implementation of the IEventHandler<T> interface:

```
public interface IEventHandler<T>: IEventHandler
    where T: IEventNotification
{

    Task HandleAsync(T ev);
}
```

Analogously, business operations can be described by the command object, which contains all the input data of the operation, while the code that implements the actual operation can be provided through the implementation of an ICommandHandler<T> interface:

```
public interface ICommandHandler<T>: ICommandHandler
    where T: ICommand
{
    Task HandleAsync(T command);
}
```

Here, ICommand is an empty interface that's used to mark classes as commands. ICommandHandler<T> and IEventHandler<T> are examples of the command pattern we described in *Chapter 11, Design Patterns and .NET 5 Implementation.*

Each ICommandHandler<T> can be registered in the dependency injection engine so that classes that need to execute a command, T, can use ICommandHandler<T> in their constructor. This way, we decouple the abstract definition of a command (the command class) from the way it is executed.

The same construction can't be applied to events, T, and their IEventHandler<T> because when an event is triggered, we need to retrieve several instances of IEventHandler<T> and not just one. We need to do this since each event may have several subscriptions. However, a few lines of code can easily solve this difficulty. First, we need to define a class that hosts all the handlers for a given event type:

```
public class EventTrigger<T>
        where T: IEventNotification
    {

        private IEnumerable<IEventHandler<T>> handlers;
        public EventTrigger(IEnumerable<IEventHandler<T>> handlers)
        {
            this.handlers = handlers;
        }
        public async Task Trigger(T ev)
        {
            foreach (var handler in handlers)
                await handler.HandleAsync(ev);
        }
    }
```

The idea is that each class that needs to trigger event T requires EventTrigger<T> and then passes the event to be triggered to its Trigger method, which, in turn, invokes all the handlers.

Then, we need to register EventTrigger<T> in the dependency injection engine. A good idea is to define the dependency injection extensions that we can invoke to declare each event, as follows:

```
service.AddEventHandler<MyEventType, MyHandlerType>()
```

This AddEventHandler extension must automatically produce a dependency injection definition for EventTrigger<T> and must process all the handlers that are declared with AddEventHandler for each type, T.

The following extension class does this for us:

```
public static class EventDIExtensions
{
    public static IServiceCollection AddEventHandler<T, H>
        (this IServiceCollection services)
        where T : IEventNotification
        where H: class, IEventHandler<T>
    {
        services.AddScoped<H>();
```

```
        services.TryAddScoped(typeof(EventTrigger<>));
        return services;
    }
    ...
    ...
}
```

The H type passed to AddEventHandler is recorded in the dependency injection engine, and the first time AddEventHandler is called, EventTrigger<> is also added to the dependency injection engine. Then, when an EventTrigger<T> instance is required by the dependency injection engine, all IEventHandler<T> types added to the dependency injection engine are created, collected, and passed to the EventTrigger(IEnumerable<IEventHandler<T>> handlers) constructor.

When the program starts up, all the ICommandHandler<T> and IEventHandler<T> implementations can be retrieved with reflection and registered automatically. To help with automatic discovery, they inherit from ICommandHandler and IEventHandler, which are both empty interfaces. The EventDIExtensions class, which is available in this book's GitHub repository, contains methods for the automatic discovery and registration of command handlers and event handlers. The GitHub repository also contains an IEventMediator interface and its EventMediator implementation, whose TriggerEvents(IEnumerable<IEventNotification> events) method retrieves all the handlers associated with the events it receives in its argument from the dependency injection engine and executes them. It is sufficient to have IEventMediator injected into a class so that it can trigger events. EventDIExtensions also contains an extension method that discovers all the queries that implement the empty IQuery interface and adds them to the dependency injection engine.

A more sophisticated implementation is given by the MediatR NuGet package. The next subsection is dedicated to an extreme implementation of the CQRS pattern.

Event sourcing

Event sourcing is an extreme implementation of the stronger form of CQRS. It is useful when the original Bounded Context database isn't used at all to retrieve information but just as a **source of truth**, that is, for recovering from failures and for software maintenance. In this case, instead of updating data, we simply add events that describe the operation that was performed: deleted record Id 15, changed the name to John in Id 21, and so on. These events are immediately sent to all the dependent Bounded Contexts, and in the case of failures and/or the addition of new queries, all we have to do is to reprocess some of them. Event reprocessing can't cause problems if events are idempotent, that is, if processing the same event several times has the same effect of processing it once.

As discussed in *Chapter 5, Applying a Microservice Architecture to Your Enterprise Application*, idempotency is a standard requirement for microservices that communicate through events.

While all of the techniques we've described up until now can be used in every type of project if minor modifications are made, event sourcing requires a deep analysis to be performed before it can be adopted since, in several cases, it may create bigger problems than the ones it can solve. To get an idea of the problems it may cause when it's misused, imagine that we apply it to purchase orders that have been modified and validated by several users before being approved. Since purchase orders need to be retrieved before they're updated/validated, the purchase order's Bounded Context isn't used just as a source of truth, so event sourcing should not be applied to it. If this isn't the case, then we can apply event sourcing to it, in which case our code would be forced to rebuild the whole order from the recorded events each time the order is updated.

An example of its usage is the revenue logging system we described at the end of *Chapter 5, Applying a Microservice Architecture to Your Enterprise Application*. Single revenues are recorded with event sourcing and then sent to the microservice we described in *Chapter 5, Applying a Microservice Architecture to Your Enterprise Application*, which, in turn, uses them to preprocess future queries, that is, to compute daily revenues.

In the next section, we will learn how DDD can be applied to define the Bounded Contexts of this book's WWTravelClub use case. A complete example of how to implement a Bounded Context that uses most of the patterns and code described in this book can be found in the *Use case – implementing a web app in ASP.NET Core MVC* section of *Chapter 15, Presenting ASP.NET Core MVC*.

Use case – understanding the domains of the use case

From the requirements listed in the *Case study – introducing World Wild Travel Club* section of *Chapter 1, Understanding the Importance of Software Architecture*, and for the analysis in the *Use case – storing data* section of *Chapter 9, How to Choose Your Data Storage in the Cloud*, we know that the WWTravelClub system is composed of the following parts:

- Information about the available destinations and packages. We implemented the first prototype of this subsystem's data layer in *Chapter 9, How to Choose Your Data Storage in the Cloud*.

- Reservation/purchase orders subsystem.

- Communication with the experts/reviews subsystem.

- Payment subsystem. We briefly analyzed the features of this subsystem and its relationship with the reservation purchase subsystem at the beginning of the *Understanding domain-driven design* section of this chapter.

- User accounts subsystem.

- Statistics reporting subsystem.

Do the preceding subsystems represent different **Bounded Contexts**? Can some subsystems be split into different Bounded Contexts? The answers to these questions are given by the languages that are spoken in each subsystem:

- The language that's spoken in subsystem 1 is the language of **travel agencies**. There is no concept of a customer; just of locations, packages, and their features.

- The language that's spoken in subsystem 2 is common to all service purchases, such as the available resources, reservations, and purchase orders. This is a separate Bounded Context.

- The language that's spoken in subsystem 3 has a lot in common with subsystem 1's language. However, there are also typical **social media** concepts, such as ratings, chats, post sharing, media sharing, and so on. This subsystem can be split into two parts: a social media subsystem that has a new bounded context and an available information subsystem that is part of the Bounded Context of subsystem 1.

- As we pointed out in the *Understanding domain-driven design* section, in subsystem 4, we speak the language of **banking**. This subsystem communicates with the reservation purchase subsystem and executes tasks that are needed to carry out a purchase. From these observations, we can see that it is a different Bounded Context and has a customer/supplier relationship with the purchase/reservation system.

- Subsystem 5 is definitely a separate Bounded Context (as in almost all web applications). It has a relationship with all the Bounded Contexts that either have a concept of a user or a concept of a customer because the concept of user accounts always maps to these concepts. But how? Simple—the currently logged-in user is assumed to be the social media user of the social media Bounded Context, the customer of the reservation/purchase Bounded Context, and the payer of the payment Bounded Context.

- The query-only subsystem, that is, 6, speaks the language of analytics and statistics and differs a lot from the languages that are spoken in the other subsystems. However, it has a connection with almost all the Bounded Contexts since it takes all its input from them. The preceding constraints force us to adopt CQRS in its strong form, thereby considering it a query-only separated Bounded Context. We implemented a part of it in *Chapter 5, Applying a Microservice Architecture to Your Enterprise Application,* by using a microservice that conforms to a strong form of CQRS.

In conclusion, each of the listed subsystems defines a different Bounded Context, but part of the communication with the experts/reviews subsystem must be included in the information about available destinations and packages Bounded Context.

As the analysis continues and a prototype is implemented, some Bounded Contexts may split and some others may be added, but it is fundamental to immediately start modeling the system and to immediately start analyzing the relations among the Bounded Contexts with the partial information we have since this will drive further investigations and will help us define the communication protocols and Ubiquitous Languages that are needed so that we can interact with the domain experts.

The following is a basic first sketch of the domain map:

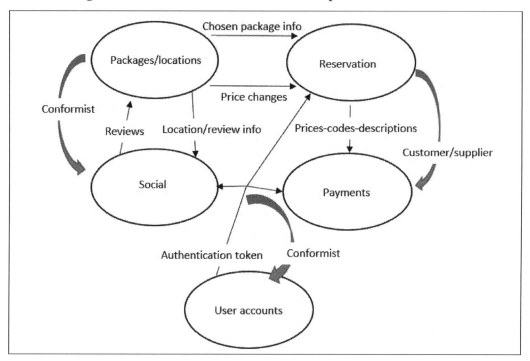

Figure 12.6: WWTravelClub domain map

For simplicity, we've omitted the **Statistics reporting** Bounded Context. Here, we're assuming that the **User accounts** and **Social** Bounded Contexts have a **conformist** relationship with all the other Bounded Contexts that communicate with them because they are implemented with already existing software, so all the other components must adapt to them.

As we mentioned previously, the relationship between **Reservation** and **Payments** is **customer/supplier** because **Payments** provides services that are used to execute the tasks of **Reservation**. All the other relationships are classified as **Partners**. The various concepts of customer/user that most Bounded Contexts have are coordinated by the **User accounts** authorization token, which indirectly takes care of mapping these concepts between all the Bounded Contexts.

The **Packages/locations** subsystem not only communicates the packages information that's needed to carry out a reservation/purchase—it also takes care of informing pending purchase orders of possible price changes. Finally, we can see that social interactions are started from an existing review or location, thereby creating communication with the **Packages/locations** Bounded Context.

Summary

In this chapter, we analyzed the main reasons for the adoption of DDD and why and how it meets the needs of the market. We described how to identify domains and how to coordinate the teams that work on different domains of the same application with domain maps. Then, we analyzed the way DDD represents data with entities, value objects, and aggregates, providing advice and code snippets so that we can implement them in practice.

We also covered some typical patterns that are used with DDD, that is, the repository and Unit of Work patterns, domain event patterns, CQRS, and event sourcing. Then, we learned how to implement them in practice. We also showed you how to implement domain events and the command pattern with decoupled handling so that we can add code snippets to real-world projects.

Finally, we used the principles of DDD in practice to define domains and to create the first sketch of a domain map for this book's WWTravelClub use case.

In the next chapter, you will learn how to maximize code reuse in your projects.

Questions

1. What provides the main hints so that we can discover domain boundaries?

2. What is the main tool that's used for coordinating the development of a separate Bounded Context?

3. Is it true that each entry that composes an aggregate communicates with the remainder of the system with its own methods?

4. Why is there a single aggregate root?

5. How many repositories can manage an aggregate?

6. How does a repository interact with the application layer?

7. Why is the Unit of Work pattern needed?

8. What are the reasons for the light form of CQRS? What about the reasons for its strongest form?

9. What is the main tool that allows us to couple commands/domain events with their handlers?

10. Is it true that event sourcing can be used to implement any Bounded Context?

Further reading

*   More resources on DDD can be found here: `https://domainlanguage.com/ddd/`

*   A detailed discussion of CQRS design principles can be found here: `http://udidahan.com/2009/12/09/clarified-cqrs/`

*   More information on MediatR can be found on MediatR's GitHub repository: `https://github.com/jbogard/MediatR`

*   A good description of event sourcing, along with an example of it, can be seen in the following blog post by Martin Fowler: `https://martinfowler.com/eaaDev/EventSourcing.html`

13
Implementing Code Reusability in C# 9

Code reusability is one of the most important topics in software architecture. This chapter aims to discuss ways to enable code reuse, as well as to help you understand how .NET 5 goes in this direction to solve the problem of managing and maintaining a reusable library.

The following topics will be covered in this chapter:

- Understanding the principles of code reuse
- The advantages of working with .NET 5 versus .NET Standard
- Creating reusable libraries using .NET Standard

Although code reuse is an exceptional practice, as a software architect you must be aware when this is important for the scenario you are dealing with. Many good software architects agree that there is a lot of overengineering due to trying to make things reusable even though they are often single-use or not understood well enough.

Technical requirements

This chapter requires the following things:

- You need the free Visual Studio 2019 Community edition or better with all the database tools installed.

- You can find the sample code for this chapter at `https://github.com/ PacktPublishing/Software-Architecture-with-C-9-and-.NET-5`.

Understanding the principles of code reusability

There is a single reason that you can always use to justify code reuse – you cannot spend your valuable time recreating the wheel if it is already running well in other scenarios. That is why most engineering domains are based on reusability principles. Think about the light switches you have in your house.

Can you imagine the number of applications that can be made with the same interface components? The fundamentals of code reuse are the same. Again, it is a matter of planning a good solution so part of it can be reused later.

In software engineering, code reuse is one of the techniques that can bring a software project a bunch of advantages, such as the following:

- There is confidence in the software, considering that the reused piece of code was already tested in another application.
- There is better usage of software architects and the senior team since they can be dedicated to solving this kind of problem.
- There is the possibility of bringing to the project a pattern that is already accepted by the market.
- Development speed goes up due to the already implemented components.
- Maintenance is easier.

These aspects indicate that code reuse should be done whenever it is possible. It is your responsibility, as a software architect, to ensure the preceding advantages are utilized and, more than that, that you incentivize your team to enable reuse in the software they are creating.

What is not code reuse?

The first thing you must understand is that code reuse does not mean copying and pasting code from one class to another. Even if this code was written by another team or project, this does not indicate that you are properly working with reusability principles. Let us imagine a scenario that we will find in this book's use case, the WWTravelClub evaluation.

In this project scenario, you may want to evaluate different kinds of subjects, such as the **Package**, **DestinationExpert**, **City**, **Comments**, and so on. The process for getting the evaluation average is the same, no matter which subject you are referring to. Due to this, you may want to *enable* reuse by copying and pasting the code for each evaluation. The (bad) result will be something like this:

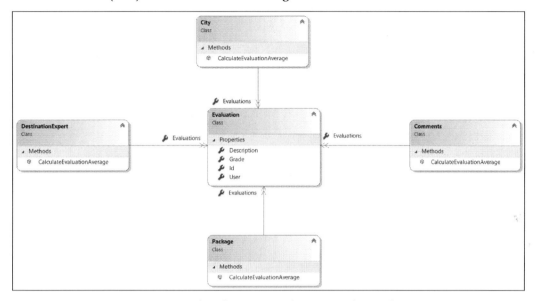

Figure 13.1: Bad implementation – there is no code reuse here

In the preceding diagram, the process of calculating the evaluation average is decentralized, which means that the same code will be duplicated in different classes. This will cause a lot of trouble, especially if the same approach is used in other applications. For instance, if there is a new specification about how you have to calculate the average or if you just get a bug in the calculation formula, you will have to fix it in all instances of code. If you do not remember to update it in all places, you will possibly end up with an inconsistent implementation.

What is code reuse?

The solution to the problem mentioned in the previous section is quite simple: you must analyze your code and select the parts of it that would be good to decouple from your application.

The greatest reason why you should decouple them is related to how you are sure that this code can be reused in other parts of the application, or even in another application:

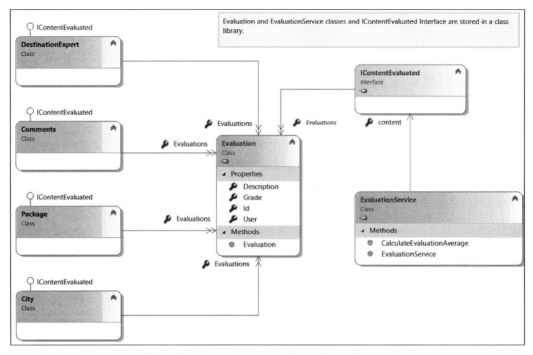

Figure 13.2: An implementation focused on code reuse

The centralization of the code brings to you, as a software architect, a different responsibility for it. You will have to keep in mind that a bug or incompatibility in this code could cause damage to many parts of the application or different applications. On the other hand, once you have this code tested and running, you will be able to propagate its usage with no worries. Besides, if you need to evolve the average calculation process, you will have to change the code in a single class.

It is worth mentioning that the more you use the same code, the cheaper this development will become. Cost needs to be mentioned because, in general, the conception of reusable software costs more in the beginning.

Reusability in the development life cycle

If you understood that reusability will take you to another level of code implementation, you should have been thinking about how to make this technique available in your development life cycle.

As a matter of fact, creating and maintaining a component library is not very easy, due to the responsibility you will have and the lack of good tools to support the search for existing components.

On the other hand, there are some things that you may consider implementing in your software development process every time you initiate a new development:

- **Use** already implemented components from your user library, selecting features in the software requirements specification that need them.

- **Identify** features in the software requirements specification that are candidates to be designed as library components.

- **Modify** the specification, considering that these features will be developed using reusable components.

- **Design** the reusable components and be sure that they have the appropriate interfaces to be used in many projects.

- **Build** the project architecture with the new component library version.

- **Document** the component library version so that every developer and team knows about it.

The *use-identify-modify-design-build* process is a technique that you may consider implementing every time you need to enable software reuse. As soon as you have the components you need to write for this library, you will need to decide on the technology that will provide these components.

During the history of software development, there have been many approaches to doing this; some of them were discussed in *Chapter 5*, *Applying a Microservice Architecture to Your Enterprise Application*, in the *Microservices and the evolution of the concept of modules* section.

Using .NET 5 or .NET Standard for code reuse

.NET has evolved a lot since its first version. This evolution is not only related to the number of commands and performance issues, but the supported platforms too. As we discussed in *Chapter 1*, *Understanding the Importance of Software Architecture*, you can run C# .NET on billions of devices, even if they are running Linux, Android, macOS, or iOS. For this reason, .NET Standard was first announced together with .NET Core 1.0, but .NET Standard became particularly important with .NET Standard 2.0, when .NET Framework 4.6, .NET Core, and Xamarin were compatible with it.

The key point is that .NET Standard was not only a kind of Visual Studio project. More than that, it was a formal specification available to all .NET implementations. As you can see in the following table, it covers everything from .NET Framework to Unity:

.NET Standard	1.0	1.1	1.2	1.3	1.4	1.5	1.6	2.0	2.1
.NET Core and .NET 5	1.0	1.0	1.0	1.0	1.0	1.0	1.0	2.0	3.0
.NET Framework	4.5	4.5	4.5.1	4.6	4.6.1	4.6.1	4.6.1	4.6.1	N/A

 You can find a full .NET Standard overview at `https://docs.` `microsoft.com/en-us/dotnet/standard/net-standard`.

The preceding table indicates that if you build a class library that is compatible with this standard, you will be able to reuse it in any of the platforms presented. Think about how fast your development process could become if you plan to do this in all your projects.

Obviously, some components are not included in .NET Standard, but its evolution is continuous. It is worth mentioning that Microsoft's official documentation indicates that *the higher the version, the more APIs are available to you.*

The initiative of having a single framework for all platforms brought us to .NET 5. Microsoft indicates that from now, net5.0 or later will run everywhere. The next question you, as a software architect, might have is: what is going to happen to .NET Standard?

The answer to this question is well explained by Immo Landwerth at the dotnet blog: `https://devblogs.microsoft.com/dotnet/the-future-of-net-standard/`. The basic answer is that .NET 5.0 (and future versions) needs to be thought of as the foundation for sharing code moving forward.

Creating a .NET Standard library

It is quite simple to create a class library compatible with .NET Standard. Basically, you need to choose the following project when creating the library:

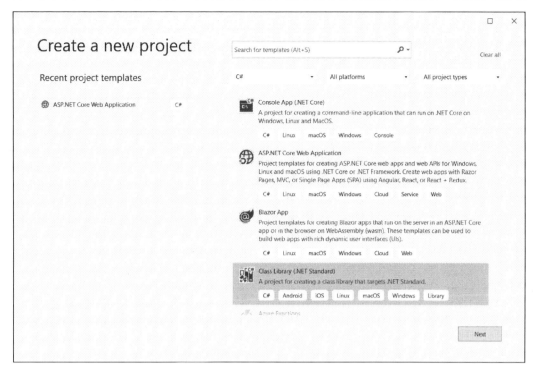

Figure 13.3: Creating a .NET Standard library

Once you have concluded this part, you will notice that the only difference between a common class library and the one you created is the target framework defined in the project file:

```
<Project Sdk="Microsoft.NET.Sdk">
<PropertyGroup>
<TargetFramework>netstandard2.0</TargetFramework>
</PropertyGroup>
</Project>
```

As soon as your project is loaded, you can start coding the classes that you intend to reuse. The advantage of building reusable classes using this approach is that you will be able to reuse the written code in all the project types we checked previously. On the other hand, you will find out that some APIs that are available in .NET Framework do not exist in this type of project.

How does C# deal with code reuse?

There are many approaches where C# helps us deal with code reuse. The ability to build libraries, as we did in the previous section, is one of them. The most important one is the fact that the language is object-oriented. Besides, it is worth mentioning the facilities that generics brought to the C# language. This section will discuss the last two we mentioned.

Object-oriented analysis

The object-oriented analysis approach gives us the ability to reuse code in different ways, from the facility of inheritance to the changeability of polymorphism. Complete adoption of object-oriented programming will let you implement abstraction and encapsulation too.

The following diagram shows how using the object-oriented approach makes reuse easier. As you can see, there are different ways to calculate the grades of an evaluation, considering you can be a basic or a prime user of the system:

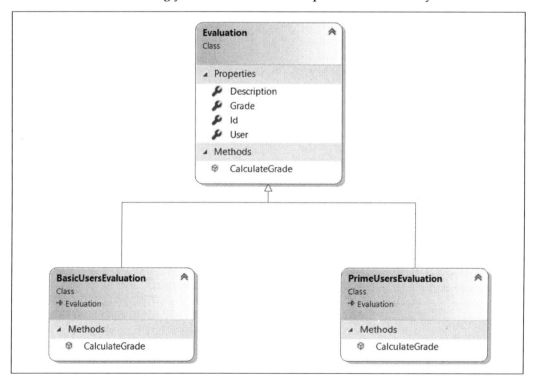

Figure 13.4: Object-oriented case analysis

There are two aspects to be analyzed as code reuse in this design. The first is that there is no need to declare the properties in each child class since inheritance is doing it for you.

The second is the opportunity to use polymorphism, enabling different behaviors for the same method:

```
public class PrimeUsersEvaluation : Evaluation
{
    /// <summary>
    /// The business rule implemented here indicates that grades that
    /// came from prime users have 20% of increase
    /// </summary>
    /// <returns>the final grade from a prime user</returns>
    public override double CalculateGrade()
    {
        return Grade * 1.2;
    }
}
```

In the preceding code, you can see the usage of the polymorphism principle, where the calculation of evaluation for prime users will increase by 20%. Now, look at how easy it is to call different objects inherited by the same class. Since the collection content implements the same interface, `IContentEvaluated`, it can have basic and prime users too:

```
public class EvaluationService
{
    public IContentEvaluated content { get; set; }
    /// <summary>
    /// No matter the Evaluation, the calculation will always get
    /// values from the method CalculateGrade
    /// </summary>
    /// <returns>The average of the grade from Evaluations</returns>
    public double CalculateEvaluationAverage()
    {
        return content.Evaluations
            .Select(x => x.CalculateGrade())
            .Average();
    }
}
```

Object-oriented adoption can be considered mandatory when using C#. However, more specific usage will need study and practice. You, as a software architect, should always incentivize your team to study object-oriented analysis. The more abstraction abilities they have, the easier code reuse will become.

Generics

Generics were introduced in C# in version 2.0, and it is considered an approach that increases code reuse. It also maximizes type safety and performance.

The basic principle of generics is that you can define in an interface, class, method, property, event, or even a delegate, a placeholder that will be replaced with a specific type at a later time when one of the preceding entities is used. The opportunity you have with this feature is incredible since you can use the same code to run different versions of the type, generically.

The following code is a modification of EvaluationService, which was presented in the previous section. The idea here is to enable the generalization of the service, giving us the opportunity to define the goal of evaluation since its creation:

```
public class EvaluationService<T> where T: IContentEvaluated
```

This declaration indicates that any class that implements the IContentEvaluaded interface can be used for this service. Besides, the service will be responsible for creating the evaluated content.

The following code implements the evaluated content that was created since the construction of the service. This code uses System.Reflection and the generic definition from the class:

```
public EvaluationService()
{
    var name = GetTypeOfEvaluation();
    content = (T)Assembly.GetExecutingAssembly().CreateInstance(name);
}
```

It is worth mentioning that this code will work because all the classes are in the same assembly. Besides, reflection is not mandatory while using generics. The result of this modification can be checked in the instance creation of the service:

```
var service = new EvaluationService<CityEvaluation>();
```

The good news is that, now, you have a generic service that will automatically instantiate the list object with the evaluations of the content you need. It's worth mentioning that generics will obviously need more time dedicated to the first project's construction. However, once the design is done, you will have good, fast, and easy-to-maintain code. This is what we call reuse!

What if the code is not reusable?

In fact, any code can be reusable. The key point here is if the code you intend to reuse is well-written and follows good patterns for reuse. There are several reasons why code should be considered not ready for reuse:

- **The code was not tested before**: Before reusing code, it is a good approach to guarantee that it works.

- **The code is duplicated**: If you have duplicate code, you will need to find each place where it is being used so you only have a single version of the code being reused.

- **The code is too complex to understand**: Code that is reused in many places needs to be written with simplicity to enable easy understanding.

- **The code has tight coupling**: This is a discussion related to composition versus inheritance when building separate class libraries. Classes (with interfaces) are usually much easier to reuse than base classes that can be inherited.

In any of these cases, considering a refactoring strategy can be a great approach. When you are refactoring code, you are writing it in a better way while respecting the input and output data that this code will process. This enables more comprehensive and lower-cost code when it comes to changing it. Martin Fowler indicates some reasons why we should consider refactoring:

- **It improves software design**: The more expert your team becomes, the better the design will be. A better software design will deliver not only faster coding, but it will bring us the opportunity to process more tasks in less time.

- **It makes the software easier to understand**: Regardless of whether we are talking about juniors or seniors, good software needs to be understood by each developer you have in the team.

- **It helps us find bugs**: While you are refactoring, you will find business rules that may have not been well-programmed, so you will find bugs.

- **It makes us program quicker**: The result of refactoring will be code that will enable faster development in the future.

The process of refactoring depends on some steps that we shall follow to guarantee good results and minimize errors during the journey:

- **Be sure you have a set of tests to guarantee the correct processing**: The set of tests you have will eliminate the fear of having to clean code.

- **Eliminate duplication**: Refactoring is a good opportunity to eliminate code duplication.

- **Minimize complexity**: Considering you will have the goal of making the code more understandable, following the best practices of programming, as mentioned in *Chapter 17, Best practices in Coding C# 9*, will reduce the complexity of the code.

- **Clean up the design**: Refactoring is a good time for reorganizing the design of your libraries too. Do not forget to update them too. This can be a great way to eliminate bugs and security issues.

As a software architect, you will receive many refactoring demands from your team. The incentive for doing so must be continuous. But you must remind your team that refactoring without following the preceding steps might be risky. So, it is your responsibility to make it happen in a way that can both enable fast programming and less impact, thus delivering real business value.

I have my libraries. How do I promote them?

Considering you have made all the necessary effort to guarantee you have good libraries that must be reused in many of your projects, you will find another difficult situation arises when enabling reusability: it is not simple to let programmers know you have libraries ready to reuse.

There are some simple approaches to documenting a library. As we mentioned when we talked about the development life cycle, documenting is a good way to help developers take notice of the libraries they have. There are two examples of documenting reusable code that we would like to mention here.

Documenting .NET libraries using DocFX

This tool is a good alternative for documenting a library using comments made in its code. By simply adding the NuGet package `docfx.console`, the tool allows you to create a task that will run once your library has been built:

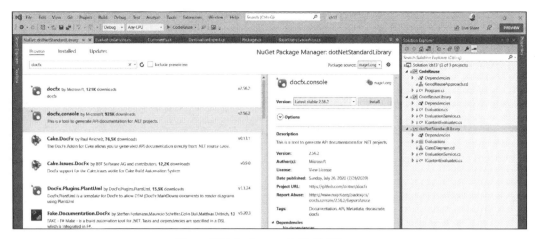

Figure 13.5: docfx.console NuGet library

The output of this compilation is a stylish static website that contains the documentation of your code:

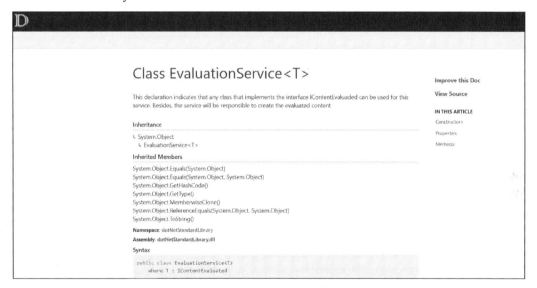

Figure 13.6: DocFx result

This website is useful because you can distribute the documentation to your team so that they can search for the libraries you have. You can check the customizations of the output and find more information about it at `https://dotnet.github.io/docfx/`.

Documenting a Web API using Swagger

There is no doubt that a Web API is one of the technologies that facilitates and promotes code reuse. For this reason, having its documentation well done and, more than that, respecting a standard is good practice and indicates that you are up to date on to this approach. To do this, we have Swagger, which respects the OpenAPI Specification.

The OpenAPI Specification is known as the standard for describing modern APIs. One of the most widely used tools for documenting it in an ASP.NET Core Web API is `Swashbuckle.AspNetCore`.

The good thing about implementing the `Swashbuckle.AspNetCore` library is that you can set the Swagger UI viewer for your Web API, which is a good, graphical way to distribute the APIs.

We will learn how to use this library in ASP.NET Core Web APIs in the next chapter. Until then, it is important to understand that this documentation will help not only your team, but any developer who might use the APIs you are developing.

Use case – reusing code as a fast way to deliver good and safe software

The final design of the solution for evaluating content for WWTravelClub can be checked as follows. This approach consists of using many topics that were discussed in this chapter. First, all the code is placed in a .NET Standard class library. This means that you can add this code to different types of solutions, such as .NET Core web apps and Xamarin apps for the Android and iOS platforms:

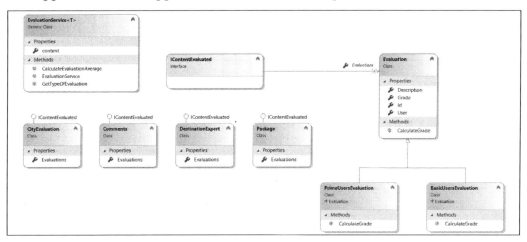

Figure 13.7: WWTravelClub reuse approach

This design makes use of object-oriented principles such as inheritance, so you do not need to write properties and methods more than once that can be used in many classes; and polymorphism, so that you can change the behavior of the code without changing the name of the method.

To finish, the design abstracts the idea of the content by introducing generics as a tool that can facilitate the manipulation of similar classes, such as the ones we have in WWTravelClub to evaluate content regarding cities, comments, destination experts, and travel packages.

The big difference between a team that incentivizes code reuse and one that does not is the velocity of delivering good software to end users. Of course, beginning this approach is not easy, but rest assured that you will get good results after some time working with it.

Summary

This chapter aimed to help you understand the advantages of code reuse. It also gave you an idea about what is not properly reused code. This chapter also presented approaches for reusing and refactoring code.

Considering that technology without processes does not take you anywhere, a process was presented that helps enable code reuse. This process is related to using already completed components from your library; identifying features in the software requirements specification that are candidates to be designed as library components; modifying the specification considering these features; designing the reusable components; and building the project architecture with the new component library version.

To finish, this chapter presented .NET Standard libraries as an approach to reusing code for different C # platforms, indicating that .NET 5 and new versions shall be used for reusing code in different platforms. This chapter also reinforced the principles of object-oriented programming when reusing code and presented generics as a sophisticated implementation to simplify the treatment of objects with the same characteristics. In the next chapter, we will learn how to apply a **service-oriented architecture (SOA)** with .NET Core.

It is worth mentioning that SOA is considered a way to implement code reuse in sophisticated environments.

Questions

1. Can copy-and-paste be considered code reuse? What are the impacts of this approach?

2. How can you make use of code reuse without copying and pasting code?

3. Is there a process that can help with code reuse?

4. What is the difference between .NET Standard and .NET Core?

5. What are the advantages of creating a .NET Standard library?

6. How does object-oriented analysis help with code reuse?

7. How do generics help with code reuse?

8. Will .NET Standard be replaced with .NET 5?

9. What are the challenges related to refactoring?

Further reading

These are some books and websites where you will find more information about this chapter:

- *Clean Code: A Handbook of Agile Software Craftmanship by* Martin, Robert C. Pearson Education, 2012.

- *Clean Architecture: A Craftsman's Guide to Software Structure and Design* by Martin, Robert C. Pearson Education, 2018.

- *Design Patterns: Elements of Reusable Object-Oriented Software* by Erica Gamma [et al.] Addison-Wesley, 1994.

- *Design Principles and Design Patterns* by Robert C. Martin, 2000.

- *Refactoring* by Martin Fowler, 2018.

- https://devblogs.microsoft.com/dotnet/introducing-net-standard/

- https://www.packtpub.com/application-development/net-standard-20-cookbook

- https://github.com/dotnet/standard/blob/master/docs/versions.md

- https://docs.microsoft.com/pt-br/dotnet/csharp/programming-guide/generics/

- https://devblogs.microsoft.com/dotnet/the-future-of-net-standard/
- https://dotnet.github.io/docfx/
- https://github.com/domaindrivendev/Swashbuckle.AspNetCore
- https://docs.microsoft.com/en-us/aspnet/core/tutorials/web-api-help-pages-using-swagger

14

Applying Service-Oriented Architectures with .NET Core

The term **Service-Oriented Architecture (SOA)** refers to a modular architecture where interaction between system components is achieved through communication. SOA allows applications from different organizations to exchange data and transactions automatically and allows organizations to offer services on the internet.

Moreover, as we discussed in the *Microservices and the evolution of the concept of modules* section of *Chapter 5, Applying a Microservice Architecture to Your Enterprise Application*, communication-based interaction solves binary compatibility and version mismatch problems that inevitably appear in complex systems made up of modules that share the same address space. Moreover, with SOA, you do not need to deploy different copies of the same component in the various systems/subsystems that use it – each component only needs to be deployed in just one place. This can be a single server, a cluster located in a single data center, or a geographically distributed cluster. Here, each version of your component is deployed just once, and the server/cluster logic automatically creates all the necessary replicas, thus simplifying the overall **Continuous Integration/Continuous Delivery (CI/CD)** cycle.

If a newer version conforms to the communication interface that is declared to the clients, no incompatibilities can occur. On the other hand, with DLLs/packages, when the same interface is maintained, incompatibilities may arise because of possible version mismatches in terms of the dependencies of other DLLs/packages that the library module might have in common with its clients.

Organizing clusters/networks of cooperating services was discussed in *Chapter 5, Applying a Microservice Architecture to Your Enterprise Application*. In this chapter, we will mainly focus on the communication interface offered by each service. More specifically, we will discuss the following topics:

- Understanding the principles of the SOA approach
- SOAP and REST web services
- How does .NET 5 deal with SOA?
- Use case – exposing WWTravelClub packages

By the end of this chapter, you will know how to publicly expose data from the WWTravelClub book use case through an ASP.NET Core service.

Technical requirements

This chapter requires the Visual Studio 2019 free Community edition or better with all the database tools installed.

All the concepts in this chapter will be clarified with practical examples based on this book's WWTravelClub book use case. You will find the code for this chapter at `https://github.com/PacktPublishing/Software-Architecture-with-C-9-and-.NET-5`.

Understanding the principles of the SOA approach

Like classes in an object-oriented architecture, services are implementations of interfaces that, in turn, come from a system's functional specifications. Therefore, the first step in a *service* design is the definition of its *abstract interface*. During this stage, you define all the service operations as interface methods that operate on the types of your favorite language (C#, Java, C++, JavaScript, and so on) and decide which operations to implement with synchronous communication and which ones to implement with asynchronous communication.

The interfaces that are defined in this initial stage will not necessarily be used in the actual service implementation and are just useful design tools. Once we have decided on the architecture of the services, these interfaces are usually redefined so that we can adapt them to the peculiarity of the architecture.

It is worth pointing out that SOA messages must keep the same kind of semantics as method calls/answers; that is, the reaction to a message must not depend on any previously received messages. Here, the messages must be independent of each other, and the service *must not remember* any previously received messages. This is what we call stateless development.

For instance, if the purpose of messages is to create a new database entry, this semantic must not change with the context of other messages, and the way the database entry is created must depend on the content of the current message and not on other previously received messages. Consequently, a client cannot create sessions and cannot log in to a service, perform some operations, and then log out. An authentication token must be repeated in each message.

The reasons for this constraint are modularity, testability, and maintainability. In fact, a session-based service would be very hard to test and modify due to the interactions that are *hidden* in the session data.

Once you have decided on the interface that is going to be implemented by a service, you must decide which communication stack/SOA architecture to adopt. The communication stack must be part of some official or *de facto* standard to ensure the interoperability of the service. Interoperability is the main constraint prescribed by SOA: services must offer a communication interface that does not depend on the specific communication library used, on the implementation language, or on the deployment platform.

Considering you have decided on the communication stack/architecture, you need to adapt your previous interfaces to the peculiarities of the architecture (see the *REST web services* subsection of this chapter for more details). Then, you must translate these interfaces into the chosen communication language. This means that you must map all the programming language types into types that are available in the chosen communication language.

The actual translation of data is usually performed automatically by the SOA libraries that are used by your development environment. However, some configuration might be needed, and, in any case, we must be aware of how our programming language types are transformed before each communication. For instance, some numeric types might be transformed into types with less precision or with different ranges of values.

The interoperability constraint can be interpreted in a lighter form in the case of microservices that are not accessible outside of their clusters, since they need to communicate with other microservices that belong to the same cluster. In this case, this means that the communication stack might be platform-specific so that it can increase performance, but it must be standard to avoid compatibility problems with other microservices that might be added to the cluster as the application evolves.

We have spoken of the *communication stack* and not of the *communication protocol* because SOA communication standards usually define the format of the message's content and provide different possibilities for the specific protocol that is used to embed those messages. For instance, the SOAP protocol just defines an XML-based format for the various kinds of messages, but SOAP messages can be conveyed by various protocols. Usually, the most common protocol that is used for SOAP is HTTP, but you may decide to jump to the HTTP level and send SOAP messages directly over TCP/IP for better performance.

The choice of communication stack you should adopt depends on several factors:

- **Compatibility constraints**: If your service must be publicly available on the internet to business clients, then you must conform to the most common choices, which means using either SOAP over HTTP or JSON REST services. The most common choices are different if your clients are not business clients but **Internet of Things (IoT)** clients. Also, within IoT, the protocols that are used in different application areas can be different. For instance, marine vehicle status data is not typically exchanged with *Signal K*.

- **Development/deployment platform**: Not all communication stacks are available on all development frameworks and on all deployment platforms, but luckily, all the most common communication stacks that are used in public business services, such as SOAP and JSON-based REST communication, are available on all the main development/deployment platforms.

- **Performance**: If your system is not exposed to the outside world and is a private part of your microservice cluster, performance considerations have a higher priority. In this scenario, gRPC, which we will discuss soon in this chapter, can be mentioned as a good option.

- **Availability of tools and knowledge in your team**: Having knowledge and knowing about the availability of tools in your team/organization has an important weight when it comes to choosing between acceptable communication stacks. However, this kind of constraint always has less priority than compatibility constraints since it makes no sense to conceive a system that is easy to implement for your team but that almost nobody can use.

- **Flexibility versus available features**: Some communication solutions, while less complete, offer a higher degree of flexibility, while other solutions, while being more complete, offer less flexibility. The need for flexibility started a movement from SOAP-based services to the more flexible REST services in the last few years. This point will be discussed in more detail when we describe SOAP and REST services in the remainder of this section.

- **Service description**: When services must be exposed on the internet, client applications need a publicly available description of the service specifications to design their communication clients. Some communication stacks include languages and conventions to describe service specifications. Formal service specifications that are exposed this way can be processed so that they automatically create communication clients. SOAP goes further and allows service discoverability by means of a public XML-based directory containing information about the tasks each web service can carry out.

Once you have chosen the communication stack you wish to use, you must use the tools that are available in your development environment to implement the service in a way that conforms to the chosen communication stack. Sometimes, communication stack compliance is automatically ensured by the development tools, but sometimes, it may require some development effort. For instance, in the .NET world, the compliance of SOAP services is automatically ensured by development tools if you use WCF, while the compliance of REST services falls under the developer's responsibility. Some of the fundamental features of SOA solutions are as follows:

- **Authentication**: Allows the client to authenticate to access service operations.
- **Authorization**: Handles the client's permissions.
- **Security**: This is how communication is kept safe, that is, how to prevent unauthorized systems from reading and/or modifying the content of the communication. Typically, encryption prevents both unauthorized modifications and reading, while electronic signature algorithms prevent just modifications.
- **Exceptions**: Returns exceptions to the client.
- **Message reliability**: Ensures that messages reliably reach their destination in case of possible infrastructure faults.

Though sometimes desirable, the following features are not always necessary:

- **Distributed transactions**: The capability to handle distributed transactions, thus undoing all the changes you have made whenever the distributed transactions fail or are aborted.
- **Support for the Publisher/Subscriber pattern**: If and how events and notifications are supported.
- **Addressing**: If and how references to other services and or service/methods are supported.
- **Routing**: If and how messages can be routed through a network of services.

The remainder of this section is dedicated to describing SOAP and REST services since they are the *de facto* standard for business services that are exposed outside of their clusters/servers. For performance reasons, microservices use other protocols, discussed in *Chapter 5, Applying a Microservice Architecture to Your Enterprise Application; Chapter 6, Azure Service Fabric;* and *Chapter 7, Azure Kubernetes Service.* For inter-cluster communication, **Advanced Message Queuing Protocol (AMQP)** is used, and links are given in the *Further reading* section.

SOAP web services

The **Simple Object Access Protocol (SOAP)** allows both one-way messages and answer/response messages. Communication can be both synchronous and asynchronous, but, if the underlying protocol is synchronous, such as in the case of HTTP, the sender receives an acknowledgment saying that the message was received (but not necessarily processed). When asynchronous communication is used, the sender must listen for incoming communications. Often, asynchronous communication is implemented with the Publisher/Subscriber pattern that we described in *Chapter 11, Design Patterns and .NET 5 Implementation.*

Messages are represented as XML documents called **envelopes**. Each envelope contains a header, a body, and a fault element. The body is where the actual content of the message is placed. The fault element contains possible errors, so it is the way exceptions are exchanged when communication occurs. Finally, the header contains any auxiliary information that enriches the protocol but does not contain domain data. For example, the header may contain an authentication token, and/or a signature if the message is signed.

The underlying protocol that is used to send the XML envelopes is usually HTTP, but the SOAP specification allows any protocol, so we can use TCP/IP or SMTP directly. As a matter of fact, the more diffused underlying protocol is HTTP, so, if you do not have a good reason to choose another protocol, you should use HTTP in order to maximize the interoperability of the service.

SOAP specifications contain the basics of message exchange, while other auxiliary features are described in separate specification documents called WS- * and are usually handled by adding extra information in the SOAP header. WS-* specifications handle all the fundamental and desirable features of SOA we listed previously. For instance, WS-Security takes care of security, including authentication, authorization, and encryption/signatures; WS-Eventing and WS-Notification are two alternative ways of implementing the Publisher/Subscriber pattern; WS-ReliableMessaging is concerned with the reliable delivery of messages in case of possible faults; and WS-Transaction is concerned with distributed transactions.

The preceding WS-* specifications are in no way exhaustive but are the more relevant and supported features. In fact, actual implementations in various environments (such as Java and .NET) furnish the more relevant WS-* services, but no implementation supports all the WS-* specifications.

All the XML documents/document parts involved in the SOAP protocol are formally defined in XSD documents, which are special XML documents whose content provides a description of XML structures. Also, all your custom data structures (classes and interfaces in an object-oriented language) must be translated into XSD if they are going to be part of a SOAP envelope.

Each XSD specification has an associated namespace that identifies the specification and a physical location where it can be found. Both the namespace and the physical location are URIs. The location URI does not need to be publicly accessible if the web service is accessible just from within an intranet.

The whole definition of a service is an XSD specification that may contain references to other namespaces, that is, to other XSD documents. Simply put, all the messages of a SOAP communication must be defined in an XSD specification. Then, a server and a client can communicate if they refer to the same XSD specifications. This means, for instance, that you need to create a new XSD specification each time you add another field to a message. After that, you need to update all the XSD files that reference the old message definition to the new message definition by creating a new version of them. In turn, these modifications require the creation of other versions for other XSD files, and so on. Therefore, simple modifications that maintain compatibility with the previous behavior (clients could simply ignore the field that was added) may cause an exponential chain of version changes.

In the last few years, the difficulty in handling modifications, along with the complexity of handling the configuration of all the WS-* specifications and performance problems, caused a gradual move toward the simpler REST services that we will describe in the upcoming sections. This move started with services that were called from JavaScript due to the difficulty of implementing complete SOAP clients that were able to run efficiently in a web browser. Moreover, the complex SOAP machinery was oversized for the simple needs of the typical clients running in a browser and may have caused a complete waste of development time.

For this reason, services aimed at non-JavaScript clients started a massive move toward REST services, and nowadays the preferred choice is REST services, with SOAP being used either for compatibility with legacy systems or when features that are not supported by REST services are needed. A typical application area that continues to prefer the SOAP system is that of payment/banking systems because these systems need the transactional support that is offered by the WS-Transaction SOAP specification. There is no equivalent in the REST services world.

REST web services

REST services were initially conceived to avoid the complex machinery of SOAP in simple cases such as calls to a service from the JavaScript code of a web page. Then, they gradually became the preferred choice for complex systems. REST services use HTTP to exchange data in JSON or, less commonly, in XML format. Simply put, they replace the SOAP body with the HTTP body, the SOAP header with the HTTP header, and the HTTP response code replaces the fault element and furnishes further auxiliary information on the operation that was performed.

The main reason for the success of REST services is that HTTP already offers most of the SOAP features natively, which means we can avoid building a SOAP level on top of HTTP. Moreover, the whole HTTP machinery is simpler than SOAP: simpler to program, simpler to configure, and simpler to implement efficiently.

Moreover, REST services impose fewer constraints on the clients. Type compatibility between servers and clients conforms to the more flexible JavaScript type compatibility model because JSON is a subset of JavaScript. Moreover, when XML is used in place of JSON, it maintains the same JavaScript type compatibility rules. No XML namespaces need to be specified.

When using JSON and XML, if the server adds some more fields to the response while keeping the same semantic of all the other fields compatible with the previous client, they can simply ignore the new fields. Accordingly, changes that are made to a REST service definition only need to be propagated to previous clients in case of breaking changes that cause actual incompatible behavior in the server.

Moreover, it is likely that changes will be self-limited and won't result in an exponential chain of changes because type compatibility does not require the reference to a specific type to be defined in a unique shared place and simply requires that the shape of types is compatible.

Service type compatibility rules

Let's clarify the REST service type compatibility rules with an example. Imagine that several services use a `Person` object that contains `Name`, `Surname`, and `Address` string fields. This object is served by **S1**:

```
{
    Name: string,
    Surname: string,
    Address: string
}
```

Type compatibility is ensured if the service and client refer to different copies of the preceding definition. It is also acceptable for the client to use a definition with fewer fields, since it can simply ignore all the other fields:

```
{
    Name: string,
    Surname: string,
}
```

 You can only use a definition with fewer fields within your "own" code. Attempting to send information back to the server without the expected fields may cause problems.

Now, imagine the scenario where you have an **S2** service that takes `Person` objects from **S1** and adds them to the responses it returns on some of its methods. Suppose the **S1** service that handles the `Person` object replaces the `Address` string with a complex object:

```
{
    Name: string,
    Surname: string,
    Address:
        {
            Country: string,
            Town: string,
            Location: string
        }
}
```

After the breaking change, the **S2** service will have to adapt its communication client that calls the **S1** service to the new format. Then, it can convert the new `Person` format into the older one before using `Person` objects in its responses. This way, the **S2** service avoids propagating the breaking change of **S1**.

In general, basing type compatibility on the object shape (tree of nested properties), instead of a reference to the same formal type definition, increases flexibility and modifiability. The price we pay for this increased flexibility is that type compatibility cannot be computed automatically by comparing the formal definition of server and client interfaces. In fact, in absence of a univocal specification, each time a new version of the service is released, the developer must verify that the semantics of all the fields that the client and server have in common remain unchanged from the previous version.

The basic idea behind REST services is to give up the severity checks and complex protocols for greater flexibility and simplicity, while SOAP does exactly the opposite.

Rest and native HTTP features

The REST services manifesto states that REST uses native HTTP features to implement all the required service features. So, for instance, authentication will be performed directly with the HTTP Authorization field, encryption will be achieved with HTTPS, exceptions will be handled with an HTTP error status code, and routing and reliable messaging will be handled by the machinery the HTTP protocol relies on. Addressing is achieved by using URLs to refer to services, their methods, and other resources.

There is no native support for asynchronous communication since HTTP is a synchronous protocol. There is also no native support for the Publisher/Subscriber pattern, but two services can interact with the Publisher/Subscriber pattern by each exposing an endpoint to the other. More specifically, the first service exposes a subscription endpoint, while the second one exposes an endpoint where it receives its notifications, which are authorized through a common secret that is exchanged during the subscription. This pattern is quite common. GitHub also allows us to send our REST services to repository events.

REST services offer no easy options when it comes to implementing distributed transactions, which is why payment/banking systems still prefer SOAP. Luckily, most application areas do not need the strong form of consistency that is ensured by distributed transactions. For them, lighter forms of consistency, such as *eventual consistency*, are enough and are preferred for performance reasons. Please refer to *Chapter 9*, *How to Choose Your Data Storage in the Cloud*, for a discussion on the various types of consistencies.

The REST manifesto not only prescribes the usage of the predefined solutions that are already available in HTTP but also the usage of a web-like semantic. More specifically, all the service operations must be conceived as CRUD operations on resources that are identified by URLs (the same resource may be identified by several URLs). In fact, REST is the acronym for **Representational State Transfer**, meaning that each URL is the representation of some sort of object. Each kind of service request needs to adopt the appropriate HTTP verb, as follows:

- GET (Read operation): The URL represents the resource that is returned by the read operation. Thus, GET operations mimic pointer dereferencing. In the case of a successful operation, a 200 (OK) status code is returned.

- POST (Creation operation): The JSON/XML object that is contained in the request body is added as a new resource to the object represented by the operation URL. If the new resource is successfully created immediately, a 201 (created) status code is returned, along with a response object that depends on the operation and the indicative about where the created resource can be retrieved from. The response object should contain the most specific URL that identifies the created resource. If creation is deferred to a later time, a 202 (accepted) status code is returned.

- PUT (Edit operation): The JSON/XML object contained in the request body replaces the object referenced by the request URL. In the case of successful operation, a 200 (OK) status code is returned. This operation is idempotent, meaning that repeating the same request twice causes the same modification.

- PATCH: The JSON/XML object contained in the request body contains instructions on how to modify the object referenced by the request URL. This operation is not idempotent since the modification may be an increment of a numeric field. In the case of successful operation, a 200 (OK) status code is returned.

- DELETE: The resource referenced by the request URL is removed. In the case of successful operation, a 200 (OK) status code is returned.

If the resource has been moved from the request URL to another URL, a redirect code is returned:

- 301 (moved permanently), plus the new URL where we can find the resource
- 307 (moved temporarily), plus the new URL where we can find the resource

If the operation fails, a status code that depends on the kind of failure is returned. Some examples of failures codes are as follows:

- 400 (bad request): The request that was sent to the server is ill-formed.
- 404 (not found): When the request URL does not refer to any known object.
- 405 (method not allowed): When the request verb is not supported by the resource referenced by the URL.
- 401 (unauthorized): The operation requires authentication, but the client has not furnished any valid authorization header.
- 403 (forbidden): The client is correctly authenticated but has no right to perform the operation.

The preceding list of status codes is not exhaustive. References to an exhaustive list will be provided in the *Further reading* section.

It is fundamental to point out that POST/PUT/PATCH/DELETE operations may have – and usually have – side effects on other resources. Otherwise, it would be impossible to code operations that act simultaneously on several resources.

In other words, the HTTP verb must conform with the operation that is performed on the resource and referenced by the request URL, but the operation might affect other resources. The same operation might be performed with a different HTTP verb on one of the other involved resources. It is the developer's responsibility to choose which way to perform the same operation to implement it in the service interface.

Thanks to the side effects of HTTP verbs, REST services can encode all these operations as CRUD operations on resources represented by URLs.

Often, moving an existing service to REST requires us to split the various inputs between the request URL and the request body. More specifically, we extract the input fields that univocally define one of the objects involved in the method's execution and use them to create a URL that univocally identifies that object. Then, we decide on which HTTP verb to use based on the operation that is performed on the selected object. Finally, we place the remainder of the input in the request body.

If our services were designed with an object-oriented architecture focused on the business domain objects (such as DDD, as described in *Chapter 12, Understanding the Different Domains in Software Solutions*), the REST translation of all the service methods should be quite immediate, since services should already be organized around domain resources. Otherwise, moving to REST might require some service interface redefinitions.

The adoption of full REST semantics has the advantage that services can be extended with or without small modifications being made to the preexisting operation definitions. In fact, extensions should mainly manifest as additional properties of some objects and as additional resource URLs with some associated operations. Therefore, preexisting clients can simply ignore them.

Example of methods in the REST language

Now, let's learn how methods can be expressed in the REST language with a simple example of an intra-bank money transfer. A bank account can be represented by a URL, as follows:

```
https://mybank.com/bankaccounts/{bank account number}
```

A transfer might be represented as a PATCH request whose body contains an object with properties representing the amount of money, time of transfer, description, and the account receiving the money.

The operation modifies the account mentioned in the URL, but also the receiving account as a *side effect*. If the account doesn't have enough money, a 403 (Forbidden) status code is returned, along with an object with all the error details (an error description, the available funds, and so on).

However, since all the bank operations are recorded in the account statement, the creation and addition of a new transfer object for a *bank account operations* collection associated with the bank account is a better way to represent the transfer. In this case, the URL might be something like the following:

```
https://mybank.com/bankaccounts/{bank account number}/transactions
```

Here, the HTTP verb is POST since we are creating a new object. The body content is the same and a 422 status code is returned if there is a lack of funds.

Both representations of the transfer cause the same changes in the database. Moreover, once the inputs are extracted from the different URLs and from the possibly different request bodies, the subsequent processing is the same. In both cases, we have the same inputs and the same processing – it is just the exterior appearance of the two requests that is different.

However, the introduction of the virtual *operations* collection allows us to extend the service with several more *operations* collection-specific methods. It is worth pointing out that the *operations* collection does not need to be connected with a database table or with any physical object: it lives in the world of URLs and creates a convenient way for us to model the transfer.

The increased usage of REST services leads to a description of REST service interfaces to be created, like the ones developed for SOAP. This standard is called **OpenAPI**. We will talk about this in the following subsection.

The OpenAPI standard

OpenAPI is a standard that is used for describing the REST API. It is currently version 3. The whole service is described by a JSON endpoint, that is, an endpoint that describes the service with a JSON object. This JSON object has a general section that applies to the whole service and contains the general features of the service, such as its version and description, as well as shared definitions.

Then, each service endpoint has a specific section that describes the endpoint URL or URL format (in case some inputs are included in the URL), all its inputs, all the possible output types and status codes, and all the authorization protocols. Each endpoint-specific section can reference the definitions contained in the general section.

A description of the OpenAPI syntax is out of the scope of this book, but references are provided in the *Further reading* section. Various development frameworks automatically generate OpenAPI documentation by processing the REST API code and further information is provided by the developer, so your team does not need to have in-depth knowledge of OpenAPI syntax. An example of it is the `Swashbuckle.AspNetCore` NuGet package that we will present in this chapter.

The *How does .NET 5 deal with SOA?* section explains how we can automatically generate OpenAPI documentation in ASP.NET Core REST API projects, while the use case at the end of this chapter provides a practical example of its usage.

We will end this subsection by talking about how to handle authentication and authorization in REST services.

REST service authorization and authentication

Since REST services are sessionless, when authentication is required, the client must send an authentication token in every single request. That token is usually placed in the HTTP authorization header, but this depends on the type of authentication protocol you are using. The simplest way to authenticate is through the explicit transmission of a shared secret. This can be done with the following code:

```
Authorization: Api-Key <string known by both server and client>
```

The shared secret is called an API key. Since, at the time of writing, there is no standard on how to send it, API keys can also be sent in other headers, as shown in the following code:

```
X-API-Key: <string known by both server and client>
```

It is worth mentioning that API key-based authentication needs HTTPS to stop shared secrets from being stolen. API keys are very simple to use, but they do not convey information about user authorizations, so they can be adopted when the operations allowed by the client are quite standard and there are no complex authorization patterns. Moreover, when exchanged in requests, API keys are susceptible to being attacked on the server or client side. A common pattern to mitigate this is to create a "service account" user and restrict their authorizations to just those needed and use the API keys from that specific account when interacting with the API.

Safer techniques use shared secrets that are valid for a long period of time, just by the user logging in. Then, the login returns a short-life token that is used as a shared secret in all the subsequent requests. When the short-life secret is going to expire, it can be renewed with a call to a renew endpoint.

The whole logic is completely decoupled from the short-life token-based authorization logic. The login is usually based on login endpoints that receive long-term credentials and return short-life tokens. Login credentials are either usual username-password pairs that are passed as input to the login method or other kinds of authorization tokens that are converted into short-life tokens that are served by the login endpoint. Login can also be achieved with various authentication protocols based on X.509 certificates.

The most widespread short-life token type is the so-called bearer token. Each bearer token encodes information about how long it lasts and a list of assertions, called claims, that can be used for authorization purposes. Bearer tokens are returned by either login operations or renewal operations. Their characteristic feature is that they are not tied to the client that receives them or to any other specific client.

No matter how a client gets a bearer token, this is all a client needs to be granted all the rights implied by its claims. It is enough to transfer a bearer token to another client to empower that client with all the rights implied by all the bearer token claims, since no proof of identity is required by bearer token-based authorization.

Therefore, once a client gets a bearer token, it can delegate some operations to third parties by transferring its bearer token to them. Typically, when a bearer token must be used for delegation, during the login phase, the client specifies the claims to include to restrict what operations can be authorized by the token.

Compared to API key authentication, bearer token-based authentication is disciplined by standards. They must use the following `Authorization` header:

```
Authorization: Bearer <bearer token string>
```

Bearer tokens can be implemented in several ways. REST services typically use JWT tokens that are strung with a Base64URL encoding of JSON objects. More specifically, JWT creation starts with a JSON header, as well as a JSON payload. The JSON header specifies the kind of token and how it is signed, while the payload consists of a JSON object that contains all the claims as property/value pairs. The following is an example header:

```
{
    "alg": "RS256",
    "typ": "JWT"
}
```

The following is an example payload:

```
{
  "iss": "wwtravelclub.com"
  "sub": "example",
  "aud": ["S1", "S2"],
  "roles": [
    "ADMIN",
    "USER"
  ],
  "exp": 1512975450,
  "iat": 1512968250230
}
```

Then, the header and payload are Base64URL-encoded and the corresponding string is concatenated as follows:

```
<header BASE64 string>.<payload base64 string>
```

The preceding string is then signed with the algorithm specified in the header, which, in our example, is RSA +SHA256, and the signature string is concatenated with the original string as follows:

```
<header BASE64 string>.<payload base64 string>.<signature string>
```

The preceding code is the final bearer token string. A symmetric signature can be used instead of RSA, but, in this case, both the JWT issuer and all the services using it for authorization must share a common secret, while, with RSA, the private key of the JWT issuer does not need to be shared with anyone, since the signature can be verified with just the issuer public key.

Some payload properties are standard, such as the following:

- iss: Issuer of the JWT.
- aud: The audience, that is, the services and/or operations that can use the token for authorization. If a service does not see its identifier within this list, it should reject the token.
- sub: A string that identifies the *principal* (that is, the user) to which the JWT was issued.
- iat, exp, and nbf: These are for the time the JWT was issued, its expiration time, and, if set, the time after which the token is valid, respectively. All the times are expressed as seconds from midnight UTC on January 1, 1970. Here, all the days are considered as having exactly 86,400 seconds in them.

Other claims may be defined as public if we represent them with a unique URI; otherwise, they are considered private to the issuer and to the services known to the issuer.

How does .NET 5 deal with SOA?

WCF technology has not been ported to .NET 5 and there are no plans to perform a complete port of it. Instead, Microsoft is investing in gRPC, Google's open source technology. Besides, .NET 5 has excellent support for REST services through ASP. NET Core.

The main reasons behind the decision to abandon WCF in .NET 5 are as follows:

- As we have already discussed, SOAP technology has been overtaken by REST technology in most application areas.

- WCF technology is strictly tied to Windows, so it would be very expensive to reimplement all its features from scratch in .NET 5. Since support for full .NET will continue, users that need WCF can still rely on it.

- As a general strategy, with .NET 5, Microsoft prefers investing in open source technologies that can be shared with other competitors. That is why, instead of investing in WCF, Microsoft provided a gRPC implementation starting from .NET Core 3.0.

The next subsections will cover the support provided inside Visual Studio for each technology we have mentioned.

SOAP client support

In WCF, service specifications are defined through .NET interfaces and the actual service code is supplied in classes that implement those interfaces. Endpoints, underlying protocols (HTTP and TCP/IP), and any other features are defined in a configuration file. In turn, the configuration file can be edited with an easy to use configuration tool. Therefore, the developer is responsible for providing just the service behavior as a standard .NET class and for configuring all the service features in a declarative way. This way, the service configuration is completely decoupled from the actual service behavior and each service can be reconfigured so that it can be adapted to a different environment without the need to modify its code.

While .NET 5 does not support SOAP technology, it does support SOAP clients. More specifically, it is quite easy to create a SOAP service proxy for an existing SOAP service in Visual Studio (please refer to *Chapter 11*, *Design Patterns and .NET 5 Implementation*, for a discussion of what a proxy is and of the proxy pattern).

In the case of services, a proxy is a class that implements the service interface and whose methods perform their jobs by calling the analogous methods of the remote service.

To create a service proxy, right-click **Dependencies** in your project in **Solution Explorer**, and then select **Add connected service**. Then, in the form that appears, select **Microsoft WCF Service Reference Provider**. There, you can specify the URL of the service (where the WSDL service description is contained), the namespace where you wish to add the proxy class, and much more. At the end of the wizard, Visual Studio automatically adds all the necessary NuGet packages and scaffolds the proxy class. This is enough to create an instance of this class and to call its methods so that we can interact with the remote SOAP service.

There are also third parties, such as NuGet packages that provide limited support for SOAP services, but at the moment, they aren't very useful, since such limited support does not include features that aren't available in REST services.

gRPC support

Visual Studio 2019 supports the gRPC project template, which scaffolds both a gRPC server and a gRPC client. gRPC implements a remote procedure call pattern that offers both synchronous and asynchronous calls, reducing the traffic of messages between client and server.

 Although at the time of writing this book, gRPC is not available for IIS and App Service in Azure, there are great initiatives related to it. One of them is gRPC-Web (https://devblogs.microsoft.com/aspnet/grpc-web-for-net-now-available/).

It is configured in a way that is similar to WCF and to .NET remoting, as we described at the end of *Chapter 6, Azure Service Fabric*. That is, services are defined through interfaces and their code is provided in classes that implement those interfaces, while clients interact with those services through proxies that implement the same service interfaces.

gRPC is a good option for internal communications within a microservices cluster, especially if the cluster is not fully based on Service Fabric technology and cannot rely on .NET remoting. Since there are gRPC libraries for all the main languages and development frameworks, it can be used in Kubernetes-based clusters, as well as in Service Fabric clusters that host Docker images that have been implemented in other frameworks.

gRPC is more efficient than the REST services protocol due to its more compact representation of data and it being easier to use, since everything to do with the protocol is taken care of by the development framework. However, at the time of writing, none of its features rely on well-established standards, so it cannot be used for publicly exposed endpoints – it can only be used for intra-cluster communication. For this reason, we will not describe gRPC in detail, but the *Further reading* section of this chapter contains references to both gRPC in general and to its .NET Core implementation.

Using gRPC is super easy since Visual Studio's gRPC project template scaffolds everything so that the gRPC service and its clients are working. The developer just needs to define the application-specific C# service interface and a class that implements it.

 You can check details about this implementation at `https://docs.microsoft.com/en-us/aspnet/core/tutorials/grpc/grpc-start?view=aspnetcore-5.0`.

The remainder of the section is dedicated to .NET Core support for REST services from both the server and client side.

A short introduction to ASP.NET Core

ASP.NET Core applications are .NET Core applications based on the *Host* concept we described in the *Using generic hosts* subsection of *Chapter 5*, *Applying a Microservice Architecture to Your Enterprise Application*. The `program.cs` file of each ASP.NET application creates a Host, builds it, and runs it with the following code:

```
public class Program
{
    public static void Main(string[] args)
    {
        CreateHostBuilder(args).Build().Run();
    }

    public static IHostBuilder CreateHostBuilder(string[] args) =>
        Host
        .CreateDefaultBuilder(args)
        .ConfigureWebHostDefaults(webBuilder =>
        {
            webBuilder.UseStartup<Startup>();
        });
}
```

CreateDefaultBuilder sets up a standard Host, while ConfigureWebHostDefaults configures it so that it can handle an HTTP pipeline. More specifically, it sets the ContentRootPath property of the IWebHostEnvironment interface for the current directory.

Then, it loads the configuration information from appsettings.json and appsettings.[EnvironmentName].json. Once loaded, the configuration information contained in the JSON object properties can be mapped to .NET object properties with the ASP.NET Core options framework. More specifically, appsettings.json and appsettings.[EnvironmentName].json are merged and the file's environment-specific information overrides the corresponding appsettings.json settings.

EnvironmentName is taken from the ASPNETCORE_ENVIRONMENT environment variable. In turn, it is defined in the Properties\launchSettings.json file when the application runs in Visual Studio, over **Solution Explorer**. In this file, you can define several environments that can be selected with the dropdown next to Visual Studio's run button **IIS Express**. By default, the **IIS Express** setting sets ASPNETCORE_ENVIRONMENT to Development. The following is a typical launchSettings.json file:

```
{
  "iisSettings": {
    "windowsAuthentication": false,
    "anonymousAuthentication": true,
    "iisExpress": {
      "applicationUrl": "http://localhost:2575",
      "sslPort": 44393
    }
  },
  "profiles": {
    "IIS Express": {
      "commandName": "IISExpress",
      "launchBrowser": true,
      "environmentVariables": {
        "ASPNETCORE_ENVIRONMENT": "Development"
      }
    },
    ...
    ...
    }
  }
}
```

The value to use for ASPNETCORE_ENVIRONMENT when the application is published can be added to the published XML file after it has been created by Visual Studio. This value is <EnvironmentName>Staging</EnvironmentName>. It can also be specified in your Visual Studio ASP.NET Core project file (.csproj):

```
<PropertyGroup>
<EnvironmentName>Staging</EnvironmentName>
</PropertyGroup>
```

Later, the application configures Host logging so that it can write to the console and debug output. This setting can be changed with further configuration. Then, it sets up/connects a web server to the ASP.NET Core pipeline.

When the application runs in Linux, the ASP.NET Core pipeline connects to the .NET Core Kestrel web server. Since Kestrel is a minimal web server, you are responsible for reverse proxying requests to it from a complete web server, such as Apache or NGINX, that adds features that Kestrel does not have. When the application runs in Windows, by default, ConfigureWebHostDefaults connects the ASP.NET Core pipeline directly to **Internet Information Services (IIS)**. However, you can also use Kestrel in Windows and you can reverse proxy IIS requests to Kestrel by changing the AspNetCoreHostingModel setting of your Visual Studio project file like so:

```
<PropertyGroup>
    ...
<AspNetCoreHostingModel>OutOfProcess</AspNetCoreHostingModel>
</PropertyGroup>
```

UseStartup<Startup>() lets Host services (see the *Using generic hosts* subsection in *Chapter 5, Applying a Microservice Architecture to Your Enterprise Application*) and the definition of the ASP.NET Core pipeline be taken from the methods of the project's Startup.cs class. More specifically, services are defined in its ConfigureServices(I ServiceCollection services) method, while the ASP.NET Core pipeline is defined in the Configure method. The following code shows the standard Configure method scaffolded with an API REST project:

```
public void Configure(IApplicationBuilder app,
    IWebHostEnvironment env)
{
    if (env.IsDevelopment())
    {
        app.UseDeveloperExceptionPage();
    }
    app.UseHsts();
    app.UseHttpsRedirection();
```

```
    app.UseRouting();
    app.UseAuthorization();
    app.UseEndpoints(endpoints =>
    {
        endpoints.MapControllers();
    });
}
```

Each middleware in the pipeline is defined by an `app.Use<something>` method, which often accepts some options. Each of them processes the requests and then either forwards the modified request to the next one in the pipeline or returns an HTTP response. When an HTTP response is returned, it is processed by all the previous ones in reverse order.

Modules are inserted in the pipeline in the order they are defined by the `app.Use<something>` method calls. The preceding code adds an error page if `ASPNETCORE_ENVIRONMENT` is `Development`; otherwise, `UseHsts` negotiates a security protocol with the client. Finally, `UseEndpoints` adds the MVC controllers that create the actual HTTP response. A complete description of the ASP.NET Core pipeline will be given in the *Understanding the presentation layers of web applications* section of *Chapter 15, Presenting ASP.NET Core MVC*.

In the next subsection, we will explain how the MVC framework lets you implement REST services.

Implementing REST services with ASP.NET Core

Today, we can guarantee that the use of MVC and a Web API is consolidated. In the MVC framework, HTTP requests are processed by classes called controllers. Each request is mapped to the call of a controller public method. The selected controller and controller methods depend on the shape of the request path, and they are defined by routing rules, that, for the REST API, are usually provided through attributes associated with both the `Controller` class and its methods.

`Controller` methods that process HTTP requests are called action methods. When the controller and action methods are selected, the MVC framework creates a controller instance to serve the request. All the parameters of the controller constructors are resolved with dependency injection with types defined in the `ConfigureServices` method of the `Startup.cs` class.

Please refer to the *Using generic hosts* subsection of *Chapter 5, Applying a Microservice Architecture to Your Enterprise Application,* for a description of how to use dependency injection with .NET Core Hosts, and to the *Dependency Injection pattern* subsection of *Chapter 11, Design Patterns and .NET 5 Implementation,* for a general discussion of dependency injection.

The following is a typical REST API controller and its controller method definitions:

```
[Route("api/[controller]")]
    [ApiController]
    public class ValuesController : ControllerBase
    {
        // GET api/values/5
        [HttpGet("{id}")]
        public ActionResult<string> Get(int id)
        {
            ...
```

The [ApiController] attribute declares that the controller is a REST API controller. [Route("api/[controller]")] declares that the controller must be selected on paths that start with api/<controller name>. The controller name is the name of the controller class without the Controller postfix. Thus, in this case, we have api/values.

[HttpGet("{id}")] declares that the method must be invoked on GET requests of the api/values/<id> type, where id must be a number that's passed as an argument to the method invocation. This can be done with Get(int id). There is also an Http<verb> attribute for each HTTP verb: HttpPost and HttpPatch.

We may also have another method defined like so:

```
[HttpGet]
public ... Get()
```

This method is invoked on GET requests of the api/values type, that is, on GET requests without id after the controller name.

Several action methods can have the same name, but only one should be compatible with each request path; otherwise, an exception is thrown. In other words, routing rules and Http<verb> attributes must univocally define which controller and which of its action methods to select for each request.

By default, parameters are passed to the action methods of API controllers according to the following rules:

- Simple types (`integers`, `floats`, and `DateTimes`) are taken from the request path if routing rules specify them as parameters, as in the case of the previous example's [`HttpGet("{id}")`] attribute. If they are not found in the routing rules, the MVC framework looks for query string parameters with the same name. Thus, for instance, if we replace [`HttpGet("{id}")`] with [`HttpGet`], the MVC framework will look for something like api/values?id=<an integer>.

- Complex types are extracted from the request body by formatters. The right formatter is chosen according to the value of the request's `Content-Type` header. If no `Content-Type` header is specified, the JSON formatter is taken. The JSON formatter tries to parse the request body as a JSON object and then tries to transform this JSON object into an instance of the .NET Core complex type. If either the JSON extraction or the subsequent conversion fails, an exception is thrown. By default, just the JSON input formatter is supported, but you can also add an XML formatter that can be used when `Content-Type` specifies XML content. It is enough to add the `Microsoft.AspNetCore.Mvc.Formatters.Xml` NuGet package and replace `services.AddControllers()` with `services.AddControllers().AddXmlSerializerFormatters()` in the `ConfigureServices` method of `Startup.cs`.

You can customize the source that is used to fill an action method parameter by prefixing the parameter with an adequate attribute. The following code shows some examples of this:

```
...MyActionMethod(....[FromHeader] string myHeader....)
// x is taken from a request header named myHeader

...MyActionMethod(....[FromServices] MyType x....)
// x is filled with an instance of MyType through dependency injection
```

The return type of an `Action` method must be an `IActionResult` interface or a type that implements that interface. In turn, `IActionResult` has just the following method:

```
Task ExecuteResultAsync(ActionContext context);
```

This method is called by the MVC framework at the right time to create the actual response and response headers. The `ActionContext` object, when passed to the method, contains the whole context of the HTTP request, which includes a request object with all the necessary information about the original HTTP requests (headers, body, and cookies), as well as a response object that collects all the pieces of the response that is being built.

You do not have to create an implementation of `IActionResult` manually, since `ControllerBase` already has methods to create `IActionResult` implementations so that all the necessary HTTP responses are generated. Some of these methods are as follows.

- `OK`: This returns a 200 status code, as well as an optional result object. It is used either as return `OK()` or as return `OK(myResult)`.

- `BadRequest`: This returns a 400 status code, as well as an optional response object.

- `Created(string uri, object o)`: This returns a 201 status code, as well as a result object and the URI of the created resource.

- `Accepted`: This returns a 202 status result, as well as an optional result object and resource URI.

- `Unauthorized`: This returns a 401 status result, as well as an optional result object.

- `Forbid`: This returns a 403 status result, as well as an optional list of failed permissions.

- `StatusCode(int statusCode, object o = null)`: This returns a custom status code, as well as an optional result object.

An action method can return a result object directly with return `myObject`. This is equivalent to returning `OK(myObject)`.

When all the result paths return a result object of the same type, say, `MyType`, the action method can be declared as returning `ActionResult<MyType>`. You may also return responses like `NotFound`, but for sure you will get a better type check with this approach.

By default, result objects are serialized in JSON in the response body. However, if an XML formatter has been added to the MVC framework processing pipeline, as shown previously, the way the result is serialized depends on the `Accept` header of the HTTP request. More specifically, if the client explicitly requires XML format with the `Accept` header, the object will be serialized in XML; otherwise, it will be serialized in JSON.

Complex objects that are passed as input to action methods can be validated with validation attributes, as follows:

```
public record MyType
{
    [Required]
    public string Name{get; set;}
```

```
    ...
    [MaxLength(64)]
    public string Description{get; set;}
}
```

 If the controller has been decorated with the [ApiController] attribute and if validation fails, the MVC framework automatically creates a BadRequest response containing a dictionary with all the validation errors detected, without executing the action method. Therefore, you do not need to add further code to handle validation errors.

Action methods can also be declared as async methods, as follows:

```
public async Task<IActionResult>MyMethod(......)
{
    await MyBusinessObject.MyBusinessMethod();
    ...
}

public async Task<ActionResult<MyType>>MyMethod(......)
{
    ...
}
```

Practical examples of controllers/action methods will be shown in the *Use case* section of this chapter. In the next subsection, we will explain how to handle authorization and authentication with JWT tokens.

ASP.NET Core service authorization

When using a JWT token, authorizations are based on the claims contained in the JWT token. All the token claims in any action method can be accessed through the User.Claims controller property. Since User.Claims is an IEnumerable<Claim>, it can be processed with LINQ to verify complex conditions on claims. If authorization is based on *role* claims, you can simply use the User.IsInRole function, as shown in the following code:

```
If(User.IsInRole("Administrators") || User.IsInRole("SuperUsers"))
{
    ...
}
else return Forbid();
```

However, permissions are not usually checked from within action methods and are automatically checked by the MVC framework, according to authorization attributes that decorate either the whole controller or a single action method. If an action method or the whole controller is decorated with [Authorize], then access to the action method is possible only if the request has a valid authentication token, which means we don't have to perform a check on the token claims. It is also possible to check whether the token contains a set of roles using the following code:

```
[Authorize(Roles = "Administrators,SuperUsers")]
```

More complex conditions on claims require that authorization policies be defined in the ConfigureServices method of Startup.cs, as shown in the following code:

```
public void ConfigureServices(IServiceCollection services)
{
    services.AddControllers();
    ...
    services.AddAuthorization(options =>
    {
        options.AddPolicy("CanDrive", policy =>
            policy.RequireAssertion(context =>
            context.User.HasClaim(c =>c.Type == "HasDrivingLicense"));
    });
}
```

After that, you can decorate the action methods or controllers with [Authorize(Policy = "Father")].

Before using JWT-based authorization, you must configure it in Startup.cs. First, you must add the middleware that processes authentication tokens in the ASP.NET Core processing pipeline defined in the Configure method, as shown here:

```
public void Configure(IApplicationBuilder app, IWebHostEnvironment env)
{
    ...
    app.UseAuthorization();
    ...
    app.UseEndpoints(endpoints =>
    {
    endpoints.MapControllers();
    });

}
```

Then, you must configure the authentication services in the `ConfigureServices` section. Here, you define the authentication options that will be injected through dependency injection into the authentication middleware:

```
services.AddAuthentication(JwtBearerDefaults.AuthenticationScheme)
    .AddJwtBearer(options => {
      options.TokenValidationParameters =
        new TokenValidationParameters
        {
            ValidateIssuer = true,
            ValidateAudience = true,
            ValidateLifetime = true,
            ValidateIssuerSigningKey = true,
            ValidIssuer = "My.Issuer",
            ValidAudience = "This.Website.Audience",
            IssuerSigningKey = new
                SymmetricSecurityKey(Encoding.ASCII.GetByte
                ("MySecret"))
        };
    });
```

The preceding code provides a name to the authentication scheme, that is, a default name. Then, it specifies JWT authentication options. Usually, we require that the authentication middleware verifies that the JWT token is not expired (`ValidateLifetime = true`), that it has the right issuer and audience (see the *REST services authorization and authentication* section of this chapter), and that its signature is valid.

The preceding example uses a symmetric signing key generated from a string. This means that the same key is used to sign and to verify the signature. This is an acceptable choice if JWT tokens are created by the same website that uses them, but it is not an acceptable choice if there is a unique JWT issuer that controls access to several Web API sites.

Here, we should use an asymmetric key (typically, an `RsaSecurityKey`), so JWT verification requires just the knowledge of the public key associated with the actual private signing key. Identity Server 4 can be used to quickly create a website that works as an authentication server. It emits a JWT token with the usual username/password credentials or converts other authentication tokens. If you use an authentication server such as Identity Server 4, you do not need to specify the `IssuerSigningKey` option, since the authorization middleware is able to retrieve the required public key from the authorization server automatically.

It is enough to provide the authentication server URL, as shown here:

```
.AddJwtBearer(options => {
options.Authority = "https://www.MyAuthorizationserver.com";
options.TokenValidationParameters =...
        ...
```

On the other hand, if you decide to emit JWT in your Web API's site, you can define a Login action method that accepts an object with a username and password, and that, while relying on database information, builds the JWT token with code similar to the following:

```
var claims = new List<Claim>
{
    new Claim(...),
    new Claim(...) ,
    ...
};

var token = new JwtSecurityToken(
        issuer: "MyIssuer",
        audience: ...,
        claims: claims,
        expires: DateTime.UtcNow.AddMinutes(expiryInMinutes),
signingCredentials:
new SymmetricSecurityKey(Encoding.ASCII.GetBytes("MySecret"));
return OK(new JwtSecurityTokenHandler().WriteToken(token));
```

Here, JwtSecurityTokenHandler().WriteToken(token) generates the actual token string from the token properties contained in the JwtSecurityToken instance.

In the next subsection, we will learn how to empower our Web API with an OpenAPI documentation point so that proxy classes for communicating with our services can be generated automatically.

ASP.NET Core support for OpenAPI

Most of the information that is needed to fill in an OpenAPI JSON document can be extracted from Web API controllers through reflection, that is, input types and sources (path, request body, and header) and endpoint paths (these can be extracted from routing rules). Returned output types and status codes, in general, cannot be easily computed since they can be generated dynamically.

Therefore, the MVC framework provides the `ProducesResponseType` attribute so that we can declare a possible return type – a status code pair. It is enough to decorate each action method with as many `ProducesResponseType` attributes as there are possible types, that is, possible status code pairs, as shown in the following code:

```
[HttpGet("{id}")]
[ProducesResponseType(typeof(MyReturnType), StatusCodes.Status200OK)]
[ProducesResponseType(typeof(MyErrorReturnType), StatusCodes.
Status404NotFound)]
public IActionResult GetById(int id)...
```

If no object is returned along a path, we can just declare the status code, as follows:

```
[ProducesResponseType(StatusCodes.Status403Forbidden)]
```

We can also specify just the status code when all the paths return the same type and when that type is specified in the action method return type as `ActionResult<CommonReturnType>`.

Once all the action methods have been documented, to generate any actual documentation for the JSON endpoints, we must install the `Swashbuckle.AspNetCore` NuGet package and place some code in the `Startup.cs` file. More specifically, we must add some middleware in the `Configure` method, as shown here:

```
app.UseSwagger(); //open api middleware
...
app.UseEndpoints(endpoints =>
{
    endpoints.MapControllers();
});
```

Then, we must add some configuration options in the `ConfigureServices` method, as follows:

```
services.AddSwaggerGen(c =>
{
c.SwaggerDoc("MyServiceName", new OpenApiInfo
    {
        Version = "v1",
        Title = "ToDo API",
        Description = "My service description",
    });
});
```

The first argument of the SwaggerDoc method is the documentation endpoint name. By default, the documentation endpoint is accessible through the <webroot>// swagger/<endpoint name>/swagger.json path, but this can be changed in several ways. The rest of the information contained in the Info class is self-explanatory.

We can add several SwaggerDoc calls to define several documentation endpoints. However, by default, all the documentation endpoints will contain the same documentation, which includes a description of all the REST services included in the project. This default can be changed by calling the c.DocInclusionPredic ate(Func<string, ApiDescription> predicate) method from within services. AddSwaggerGen(c => {...}).

DocInclusionPredicate must be passed a function that receives a JSON document name and an action method description and must return true if the documentation of the action must be included in that JSON document.

To declare that your REST APIs need a JWT token, you must add the following code within services.AddSwaggerGen(c => {...}):

```
var security = new Dictionary<string, IEnumerable<string>>
{
    {"Bearer", new string[] { }},
};

c.AddSecurityDefinition("Bearer", new ApiKeyScheme
{
    Description = "JWT Authorization header using the Bearer scheme.
    Example: \"Authorization: Bearer {token}\"",
    Name = "Authorization",
    In = "header",
    Type = "apiKey"
});
c.AddSecurityRequirement(security);
```

You can enrich the JSON documentation endpoint with information that has been extracted from triple-slash comments, which are usually added to generate automatic code documentation. The following code shows some examples of this. The following snippet shows how we can add a method description and parameter information:

```
/// <summary>
/// Deletes a specific TodoItem.
/// </summary>
/// <param name="id">id to delete</param>
```

```
[HttpDelete("{id}")]
public IActionResultDelete(long id)
```

The following snippet shows how we can add an example of usage:

```
/// <summary>
/// Creates an item.
/// </summary>
/// <remarks>
/// Sample request:
///
/// POST /MyItem
/// {
/// "id": 1,
/// "name": "Item1"
/// }
///
/// </remarks>
```

The following snippet shows how we can add parameter descriptions and return type descriptions for each HTTP status code:

```
/// <param name="item">item to be created</param>
/// <returns>A newly created TodoItem</returns>
/// <response code="201">Returns the newly created item</response>
/// <response code="400">If the item is null</response>
```

To enable extraction from triple-slash comments, we must enable code documentation creation by adding the following code in our project file (.csproj):

```
<PropertyGroup>
<GenerateDocumentationFile>true</GenerateDocumentationFile>
<NoWarn>$(NoWarn);1591</NoWarn>
</PropertyGroup>
```

Then, we must enable code documentation processing from within services. AddSwaggerGen(c => {...}) by adding the following code:

```
var xmlFile = $"{Assembly.GetExecutingAssembly().GetName().Name}.xml";
var xmlPath = Path.Combine(AppContext.BaseDirectory, xmlFile);
c.IncludeXmlComments(xmlPath);
```

Once our documentation endpoints are ready, we can add some more middleware that is contained in the same `Swashbuckle.AspNetCore` NuGet package to generate a friendly user interface that we can test our REST API on:

```
app.UseSwaggerUI(c =>
{
    c.SwaggerEndpoint("/swagger/<documentation name>/swagger.json", "
    <api name that appears in dropdown>");
});
```

If you have several documentation endpoints, you need to add a `SwaggerEndpoint` call for each of them. We will use this interface to test the REST API defined in this chapter's use case.

Once you have a working JSON documentation endpoint, you can automatically generate the C# or TypeScript code of a proxy class with one of the following methods:

- The NSwagStudio Windows program, which is available at `https://github.com/RicoSuter/NSwag/wiki/NSwagStudio`.

- The `NSwag.CodeGeneration.CSharp` or `NSwag.CodeGeneration.TypeScript` NuGet packages if you want to customize code generation.

- The `NSwag.MSBuild` NuGet package if you want to tie code generation to Visual Studio build operations. The documentation for this can be found at `https://github.com/RicoSuter/NSwag/wiki/MSBuild`.

In the next subsection, you will learn how to invoke a REST API from another REST API or from a .NET Core client.

.Net Core HTTP clients

The `HttpClient` class in the `System.Net.Http` namespace is a .NET standard 2.0 built-in HTTP client class. While it could be used directly whenever we need to interact with a REST service, there are some problems in creating and releasing `HttpClient` instances repeatedly, as follows:

- Their creation is expensive.

- When an `HttpClient` is released, for instance, in a `using` statement, the underlying connection is not closed immediately but at the first garbage collection session, which is a repeated creation. Release operations quickly exhaust the maximum number of connections the operating system can handle.

Therefore, either a single HttpClient instance is reused, such as a singleton, or HttpClient instances are somehow pooled. Starting from the 2.1 version of .NET Core, the HttpClientFactory class was introduced to pool HTTP clients. More specifically, whenever a new HttpClient instance is required for an HttpClientFactory object, a new HttpClient is created. However, the underlying HttpClientMessageHandler instances, which are expensive to create, are pooled until their maximum lifetime expires.

HttpClientMessageHandler instances must have a finite duration since they cache DNS resolution information that may change over time. The default lifetime of HttpClientMessageHandler is 2 minutes, but it can be redefined by the developer.

Using HttpClientFactory allows us to automatically pipeline all the HTTP operations with other operations. For instance, we can add a Polly retry strategy to handle all the failures of all our HTTP operations automatically. For an introduction to Polly, please refer to the *Resilient task execution* subsection of *Chapter 5, Applying a Microservice Architecture to Your Enterprise Application.*

The simplest way to exploit the advantages offered by the HttpClientFactory class is to add the Microsoft.Extensions.Http NuGet package and then to follow these steps:

1. Define a proxy class, say, MyProxy, to interact with the desired REST service.

2. Let MyProxy accept an HttpClient instance in its constructor.

3. Use the HttpClient that was injected into the constructor to implement all the necessary operations.

4. Declare your proxy in the services configuration method of your Host which, in the case of an ASP.NET Core application, is the ConfigureServices method of the Startup.cs class, while, in the case of a client application, this is the ConfigureServices method of the HostBuilder instance. In the simplest case, the declaration is something similar to services. AddHttpClient<MyProxy>(). This will automatically add MyProxy to the services that are available for dependency injection, so you can easily inject it, for instance, in your controller's constructors. Moreover, each time an instance of MyProxy is created, an HttpClient is returned by an HttpClientFactory and is automatically injected into its constructor.

In the constructors of the classes that need to interact with a REST service, we may also need an interface instead of a specific proxy implementation with a declaration of the type:

```
services.AddHttpClient<IMyProxy, MyProxy>()
```

A Polly resilient strategy (see the *Resilient task execution* subsection of *Chapter 5, Applying a Microservice Architecture to Your Enterprise Application*) can be applied to all the HTTP calls issued by our proxy class, as shown here:

```
var myRetryPolicy = Policy.Handle<HttpRequestException>()
    ...//policy definition
    ...;
services.AddHttpClient<IMyProxy, MyProxy>()
    .AddPolicyHandler(myRetryPolicy );
```

Finally, we can preconfigure some of the properties of all the `HttpClient` instances that are passed to our proxy, as shown here:

```
services.AddHttpClient<IMyProxy, MyProxy>(clientFactory =>
{
   clientFactory.DefaultRequestHeaders.Add("Accept", "application/
json");
   clientFactory.BaseAddress = new Uri("https://www.myService.com/");
})
  .AddPolicyHandler(myRetryPolicy );
```

This way, each client that is passed to the proxy is preconfigured so that they require a JSON response and must work with a specific service. Once the base address has been defined, each HTTP request needs to specify the relative path of the service method to call.

The following code shows how to perform a `POST` to a service. This requires an extra package, `System.Net.Http.Json`. Here, we are stating that the `HttpClient` that was injected into the proxy constructor has been stored in the `webClient` private field:

```
//Add a bearer token to authenticate the call
webClient.DefaultRequestHeaders.Add("Authorization", "Bearer " +
token);
...
//Call service method with a POST verb and get response
var response = await webClient.PostAsJsonAsync<MyPostModel>("my/method/
relative/path",
    new MyPostModel
    {
        //fill model here
        ...
    });
//extract response status code
var status = response.StatusCode;
```

```
...
//extract body content from response
string stringResult = await response.Content.ReadAsStringAsync();
```

If you use Polly, you do not need to intercept and handle communication errors since this job is performed by Polly. First, you need to verify the status code to decide what to do next. Then, you can parse the JSON string contained in the response body to get a .NET instance of a type that, in general, depends on the status code. The code to perform the parsing is based on the `System.Text.Json` NuGet package's `JsonSerializer` class and is as follows:

```
var result =
  JsonSerializer.Deserialize<MyResultClass>(stringResult);
```

Performing a GET request is similar but, instead of calling `PostAsJsonAsync`, you need to call `GetAsync`, as shown here. The use of other HTTP verbs is completely analogous:

```
var response =
  await webClient.GetAsync("my/getmethod/relative/path");
```

As you can check in this topic, accessing HTTP APIs is quite simple and requires the implementation of some .NET 5 libraries. Since the beginning of .NET Core, Microsoft has been working a lot on the improvement of the performance and the simplicity of this part of the framework. It is up to you to keep in touch with the documentation and facilities they keep implementing.

Use case – exposing WWTravelClub packages

In this section, we will implement an ASP.NET REST service that lists all the packages that are available for a given vacation's start and end dates. For didactic purposes, we will not structure the application according to the best practices described in *Chapter 12, Understanding the Different Domains in Software Solutions*; instead, we will simply generate the results with a LINQ query that will be directly placed in the controller action method. A well-structured ASP.NET Core application will be presented in *Chapter 15, Presenting ASP.NET Core MVC*, which is dedicated to the MVC framework.

Let's make a copy of the WWTravelClubDB solution folder and rename the new folder WWTravelClubREST. The WWTravelClubDB project was built step by step in the various sections of *Chapter 8, Interacting with Data in C# – Entity Framework Core.* Let's open the new solution and add a new ASP.NET Core API project to it named WWTravelClubREST (the same name as the new solution folder). For simplicity, select no authentication. Right-click on the newly created project and select **Set as StartUp project** to make it the default project that is launched when the solution is run.

Finally, we need to add a reference to the WWTravelClubDB project.

ASP.NET Core projects store configuration constants in the appsettings.json file. Let's open this file and add the database connection string for the database we created in the WWTravelClubDB project to it, as shown here:

```
{
    "ConnectionStrings": {
        "DefaultConnection": "Server=
    (localdb)\\mssqllocaldb;Database=wwtravelclub;
 Trusted_Connection=True;MultipleActiveResultSets=true"
    },
    ...
    ...
}
```

Now, we must add the WWTravelClubDB entity framework database context to the ConfigureServices method in Startup.cs, as shown here:

```
services.AddDbContext<WWTravelClubDB.MainDBContext>(options =>
options.UseSqlServer(
Configuration.GetConnectionString("DefaultConnection"),
            b =>b.MigrationsAssembly("WWTravelClubDB")));
```

The option object settings that are passed to AddDbContext specify the usage of SQL server with a connection string that is extracted from the ConnectionStrings section of the appsettings.json configuration file with the Configuration.GetConnectionString("DefaultConnection") method. The b =>b.MigrationsAssembly("WWTravelClubDB") lambda function declares the name of the assembly that contains the database migrations (see *Chapter 8, Interacting with Data in C# – Entity Framework Core*) which, in our case, is the DLL that was generated by the WWTravelClubDB project. For the preceding code to compile, you should add Microsoft.EntityFrameworkCore.

Since we want to enrich our REST service with OpenAPI documentation, let's add a reference to the `Swashbuckle.AspNetCore` NuGet package. Now, we can add the following very basic configuration to the `ConfigureServices` method:

```
services.AddSwaggerGen(c =>
{
c.SwaggerDoc("WWWTravelClub", new OpenAPIInfo
    {
        Version = "WWWTravelClub 1.0.0",
        Title = "WWWTravelClub",
        Description = "WWWTravelClub Api",
TermsOfService = null
    });
});
```

Then, we can add the middleware for the OpenAPI endpoint and for adding a user interface for our API documentation, as shown here:

```
app.UseSwagger();
app.UseSwaggerUI(c =>
{
    c.SwaggerEndpoint(
        "/swagger/WWWTravelClub/swagger.json",
        "WWWTravelClub Api");
});

app.UseEndpoints(endpoints => //preexisting code//
{
    endpoints.MapControllers();
});
```

Now, we are ready to encode our service. Let's delete `ValuesController`, which is automatically scaffolded by Visual Studio. Then, right-click on the `Controller` folder and select **Add | Controller**. Now, choose an empty API controller called `PackagesController`. First, let's modify the code, as follows:

```
[Route("api/packages")]
[ApiController]
public class PackagesController : ControllerBase
{
    [HttpGet("bydate/{start}/{stop}")]
    [ProducesResponseType(typeof(IEnumerable<PackagesListDTO>), 200)]
    [ProducesResponseType(400)]
```

```
    [ProducesResponseType(500)]
    public async Task<IActionResult> GetPackagesByDate(
        [FromServices] WWTravelClubDB.MainDBContext ctx,
        DateTime start, DateTime stop)
    {

    }
}
```

The Route attribute declares that the basic path for our service will be api/
packages. The unique action method that we implement is GetPackagesByDate,
which is invoked on HttpGet requests on paths of the bydate/{start}/{stop} type,
where start and stop are the DateTime parameters that are passed as input to
GetPackagesByDate. The ProduceResponseType attributes declare the following:

- When a request is successful, a 200 code is returned, and the body contains
  an IEnumerable of the PackagesListDTO (which we will soon define) type
  containing the required package information.

- When the request is ill-formed, a 400 code is returned. We don't specify
  the type returned since bad requests are automatically handled by the
  MVC framework through the ApiController attribute.

- In the case of unexpected errors, a 500 code is returned with an empty body.

Now, let's define the PackagesListDTO class in a new DTOs folder:

```
namespace WWTravelClubREST.DTOs
{
    public record PackagesListDTO
    {
        public int Id { get; set; }
        public string Name { get; set; }
        public decimal Price { get; set; }
        public int DurationInDays { get; set; }
        public DateTime? StartValidityDate { get; set; }
        public DateTime? EndValidityDate { get; set; }
        public string DestinationName { get; set; }
        public int DestinationId { get; set; }
    }
}
```

Finally, let's add the following using clauses to our controller code so that we can easily refer to our DTO and to Entity Framework LINQ methods:

```
using Microsoft.EntityFrameworkCore;
using WWTravelClubREST.DTOs;
```

Now, we are ready to fill the body of the GetPackagesByDate method with the following code:

```
try
{
    var res = await ctx.Packages
        .Where(m => start >= m.StartValidityDate
        && stop <= m.EndValidityDate)
        .Select(m => new PackagesListDTO
        {
            StartValidityDate = m.StartValidityDate,
            EndValidityDate = m.EndValidityDate,
            Name = m.Name,
            DurationInDays = m.DurationInDays,
            Id = m.Id,
            Price = m.Price,
            DestinationName = m.MyDestination.Name,
            DestinationId = m.DestinationId
        })
        .ToListAsync();
    return Ok(res);
}
catch (Exception err)
{
    return StatusCode(500, err);
}
```

The LINQ query is similar to the one contained in the `WWTravelClubDBTest` project we tested in *Chapter 8, Interacting with Data in C# – Entity Framework Core*. Once the result has been computed, it is returned with an `OK` call. The method's code handles internal server errors by catching exceptions and returning a 500 status code since bad requests are automatically handled before the `Controller` method is called by the `ApiController` attribute.

Let's run the solution. When the browser opens, it is unable to receive any result from our ASP.NET Core website. Let's modify the browser URL so that it is `https://localhost:<previous port>/swagger`. The user interface of the OpenAPI documentation will look as follows:

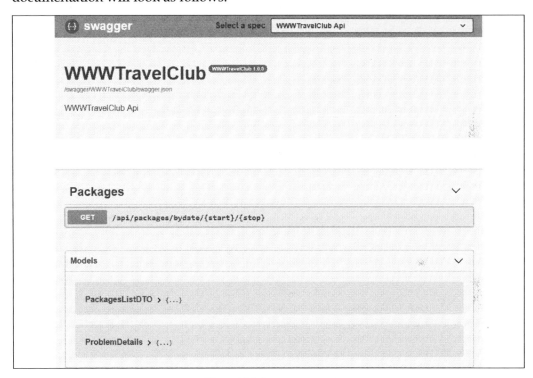

Figure 14.1: Swagger output

PackagesListDTO is the model we defined to list the packages, while ProblemDetails is the model that is used to report errors in the event of bad requests. By clicking the **GET** button, we can get more details about our GET method and we can also test it, as shown in the following screenshot:

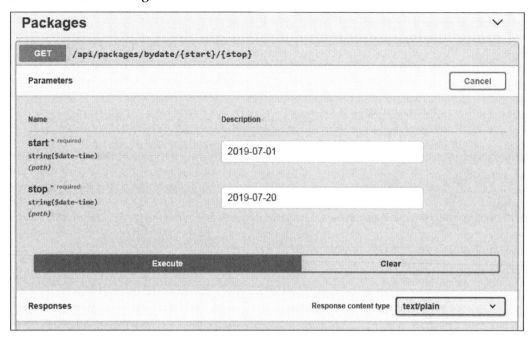

Figure 14.2: GET method details

Pay attention when it comes to inserting dates that are covered by packages in the database; otherwise, an empty list will be returned. The ones shown in the preceding screenshot should work.

Dates must be entered in a correct JSON format; otherwise, a 400 Bad Request error is returned, like the one shown in the following code:

```
{
  "errors": {
    "start": [
      "The value '2019' is not valid."
    ]
  },
  "title": "One or more validation errors occurred.",
  "status": 400,
  "traceId": "80000008-0000-f900-b63f-84710c7967bb"
}
```

If you insert the correct input parameters, the Swagger UI returns the packages that satisfy the query in JSON format.

That is all! You have implemented your first API with OpenAPI documentation!

Summary

In this chapter, we introduced SOA, its design principles, and its constraints. Among them, it is worth remembering interoperability.

Then, we focused on well-established standards for business applications that achieve the interoperability that is needed for publicly exposed services. Therefore, SOAP and REST services were discussed in detail, along with the transition from SOAP services to REST services, which has taken place in most application areas in the last few years. Then, REST service principles, authentication/authorization, and its documentation were described in greater detail.

Finally, we looked at the tools that are available in .NET 5 that we can use to implement and interact with services. We looked at a variety of frameworks for intra-cluster communication, such as .NET remoting and gRPC, and tools for SOAP and REST-based public services.

Here, we mainly focused on REST services. Their ASP.NET Core implementations were described in detail, along with the techniques we can use to authenticate/authorize them and their documentation. We also focused on how to implement efficient .NET Core proxies so that we can interact with REST services.

In the next chapter, we will learn how to use .NET 5 while building an application on ASP .NET Core MVC.

Questions

1. Can services use cookie-based sessions?
2. Is it good practice to implement a service with a custom communication protocol? Why or why not?
3. Can a POST request to a REST service cause a deletion?
4. How many dot-separated parts are contained in a JWT bearer token?
5. By default, where are the complex type parameters of a REST service's action methods taken from?
6. How is a controller declared as a REST service?
7. What are the main documentation attributes of ASP.NET Core services?

8. How are ASP.NET Core REST service routing rules declared?

9. How should a proxy be declared so that we can take advantage of .NET Core's `HttpClientFactory` class features?

Further reading

This chapter mainly focused on the more commonly used REST service. If you are interested in SOAP services, a good place to start is the Wikipedia page regarding SOAP specifications: `https://en.wikipedia.org/wiki/List_of_web_service_specifications`. On the other hand, if you are interested in the Microsoft .NET WCF technology for implementing SOAP services, you can refer to WCF's official documentation here: `https://docs.microsoft.com/en-us/dotnet/framework/wcf/`.

This chapter mentioned the AMQP protocol as an option for intra-cluster communication without describing it. Detailed information on this protocol is available on AMQP's official site: `https://www.amqp.org/`.

More information on gRPC is available on Google gRPC's official site: `https://grpc.io/`. More information on the Visual Studio gRPC project template can be found here: `https://docs.microsoft.com/en-US/aspnet/core/grpc/`. You may also want to check out gRPC-Web at `https://devblogs.microsoft.com/aspnet/grpc-web-for-net-now-available/`.

More details on ASP.NET Core services are available in the official documentation: `https://docs.microsoft.com/en-US/aspnet/core/web-api/`. More information on .NET Core's HTTP client is available here: `https://docs.microsoft.com/en-US/aspnet/core/fundamentals/http-requests`.

More information on JWT token authentication is available here: `https://jwt.io/`. If you would like to generate JWT tokens with Identity Server 4, you may refer to its official documentation page: `http://docs.identityserver.io/en/latest/`.

More information on OpenAPI is available at `https://swagger.io/docs/specification/about/`, while more information on Swashbuckle can be found on its GitHub repository page: `https://github.com/domaindrivendev/Swashbuckle`.

15
Presenting ASP.NET Core MVC

In this chapter, you will learn how to implement an application presentation layer. More specifically, you will learn how to implement a web application based on ASP. NET Core MVC.

ASP.NET Core is a .NET framework for implementing web applications. ASP. NET Core has been partially described in previous chapters, so this chapter will focus mainly on ASP.NET Core MVC. More specifically, this chapter will cover the following topics:

- Understanding the presentation layers of web applications
- Understanding the ASP.NET Core MVC structure
- What is new in the latest versions of ASP.NET Core?
- Understanding the connection between ASP.NET Core MVC and design principles
- Use case – implementing a web app in ASP.NET Core MVC

We will review and give further details on the structure of the ASP.NET Core framework, which, in part, was discussed in *Chapter 14, Applying Service-Oriented Architectures with .NET Core*, and *Chapter 4, Deciding the Best Cloud-Based Solution*. Here, the main focus is on how to implement web-based presentation layers based on the so-called **Model View Controller** (**MVC**) architectural pattern.

We will also analyze all of the new features available in the last ASP.NET Core 5.0 version, as well as the architectural patterns included in the ASP.NET Core MVC framework and/or used in typical ASP.NET Core MVC projects. Some of these patterns were discussed in *Chapter 11, Design Patterns and .NET 5 Implementation*, and *Chapter 12, Understanding the Different Domains in Software Solutions*, whereas some others, such as the MVC pattern itself, are new.

You will learn how to implement an ASP.NET Core MVC application, as well as how to organize the whole Visual Studio solution, by going through a practical example at the end of this chapter. This example describes a complete ASP.NET Core MVC application for editing the packages of the WWTravelClub book use case.

Technical requirements

This chapter requires the free Visual Studio 2019 Community edition or better with all database tools installed.

All the concepts in this chapter will be clarified with practical examples based on the WWTravelClub book use case. The code for this chapter is available at https://github.com/PacktPublishing/Software-Architecture-with-C-9-and-.NET-5.

Understanding the presentation layers of web applications

This chapter discusses an architecture for implementing the presentation layers of web-based applications based on the ASP.NET Core framework. The presentation layers of web applications are based on three techniques:

- **Mobile or desktop native applications that exchange data with servers through REST or SOAP services**: We have not discussed them since they are strictly tied to the client device and its operating system. Therefore, analyzing them, which would require a dedicated book, is completely beyond the scope of this book.

- **Single-Page Applications (SPAs)**: These are HTML-based applications whose dynamic HTML is created on the client either in JavaScript or with the help of WebAssembly (a kind of cross-browser assembly that can be used as a high-performance alternative to JavaScript). Like native applications, SPAs exchange data with the server through REST or SOAP services, but they have the advantage of being independent of the device and its operating system since they run in a browser. *Chapter 16, Blazor WebAssembly*, describes the Blazor SPA framework, which is based on WebAssembly, since it is based itself on a .NET runtime compiled in WebAssembly.

- **HTML pages created by the server whose content depends on the data to be shown to the user**: The ASP.NET Core MVC framework, which will be discussed in this chapter, is a framework for creating such dynamic HTML pages.

The remainder of this chapter focuses on how to create HTML pages on the server side and, more specifically, on ASP.NET Core MVC, which will be introduced in the next section.

Understanding the ASP.NET Core MVC structure

ASP.NET Core is based on the concept of the Generic Host, as explained in the *Using generic hosts* subsection of *Chapter 5, Applying a Microservice Architecture to Your Enterprise Application*. The basic architecture of ASP.NET Core was outlined in the *A short introduction to ASP.NET Core* subsection of *Chapter 14, Applying Service-Oriented Architectures with .NET Core*.

It is worth reminding you that the host configuration is delegated to the Startup class defined in the Startup.cs file by calling the .UseStartup<Startup>() method of the IWebHostBuilder interface. ConfigureServices(IServiceCollection services) of the Startup class defines all services that can be injected into object constructors through **Dependency Injection (DI)**. DI was described in detail in the *Using generic hosts* subsection of *Chapter 5, Applying a Microservice Architecture to Your Enterprise Application*.

On the other hand, the Configure(IApplicationBuilder app, IWebHostEnvironment env) startup method defines the so-called ASP.NET Core pipeline, which was briefly described in the *A short introduction to ASP.NET Core* subsection of *Chapter 14, Applying Service-Oriented Architectures with .NET Core*, and which will be described in more detail in the next subsection.

How the ASP.NET Core pipeline works

ASP.NET Core furnishes a set of configurable modules you can assemble according to your needs. Each module takes care of a functionality that you may or may not need. Examples of such functionalities are authorization, authentication, static file processing, protocol negotiation, CORS handling, and so on. Since most of the modules apply transformations to the incoming request and the final response, these modules are usually referred to as **middleware**.

You can put together all of the modules you need by inserting them into a common processing framework called the **ASP.NET Core pipeline**.

More specifically, ASP.NET Core requests are processed by pushing a context object through a pipeline of ASP.NET Core modules, as shown in the following diagram:

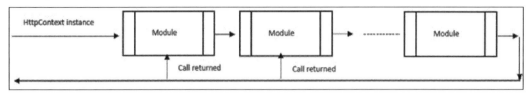

Figure 15.1: ASP.NET Core pipeline

The object that is inserted into the pipeline is an HttpContext instance that contains the data of the incoming request. More specifically, the Request property of HttpContext contains an HttpRequest object whose properties represent the incoming request in a structured way. There are properties for headers, cookies, request path, parameters, form fields, and the request body.

The various modules can contribute to the construction of the final response if we write them in an HttpResponse object contained in the Response property of the HttpContext instance. The HttpResponse class is similar to the HttpRequest class, but its properties refer to the response being built.

Some modules can build an intermediate data structure that is then used by other modules in the pipeline. In general, such intermediary data can be stored in custom entries of IDictionary<object, object>, which is contained in the Items property of the HttpContext object. However, there is a predefined property, User, that contains information about the currently logged-in user. The logged-in user is not computed automatically, so they must be computed by an authentication module. The *ASP.NET Core service authorization* subsection of *Chapter 14, Applying Service-Oriented Architectures with .NET Core*, explained how to add the standard module that performs JWT token-based authentication to the ASP.NET Core pipeline.

HttpContext also has a Connection property that contains information on the underlying connection established with the client, as well as a WebSockets property that contains information on possible WebSocket-based connections established with the clients.

HttpContext also has a Features property that contains IDictionary<Type, object>, which specifies the features supported by the web server that hosts the web application and the modules of the pipeline. Features can be set with the .Set<TFeature>(TFeature o) method and can be retrieved with the .Get<TFeature>() method.

Web server features are automatically added by the framework, while all other features are added by pipeline modules when they process HttpContext.

HttpContext also gives us access to the dependency injection engine through its RequestServices property. You can get an instance of a type managed by the dependency engine by calling the .RequestService.GetService(Type t) method or, even better, the .GetRequiredService<TService>() extension method that is built on top of it. However, as we will see in the remainder of this chapter, all types managed by the dependency injection engine are usually automatically injected into constructors, so these methods are only used when we're building custom **middleware** or other customizations of the ASP.NET Core engine.

The HttpContext instance that is created for processing a web request is not only available to modules, but also to the application code through DI. It is enough to insert an IHttpContextAccessor parameter into the constructor of a class that is automatically dependency injected, such as a service passed to a controller (see later on in this section), and then access its HttpContext property.

A module is any class with the following structure:

```
public class CoreMiddleware
{
    private readonly RequestDelegate _next;
    public CoreMiddleware(RequestDelegate next, ILoggerFactory
    loggerFactory)
    {
        ...
        _next = next;
        ...
    }

    public async Task Invoke(HttpContext context)
    {
        /*

            Insert here the module specific code that processes the
            HttpContext instance before it is passed to the next
            module.

        */

        await _next.Invoke(context);
```

```
        /*
            Insert here other module specific code that processes the
            HttpContext instance, after all modules that follow this
            module finished their processing.
        */
    }
}
```

In general, each module processes the HttpContext instance that was passed by the previous module in the pipeline, then calls await _next.Invoke(context) to invoke the modules in the remainder of the pipeline. When the other modules have finished their processing and the response for the client has been prepared, each module can perform further post-processing of the response in the code that follows the _next. Invoke(context) call.

Modules are registered in the ASP.NET Core pipeline by calling the UseMiddleware<T> method in the Startup.cs file's Configure method, as shown here:

```
public void Configure(IApplicationBuilder app, IWebHostEnvironment env,
IServiceProvider serviceProvider)
{
    ...
    app.UseMiddleware<MyCustomModule>
    ...
}
```

Modules are inserted into the pipeline in the same order when UseMiddleware is called. Since each functionality that's added to an application might require several modules and might require operations other than adding modules, you usually define an IApplicationBuilder extension such as UseMyFunctionality, as shown in the following code:

```
public static class MyMiddlewareExtensions
{
    public static IApplicationBuilder UseMyFunctionality(this
    IApplicationBuilder builder,...)
    {
        //other code
        ...
        builder.UseMiddleware<MyModule1>();
        builder.UseMiddleware<MyModule2>();
```

```
        ...
        //Other code
        ...
        return builder;
    }
}
```

After that, the whole functionality can be added to the application by calling app. UseMyFunctionality(...). For instance, the ASP.NET Core MVC functionality can be added to the ASP.NET Core pipeline by calling app.UseEndpoints(....).

Often, functionalities that are added with each app.Use... require that some .NET types are added to the application DI engine. In these cases, we also define an IServiceCollection extension named AddMyFunctionality, which must be called in the Startup.cs file's ConfigureServices(IServiceCollection services) method. For instance, ASP.NET Core MVC requires a call like the following:

```
services.AddControllersWithViews(o =>
{
    //set here MVC options by modifying the o option parameter
}
```

If you don't need to change the default MVC options, you can simply call services. AddControllersWithViews().

The next subsection describes another important feature of the ASP.NET Core framework; namely, how to handle application configuration data.

Loading configuration data and using it with the options framework

When an ASP.NET Core application starts, it reads configuration information (such as a database connection string) from the appsettings.json and appsettings. [EnvironmentName].json files, where EnvironmentName is a string value that depends on where the application is deployed. Typical values for EnvironmentName are as follows:

- Production is used for production deployment
- Development is used during development
- Staging is used when the application is tested in staging

The two JSON trees that were extracted from the appsettings.json and
appsettings.[EnvironmentName].json files are merged into a unique tree, where
the values contained in [EnvironmentName].json override the values contained in
the corresponding paths of appsettings.json. This way, the application can be run
with different configurations in different deployment environments. In particular,
you may use a different database connection string, and hence, a different database
instance in each different environment.

The [EnvironmentName] string is taken from the ASPNETCORE_ENVIRONMENT operating
system environment variable. In turn, ASPNETCORE_ENVIRONMENT can be automatically
set during the application's deployment with Visual Studio in two ways:

- During Visual Studio deployment, Visual Studio's **Publish** wizard creates an
  XML publish profile. If the **Publish** wizard allows you to choose ASPNETCORE_
  ENVIRONMENT from its drop-down list, you are done:

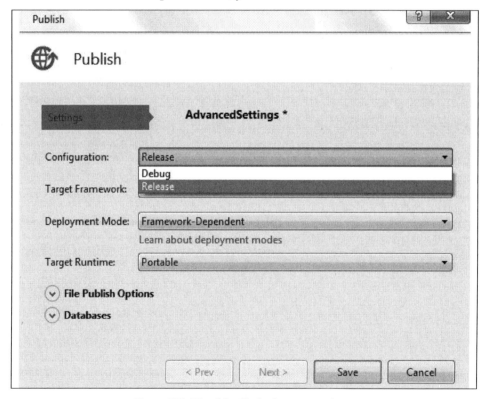

Figure 15.2: Visual Studio deployment settings

Otherwise, you may proceed as follows:

1. Once you've filled in the information in the wizard, save the publish
   profile without publishing it.

2. Then, edit the profile with a text editor and add an XML property such as `<EnvironmentName>Staging</EnvironmentName>`. Since all the already defined publish profiles can be selected during the application's publication, you may define a different publish profile for each of your environments, and then you may select the one you need during each publication.

- The value you must set `ASPNETCORE_ENVIRONMENT` to during deployment can also be specified in the Visual Studio ASP.NET Core project file (`.csproj`) of your application by adding the following code:

```
<PropertyGroup>
    <EnvironmentName>Staging</EnvironmentName>
</PropertyGroup>
```

During development in Visual Studio, the value to give to `ASPNETCORE_ENVIRONMENT` when the application is run can be specified in the `Properties\launchSettings.json` file of the ASP.NET Core project. The `launchSettings.json` file contains several named groups of settings. These settings configure how to launch the web application when it is run from Visual Studio. You may choose to apply all the settings of a group by selecting the group name with the drop-down list next to Visual Studio's run button:

Figure 15.3: Choice of launch settings group

Your selection from this drop-down list will be shown in the run button, with the default selection being **IIS Express**.

The following code shows a typical `launchSettings.json` file in which you can either add a new group of settings or change the settings of the existing default groups:

```
{
  "iisSettings": {
    "windowsAuthentication": false,
    "anonymousAuthentication": true,
    "iisExpress": {
      "applicationUrl": "http://localhost:2575",
      "sslPort": 44393
    }
  },
  "profiles": {
    "IIS Express": {
      "commandName": "IISExpress",
```

```
        "launchBrowser": true,
        "environmentVariables": {
          "ASPNETCORE_ENVIRONMENT": "Development"
        }
      },
      ...
      ...
      }
    }
  }
```

The named groups of settings are under the `profiles` properties. There, you may choose where to host the application (`IISExpress`), where to launch the browser, and the values of some environment variables.

The current environment that's been loaded from the `ASPNETCORE_ENVIRONMENT` operating system environment variable can be tested through the `IWebHostEnvironment` interface during the ASP.NET Core pipeline definition. This is because an `IWebHostEnvironment` instance is passed as a parameter to the `Startup.cs` file's `Configure` method. `IWebHostEnvironment` is also available to the remainder of the user code through DI.

`IWebHostEnvironment.IsEnvironment(string environmentName)` checks whether the current value of `ASPNETCORE_ENVIRONMENT` is `environmentName`. There are also specific shortcuts for testing development (`.IsDevelopment()`), production (`.IsProduction()`), and staging (`.IsStaging()`). `IWebHostEnvironment` also contains the current root directory of the ASP.NET Core application (`.WebRootPath`) and the directory reserved for the static files (`.ContentRootPath`) that are served as-is by the web server (CSS, JavaScript, images, and so on).

Both `launchSettings.json` and all publish profiles can be accessed as children of the **Properties** node in Visual Studio Explorer, as shown in the following screenshot:

Figure 15.4: Launch settings file

Once `appsettings.json` and `appsettings.[EnvironmentName].json` have been loaded, the configuration tree resulting from their merge can be mapped to the properties of .NET objects. For example, let's suppose we have an `Email` section of the `appsettings` file that contains all of the information needed to connect to an email server, as shown here:

```
{
    "ConnectionStrings": {
        "DefaultConnection": "...."
    },
    "Logging": {
        "LogLevel": {
            "Default": "Warning"
        }
    },
    "Email": {
        "FromName": "MyName",
        "FromAddress": "info@MyDomain.com",
        "LocalDomain": "smtps.MyDomain.com",
        "MailServerAddress": "smtps.MyDomain.com",
        "MailServerPort": "465",
        "UserId": "info@MyDomain.com",
        "UserPassword": "mypassword"
```

Then, the whole Email section can be mapped to an instance of the following class:

```
public class EmailConfig
{
    public String FromName { get; set; }
    public String FromAddress { get; set; }
    public String LocalDomain { get; set; }

    public String MailServerAddress { get; set; }
    public String MailServerPort { get; set; }

    public String UserId { get; set; }
    public String UserPassword { get; set; }
}
```

The code that performs the mapping must be inserted into the ConfigureServices method in the Startup.cs file since the EmailConfig instance will be available through DI. The code we need is shown here:

```
public Startup(IConfiguration configuration)
{
    Configuration = configuration;
}
....
public void ConfigureServices(IServiceCollection services)
```

```
{
    ...
    services.Configure<EmailConfig>(Configuration.GetSection("Email"));
    ..
```

Once we've configured the preceding settings, classes that need `EmailConfig` data must declare an `IOptions<EmailConfig>` options parameter that will be provided by the DI engine. An `EmailConfig` instance is contained in `options.Value`.

It is worth mentioning that the option classes' properties can be applied to the same validation attributes we will use for ViewModels (see the *Server-side and client-side validation* subsection).

The next subsection describes the basic ASP.NET Core pipeline modules needed by an ASP.NET Core MVC application.

Defining the ASP.NET Core MVC pipeline

If you create a new ASP.NET Core MVC project in Visual Studio, a standard pipeline is created in the `Startup.cs` file's `Configure` method. There, if needed, you may add further modules or change the configuration of the existing modules.

The initial code of the `Configure` method handles errors and performs basic HTTPS configuration:

```
if (env.IsDevelopment())
{
    app.UseDeveloperExceptionPage();
}
else
{
    app.UseExceptionHandler("/Home/Error");
    app.UseHsts();
}
app.UseHttpsRedirection();
```

If there are errors, if the application is in a development environment, the module installed by `UseDeveloperExceptionPage` adds a detailed error report to the response. This module is a valuable debugging tool.

If an error occurs when the application is not in development mode, UseExceptionHandler restores the request processing from the path it receives as an argument; that is, from /Home/Error. In other words, it simulates a new request with the /Home/Error path. This request is pushed into the standard MVC processing until it reaches the endpoint associated with the /Home/Error path, where the developer is expected to place the custom code that handles the error.

When the application is not in development, UseHsts adds the Strict-Transport-Security header to the response, which informs the browser that the application must only be accessed with HTTPS. After this declaration, compliant browsers should automatically convert any HTTP request of the application into an HTTPS request for the time specified in the Strict-Transport-Security header. By default, UseHsts specifies 30 days as the time in the header, but you may specify a different time and other header parameters by adding an options object to the ConfigureServices method of Startup.cs:

```
services.AddHsts(options =>      {
    ...
    options.MaxAge = TimeSpan.FromDays(60);
    ...
});
```

UseHttpsRedirection causes an automatic redirection to an HTTPS URL when an HTTP URL is received, in a way that forces a secure connection. Once the first HTTPS secure connection is established, the Strict-Transport-Security header prevents future redirections that might be used to perform man-in-the-middle attacks.

The following code shows the remainder of the default pipeline:

```
app.UseStaticFiles();
app.UseCookiePolicy();

app.UseRouting();

app.UseAuthentication();
app.UseAuthorization();

...
```

UseStaticFiles makes all files contained in the wwwroot folder of the project (typically CSS, JavaScript, images, and font files) accessible from the web through their actual path.

UseCookiePolicy has been removed in the .NET 5 template, but you can still add it manually. It ensures that cookies are processed by the ASP.NET Core pipeline, but only if the user has given consent for cookie usage. Consent to cookie usage is given through a consent cookie; that is, cookie processing is enabled only if this consent cookie is found among the request cookies. This cookie must be created by JavaScript when the user clicks a consent button. The whole string that contains both the consent cookie's name and its contents can be retrieved from HttpContext.Features, as shown in the following snippet:

```
var consentFeature = context.Features.Get<ITrackingConsentFeature>();
var showBanner = !consentFeature?.CanTrack ?? false;
var cookieString = consentFeature?.CreateConsentCookie();
```

CanTrack is true only if consent is required and has not been given yet. When the consent cookie is detected, CanTrack is set to false. This way, showBanner is true only if consent is required and it has not been given yet. Therefore, it tells us whether to ask the user for consent or not.

The options for the consent module are contained in a CookiePolicyOptions instance that must be configured manually with the options framework. The following code snippet shows the default configuration code scaffolded by Visual Studio that configures CookiePolicyOptions in the code instead of using the configuration file:

```
services.Configure<CookiePolicyOptions>(options =>
{
    options.CheckConsentNeeded = context => true;
});
```

UseAuthentication enables authentication schemes and only appears if you select an authentication scheme when the project is created.

Specific authentication schemes can be enabled by configuring the options objects in the ConfigureServices method, as shown here:

```
services.AddAuthentication(o =>
{
    o.DefaultScheme =
    CookieAuthenticationDefaults.AuthenticationScheme;
})
.AddCookie(o =>
```

```
{
    o.Cookie.Name = "my_cookie";
})
.AddJwtBearer(o =>
{
    ...
});
```

The preceding code specifies a custom authentication cookie name and adds JWT-based authentication for the REST service contained in the application. Both AddCookie and AddJwtBearer have overloads that accept the name of the authentication scheme before the action, which is where you can define the authentication scheme options. Since the authentication scheme name is necessary for referring to a specific authentication scheme, when it is not specified, a default name is used:

- The standard name contained in CookieAuthenticationDefaults. AuthenticationScheme for cookie authentication.

- The standard name contained in JwtBearerDefaults.AuthenticationScheme for JWT authentication.

The name that's passed into o.DefaultScheme selects the authentication scheme used for filling the User property of HttpContext. Together with DefaultScheme, there are other properties that allow more advanced customizations.

> For more information about JWT authentication, please refer to the *ASP.NET Core service authorization* subsection of *Chapter 14, Applying Service-Oriented Architectures with .NET Core.*

If you just specify services.AddAuthentication(), a cookie-based authentication with default parameters is assumed.

UseAuthorization enables authorization based on the Authorize attribute. Options can be configured by placing the AddAuthorization method in the ConfigureServices method. These options allow you to define the policies for claims-based authorization.

> For more information on authorization, please refer to the *ASP. NET Core service authorization* subsection of *Chapter 14, Applying Service-Oriented Architectures with .NET Core.*

`UseRouting` and `UseEndpoints` handle the so-called ASP.NET Core endpoints. An endpoint is an abstraction of a handler that serves specific classes of URLs. These URLs are transformed into an `Endpoint` instance with patterns. When a pattern matches a URL, an `Endpoint` instance is created and filled with both the pattern's name and the data that was extracted from the URL. This is a consequence of matching URL parts with named parts of the pattern. This can be seen in the following code snippet:

```
Request path: /UnitedStates/NewYork
Pattern: Name="location", match="/{Country}/{Town}"


Endpoint: DisplayName="Location", Country="UnitedStates",
Town="NewYork"
```

`UseRouting` adds a module that processes the request path to get the request `Endpoint` instance and adds it to the `HttpContext.Features` dictionary under the `IEndpointFeature` type. The actual `Endpoint` instance is contained in the `Endpoint` property of `IEndpointFeature`.

Each pattern also contains the handler that should process all the requests that match the pattern. This handler is passed to `Endpoint` when it is created.

On the other hand, `UseEndpoints` adds the middleware that executes the route determined by the `UseRouting` logic. It is placed at the end of the pipeline since its middleware produces the final response. Splitting the routing logic into two separate middleware modules enables authorization middleware to sit in-between them and, based on the matched endpoint, to decide whether to pass the request to the `UseEndpoints` middleware for its normal execution, or whether to return a 401 (Unauthorized)/403 (Forbidden) response immediately.

As the following code snippet shows, patterns are processed in the `UseRouting` middleware, but they are listed in the `UseEndpoints` method. While it might appear strange that URL patterns are not defined directly in the middleware that uses them, this was done mainly for coherence with the previous ASP.NET Core versions. In fact, previous versions contained no method analogous to `UseRouting`, but a unique middleware at the end of the pipeline. In the new version, patterns are still defined at the end of the pipeline for coherence with previous versions, but now, `UseEndpoints` just creates a data structure containing all patterns when the application starts. Then, this data structure is processed by the `UseRouting` middleware, as shown in the following code:

```
app.UseRouting();


app.UseAuthentication();
```

```
app.UseAuthorization();

app.UseEndpoints(endpoints =>
{
    endpoints.MapControllerRoute(
        name: "default",
        pattern: "{controller=Home}/{action=Index}/{id?}");


});
```

`MapControllerRoute` defines the patterns associated with the MVC engine, which will be described in the next subsection. There are other methods that define other types of patterns. A call such as `.MapHub<MyHub>("/chat")` maps paths to hubs that handle **SignalR**, an abstraction built on top of `WebSocket`, whereas `.MapHealthChecks("/health")` maps paths to ASP.NET Core components that return application health data. You can also directly map a pattern to a custom handler with `.MapGet`, which intercepts GET requests, and `.MapPost`, which intercepts POST requests. This is called **route to code**. The following is an example of `MapGet`:

```
MapGet("hello/{country}", context =>
    context.Response.WriteAsync(
    $"Selected country is {context.GetRouteValue("country")}"));
```

Patterns are processed in the order in which they are defined until a matching pattern is found. Since the authentication/authorization middleware is placed after the routing middleware, it can process the `Endpoint` request to verify whether the current user has the required authorizations to execute the `Endpoint` handler. Otherwise, a 401 (Unauthorized) or 403 (Forbidden) response is immediately returned. Only requests that survive authentication and authorization have their handlers executed by the `UseEndpoints` middleware.

With the ASP.NET Core RESTful API described in *Chapter 14, Applying Service-Oriented Architectures with .NET Core*, ASP.NET Core MVC also uses attributes placed on controllers or controller methods to specify authorization rules. However, an instance of `AuthorizeAttribute` can be also added to a pattern to apply its authorization constraints to all the URLs matching that pattern, as shown in the following example:

```
endpoints
  .MapHealthChecks("/health")
  .RequireAuthorization(new AuthorizeAttribute(){ Roles = "admin", });
```

The preceding code makes the health check path available only to administrative users.

Having described the basic structure of the ASP.NET Core framework, we can now move toward more MVC-specific features. The next subsection describes controllers and explains how they interact with the UI components known as Views through ViewModels.

Defining controllers and ViewModels

The various `.MapControllerRoute` calls in `UseEndpoints` associate URL patterns with controllers and with the methods of these controllers, where controllers are classes that inherit from the `Microsoft.AspNetCore.Mvc.Controller` class. Controllers are discovered by inspecting all of the application's `.dll` files and are added to the DI engine. This job is performed by the call to `AddControllersWithViews` in the `ConfigureServices` method of the `startup.cs` file.

The pipeline module that's added by `UseEndpoints` takes the controller name from the `controller` pattern variable, and the name of the controller method to invoke from the `action` pattern variable. Since, by convention, all controller names are expected to end with the `Controller` suffix, the actual controller type name is obtained from the name found in the `controller` variable by adding this suffix. Hence, for instance, if the name found in `controller` is `"Home"`, then the `UseEndpoints` module tries to get an instance of the `HomeController` type from the DI engine. All of the controller public methods can be selected by the routing rules. Use of a controller public method can be prevented by decorating it with the `[NonAction]` attribute. All controller methods available to the routing rules are called action methods.

MVC controllers work like the API controllers that we described in the *Implementing REST services with ASP.NET Core* subsection of *Chapter 14, Applying Service-Oriented Architectures with .NET Core*. The only difference is that API controllers are expected to produce JSON or XML, while MVC controllers are expected to produce HTML. For this reason, while API controllers inherit from the `ControllerBase` class, MVC controllers inherit from the `Controller` class, which, in turn, inherits from the `ControllerBase` class and adds its methods that are useful for HTML generation, such as invoking views, which are described in the next subsection, and creating a redirect response.

MVC controllers may also use a routing technique similar to one of the API controllers; that is, routing based on controllers and controller method attributes. This behavior is enabled by calling the `MapControllerRoute()` method in `UseEndpoints`. If this call is placed before all other `MapControllerRoute` calls, then the controller routes have priority on `MapControllerRoute` patterns; otherwise, the opposite is true.

All the attributes we have seen for API controllers can be also used with MVC controllers and action methods (HttpGet, HttpPost, ...Authorize, and so on). Developers can write their own custom attributes by inheriting from the ActionFilter class or other derived classes. I will not give details on this right now, but these details can be found in the official documentation, which is referred to in the *Further reading* section.

When the UseEndpoints module invokes a controller, all of its constructor parameters are filled by the DI engine since the controller instance itself is returned by the DI engine, and since DI automatically fills constructor parameters with DI in a recursive fashion.

Action method parameters, on the other hand, are taken from the following sources:

- Request headers
- Variables in the pattern matched by the current request
- Query string parameters
- Form parameters (in the case of POST requests)
- Dependency injection (DI)

While the parameters filled with DI are matched by type, all other parameters are matched by *name* while ignoring the letter casing. That is, the action method parameter name must match the header, query string, form, or pattern variable. When the parameter is a complex type, a match is searched for in each property, using the property name for the match. In the case of nested complex types, a match is searched for each nested property's path, and the name associated with the path is obtained by chaining all the property names in the path and separating them with dots. For instance, Property1.Property2.Property3...Propertyn is the name associated with a path composed by the nested properties Property1, Property2, ..., Propertyn. The name that's obtained this way must match a header name, pattern variable name, query string parameter name, and so on. For instance, an OfficeAddress property containing a complex Address object would generate names like OfficeAddress.Country, OfficeAddress.Town, and so on.

By default, simple type parameters are matched with pattern variables and query string variables, while complex types parameters are matched with form parameters. However, the preceding defaults can be changed by prefixing the parameters with attributes, as detailed here:

- [FromForm] forces a match with form parameters
- [FromHeader] forces a match with a request header
- [FromRoute] forces a match with pattern variables

- [FromQuery] forces a match with a query string variable
- [FromServices] forces the use of DI

During the match, the string that was extracted from the selected source is converted into the type of the action method parameter using the current thread culture. If either a conversion fails or no match is found for an obligatory action method parameter, then the whole action method invocation process fails, and a 404 response is automatically returned. For instance, in the following example, the id parameter is matched with query string parameters or pattern variables since it is a simple type, while myclass properties and nested properties are matched with form parameters since MyClass is a complex type. Finally, myservice is taken from DI since it is prefixed with the [FromServices] attribute:

```
public class HomeController : Controller
{
    public IActionResult MyMethod(
        int id,
        MyClass myclass,
        [FromServices] MyService myservice)
    {
        ...
```

If no match is found for the id parameter and if the id parameter is declared as obligatory in the UseEndpoints pattern, a 404 response is automatically returned since pattern matching fails. It is common to declare parameters as not optional when they must match not nullable single types. If, instead, no MyService instance is found in the DI container, an exception is thrown because in this case, the failure doesn't depend on a wrong request but a design error.

MVC controllers return an IActionResult interface or a Task<IActionResult> result if they are declared as async. IActionResult defines the unique method with the Exec uteResultAsync(ActionContext) signature, which, when invoked by the framework, produces the actual response.

For each different IActionResult, MVC controllers have methods that return them. The most commonly used IActionResult is ViewResult, which is returned by a View method:

```
public IActionResult MyMethod(...)
{
    ...
    return View("myviewName", MyViewModel)
}
```

ViewResult is a very common way for a controller to create an HTML response. More specifically, the controller interacts with business/data layers to produce an abstraction of the data that will be shown in the HTML page. This abstraction is an object called a **ViewModel**. The ViewModel is passed as a second argument to the View method, while the first argument is the name of an HTML template, called View, that is instantiated with the data contained in the ViewModel.

Summing this up, the MVC controllers' processing sequence is as follows:

1. The controllers perform some processing to create the ViewModel, which is an abstraction of the data to show on the HTML page.

2. Then, the controllers create ViewResult by passing a View name and ViewModel to the View method.

3. The MVC framework invokes ViewResult and causes the template contained in the View to be instantiated with the data contained in the ViewModel.

4. The result of the template's instantiation is written in the response with adequate headers.

This way, the controller performs the conceptual job of HTML generation by building a ViewModel, while the View – that is, the template – takes care of all the graphical details.

Views will be described in greater detail in the next subsection, while the Model (ViewModel) View Controller pattern will be discussed in more detail in the *Understanding the connection between ASP.NET Core MVC and design principles* section of this chapter. Finally, a practical example will be provided in the *Use case – implementing a web app in ASP.NET Core MVC* section of this chapter.

Another common IActionResult is RedirectResult, which creates a redirect response, hence forcing the browser to move to a specific URL. Redirects are often used once the user has successfully submitted a form that completes a previous operation. In this case, it is common to redirect the user to a page where they can select another operation.

The simplest way to return RedirectResult is by passing a URL to the Redirect method. This is the advised way to perform a redirect to a URL that is outside the web application. On the other hand, when the URL is within the web application, it is advisable to use the RedirectToAction method, which accepts the controller name, the action method name, and the desired parameters for the target action method. The framework uses this data to compute a URL that causes the desired action method to be invoked with the provided parameters. This way, if the routing rules are changed during the application's development or maintenance, the new URL is automatically updated by the framework with no need to modify all occurrences of the old URL in the code.

The following code shows how to call `RedirectToAction`:

```
return RedirectToAction("MyActionName", "MyControllerName",
        new {par1Name=par1Value,..parNName=parNValue});
```

Another useful `IActionResult` is `ContentResult`, which can be created by calling the `Content` method. `ContentResult` allows you to write any string to the response and specify its MIME type, as shown in the following example:

```
return Content("this is plain text", "text/plain");
```

Finally, the `File` method returns `FileResult`, which writes binary data in the response. There are several overloads of this method that allow the specification of a byte array, a stream, or the path of a file, plus the MIME type of the binary data.

Now, let's move on to describing how actual HTML is generated in Views.

Understanding Razor Views

ASP.NET Core MVC uses a language called Razor to define the HTML templates contained in the Views. Razor views are files that are compiled into .NET classes when they're first used, when the application has been built, or when the application has been published. By default, both pre-compilation on each build and on publish are enabled, but you can also enable runtime compilation so that the Views can be modified once they have been deployed. This option can be enabled by checking the **Enable Razor runtime compilation** checkbox when the project is created in Visual Studio. You can also disable compilation on each build and on publish by adding the following code to the web application project file:

```
<PropertyGroup>
  <TargetFramework> net5.0 </TargetFramework>
  <!-- add code below -->
  <RazorCompileOnBuild>false</RazorCompileOnBuild>
  <RazorCompileOnPublish>false</RazorCompileOnPublish>
  <!-- end of code to add -->
    ...
</PropertyGroup>
```

Views can also be precompiled into views libraries if you choose a Razor view library project in the window that appears once you have chosen an ASP.NET Core project.

Also, after the compilation, views remain associated with their paths, which become their full names. Each controller has an associated folder under the **Views** folder with the same name as the controller, which is expected to contain all the views used by that controller.

The following screenshot shows the folder associated with `HomeController` and its Views:

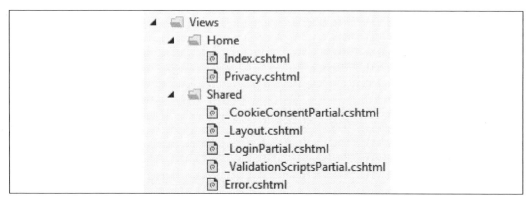

Figure 15.5: View folders associated with controllers and the shared folder

The preceding screenshot also shows the **Shared** folder, which is expected to contain all the views or partial views used by several controllers. The controller refers to views in the `View` method through their paths without the `.cshtml` extension. If the path starts with /, the path is interpreted as relative to the application root. Otherwise, as a first attempt, the path is interpreted as relative to the folder associated with the controller. If no view is found there, the view is searched for in the **Shared** folder.

Hence, for instance, the `Privacy.cshtml` View file in the preceding screenshot can be referred to from within `HomeController` as `View("Privacy", MyViewModel)`. If the name of the View is the same as the name of the action method, we can simply write `View(MyViewModel)`.

Razor views are a mix of HTML code with C# code, plus some Razor-specific statements. They all begin with a header that contains the type of ViewModel that the View is expected to receive:

```
@model MyViewModel
```

Each view may also contain some `using` statements whose effect is the same as the `using` statements of standard code files:

```
@model MyViewModel
@using MyApplication.Models
```

`@using` statements declared in the special `_ViewImports.cshtml` file – that is, in the root of the `Views` folder – are automatically applied to all views.

Each view can also require instances of types from the DI engine in its header with the syntax shown here:

```
@model MyViewModel
@using MyApplication.Models
@inject IViewLocalizer Localizer
```

The preceding code requires an instance of the IViewLocalizer interface and places it in the Localizer variable. The remainder of the View is a mix of C# code, HTML, and Razor control flow statements. Each area of a view can be either in HTML mode or C# mode. The code in a View area that is in HTML mode is interpreted as HTML, while the code in a View area that is in C# mode is interpreted as C#.

The topic that follows explains the Razor flow of control statements.

Learning the Razor flow of control statements

If you want to write some C# code in an HTML area, you can create a C# area with the @{..} Razor flow of control statement, as shown here:

```
@{
    //place C# code here
    var myVar = 5;
    ...
    <div>
        <!-- here you are in HTML mode again -->
        ...
    </div>
    //after the HTML block you are still in C# mode
    var x = "my string";
}
```

The preceding example shows that it is enough to write an HTML tag to create an HTML area inside of the C# area and so on recursively. As soon as the HTML tag closes, you are in C# mode again.

C# code produces no HTML, while HTML code is added to the response in the same order it appears. You can add text computed with C# code while in HTML mode by prefixing any C# expression with @. If the expression is complex in that it is composed of a chain of properties and method calls, it must be enclosed by parentheses. The following code shows some examples:

```
<span>Current date is: </span>
<span>@DateTime.Today.ToString("d")</span>
...
<p>
  User name is: @(myName+ " "+mySurname)
</p>
...
<input type="submit" value="@myUserMessage" />
```

Types are converted into strings using the current culture settings (see the *Understanding the connection between ASP.NET Core MVC and design principles* section for details on how to set the culture of each request). Moreover, strings are automatically HTML encoded to avoid the < and > symbols, which might interfere with the view HTML. HTML encoding can be prevented with the @HTML.Raw function, as shown here:

```
@HTML.Raw(myDynamicHtml)
```

In an HTML area, alternative HTML can be selected with the @if Razor statement:

```
@if(myUser.IsRegistered)
{
    //this is a C# code area
    var x=5;
    ...
    <p>
     <!-- This is an HTML area -->
    </p>
    //this is a C# code area again
}
else if(callType == CallType.WebApi)
{
    ...
}
else
{
  ..
}
```

As shown in the preceding code, the beginning of each block of a Razor control flow statement is in C# mode and remains in C# mode until the first HTML open tag is encountered, and then HTML mode starts. C# mode is resumed after the corresponding HTML close tag.

An HTML template can be instantiated several times with the for, foreach, while, and do Razor statements, as shown in the following examples:

```
@for(int i=0; i< 10; i++)
{

}

@foreach(var x in myIEnumerable)
{

}

@while(true)
{

}
@do
{

}
while(true)
```

Razor views can contain comments that do not generate any code. Any text included within @*...*@ is considered a comment and is removed when the page is compiled. The next topic describes properties that are available in all Views.

Understanding Razor View properties

Some standard variables are predefined in each view. The most important variable is Model, which contains the ViewModel that was passed to the view. For instance, if we pass a Person model to a view, then @Model.Name displays the name of the Person model that was passed to the view.

The ViewData variable contains IDictionary<string, object>, which is shared with the controller that invoked the view. That is, all controllers also have a ViewData property containing IDictionary<string, object>, and every entry that is set in the controller is also available in the ViewData variable of the invoked view. ViewData is an alternative to the ViewModel for a controller for passing information to its invoked view. It is worth mentioning that the ViewState dictionary can also be accessed as a dynamic object through the ViewBag property. This means that dynamic ViewBag properties are mapped to ViewData string indices and that their values are mapped to the ViewState entries corresponding to those indices.

The User variable contains the currently logged user; that is, the same instance contained in the current request's Http.Context.User property. The Url variable contains an instance of the IUrlHelper interface whose methods are utilities for computing the URLs of application pages. For instance, Url.Action("action", "controller", new {par1=valueOfPar1,...}) computes the URL that causes the action method, *action*, of the *controller* to be invoked with all the parameters specified in the anonymous object passed as its parameters.

The Context variable contains the whole request's HttpContext. The ViewContext variable contains data about the context of the view invocation, including metadata about the action method that invoked the view.

The next topic describes how Razor enhances HTML tag syntax.

Using Razor tag helpers

In ASP.NET Core MVC, the developer can define so-called tag helpers, which either enhance existing HTML tags with new tag attributes or define new tags. While Razor views are compiled, any tag is matched against existing tag helpers. When a match is found, the source tag is replaced with HTML created by the tag helpers. Several tag helpers may be defined for the same tag. They are all executed in an order that can be configured with a priority attribute associated with each tag helper.

All tag helpers defined for the same tag may cooperate while each tag instance is being processed. This is because they are passed a shared data structure where each of them may apply a contribution. Usually, the final tag helper that is invoked processes this shared data structure to produce the output HTML.

Tag helpers are classes that inherit from the TagHelper class. This topic doesn't discuss how to create new tag helpers but introduces the main predefined tag helpers that come with ASP.NET Core MVC. A complete guide on how to define tag helpers is available in the official documentation, which is referenced in the *Further reading* section.

To use a tag helper, you must declare the .dll file containing it with a declaration like the following:

```
@addTagHelper *, Dll.Complete.Name
```

If you would like to use just one of the tag helpers defined in the .dll file, you must replace * with the tag name.

The preceding declaration can be placed either in each view that uses the tag helpers defined in the library or, once and for all, in the _ViewImports.cshtml file in the root of the Views folder. By default, _ViewImports.cshtml adds all predefined ASP.NET Core MVC tag helpers with the following declaration:

```
@addTagHelper *, Microsoft.AspNetCore.Mvc.TagHelpers
```

The anchor tag is enhanced with attributes that automatically compute the URL and that invoke a specific action method with given parameters, as shown here:

```
<a asp-controller="{controller name}"
asp-action="{action method name}"
asp-route-{action method parameter1}="value1"
...
asp-route-{action method parametern}="valuen">
    put anchor text here
</a>
```

A similar syntax is added to the form tags:

```
<form asp-controller="{controller name}"
asp-action="{action method name}"
asp-route-{action method parameter1}="value1"
...
asp-route-{action method parametern}="valuen"
...
>
    ...
```

The script tag is enhanced with attributes that allow us to fall back to a different source if the download fails. Typical usage is to download scripts from some cloud service to optimize the browser cache and to fall back to a local copy of the script in case of failure. The following code uses the fallback technique to download the bootstrap JavaScript file:

```
<script src="https://stackpath.bootstrapcdn.com/
bootstrap/4.3.1/js/bootstrap.bundle.min.js"
asp-fallback-src="~/lib/bootstrap/dist/js/
bootstrap.bundle.min.js"
asp-fallback-test="window.jQuery && window.jQuery.fn && window.jQuery.
fn.modal" crossorigin="anonymous"
integrity="sha384-xrRywqdh3PHs8keKZN+8zzc5TX0GRTLCcmivcbNJWm2rs5C8PRhcE
n3czEjhAO9o">
</script>
```

`asp-fallback-test` contains a JavaScript test that verifies whether the download succeeded. In the preceding example, the test verifies whether a JavaScript object has been created.

The environment tag can be used to select different HTML for different environments (development, staging, and production). Its typical usage is selecting the debug versions of JavaScript files during development, as shown in this example:

```
<environment include="Development">
        @*development version of JavaScript files*@
</environment>
<environment exclude="Development">
        @*development version of JavaScript files *@
</environment>
```

There is also a `cache` tag, which caches its content in memory to optimize rendering speed:

```
<cache>
    @* heavy to compute content to cache *@
</cache>
```

By default, content is cached for 20 minutes, but the tag has attributes that must be defined when the cache expires, such as `expires-on="{datetime}"`, `expires-after="{timespan}"`, and `expires-sliding="{timespan}"`. Here, the difference between `expires-sliding` and `expires-after` is that, in the second attribute, the expiration time count is reset each time the content is requested. The `vary-by` attribute causes the creation of a different cache entry for each different value passed to `vary-by`. There are also attributes such as `vary-by-header`, which creates a different entry for each different value assumed by the request header specified in the attribute; `vary-by-cookie`; and so on.

All input tags – that is, `textarea`, `input`, and `select` – have an `asp-for` attribute that accepts a properties path rooted in the view's ViewModel as their value. For instance, if the view has a `Person` ViewModel, we may have something like this:

```
<input type="text" asp-for"Address.Town"/>
```

The first thing the preceding code does is assign the value of the `Town` nested property to the `value` attribute of the `input` tag. In general, if the value is not a string, it is converted into a string using the current request culture.

However, it also sets the name of the input field to `Address.Town` and the ID of the input field to `Address_Town`. This is because dots are not allowed in tag IDs.

A prefix can be added to these standard names by specifying it in `ViewData.TemplateInfo.HtmlFieldPrefix`. For instance, if the previous property is set to `MyPerson`, the name becomes `MyPerson.Address.Town`.

If the form is submitted to an action method that has the same `Person` class as one of its parameters, the name of `Address.Town` that's given to the input field will cause the `Town` property of this parameter to be filled with the input field. In general, the string contained in the input field is converted into the type of property it has been matched with using the current request culture. Summing this up, names of input fields are created in such a way that a complete `Person` model can be recovered in the action method when the HTML page is posted.

The same `asp-for` attribute can be used in a `label` tag to cause the label to refer to the input field with the same `asp-for` value.

The following code is an example of an `input`/`label` pair:

```
<label asp-for="Address.Town"></label
<input type="text" asp-for="Address.Town"/>
```

When no text is inserted into the label, the text shown in the label is taken from a `Display` attribute that decorates the property (`Town`, in this example), if any; otherwise, the name of the property is used.

If span or div contains an `asp-validation-for` =`"Address.Town"` error attribute, then validation messages concerning the `Address.Town` input will be inserted automatically inside that tag. The validation framework will be described in the *Understanding the connection between ASP.NET Core MVC and design principles* section.

It is also possible to automatically create a validation error summary by adding the attribute that follows a div or a span:

```
asp-validation-summary="ValidationSummary.{All, ModelOnly}"
```

If the attribute is set to `ValidationSummary.ModelOnly`, only messages that are not associated with specific input fields will be shown in the summary, while if the value is `ValidationSummary.All`, all error messages will be shown.

The `asp-items` attribute can be applied to any `select` tag in order to automatically generate all `select` options. It must be passed an `IEnumerable<SelectListItem>`, where each `SelectListItem` contains both the text and value of an option. `SelectListItem` also contains an optional `Group` property you can use to organize the options shown in `select` into groups.

The next topic shows how to reuse view code.

Reusing view code

ASP.NET Core MVC includes several techniques for reusing view code. The most important is the layout page.

In each web application, several pages share the same structure; for instance, the same main menu or the same left or right bar. In ASP.NET Core, this common structure is factored out in views called layout pages/views.

Each view can specify the view to be used as its layout page with the following code:

```
@{
    Layout = "_MyLayout";
}
```

If no layout page is specified, a default layout page, defined in the _ViewStart. cshtml file located in the Views folder, is used. The default content of _ViewStart. cshtml is as follows:

```
@{
    Layout = "_Layout";
}
```

Therefore, the default layout page in the files scaffolded by Visual Studio is _Layout. cshtml, which is contained in the Shared folder.

The layout page contains the HTML that's shared with all of its children pages, the HTML page headers, and the page references to CSS and JavaScript files. The HTML produced by each view is placed inside of its layout place, where the layout page calls the @RenderBody() method, as shown in the following example:

```
...
<main role="main" class="pb-3">
    ...
    @RenderBody()
    ...
</main>
...
```

ViewState of each View is copied into ViewState of its layout page, so ViewState can be used to pass information to the view layout page. Typically, it is used to pass the view title to the layout page, which then uses it to compose the page's title header, as shown here:

```
@*In the view *@

@{
```

```
    ViewData["Title"] = "Home Page";
}


@*In the layout view*@
<head>
    <meta charset="utf-8" />
    ...
    <title>@ViewData["Title"] - My web application</title>
    ...
```

While the main content produced by each view is placed in a single area of its layout page, each layout page can also define several sections placed in different areas where each view can place further secondary content.

For instance, suppose a layout page defines a Scripts section, as shown here:

```
...
<script src="~/js/site.js" asp-append-version="true"></script>

@RenderSection("Scripts", required: false)
...
```

Then, the view can use the previously defined section to pass some view-specific JavaScript references, as shown here:

```
.....
@section scripts{
    <script src="~/js/pages/pageSpecificJavaScript.min.js"></script>
}
.....
```

If an action method is expected to return HTML to an AJAX call, it must produce an HTML fragment instead of a whole HTML page. Therefore, in this case, no layout page must be used. This is achieved by calling the PartialView method instead of the View method in the controller action method. PartialView and View have exactly the same overloads and parameters.

Another way to reuse view code is to factor out a view fragment that's common to several views into another view that is called by all previous views. A view can call another view with the partial tag, as shown here:

```
<partial name="_viewname" for="ModelProperty.NestedProperty"/>
```

The preceding code invokes _viewname and passes it the object contained in Model. ModelProperty.NestedProperty as its ViewModel. When a view is invoked by the partial tag, no layout page is used since the called view is expected to return an HTML fragment.

The ViewData.TemplateInfo.HtmlFieldPrefix property of the called view is set to the "ModelProperty.NestedProperty" string. This way, possible input fields rendered in _viewname.cshtml will have the same name as if they had been rendered directly by the calling view.

Instead of specifying the ViewModel of _viewname through a property of the caller view (ViewModel), you can also directly pass an object that is contained in a variable or returned by a C# expression by replacing for with model, as shown in this example:

```
<partial name="_viewname" model="new MyModel{...})" />
```

In this case, the ViewData.TemplateInfo.HtmlFieldPrefix property of the called view keeps its default value; that is, the empty string.

A view can also call something more complex than another view; that is, another controller method that, in turn, renders a view. Controllers that are designed to be invoked by views are called **view components**. The following code is an example of component invocation:

```
<vc:[view-component-name] par1="par1 value" par2="parameter2 value"> </
vc:[view-component-name]>
```

Parameter names must match the ones used in the view component method. However, both the component's name and parameter names must be translated into kebab case; that is, all the characters must be transformed into lowercase if all the characters that were in the original name were in uppercase, though the first one word must be preceded by a -. For instance, MyParam must be transformed into my-param.

Actually, view components are classes that derive from the ViewComponent class. When a component is invoked, the framework looks for either an Invoke method or an InvokeAsync method and passes it all the parameters that were defined in the component's invocation. InvokeAsync must be used if the method is defined as async; otherwise, we must use Invoke.

The following code is an example of a view component definition:

```
public class MyTestViewComponent : ViewComponent
    {

        public async Task<IViewComponentResult> InvokeAsync(
        int par1, bool par2)
        {
            var model= ....
            return View("ViewName", model);
        }


    }
```

The previously defined component must be invoked with a call such as the following:

```
<vc:my-test par1="10" par2="true"></my-test>
```

If the component is invoked by a view of a controller called `MyController`, `ViewName` is searched for in the following paths:

- `/Views/MyController/Components/MyTest/ViewName`
- `/Views/Shared/Components/MyTest/ViewName`

Now, let's look at the more recent relevant features of ASP.NET Core.

What is new in the latest versions of ASP. NET Core?

The main change for ASP.NET Core took place in version 3.0: the routing engine was factored out of the MVC engine and is now also available for other handlers. In previous versions, routes and routing were a part of the MVC handler and were added with `app.UseMvc(....)`; this has now been replaced with `app.UseRouting()` and `UseEndpoints(...)`, which can route requests not only to controllers but also to other handlers.

Endpoints and their associated handlers are now defined in `UseEndpoints`, as shown here:

```
app.UseEndpoints(endpoints =>
    {
```

```
        ...
        endpoints.MapControllerRoute("default", "
        {controller=Home}/{action=Index}/{id?}");
        ...
    });
```

MapControllerRoute associates patterns with controllers, but we may also use something such as endpoints.MapHub<ChatHub>("/chat"), which associates a pattern with a hub that handles WebSocket connections. In the previous section, we saw that patterns can also be associated with custom handlers using MapPost and MapGet.

An independent router also allows us to add authorizations not only to controllers but also to any handler, as shown here:

```
MapGet("hello/{country}", context =>
    context.Response.WriteAsync(
    $"Selected country is {context.GetRouteValue("country")}"))
    .RequireAuthorization(new AuthorizeAttribute(){ Roles = "admin" });
```

Moreover, ASP.NET Core now has an independent JSON formatter and doesn't depend on the third-party Newtonsoft JSON serializer anymore. However, if you have compatibility issues, you still have the option to replace the minimal ASP. NET Core JSON formatter with the Newtonsoft JSON serializer by installing the Microsoft.AspNetCore.Mvc.NewtonsoftJson NuGet package and configuring the controllers, as shown here:

```
services.AddControllersWithViews()
    .AddNewtonsoftJson();
```

Here, AddNewtonsoftJson also has an overload that accepts the configuration options for the Newtonsoft JSON serializer:

```
.AddNewtonsoftJson(options =>
        options.SerializerSettings.ContractResolver =
        new CamelCasePropertyNamesContractResolver());
```

Microsoft's JSON serializer was introduced in version 3, but at the beginning, its implementation was minimal. Now, in .NET 5, it offers options that are comparable to the ones of the Newtonsoft JSON serializer.

In versions previous to 3.0, you were forced to add both controllers and views to the DI engine. Now, you can still inject both controllers and views with services. AddControllersWithViews, but you can also add controllers with AddControllers if you are going to implement REST endpoints only.

Version 5 brought significant performance improvements due to improvements in .NET performance, improvements in the JIT compiler, which now generate shorter and more optimized code, and due to improvements in the HTTP/2 protocol implementation. Basically, you can rely on a doubled computation speed, along with more efficient memory and garbage collection handling.

Understanding the connection between ASP.NET Core MVC and design principles

The whole ASP.NET Core framework is built on top of the design principles and patterns that we analyzed in *Chapter 5, Applying a Microservice Architecture to Your Enterprise Application, Chapter 8, Interacting with Data in C# – Entity Framework Core, Chapter 11, Design Patterns and .NET 5 Implementation, Chapter 12, Understanding the Different Domains in Software Solutions*, and *Chapter 13, Implementing Code Reusability in C# 9*.

Moreover, all framework functionalities are provided through DI so that each of them can be replaced by a customized counterpart without it affecting the remainder of the code. However, these providers are not added individually to the DI engine; instead, they are grouped into option objects (see the *Loading configuration data and using it with the options framework* subsection) in order to conform to the SOLID Single Responsibility Principle. This is the case, for instance, for all model binders, validation providers, and data annotation providers.

Moreover, configuration data, instead of being available from a unique dictionary created from a configuration file, is organized into option objects thanks to the options framework we described in the first section of this chapter. This is also an application of the SOLID Interface Segregation Principle.

However, ASP.NET Core also applies other patterns that are specific instances of the general Separation of Concerns principle, which is a generalization of the Single Responsibility Principle. They are as follows:

- The middleware modules architecture (ASP.NET Core pipeline)
- Factoring out validation and globalization from the application code
- The MVC pattern itself

We will analyze each of these in the various subsections that follow.

Advantages of the ASP.NET Core pipeline

The ASP.NET Core pipeline architecture has two important advantages:

- All the different operations that are performed on the initial request are factored out into different modules, according to the Single Responsibility Principle.

- The modules that perform these different operations don't need to call each other because each module is invoked once and for all by the ASP.NET Core framework. This way, the code for each module is not required to perform any action that is connected to responsibilities that have been assigned to other modules.

This ensures maximum independence of functionalities and simpler code. For instance, once authorization and authentication modules are on, no other module needs to worry about authorization anymore. Each controller code can focus on application-specific business stuff.

Server-side and client-side validation

Validation logic has been completely factored out from the application code and has been confined to the definition of validation attributes. The developer just needs to specify the validation rule to apply to each model property by decorating the property with an adequate validation attribute.

Validation rules are checked automatically when action method parameters are instantiated. Both errors and paths in the model (where they occurred) are then recorded in a dictionary that is contained in the ModelState controller property. The developer has the responsibility of verifying whether there are errors by checking ModelState.IsValid, in which case the developer must return the same ViewModel to the same view so that the user can correct all errors.

Error messages are automatically shown in the view with no action required from the developer. The developer is only required to do the following:

- Add span or div with an asp-validation-for attribute next to each input field, which will be automatically filled with the possible error.

- Add div with an asp-validation-summary attribute that will be automatically filled with the validation error summary. See the *Using Razor tag helpers* section for more details.

It is enough to add some JavaScript references by invoking the _
ValidationScriptsPartial.cshtml view with the partial tag to enable the same
validation rules on the client side, so that errors are shown to the user before the
form is posted to the server. Some predefined validation attributes are contained
in the System.ComponentModel.DataAnnotations and Microsoft.AspNetCore.Mvc
namespaces and include the following attributes:

- The Required attribute requires the user to specify a value for the property
  that it decorates. An implicit Required attribute is automatically applied to all
  non-nullable properties, such as all floats, integers, and decimals, since they
  can't have a null value.

- The Range attribute constrains numeric quantities within a range.

- They also include attributes that constrain string lengths.

Custom error messages can be inserted directly into the attributes, or attributes can
refer to the property of resource types containing them.

The developer can define their custom attributes by providing the validation code
both in C# and in JavaScript for client-side validation.

Attribute-based validation can be replaced by other validation providers, such
as fluent validation that defines validation rules for each type using a fluent
interface. It is enough to change a provider in a collection contained in the MVC
options object. This can be configured through an action passed to the services.
AddControllersWithViews method. MVC options can be configured as follows:

```
services.AddControllersWithViews(o => {
    ...
    // code that modifies o properties
});
```

The validation framework automatically checks whether numeric and date inputs
are well-formatted according to the selected culture.

ASP.NET Core globalization

In multicultural applications, pages must be served according to the language and
culture preferences of each user. Typically, multicultural applications can serve
their content in a few languages, and they can handle dates and numeric formats in
several more languages. In fact, while the content in all supported languages must be
produced manually, .NET Core has the native capability of formatting and parsing
dates and numbers in all cultures.

For instance, a web application might not support unique content for all English-based cultures (en), but might support all known English-based cultures for numbers and dates formats (en-US, en-GB, en-CA, and so on).

The culture used for numbers and dates in a .NET thread is contained in the `Thread.CurrentThread.CurrentCulture` property. Hence, by setting this property to new `CultureInfo("en-CA")`, numbers and dates will be formatted/parsed according to the Canadian culture. `Thread.CurrentThread.CurrentUICulture`, instead, decides on the culture of the resource files; that is, it selects a culture-specific version of each resource file or view. Accordingly, a multicultural application is required to set the two cultures associated with the request thread and organize multilingual content into language-dependent resource files and/or views.

According to the Separation of Concerns principle, the whole logic used to set the request culture according to the user's preferences is factored out into a specific module of the ASP.NET Core pipeline. To configure this module, as a first step, we set the supported date/numbers cultures, as in the following example:

```
var supportedCultures = new[]
{

    new CultureInfo("en-AU"),
    new CultureInfo("en-GB"),
    new CultureInfo("en"),
    new CultureInfo("es-MX"),
    new CultureInfo("es"),
    new CultureInfo("fr-CA"),
    new CultureInfo("fr"),
    new CultureInfo("it-CH"),
    new CultureInfo("it")
};
```

Then, we set the languages supported for the content. Usually, a version of the language that is not specific for any country is selected to keep the number of translations small enough, as shown here:

```
var supportedUICultures = new[]
{
    new CultureInfo("en"),
    new CultureInfo("es"),
    new CultureInfo("fr"),
    new CultureInfo("it")
};
```

Then, we add the culture middleware to the pipeline, as shown here:

```
app.UseRequestLocalization(new RequestLocalizationOptions
{
    DefaultRequestCulture = new RequestCulture("en", "en"),

    // Formatting numbers, dates, etc.
    SupportedCultures = supportedCultures,
    // UI strings that we have localized.
    SupportedUICultures = supportedUICultures,
    FallBackToParentCultures = true,
    FallBackToParentUICultures = true
});
```

If the culture requested by the user is explicitly found among the ones listed in supportedCultures or supportedUICultures, it is used without modifications. Otherwise, since FallBackToParentCultures and FallBackToParentUICultures are true, the parent culture is tried; that is, for instance, if the required fr-FR culture is not found among those listed, then the framework searches for its generic version, fr. If this attempt also fails, the framework uses the cultures specified in DefaultRequestCulture.

By default, the culture middleware searches the culture selected for the current user with three providers that are tried in the order shown here:

1. The middleware looks for the culture and ui-culture query string parameters.

2. If the previous step fails, the middleware looks for a cookie named .AspNetCore.Culture, the value of which is expected to be as in this example: c=en-US|uic=en.

3. If both previous steps fail, the middleware looks for the Accept-Language request header sent by the browser, which can be changed in the browser settings, and which is initially set to the operating system culture.

With the preceding strategy, the first time a user requests an application page, the browser culture is taken (the provider listed in *step 3*). Then, if the user clicks a language-change link with the right query string parameters, a new culture is selected by provider 1. Usually, once a language link has been clicked, the server also generates a language cookie to remember the user's choice through provider 2.

The simplest way to provide content localization is to provide a different view for each language. Hence, if we would like to localize the Home.cshtml view for different languages, we must provide views named Home.en.cshtml, Home.es.cshtml, and so on. If no view specific to the ui-culture thread is found, the not localized Home.cshtml version of the view is chosen.

View localization must be enabled by calling the `AddViewLocalization` method, as shown here:

```
services.AddControllersWithViews()
    .AddViewLocalization(LanguageViewLocationExpanderFormat.Suffix)
```

Another option is to store simple strings or HTML fragments in resource files specific for all supported languages. The usage of resource files must be enabled by calling the `AddLocalization` method in the configure services section, as shown here:

```
services.AddLocalization(options =>
    options.ResourcesPath = "Resources");
```

`ResourcesPath` is the root folder where all resource files will be placed. If it is not specified, an empty string is assumed, and the resource files will be placed in the web application root. Resource files for a specific view, say, the /Views/Home/Index.cshtml view, must have a path like this:

```
<ResourcesPath >/Views/Home/Index.<culture name>.resx
```

Hence, if `ResourcesPath` is empty, resources must have the /Views/Home/Index.<culture name>.resx path; that is, they must be placed in the same folder as the view.

Once the key-value pairs for all the resource files associated with a view have been added, localized HTML fragments can be added to the view, as follows:

- Inject `IViewLocalizer` into the view with `@inject IViewLocalizer Localizer`.

- Where needed, replace the text in the View with accesses to the `Localizer` dictionary, such as `Localizer["myKey"]`, where `"myKey"` is a key used in the resource files.

The following code shows an example of the `IViewLocalizer` dictionary:

```
@{
    ViewData["Title"] = Localizer["HomePageTitle"];
}
<h2>@ViewData["MyTitle"]</h2>
```

If localization fails because the key is not found in the resource file, the key itself is returned. Strings used in data annotation, such as validation attributes, are used as keys in resource files if data annotation localization is enabled, as shown here:

```
services.AddControllersWithViews()
    .AddViewLocalization(LanguageViewLocationExpanderFormat.Suffix)
    .AddDataAnnotationsLocalization();
```

Resource files for data annotations applied to a class whose full name is, say, `MyWebApplication.ViewModels.Account.RegisterViewModel`, must have the following path:

```
<ResourcesPath >/ViewModels/Account/RegisterViewModel.<culture name>.
resx
```

It is worth pointing out that the first segment of the namespace that corresponds to the `.dll` application name is replaced with `ResourcesPath`. If `ResourcesPath` is empty and if you use the default namespaces created by Visual Studio, then the resource files must be placed in the same folder that contains the classes they are associated with.

It is possible to localize strings and HTML fragments in controllers, or wherever dependencies can be injected, by associating each group of resource files with a type, such as `MyType`, and then injecting either `IHtmlLocalizer<MyType>` for HTML fragments or `IStringLocalizer<MyType>` for strings that need to be HTML encoded.

Their usage is identical to the usage of `IViewLocalizer`. The path of the resource files associated with `MyType` is computed as in the case of data annotations. If you would like to use a unique group of resource files for the whole application, a common choice is to use the `Startup` class as the reference type (`IStringLocalizer<Startup >` and `IHtmlLocalizer<Startup >`). Another common choice is to create various empty classes to use as reference types for various groups of resource files.

Now that we've learned how to manage globalization in your ASP.NET Core projects, in the next subsection, we will describe the more important pattern used by ASP.NET Core MVC to enforce *Separation of Concerns*: the MVC pattern itself.

The MVC pattern

MVC is a pattern used to implement the presentation layers of a web application. The basic idea is to apply a *Separation of Concerns* between the logic of the presentation layer and its graphics. Logic is taken care of by controllers, while graphics are factored out into views. Controllers and views communicate through the model, which is often called the ViewModel to distinguish it from the models of the business and data layers.

However, what is the logic of a presentation layer? In *Chapter 1, Understanding the Importance of Software Architecture*, we saw that software requirements can be documented with use cases that describe the interaction between the user and the system.

Roughly speaking, the logic of the presentation layer consists of the management of use cases; hence, roughly, use cases are mapped to controllers and every single operation of a use case is mapped to an action method of those controllers. Hence, controllers take care of managing the protocol of interaction with the user and rely on the business layer for any business processing involved during each operation.

Each action method receives data from the user, performs some business processing, and, depending on the results of this processing, decides what to show to the user and encodes it in the ViewModel. Views receive ViewModels that describe what to show to the user and decide the graphics to use; that is, the HTML to use.

What are the advantages of separating logic and graphics into two different components? The main advantages are listed here:

- Changes in graphics do not affect the remainder of the code, so you can experiment with various graphic options to optimize the interaction with the user without putting the reliability of the remainder of the code at risk.

- The application can be tested by instantiating controllers and passing the parameters, with no need to use testing tools that operate on the browser pages. In this way, tests are easier to implement. Moreover, they do not depend on the way graphics are implemented, so they do not need to be updated each time the graphics change.

- It is easier to split the job between developers that implement controllers and graphic designers that implement views. Often, graphic designers have difficulties with Razor, so they might just furnish an example HTML page that developers transform into Razor views that operate on the actual data.

Now, let's look at how to create a web app in ASP.NET Core MVC.

Use case – implementing a web app in ASP.NET Core MVC

In this section, as an example of the ASP.NET Core application, we will implement the administrative panel for managing the destinations and packages of the WWTravelClub book use case. The application will be implemented with the **Domain-Driven Design (DDD)** approach described in *Chapter 12, Understanding the Different Domains in Software Solutions*. So, having a good understanding of that chapter is a fundamental prerequisite to reading this section. The subsections that follow describe the overall application specifications and organization, and then the various application parts.

Defining application specifications

The destinations and packages were described in *Chapter 8, Interacting with Data in C# – Entity Framework Core*. Here, we will use exactly the same data model, with the necessary modifications to adapt it to the DDD approach. The administrative panel must allow packages, a destinations listing, and CRUD operations on it. To simplify the application, the two listings will be quite simple: the application will show all destinations sorted according to their names, while all packages will be sorted starting from the ones with a higher-end validity date.

Moreover, we suppose the following things:

- The application that shows destinations and packages to the user shares the same database used by the administrative panel. Since only the administrative panel application needs to modify data, there will be just one write copy of the database with several read-only replicas.

- Price modifications and package deletions are immediately used to update the user's shopping carts. For this reason, the administrative application must send asynchronous communications about price changes and package removals. We will not implement the whole communication logic here, but we will just add all such events to an event table, which should be used as input to a parallel thread that's in charge of sending these events to all relevant microservices.

Here, we will give the full code for just package management; most of the code for destination management is left as an exercise for you. The full code is available in the ch15 folder of the GitHub repository associated with this book. In the remainder of this section, we will describe the application's overall organization and discuss some relevant samples of code.

Defining the application architecture

The application is organized based on the guidelines described in *Chapter 12, Understanding the Different Domains in Software Solution*, while considering the DDD approach and using SOLID principles to map your domain sections. That is, the application is organized into three layers, each implemented as a different project:

- There's a data layer that contains the repository's implementation and the classes describing database entities. It is a .NET Core library project. However, since it needs some interfaces like IServiceCollection, which are defined in Microsoft.NET.Sdk.web, we must add a reference not only to the .NET Core SDK but also to the ASP.NET Core SDK. This can be done as follows:
    1. Right-click on the project icon in the solution explorer and select **Edit project file**.

2. In the edit window add:

```
<ItemGroup>
    <FrameworkReference Include="Microsoft.AspNetCore.App" />
</ItemGroup>
```

- There's also a domain layer that contains repository specifications; that is, interfaces that describe repository implementations and DDD aggregates. In our implementation, we decided to implement aggregates by hiding the forbidden operations/properties of root data entities behind interfaces. Hence, for instance, the Package data layer class, which is an aggregate root, has a corresponding IPackage interface in the domain layer that hides all the property setters of the Package entity. The domain layer also contains the definitions of all the domain events, while the corresponding event handlers are defined in the application layer.

- Finally, there's the application layer – that is, the ASP.NET Core MVC application – where we define DDD queries, commands, command handlers, and event handlers. Controllers fill query objects and execute them to get ViewModels they can pass to views. They update storage by filling command objects and executing their associated command handlers. In turn, command handlers use IRepository interfaces and IUnitOfWork coming from the domain layer to manage and coordinate transactions.

The application uses the Query Command Segregation pattern; therefore, it uses command objects to modify the storage and the query object to query it.

The query is simple to use and implement: controllers fill their parameters and then call their execution methods. In turn, query objects have direct LINQ implementations that project results directly onto the ViewModels used by the controller Views with Select LINQ methods. You may also decide to hide the LINQ implementation behind the same repository classes used for the storage update operations, but this would turn the definition and modification of simple queries into very time-consuming tasks.

In any case, it is good practice to hide query objects behind interfaces so that their implementations can be replaced by fake implementations when you test controllers.

However, the chain of objects and calls involved in the execution of commands is more complex. This is because it requires the construction and modification of aggregates, as well as a definition of the interaction between several aggregates and between aggregates and other applications through domain events to be provided.

The following diagram is a sketch of how storage update operations are performed. The circles are data being exchanged between the various layers, while rectangles are the procedures that process them. Moreover, dotted arrows connect interfaces with types that implement them:

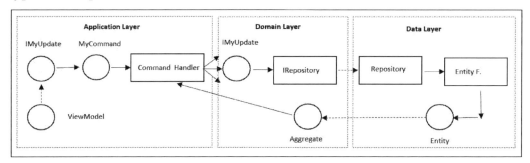

Figure 15.6: Diagram of command execution

Here's the flow of action through *Figure 15.6* as a list of steps:

1. A controller's action method receives one or more ViewModels and performs validation.

2. One or more ViewModels containing changes to apply are hidden behind interfaces (IMyUpdate) defined in the domain layer. They are used to fill the properties of a command object. These interfaces must be defined in the domain layer since they will be used as arguments of the repository methods defined there.

3. A command handler matching the previous command is retrieved via DI in the controller action method (through the[FromServices] parameter attribute we described in the *Defining Controllers and ViewModels* subsection). Then, the handler is executed. During its execution, the handler interacts with various repository interface methods and with the aggregates they return.

4. When creating the command handler discussed in *step 3*, the ASP.NET Core DI engine automatically injects all parameters declared in its constructor. In particular, it injects all IRepository implementations needed to perform all command handler transactions. The command handler performs its job by calling the methods of these IRepository implementations received in its constructor to build aggregates and modify the built aggregates. Aggregates either represent already-existing entities or newly created ones. Handlers use the IUnitOfWork interface contained in each IRepository, as well as the concurrency exceptions returned by the data layer, to organize their operations as transactions. It is worth pointing out that each aggregate has its own IRepository, and that the whole logic for updating each aggregate is defined in the aggregate itself, not in its associated IRepository, to keep the code more modular.

5. Behind the scenes, in the data layer, IRepository implementations use Entity Framework to perform their job. Aggregates are implemented by root data entities hidden behind interfaces defined in the domain layer, while IUnitOfWork methods, which handle transactions and pass changes to the database, are implemented with DbContext methods. In other words, IUnitOfWork is implemented with the application's DbContext.

6. Domain events are generated during each aggregate process and are added to the aggregates themselves by us calling their AddDomainEvent methods. However, they are not triggered immediately. Usually, they are triggered at the end of all the aggregates' processing and before changes are passed to the database; however, this is not a general rule.

7. The application handles errors by throwing exceptions. A more efficient approach would be to define a request-scoped object in the dependency engine, where each application subpart may add its errors as domain events. However, while this approach is more efficient, it increases the complexity of the code and the application development time.

The Visual Studio solution is composed of three projects:

- There's a project containing the domain layer called PackagesManagementDomain, which is a .NET Standard 2.0 library.

- There's a project containing the whole data layer called PackagesManagementDB, which is a .NET 5.0 library.

- Finally, there's an ASP.NET Core MVC 5.0 project called PackagesManagement that contains both application and presentation layers. When you define this project, select **no authentication**; otherwise, the user database will be added directly to the ASP.NET Core MVC project instead of to the database layer. We will add the user database manually in the data layer.

Let's start by creating the PackagesManagement ASP.NET Core MVC project so that the whole solution has the same name as the ASP.NET Core MVC project. Then, we'll add the other two library projects to the same solution.

Finally, let the ASP.NET Core MVC project reference both projects, while PackagesManagementDB references PackagesManagementDomain. We suggest you define your own projects and then copy the code of this book's GitHub repository into them as you read this section.

The next subsection describes the code of the PackagesManagementDomain data layer project.

Defining the domain layer

Once the `PackagesManagementDomain` standard 2.0 library project has been added to the solution, we'll add a `Tools` folder to the project root. Then, we'll place all the `DomainLayer` tools contained in the code associated with chapter 12. Since the code contained in this folder uses data annotations and defines DI extension methods, we must also add references to the `System.ComponentModel.Annotations` and `Microsoft.Extensions.DependencyInjection` NuGet packages.

Then, we need an `Aggregates` folder containing all the aggregate definitions (remember, we implemented aggregates as interfaces); namely, `IDestination`, `IPackage`, and `IPackageEvent`. Here, `IPackageEvent` is the aggregate associated with the table where we will place events to be propagated to other applications.

As an example, let's analyze `IPackage`:

```
public interface IPackage : IEntity<int>
{
    void FullUpdate(IPackageFullEditDTO o);
    string Name { get; set; }

    string Description { get;}
    decimal Price { get; set; }
    int DurationInDays { get; }
    DateTime? StartValidityDate { get;}
    DateTime? EndValidityDate { get; }
    int DestinationId { get; }

}
```

It contains the same properties of the `Package` entity, which we saw in *Chapter 8, Interacting with Data in C# – Entity Framework Core*. The only differences are the following:

- It inherits from `IEntity<int>`, which furnishes all basic functionalities of aggregates.
- It has no `Id` property since it is inherited from `IEntity<int>`.
- All properties are read-only, and it has a `FullUpdate` method since all aggregates can only be modified through update operations defined in the user domain (in our case, the `FullUpdate` method).

Now, let's also add a DTOs folder. Here, we place all interfaces used to pass updates to the aggregates. Such interfaces are implemented by the application layer ViewModels used to define such updates. In our case, it contains IPackageFullEditDTO, which we can use to update existing packages. If you would like to add the logic to manage destinations, you must define an analogous interface for the IDestination aggregate.

An IRepository folder contains all repository specifications; namely, IDestinationRepository, IPackageRepository, and IPackageEventRepository. Here, IPackageEventRepository is the repository associated with the IPackageEvent aggregate. As an example, let's have a look at the IPackageRepository repository:

```
public interface IPackageRepository:
        IRepository<IPackage>
{
    Task<IPackage> Get(int id);
    IPackage New();
    Task<IPackage> Delete(int id);
}
```

Repositories always contain just a few methods since all business logic should be represented as aggregate methods – in our case, just the methods to create a new package, to retrieve an existing package, and to delete an existing package. The logic to modify an existing package is included in the FullUpdate method of IPackage.

Finally, as with all domain layer projects, PackagesManagementDomain contains an event folder containing all domain event definitions. In our case, the folder is named Events and contains the package-deleted event and the price-changed event:

```
public class PackageDeleteEvent: IEventNotification
{
    public PackageDeleteEvent(int id, long oldVersion)
    {
        PackageId = id;
        OldVersion = oldVersion;
    }
    public int PackageId { get; }
    public long OldVersion { get; }


}
```

```
public class PackagePriceChangedEvent: IEventNotification
{
    public PackagePriceChangedEvent(int id, decimal price,
        long oldVersion, long newVersion)
    {
            PackageId = id;
            NewPrice = price;
            OldVersion = oldVersion;
            NewVersion = newVersion;
     }
    public int PackageId { get; }
    public decimal NewPrice { get; }
    public long OldVersion { get; }
    public long NewVersion { get; }
}
```

When an aggregate sends all its changes to another application, it must have a version property. The application that receives the changes uses this version property to apply all changes in the right order. An explicit version number is necessary because changes are sent asynchronously, so the order they are received in may differ from the order they were sent in. For this purpose, events that are used to publish changes outside of the application have both OldVersion (the version before the change) and NewVersion (the version after the change) properties. Events associated with delete events have no NewVersion since after being deleted, an entity can't store any versions.

The next subsection explains how all interfaces defined in the domain layer are implemented in the data layer.

Defining the data layer

The data layer project contains references to the Microsoft.AspNetCore.Identity. EntityFrameworkCore and Microsoft.EntityFrameworkCore.SqlServer NuGet packages, since we use Entity Framework Core with SQL server. It references Microsoft.EntityFrameworkCore.Tools and Microsoft.EntityFrameworkCore. Design, which are needed to generate database migrations, as explained in the *Entity Framework Core migrations* section of *Chapter 8, Interacting with Data in C# – Entity Framework Core*.

We have a Models folder that contains all database entities. They are similar to the ones in *Chapter 8, Interacting with Data in C# – Entity Framework Core*. The only differences are as follows:

- They inherit from `Entity<T>`, which contains all basic features of aggregates. Please notice that inheriting from `Entity<T>` is only needed for aggregate roots; all other entities must be defined as explained in *Chapter 8, Interacting with Data in C# – Entity Framework Core*. In our example, all entities are aggregate roots.

- They have no `Id` since it is inherited from `Entity<T>`.

- Some of them have an `EntityVersion` property that is decorated with the `[ConcurrencyCheck]` attribute. It contains the entity version that is needed for sending a property all entity changes to other applications. The `ConcurrencyCheck` attribute is needed to prevent concurrency errors while updating the entity version. This prevents suffering the performance penalty implied by a transaction.

More specifically, when saving entity changes, if the value of a field marked with the `ConcurrencyCheck` attribute is different from the one that was read when the entity was loaded in memory, a concurrency exception is thrown to inform the calling method that someone else modified this value after the entity was read, but before we attempted to save its changes. This way, the calling method can repeat the whole operation with the hope that, this time, no one will write the same entity in the database during its execution.

It is worth analyzing the `Package` entity:

```
public class Package: Entity<int>, IPackage
{
    public void FullUpdate(IPackageFullEditDTO o)
    {
        if (IsTransient())
        {
            Id = o.Id;
            DestinationId = o.DestinationId;
        }
        else
        {
            if (o.Price != this.Price)
                this.AddDomainEvent(new PackagePriceChangedEvent(
                        Id, o.Price, EntityVersion, EntityVersion+1));
        }
        Name = o.Name;
        Description = o.Description;
        Price = o.Price;
```

```
        DurationInDays = o.DurationInDays;
        StartValidityDate = o.StartValidityDate;
        EndValidityDate = o.EndValidityDate;
    }
    [MaxLength(128), Required]
    public string Name { get; set; }
    [MaxLength(128)]
    public string Description { get; set; }
    public decimal Price { get; set; }
    public int DurationInDays { get; set; }
    public DateTime? StartValidityDate { get; set; }
    public DateTime? EndValidityDate { get; set; }
    public Destination MyDestination { get; set; }
    [ConcurrencyCheck]
    public long EntityVersion{ get; set; }

    public int DestinationId { get; set; }
}
```

The `FullUpdate` method is the only way to update the `IPackage` aggregate when the price changes add `PackagePriceChangedEvent` to the entity list of events.

The `MainDBContext.cs` file contains the data layer database context definition. It doesn't inherit from `DBContext` but from the following predefined context class:

```
IdentityDbContext<IdentityUser<int>, IdentityRole<int>, int>
```

This context defines the user's tables needed for the authentication. In our case, we opted for the `IdentityUser<T>` standard and `IdentityRole<S>` for users and roles, respectively, and used integers for both the `T` and `S` Entity keys. However, we may also use classes that inherit from `IdentityUser` and `IdentityRole` and then add further properties.

In the `OnModelCreating` method, we must call `base.OnModelCreating(builder)` in order to apply the configuration defined in `IdentityDbContext`.

`MainDBContext` implements `IUnitOfWork`. The following code shows the implementation of all methods that start, roll back, and commit a transaction:

```
public async Task StartAsync()
{
    await Database.BeginTransactionAsync();
}
```

```
public Task CommitAsync()
{
    Database.CommitTransaction();
    return Task.CompletedTask;
}

public Task RollbackAsync()
{
    Database.RollbackTransaction();
    return Task.CompletedTask;
}
```

However, they are rarely used by command classes in a distributed environment. This is because retrying the same operation until no concurrency exception is returned usually ensures better performance than transactions.

It is worth analyzing the implementation of the method that passes all changes applied to DbContext to the database:

```
public async Task<bool> SaveEntitiesAsync()
{
    try
    {
        return await SaveChangesAsync() > 0;
    }
    catch (DbUpdateConcurrencyException ex)
    {
        foreach (var entry in ex.Entries)
        {

            entry.State = EntityState.Detached;

        }
        throw;
    }
}
```

The preceding implementation just calls the SaveChangesAsync DbContext context method, which saves all changes to the database, but then it intercepts all concurrency exceptions and detaches all the entities involved in the concurrency error from the context. This way, next time a command retries the whole failed operation, their updated versions will be reloaded from the database.

The Repositories folder contains all repository implementations. It is worth analyzing the implementation of the IPackageRepository.Delete method:

```
public async Task<IPackage> Delete(int id)
{
    var model = await Get(id);
    if (model is not Package package) return null;
    context.Packages.Remove(package);
    model.AddDomainEvent(
        new PackageDeleteEvent(
            model.Id, package.EntityVersion));
    return model;
}
```

It reads the entity from the database and formally removes it from the Packages dataset. This will force the entity to be deleted in the database when changes are saved to the database. Moreover, it adds PackageDeleteEvent to the aggregate list of events.

The Extensions folder contains the DBExtensions static class, which, in turn, defines two extension methods to be added to the application DI engine and the ASP.NET Core pipeline, respectively. Once added to the pipeline, these two methods will connect the database layer to the application layer.

The IServiceCollection extension of AddDbLayer accepts (as its input parameters) the database connection string and the name of the .dll file that contains all migrations. Then, it does the following:

```
services.AddDbContext<MainDbContext>(options =>
            options.UseSqlServer(connectionString,
            b => b.MigrationsAssembly(migrationAssembly)));
```

That is, it adds the database context to the DI engine and defines its options; namely, that it uses SQL Server, the database connection string, and the name of the .dll file that contains all migrations.

Then, it does the following:

```
services.AddIdentity<IdentityUser<int>, IdentityRole<int>>()
            .AddEntityFrameworkStores<MainDbContext>()
            .AddDefaultTokenProviders();
```

That is, it adds and configures all the types needed to handle database-based authentication. In particular, it adds the UserManager and RoleManager types, which the application layer can use to manage users and roles. AddDefaultTokenProviders adds the provider that creates the authentication tokens using data contained in the database when users log in.

Finally, it discovers and adds to the DI engine all repository implementations by calling the `AddAllRepositories` method, which is defined in the DDD tools we added to the domain layer project.

The `UseDBLayer` extension method ensures migrations are applied to the database by calling `context.Database.Migrate()` and then populates the database with some initial objects. In our case, it uses `RoleManager` and `UserManager` to create an administrative role and an initial administrator, respectively. Then, it creates some sample destinations and packages.

 `context.Database.Migrate()`is useful to quickly set up and update staging and test environments. When deploying in production, instead, an SQL script should be produced from the migrations using the migration tools. Then, this script should be examined before being applied by the person in charge of maintaining the database.

To create migrations, we must add the aforementioned extension methods to the ASP.NET Core MVC `Startup.cs` file, as shown here:

```
public void ConfigureServices(IServiceCollection services)
{
    ...
    services.AddRazorPages();
    services.AddDbLayer(
        Configuration.GetConnectionString("DefaultConnection"),
        "PackagesManagementDB");


public void Configure(IApplicationBuilder app,
    IWebHostEnvironment env)
    ...
    app.UseAuthentication();
    app.UseAuthorization();
    ...
}
```

Please be sure that both the authorization and authentication modules have been added to the ASP.NET Core pipeline; otherwise, the authentication/authorization engine will not work.

Then, we must add the connection string to the `appsettings.json` file, as shown here:

```
{
    "ConnectionStrings": {
        "DefaultConnection": "Server=(localdb)\\
mssqllocaldb;Database=package-management;Trusted_Connection=True;Multip
leActiveResultSets=true"

    },
    ...
}
```

Finally, let's add `Microsoft.EntityFrameworkCore.Design` to the ASP.NET Core project.

At this point, let's open Visual Studio Package Manager Console, select `PackageManagementDB` as the default project, and then launch the following command:

```
Add-Migration Initial -Project PackageManagementDB
```

The preceding command will scaffold the first migration. We may apply it to the database with the `Update-Database` command. Please note that if you copy the project from GitHub, you don't need to scaffold migrations since they have already been created, but you still need to update the database.

The next subsection describes the application layer.

Defining the application layer

As a first step, for simplicity, let's freeze the application culture to en-US by adding the code that follows to the ASP.NET Core pipeline:

```
app.UseAuthorization();

// Code to add: configure the Localization middleware
var ci = new CultureInfo("en-US");
app.UseRequestLocalization(new RequestLocalizationOptions
{
    DefaultRequestCulture = new RequestCulture(ci),
    SupportedCultures = new List<CultureInfo>
    {
        ci,
    },
     SupportedUICultures = new List<CultureInfo>
```

```
    {
        ci,
    }
});
```

Then, let's create a `Tools` folder and place the `ApplicationLayer` code there, which you may find in the `ch12` code of the GitHub repository associated with this book. With these tools in place, we can add the code that automatically discovers and adds all queries, command handlers, and event handlers to the DI engine, as shown here:

```
public void ConfigureServices(IServiceCollection services)
{
    ...
    ...
    services.AddAllQueries(this.GetType().Assembly);
    services.AddAllCommandHandlers(this.GetType().Assembly);
    services.AddAllEventHandlers(this.GetType().Assembly);
}
```

Then, we must add a `Queries` folder to place all queries and their associated interfaces. As an example, let's have a look at the query that lists all packages:

```
public class PackagesListQuery:IPackagesListQuery
{
    private readonly MainDbContext ctx;
    public PackagesListQuery(MainDbContext ctx)
    {
        this.ctx = ctx;
    }
    public async Task<IEnumerable<PackageInfosViewModel>>
GetAllPackages()
    {
        return await ctx.Packages.Select(m => new PackageInfosViewModel
        {
            StartValidityDate = m.StartValidityDate,
            EndValidityDate = m.EndValidityDate,
            Name = m.Name,
            DurationInDays = m.DurationInDays,
            Id = m.Id,
            Price = m.Price,
            DestinationName = m.MyDestination.Name,
            DestinationId = m.DestinationId
```

```
    })
            .OrderByDescending(m=> m.EndValidityDate)
            .ToListAsync();
    }
}
```

The query object is automatically injected into the application DB context. The
GetAllPackages method uses LINQ to project all of the required information
into PackageInfosViewModel and sorts all results in descending order on the
EndValidityDate property.

PackageInfosViewModel is placed in the Models folder together with all other
ViewModels. It is good practice to organize ViewModels into folders by defining
a different folder for each controller. It is worth analyzing the ViewModel used for
editing packages:

```
public class PackageFullEditViewModel: IPackageFullEditDTO
    {
        public PackageFullEditViewModel() { }
        public PackageFullEditViewModel(IPackage o)
        {
            Id = o.Id;
            DestinationId = o.DestinationId;
            Name = o.Name;
            Description = o.Description;
            Price = o.Price;
            DurationInDays = o.DurationInDays;
            StartValidityDate = o.StartValidityDate;
            EndValidityDate = o.EndValidityDate;
        }
        ...
        ...
```

It has a constructor that accepts an IPackage aggregate. This way, package data is
copied into the ViewModel that is used to populate the edit view. It implements the
IPackageFullEditDTO DTO interface defined in the domain layer. This way, it can be
directly used to send IPackage updates to the domain layer.

All properties contain validation attributes that are automatically used by client-side
and server-side validation engines. Each property contains a Display attribute that
defines the label to give to the input field that will be used to edit the property. It is
better to place the field labels in the ViewModels than placing them directly into the
views since, this way, the same names are automatically used in all views that use
the same ViewModel. The following code block lists all its properties:

```
public int Id { get; set; }
[StringLength(128, MinimumLength = 5), Required]
[Display(Name = "name")]
public string Name { get; set; }
[Display(Name = "package infos")]
[StringLength(128, MinimumLength = 10), Required]
public string Description { get; set; }
[Display(Name = "price")]
[Range(0, 100000)]
public decimal Price { get; set; }
[Display(Name = "duration in days")]
[Range(1, 90)]
public int DurationInDays { get; set; }
[Display(Name = "available from"), Required]
public DateTime? StartValidityDate { get; set; }
[Display(Name = "available to"), Required]
public DateTime? EndValidityDate { get; set; }
[Display(Name = "destination")]
public int DestinationId { get; set; }
```

The `Commands` folder contains all commands. As an example, let's have a look at the command used to modify packages:

```
public class UpdatePackageCommand: ICommand
{
    public UpdatePackageCommand(IPackageFullEditDTO updates)
    {
        Updates = updates;
    }
    public IPackageFullEditDTO Updates { get; private set; }
}
```

Its constructor must be invoked with an implementation of the `IPackageFullEditDTO` DTO interface, which, in our case, is the edit ViewModel we described previously. Command handlers are placed in the `Handlers` folder. It is worth analyzing the command that updates packages:

```
IPackageRepository repo;
IEventMediator mediator;
public UpdatePackageCommandHandler(IPackageRepository repo,
IEventMediator mediator)
{
    this.repo = repo;
    this.mediator = mediator;
}
```

Its constructor has automatically injected the IPackageRepository repository and an IEventMediator instance needed to trigger event handlers. The following code also shows the implementation of the standard HandleAsync command handler method:

```
public async Task HandleAsync(UpdatePackageCommand command)
{
    bool done = false;
    IPackage model;
    while (!done)
    {
        try
        {
            model = await repo.Get(command.Updates.Id);
            if (model == null) return;
            model.FullUpdate(command.Updates);
            await mediator.TriggerEvents(model.DomainEvents);
            await repo.UnitOfWork.SaveEntitiesAsync();
            done = true;
        }
        catch (DbUpdateConcurrencyException)
        {
            // add some logging here
        }
    }
}
```

Command operations are repeated until no concurrency exception is returned. HandleAsync uses the repository to get an instance of the entity to modify. If the entity is not found (it has been deleted), the commands stop its execution. Otherwise, all changes are passed to the retrieved aggregate. Immediately after the update, all events contained in the aggregate are triggered. In particular, if the price has changed, the event handler associated with the price change is executed. The concurrency check declared with the [ConcurrencyCheck] attribute on the EntityVersion property of the Package entity ensures that the package version is updated properly (by incrementing its previous version number by 1), as well as that the price changed event is passed the right version numbers.

Also, event handlers are placed in the Handlers folder. As an example, let's have a look at the price changed event handler:

```
public class PackagePriceChangedEventHandler :
    IEventHandler<PackagePriceChangedEvent>
{
```

```
    private readonly IPackageEventRepository repo;
    public PackagePriceChangedEventHandler(IPackageEventRepository
repo)
    {
        this.repo = repo;
    }
    public Task HandleAsync(PackagePriceChangedEvent ev)
    {
        repo.New(PackageEventType.CostChanged, ev.PackageId,
            ev.OldVersion, ev.NewVersion, ev.NewPrice);
      return Task.CompletedTask;
    }
}
```

The constructor has automatically injected the IPackageEventRepository repository that handles the database table and all the events to send to other applications. The HandleAsync implementation simply calls the repository method that adds a new record to this table.

All records in the table are handled by IPackageEventRepository, which can be retrieved and sent to all interested microservices by a parallel task defined in the DI engine with a call such as services.AddHostedService<MyHostedService>(); , as detailed in the *Using generic hosts* subsection of *Chapter 5, Applying Microservice Architecture to Your Enterprise Application*. However, this parallel task is not implemented in the GitHub code associated with this chapter.

The next subsection describes how controllers and views are designed.

Controllers and views

We need to add two more controllers to the one automatically scaffolded by Visual Studio; namely, AccountController, which takes care of user login/logout and registration, and ManagePackageController, which handles all package-related operations. It is enough to right-click on the Controllers folder and then select **Add | Controller**. Then, choose the controller name and select the empty MVC controller to avoid the possibility of Visual Studio scaffolding code you don't need.

For simplicity, AccountController just has login and logout methods, so you can log in just with the initial administrator user. However, you can add further action methods that use the UserManager class to define, update, and delete users. The UserManager class can be provided through DI, as shown here:

```
private readonly UserManager<IdentityUser<int>> _userManager;
private readonly SignInManager<IdentityUser<int>> _signInManager;
```

```
public AccountController(
    UserManager<IdentityUser<int>> userManager,
    SignInManager<IdentityUser<int>> signInManager)
{
    _userManager = userManager;
    _signInManager = signInManager;
}
```

SignInManager takes care of login/logout operations. The Logout action method is quite simple and is shown here:

```
[HttpPost]
public async Task<IActionResult> Logout()
{
    await _signInManager.SignOutAsync();
    return RedirectToAction(nameof(HomeController.Index), "Home");
}
```

It just calls the signInManager.SignOutAsync method and then redirects the browser to the home page. To avoid it being called by clicking a link, it is decorated with HttpPost, so it can only be invoked via a form submit.

Login, on the other hand, requires two action methods. The first one is invoked via Get and shows the login form, where the user must place their username and password. It is shown here:

```
[HttpGet]
public async Task<IActionResult> Login(string returnUrl = null)
{
    // Clear the existing external cookie
    //to ensure a clean login process
    await HttpContext
        .SignOutAsync(IdentityConstants.ExternalScheme);
    ViewData["ReturnUrl"] = returnUrl;
    return View();
}
```

It receives returnUrl as its parameter when the browser is automatically redirected to the login page by the authorization module. This happens when an unlogged user tries to access a protected page. returnUrl is stored in the ViewState dictionary that is passed to the login view. The form in the login view passes it back, together with the username and password, to the controller when it is submitted, as shown in this code:

```
<form asp-route-returnurl="@ViewData["ReturnUrl"]" method="post">
...
</form>
```

The form post is intercepted by an action method with the same Login name but decorated with the [HttpPost] attribute, as shown here:

```
[ValidateAntiForgeryToken]
public async Task<IActionResult> Login(
    LoginViewModel model,
    string returnUrl = null)
        {
            ...
```

The preceding method receives the Login model used by the login view, together with the returnUrl query string parameter. The ValidateAntiForgeryToken attribute verifies a token (called an anti-forgery token) that MVC forms automatically. This is then added to a hidden field to prevent cross-site attacks.

As a first step, the action method logs the user out if they are already logged in:

```
if (User.Identity.IsAuthenticated)
{
        await _signInManager.SignOutAsync();

}
```

Otherwise, it verifies whether there are validation errors, in which case it shows the same view filled with the data of the ViewModel to let the user correct their errors:

```
if (ModelState.IsValid)
{
    ...
}
else
// If we got this far, something failed, redisplay form
 return View(model);
```

If the model is valid, _signInManager is used to log the user in:

```
var result = await _signInManager.PasswordSignInAsync(
    model.UserName,
    model.Password, model.RememberMe,
    lockoutOnFailure: false);
```

If the result returned by the operation is successful, the action method redirects the browser to `returnUrl` if it's not null; otherwise, it redirects the browser to the home page:

```
if (result.Succeeded)
{
    if (!string.IsNullOrEmpty(returnUrl))
        return LocalRedirect(returnUrl);
    else
        return RedirectToAction(nameof(HomeController.Index), "Home");
}
else
{
    ModelState.AddModelError(string.Empty,
        "wrong username or password");
    return View(model);
}
```

If the login fails, it adds an error to `ModelState` and shows the same form to let the user try again.

`ManagePackagesController` contains an `Index` method that shows all packages in table format:

```
[HttpGet]
public async Task<IActionResult> Index(
    [FromServices]IPackagesListQuery query)
{
    var results = await query.GetAllPackages();
    var vm = new PackagesListViewModel { Items = results };
    return View(vm);
}
```

The query object is injected into the action method by DI. Then, the action method invokes it and inserts the resulting `IEnumerable` into the `Items` property of a `PackagesListViewModel` instance. It is a good practice to include `IEnumerables` in ViewModels instead of passing them directly to the views so that, if necessary, other properties can be added without the need to modify the existing view code. Results are shown in a Bootstrap 4 table since Bootstrap 4 CSS is automatically scaffolded by Visual Studio.

The result is shown here:

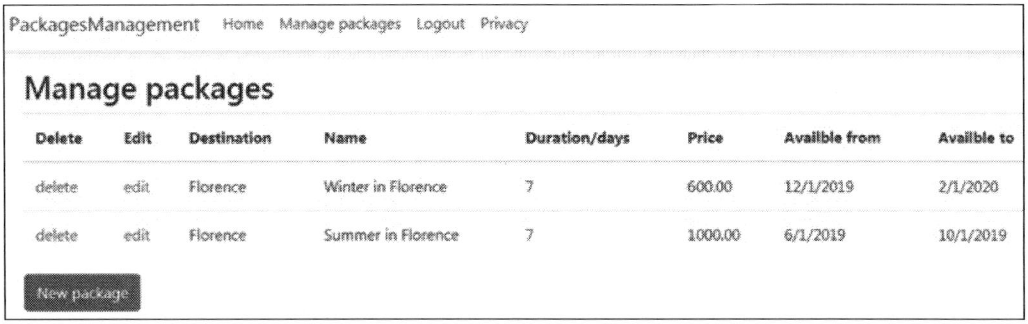
PackagesManagement
Home
Manage packages
Logout
Privacy
Manage packages
Delete
Edit
Destination
Name
Duration/days
Price
Availble from
Availble to
delete
edit
Florence
Winter in Florence
7
600.00
12/1/2019
2/1/2020
delete
edit
Florence
Summer in Florence
7
1000.00
6/1/2019
10/1/2019
New package

Figure 15.7: Application packages handling page

The **New package** link (it is shaped like a **Bootstrap 4** button, but it is a link) invokes a controller `Create` action method, while the **delete** and **edit** links in each row invoke a `Delete` and `Edit` action method, respectively, and pass them the ID of the package shown in the row. Here is the implementation of the two-row links:

```
@foreach(var package in Model.Items)
{
<tr>
    <td>
        <a asp-controller="ManagePackages"
            asp-action="@nameof(ManagePackagesController.Delete)"
            asp-route-id="@package.Id">
            delete
        </a>
    </td>
    <td>
        <a asp-controller="ManagePackages"
            asp-action="@nameof(ManagePackagesController.Edit)"
            asp-route-id="@package.Id">
            edit
        </a>
    </td>
    ...
    ...
```

It is worth describing the code of the `HttpGet` and `HttpPost` `Edit` action methods:

```
[HttpGet]
public async Task<IActionResult> Edit(
```

```
        int id,
        [FromServices] IPackageRepository repo)
    {

        if (id == 0) return RedirectToAction(
            nameof(ManagePackagesController.Index));
        var aggregate = await repo.Get(id);
        if (aggregate == null) return RedirectToAction(
            nameof(ManagePackagesController.Index));
        var vm = new PackageFullEditViewModel(aggregate);
        return View(vm);
    }
```

The `Edit` method of `HttpGet` uses `IPackageRepository` to retrieve the existing package. If the package is not found, that means it has been deleted by some other user, and the browser is redirected again to the list page to show the updated list of packages. Otherwise, the aggregate is passed to the `PackageFullEditViewModel` ViewModel, which is rendered by the `Edit` view.

The view used to render the package must render `select` with all possible package destinations, so it needs an instance of the `IDestinationListQuery` query that was implemented to assist with the destination selection HTML logic. This query is injected directly into the view since it is the view's responsibility to decide how to enable the user to select a destination. The code that injects the query and uses it is shown here:

```
@inject PackagesManagement.Queries.IDestinationListQuery
destinationsQuery
@{
    ViewData["Title"] = "Edit/Create package";
    var allDestinations =
        await destinationsQuery.AllDestinations();
}
```

The action method that processes the post of the view form is given here:

```
[HttpPost]
public async Task<IActionResult> Edit(
    PackageFullEditViewModel vm,
    [FromServices] ICommandHandler<UpdatePackageCommand> command)
{
    if (ModelState.IsValid)
    {
        await command.HandleAsync(new UpdatePackageCommand(vm));
```

```
        return RedirectToAction(
            nameof(ManagePackagesController.Index));
    }
    else
        return View(vm);
}
```

If `ModelState` is valid, `UpdatePackageCommand` is created and its associated handler is invoked; otherwise, the View is displayed again to the user to enable them to correct all the errors.

The new links to the package list page and login page must be added to the main menu, which is in the _Layout view, as shown here:

```
<li class="nav-item">
    <a class="nav-link text-dark"
        asp-controller="ManagePackages"
            asp-action="Index">Manage packages</a>
</li>
@if (User.Identity.IsAuthenticated)
{
    <li class="nav-item">
        <a class="nav-link text-dark"
            href="javascript:document.getElementById('logoutForm').
submit()">
            Logout
        </a>
    </li>
}
else
{
    <li class="nav-item">
        <a class="nav-link text-dark"
            asp-controller="Account" asp-action="Login">Login</a>
    </li>
}
```

`logoutForm` is an empty form whose only purpose is to send a post to the `Logout` action method. It has been added to the end of the body, as shown here:

```
@if (User.Identity.IsAuthenticated)
{
    <form asp-area="" asp-controller="Account"
```

```
            asp-action="Logout" method="post"
            id="logoutForm" ></form>
}
```

Now, the application is ready! You can run it, log in, and start to manage packages.

Summary

In this chapter, we analyzed the ASP.NET Core pipeline and various modules that comprise an ASP.NET Core MVC application in detail, such as authentication/authorization, the options framework, and routing. Then, we described how controllers and Views map requests to response HTML. We also analyzed all the improvements introduced in the latest versions.

Finally, we analyzed all the design patterns implemented in the ASP.NET Core MVC framework and, in particular, the importance of the Separation of Concerns principle and how ASP.NET Core MVC implements it in the ASP.NET Core pipeline, as well as in its validation and globalization modules. We focused in more detail on the importance of Separation of Concerns between the presentation layer logic and graphics, as well as how the MVC pattern ensures it.

The next chapter explains how to implement a presentation layer as a **Single-Page Application (SPA)** with the new Blazor WebAssembly framework.

Questions

1. Can you list all the middleware modules scaffolded by Visual Studio in an ASP.NET Core project?

2. Does the ASP.NET Core pipeline module need to inherit from a base class or implement some interface?

3. Is it true that a tag must have just one tag helper defined for it, otherwise an exception is thrown?

4. Do you remember how to test if validation errors have occurred in a controller?

5. What is the instruction in a layout view for including the output of the main view that's called?

6. How are secondary sections of the main view invoked in a layout view?

7. How does a controller invoke a view?

8. By default, how many providers are installed in the globalization module?

9. Are ViewModels the only way for controllers to communicate with their invoked views?

Further reading

- More details on the ASP.NET MVC framework are available in its official documentation at `https://docs.microsoft.com/en-US/aspnet/core/`

- More details on the Razor syntax can be found at `https://docs.microsoft.com/en-us/aspnet/core/razor-pages/?tabs=visual-studio`.

- Documentation on the creation custom tag helpers that were not discussed in this chapter can be found at `https://docs.microsoft.com/en-US/aspnet/core/mvc/views/tag-helpers/authoring`.

- Documentation on the creation of custom controller attributes can be found at `https://docs.microsoft.com/en-US/aspnet/core/mvc/controllers/filters`.

- The definition of custom validation attributes is discussed in this article: `https://blogs.msdn.microsoft.com/mvpawardprogram/2017/01/03/asp-net-core-mvc/`.

16

Blazor WebAssembly

In this chapter, you will learn how to implement a presentation layer with Blazor WebAssembly. Blazor WebAssembly applications are C# applications that can run in any browser that supports the WebAssembly technology. They can be accessed by navigating to a specific URL and are downloaded in the browser as standard static content, made of HTML pages and downloadable files.

Blazor applications use many technologies we already analyzed in *Chapter 15, Presenting ASP.NET Core MVC*, such as dependency injection and Razor. Therefore, we strongly recommend studying *Chapter 15, Presenting ASP.NET Core MVC*, before reading this chapter.

More specifically, in this chapter, you will learn about the following subjects:

- Blazor WebAssembly architecture
- Blazor pages and components
- Blazor forms and validation
- Blazor advanced features, such as globalization, authentication, and JavaScript interoperability
- Third-party tools for Blazor WebAssembly
- Use case: implementing a simple application in Blazor WebAssembly

While there is also server-side Blazor, which runs on the server like ASP.NET Core MVC, this chapter discusses just Blazor WebAssembly, which runs entirely in the user's browser, since the main purpose of the chapter is to furnish a relevant example of how to implement a presentation layer with client-side technology. Moreover, as a server-side technology, Blazor can't furnish a performance that is comparable with other server-side technologies like ASP.NET Core MVC, which we already analyzed in *Chapter 15, Presenting ASP.NET Core MVC*.

The first section gives a sketch of the general Blazor WebAssembly architecture, while the remaining sections describe specific features. When needed, concepts are clarified by analyzing and modifying the example code that Visual Studio generates automatically when one selects the Blazor WebAssembly project template. The last section shows how to use all the concepts learned in practice with the implementation of a simple application based on the WWTravelClub book use case.

Technical requirements

This chapter requires the free Visual Studio 2019 Community edition or better with all database tools installed. All concepts are clarified with a simple example application, based on the WWTravelClub book use case. The code for this chapter is available at https://github.com/PacktPublishing/Software-Architecture-with-C-9-and-.NET-5.

Blazor WebAssembly architecture

Blazor WebAssembly exploits the new WebAssembly browser feature to execute the .NET runtime in the browser. This way, it enables all developers to use the whole .NET code base and ecosystem in the implementation of applications capable of running in any WebAssembly compliant browser. WebAssembly was conceived as a high-performance alternative to JavaScript. It is an assembly capable of running in a browser and obeying the same limitations as JavaScript code. This means that WebAssembly code, like JavaScript code, runs in an isolated execution environment that has very limited access to all machine resources.

WebAssembly differs from similar options of the past, like Flash and Silverlight, since it is an official W3C standard. More specifically, it became an official standard on December 5, 2019, so it is expected to have a long life. As a matter of fact, all mainstream browsers already support it.

However, WebAssembly doesn't bring just performance with it! It also creates the opportunity to run whole code bases associated with modern and advanced object-oriented languages such as C++ (direct compilation), Java (bytecode), and C# (.NET) in browsers.

Microsoft advises running .NET code in the browser with the Unity 3D graphic framework and Blazor.

Before WebAssembly, presentation layers running in a browser could be implemented only in JavaScript, with all the problems implied by the maintenance of big code bases the language brings with it.

Now, with Blazor we can implement complex applications in the modern and advanced C#, with all the comforts offered to this language by the C# compiler and Visual Studio.

Moreover, with Blazor, all .NET developers can use the full power of the .NET framework to implement presentation layers that run in the browser and that share libraries and classes with all other layers that run on the server side.

The subsections that follow describe the overall Blazor architectures. The first subsection explores the general concept of a Single-Page Application, pointing out Blazor peculiarities.

What is a Single-Page Application?

A **Single-Page Application (SPA)** is an HTML-based application, where the HTML is changed by code that runs in the browser itself instead of issuing a new request to the server and rendering a new HTML page from scratch. SPAs are able to simulate a multi-page experience by replacing complete page areas with new HTML.

SPA frameworks are frameworks explicitly designed for implementing SPAs. Before WebAssembly, all SPA frameworks were based on JavaScript. The most famous JavaScript-based SPA frameworks are Angular, React.js, and Vue.js.

All SPA frameworks furnish ways to transform data into HTML to show to the user and rely on a module called *router* to simulate page changes. Typically, data fills in the placeholders of HTML templates and selects which parts of a template to render (if-like constructs), and how many times to render it (for-like constructs).

The Blazor template language is Razor, which we already described in *Chapter 15, Presenting ASP.NET Core MVC*.

In order to increase modularity, code is organized into components that are a kind of virtual HTML tag that, once rendered, generates actual HTML markup. Like HTML tags, components have their attributes, which are usually called parameters, and their custom events. It is up to the developer to ensure that each component uses its parameters to create proper HTML and to ensure that it generates adequate events. Components can be used inside other components in a hierarchical fashion.

The application router performs its job by selecting components, acting as pages, and placing them in predefined areas. Each page component has a web address path that is somehow associated with it. This path concatenated with the web application domain becomes a URL that univocally identifies the page. As in usual web applications, page URLs are used to communicate to the router which page to load, either with usual links or with routing methods/functions.

Some SPA frameworks also furnish a predefined dependency injection engine in order to ensure better separation between components from one side and general-purpose services plus business code that runs in the browser on the other side. Among the frameworks listed in this subsection, only Blazor and Angular have an out-of-the-box dependency injection engine.

SPA frameworks based on JavaScript usually compile all JavaScript code in a few JavaScript files and then perform so-called tree-shaking, that is, the removal of all unused code.

At the moment, instead, Blazor keeps all DLLs referenced by the main application separate, and performs tree-shaking on each of them separately.

The next subsection starts to describe the Blazor architecture. You are encouraged to create a Blazor WebAssembly project called BlazorReview, so you can inspect the code and the constructs explained throughout the chapter. Please select **Individual User Accounts** as authentication, and **ASP.NET Core hosted**. This way, Visual Studio will also create an ASP.NET Core project that communicates with the Blazor client application, with all the authentication and authorization logic.

Figure 16.1: Creating the BlazorReview application

If you start the application and try to log in or try to access a page that requires login, an error should appear saying database migrations have not been applied. It should be enough to click the link next to the message to apply the pending migrations. Otherwise, as explained in the *Entity Framework Core migrations* section of *Chapter 8, Interacting with Data in C# – Entity Framework Core*, go to the Visual Studio Package Manager Console and run the Update-Database command.

Loading and starting the application

The URL of a Blazor WebAssembly application always includes an index.html static HTML page. In our BlazorReview project, index.html is in BlazorReview.Client->wwwroot->index.html. This page is the container where the Blazor application will create its HTML. It contains an HTML header with a viewport meta declaration, title, and the overall application's CSS. The Visual Studio default project template adds an application-specific CSS file and Bootstrap CSS, with a neutral style. You can replace the default Bootstrap CSS either with Bootstrap CSS with a customized style or with a completely different CSS framework.

The body contains the code that follows:

```
<body>
<div id="app">Loading...</div>

<div id="blazor-error-ui">
        An unhandled error has occurred.
<a href="" class="reload">Reload</a>
<a class="dismiss">✖</a>
</div>
<script
src="_content/Microsoft.AspNetCore.Components.WebAssembly.
Authentication/AuthenticationService.js">
</script>
<script src="_framework/blazor.webassembly.js"></script>
</body>
```

The initial div is where the application will place the code it generates. Any markup placed inside this div will appear just while the Blazor application is loading and starting, then it will be replaced by the application-generated HTML. The second div is normally invisible and appears only when Blazor intercepts an unhandled exception.

blazor.webassembly.js contains the JavaScript part of the Blazor framework. Among other things, it takes care of downloading the .NET runtime, together with all application DLLs. More specifically, blazor.webassembly.js downloads the blazor.boot.json file that lists all application files with their hashes. Then, blazor.webassembly.js downloads all resources listed in this file and verifies their hashes. All resources downloaded by blazor.webassembly.js are created when the application is built or published.

`AuthenticationService.js` is added only when the project enables authentication and takes care of the `OpenID Connect` protocol used by Blazor to exploit other authentication credentials like cookies to get bearer tokens, which are the preferred authentication credentials for clients that interact with a server through Web APIs. Authentication is discussed in more detail in the *Authentication and authorization* subsection later on in this chapter, while bearer tokens are discussed in the *REST services authorization and authentication* section of *Chapter 14, Applying Service-Oriented Architectures with .NET Core*.

The Blazor application entry point is in the `BlazorReview.Client->Program.cs` file. It has the following structure:

```
public class Program
{
    public static async Task Main(string[] args)
        {
            var builder = WebAssemblyHostBuilder.CreateDefault(args);
            builder.RootComponents.Add<App>("#app");

            // Services added to the application
            // Dependency Injection engine declared with statements
    like:
            // builder.Services.Add...

            await builder.Build().RunAsync();
        }
    }
}
```

`WebAssemblyHostBuilder` is a builder for creating a `WebAssemblyHost`, which is a WebAssembly-specific implementation of the generic host discussed in the *Using generic hosts* subsection of *Chapter 5, Applying a Microservice Architecture to Your Enterprise Application* (you are encouraged to review that subsection). The first builder configuration instruction declares the Blazor root component (`App`), which will contain the whole components tree, and in which HTML tag of the `Index.html` page to place it (`#app`). More specifically, `RootComponents.Add` adds a hosted service that takes care of handling the whole Blazor components tree. We can run several Blazor WebAssembly user interfaces in the same HTML page by calling `RootComponents.Add` several times, each time with a different HTML tag reference.

`builder.Services` contains all the usual methods and extension methods to add services to the Blazor application dependency engine: `AddScoped`, `AddTransient`, `AddSingleton`, and so on. Like in ASP.NET Core MVC applications (*Chapter 15, Presenting ASP.NET Core MVC*), services are the preferred places to implement business logic and to store shared state. While in ASP.NET Core MVC, services were usually passed to controllers, in Blazor WebAssembly, they are injected into components.

The next subsection explains how the root App component simulates page changes.

Routing

The root App class referenced by the host building code is defined in the BlazorReview.Client->App.razor file. App is a Blazor component, and like all Blazor components, it is defined in a file with a .razor extension and uses Razor syntax enriched with component notation, that is, with HTML-like tags that represent other Blazor components. It contains the whole logic for handling application pages:

```
<CascadingAuthenticationState>
<Router AppAssembly="@typeof(Program).Assembly">
<Found Context="routeData">
<AuthorizeRouteView RouteData="@routeData"
                    DefaultLayout="@typeof(MainLayout)">
<NotAuthorized>
@*Template that specifies what to show
when user is not authorized *@
</NotAuthorized>
</AuthorizeRouteView>
</Found>
<NotFound>
<LayoutView Layout="@typeof(MainLayout)">
<p>Sorry, there's nothing at this address.</p>
</LayoutView>
</NotFound>
</Router>
</CascadingAuthenticationState>
```

All tags in the preceding code represent either components or particular component parameters, called templates. Components will be discussed in detail throughout the chapter. For the moment, imagine them as a kind of custom HTML tag that we can define somehow with C# and Razor code. Templates, instead, are parameters that accept Razor markup as values. Templates are discussed in the *Templates and cascading parameters* subsection later on in this section.

The CascadingAuthenticationState component has the only function of passing authentication and authorization information to all components of the component tree that is inside of it. Visual Studio generates it only if one chooses to add authorization during project creation.

The `Router` component is the actual application router. It scans the assembly passed in the `AppAssembly` parameter looking for components containing routing information, that is, for components that can work as pages. Visual studio passes it the assembly that contains the `Program` class, that is, the main application. Pages contained in other assemblies can be added through the `AdditionalAssemblies` parameter, which accepts an `IEnumerable` of assemblies.

After that, the router intercepts all page changes performed either by code or through the usual `<a>` HTML tags that point to an address inside of the application base address. Navigation can be handled by code by requiring a `NavigationManager` instance from dependency injection.

The `Router` component has two templates, one for the case where a page for the requested URI is found (`Found`), and the other for the case where it is not found (`NotFound`). When the application uses authorization, the `Found` template consists of the `AuthorizeRouteView` components, which further distinguish whether the user is authorized to access the selected page or not. When the application doesn't use authorization, the `Found` template consists of the `RouteView` component:

```
<RouteView RouteData="@routeData" DefaultLayout="@typeof(MainLayout)"
/>
```

`RouteView` takes the selected page and renders it inside the layout page specified by the `DefaultLayout` parameter. This specification acts just as a default since each page can override it by specifying a different layout page. Blazor layout pages work similarly to ASP.NET Core MVC layout pages described in the *Reusing view code* subsection of *Chapter 15, Presenting ASP.NET Core MVC*, the only difference being that the place to add the page markup is specified with `@Body`:

```
<div class="content px-4">
    @Body
</div>
```

In the Visual Studio template, the default layout page is in the `BlazorReview.Client->Shared->MainLayout.razor` file.

If the application uses authorization, `AuthorizeRouteView` works like `RouteView`, but it also allows the specification of a template for a case where the user is not authorized:

```
<NotAuthorized>
@if (!context.User.Identity.IsAuthenticated)
{
<RedirectToLogin />
}
```

```
else
{
<p>You are not authorized to access this resource.</p>
}
</NotAuthorized>
```

If the user is not authenticated, the RedirectToLogin component uses a NavigationManager instance to move to the login logic page, otherwise, it informs the user they haven't got enough privileges to access the selected page.

Blazor WebAssembly also allows assemblies lazy loading to reduce the initial application loading time, but we will not discuss it here for lack of space. The *Further reading* section contains references to the official Blazor documentation.

Blazor pages and components

In this section, you will learn the basics of Blazor components, how to define a component, its structure, how to attach events to HTML tags, how to define their attributes, and how to use other components inside your components. We have organized all content into different subsections. The first subsection describes the basics of component structure.

Component structure

Components are defined in files with a .razor extension. Once compiled, they become classes that inherit from ComponentBase. Like all other Visual Studio project elements, Blazor components are available through the **add new item** menu. Usually, components to be used as pages are defined in the Pages folder, or in its subfolders, while other components are organized in different folders. Default Blazor projects add all their non-page components inside the Shared folder, but you can organize them differently.

By default, pages are assigned a namespace that corresponds to the path of the folder they are in. Thus, for instance, in our example project, all pages that are in the BlazorReview.Client->Pages path are assigned to the BlazorReview.Client.Pages namespace. However, you can change this default namespace with an @namespace declaration placed in the declaration area that is at the top of the file. This area may also contain other important declarations. Following is an example that shows all declarations:

```
@page "/counter"
@layout MyCustomLayout
```

```
@namespace BlazorApp2.Client.Pages
@using Microsoft.AspNetCore.Authorization
@implements MyInterface
@inherits MyParentComponent
@typeparam T
@attribute [Authorize]
@inject NavigationManager navigation
```

The first two directives make sense only for components that must work as pages. More specifically, the @layout directive overrides the default layout page with another component, while the @page directive defines the path of the page (**route**) within the application base URL. Thus, for instance, if our application runs at https://localhost:5001, then the URL of the above page will be https://localhost:5001/counter. Page routes can also contain parameters like in this example: /orderitem/{customer}/{order}. Parameter names must match public properties defined as parameters by the components. The match is case-insensitive, and parameters will be explained later on in this subsection.

The string that instantiates each parameter is converted into the parameter type and if this conversion fails an exception is thrown. This behavior can be prevented by associating a type with each parameter, in which case, if the conversion to the specified type fails, the match with the page URL fails. Only elementary types are supported: /orderitem/{customer:int}/{order:int}. Parameters are obligatory, that is, if they are not found, the match fails and the router tries other pages. However, you can make a parameter optional by specifying two @page directives, one with the parameter, and the other without the parameter.

@namespace overrides the default namespace of the component, while @using is equivalent to the usual C# using. @using declared in the special {project folder}->_ Imports.razor folder is automatically applied to all components.

@inherits declares that the component is a subclass of another component, while @ implements declares it implements an interface.

@typeparam is used if the component is a generic class, and declares the name of the generic parameter, while @attribute declares any attribute applied to the component class. Property-level attributes are applied directly to properties defined in the code area, so they don't need special notation. The [Authorize] attribute, applied to a component class used as a page, prevents unauthorized users from accessing the page. It works exactly in the same way as when it is applied to a controller or to an action method in ASP.NET Core MVC.

Finally, the @inject directive requires a type instance to the dependency injection engine and inserts it in the field declared after the type name; in the previous example, in the navigation parameter.

The middle part of the component file contains the HTML that will be rendered by the component with Razor markup, enriched with the possible invocation of children components.

The bottom part of the file is enclosed by an @code construct and contains fields, properties, and methods of the class that implements the component:

```
@code{
...
private string myField="0";
[Parameter]
public int Quantity {get; set;}=0;
private void IncrementQuantity ()
{
        Quantity++;
}
private void DecrementQuantity ()
{
        Quantity--;
        if (Quantity<0) Quantity=0;
}
...
}
```

Public properties decorated with the [Parameter] attribute work as component parameters; that is, when the component is instantiated into another component, they are used to pass values to the decorated properties, like values are passed to HTML elements in HTML markup:

```
<OrderItem Quantity ="2" Id="123"/>
```

Values can also be passed to component parameters by page route parameters that match the property name in a case invariant match:

```
OrderItem/{id}/{quantity}
```

Component parameters can also accept complex types and functions:

```
<modal title='() => "Test title" ' ...../>
```

If components are generic, they must be passed type values for each generic parameter declared with `typeparam`:

```
<myGeneric T= "string"……/>
```

However, often, the compiler is able to infer generic types from the type of other parameters.

Finally, the code enclosed in the @code directive can be also declared in a partial class with the same name and namespace as the component:

```
public partial class Counter
{
   [Parameter]
public int CurrentCounter {get; set;}=0;

   . . .

   . . .
}
```

Usually, these partial classes are declared in the same folder of the component and with a filename equal to the component file name with a `.cs` postfix added. Thus, for instance, the partial class associated with the `counter.razor` component will be `counter.razor.cs`.

Each component may also have an associated CSS file, whose name must be the name of the component file plus the `.css` postfix. Thus, for instance, the CSS file associated with the `counter.razor` component will be `counter.razor.css`. The CSS contained in this file is applied only to the component and has no effect on the remainder of the page. This is called CSS isolation, and at the moment, it is implemented by adding a unique attribute to all component HTML roots. Then, all selectors of the component CSS file are scoped to this attribute, so that they can't affect other HTML.

Whenever a component decorates an `IDictionary<string, object>` parameter with `[Parameter(CaptureUnmatchedValues = true)]`, then all unmatched parameters inserted into the tag, that is, all parameters without a matching component property, are added to the `IDictionary` as key-value pairs.

This feature furnishes an easy way to forward parameters to HTML elements or other children components contained in the component markup. For instance, if we have a `Detail` component that displays a detail view of the object passed in its `Value` parameter, we can use this feature to forward all usual HTML attributes to the root HTML tag of the component, as shown in the following example:

```
<div  @attributes="AdditionalAttributes">
...
</div>
@code{
[Parameter(CaptureUnmatchedValues = true)]
public Dictionary<string, object>
AdditionalAttributes { get; set; }
 [Parameter]
 Public T Value {get; set;}
}
```

This way, usual HTML attributes added to the component tag such as, for instance, class, are forwarded to the root div of the components and somehow used to style the component:

```
<Detail Value="myObject" class="my-css-class"/>
```

The next subsection explains how to pass markup generating functions to components.

Templates and cascading parameters

Blazor works by building a data structure called a **render tree**, which is updated as the UI changes. At each change, Blazor locates the part of the HTML that must be rendered and uses the information contained in the **render tree** to update it.

The RenderFragment delegate defines a function that is able to add further markup to a specific position of the **render tree**. There is also a RenderFragment<T> that accepts a further argument you can use to drive the markup generation. For instance, you can pass a Customer object to a RenderFragment<T> so that it can render all the data for that specific customer.

You can define a RenderFragment or a RenderFragment<T> with C# code, but the simplest way is to define it in your components with Razor markup. The Razor compiler will take care of generating the proper C# code for you:

```
RenderFragment myRenderFragment = @<p>The time is @DateTime.Now.</p>;
RenderFragment<Customer> customerRenderFragment =
(item) => @<p>Customer name is @item.Name.</p>;
```

The information on the location to add the markup is passed in the RenderTreeBuilder argument it receives as an argument. You can use a RenderFragment in your component Razor markup by simply invoking it as shown in the following example:

```
RenderFragment myRenderFragment = ...
  ...
<div>
  ...
  @myRenderFragment
  ...
</div>
  ...
```

The position where you invoke the RenderFragment defines the location where it will add its markup, since the component compiler is able to generate the right RenderTreeBuilder argument to pass to it. RenderFragment<T> delegates are invoked as shown here:

```
Customer myCustomer = ...
  ...
<div>
  ...
  @myRenderFragment(myCustomer)
  ...
</div>
  ...
```

Being functions, render fragments can be passed to component parameters like all other types. However, Blazor has a specific syntax to make it easier to simultaneously define and pass render fragments to components, the **template** syntax. First, you define the parameters in your component:

```
[Parameter]
Public RenderFragment<Customer>CustomerTemplate {get; set;}
[Parameter]
Public RenderFragment Title {get; set;}
```

Then, when you call the customer, you can do the following:

```
<Detail>
<Title>
<h5>This is a title</h5>
</Title>
```

```
<CustomerTemplate Context=customer>
<p>Customer name is @customer.Name.</p>
</CustomerTemplate >
</Detail>
```

Each render fragment parameter is represented by a tag with the same name as the parameter. You can place the markup that defines the render fragment inside of it. For the `CustomerTemplate` that has a parameter, the `Context` keyword defines the parameter name inside the markup. In our example, the chosen parameter name is `customer`.

When a component has just one render fragment parameter, if it is named `ChildContent`, the template markup can be enclosed directly between the open and end tag of the component:

```
[Parameter]
Public RenderFragment<Customer> ChildContent {get; set;}
................

................
<IHaveJustOneRenderFragment Context=customer>
<p>Customer name is @customer.Name.</p>
</IHaveJustOneRenderFragment>
```

In order to familiarize ourselves with component templates, let's modify the `Pages->FetchData.razor` page so that, instead of using a `foreach`, it uses a `Repeater` component.

Let's right-click on the `Shared` folder, select **Add**, then **Razor Component**, and add a new **Repeater.razor** component. Then, replace the existing code with this:

```
@typeparam T

@foreach(var item in Values)
{
@ChildContent(item)
}

@code {
    [Parameter]
public RenderFragment<T> ChildContent { get; set; }
    [Parameter]
public IEnumerable<T> Values { get; set; }
}
```

The component is defined with a generic parameter so that it can be used with any IEnumerable. Now let's replace the markup in the tbody of the **FetchData.razor** component with this:

```
<Repeater Values="forecasts" Context="forecast">
<tr>
<td>@forecast.Date.ToShortDateString()</td>
<td>@forecast.TemperatureC</td>
<td>@forecast.TemperatureF</td>
<td>@forecast.Summary</td>
</tr>
</Repeater>
```

Since the Repeater component has just one template, and since we named it ChildContent, we can place our template markup directly within the component open and close tags. Run it and verify that the page works properly. You have learned how to use templates, and that markup placed inside a component defines a template.

An important predefined templated Blazor component is the CascadingValue component. It renders the content placed inside of it with no changes, but passes a type instance to all its descendant components:

```
<CascadingValue  Value="new MyOptionsInstance{...}">
......
</CascadingValue >
```

All components placed inside of the CascadingValue tag and all their descendant components can now capture the instance of MyOptionsInstance passed in the CascadingValueValue parameter. It is enough that the component declares a public or private property with a type that is compatible with MyOptionsInstance and that decorates it with the CascadingParameter attribute:

```
[CascadingParameter]
privateMyOptionsInstance options {get; set;}
```

Matching is performed by type compatibility. In case of ambiguity with other cascaded parameters with a compatible type, we can specify the Name optional parameter of the CascadingValue component and pass the same name to the CascadingParameter attribute: [CascadingParameter("myUnique name")].

The CascadingValue tag also has an IsFixed parameter that should be set to true whenever possible for performance reasons. In fact, propagating cascading values is very useful for passing options and settings, but it has a very high computational cost.

When IsFixed is set to true, propagation is performed just once, the first time that each piece of involved content is rendered, and then no attempt is made to update the cascaded value during the content's lifetime. Thus, IsFixed can be used whenever the pointer of the cascaded object is not changed during the content's lifetime.

An example of a cascading value is the CascadingAuthenticationState component we encountered in the *Routing* subsection, which cascades authentications and authorization information to all rendered components.

Events

Both HTML tags and Blazor components use attributes/parameters to get input. HTML tags provide output to the remainder of the page through events, and Blazor allows C# functions to be attached to HTML on{event name} attributes. The syntax is shown in the Pages->Counter.razor component:

```
<p>Current count: @currentCount</p>

<button class="btn btn-primary" @onclick="IncrementCount">Click me</
button>

@code {
private int currentCount = 0;

private void IncrementCount()
    {
        currentCount++;
    }
}
```

The function can also be passed inline as a lambda. Moreover, it accepts the C# equivalent of the usual event argument. The *Further reading* section contains a link to the Blazor official documentation page that lists all supported events and their arguments.

Blazor also allows events in components, so they can return output, too. Component events are parameters whose type is either EventCallBack or EventCallBack<T>. EventCallBack is the type of component event with no arguments while EventCallBack<T> is the type of component event with an argument of type T. In order to trigger an event, say MyEvent, the component calls:

```
awaitMyEvent.InvokeAsync()
```

or

```
awaitMyIntEvent.InvokeAsync(arg)
```

These calls execute the handlers bound to the events or do nothing if no handler has been bound.

Once defined, component events can be used exactly in the same way as HTML element events, the only difference being that there is no need to prefix the event name with an @, since @ in HTML events is needed to distinguish between the HTML attribute and the Blazor-added parameter with the same name:

```
[Parameter]
publicEventCallback MyEvent {get; set;}
[Parameter]
publicEventCallback<int> MyIntEvent {get; set;}
...
...
<ExampleComponent
MyEvent="() => ..."
MyIntEvent = "(i) =>..." />
```

Actually, HTML element events are also `EventCallBack<T>`, that is why both event types behave in exactly the same way. `EventCallBack` and `EventCallBack<T>` are structs, not delegates, since they contain a delegate, together with a pointer to the entity that must be notified that the event has been triggered. Formally, this entity is represented by a `Microsoft.AspNetCore.Components.IHandleEvent` interface. Needless to say, all components implement this interface. The notification informs `IHandleEvent` that a state change took place. State changes play a fundamental role in the way Blazor updates the page HTML. We will analyze them in detail in the next subsection.

For HTML elements, Blazor also provides the possibility to stop the event's default action and the event bubbling by adding the `:preventDefault` and `:stopPropagation` directives to the attribute that specifies the event, like in these examples:

```
@onkeypress="KeyHandler" @onkeypress:preventDefault="true"

@onkeypress="KeyHandler" @onkeypress:preventDefault="true" @
onkeypress:stopPropagation   ="true"
```

Bindings

Often a component parameter value must be kept synchronized with an external variable, property, or field. The typical application of this kind of synchronization is an object property being edited in an input component or HTML tag. Whenever the user changes the input value, the object property must be updated coherently, and vice versa. The object property value must be copied into the component as soon as the component is rendered so that the user can edit it.

Similar scenarios are handled by parameter-event pairs. More specifically, from one side, the property is copied in the input component parameter. From the other side, each time the input changes value, a component event that updates the property is triggered. This way, property and input values are kept synchronized.

This scenario is so common and useful that Blazor has a specific syntax for simultaneously defining the event and the copying of the property value into the parameter. This simplified syntax requires that the event has the same name as the parameter involved in the interaction but with a Changed postfix.

Suppose, for instance, that a component has a Value parameter. Then the corresponding event must be ValueChanged. Moreover, each time the user changes the component value, the component must invoke the ValueChanged event by calling await ValueChanged.InvokeAsync(arg). With this in place, a property MyObject.MyProperty can be synchronized with the Value property with the syntax shown here:

```
<MyComponent @bind-Value="MyObject.MyProperty"/>
```

The preceding syntax is called **binding**. Blazor takes care of automatically attaching an event handler that updated the MyObject.MyProperty property to the ValueChanged event.

Bindings of HTML elements work in a similar way, but since the developer can't decide the names of parameters and events, a slightly different convention must be used. First of all, there is no need to specify the parameter name in the binding, since it is always the HTML input value attribute. Therefore, the binding is written simply as @bind="object.MyProperty". By default, the object property is updated on the change event, but you can specify a different event by adding the @bind-event: @bind-event="oninput" attribute.

Moreover, bindings of HTML inputs try to automatically convert the input string into the target type. If the conversion fails, the input reverts to its initial value. This behavior is quite primitive since, in the event of errors, no error message is provided to the user, and the culture settings are not taken into account properly (HTML5 inputs use invariant culture but text input must use the current culture). We advise binding inputs only to string target types. Blazor has specific components for handling dates and numbers that should be used whenever the target type is not a string. We will describe them in the *Blazor forms and validation* section.

In order to familiarize ourselves with events, let's write a component that synchronizes the content of an input type text when the user clicks a confirmation button. Let's right-click on the Shared folder and add a new **ConfirmedText.razor** component. Then replace its code with this:

```
<input type="text" @bind="Value" @attributes="AdditionalAttributes"/>
<button class="btn btn-secondary" @onclick="Confirmed">@ButtonText</
button>

@code {
    [Parameter(CaptureUnmatchedValues = true)]
    public Dictionary<string, object> AdditionalAttributes { get; set; }
    [Parameter]
    public string Value {get; set;}
    [Parameter]
    public EventCallback<string> ValueChanged { get; set; }
    [Parameter]
    public string ButtonText { get; set; }
    async Task Confirmed()
    {
        await ValueChanged.InvokeAsync(Value);
    }
}
```

The ConfirmedText component exploits the button-click event to trigger the ValueChanged event. Moreover, the component itself uses @bind to synchronize its Value parameter with the HTML input. It is worth pointing out that the component uses CaptureUnmatchedValues to forward all HTML attributes applied to its tag to the HTML input. This way, users of the ConfirmedText component can style the input field by simply adding class and/or style attributes to the component tag.

Now let's use this component in the Pages->Index.razor page by placing the following code at the end of Index.razor:

```
<ConfirmedText @bind-Value="textValue" ButtonText="Confirm" />
<p>
```

```
    Confirmed value is: @textValue
</p>

@code{
private string textValue = null;
}
```

If you run the project and play with the input and its **Confirm** button, you will see that each time the **Confirm** button is clicked, not only are the input values copied in the textValue page property but also the content of the paragraph that is behind the component is coherently updated.

We explicitly synchronized textValue with the component with @bind-Value, but who takes care of keeping textValue synchronized with the content of the paragraph? The answer is in the next subsection.

How Blazor updates HTML

When we write the content of a variable, property, or field in Razor markup with something like @model.property, Blazor, not only renders the actual value of the variable, property, or field when the component is rendered but tries also to update the HTML each time that this value changes, with a process called **change detection**. Change detection is a feature of all main SPA frameworks, but the way Blazor implements it is very simple and elegant.

The basic idea is that, once all HTML has been rendered, changes may occur only because of code executed inside of events. That is why EventCallBack and EventCallBack<T> contain a reference to an IHandleEvent. When a component binds a handler to an event, the Razor compiler creates an EventCallBackorEventCallBack<T> passing in its struct constructor the function bound to the event, and the component where the function was defined (IHandleEvent).

Once the code of the handler has been executed, the Blazor runtime is notified that the IHandleEvent might have changed. In fact, the handler code can only change the values of variables, properties, or fields of the component where the handler was defined. In turn, this triggers a change detection rooted in the component. Blazor verifies which variables, properties, or fields used in the component Razor markup changed and updates the associated HTML.

If a changed variable, property, or field is an input parameter of another component, then, the HTML generated by that component might also need updates. Accordingly, another change-detection process rooted in that component is recursively triggered.

The algorithm sketched previously discovers all relevant changes only if the following conditions listed are met:

1. No component references data structures belonging to other components in an event handler.
2. All inputs to a component arrive through its parameters and not through method calls or other public members.

When there is a change that is not detected because of the failure of one of the preceding conditions, the developer must manually declare the possible change of the component. This can be done by calling the StateHasChanged() component method. Since this call might result in changes to the page HTML, its execution cannot take place asynchronously but must be queued in the HTML page UI thread. This is done by passing the function to be executed to the InvokeAsync component method.

Summing up, the instruction to execute is await InvokeAsync(StateHasChanged).

The next subsection concludes the description of components with an analysis of their lifecycle and of the associated lifecycle methods.

Component lifecycle

Each component lifecycle event has an associated method. Some methods have both synchronous and asynchronous versions, some have just an asynchronous version, and some others have just a synchronous version.

The component lifecycle starts with parameters passed to the component being copied in the associated component properties. You can customize this step by overriding the following method:

```
public override async Task SetParametersAsync(ParameterView parameters)
{
await ...

await base.SetParametersAsync(parameters);
}
```

Typically, customization consists of the modification of additional data structures, so the base method is called to also perform the default action of copying parameters in the associated properties.

After that, there is the component initialization that is associated with the two methods:

```
protected override void OnInitialized()
{
    ...
}
protected override async Task OnInitializedAsync()
{
await ...
}
```

They are called once in the component lifetime, immediately after the component has been created and added to the render tree. Please place any initialization code there, and not in the component constructor because this will improve component testability, because, there, you have all parameters set, and because future Blazor versions might pool and reuse component instances.

If the initialization code subscribes to some events or performs actions that need a cleanup when the component is destroyed, implement IDisposable, and place all cleanup code in its Dispose method. In fact, whenever a component implements IDisposable, Blazor calls its Dispose method before destroying it.

After the component has been initialized and each time a component parameter changes, the following two methods are called:

```
protected override async Task OnParametersSetAsync()
{
await ...
}
protected override void OnParametersSet()
{
    ...
}
```

They are the right place to update data structures that depend on the values of the component parameters.

After that, the component is rendered or re-rendered. You can prevent component re-rendering after an update by overriding the ShouldRender method:

```
protected override bool ShouldRender()
{
    ...
}
```

Letting a component re-render only if you are sure its HTML code will change is an advanced optimization technique used in the implementation of component libraries.

The component rendering stage also involves the invocation of its children components. Therefore, component rendering is considered complete only after all its descendant components have completed their rendering, too. When rendering is complete, the following methods are called:

```
protected override void OnAfterRender(bool firstRender)
{
if (firstRender)
    {

    }
...
}
protected override async Task OnAfterRenderAsync(bool firstRender)
{
if (firstRender)
    {
    await...
        ...
    }
    await ...
}
```

Since when the preceding methods are called, all component HTML has been updated and all children components have executed all their lifetime methods, the preceding methods are the right places for performing the following operations:

- Calling JavaScript functions that manipulate the generated HTML. JavaScript calls are described in the *JavaScript interoperability* subsection.

- Processing information attached to parameters or cascaded parameters by descendant components. In fact, Tabs-like components and other components might have the need to register some of their subparts in the root component, so the root component typically cascades a data structure where some children components can register. Code written in `AfterRender` and `AfterRenderAsync` can rely on the fact that all subparts have completed their registration.

The next section describes Blazor tools for collecting user input.

Blazor forms and validation

Similar to all major SPA frameworks, Blazor also offers specific tools for processing user input while providing valid feedback to the user with error messages and immediate visual clues. The whole toolset is known as **Blazor Forms** and consists of a form component called EditForm, various input components, a data annotation validator, a validation error summary, and validation error labels.

EditForm takes care of orchestrating the state of all input components, through an instance of the EditContext class that is cascaded inside of the form. The orchestration comes from the interaction of both input components and the data annotation validator with this EditContext instance. A validation summary and error message labels don't take part in the orchestration but register to some EditContext events to be informed about errors.

EditForm must be passed the object whose properties must be rendered in its Model parameter. It is worth pointing out that input components bound to nested properties are not validated, so EditForm must be passed a flattened ViewModel. EditForm creates a new EditContext instance, passes the object received in its Model parameter in its constructor, and cascades it so it can interact with the form content.

You can also directly pass an EditContext custom instance in the EditContext parameter of EditForm instead of passing the object in its Model parameter, in which case EditForm will use your custom copy instead of creating a new instance. Typically, you do this when you need to subscribe to the EditContextOnValidationStateChanged and OnFieldChanged events.

When EditForm is submitted with a **Submit** button and there are no errors, the form invokes its OnValidSubmit callback, where you can place the code that uses and processes the user input. If instead, there are validation errors, they are shown, and the form invokes its OnInvalidSubmit callback.

The state of each input is reflected in some CSS classes that are automatically added to them, namely: valid, invalid, and modified. You can use these classes to furnish adequate visual feedback to the user. The default Blazor Visual Studio template already furnishes some CSS for them.

Following is a typical form:

```
<EditForm Model="FixedInteger"OnValidSubmit="@HandleValidSubmit" >
<DataAnnotationsValidator />
<ValidationSummary />
<div class="form-group">
<label for="integerfixed">Integer value</label>
<InputNumber @bind-Value="FixedInteger.Value"
```

```
id="integerfixed" class="form-control" />
<ValidationMessage For="@(() => FixedInteger.Value)" />
</div>
<button type="submit" class="btn btn-primary"> Submit</button>
</EditForm>
```

The label is a standard HTML label, while `InputNumber` is a Blazor-specific component for number properties. `ValidationMessage` is the error label that appears only in the event of a validation error. As a default, it is rendered with a `validation-message` CSS class. The property associated with the error message is passed in the `for` parameter with a parameterless lambda as shown in the example.

The `DataAnnotationsValidator` component adds a validation based on the usual .NET validation attributes, such as `RangeAttribute`, `RequiredAttribute`, and so on. You can also write your custom validation attributes by inheriting from the `ValidationAttribute` class.

You can provide custom error messages in the validation attributes. If they contain a `{0}` placeholder, this will be filled with the property display name declared in a `DisplayAttribute`, if one is found, otherwise with the property name.

Together with the `InputNumber` component, Blazor also supports an `InputText` component for `string` properties, an `InputTextArea` component for `string` properties to be edited in an HTML textarea, an `InputCheckbox` component for `bool` properties, and an `InputDate` component that renders `DateTime` and `DateTimeOffset` as dates. They all work in exactly the same way as the `InputNumber` component. No component is available for other HTML5 input types. In particular, no component is available for rendering time or date and time, or for rendering numbers with a range widget.

You can implement rendering time or date and time by inheriting from the `InputBase<TValue>` class and overriding the `BuildRenderTree`, `FormatValueAsString`, and `TryParseValueFromString` methods. The sources of the `InputNumber` component show how to do it: https://github.com/dotnet/aspnetcore/blob/15f341f8ee556 fa0c2825cdddfe59a88b35a87e2/src/Components/Web/src/Forms/InputNumber.cs. You can also use the third-party libraries described in the *Third-party tools for Blazor WebAssembly* section.

Blazor also has a specific component for rendering a `select`, which works as in the following example:

```
<InputSelect @bind-Value="order.ProductColor">
<option value="">Select a color ...</option>
<option value="Red">Red</option>
<option value="Blue">Blue</option>
```

```
<option value="White">White</option>
</InputSelect>
```

You can also render enumerations with a radio group thanks to the `InputRadioGroup` and `InputRadio` components, as shown in the following example:

```
<InputRadioGroup Name="color" @bind-Value="order.Color">
<InputRadio Name="color" Value="AllColors.Red" /> Red<br>
<InputRadio Name="color" Value="AllColors.Blue" /> Blue<br>
<InputRadio Name="color" Value="AllColors.White" /> White<br>
</InputRadioGroup>
```

Finally, Blazor also offers an `InputFile` component together with all the tools for processing and uploading the file. We will not cover this here, but the *Further reading* section contains links to the official documentation.

This subsection finishes the description of Blazor basics; the next section analyzes some advanced features.

Blazor advanced features

This section collects short descriptions of various Blazor advanced features organized in subsections. For lack of space, we can't give all the details of each feature, but the lacking details are covered by links in the *Further reading* section. We start with how to reference components and HTML elements defined in Razor markup.

References to components and HTML elements

Sometimes we might need a reference to a component in order to call some of its methods. This is the case, for instance, for a component that implements a modal window:

```
<Modal @ref="myModal">
...
</Modal>
...
<button type="button" class="btn btn-primary"
@onclick="() => myModal.Show()">
Open modal
</button>
...
```

```
@code{
private Modal  myModal {get; set;}
 ...
}
```

As the preceding example shows, references are captured with the @ref directive. The same @ref directive can also be used to capture references to HTML elements. HTML references have an ElementReference type and are typically used to call JavaScript functions on HTML elements, as explained in the next subsection.

JavaScript interoperability

Since Blazor doesn't expose all JavaScript features to C# code, and since it is convenient to take advantage of the huge JavaScript code base available, sometimes it is necessary to invoke JavaScript functions. Blazor allows this through the IJSRuntime interface that can be injected into a component via dependency injection.

Once one has an IJSRuntime instance, a JavaScript function that returns a value can be called as shown here:

```
T result = await jsRuntime.InvokeAsync<T>(
 "<name of JavaScript function or method>", arg1, arg2....);
```

Functions that do not return any argument can be invoked as shown here:

```
awaitjsRuntime.InvokeAsync(
 "<name of JavaScript function or method>", arg1, arg2....);
```

Arguments can be either basic types or objects that can be serialized in JSON, while the name of the JavaScript function is a string that can contain dots that represent access to properties, sub-properties, and method names, like, for instance, the "myJavaScriptObject.myProperty.myMethod" string.

Arguments can also be ElementReference instances captured with the @ref directive, in which case they are received as HTML elements on the JavaScript side.

The JavaScript functions invoked must be defined either in the Index.html file or in JavaScript files referenced in Index.html.

If you are writing a component library with a Razor library project, JavaScript files can be embedded together with CSS files as resources in the DLL library. It is enough to add a wwwroot folder in the project root and to place the needed CSS and JavaScript files in that folder or in some subfolder of it. After that, these files can be referenced as:

```
_content/<dll name>/<file path in wwwroot>
```

Accordingly, if the filename is `myJsFile.js`, the dll name is `MyCompany.MyLibrary`, and the file is placed in the `js` folder inside `wwwroot`, then its reference will be:

```
_content/MyCompany.MyLibrary/js/myJsFile.js
```

If your JavaScript files are organized as ES6 modules, you can avoid referencing them in `Index.html`, and can load the modules directly as shown here:

```
// _content/MyCompany.MyLibrary/js/myJsFile.js  JavaScript file
export function myFunction ()
{
...
}
...
//C# code
var module = await jsRuntime.InvokeAsync<JSObjectReference>(
    "import", "./_content/MyCompany.MyLibrary/js/myJsFile.js");
...
T res= await module.InvokeAsync<T>("myFunction")
```

In addition, instance methods of C# objects can be called from JavaScript code, taking the following steps:

1. Say the C# method is called `MyMethod`. Decorate the `MyMethod` method with the `[JSInvokable]` attribute.

2. Enclose the C# object in a `DotNetObjectReference` instance and pass it to JavaScript with a JavaScript call:

   ```
   var objRef = DotNetObjectReference.Create(myObjectInstance);
   //pass objRef to JavaScript
   ....
   //dispose the DotNetObjectReference
   objRef.Dispose()
   ```

3. On the JavaScript side, say the C# object is in a variable called `dotnetObject`. Then it is enough to invoke:

   ```
   dotnetObject.invokeMethodAsync("<dll name>", "MyMethod", arg1,
   ...).
   then(result => {...})
   ```

The next section explains how to handle contents and number/date localization.

Globalization and localization

As soon as the Blazor application starts, both the application culture and the application UI culture are set to the browser culture. However, the developer can change both of them by assigning the chosen cultures to CultureInfo. DefaultThreadCurrentCulture and CultureInfo.DefaultThreadCurrentUICulture. Typically, the application lets the user choose one of its supported cultures, or it accepts the browser culture only if it is supported, otherwise, it falls back to a supported culture. In fact, it is possible to support just a reasonable number of cultures because all application strings must be translated in all supported cultures.

Once the CurrentCulture is set, dates and numbers are automatically formatted according to the conventions of the chosen culture. For the UI culture, the developer must manually provide resource files with the translations of all application strings in all supported cultures.

There are two ways to use resource files. With the first option, you create a resource file, say, myResource.resx, and then add all language-specific files: myResource. it.resx, myResource.pt.resx, and so on. In this case, Visual Studio creates a static class named myResource whose static properties are the keys of each resource file. These properties will automatically contain the localized strings corresponding to the current UI culture. You can use these static properties wherever you like, and you can use pairs composed of a resource type and a resource name to set the ErrorMessageResourceType and the ErrorMessageResourceName properties of validation attributes or similar properties of other attributes. This way, the attributes will use an automatically localized string.

With the second option, you add only language-specific resource files (myResource. it.resx, myResource.pt.resx, and so on). In this case, Visual Studio doesn't create any class associated with the resource file, and you can use resource files together with IStringLocalizer and IStringLocalizer<T> injected in components as you use them in ASP.NET Core MVC views (see the *ASP.NET Core globalization* section of *Chapter 15, Presenting ASP.NET Core MVC*).

Authentication and authorization

In the *Routing* subsection, we sketched how the CascadingAuthenticationState and AuthorizeRouteView components prevent unauthorized users from accessing pages protected with an [Authorize] attribute. Let's go deeper into the details of how page authorization works.

In .NET applications, authentication and authorization information is usually contained in a ClaimsPrincipal instance. In server applications, this instance is built when the user logs in, taking the required information from a database. In Blazor WebAssembly, such information must be provided by some remote server that takes care of SPA authentication, too. Since there are several ways to provide authentication and authorization to a Blazor WebAssembly application, Blazor defines the AuthenticationStateProvider abstraction.

Authentication and authorization providers inherit from the AuthenticationStateProvider abstract class and override its GetAuthenticationStateAsync method, which returns a Task<AuthenticationState>, where the AuthenticationState contains the authentication and authorization information. Actually, AuthenticationState contains just a User property with a ClaimsPrincipal.

Once we've defined a concrete implementation of AuthenticationStateProvider, we must register it in the dependency engine container in the application program.cs file:

```
services.AddScoped<AuthenticationStateProvider, MyAuthStateProvider>();
```

We will return to the predefined implementations of AuthenticationStateProvider offered by Blazor after having described how Blazor uses authentication and authorization information furnished by a registered AuthenticationStateProvider.

The CascadingAuthenticationState component calls the GetAuthenticationStateAsync method of the registered AuthenticationStateProvider and cascades the returned Task<AuthenticationState>. You can intercept this cascading value with a [CascadingParameter] defined as follows in your components:

```
[CascadingParameter]
private Task<AuthenticationState>myAuthenticationStateTask { get; set;
}
......
ClaimsPrincipal user = (await myAuthenticationStateTask).User;
```

However, Blazor applications typically use AuthorizeRouteView and AuthorizeView components to control user access to content.

AuthorizeRouteView prevents access to pages if the user doesn't satisfy the prescriptions of the page [Authorize] attribute, otherwise, the content in the NotAuthorized template is rendered. AuthorizeRouteView also has an Authorizing template that is shown while user information is being retrieved.

`AuthorizeView` can be used within components to show the markup it encloses only to authorized users. It contains the same `Roles` and `Policy` parameters of the `[Authorize]` attribute that you can use to specify the constraints the user must satisfy to access the content:

```
<AuthorizeView Roles="Admin,SuperUser">
//authorized content
</AuthorizeView>
```

`AuthorizeView` can also specify `NotAuthorized` and an `Authorizing` template:

```
<AuthorizeView>
<Authorized>
...
</Authorized>
<Authorizing>
        ...
</Authorizing>
<NotAuthorized>
        ...
</NotAuthorized>
</AuthorizeView>
```

If one adds authorization while creating a Blazor WebAssembly project, the following method call is added to the application dependency engine:

```
builder.Services.AddApiAuthorization();
```

This method adds an `AuthenticationStateProvider` that extracts the user information from the usual ASP.NET Core authentication cookie. Since authentication cookies are encrypted, this operation must be performed by contacting an endpoint exposed by the server. The operation is performed with the help of the `AuthenticationService.js` JavaScript file we saw in the *Loading and starting the application* subsection of this chapter. The server endpoint returns user information in the form of a bearer token that can be used also to authenticate communications with the server's WEB API. Bearer tokens are described in detail in the *REST services authorization and authentication* and *ASP.NET Core service authorization* sections of *Chapter 14, Applying Service-Oriented Architectures with .NET Core*. Blazor WebAssembly communication is described in the next subsection.

If no valid authentication cookie is found, the provider creates an unauthenticated `ClaimsPrincipal`. This way, when the user tries to access a page that is protected by an `[Authorize]` attribute, the `AuthorizeRouteView` component invokes the `RedirectToLogin` component, which, in turn, navigates to the `Authentication.razor` page, passing it a login request in its `action` route parameter:

```
@page "/authentication/{action}"
@using Microsoft.AspNetCore.Components.WebAssembly.Authentication
<RemoteAuthenticatorView Action="@Action" />

@code{
    [Parameter] public string Action { get; set; }
}
```

The RemoteAuthenticatorView acts as an interface with the usual ASP.NET Core user login/registration system, and whenever it receives an "action" to perform redirects the user from the Blazor application to the proper ASP.NET Core server page (login, registration, logout, user profile).

All information needed to communicate with the server is based on name conventions, but they can be customized with the options argument of the AddApiAuthorization method. There, for instance, you can change the URL where the user can register, and also the address of the endpoint contacted by Blazor to collect information on the server settings. This endpoint is in the BlazorReview. Server->Controller->OidcConfigurationController.cs file.

Once the user logs in, they are redirected to the Blazor application page that caused the login request. The redirect URL is computed by the BlazorReview. Client->Shared->RedirectToLogin.razor component, which extracts it from the NavigationManager and passes it to the RemoteAuthenticatorView component. This time, the AuthenticationStateProvider is able to get the user information from the authentication cookie that has been created by the login operation.

More details on the authentication process are available in the official documentation reference in the *Further reading* section

The next subsection describes a Blazor WebAssembly-specific implementation of the HttpClient class and related types.

Communication with the server

Blazor WebAssembly supports the same .NET HttpClient and HttpClientFactory classes described in the *.NET Core HTTP clients* section of *Chapter 14, Applying Service-Oriented Architectures with .NET Core*. However, due to the communication limitations of browsers, their implementations are different and rely on the browser **fetch API**.

In *Chapter 14, Applying Service-Oriented Architectures with .NET Core*, we analyzed how to take advantage of HttpClientFactory to define typed clients. You can also define typed clients in Blazor with exactly the same syntax.

However, since Blazor needs to send the bearer token created during the authentication process in each request to the application server, it is common to define a named client as shown here:

```
builder.Services.AddHttpClient("BlazorReview.ServerAPI", client =>
    client.BaseAddress = new Uri(builder.HostEnvironment.BaseAddress)
.AddHttpMessageHandler<BaseAddressAuthorizationMessageHandler>();
```

AddHttpMessageHandler adds a DelegatingHandler, that is, a subclass of the DelegatingHandler abstract class. Implementations of DelegatingHandler override its SendAsync method in order to process each request and each relative response:

```
protected override async Task<HttpResponseMessage> SendAsync(
        HttpRequestMessage request,
        CancellationToken cancellationToken)
{
//modify request
    ...
HttpResponseMessage= response = await base.SendAsync(
request, cancellationToken);
//modify response
    ...
return response;
}
```

BaseAddressAuthorizationMessageHandler is added to the dependency injection engine by the AddApiAuthorization call we saw in the previous section. It adds the bearer token produced by the authorization process to each request addressed to the application server domain. If either this bearer token is expired or is not found at all, it tries to get a new bearer token from the user authentication cookie. If this attempt also fails, an AccessTokenNotAvailableException is thrown. Typically, similar exceptions are captured and trigger a redirection to the login page (as the default, to /authentication/{action}):

```
try
    {
        //server call here
    }
catch (AccessTokenNotAvailableException exception)
    {
        exception.Redirect();
    }
```

Since most requests are directed to the application server, and just a few calls might contact other servers with CORS, the `BlazorReview.ServerAPI` named `client` is also defined to be the default `HttpClient` instance:

```
builder.Services.AddScoped(sp =>
            sp.GetRequiredService<IHttpClientFactory>()
                .CreateClient("BlazorReview.ServerAPI"));
```

The default client can be obtained by requiring an `HttpClient` instance to the dependency injection engine. CORS requests to other servers can be handled by defining other named clients that use other bearer tokens. One can get a named client by first getting an `IHttpClientFactory` instance from dependency injection, and then calling its `CreateClient("<named client name>")` method. Blazor offers packages for getting bearer tokens and connecting with well-known services. They are described in the authorization documentation referenced in the *Further reading* section.

The next section briefly discusses some of the most relevant third-party tools and libraries that complete Blazor's official features, and help increase productivity in Blazor projects.

Third-party tools for Blazor WebAssembly

Notwithstanding Blazor is a young product, its third-party tool and product ecosystem is already quite rich. Among the open source, free products, it is worth mentioning the **Blazorise** project (`https://github.com/stsrki/Blazorise`), which contains various free basic Blazor components (inputs, tabs, modals, and so on) that can be styled with various CSS frameworks, such as Bootstrap and Material. It also contains a simple editable grid and a simple tree view.

Also worth mentioning is **BlazorStrap** (`https://github.com/chanan/BlazorStrap`), which contains pure Blazor implementations of all Bootstrap 4 components and widgets.

Among all the commercial products, it is worth mentioning **Blazor Controls Toolkit** (`http://blazor.mvc-controls.com/`), which is a complete toolset for implementing commercial applications. It contains all input types with their fallbacks in case they are not supported by the browser; all Bootstrap components; other basic components; and a complete, advanced drag-and-drop framework; advanced customizable and editable components, like detail views, detail lists, grids, a tree-repeater (a generalization of the tree-view). All components are based on a sophisticated metadata representation system that enables the user to design the markup in a declarative way using data annotations and inline Razor declarations.

Moreover, it contains additional sophisticated validation attributes, tools for undoing user input, tools for computing changes to send to the server, sophisticated client-side and server-side query tools based on the OData protocol, and tools to maintain and save the whole application state.

It is worth also mentioning the **bUnit** open source project (`https://github.com/egil/bUnit`), which furnishes all tools for testing Blazor components.

The next section shows how to put into practice what you have learned by implementing a simple application.

Use case – implementing a simple application in Blazor WebAssembly

In this section, we will implement a package search application for the *WWTravelClub* book use case. The first subsection explains how to set up the solution exploiting the domain layer and data layer we already implemented in *Chapter 15, Presenting ASP.NET Core MVC*.

Preparing the solution

First of all, create a copy of the **PackagesManagement** solution folder we created in *Chapter 15, Presenting ASP.NET Core MVC*, and rename it **PackagesManagementBlazor**.

Open the solution, right-click on the Web project (the one named **PackagesManagement**) and remove it. Then, go to the solution folder and delete the whole Web project folder (the one named **PackagesManagement**).

Now right-click on the solution and select **Add New project**. Add a new Blazor WebAssembly project called **PackagesManagementBlazor**. Select **no authentication** and **ASP.NET Core hosted**. We don't need authentication since the search-by-location feature we are going to implement must also be available to unregistered users.

Ensure that the **PackagesManagementBlazor.Server** project is the start project (its name should be in bold). If it is not, right-click on it and click on **Set as Start Project**.

The server project needs to reference both the data (**PackagesManagementDB**) and the domain (**PackagesManagementDomain**) projects, so please add them as references.

Let's also copy the same connection string of the old web project into the
PackagesManagementBlazor.Serverappsettings.json file:

```
"ConnectionStrings": {
        "DefaultConnection": "Server=(localdb)\\
mssqllocaldb;Database=package-management;Trusted_Connection=True;Multip
leActiveResultSets=true"

},
```

This way, we can reuse the database we already created. We also need to add the
same DDD tools we added to the old web project. Add a folder named Tools in
the project root and copy the content of the ch12->ApplicationLayer folder of the
GitHub repository associated with the book there.

In order to finish the solution setup, we just need to connect
PackagesManagementBlazor.Server with the domain layer by adding the following
code at the end of the ConfigureServices method in the Startup.cs file:

```
services.AddDbLayer(Configuration
                .GetConnectionString("DefaultConnection"),
                "PackagesManagementDB");
```

It is the same method we added to the old Web project. Finally, we can also add the
AddAllQueries extension method, which discovers all queries in the Web project:

```
services.AddAllQueries(this.GetType().Assembly);
```

We don't need other automatic discovery tools since this is a query-only application.

The next subsection explains how to design the server-side REST API.

Implementing the required ASP.NET Core REST APIs

As the first step, let's define the ViewModels used in the communication
between the server and the client applications. They must be defined in the
PackagesManagementBlazor.Shared project that is referenced by both applications.

Let's start with the `PackageInfosViewModel` ViewModel:

```
using System;
namespace PackagesManagementBlazor.Shared
{
    public class PackageInfosViewModel
    {
        public int Id { get; set; }
        public string Name { get; set; }
        public decimal Price { get; set; }
        public int DurationInDays { get; set; }
        public DateTime? StartValidityDate { get; set; }
        public DateTime? EndValidityDate { get; set; }
        public string DestinationName { get; set; }
        public int DestinationId { get; set; }
        public override string ToString()
        {
            return string.Format("{0}. {1} days in {2}, price: {3}",
                Name, DurationInDays, DestinationName, Price);
        }
    }
}
```

Then, add also the ViewModel that encloses all packages to return to the Blazor application:

```
using System.Collections.Generic;
namespace PackagesManagementBlazor.Shared
{
    public class PackagesListViewModel
    {
        public IEnumerable<PackageInfosViewModel>
            Items { get; set; }
    }
}
```

Now we can also add our query that searches packages by location. Let's add a Queries folder in the root of the **PackagesManagementBlazor.Server** project, and then add the interface that defines our query, `IPackagesListByLocationQuery`:

```
using DDD.ApplicationLayer;
using PackagesManagementBlazor.Shared;
using System.Collections.Generic;
```

```
using System.Threading.Tasks;

namespace PackagesManagementBlazor.Server.Queries
{
    public interface IPackagesListByLocationQuery: IQuery
    {
        Task<IEnumerable<PackageInfosViewModel>>
            GetPackagesOf(string location);
    }
}
```

Finally, let's also add the query implementation:

```
public class PackagesListByLocationQuery:IPackagesListByLocationQuery
    {
        private readonly MainDbContext ctx;
        public PackagesListByLocationQuery(MainDbContext ctx)
        {
            this.ctx = ctx;
        }
        public async Task<IEnumerable<PackageInfosViewModel>>
GetPackagesOf(string location)
        {
            return await ctx.Packages
                .Where(m => m.MyDestination.Name.StartsWith(location))
                .Select(m => new PackageInfosViewModel
            {
                StartValidityDate = m.StartValidityDate,
                EndValidityDate = m.EndValidityDate,
                Name = m.Name,
                DurationInDays = m.DurationInDays,
                Id = m.Id,
                Price = m.Price,
                DestinationName = m.MyDestination.Name,
                DestinationId = m.DestinationId
            })
                .OrderByDescending(m=> m.EndValidityDate)
                .ToListAsync();
        }
    }
```

We are finally ready to define our `PackagesController`:

```
using Microsoft.AspNetCore.Mvc;
using PackagesManagementBlazor.Server.Queries;
using PackagesManagementBlazor.Shared;
using System.Threading.Tasks;

namespace PackagesManagementBlazor.Server.Controllers
{
    [Route("[controller]")]
    [ApiController]
    public class PackagesController : ControllerBase
    {
        // GET api/<PackagesController>/Flor
        [HttpGet("{location}")]
        public async Task<PackagesListViewModel> Get(string location,
            [FromServices] IPackagesListByLocationQuery query )
        {
            return new PackagesListViewModel
            {
                Items = await query.GetPackagesOf(location)
            };
        }
    }
}
```

The server-side code is finished! Let's move on to the definition of the Blazor service that communicates with the server.

Implementing the business logic in a service

Let's add a `ViewModels` and a `Services` folder to the **PackagesManagementBlazor. Client** project. Most of the ViewModels we need were already defined in the **PackagesManagementBlazor.Shared** project. We only need a ViewModel for the search form. Let's add it to the `ViewModels` folder:

```
using System.ComponentModel.DataAnnotations;
namespace PackagesManagementBlazor.Client.ViewModels
{
    public class SearchViewModel
    {
        [Required]
```

```
                public string Location { get; set; }
        }
}
```

Let's call our service `PackagesClient`, and let's add it to the `Services` folder:

```
namespace PackagesManagementBlazor.Client.Services
{
    public class PackagesClient
    {
        private HttpClient client;
        public PackagesClient(HttpClient client)
        {
            this.client = client;
        }
        public async Task<IEnumerable<PackageInfosViewModel>>
            GetByLocation(string location)
        {
            var result =
                await client.GetFromJsonAsync<PackagesListViewModel>
                    ("Packages/" + Uri.EscapeDataString(location));
            return result.Items;
        }
    }
}
```

The code is straightforward! The `Uri.EscapeDataString` method url-encodes the parameter so it can be safely appended to the URL.

Finally, let's register the service in the dependency injection:

```
builder.Services.AddScoped<PackagesClient>();
```

It is worth pointing out that in a commercial application, we should have registered the service through an `IPackagesClient` interface, in order to be able to mock it in the tests (`.AddScoped<IPackagesClient, PackagesClient>()`).

Everything is in place; we just need to build the UI.

Implementing the user interface

As the first step, let's delete application pages we don't need, namely, Pages->Counter.razor and Pages->FetchData.razor. Let's also remove their links from the side menu in Shared->NavMenu.razor.

We will put our code in the Pages->Index.razor page. Let's replace the code of this page with this:

```
@using PackagesManagementBlazor.Client.ViewModels
@using PackagesManagementBlazor.Shared
@using PackagesManagementBlazor.Client.Services
@inject PackagesClient client
@page "/"

<h1>Search packages by location</h1>
<EditForm Model="search"
          OnValidSubmit="Search">
<DataAnnotationsValidator />
<div class="form-group">
<label for="integerfixed">Insert location starting chars</label>
<InputText @bind-Value="search.Location" />
<ValidationMessage For="@(() => search.Location)" />
</div>
<button type="submit" class="btn btn-primary">
        Search
</button>
</EditForm>
@code{
    SearchViewModel search { get; set; }
= new SearchViewModel();
    async Task Search()
    {
        ...
    }
}
```

The preceding code adds the needed @using, injects our PackagesClient service in the page, and defines the search form. When the form is successfully submitted, it invokes the Search callback where we will place the code that retrieves all the results.

It is time to add the logic to display all the results and to complete the @code block. The following code must be placed immediately after the search form:

```
@if (packages != null)
{
...
}
else if (loading)
```

```
{
    <p><em>Loading...</em></p>
}
@code{
    SearchViewModel search { get; set; } = new SearchViewModel();
    private IEnumerable<PackageInfosViewModel> packages;
    bool loading;
    async Task Search()
    {
        packages = null;
        loading = true;
        await InvokeAsync(StateHasChanged);
        packages = await client.GetByLocation(search.Location);
        loading = false;


    }
}
```

The omitted code in the if block is responsible for rendering a table with all the results. We will show it after having commented the preceding code.

Before retrieving the results with the PackagesClient service, we remove all previous results and set the loading field, so the Razor code selects the else if path that replaces the previous table with a loading message. Once we've set these variables, we are forced to call StateHasChanged to trigger change detection and to refresh the page. After all the results have been retrieved and the callback returns, there is no need to call StateHasChanged again because the termination of the callback itself triggers change detection and causes the required page refresh.

Following is the code that renders the table with all the results:

```
<div class="table-responsive">
  <table class="table">
    <thead>
      <tr>
        <th scope="col">Destination</th>
        <th scope="col">Name</th>
        <th scope="col">Duration/days</th>
        <th scope="col">Price</th>
        <th scope="col">Available from</th>
        <th scope="col">Available to</th>
      </tr>
    </thead>
```

```
    <tbody>
      @foreach (var package in packages)
      {
        <tr>
          <td>
            @package.DestinationName
          </td>
          <td>
            @package.Name
          </td>
          <td>
            @package.DurationInDays
          </td>
          <td>
            @package.Price
          </td>
          <td>
            @(package.StartValidityDate.HasValue ?
              package.StartValidityDate.Value.ToString("d")
              :
              String.Empty)
          </td>
          <td>
            @(package.EndValidityDate.HasValue ?
              package.EndValidityDate.Value.ToString("d")
              :
              String.Empty)
          </td>
        </tr>
      }
    </tbody>
  </table>
</div>
```

Run the project and write the initial characters of Florence. Since in previous chapters, we inserted Florence as a location in the database, some results should appear!

Summary

In this chapter, you learned what a SPA is and learned how to build a SPA based on the Blazor WebAssembly framework. The first part of the chapter described Blazor WebAssembly architecture, and then the chapter explained how to exchange input/output with Blazor components, and the concept of binding.

After having explained Blazor's general principles, the chapter focused on how to get user input while furnishing the user with adequate feedback and visual clues in the event of errors. Then, the chapter furnished a short description of advanced features, such as JavaScript interoperability, globalization, authentication with authorization, and client-server communication.

Finally, a practical example taken from the book user case shows how to use Blazor in practice to implement a simple touristic package search application.

Questions

1. What is WebAssembly?
2. What is an SPA?
3. What is the purpose of the Blazor router component?
4. What is a Blazor page?
5. What is the purpose of the @namespace directive?
6. What is an EditContext?
7. What is the right place to initialize a component?
8. What is the right place to process the user input?
9. What is the IJSRuntime interface?
10. What is the purpose of @ref?

Further reading

- Blazor official documentation is available at: https://docs.microsoft.com/en-US/aspnet/core/blazor/webassembly-lazy-load-assemblies.
- Assemblies' lazy loading is described at: https://docs.microsoft.com/en-US/aspnet/core/blazor/webassembly-lazy-load-assemblies.

- All HTML events supported by Blazor together with their event arguments are listed at: `https://docs.microsoft.com/en-US/aspnet/core/blazor/components/event-handling?#event-argument-types`.

- Blazor supports the same validation attributes as ASP.NET MVC, with the exception of the `RemoteAttribute`: `https://docs.microsoft.com/en-us/aspnet/core/mvc/models/validation#built-in-attributes`.

- A description of the `InputFile` component, and how to use it, can be found here: `https://docs.microsoft.com/en-US/aspnet/core/blazor/file-uploads`.

- More details on Blazor localization and globalization are available here: `https://docs.microsoft.com/en-US/aspnet/core/blazor/globalization-localization`.

- More details on Blazor authentication are available here, and on all its related URLs: `https://docs.microsoft.com/en-US/aspnet/core/blazor/security/webassembly/`.

17

Best Practices in Coding C# 9

When you act as a software architect on a project, it is your responsibility to define and/or maintain a coding standard that will direct the team to program according to the expectations of the company. This chapter covers some of the best practices in coding that will help developers like you program safe, simple, and maintainable software. It also includes tips and tricks for coding in C#.

The following topics will be covered in this chapter:

- How the complexity of your code can affect performance
- The importance of using a version control system
- Writing safe code in C#
- .NET core tips and tricks for coding
- Book use case – DOs and DON'Ts in writing code

C# 9 was launched together with .NET 5. However, the practices presented here can be used in many versions of .NET, but they refer to the basics of programming C#.

Technical requirements

This chapter requires the Visual Studio 2019 free Community Edition or better with all database tools installed. You will find the sample code for this chapter at https://github.com/PacktPublishing/Software-Architecture-with-C-9-and-.NET-5.

The more complex your code, the worse a programmer you are

For many people, a good programmer is one who writes complex code. However, the evolution of maturity in software development means there is a different way of thinking about it. Complexity does not mean a good job; it means poor code quality. Some incredible scientists and researchers have confirmed this theory and emphasize that professional code needs to be focused on time, high quality, and within budget.

Even when you have a complex scenario on your hands, if you reduce ambiguities and clarify the process of what you are coding, especially using good names for methods and variables, and respecting SOLID principles, you will turn complexity into simple code.

So, if you want to write good code, you need to keep the focus on how to do it, considering you are not the only one who will read it later. This is a good tip that changes the way you write code. This is how we will discuss each point of this chapter.

If your understanding of the importance of writing good code is aligned to the idea of simplicity and clarity while writing it, you should look at the Visual Studio tool **Code Metrics**:

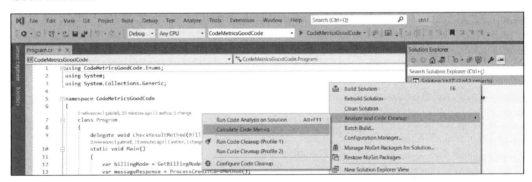

Figure 17.1: Calculating code metrics in Visual Studio

The **Code Metrics** tool will deliver metrics that will give you insights regarding the quality of the software you are delivering. The metrics that the tool provides can be found at this link: https://docs.microsoft.com/en-us/visualstudio/code-quality/code-metrics-values?view=vs-2019. The following subsections are focused on describing how they are useful in some real-life scenarios.

Maintainability index

This index indicates how easy it is to maintain the code – the easier the code, the higher the index (limited to 100). Easy maintenance is one of the key points to keep software in good health. It is obvious that any software will require changes in the future, since change is inevitable. For this reason, consider refactoring your code if you have low levels of maintainability. Writing classes and methods dedicated to a single responsibility, avoiding duplicate code, and limiting the number of lines of code of each method are examples of how you can improve the maintainability index.

Cyclomatic complexity

The author of *Cyclomatic Complexity Metric* is Thomas J. McCabe. He defines the complexity of a software function according to the number of code paths available (graph nodes). The more paths you have, the more complex your function is. McCabe considers that each function must have a complexity score of less than 10. That means that, if the code has more complex methods, you must refactor it, transforming parts of these codes into separate methods. There are some real scenarios where this behavior is easily detected:

- Loops inside loops
- Lots of consecutive if-else
- switch with code processing for each case inside the same method

For instance, look at the first version of this method for processing different responses of a credit card transaction. As you can see, the cyclomatic complexity is bigger than the number considered by McCabe as a basis. The reason why this happens is because of the number of if-else inside each case of the main switch:

```
/// <summary>
/// This code is being used just for explaining the concept of
cyclomatic complexity.
/// It makes no sense at all. Please Calculate Code Metrics for
understanding
/// </summary>
private static void CyclomaticComplexitySample()
{
  var billingMode = GetBillingMode();
  var messageResponse = ProcessCreditCardMethod();
  switch (messageResponse)
    {
      case "A":
```

```csharp
      if (billingMode == "M1")
        Console.WriteLine($"Billing Mode {billingMode} for " +
          $"Message Response {messageResponse}");
      else
        Console.WriteLine($"Billing Mode {billingMode} for " +
          $"Message Response {messageResponse}");
      break;
  case "B":
      if (billingMode == "M2")
        Console.WriteLine($"Billing Mode {billingMode} for " +
          $"Message Response {messageResponse}");
      else
        Console.WriteLine($"Billing Mode {billingMode} for " +
          $"Message Response {messageResponse}");
      break;
  case "C":
      if (billingMode == "M3")
        Console.WriteLine($"Billing Mode {billingMode} for " +
          $"Message Response {messageResponse}");
      else
        Console.WriteLine($"Billing Mode {billingMode} for " +
          $"Message Response {messageResponse}");
      break;
  case "D":
      if (billingMode == "M4")
        Console.WriteLine($"Billing Mode {billingMode} for " +
          $"Message Response {messageResponse}");
      else
        Console.WriteLine($"Billing Mode {billingMode} for " +
          $"Message Response {messageResponse}");
      break;
  case "E":
      if (billingMode == "M5")
        Console.WriteLine($"Billing Mode {billingMode} for " +
          $"Message Response {messageResponse}");
      else
        Console.WriteLine($"Billing Mode {billingMode} for " +
          $"Message Response {messageResponse}");
      break;
  case "F":
      if (billingMode == "M6")
        Console.WriteLine($"Billing Mode {billingMode} for " +
          $"Message Response {messageResponse}");
      else
```

```
        Console.WriteLine($"Billing Mode {billingMode} for " +
          $"Message Response {messageResponse}");
      break;
    case "G":
      if (billingMode == "M7")
        Console.WriteLine($"Billing Mode {billingMode} for " +
          $"Message Response {messageResponse}");
      else
        Console.WriteLine($"Billing Mode {billingMode} for " +
          $"Message Response {messageResponse}");
      break;
    case "H":
      if (billingMode == "M8")
        Console.WriteLine($"Billing Mode {billingMode} for " +
          $"Message Response {messageResponse}");
      else
        Console.WriteLine($"Billing Mode {billingMode} for " +
          $"Message Response {messageResponse}");
      break;
    default:
      Console.WriteLine("The result of processing is unknown");
      break;
  }
}
```

If you calculate the code metrics of this code, you will find a bad result when it comes to cyclomatic complexity, as you can see in the following screenshot:

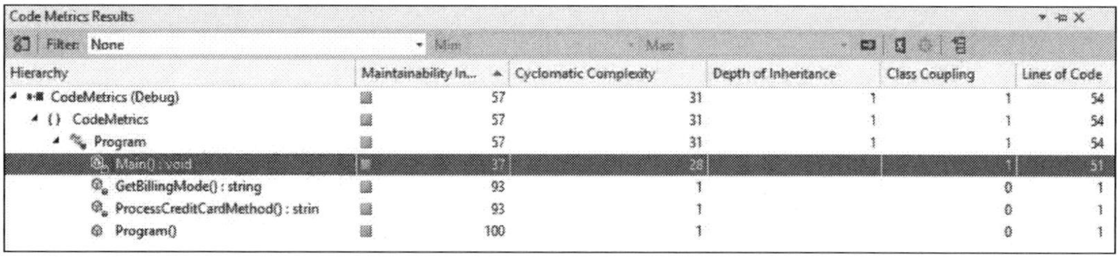

Hierarchy	Maintainability In...	Cyclomatic Complexity	Depth of Inheritance	Class Coupling	Lines of Code
▲ ◼◼ CodeMetrics (Debug)	57	31	1	1	54
▲ {} CodeMetrics	57	31	1	1	54
▲ ◥ Program	57	31	1	1	54
◉◦ Main() : void	37	28	1	1	51
◉◦ GetBillingMode() : string	93	1		0	1
◉◦ ProcessCreditCardMethod() : strin	93	1		0	1
◉ Program()	100	1		0	1

Figure 17.2: High level of cyclomatic complexity

The code itself makes no sense, but the point here is to show you the number of improvements that can be made with a view to writing better code:

- The options from switch-case could be written using Enum
- Each case processing can be done in a specific method
- switch-case can be substituted with Dictionary<Enum, Method>

By refactoring this code with the preceding techniques, the result is a piece of code that is much easier to understand, as you can see in the following code snippet of its main method:

```csharp
static void Main()
{
    var billingMode = GetBillingMode();
    var messageResponse = ProcessCreditCardMethod();
Dictionary<CreditCardProcessingResult, CheckResultMethod>
methodsForCheckingResult =GetMethodsForCheckingResult();
    if (methodsForCheckingResult.ContainsKey(messageResponse))
        methodsForCheckingResult[messageResponse](billingMode,
        messageResponse);
    else
        Console.WriteLine("The result of processing is unknown");
}
```

The full code can be found on the GitHub repository of this chapter and demonstrates how lower-complexity code can be achieved. The following screenshot shows these results according to code metrics:

Hierarchy ▲	Maintainability Index	Cyclomatic Complexity	Depth of Inheritance	Class Coupling	Lines of Code
▲ ▪◼ CodeMetricsGoodCode (Debug)	91	24	1	5	146
▲ {} CodeMetricsGoodCode	90	22	1	5	116
▲ ⁿ◆ Program	80	21	1	5	112
◆ Main() : void	73	2		5	11
◆ GetMethodsForCheckingResult() : Dictionary<CreditCardProce:	62	1		3	15
◆ CheckResultSucceed(BillingMode, CreditCardProcessingResult)	90	2		3	8
◆ CheckResultG(BillingMode, CreditCardProcessingResult) : void	90	2		3	8
◆ CheckResultF(BillingMode, CreditCardProcessingResult) : void	90	2		3	8
◆ CheckResultE(BillingMode, CreditCardProcessingResult) : void	90	2		3	8
◆ CheckResultD(BillingMode, CreditCardProcessingResult) : void	90	2		3	8
◆ CheckResultC(BillingMode, CreditCardProcessingResult) : void	90	2		3	8
◆ CheckResultB(BillingMode, CreditCardProcessingResult) : void	90	2		3	8
◆ CheckResultA(BillingMode, CreditCardProcessingResult) : void	90	2		3	8
◆ GetBillingMode() : BillingMode	100	1		1	9
◆ ProcessCreditCardMethod() : CreditCardProcessingResult	100	1		1	9
◆ Program.CheckResultMethod	100	1	1	2	1
▷ {} CodeMetricsGoodCode.Enums	93	2	1	0	30

Figure 17.3: Cyclomatic complexity reduction after refactoring

As you can see in the preceding screenshot, there is a considerable reduction in complexity after refactoring. In *Chapter 13, Implementing Code Reusability in C# 9*, we discussed the importance of refactoring for code reuse. The reason why we are doing this here is the same – we want to eliminate duplication.

The key point here is that with the techniques applied, the understanding of the code increased and the complexity decreased, proving the importance of cyclomatic complexity.

Depth of inheritance

This metric represents the number of classes connected to the one that is being analyzed. The more classes you have inherited, the worse the metric will be. This is like class coupling and indicates how difficult it is to change your code. For instance, the following screenshot has four inherited classes:

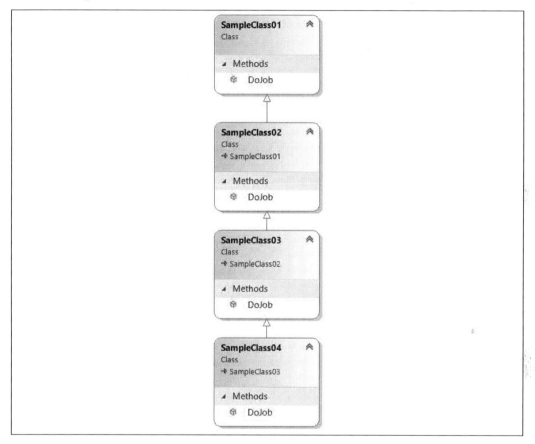

Figure 17.4: Depth of inheritance sample

You can see in the following screenshot that the deeper class has the worse metric, considering there are three other classes that can change its behavior:

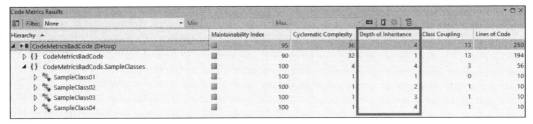

Figure 17.5: Depth of inheritance metric

Inheritance is one of the basic object-oriented analysis principles. However, it can sometimes be bad for your code in that it can cause dependencies. So, if it makes sense to do so, instead of using inheritance, consider using composition.

Class coupling

When you connect too many classes in a single class, obviously you will get coupling, and this can cause bad maintenance of your code. For instance, refer to the following screenshot. It shows a design where aggregation has been performed a lot. There is no sense to the code itself:

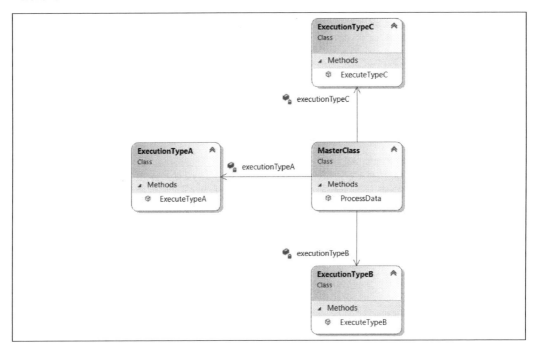

Figure 17.6: Class coupling sample

Once you have calculated the code metrics for the preceding design, you will see that the number of class coupling instances for the `ProcessData()` method, which calls `ExecuteTypeA()`, `ExecuteTypeB()`, and `ExecuteTypeC()`, equals three (3):

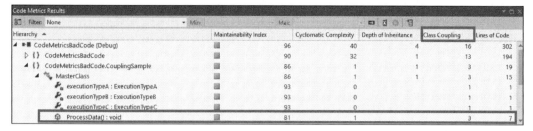

Figure 17.7: Class coupling metric

Some papers indicate that the maximum number of class coupling instances should be nine (9). With aggregation being a better practice than inheritance, the use of interfaces will solve class coupling problems. For instance, the same code with the following design will give you a better result:

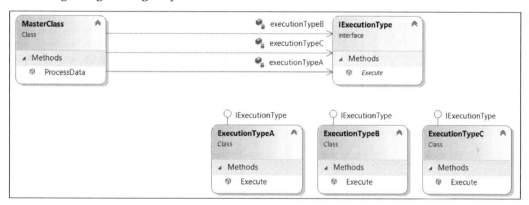

Figure 17.8: Reducing class coupling

Notice that using the interface in the design will allow you the possibility of increasing the number of execution types without increasing the class coupling of the solution:

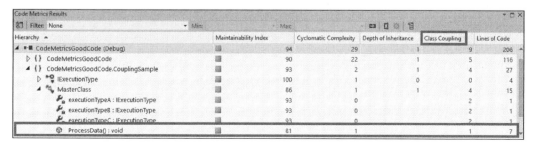

Figure 17.9: Class coupling results after applying aggregations

As a software architect, you must consider designing your solution to have more cohesion than coupling. The literature indicates that good software has low coupling and high cohesion. In software development, high cohesion indicates a scenario where you should have a software in which each class must have its methods and data with good relationships between them. On the other hand, low coupling indicates software where the classes are not closely and directly connected. This is a basic principle that can guide you to a better architectural model.

Lines of code

This metric is useful in terms of making you understand the size of the code you are dealing with. There is no way to connect lines of code and complexity since the number of lines is not indicative of that. On the other hand, the lines of code show the software size and software design. For instance, if you have too many lines of code in a single class (more than 1,000 lines of code – 1KLOC), this indicates that it is a bad design.

Using a version control system

You may find this topic in this book a bit obvious, but many people and companies still do not regard having a version control system as a basic tool for software development! The idea of writing about it is to force you to understand it. There is no architectural model or best practice that can save software development if you do not use a version control system.

In the last few years, we have been enjoying the advantages of online version control systems, such as GitHub, BitBucket, and Azure DevOps. The fact is, you must have a tool like that in your software development life cycle and there is no reason to not have it anymore since most providers offer free versions for small groups. Even if you develop by yourself, these tools are useful for tracking your changes, managing your software versions, and guaranteeing the consistency and integrity of your code.

Dealing with version control systems in teams

The use of a version control system tool when you are alone is obvious. You want to keep your code safe. But this kind of system was developed to solve team problems while writing code. For this reason, some features, such as branching and merging, were introduced to keep code integrity even in scenarios where the number of developers is quite large.

As a software architect, you will have to decide which branch strategy you will conduct in your team. Azure DevOps and GitHub suggest different ways to deliver that, and both are useful in some scenarios.

Information about how the Azure DevOps team deals with this can be found here: `https://devblogs.microsoft.com/devops/release-flow-how-we-do-branching-on-the-vsts-team/`. GitHub describes its process at `https://guides.github.com/introduction/flow/`. We have no idea of which is the one that best fits your needs, but we do want you to understand that you need to have a strategy for controlling your code.

In *Chapter 20, Understanding DevOps Principles*, we will discuss this in more detail.

Writing safe code in C#

C# can be considered a safe programming language by design. Unless you force it, there is no need for pointers, and memory release is, in most cases, managed by the garbage collector. Even so, some care should be taken so you can get better and safe results from your code. Let us have a look at some common practices to ensure safe code in C#.

try-catch

Exceptions in coding are so frequent that you should have a way to manage them whenever they happen. `try-catch` statements are built to manage exceptions and they are important for keeping your code safe. There are a lot of cases where an application crashes and the reason for that is the lack of using `try-catch`. The following code shows an example of the lack of usage of the `try-catch` statement. It is worth mentioning that this is just an example for understanding the concept of an exception thrown without correct treatment. Consider using `int.TryParse(textToConvert, out int result)` to handle cases where a parse is unsuccessful:

```
private static int CodeWithNoTryCatch(string textToConvert)
{
    return Convert.ToInt32(textToConvert);
}
```

On the other hand, bad `try-catch` usage can cause damage to your code too, especially because you will not see the correct behavior of that code and may misunderstand the results provided.

The following code shows an example of an empty try-catch statement:

```csharp
private static int CodeWithEmptyTryCatch(string textToConvert)
{
    try
    {
        return Convert.ToInt32(textToConvert);
    }
    catch
    {
        return 0;
    }
}
```

try-catch statements must always be connected to logging solutions, so that you can have a response from the system that will indicate the correct behavior and, at the same time, will not cause application crashes. The following code shows an ideal try-catch statement with logging management. It is worth mentioning that specific exceptions should be caught whenever possible, since catching a general exception will hide unexpected exceptions:

```csharp
private static int CodeWithCorrectTryCatch(string textToConvert)
{
    try
    {
        return Convert.ToInt32(textToConvert);
    }
    catch (FormatException err)
    {
        Logger.GenerateLog(err);
        return 0;
    }
}
```

As a software architect, you should conduct code inspections to fix this kind of behavior found in the code. Instability in a system is often connected to the lack of try-catch statements in the code.

try-finally and using

Memory leaks can be considered one of software's worst behaviors. They cause instability, bad usage of computer resources, and undesired application crashes. C# tries to solve this with Garbage Collector, which automatically releases objects from memory as soon as it realizes the object can be freed.

Objects that interact with I/O are the ones that generally are not managed by Garbage Collector: filesystem, sockets, and so on. The following code is an example of the incorrect usage of a FileStream object, because it thinks Garbage Collector will release the memory used, but it will not:

```
private static void CodeWithIncorrectFileStreamManagement()
{
    FileStream file = new FileStream("C:\\file.txt",
        FileMode.CreateNew);
    byte[] data = GetFileData();
    file.Write(data, 0, data.Length);
}
```

Besides, it takes a while for Garbage Collector to interact with objects that need to be released and sometimes you may want to do it yourself. For both cases, the use of try-finally or using statements is the best practice:

```
private static void CorrectFileStreamManagementFirstOption()
{
    FileStream file = new FileStream("C:\\file.txt",
        FileMode.CreateNew);
    try
    {
        byte[] data = GetFileData();
        file.Write(data, 0, data.Length);
    }
    finally
    {
        file.Dispose();
    }
}

private static void CorrectFileStreamManagementSecondOption()
{
    using (FileStream file = new FileStream("C:\\file.txt",
        FileMode.CreateNew))
    {
        byte[] data = GetFileData();
        file.Write(data, 0, data.Length);
    }
}

private static void CorrectFileStreamManagementThirdOption()
```

```
{
    using FileStream file = new FileStream("C:\\file.txt",
        FileMode.CreateNew);
    byte[] data = GetFileData();
    file.Write(data, 0, data.Length);
}
```

The preceding code shows exactly how to deal with objects that are not managed by Garbage Collector. You have both try-finally and using being implemented. As a software architect, you do need to pay attention to this kind of code. The lack of try-finally or using statements can cause huge damage to software behavior when it is running. It is worth mentioning that using code analysis tools (now distributed with .NET 5) will automatically alert you to these sorts of problems.

The IDisposable interface

In the same way that you will have trouble if you do not manage objects created inside a method with try-finally/using statements, objects created in a class that does not properly implement the IDisposable interface may cause memory leaks in your application. For this reason, when you have a class that deals with and creates objects, you should implement the disposable pattern to guarantee the release of all resources created by it:

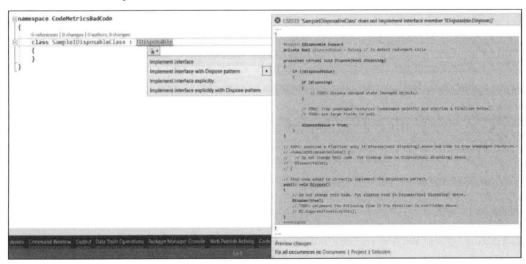

Figure 17.10: IDisposable interface implementation

The good news is that Visual Studio gives you the code snippet to implement this interface by just indicating it in your code and right-clicking on the **Quick Actions** and **Refactoring** option, as you can see in the preceding screenshot.

Once you have the code inserted, you need to follow the TODO instructions so that you have the correct pattern implemented.

.NET 5 tips and tricks for coding

.NET 5 implements some good features that help us to write better code. One of the most useful for having safer code is **dependency injection** (**DI**), which was already discussed in *Chapter 11*, *Design Patterns and .NET 5 Implementation*. There are some good reasons for considering this. The first one is that you will not need to worry about disposing the injected objects since you are not going to be the creator of them.

Besides, DI enables you to inject `ILogger`, a useful tool for debugging exceptions that will need to be managed by `try-catch` statements in your code. Furthermore, programming in C# with .NET 5 must follow the common good practices of any programming language. The following list shows some of these:

- **Classes, methods, and variables should have understandable names**: The name should explain everything that the reader needs to know. There should be no need for an explanatory comment unless these declarations are public.

- **Methods cannot have high complexity levels**: Cyclomatic complexity should be checked so that methods do not have too many lines of code.

- **Members must have the correct visibility**: As an object-oriented programming language, C# enables encapsulation with different visibility keywords. C# 9.0 is presenting *Init-only setters* so you can create `init` property/index accessors instead of `set`, defining these members as read-only following construction of the object.

- **Duplicate code should be avoided**: There is no reason for having duplicate code in a high-level programming language such as C#.

- **Objects should be checked before usage**: Since null objects can exist, the code must have null-type checking. It is worth mentioning that since C# 8, we have nullable reference types to avoid errors related to nullable objects.

- **Constants and enumerators should be used**: A good way of avoiding magic numbers and text inside code is to transform this information into constants and enumerators, which generally are more understandable.

- **Unsafe code should be avoided**: Unsafe code enables you to deal with pointers in C#. Unless there is no other way to implement the solution, unsafe code should be avoided.

- **try-catch statements cannot be empty**: There is no reason for a try-catch statement without treatment in the catch area. More than that, the caught exceptions should be as specific as possible, and not just an "exception," to avoid swallowing unexpected exceptions.

- **Dispose of the objects that you have created, if they are disposable**: Even for objects where Garbage Collector will take care of the disposed-of object, consider disposing of objects that you were responsible for creating yourself.

- **At least public methods should be commented**: Considering that public methods are the ones used outside your library, they must be explained for their correct external usage.

- **switch-case statements must have a default treatment**: Since the switch-case statement may receive an entrance variable unknown in some cases, the default treatment will guarantee that the code will not break in such a situation.

 You may refer to https://docs.microsoft.com/en-us/dotnet/csharp/language-reference/builtin-types/nullable-reference-types for more information about nullable reference types.

As a software architect, you may consider a good practice of providing a code pattern for your developers that will be used to keep the style of the code consistent. You can also use this code pattern as a checklist for coding inspection, which will enrich software code quality.

WWTravelClub – DOs and DON'Ts in writing code

As a software architect, you must define a code standard that matches the needs of the company you are working for.

In the sample project of this book (check out more about the WWTravelClub project in *Chapter 1, Understanding the Importance of Software Architecture*), this is no different. The way we decided to present the standard for it is by describing a list of DOs and DON'Ts that we followed while writing the samples we produced. It is worth mentioning that the list is a good way to start your standard and, as a software architect, you should discuss this list with the developers you have in the team so that you can evolve it in a practical and good manner.

In addition, these statements are designed to clarify the communication between team members and improve the performance and maintenance of the software you are developing:

- DO write your code in English
- DO follow C# coding standards with CamelCase
- DO write classes, methods, and variables with understandable names
- DO comment public classes, methods, and properties
- DO use the `using` statement whenever possible
- DO use `async` implementation whenever possible
- DON'T write empty `try-catch` statements
- DON'T write methods with a cyclomatic complexity score of more than 10
- DON'T use `break` and `continue` inside `for/while/do-while/foreach` statements

These DOs and DON'Ts are simple to follow and, better than that, will yield great results for the code your team produces. In *Chapter 19, Using Tools to Write Better Code*, we will discuss the tools to help you implement these rules.

Summary

During this chapter, we discussed some important tips for writing safe code. This chapter introduced a tool for analyzing code metrics so that you can manage the complexity and maintainability of the software you are developing. To finish, we presented some good tips to guarantee that your software will not crash due to memory leaks and exceptions. In real life, a software architect will always be asked to solve this kind of problem.

In the next chapter, we will learn about some unit testing techniques, the principles of unit testing, and a software process model that focuses on C# test projects.

Questions

1. Why do we need to care about maintainability?

2. What is cyclomatic complexity?

3. List the advantages of using a version control system.

4. What is Garbage Collector?

5. What is the importance of implementing the IDisposable interface?

6. What advantages do we gain from .NET 5 when it comes to coding?

Further reading

These are some books and websites where you will find more information about the topics of this chapter:

- *Clean Code: A Handbook of Agile Software Craftmanship*, by Martin, Robert C. Pearson Education, 2012.

- *The Art of Designing Embedded Systems*, by Jack G. Ganssle. Elsevier, 1999.

- *Refactoring*, by Martin Fowler. Addison-Wesley, 2018.

- *A Complexity Measure*, by Thomas J. McCabe. IEEE Trans. Software Eng. 2(4): 308-320, 1976 (https://dblp.uni-trier.de/db/journals/tse/tse2.html).

- https://blogs.msdn.microsoft.com/zainnab/2011/05/25/code-metrics-class-coupling/

- https://docs.microsoft.com/en-us/visualstudio/code-quality/code-metrics-values?view=vs-2019

- https://github.com/

- https://bitbucket.org/

- https://azure.microsoft.com/en-us/services/devops/

- https://guides.github.com/introduction/flow/

- https://blogs.msdn.microsoft.com/devops/2018/04/19/release-flow-how-we-do-branching-on-the-vsts-team/

- https://docs.microsoft.com/aspnet/core/fundamentals/logging/

- https://docs.microsoft.com/en-us/dotnet/csharp/whats-new/csharp-9

18

Testing Your Code with Unit Test Cases and TDD

When developing software, it is essential to ensure that an application is bug-free and that it satisfies all requirements. This can be done by testing all the modules while they are being developed, or when the overall application has been either completely or partially implemented.

Performing all the tests manually is not a feasible option since most of the tests must be executed each time the application is modified and, as explained throughout this book, modern software is being continuously modified to adapt the applications to the needs of a fast-changing market. This chapter discusses all the types of tests needed to deliver reliable software, and how to organize and automate them.

More specifically, this chapter covers the following topics:

- Understanding unit and integration tests and their usage
- Understanding the basics of **Test-Driven Development** (TDD)
- Defining C# test projects in Visual Studio
- Use case – Automating unit tests in DevOps Azure

In this chapter, we'll see which types of tests are worth implementing, and what unit tests are. We'll see the different types of projects available and how to write unit tests in them. By the end of the chapter, the book use case will help us to execute our tests in Azure DevOps during the **Continuous Integration/Continuous Delivery** (CI/CD) cycle of our applications automatically.

Technical requirements

This chapter requires the Visual Studio 2019 free Community Edition or better with all database tools installed. It also requires a free Azure account. If you have not already created one, refer to the *Creating an Azure account* section in *Chapter 1, Understanding the Importance of Software Architecture*.

All concepts in this chapter are clarified with practical examples based on the WWTravelClub book use case. The code for this chapter is available at `https://github.com/PacktPublishing/Software-Architecture-with-C-9-and-.NET-5`.

Understanding unit and integration tests

Delaying the application testing until immediately after most of its functionalities have been completely implemented must be avoided for the following reasons:

- If a class or module has been incorrectly designed or implemented, it might have already influenced the way other modules were implemented. Therefore, at this point, fixing the problem might have a very high cost.

- The possible combination of input that is needed to test all possible paths that execution can take grows exponentially with the number of modules or classes that are tested together. Thus, for instance, if the execution of a class method A can take three different paths, while the execution of another method B can take four paths, then testing A and B together would require 3 x 4 different inputs. In general, if we test several modules together, the total number of paths to test is the product of the number of paths to test in each module. If modules are tested separately, instead, the number of inputs required is just the sum of the paths needed to test each module.

- If a test of an aggregate made of N modules fails, then locating the origin of the bug among the N modules is usually a very time-consuming activity.

- When N modules are tested together, we have to redefine all tests involving the N modules, even if just one of the N modules changes during the application's CI/CD cycle.

These considerations show that it is more convenient to test each module method separately. Unluckily, a battery of tests that verifies all methods independently from their context is incomplete because some bugs may be caused by incorrect interactions between modules.

Therefore, tests are organized into two stages:

- **Unit tests**: These verify that all execution paths of each module behave properly. They are quite complete and usually cover all possible paths. This is feasible because there are not many possible execution paths of each method or module compared to the possible execution paths of the whole application.

- **Integration tests**: These are executed once the software passes all its unit tests. Integration tests verify that all modules interact properly to get the expected results. Integration tests do not need to be complete since unit tests will have already verified that all execution paths of each module work properly. They need to verify all patterns of interaction, that is, all the possible ways in which the various modules may cooperate.

Usually, each interaction pattern has more than one test associated with it: a typical activation of a pattern, and some extreme cases of activation. For instance, if a whole pattern of interaction receives an array as input, we will write a test for the typical size of the array, a test with a `null` array, a test with an empty array, and a test with a very big array. This way, we verify that the way the single module was designed is compatible with the needs of the whole interaction pattern.

With the preceding strategy in place, if we modify a single module without changing its public interface, we need to change the unit tests for that module.

If, instead, the change involves the way some modules interact, then we also have to add new integration tests or to modify existing ones. However, usually, this is not a big problem since most of the tests are unit tests, so rewriting a large percentage of all integration tests does not require too big an effort. Moreover, if the application was designed according to the **Single Responsibility, Open/Closed, Liskov Substitution, Interface Segregation,** or **Dependency Inversion (SOLID)** principles, then the number of integration tests that must be changed after a single code modification should be small since the modification should affect just a few classes that interact directly with the modified method or class.

Automating unit and integration tests

At this point, it should be clear that both unit tests and integration tests must be reused during the entire lifetime of the software. That is why it is worth automating them. Automation of unit and integration tests avoids possible errors of manual test execution and saves time. A whole battery of several thousand automated tests can verify software integrity after each small modification in a few minutes, thereby enabling the frequent changes needed in the CI/CD cycles of modern software.

As new bugs are found, new tests are added to discover them so that they cannot reappear in future versions of the software. This way, automated tests always become more reliable and protect the software more from bugs added as a result of new changes. Thus, the probability of adding new bugs (that are not immediately discovered) is greatly reduced.

The next section will give us the basics for organizing and designing automated unit and integration tests, as well as practical details on how to write a test in C# in the *Defining C# Test Projects* section.

Writing automated (unit and integration) tests

Tests are not written from scratch; all software development platforms have tools that help us to both write tests and launch them (or some of them). Once the selected tests have been executed, all tools show a report and give the possibility to debug the code of all failed tests.

More specifically, all unit and integration test frameworks are made of three important parts:

- **Facilities for defining all tests**: They verify whether the actual results correspond to expected results. Usually, a test is organized into test classes, where each test call tests either a single application class or a single class method. Each test is split into three stages:

    1. **Test preparation**: The general environment needed by the test is prepared. This stage only prepares the global environment for tests, such as objects to inject in class constructors or simulations of database tables; it doesn't prepare the individual inputs for each of the methods we're going to test. Usually, the same preparation procedure is used in several tests, so test preparations are factored out into dedicated modules.

    2. **Test execution**: The methods to test are invoked with adequate input and all results of their executions are compared with expected results with constructs such as `Assert.Equal(x, y)` and `Assert.NotNull(x)`.

    3. **Tear-down**: The whole environment is cleaned up to avoid the execution of a test influencing other tests. This step is the converse of *step 1*.

- **Mock facilities**: While integration tests use all (or almost all) classes involved in a pattern of object cooperation, in unit tests, the use of other application classes is forbidden. Thus, if a class under test, say, A, uses a method of another application class, B, that is injected in its constructor in one of its methods, M, then in order to test M, we must inject a fake implementation of B. It is worth pointing out that only classes that do some processing are not allowed to use another class during unit tests, while pure data classes can. Mock frameworks contain facilities to define implementations of interfaces and interface methods that return data that can be defined in tests. Typically, mock implementations are also able to report information on all mock method calls. Such mock implementations do not require the definition of actual class files, but are done online in the test code by calling methods such as `new Mock<IMyInterface>()`.

- **Execution and reporting tool**: This is a visual configuration-based tool that the developer may use to decide which tests to launch and when to launch them. Moreover, it also shows the final outcome of the tests as a report containing all successful tests, all failed tests, each test's execution time, and other information that depends on the specific tool and on how it was configured. Usually, execution and reporting tools that are executed in development IDEs such as Visual Studio also give you the possibility of launching a debug session on each failed test.

Since only interfaces allow a complete mock definition of all their methods, we should inject interfaces or pure data classes (that don't need to be mocked) in class constructors and methods; otherwise, classes could not be unit tested. Therefore, for each cooperating class that we want to inject into another class, we must define a corresponding interface.

Moreover, classes should use instances that are injected in their constructors or methods, and not class instances available in the public static fields of other classes; otherwise, the hidden interactions might be forgotten while writing tests, and this might complicate the *preparation* step of tests.

The following section describes other types of tests used in software development.

Writing acceptance and performance tests

Acceptance tests define the contract between the project stakeholders and the development team. They are used to verify that the software developed actually behaves as agreed with them. Acceptance tests verify not only functional specifications, but also constraints on the software usability and user interface. Since they also have the purpose of showing how the software appears and behaves on actual computer monitors and displays, they are never completely automatic, but consist mainly of lists of recipes and verifications that must be followed by an operator.

Sometimes, automatic tests are developed to verify just the functional specifications, but such tests usually bypass the user interface and inject the test input directly in the logic that is immediately behind the user interface. For instance, in the case of an ASP.NET Core MVC application, the whole website is run in a complete environment that includes all the necessary storage filled with test data. Input is not provided to HTML pages, but is injected directly in the ASP.NET Core controllers. Tests that bypass the user interface are called subcutaneous tests. ASP.NET Core supplies various tools to perform subcutaneous tests and also tools that automate interaction with HTML pages.

Subcutaneous tests are usually preferred in the case of automated tests, while full tests are executed manually for the following reasons:

- No automatic test can verify how the user interface appears and how usable it is.

- Automating the actual interaction with the user interface is a very time-consuming task.

- User interfaces are changed frequently to improve their usability and to add new features, and small changes in a single application screen may force a complete rewrite of all tests that operate on that screen.

In a few words, user interface tests are very expansive and have low reusability, so it's rarely worth automating them. However, ASP.NET Core supplies the `Microsoft.AspNetCore.Mvc.Testing` NuGet package to run the whole website in a testing environment. Using it together with the `AngleSharp` NuGet package, which parses HTML pages into DOM trees, you can write automated full tests with an acceptable programming effort. The automated ASP.NET Core acceptance tests will be described in detail in *Chapter 22, Automation for Functional Tests*.

Performance tests apply a fake load to an application to see whether it is able to handle the typical production load, to discover its load limits, and to locate bottlenecks. The application is deployed in a staging environment that is a copy of the actual production environment in terms of hardware resources.

Then, fake requests are created and applied to the system, and response times and other metrics are collected. Fake request batches should have the same composition as the actual production batches. They can be generated from the actual production request logs if they are available.

If response times are not satisfactory, other metrics are collected to discover possible bottlenecks (low memory, slow storage, or slow software modules). Once located, a software component that is responsible for the problem can be analyzed in the debugger to measure the execution time of the various method calls involved in a typical request.

Failures in the performance tests may lead either to a redefinition of the hardware needed by the application or to the optimization of some software modules, classes, or methods.

Both Azure and Visual Studio offer tools to create fake loads and to report execution metrics. However, they have been declared obsolete and will be discontinued, and so we will not describe them. As an alternative, there are both open source and third-party tools that can be used. Some of them are listed in the *Further reading* section.

The next section describes a software development methodology that gives a central role to tests.

Understanding test-driven development (TDD)

Test-driven development (TDD) is a software development methodology that gives a central role to unit tests. According to this methodology, unit tests are a formalization of the specifications of each class, so they must be written before the code of the class. Actually, a full test that covers all code paths univocally defines the code behavior, so it can be considered a specification for the code. It is not a formal specification that defines the code behavior through some formal language, but a specification based on examples of behavior.

The ideal way to test software would be to write formal specifications of the whole software behavior and to verify with some wholly automatic tools whether the software that was actually produced conforms to them. In the past, some research effort was spent defining formal languages for describing code specifications, but expressing the behavior the developer has in mind with similar languages was a very difficult and error-prone task. Therefore, these attempts were quickly abandoned in favor of approaches based on examples. At that time, the main purpose was the automatic generation of code.

Nowadays, automatic code generation has been substantially abandoned and survives in small application areas, such as the creation of device drivers. In these areas, the effort of formalizing the behavior in a formal language is worth the time saved in trying to test difficult-to-reproduce behaviors of parallel threads.

Unit tests were initially conceived as a way to encode example-based specifications in a completely independent way, as part of a specific agile development methodology called **Extreme Programming**. However, nowadays, TDD is used independently of Extreme Programming and is included as an obligatory prescription in other agile methodologies.

While it is undoubtedly true that unit tests refined after finding hundreds of bugs act as reliable code specifications, it is not obvious that developers can easily design unit tests that can be immediately used as reliable specifications for the code to be written. In fact, generally, you need an infinite or at least an immense number of examples to univocally define a code's behavior if examples are chosen at random.

The behavior can be defined with an acceptable number of examples only after you have understood all possible execution paths. In fact, at this point, it is enough to select a typical example for each execution path. Therefore, writing a unit test for a method after that method has been completely coded is easy: it simply requires selecting a typical instance for each execution path of the already existing code. However, writing unit tests this way does not protect from errors in the design of the execution paths themselves. Arguably, writing the tests beforehand doesn't prevent someone from forgetting to test a value, or combination of values – no one is perfect! It does, however, force you to think about them explicitly prior to implementation, which is why you're less likely to accidentally omit a test case.

We may conclude that, while writing unit tests, the developer must somehow forecast all execution paths by looking for extreme cases and by possibly adding more examples than strictly needed. However, the developer can make mistakes while writing the application code, and he or she can also make mistakes in forecasting all possible execution paths while designing the unit tests.

We have identified the main drawback of TDD: unit tests themselves may be wrong. That is, not only application code, but also its associated TDD unit tests, may be incoherent with the behavior the developer has in mind. Therefore, in the beginning, unit tests can't be considered software specifications, but rather a possibly wrong and incomplete description of the software behavior. Therefore, we have two descriptions of the behavior we have in mind: the application code itself and its TDD unit tests that were written before the application code.

What makes TDD work is that the probability of making exactly the same error while writing the tests and while writing the code is very low. Therefore, whenever a test fails, there is an error either in the tests or in the application code, and, conversely, if there is an error either in the application code or in the test, there is a very high probability that a test will fail. That is, the usage of TDD ensures that most of the bugs are immediately found!

Writing a class method or a chunk of code with TDD is a loop composed of three stages:

- **Red stage**: In this stage, the developer writes empty methods that either throw NotImplementedException or have empty bodies and designs new unit tests for them that must necessarily fail because, at this time, there is no code that implements the behavior they describe.

- **Green stage**: In this stage, the developer writes the minimum code or makes the minimum modifications to existing code that are necessary to pass all unit tests.

- **Refactoring stage**: Once the test is passed, code is refactored to ensure good code quality and the application of best practices and patterns. In particular, in this stage, some code can be factored out in other methods or in other classes. During this stage, we may also discover the need for other unit tests because new execution paths or new extreme cases are discovered or created.

The loop stops as soon as all tests pass without writing new code or modifying the existing code.

Sometimes, it is very difficult to design the initial unit tests because it is quite difficult to imagine how the code might work and the execution paths it might take. In this case, you can get a better understanding of the specific algorithm to use by writing an initial sketch of the application code. In this initial stage, we need to focus just on the main execution path, completely ignoring extreme cases and input verifications. Once we get a clear picture of the main ideas behind an algorithm that should work, we can enter the standard three-stage TDD loop.

In the next section, we will list all test projects available in Visual Studio and describe xUnit in detail.

Defining C# test projects

Visual Studio contains project templates for three types of unit testing frameworks, namely, MSTest, xUnit, and NUnit. Once you start the new project wizard, in order to visualize the version of all of them that is adequate for .NET Core C# applications, set **Project type** as **Test**, **Language** as **C#**, and **Platform** as **Linux**, since .NET Core projects are the only ones that can be deployed on Linux.

The following screenshot shows the selection that should appear:

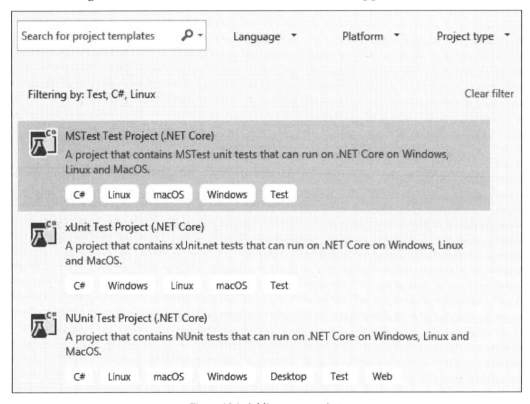

Figure 18.1: Adding a test project

All the preceding projects automatically include the NuGet package for running all the tests in the Visual Studio test user interface (Visual Studio test runner). However, they do not include any facility for mocking interfaces, so you need to add the Moq NuGet package, which contains a popular mocking framework.

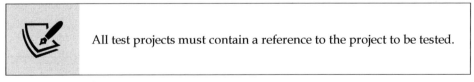

All test projects must contain a reference to the project to be tested.

In the next section, we will describe xUnit, since it is probably the most popular of the three frameworks. However, all three frameworks are quite similar and differ mainly in the names of the assert methods and in the names of the attributes used to decorate various testing classes and methods.

Using the xUnit test framework

In xUnit, tests are methods decorated with either the [Fact] or [Theory] attributes. Tests are automatically discovered by the test runner that lists all of them in the user interface so the user can run either all of them or just a selection of them.

A new instance of the test class is created before running each test, so the *test preparation* code contained in the class constructor is executed before each test of the class. If you also require *tear-down* code, the test class must implement the IDisposable interface so that the tear-down code can be included in the IDisposable.Dispose method.

The test code invokes the methods to be tested and then tests the results with methods from the Assert static class, such as Assert.NotNull(x), Assert.Equal(x, y), and Assert.NotEmpty(IEnumerable x). There are also methods that verify whether a call throws an exception of a specific type, for instance:

```
Assert.Throws<MyException>(() => {/* test code */ ...}).
```

When an assertion fails, an exception is thrown. A test fails if a not-intercepted exception is thrown either by the test code or by an assertion.

The following is an example of a method that defines a single test:

```
[Fact]
public void Test1()
{
    var myInstanceToTest = new ClassToTest();
    Assert.Equal(5, myInstanceToTest.MethodToTest(1));
}
```

The [Fact] attribute is used when a method defines just one test, while the [Theory] attribute is used when the same method defines several tests, each on a different tuple of data. Tuples of data can be specified in several ways and are injected in the test as method parameters.

The previous code can be modified to test `MethodToTest` on several inputs, as follows:

```
[Theory]
[InlineData(1, 5)]
[InlineData(3, 10)]
[InlineData(5, 20)]
public void Test1(int testInput, int testOutput)
{
    var myInstanceToTest = new ClassToTest();
    Assert.Equal(testOutput,
        myInstanceToTest.MethodToTest(testInput));
}
```

Each `InlineData` attribute specifies a tuple to be injected in the method parameters. Since just simple constant data can be included as attribute arguments, xUnit also gives you the possibility to take all data tuples from a class that implements `IEnumerable`, as shown in the following example:

```
public class Test1Data: IEnumerable<object[]>
{
    public IEnumerator<object[]> GetEnumerator()
    {
        yield return new object[] { 1, 5};
        yield return new object[] { 3, 10 };
        yield return new object[] { 5, 20 };

    }

    IEnumerator IEnumerable.GetEnumerator()=>GetEnumerator();

}
...
...
[Theory]
[ClassData(typeof(Test1Data))]
public void Test1(int testInput, int testOutput)
{
    var myInstanceToTest = new ClassToTest();
    Assert.Equal(testOutput,
        myInstanceToTest.MethodToTest(testInput));
}
```

The type of the class that provides the test data is specified with the ClassData attribute.

It is also possible to take data from a static method of a class that returns an IEnumerable with the MemberData attribute, as shown in the following example:

```
[Theory]
[MemberData(nameof(MyStaticClass.Data),
    MemberType= typeof(MyStaticClass))]
public void Test1(int testInput, int testOutput)
{
    ...
```

The MemberData attribute is passed the method name as the first parameter, and the class type in the MemberType named parameter. If the static method is part of the same test class, the MemberType parameter can be omitted.

The next section shows how to deal with some advanced preparation and tear-down scenarios.

Advanced test preparation and tear-down scenarios

Sometimes, the preparation code contains very time-consuming operations, such as opening a connection with a database, that don't need to be repeated before each test, but that can be executed once before all the tests contained in the same class. In xUnit, this kind of test preparation code can't be included in the test class constructor; since a different instance of the test class is created before every single test, it must be factored out in a separate class called a fixture class.

If we also need a corresponding tear-down code, the fixture class must implement IDisposable. In other test frameworks, such as NUnit, the test class instances are created just once instead, so they don't need the fixture code to be factored out in other classes. However, test frameworks, such as NUnit, that do not create a new instance before each test may suffer from bugs because of unwanted interactions between test methods.

The following is an example of an xUnit fixture class that opens and closes a database connection:

```
public class DatabaseFixture : IDisposable
{
    public DatabaseFixture()
    {
        Db = new SqlConnection("MyConnectionString");
    }

    public void Dispose()
    {
        Db.Close()
    }
    public SqlConnection Db { get; private set; }
}
```

Since a fixture class instance is created just once before all tests associated with the fixture are executed and the same instance is disposed of immediately after the tests, then the database connection is created just once when the fixture class is created and is disposed of immediately after the tests when the fixture object is disposed of.

The fixture class is associated with each test class by letting the test class implement the empty IClassFixture<T> interface, as follows:

```
public class MyTestsClass : IClassFixture<DatabaseFixture>
{
    private readonly DatabaseFixture fixture;

    public MyDatabaseTests(DatabaseFixture fixture)
    {
        this.fixture = fixture;
    }
    ...
    ...
}
```

A fixture class instance is automatically injected in the test class constructor in order to make all data computed in the fixture test preparation available for the tests. This way, for instance, in our previous example, we can get the database connection instance so that all test methods of the class can use it.

If we want to execute some test preparation code on all tests contained in a collection of test classes instead of a single test class, we must associate the fixture class with an empty class that represents the collection of test classes, as follows:

```
[CollectionDefinition("My Database collection")]
public class DatabaseCollection : ICollectionFixture<DatabaseFixture>
{
    // this class is empty, since it is just a placeholder
}
```

The `CollectionDefinition` attribute declares the name of the collection, and the `IClassFixture<T>` interface has been replaced with `ICollectionFixture<T>`.

Then we declare that a test class belongs to the previously defined collection by applying it to the `Collection` attribute with the name of the collection, as follows:

```
[Collection("My Database collection")]
public class MyTestsClass
{
    DatabaseFixture fixture;

    public MyDatabaseTests(DatabaseFixture fixture)
    {
        this.fixture = fixture;
    }
    ...
    ...
}
```

The `Collection` attribute declares which collection to use, while the `DataBaseFixture` argument in the test class constructor provides an actual fixture class instance, so it can be used in all class tests.

The next section shows how to mock interfaces with the `Moq` framework.

Mocking interfaces with Moq

Mocking capabilities are not included in any of the test frameworks we listed in this section as they are not included in xUnit. Therefore, they must be provided by installing a specific NuGet package. The `Moq` framework available in the `Moq` NuGet package is the most popular mock framework available for .NET. It is quite easy to use and will be briefly described in this section.

Once we've installed the NuGet package, we need to add a using Moq statement in our test files. A mock implementation is easily defined, as follows:

```
var myMockDependency = new Mock<IMyInterface>();
```

The behavior of the mock dependency on specific inputs of the specific method can be defined with the Setup/Return method pair as follows:

```
myMockDependency.Setup(x=>x.MyMethod(5)).Returns(10);
```

We can add several Setup/Return instructions for the same method. This way, we can specify an indefinite number of input/output behaviors.

Instead of specific input values, we may also use wildcards that match a specific type as follows:

```
myMockDependency.Setup(x => x.MyMethod(It.IsAny<int>()))
                    .Returns(10);
```

Once we have configured the mock dependency, we may extract the mocked instance from its Object property and use it as if it were an actual implementation, as follows:

```
var myMockedInstance=myMockDependency.Object;
...
myMockedInstance.MyMethod(10);
```

However, mocked methods are usually called by the code under test, so we just need to extract the mocked instance and use it as an input in our tests.

We may also mock properties and async methods as follows:

```
myMockDependency.Setup(x => x.MyProperty)
                    .Returns(42);
...
myMockDependency.Setup(x => x.MyMethodAsync(1))
                    .ReturnsAsync("aasas");
var res=await myMockDependency.Object
    .MyMethodAsync(1);
```

With async methods, Returns must be replaced by ReturnsAsync.

Each mocked instance records all calls to its methods and properties, so we may use this information in our tests. The following code shows an example:

```
myMockDependency.Verify(x => x.MyMethod(1), Times.AtLeast(2));
```

The preceding statement asserts that `MyMethod` has been invoked with the given arguments at least twice. There are also `Times.Never`, and `Times.Once` (which asserts that the method was called just once), and more.

The Moq documentation summarized up to now should cover 99% of the needs that may arise in your tests, but Moq also offers more complex options. The *Further reading* section contains the link to the complete documentation.

The next section shows how to define unit tests in practice and how to run them both in Visual Studio and in Azure DevOps with the help of the book use case.

Use case – Automating unit tests in DevOps Azure

In this section, we add some unit test projects to the example application we built in *Chapter 15, Presenting ASP.NET Core MVC*. If you don't have it, you can download it from the *Chapter 15, Presenting ASP.NET Core MVC*, section of the GitHub repository associated with the book.

As a first step, let's make a new copy of the solution folder and name it `PackagesManagementWithTests`. Then, open the solution and add it to an xUnit .NET Core C# test project named `PackagesManagementTest`. Finally, add a reference to the ASP.NET Core project (`PackagesManagement`), since we will test it, and a reference to the latest version of the `Moq` NuGet package, since we require mocking capabilities. At this point, we are ready to write our tests.

As an example, we will write unit tests for the `Edit` method decorated with `[HttpPost]` of the `ManagePackagesController` controller, which is shown as follows:

```
[HttpPost]
public async Task<IActionResult> Edit(
    PackageFullEditViewModel vm,
    [FromServices] ICommandHandler<UpdatePackageCommand> command)
{
    if (ModelState.IsValid)
    {
        await command.HandleAsync(new UpdatePackageCommand(vm));
        return RedirectToAction(
            nameof(ManagePackagesController.Index));
    }
```

```
    else
        return View(vm);
}
```

Before writing our test methods, let's rename the test class that was automatically included in the test project as ManagePackagesControllerTests.

The first test verifies that in case there are errors in ModelState, the action method renders a view with the same model it received as an argument so that the user can correct all errors. Let's delete the existing test method and write an empty DeletePostValidationFailedTest method, as follows:

```
[Fact]
public async Task DeletePostValidationFailedTest()
{
}
```

The method must be async and the return type must be Task since the Edit method that we have to test is async. In this test, we don't need mocked objects since no injected object will be used. Thus, as a preparation for the test, we just need to create a controller instance, and we must add an error to ModelState as follows:

```
var controller = new ManagePackagesController();
controller.ModelState
    .AddModelError("Name", "fake error");
```

Then we invoke the method, injecting ViewModel and a null command handler as its arguments, since the command handler will not be used:

```
var vm = new PackageFullEditViewModel();
var result = await controller.Edit(vm, null);
```

In the verification stage, we verify that the result is ViewResult and that it contains the same model that was injected in the controller:

```
var viewResult = Assert.IsType<ViewResult>(result);
Assert.Equal(vm, viewResult.Model);
```

Now, we also need a test to verify that in case there are no errors, the command handler is called, and then the browser is redirected to the Index controller action method. We call the DeletePostSuccessTest method:

```
[Fact]
public async Task DeletePostSuccessTest()
{
}
```

This time the preparation code must include the preparation of a command handler mock, as follows:

```
var controller = new ManagePackagesController();
var commandDependency =
    new Mock<ICommandHandler<UpdatePackageCommand>>();
commandDependency
    .Setup(m => m.HandleAsync(It.IsAny<UpdatePackageCommand>()))
    .Returns(Task.CompletedTask);
var vm = new PackageFullEditViewModel();
```

Since the handler `HandleAsync` method returns no async value, we can't use `ReturnsAsync`, but we have to return just a completed `Task` (`Task.Complete`) with the `Returns` method. The method to test is called with both `ViewModel` and the mocked handler:

```
var result = await controller.Edit(vm,
    commandDependency.Object);
```

In this case, the verification code is as follows:

```
commandDependency.Verify(m => m.HandleAsync(
    It.IsAny<UpdatePackageCommand>()),
    Times.Once);
var redirectResult=Assert.IsType<RedirectToActionResult>(result);
Assert.Equal(nameof(ManagePackagesController.Index),
    redirectResult.ActionName);
Assert.Null(redirectResult.ControllerName);
```

As the first step, we verify that the command handler has actually been invoked once. A better verification should also include a check that it was invoked with a command that includes `ViewModel` passed to the action method. We will take it up as an exercise.

Then we verify that the action method returns `RedirectToActionResult` with the right action method name and with no controller name specified.

Once all the tests are ready, if the test window does not appear on the left bar of Visual Studio, we may simply select the **Run all tests** item from the Visual Studio **Test** menu. Once the test window appears, further invocations can be launched from within this window.

If a test fails, we can add a breakpoint to its code, so we can launch a debug session on it by right-clicking on it in the test window and then selecting **Debug selected tests**.

Connecting to an Azure DevOps repository

Tests play a fundamental role in the application CI/CD cycle, and specifically in continuous integration. They must be executed at least each time the master branch of the application repository is modified in order to verify that changes don't introduce bugs.

The following steps show how to connect our solution to an Azure DevOps repository, and we will define an Azure DevOps pipeline that builds the project and launches its tests. In this way, every day after all developers have pushed their changes, we can launch the pipeline to verify that the repository code compiles and passes all the tests:

1. As a first step, we need a free DevOps subscription. If you don't already have one, please create one by clicking the **Start free** button on this page: `https://azure.microsoft.com/en-us/services/devops/`. Here, let's define an organization but stop before creating a project, since we will create the project from within Visual Studio.

2. Ensure you are logged in to Visual Studio with your Azure account (the same used in the creation of the DevOps account). At this point, you may create a DevOps repository for your solution by right-clicking on the solution and by selecting **Configure continuous delivery to Azure...**. In the window that appears, an error message will inform you that you have no repository configured for your code:

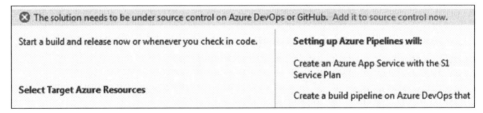

Figure 18.2: No repository error message

3. Click the **Add to source control now** link. After that, the DevOps screen will appear in the Visual Studio **Team Explorer** tab:

Figure 18.3: Publish repository to DevOps panel

As shown in *Chapter 3, Documenting Requirements with Azure DevOps*, Team Explorer is being replaced by Git Changes, but if this automatic wizard takes you to Team Explorer, use it to create your repository. Then you can use the Git Changes window.

4. Once you click the **Publish Git Repo** button, you will be prompted to select your DevOps organization and a name for the repository. After you successfully publish your code to a DevOps repository, the DevOps screen should change as follows:

Figure 18.4: DevOps button after publication

The DevOps screen shows a link to your online DevOps project. In future, when you open your solution, if the link does not appear, please click the DevOps screen **Connect** button or the **Manage connections** link (whichever appears) to select and connect your project.

5. Click this link to go to the online project. Once there, if you click the **Repos** item, on the left-hand menu, you will see the repository you just published.

6. Now, click the **Pipelines** menu item to create a DevOps pipeline to build and test your project. In the window that appears, click the button to create a new pipeline:

Figure 18.5: Pipeline page

7. You will be prompted to select where your repository is located:

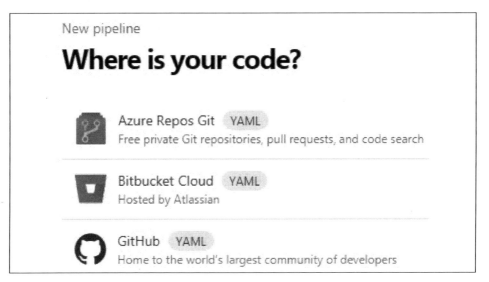

Figure 18.6: Repository selection

8. Select **Azure Repos Git** and then your repository. Then you will be prompted about the nature of the project:

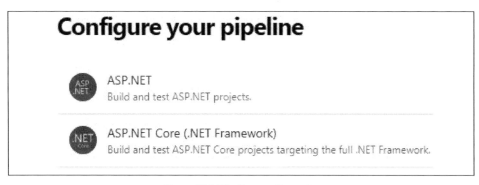

Figure 18.7: Pipeline configuration

9. Select **ASP.NET Core**. A pipeline for building and testing your project will be automatically created for you. Save it by committing the newly created .yaml file to your repository:

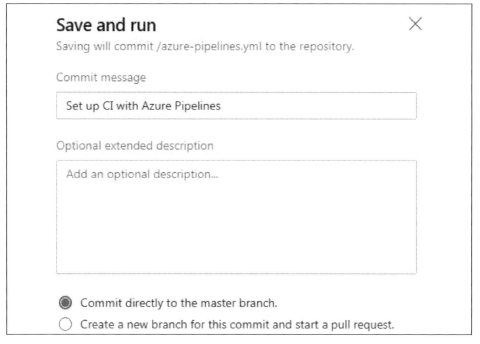

Figure 18.8: Pipeline properties

10. The pipeline can be run by selecting the **Queue** button, but since the standard pipeline scaffolded by DevOps has a trigger on the master branch of the repository, it is automatically launched each time changes to this branch are committed and each time the pipeline is modified. The pipeline can be modified by clicking the **Edit** button:

```
trigger:
- master

pool:
  vmImage: 'windows-latest'

variables:
  solution: '**/*.sln'
  buildPlatform: 'Any CPU'
  buildConfiguration: 'Release'

steps:
Settings
- task: NuGetToolInstaller@1

Settings
- task: NuGetCommand@2
  inputs:
    restoreSolution: '$(solution)'

Settings
- task: VSBuild@1
  inputs:
    solution: '$(solution)'
    msbuildArgs: '/p:DeployOnBuild=true /p:WebPublishMethod=Package /p:PackageAsSingleFile=true /p:SkipInvalidConfigurations=true
    platform: '$(buildPlatform)'
    configuration: '$(buildConfiguration)'

Settings
- task: VSTest@2
  inputs:
    testSelector: 'testAssemblies'
    testAssemblyVer2: |
      **\PackagesManagementTest.dll
      !**\*TestAdapter.dll
      !**\obj\**
    searchFolder: '$(System.DefaultWorkingDirectory)'
    platform: '$(buildPlatform)'
    configuration: '$(buildConfiguration)'
```

Figure 18.9: Pipeline code

11. Once in edit mode, all pipeline steps can be edited by clicking the **Settings** link that appears above each of them. New pipeline steps can be added as follows:

1. Write - `task:` where the new step must be added and then accept one of the suggestions that appear while you are typing the task name.

2. Once you have written a valid task name, a **Settings** link appears above the new step. Click it.

3. Insert the desired task parameters in the window that appears and then save.

12. In order to have our test working, we need to specify the criteria to locate all assemblies that contain tests. In our case, since we have a unique .dll file containing the tests, it is enough to specify its name. Click the **Settings** link of the VSTest@2 test task, and replace the content that is automatically suggested for the **Test files** field with the following:

```
**\PackagesManagementTest.dll
!**\*TestAdapter.dll
!**\obj\**
```

13. Then click **Add** to modify the actual pipeline content. As soon as you confirm your changes in the **Save and run** dialog, the pipeline is launched, and if there are no errors, test results are computed. The results of tests launched during a specific build can be analyzed by selecting the specific build in the pipeline **History** tab and by clicking the **Tests** tab on the page that appears. In our case, we should see something like the following screenshot:

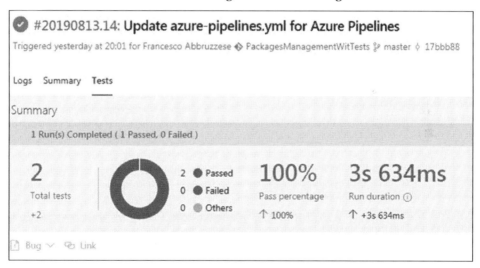

Figure 18.10: Test results

14. If you click the **Analytics** tab of the pipeline page, you will see analytics relating to all builds, including analytics about the test results:

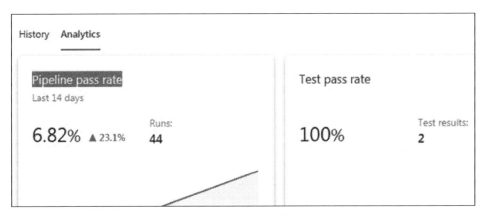

Figure 18.11: Build analytics

15. Clicking the test area of the **Analytics** page gets us a detailed report about all pipeline test results.

Summing up, we created a new Azure DevOps repository, published the solution to the new repository, and then created a build pipeline that executes our tests after each build. The build pipeline is executed as soon as we save it and will be executed each time someone commits to the master branch.

Summary

In this chapter, we explained why it is worth automating software tests, and then we focused on the importance of unit tests. We also listed all types of tests and their main features, focusing mainly on unit tests. We analyzed the advantages of TDD, and how to use it in practice. With this knowledge, you should be able to produce software that is both reliable and easy to modify.

Finally, we analyzed all test tools available for .NET Core projects, focusing on the description of xUnit and Moq, and showed how to use them in practice, both in Visual Studio and in Azure DevOps, with the help of the book's use case.

The next chapter looks at how to test and measure the quality of the code.

Questions

1. Why is it worth automating unit tests?

2. What is the main reason why TDD is able to discover most bugs immediately?

3. What is the difference between the [Theory] and [Fact] attributes of xUnit?

4. Which xUnit static class is used in test assertions?

5. Which methods allow the definition of the Moq mocked dependencies?

6. Is it possible to mock async methods with Moq? If yes, how?

Further reading

While the documentation on xUnit included in this chapter is quite complete, it doesn't include the few configuration options offered by xUnit. The full xUnit documentation is available at `https://xunit.net/`. Documentation for MSTest and NUnit can be found at `https://github.com/microsoft/testfx` and `https://github.com/nunit/docs/wiki/NUnit-Documentation`, respectively.

Full Moq documentation is available at `https://github.com/moq/moq4/wiki/Quickstart`.

Here are some links to performance test frameworks for web applications:

- `https://jmeter.apache.org/` (free and open source)
- `https://www.neotys.com/neoload/overview`
- `https://www.microfocus.com/en-us/products/loadrunner-load-testing/overview`
- `https://www.microfocus.com/en-us/products/silk-performer/overview`

19
Using Tools to Write Better Code

As we saw in *Chapter 17, Best Practices in Coding C# 9*, coding can be considered an art, but writing understandable code is surely more like philosophy. In that chapter, we discussed practices that you, as a software architect, need to observe for your developers. In this chapter, we will describe the techniques and tools for code analysis, so that you have well-written code for your projects.

The following topics will be covered in this chapter:

- Identifying well-written code
- Understanding the tools that can be used in the process to make things easier
- Applying extension tools to analyze code
- Checking the final code after analysis
- Use case — Implementing code inspection before publishing the application

By the end of the chapter, you will be able to define which tools you are going to incorporate into your software development life cycle in order to facilitate code analysis.

Technical requirements

This chapter requires the Visual Studio 2019 free Community Edition or better. You will find the sample code for this chapter at `https://github.com/PacktPublishing/Software-Architecture-with-C-9-and-.NET-5/tree/master/ch19`.

Identifying well-written code

It is not easy to define whether code is well-written. The best practices described in *Chapter 17, Best Practices in Coding C# 9,* can certainly guide you as a software architect to define a standard for your team. But even with a standard, mistakes will happen, and you will probably find them only after the code is in production. The decision to refactor code in production just because it does not follow all the standards you define is not an easy one to take, especially if the code in question is working properly. Some people conclude that well-written code is simply code that works well in production. However, this can surely cause damage to the software's life since developers can be inspired by that non-standard code.

For this reason, you – as a software architect – need to find ways to enforce adherence to the coding standard you've defined. Luckily, nowadays, we have many options for tools that can help us with this task. They are regarded as the automation of static code analysis. This technique is seen as a great opportunity to improve the software developed and to help developers.

The reason your developers will evolve with code analysis is that you start to disseminate knowledge between them during code inspections. The tools that we have now have the same purpose. Better than that, with Roslyn, they do this task while you are writing the code. Roslyn is the compiler platform for .NET, and it enables you to develop some tools for analyzing code. These analyzers can check style, quality, design, and other issues.

For instance, look at the following code. It does not make any sense, but you can still see that there are some mistakes:

```
using System;
static void Main(string[] args)
{
    try
    {
        int variableUnused = 10;
```

```
    int variable = 10;
    if (variable == 10)
    {
        Console.WriteLine("variable equals 10");
    }
    else
    {
        switch (variable)
        {
            case 0:
                Console.WriteLine("variable equals 0");
                break;
        }
    }
}
catch
{
}
}
```

The idea of this code is to show you the power of some tools to improve the code you are delivering. Let us study each of them in the next section, including how to set them up.

Understanding and applying tools that can evaluate C# code

The evolution of code analysis in Visual Studio is continuous. This means that Visual Studio 2019 certainly has more tools for this purpose than Visual Studio 2017, and so on.

One of the issues that you (as a software architect) need to deal with is the *coding style of the team*. This certainly results in a better understanding of the code. For instance, if you go to **Visual Studio Menu, Tools->Options**, and then, in the left-hand menu, you go to **Text Editor -> C#**, you will find ways to set up how to deal with different code style patterns, and a bad coding style is even indicated as an error in the **Code Style** option, as follows:

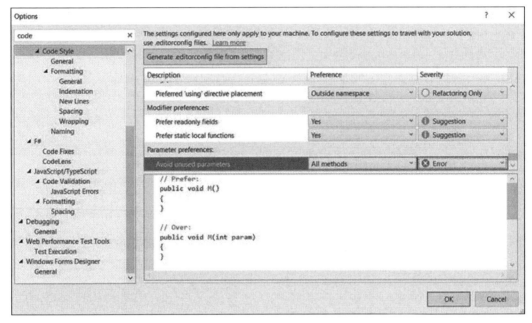

Figure 19.1: Code Style options

The preceding screenshot suggests that **Avoid unused parameters** was considered an error.

After this change, the result of the compilation of the same code presented at the beginning of the chapter is different, as you can see in the following screenshot:

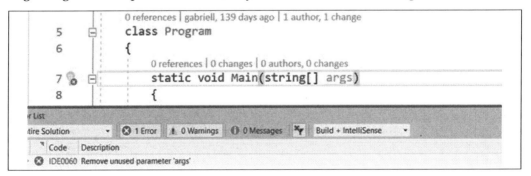

Figure 19.2: Code Style result

You can export your coding style configuration and attach it to your project so that it will follow the rules you have defined.

Another good tool that Visual Studio 2019 provides is **Analyze and Code Cleanup**. With this tool, you can set up some code standards that can clean up your code. For instance, in the following screenshot, it was set to remove unnecessary code:

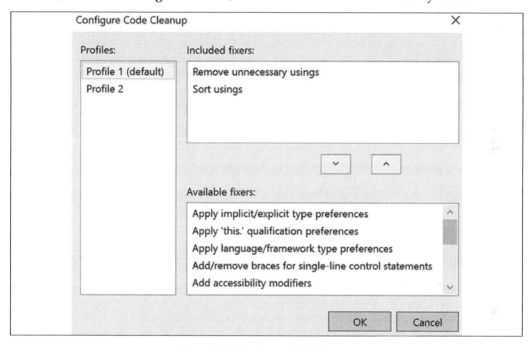

Figure 19.3: Configure Code Cleanup

The way you run code cleanup is by selecting it with the help of a right-click in the **Solution Explorer** area, over the project where you want to run it. After that, this process will run in all the code files you have:

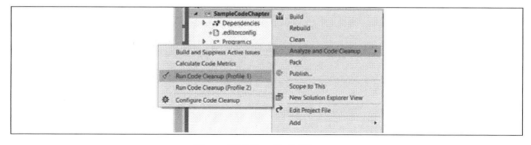

Figure 19.4: Run Code Cleanup

After solving the errors indicated by the Code Style and Code Cleanup tools, the sample code we are working on has some minimal simplifications, as follows:

```
using System;
try
{
    int variable = 10;
    if (variable == 10)
    {
        Console.WriteLine("variable equals 10");
    }
    else
    {
        switch (variable)
        {
            case 0:
                Console.WriteLine("variable equals 0");
                break;
        }
    }
}
catch
{
}
```

It is worth mentioning that the preceding code has many improvements that still need to be addressed. Visual Studio enables you to add additional tools for the IDE by installing extensions to it. These tools can help you to improve your code quality, since some of them were built to perform code analysis. This section will list some free options so that you can decide the one that best fits your needs. There are certainly other options and even paid ones. The idea here is not to indicate a specific tool but to give you an idea of their abilities.

To install these extensions, you will need to find the **Extensions** menu in Visual Studio 2019. Here is a screenshot of the **Manage Extensions** option:

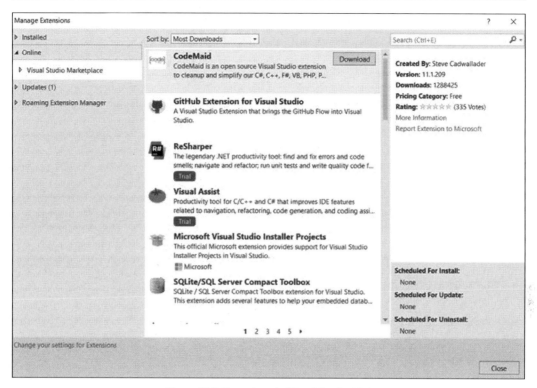

Figure 19.5: Extensions in Visual Studio 2019

 There are many other cool extensions that can improve the productivity and quality of your code and solution. Do a search for them in this manager.

After you have selected the extension that will be installed, you will need to restart Visual Studio. Most of them are easy to identify after installation since they modify the behavior of the IDE. Among them, Microsoft Code Analysis 2019 and SonarLint for Visual Studio 2019 can be considered good ones, and they will be discussed in the next section.

Applying extension tools to analyze code

Although the sample code delivered after the Code Style and Code Cleanup tools is better than the code we presented at the beginning of the chapter, it is clearly far removed from the best practices discussed in *Chapter 17, Best Practices in Coding C# 9*. In the next sections, you will be able to check the behavior of two extensions that can help you evolve this code: Microsoft Code Analysis 2019, and SonarLint for Visual Studio 2019.

Using Microsoft Code Analysis 2019

This extension is provided by Microsoft DevLabs and is an upgrade to the FxCop rules that we used to automate in the past. It can also be added to a project as a NuGet package, so it can become a part of the application CI build. Basically, it has more than 100 rules for detecting problems in the code as you type it.

For instance, just by enabling the extension and rebuilding the small sample we are using in this chapter, Code Analysis found a new issue to solve, as you can see in the following screenshot:

Figure 19.6: Code Analysis usage

It is worth mentioning that we discussed the usage of empty `try-catch` statements as an anti-pattern in *Chapter 17, Best Practices in Coding C# 9*. So, it would be good for the health of the code if this kind of problem could be exposed in this way.

Applying SonarLint for Visual Studio 2019

SonarLint is an open source initiative from the Sonar Source community to detect
bugs and quality issues while you code. There is support for C#, VB.NET, C,
C++, and JavaScript. The great thing about this extension is that it comes with
explanations for resolving detected issues, and that is why we say developers learn
how to code well while using these tools. Check out the following screenshot with
the analysis undertaken in the sample code:

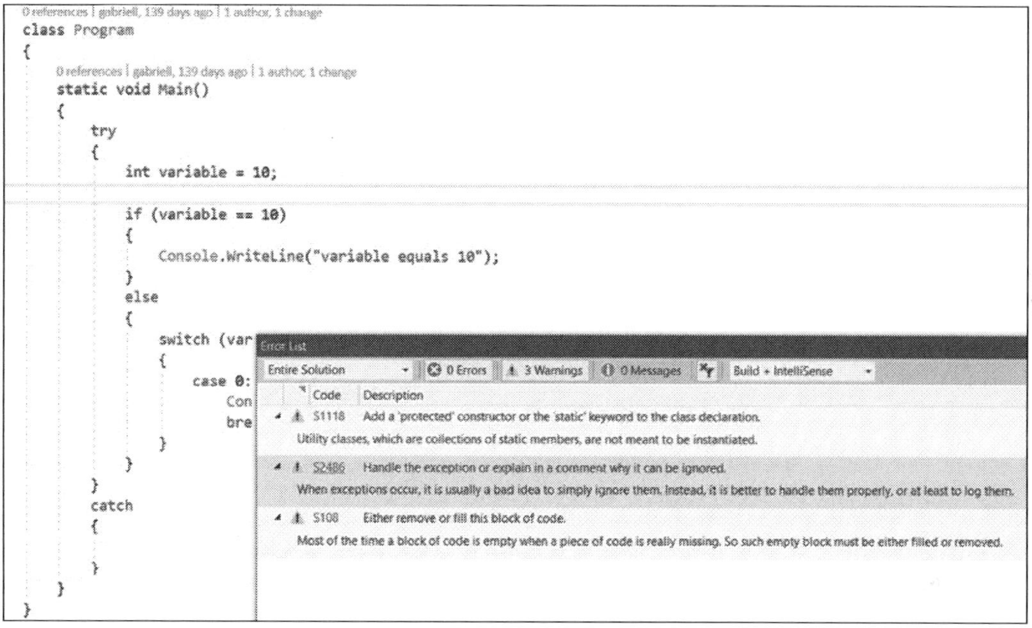

Figure 19.7: SonarLint usage

We can verify that this extension is able to point out mistakes and, as promised, there
is an explanation for each warning. This is useful not only for detecting problems,
but also for training developers in good coding practices.

Checking the final code after analysis

Following the analysis of the two extensions, we have finally solved all the issues
presented. We can check the final code, as follows:

```
using System;

try
{
```

```
    int variable = 10;

    if (variable == 10)
    {
        Console.WriteLine("variable equals 10");
    }
    else
    {
        switch (variable)
        {
            case 0:
                Console.WriteLine("variable equals 0");
                break;
            default:
                Console.WriteLine("Unknown behavior");
                break;
        }
    }
}
catch (Exception err)
{
    Console.WriteLine(err);
}
```

As you can see, the preceding code is not only easier to understand, but it is safer and is able to consider different paths of programming since the default for switch-case was programmed. This pattern was discussed in *Chapter 17, Best Practices in Coding C# 9*, too, which concludes that best practices can be easily followed by using one (or all) of the extensions mentioned in this chapter.

Use case – Evaluating C# code before publishing an application

In *Chapter 3*, *Documenting Requirements with Azure DevOps*, we created the WWTravelClub repository in the platform. As we saw there, Azure DevOps enables continuous integration, and this can be useful. In this section, we will discuss more reasons as to why the DevOps concept and the Azure DevOps platform are so useful.

For now, the only thing we would like to introduce is the possibility of analyzing code after it is committed by the developers, but has not yet been published. Nowadays, in a SaaS world for application life cycle tools, this is only possible thanks to some of the SaaS code analysis platforms that we have. This use case will use Sonar Cloud.

Sonar Cloud is free for open source code and can analyze code stored in GitHub, Bitbucket, and Azure DevOps. The user needs a registration for these platforms. As soon as you log in, assuming your code is stored in Azure DevOps, you can follow the steps described in the following article to create the connection between your Azure DevOps and Sonar Cloud: `https://sonarcloud.io/documentation/analysis/scan/sonarscanner-for-azure-devops/`.

After setting up the connection between your project in Azure DevOps and Sonar Cloud, you will have a build pipeline like the one that follows:

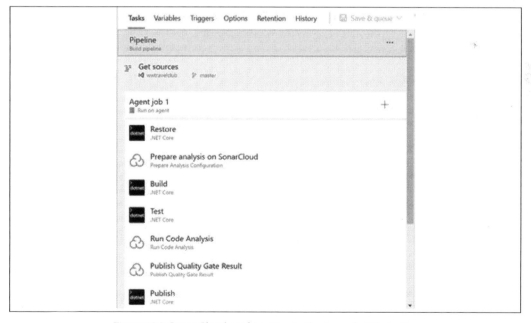

Figure 19.8: Sonar Cloud configuration in the Azure build pipeline

It is worth mentioning that C# projects do not have a GUID number, and this is required by Sonar Cloud. You can easily generate one using this link (`https://www.guidgenerator.com/`), and it will need to be placed as in the following screenshot:

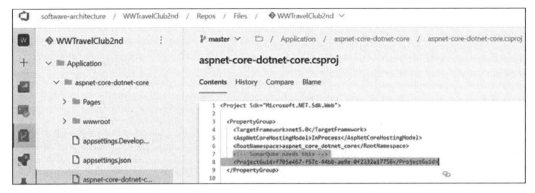

Figure 19.9: SonarQube project GUID

As soon as you finish the build, the result of the code analysis will be presented in Sonar Cloud, as can be seen in the following screenshot. If you want to navigate down to this project, you can visit `https://sonarcloud.io/dashboard?id=WWTravelClubNet50`:

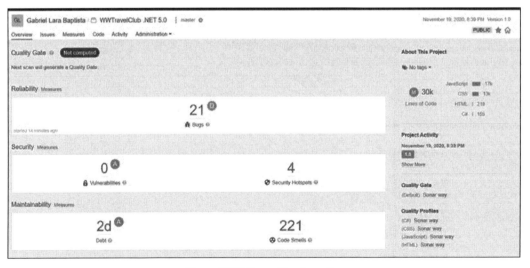

Figure 19.10: Sonar Cloud results

Also, by this time, the code analyzed is not yet in the release, so this can be really useful for getting the next step of quality before releasing your system. You can use this approach as a reference for automating code analysis during committal.

Summary

This chapter presented tools that can be used to apply the best practices of coding described in *Chapter 17, Best Practices in Coding C# 9*. We looked at the Roslyn compiler, which enables code analysis at the same time the developer is coding, and we looked at a use case, evaluating C# code prior to publishing an application, which implements code analysis during the Azure DevOps building process using Sonar Cloud.

As soon as you apply everything you have learned in this chapter to your projects, the code analysis will give you the opportunity to improve the quality of the code you are delivering to your customer. This is a very important part of your role as a software architect.

In the next chapter, you will be deploying your application with Azure DevOps.

Questions

1. How can software be described as well-written code?
2. What is Roslyn?
3. What is code analysis?
4. What is the importance of code analysis?
5. How does Roslyn help in code analysis?
6. What are Visual Studio extensions?
7. What are the extension tools presented for code analysis?

Further reading

These are some websites where you will find more information on the topics covered in this chapter:

- `https://marketplace.visualstudio.com/items?itemName=VisualStudioPlatformTeam.MicrosoftCodeAnalysis2019`
- `https://marketplace.visualstudio.com/items?itemName=SonarSource.SonarLintforVisualStudio2019`
- `https://github.com/dotnet/roslyn-analyzers`

- https://docs.microsoft.com/en-us/visualstudio/ide/code-styles-and-code-cleanup
- https://sonarcloud.io/documentation/analysis/scan/sonarscanner-for-azure-devops/
- https://www.guidgenerator.com/

20
Understanding DevOps Principles

DevOps is a process that everybody is learning and putting into practice these days. But as a software architect, you need to understand and propagate DevOps not only as a process, but as a philosophy. This chapter will cover the main concepts, principles, and tools you need to develop and deliver your software with DevOps.

In considering the DevOps philosophy, this chapter will focus on so-called **service design thinking**, that is, keeping in mind the software you are designing as a service offered to an organization/part of an organization. The main takeaway of this approach is that the highest priority is the value your software gives to the target organization. Moreover, you are not offering just working code and an agreement to fix bugs, but a solution for all the needs that your software was conceived for. In other words, your job includes everything it needs to satisfy those needs, such as monitoring users' satisfaction and adapting the software when the user needs change. Finally, it is easier to monitor the software to reveal issues and new requirements, and to modify it to adapt it quickly to ever-changing needs.

Service design thinking is strictly tied to the **Software as a Service (SaaS)** model, which we discussed in *Chapter 4, Deciding the Best Cloud-Based Solution*. In fact, the simplest way to offer solutions based on web services is to offer the usage of web services as a service instead of selling the software that implements them.

The following topics will be covered in this chapter:

- Describing what DevOps is and looking at a sample of how to apply it in the WWTravelClub project
- Understanding DevOps principles and deployment stages to leverage the deployment process
- Understanding continuous delivery with Azure DevOps
- Defining continuous feedback, and discussing the related tools in Azure DevOps
- Understanding SaaS and preparing a solution for a service scenario
- Use case – deploying our package-management application with Azure Pipelines

In contrast with other chapters, the WWTravelClub project will be presented during the topics, and we will offer an additional conclusion at the end of the chapter, giving you the opportunity to understand how the DevOps philosophy can be implemented. All the screenshots exemplifying the DevOps principles come from the main use case of the book, so you will be able to understand the DevOps principles easily. By the end of this chapter, you will be able to design software according to service design thinking principles and use Azure Pipelines to deploy your application.

Technical requirements

This chapter requires Visual Studio 2019 Community Edition or better with all Azure Tools installed. You may also need an Azure DevOps account, as described in *Chapter 3, Documenting Requirements with Azure DevOps*. It requires a free Azure account too. If you have not already created one, the *Creating an Azure account* subsection of *Chapter 1, Understanding the Importance of Software Architecture*, explains how to do so. This chapter uses the same code as *Chapter 18, Testing Your Code with Unit Test Cases and TDD*, which is available here: `https://github.com/PacktPublishing/Software-Architecture-with-C-9-and-.NET-5`.

Describing DevOps

DevOps comes from a union of the words *Development and Operations*, so this process simply unifies actions in these areas. However, when you start to study a little bit more about it, you will realize that connecting these two areas is not enough to achieve the true goals of this philosophy.

We can also say that DevOps is the process that answers the current needs of humanity regarding software delivery.

 Donovan Brown, Principal DevOps Manager of Microsoft, has a spectacular definition of what DevOps is: *DevOps is the union of people, process, and products to enable continuous delivery of value to our end users.* http://donovanbrown.com/post/what-is-devops.

A way to deliver value continuously to our end users, using process, people, and products: this is the best description of the DevOps philosophy. We need to develop and deliver customer-oriented software. As soon as all areas of the company understand that the key point is the end user, your task as a software architect is to present the technology that will facilitate the process of delivering.

It is worth mentioning that all the content of this book is connected to this approach. It is never a matter of knowing a bunch of tools and technologies. As a software architect, you must understand that it is always a way to bring faster solutions easily to your end user, linked to their real needs. For this reason, you need to learn the DevOps principles, which will be discussed during the chapter.

Understanding DevOps principles

Considering DevOps as a philosophy, it is worth mentioning that there are some principles that enable the process to work well in your team. These principles are continuous integration, continuous delivery, and continuous feedback.

 Microsoft has a specific web page for defining the DevOps overview, culture, practices, tools, and its relation to the cloud. Please check this out at https://azure.microsoft.com/en-us/overview/what-is-devops/.

DevOps is represented by the symbol of infinity in many books and technical articles. This symbol represents the necessity for a continuous approach in the software development life cycle. During the cycle, you will need to plan, build, continuously integrate, deploy, operate, get feedback, and start all over again. The process must be a collaborative one, since everybody has the same focus—to deliver value to the end user. Together with these principles, you as a software architect will need to decide the best software development process that fits this approach. We discussed these processes in *Chapter 1, Understanding the Importance of Software Architecture*.

Defining continuous integration

When you start building enterprise solutions, collaboration is the key to getting things done faster and to meeting the user needs. Version control systems, as we discussed in *Chapter 17, Best Practices in Coding C# 9*, are essential for this process, but the tool by itself does not do the job, especially if the tool is not well configured.

As a software architect, **continuous integration** (CI) will help you to have a concrete approach for software development collaboration. When you implement it, as soon as a developer commits their code, the main code is automatically built and tested.

The good thing when you apply CI is that you can motivate developers to merge their changes as fast as they can to minimize merge conflicts. Besides, they can share unit tests, which will improve the quality of software.

It is very simple to set up CI in Azure DevOps. In the build pipeline, you will find the option by editing the configuration, as you can see in the following screenshot:

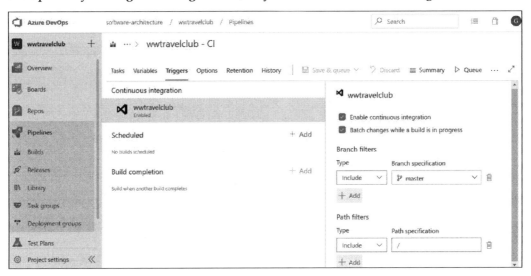

Figure 20.1: The Enable continuous integration checkbox

It is worth mentioning that if you have a solution set with unit and functional tests, as soon as you commit the code, it will automatically be compiled and tested. This will make your master branch stable and safe after every commit from your team.

The key point of CI is the ability to identify problems more quickly. You will have this opportunity when you allow the code to be tested and analyzed by others. The only thing the DevOps approach helps with is making sure this happens as quickly as possible.

Understanding continuous delivery with Azure DevOps

Once every single commit of your application is built, and this code is tested with both unit and functional tests, you may also want to deploy it continuously. Doing this is not just a matter of configuring the tool. As a software architect, you need to be sure that the team and the process are ready to go to this step. But let's check how to enable this first scenario of deployment using the book use case.

Deploying our package-management application with Azure Pipelines

In this section, we will configure an automatic deployment to the Azure App Service platform for the DevOps project that we defined in the use case at the end of *Chapter 18, Testing Your Code with Unit Test Cases and TDD*. Azure DevOps can also automatically create a new web app, but to prevent configuration errors (which might consume all your free credit), we will create it manually and let Azure DevOps just deploy the application. All the required steps are organized into various subsections as follows.

Creating the Azure Web App and the Azure database

An Azure Web App can be defined by following the simple steps that follow:

1. Go to the Azure Portal and select **App Services**, and then click the **Add** button to create a new Web App. Fill in all data as follows:

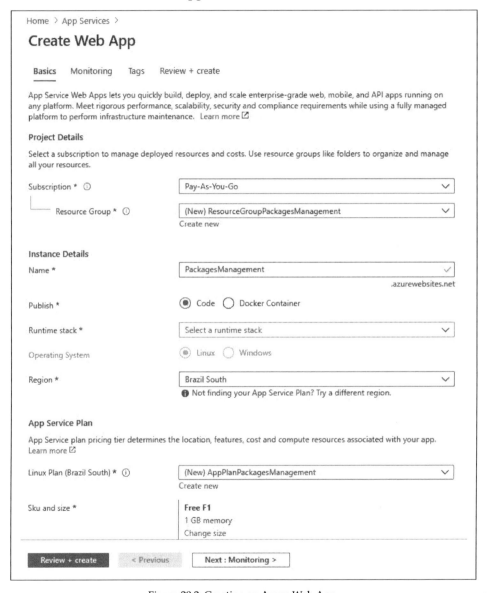

Figure 20.2: Creating an Azure Web App

2. Clearly, you may use a **Resource Group** you already have, and the most convenient region for you. For **Runtime stack**, please select the same .NET Core version you used in the Visual Studio solution.

3. Now, if you have enough credit, let's create a SQL Server database for the application, and let's call it `PackagesManagementDatabase`. If you do not have enough credit, do not worry—you can still test application deployment, but the application will return an error when it tries to access the database. Please refer to the *Relational databases* subsection of *Chapter 9, How to Choose Your Data Storage in the Cloud*, to see how to create a SQL Server database.

Configuring your Visual Studio solution

Once you have defined the Azure Web App, you need to configure the application for running in Azure by following these simple steps:

1. If you defined an Azure database, you need two different connection strings in your Visual Studio solution, one for the local databases for development and another one for your Azure Web App.

2. Now, open both `appsettings.Development.json` and `appsettings.json` in your Visual Studio solution, as follows:

Figure 20.3: Opening settings in Visual Studio

3. Then, copy the whole `ConnectionStrings` node of `appsettings.json` into `appsettings.Development.json`, as follows:

```
"ConnectionStrings": {

        "DefaultConnection": "Server=(localdb)....."

},
```

4. Now you have the local connection string in the development settings, so you can change `DefaultConnection` in `appsettings.json` to one of the Azure databases.

5. Go to the database in the Azure Portal, copy the connection string, and fill it with the username and password you got when you defined the database server.

6. Finally, commit your changes locally and then synchronize with the remote repository. Now, your changes are on DevOps Pipelines, which is already processing them to get a new build.

Configuring Azure Pipelines

Finally, you can configure an Azure pipeline for the automatic delivery of your application on Azure by following these steps:

1. Connect Visual Studio with your DevOps project by clicking the **Manage Connections** link in the **Connections** tab of the Visual Studio **Team Explorer** window. Then, click the DevOps link to go to your online project.

2. Modify the `PackagesManagementWithTest` build pipeline by adding a further step after the unit test step. In fact, we need a step that prepares all files to be deployed in a ZIP file.

3. Click the **Edit** button of the `PackagesManagementWithTest` pipeline, and then go to the end of the file and write the following:

    ```
    - task: PublishBuildArtifacts@1
    ```

4. When the **Settings** link appears above the new task, click it to configure the new task:

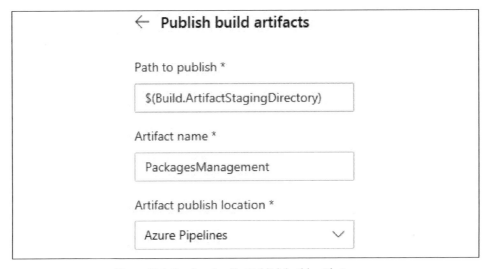

Figure 20.4: Configuring the Publish build artifacts pane

5. Accept the default **Path to publish** since it is already synchronized with the path of the task that will deploy the application, insert the artifact name, and then select **Azure Pipelines** as the location. As soon as you save, the pipeline will start, and the newly added task should succeed.

6. Deployments and other release artifacts are added to different pipelines called **Release Pipelines**, to decouple them from build-related artifacts. With **Release Pipelines**, you cannot edit a .yaml file, but you will work with a graphic interface.

7. Click the **Releases** left menu tab to create a new **Release Pipeline**. As soon as you click **Add a new pipeline**, you will be prompted to add the first task of the first pipeline stage. In fact, the whole release pipeline is composed of different stages, each grouping sequences of tasks. While each stage is just a sequence of tasks, the stages diagram can branch, and we can add several branches after each stage. This way, we can deploy to different platforms that each require different tasks. In our simple example, we will use a single stage.

8. Select the **Deploy Azure App Service** task. As soon as you add this task, you will be prompted to fill in missing information.

9. Click the **error link** and fill in the missing parameters:

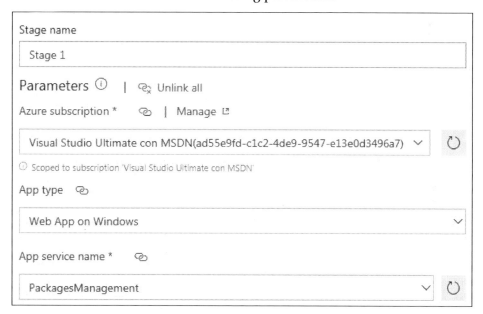

Figure 20.5: Configuring the publish stage

10. Select your subscription, and then, if an authorization button appears, please click it to **Authorize** Azure Pipelines to access your subscription. Then, select Windows as the deployment platform, and finally, select the app service you created from the **App service name** drop-down list. Task settings are automatically saved while you write them, so you need just to click the **Save** button for the whole pipeline.

11. Now, we need to connect this pipeline to a source artifact. Click the **Add Artifact** button and then select **Build** as the source type, because we need to connect the new release pipeline with the ZIP file created by our build pipeline. A settings window appears:

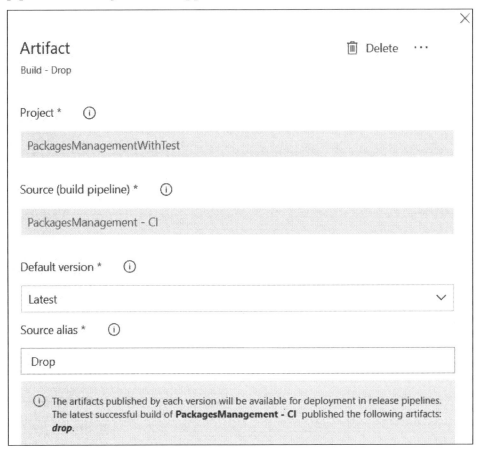

Figure 20.6: Defining the artifact to publish

12. Select our previous build pipeline from the drop-down list and keep **Latest** as the version. Accept the suggested name in **Source alias**.

13. Our release pipeline is ready and can be used as it is. The image of the source artifact you just added contains a trigger icon in its top-right corner, as follows:

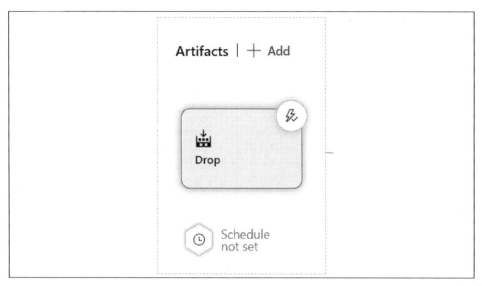

Figure 20.7: Artifact ready to publish

14. If you click on the trigger icon, you are given the option to automatically trigger the release pipeline as soon as a new build is available:

Figure 20.8: Enabling the continuous deployment trigger

15. Keep it disabled; we can enable it after we have completed and manually tested the release pipeline.

As we mentioned earlier, in preparation for an automatic trigger, we need to add a human approval task before the application is deployed.

Adding a manual approval for the release

Since tasks are usually executed by software agents, we need to embed human approval in a manual job. Let's add it with the following steps:

1. Click the three dots on the right of the **Stage 1** header:

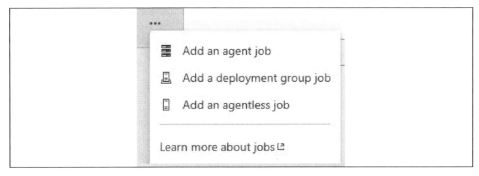

Figure 20.9: Adding human approval to a stage

2. Then, select **Add an agentless job**. Once the agentless job has been added, click the **add** button and add a **Manual intervention** task. The following screenshot shows the **Manual intervention** settings:

Figure 20.10: Configuring human approval for a stage

3. Add instructions for the operator and select your account in the **Notify users** field.

4. Now, drag the whole **Agentless job** with the mouse and place it before the application deployment task. It should look like this:

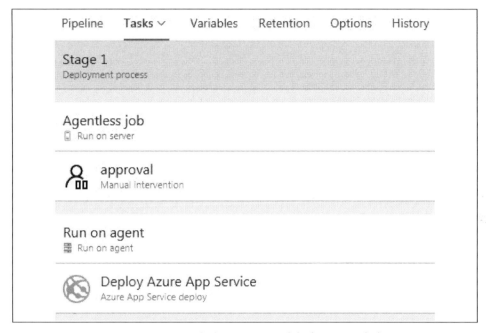

Figure 20.11: Setting the human approval deployment tasks list

5. Finished! Click the **Save** button in the top-left to save the pipeline.

Now, everything is ready to create our first automatic release.

Creating a release

Once you have everything in place, a new release can be prepared and deployed as follows:

1. Let's click the **Create release** button to start the creation of a new release, as shown in the following screenshot:

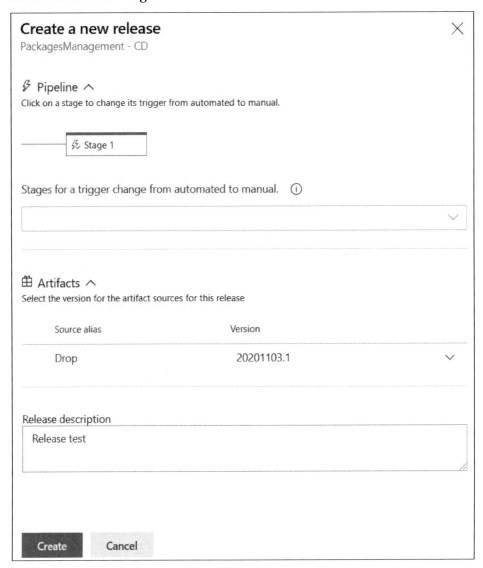

Figure 20.12: Creating a new release

2. Verify that the **Source alias** is the last available one, add a **Release description**, and then click **Create**. In a short time, you should receive an email for release approval. Click the link it contains and go to the approval page:

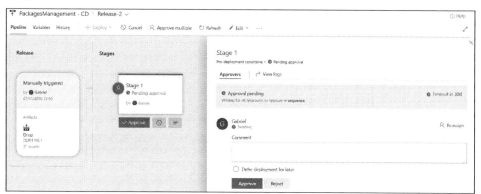

Figure 20.13: Approving a release

3. Click the **Approve** button to approve the release. Wait for the **deployment** to complete. You should have all the tasks successfully completed, as shown in the following screenshot:

Figure 20.14: Release deployed

4. You have run your first successful release pipeline!

In a real-life project, the release pipeline would contain some more tasks. In fact, applications (before being deployed in the actual production environment) are deployed in a staging environment where they are beta-tested. Hence, probably, after this first deployment, there would be some manual tests, manual authorization for the deployment in production, and the final deployment in production.

The multistage environment

The approach associated with **continuous delivery** (CD) needs to guarantee that the production environment will be kept safe in each new deployment. To do so, a multistage pipeline needs to be adopted. The following screenshot shows an approach with common stages, using the book use case as a demonstration:

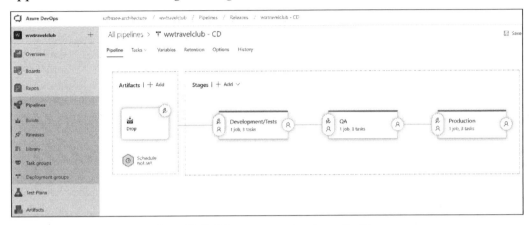

Figure 20.15: Release stages using Azure DevOps

As you can see, these stages were configured using the Azure DevOps release pipeline. Each stage has its own purpose, which will leverage the quality of the product delivered in the end. Let's look at the stages:

- **Development/tests**: This stage is used by developers and testers to build new functionality. This environment will certainly be the one that is most exposed to bugs and incomplete functions.

- **Quality assurance**: This environment gives a brief version of new functionalities to areas of the team not related to development and tests. Program managers, marketing, vendors, and others can use it as an area of study, validation, and even preproduction. Besides, the development and quality teams can guarantee that the new releases are correctly deployed, considering both functionality and infrastructure.

- **Production:** This is the stage where customers have their solution running. The goal for a good production environment, according to CD, is to have it updated as quickly as possible. The frequency will vary according to team size, but there are some approaches where this process happens more than once a day.

The adoption of these three stages of deploying your application will impact the quality of the solution. It will also enable the team to have a safer deployment process, with fewer risks and better stability of the product. This approach may look a bit expensive at first sight, but without it, the results of bad deployment will generally be more expensive than this investment.

Besides all the safety, you will have to consider the multistage scenario. You can set up the pipeline in a way where only with defined authorizations will you be able to move from one stage to another:

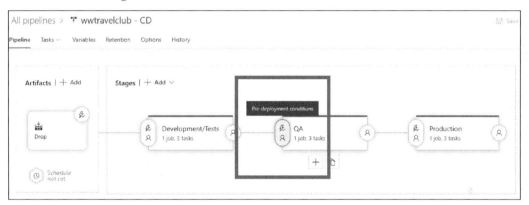

Figure 20.16: Defining pre-deployment conditions

As you can see in the preceding screenshot, it is quite simple to set up pre-deployment conditions, and you can see in the following screenshot that there is more than a single option to customize the authorization method. This gives you the possibility to refine the CD approach, exactly meeting the needs of the project you are dealing with.

The following screenshot shows the options provided by Azure DevOps for pre-deployment approval. You can define the people who can approve the stage and set policies for them, that is, revalidate the approver identity before completing the process. You, as a software architect, will need to identify the configuration that fits the project you are creating with this approach:

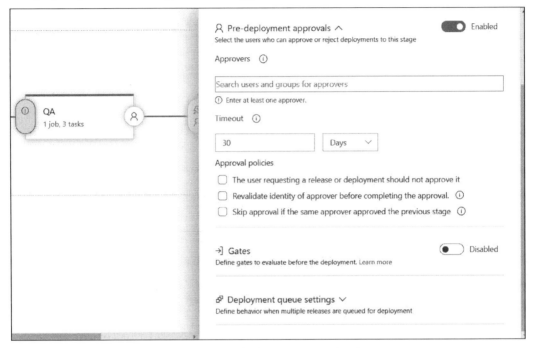

Figure 20.17: Pre-deployment approval options

It is worth mentioning that although this approach is far better than a single-stage deployment, a DevOps pipeline will direct you, as a software architect, to another stage of monitoring. Continuous feedback will be an incredible tool for this, and we will discuss this approach in the next section.

Defining continuous feedback and the related DevOps tools

Once you have a solution that is running perfectly in the deployment scenario described in the last section, feedback will be essential for your team to understand the results of the release and how the version is working for the customers. To get this feedback, some tools can help both the developers and the customers, bringing these people together to fast-track the process of feedback. Let's have a look at these tools.

Monitoring software with Azure Monitor Application Insights

Azure Monitor Application Insights is the tool a software architect needs to have for continuous feedback on their solution. It is worth mentioning that Application Insights is part of Azure Monitor, a wider suite of monitoring features that also includes alerting, dashboards, and workbooks. As soon as you connect your app to it, you start receiving feedback on each request made to the software. This enables you to monitor not only the requests made but your database performance, the errors that the application may be suffering from, and the calls that take the most time to process.

Obviously, you will have costs relating to having this tool plugged into your environment, but the facilities that the tool provides will be worth it. It might be worth noting that for simple applications it could even be free, because you pay for data ingested, for which there is a free quota. Besides, you need to understand that there is a very small performance cost since all the requests to store data in **Application Insights** run in a separate thread.

It may be worth noting that a number of services, such as App Services, Functions, and so on, will have an option to add Application Insights as part of the initial creation process, so you may have already created it while following through this book. Even so, the following screenshot shows how easily you can create a tool in your environment:

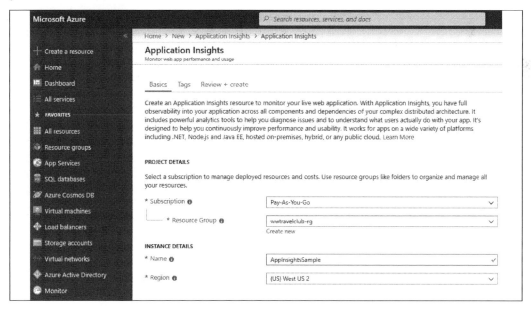

Figure 20.18: Creating Application Insights resources in Azure

If you want to set up Application Insights in your app using Visual Studio, you may find this Microsoft tutorial useful: `https://docs.microsoft.com/en-us/azure/azure-monitor/learn/dotnetcore-quick-start#configure-app-insights-sdk`.

For instance, let's suppose you need to analyze the requests that take more time in your application. The process of attaching Application Insights to your web app is quite simple: it can be done as soon as you set up your web app. If you are not sure whether Application Insights is configured for your web app, you can find out using the Azure portal. Navigate to **App Services** and look at the **Application Insights** settings, as shown in the following screenshot:

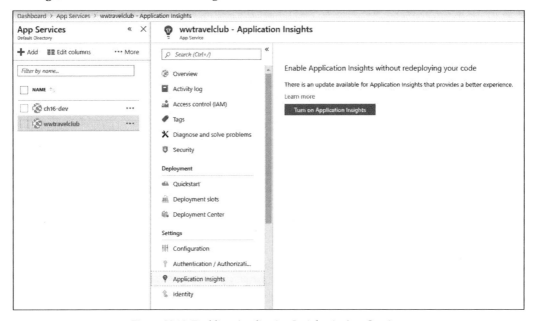

Figure 20.19: Enabling Application Insights in App Services

The interface will give you the opportunity to create or attach an already-created monitor service to your web app. It is worth mentioning that you can connect more than one web app to the same Application Insights component. The following screenshot shows how to add a web app to an already-created Application Insights resource:

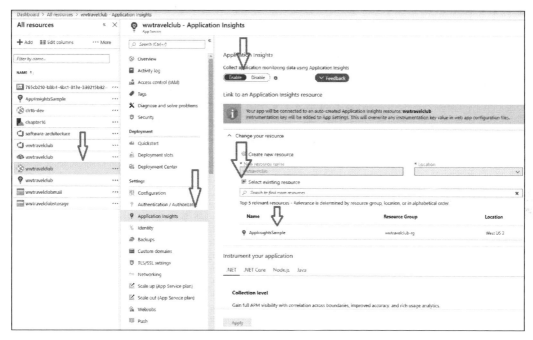

Figure 20.20: Enabling App Insights in App Services

Once you have Application Insights configured for your web app, you will find the following screen in App Services:

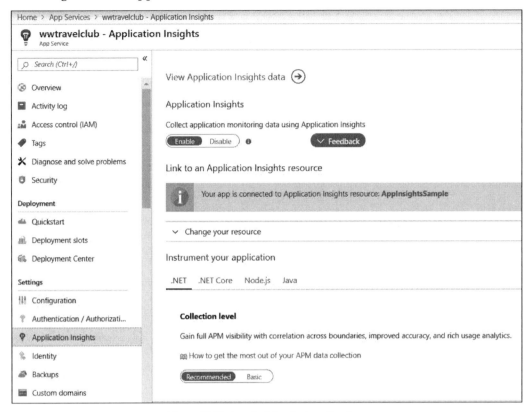

Figure 20.21: App Insights in App Services

Once it is connected to your solution, the data collection will happen continuously, and you will see the results in the dashboard provided by the component. You can find this screen in two places:

- At the same place as you configured Application Insights, inside the Web App portal

- In the Azure Portal, after navigating through the Application Insights resource:

Figure 20.22: Application Insights in action

This dashboard gives you an idea of failed requests, server response time, and server requests. You may also turn on the availability check, which will make requests to your selected URL from any of the Azure data centers.

But the beauty of Application Insights is related to how deeply it analyzes your system. In the following screenshot, for instance, it is giving you feedback on the number of requests made on the website. You can analyze it by ranking the ones that took more time to process or the ones that were called more often:

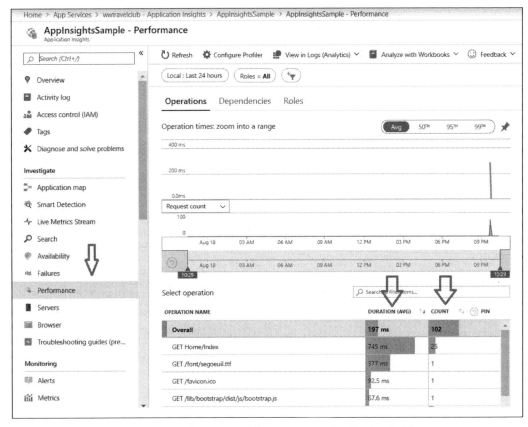

Figure 20.23: Analyzing app performance using Application Insights

Considering this view can be filtered in different ways and you receive the info just after it happens in your web app, this is certainly a tool that defines continuous feedback. This is one of the best ways you can use DevOps principles to achieve exactly what your customer needs.

Application Insights is a technical tool that does exactly what you as a software architect need to monitor modern applications in a real analytic model. It is a continuous feedback approach based on the behavior of users on the system you are developing.

Using the Test and Feedback tool to enable feedback

Another useful tool in the process of continuous feedback is the Test and Feedback tool, designed by Microsoft to help product owners and quality assurance users in the process of analyzing new features.

Using Azure DevOps, you may ask for feedback for your team by selecting an option inside each working item, as you can see in the following screenshot:

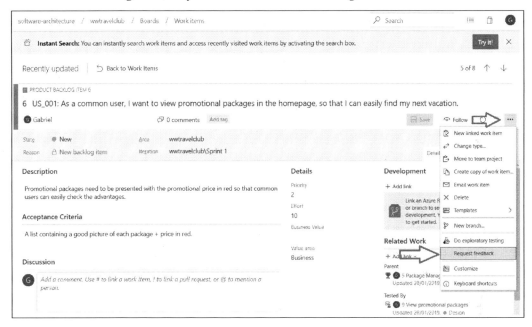

Figure 20.24: Requesting feedback using Azure DevOps

Once you receive a feedback request, you may use the Test and Feedback tool to analyze and give the correct feedback to the team. You will be able to connect the tool to your Azure DevOps project, giving you more features while analyzing the feedback request. It is worth mentioning that this tool is a web browser extension that you will need to install before use. The following screenshot shows how to set up an Azure DevOps project URL for the Test and Feedback tool:

 You can download this tool from `https://marketplace.visualstudio.com/items?itemName=ms.vss-exploratorytesting-web`.

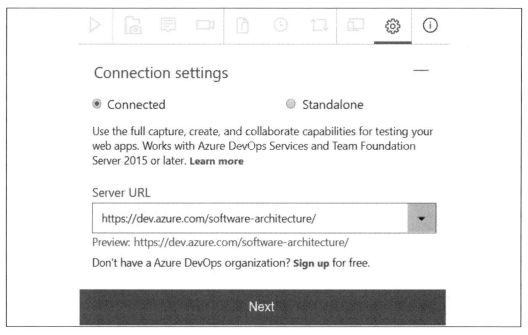

Figure 20.25: Connecting Test and Feedback to an Azure DevOps organization

The tool is quite simple. You can take screenshots, record a process, or even make a note. The following screenshot shows how easily you can write a message inside a screenshot:

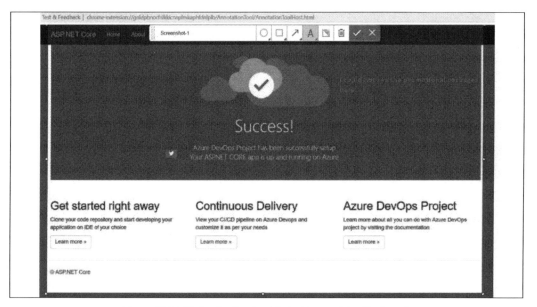

Figure 20.26: Giving feedback with the Test and Feedback tool

The good thing is that you record all this analysis in a session timeline. As you can see in the next screenshot, you can have more feedback in the same session, which is good for the analysis process:

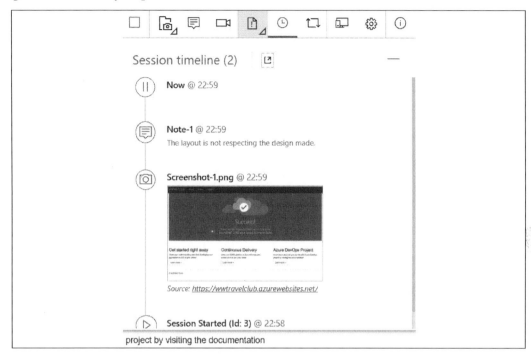

Figure 20.27: Giving feedback with the Test and Feedback tool

Once you have done the analysis and you are connected to Azure DevOps, you will be able to report a bug, create a task, or even start a new test case:

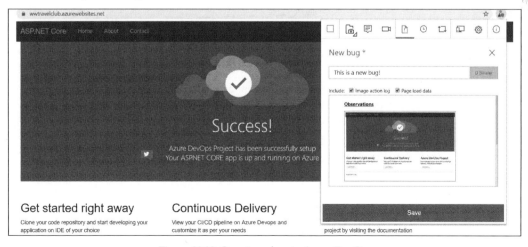

Figure 20.28: Opening a bug in Azure DevOps

The result of the bug created can be checked on the **Work items** board in Azure DevOps. It is worth mentioning that you do not need an Azure DevOps developer license to have access to this area of the environment. This enables you, as a software architect, to spread this basic and useful tool to as many key users of the solution as you have. The following screenshot shows the bug created by the tool once you have connected it to your Azure DevOps project:

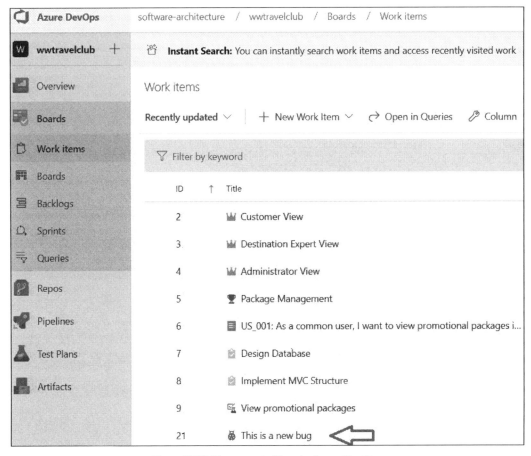

Figure 20.29: New reported bug in Azure DevOps

It is important to have a tool like this to have good feedback on your project. But, as a software architect, you may have to find the best solutions to accelerate this process. The tools explored in the book are good ways to do so. You may consider this approach every time you need to implement one more step in the development process. Continuous feedback is an important step in the process of developing software that will obtain new features continuously. Another very important approach that can take advantage of DevOps is SaaS. Let's learn about it in the next section.

Understanding SaaS

Selling/using Software as a Service relates to a wider set of solution design principles called **service design thinking**. Service design thinking is not just a software development technique and/or a software deployment approach, but it impacts several business areas, namely, organization and human resources, software development processes, and finally, hardware infrastructures and software architecture.

In the subsections that follow, we will briefly discuss the implications for each of the business areas we listed, and in the last subsection, we will focus specifically on the SaaS deployment model.

Adapting your organization to a service scenario

The first organizational implication comes from the need to optimize the value of the software for the target organization. This requires a human resource or a team to be in charge of planning and monitoring the impact of the software in the target organization in order to maximize the value added by the software. This strategic role is not needed just during the initial design stage, but during the whole lifetime of the application. In fact, this role oversees keeping the software fine-tuned with the ever-changing needs of the target organization.

Another important area of impact is human resource management. In fact, since the main priority is the value added by the software (and not exploiting existing resources and competencies), human resources must be adapted to the project needs. This means acquiring new people as soon as they are needed and developing the required competencies through adequate training.

The next subsection deals with the implications of all the processes involved in software development.

Developing software in a service scenario

The main constraint that impacts software development processes is the need to keep the software fine-tuned to the organization's needs. This need can be satisfied by any agile methodology based on a CI/CD approach. For a short review of CI/CD, please refer to the *Organizing your work using Azure DevOps* section of *Chapter 3, Documenting Requirements with Azure DevOps*. It is worth pointing out that any well-designed CI/CD cycle should include the processing of user feedback and user satisfaction reports.

Moreover, to optimize the value added by the software, it is good practice to organize stages where the development team (or part of it) is placed in close contact with the system users so that developers can better understand the impact of the software on the target organization.

Finally, the value added by the software must always be kept in mind when writing both functional and non-functional requirements. For this reason, it is useful to annotate *user stories* with a consideration of *why* and *how* they contribute to value. The process of collecting requirements is discussed in *Chapter 2, Non-Functional Requirements*.

More technical implications are discussed in the next subsection.

Technical implications of a service scenario

In a service scenario, both the hardware infrastructure and software architecture are constrained by three main principles, which are an immediate consequence of the requirement to keep the software fine-tuned to the organization's needs, namely, the following:

- The software needs to be monitored to discover any kind of issue that might have been caused by system malfunctions or changes in software usage and/ or user needs. This implies extracting health checks and load statistics from all hardware/software components. Good hints for discovering changes in the organization's needs are also given by statistics on the operations performed by the users—more specifically, the average time spent by both the user and the application on each operation instance, and the number of instances of each operation performed per unit of time (day, week, or month).

- It is also necessary to monitor user satisfaction. Feedback on user satisfaction can be obtained by adding to each application screen a link to an easy-to-fill user-satisfaction report page.

- Finally, there is the need to adapt both hardware and software quickly, both to the traffic received by each application module and to the changes in the organization's needs. This means the following:

    - Paying extreme attention to software modularity

    - Keeping the door open for changes in the database engine and preferring **Service Oriented Architecture (SOA)** or microservices-based solutions to monolithic software

    - Keeping the door open to new technologies

Making the hardware easy to adapt means allowing hardware scaling, which in turn implies either the adoption of cloud infrastructures or hardware clusters, or both. It is also important to keep the door open to changes in cloud service suppliers, which in turn means encapsulating the dependence on the cloud platform in a small number of software modules.

The maximization of the value added by the software can be achieved by choosing the best technology available for the implementation of each module, which in turn means being able to mix different technologies. This is where container-based technologies, such as Docker, come into play. Docker and related technologies were described in:

- *Chapter 5, Applying a Microservice Architecture to Your Enterprise Application*
- *Chapter 6, Azure Service Fabric*
- *Chapter 7, Azure Kubernetes Service*

Summing up, all of the requirements we have listed converge toward most of the advanced technologies we have described in this book, such as cloud services, scalable web applications, distributed/scalable databases, Docker, Kubernetes, SOA, and microservices architectures.

More details on how to prepare your software for a service environment are given in the next section, while the next subsection focuses specifically on the advantages and disadvantages of SaaS applications.

Deciding when to adopt a SaaS solution

The main attraction of SaaS solutions is their flexible payment model, which offers the following advantages:

- You can avoid abandoning big investments in favor of more affordable monthly payments
- You can start with a cheap system and then move toward more expensive solutions only when the business grows

However, SaaS solutions also offer other advantages, namely, the following:

- In all cloud solutions, you can easily scale up your solution
- The application is automatically updated
- Since SaaS solutions are delivered over the public internet, they are accessible from any location

Unfortunately, SaaS advantages come at a cost, since SaaS also has some not negligible disadvantages, namely, the following:

- Your business is strictly tied to the SaaS provider, which might discontinue the service and/or modify it in a way that is not acceptable to you anymore.

- Usually, you cannot implement any kind of customization, being limited to the few standard options offered by the SaaS supplier. However, sometimes SaaS suppliers also offer the possibility of adding custom modules written either by them or by you.

Summing up, SaaS solutions offer interesting advantages but also some disadvantages, so you, as a software architect, must perform a detailed analysis to decide how to adopt them.

The next section explains how to adapt software to be used in a service scenario.

Preparing a solution for a service scenario

First, *preparing a solution for a service scenario* means designing it specifically for the cloud and/or for a distributed environment. In turn, this means designing it with scalability, fault tolerance, and automatic fault recovery in mind.

The main implications of the preceding three points are concerned with the way the *state* is handled. Stateless module instances are easy to scale and to replace, so you should carefully plan which modules are stateless and which ones have states. Moreover, as explained in *Chapter 9, How to Choose Your Data Storage in the Cloud*, you have to keep in mind that write and read operations scale in a completely different way. Read operations are easier to scale with replication, while write operations do not scale well with relational databases and often require NoSQL solutions.

High scalability in a distributed environment prevents the usage of distributed transactions and of synchronous operations in general. Therefore, data coherence and fault tolerance can be achieved only with more complex techniques based on asynchronous messages, such as the following:

- One technique is storing all messages to send in a queue so that asynchronous transmissions can be retried in the event of errors or timeouts. Messages can be removed from the queue either when confirmation of reception is received or when the module decides to abort the operation that produced the message.

- Another is handling the possibility that the same message is received several times because timeouts caused the same message to be sent several times.

- If needed, use techniques such as optimistic concurrency and event sourcing to minimize concurrency problems in databases. Optimistic concurrency is explained in *Defining the data layer* subsection of the use case at the end of *Chapter 15*, *Presenting ASP.NET Core MVC*, while event sourcing is described together with other data layer stuff in the *Using SOLID principles to map your domains* section of *Chapter 12*, *Understanding the Different Domains in Software Solution*.

 The first two points in the preceding list are discussed in detail together with other distributed processing techniques in the *How does .NET Core deal with microservices?* section of *Chapter 5*, *Applying a Microservice Architecture to Your Enterprise Application*.

Fault tolerance and automatic fault recovery require that software modules implement health check interfaces that the cloud framework might call, to verify whether the module is working properly or whether it needs to be killed and replaced by another instance. ASP.NET Core and all Azure microservices solutions offer basic off-the-shelf health checks, so the developer does not need to take care of them. However, more detailed custom health checks can be added by implementing a simple interface.

The difficulty increases if you have the goal of possibly changing the cloud provider of some of the application modules. In this case, the dependency from the cloud platform must be encapsulated in just a few modules, and solutions that are too strictly tied to a specific cloud platform must be discarded.

If your application is conceived for a service scenario, everything must be automated: new versions testing and validation, the creation of the whole cloud infrastructure needed by the application, and the deployment of the application on that infrastructure.

All cloud platforms offer languages and facilities to automate the whole software CI/CD cycle, that is, building the code, testing it, triggering manual version approvals, hardware infrastructure creation, and application deployment.

Azure Pipelines allows the complete automatization of all the steps listed. The use case in *Chapter 18*, *Testing Your Code with Unit Test Cases and TDD*, shows how to automate all steps up to and including software testing with Azure Pipelines. The use case in the next section will show how to automate the application deployment on the Azure Web Apps platform.

Automation has a more fundamental role in SaaS applications, since the whole creation of a new tenant for each new customer must be automatically triggered by the customer subscription. More specifically, multi-tenant SaaS applications can be implemented with three fundamental techniques:

- All customers share the same hardware infrastructure and data storage. This solution is the easiest to implement since it requires the implementation of a standard web application. However, it is possible only for very simple SaaS services since, for more complex applications, it becomes increasingly difficult to ensure that storage space and computation time are split equally between users. Moreover, as the database becomes more and more complex, it is always more difficult to keep the data of different users safely isolated.

- All customers share the same infrastructure, but each customer has their own data storage. This option solves all the database problems of the previous solution, and it is quite easy to automate since the creation of a new tenant just requires the creation of a new database. This solution offers a simple way to define pricing strategies, by linking them to storage consumption.

- Each customer has their own private infrastructure and data storage. This is the most flexible strategy. From the user's point of view, its only disadvantage is the higher price. Therefore, it is convenient only above a minimum threshold of computational power required by each user. It is more difficult to automate, since a whole infrastructure must be created for each new customer and a new instance of the application must be deployed on it.

Whichever of the three strategies is chosen, you need to be able to scale out your cloud resources as your consumers increase.

If you also need the possibility to ensure your infrastructure creation scripts work across several cloud providers, then, on the one hand, you can't use features that are too specific to a single cloud platform, and on the other, you need a unique infrastructure creation language that can be translated into the native languages of the more common cloud platforms. Terraform and Ansible are two very common choices for describing hardware infrastructures.

The WWTravelClub project approach

During this chapter, screenshots from the WWTravelClub project have shown the steps needed to implement a good DevOps cycle. The WWTravelClub team has decided to use Azure DevOps because they understand that the tool is essential for getting the best DevOps experience for the whole cycle.

The requirements were written using user stories, which can be found in the **Work items** section of Azure DevOps. The code is placed in the repository of the Azure DevOps project. Both concepts were explained in *Chapter 3*, *Documenting Requirements with Azure DevOps*.

The management life cycle used for getting things done is Scrum, presented in *Chapter 1*, *Understanding the Importance of Software Architecture*. This approach divides the implementation into Sprints, which forces the need to deliver value by the end of each cycle. Using the continuous integration facilities we learned in this chapter, code will be compiled each time the team concludes a development to the master branch of the repository.

Once the code is compiled and tested, the first stage of the deployment is done. The first stage is normally named Development/Test because you enable it for internal tests. Both Application Insights and Test and Feedback can be used to get the first feedback on the new release.

If the tests and the feedback of the new release pass, it is time to go to the second stage, Quality Assurance. Application Insights and Test and Feedback can be used again, but now in a more stable environment.

The cycle ends with the authorization to deploy in the production stage. This certainly is a tough decision, but DevOps indicates that you must do it continuously so you can get better feedback from customers. Application Insights keeps being a useful tool, since you can monitor the evolution of the new release in production, even comparing it to the past releases.

The WWTravelClub project approach described here can be used in many other modern application development life cycles. As a software architect, you must oversee the process. The tools are ready to go, and it depends on you to make things right!

Summary

In this chapter, we have learned that DevOps is not only a bunch of techniques and tools used together to deliver software continuously, but a philosophy to enable continuous delivery of value to the end user of the project you are developing.

Considering this approach, we saw how continuous integration, continuous delivery, and continuous feedback are essential to the purpose of DevOps. We also saw how Azure, Azure DevOps, and Microsoft tools help you to achieve your goals.

We described *service design thinking* principles and the SaaS software deployment model. Now, you should be able to analyze all of the implications of these approaches for an organization, and you should be able to adapt pre-existing software development processes and hardware/software architectures to take advantage of the opportunities they offer.

We also explained the need for, and the techniques involved in, the automation of the software cycle, cloud hardware infrastructure configuration, and application deployment.

Once you have implemented the examples shown, you should be able to use Azure Pipelines to automate infrastructure configuration and application deployment. This chapter elucidated this approach using WWTravelClub as an example, enabling CI/CD inside Azure DevOps, and using Application Insights and the Test and Feedback tool for both technical and functional feedback. In real life, these tools will enable you to understand the current behavior of the system you are developing more quickly, as you will have continuous feedback on it.

In the next chapter, we will learn about continuous integration in detail, which plays a fundamental role in service scenarios and the maintenance of SaaS applications.

Questions

1. What is DevOps?
2. What is continuous integration?
3. What is continuous delivery?
4. What is continuous feedback?
5. What is the difference between the build and release pipelines?
6. What is the main purpose of Application Insights in the DevOps approach?
7. How can the Test and Feedback tool help in the process of DevOps?
8. What is the main goal of service design thinking?
9. Is it true that service design thinking requires the optimal usage of all competencies already available in the company?
10. Why is complete automation fundamental in the life cycle of SaaS applications?
11. Is it possible to define hardware cloud infrastructures with a platform-independent language?
12. What is the preferred Azure tool for the automation of the whole application life cycle?

13. If two SaaS suppliers offer the same software product, should you use the most reliable or the cheapest one?

14. Is scalability the only important requirement in a service scenario?

Further reading

These are some websites where you will find more information on the topics covered in this chapter:

- http://donovanbrown.com/

- https://azure.microsoft.com/en-us/overview/what-is-devops/

- https://www.packtpub.com/networking-and-servers/devops-fundamentals-video

- https://docs.microsoft.com/en-us/azure/devops/learn/what-is-devops

- https://azuredevopslabs.com/labs/devopsserver/exploratorytesting/

- https://docs.microsoft.com/en-us/azure/azure-monitor/app/app-insights-overview

- https://marketplace.visualstudio.com/items?itemName=ms.vss-exploratorytesting-web

- https://docs.microsoft.com/en-us/azure/devops/test/request-stakeholder-feedback

- https://docs.microsoft.com/en-us/azure/devops/pipelines/?view=azure-devops

- https://www.terraform.io/

- https://www.ansible.com/

21
Challenges of Applying CI Scenarios

Continuous Integration (**CI**) is sometimes stated as a prerequisite for DevOps. In the previous chapter, we discussed the basics of CI and how DevOps depends on it. Its implementation was presented in *Chapter 20, Understanding DevOps Principles*, too. But differently from the other practical chapters, the purpose of this chapter is to discuss how to enable CI in a real scenario, considering the challenges that you, as a software architect, will need to deal with.

The topics covered in this chapter are as follows:

- Understanding CI
- Continuous Integration and GitHub
- Understanding the risks and challenges when using CI
- Understanding the WWTravelClub project approach for this chapter

Like in the previous chapter, the sample of the WWTravelClub will be presented during the explanation of the chapter, since all the screens captured to exemplify CI came from it. Besides this, we will offer a conclusion at the end of the chapter so you can understand CI principles easily.

By the end of the chapter, you will be able to decide whether to use CI in your project environment. Additionally, you will be able to define the tools needed for the successful use of this approach.

Technical requirements

This chapter requires Visual Studio 2019 Community edition or better. You may also need an Azure DevOps account, as described in *Chapter 3, Documenting Requirements with Azure DevOps*. You can find the sample code for the chapter at `https://github.com/PacktPublishing/Software-Architecture-with-C-9-and-.NET-5`.

Understanding CI

As soon as you start working with a platform such as Azure DevOps, enabling CI will definitely be easy when it comes to clicking on the options for doing so, as we saw in *Chapter 20, Understanding DevOps Principles*. So, technology is not the Achilles' heel for implementing this process.

The following screenshot shows an example of how easy it is to turn on CI using Azure DevOps. By clicking in the build pipeline and editing it, you will be able to set a trigger that enables CI after some clicks:

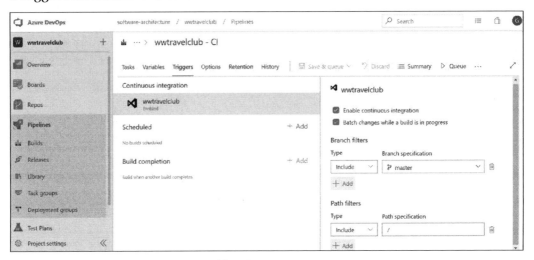

Figure 21.1: Enabling Continuous Integration trigger

The truth is that CI will help you solve some problems. For instance, it will force you to test your code, since you will need to commit the changes faster, so other developers can make use of the code you are programming.

On the other hand, you will not do CI just by enabling a CI build in Azure DevOps. For sure, you will turn on the possibility of starting a build as soon as you get a commit done and the code is done, but this is far from saying you have CI available in your solution.

The reason why you as a software architect need to worry a bit more about it is related to a real understanding of what DevOps is. As discussed in *Chapter 20, Understanding DevOps Principles*, the need to deliver value to the end user will always be a good way to decide on and draw the development life cycle. So, even if turning on CI is easy, what is the real business impact of this feature being enabled for your end user? Once you have all the answers to this question and you know how to reduce the risks of its implementation, then you will be able to say that you have a CI process implemented.

It is worth mentioning that CI is a principle that will make DevOps work better and faster, as was discussed in *Chapter 20, Understanding DevOps Principles*. However, DevOps surely can live without it, once you are not sure if your process is mature enough to enable code being continuously delivered. More than that, if you turn on CI in a team that is not mature enough to deal with its complexity, you will probably cause a bad understanding of DevOps, since you will start incurring some risks while deploying your solution. The point is, CI is not a prerequisite for DevOps. When you have CI enabled, you can make things faster in DevOps. However, you can practice DevOps without it.

This is the reason why we are dedicating an extra chapter to CI. As a software architect, you need to understand the key points of having CI switched on. But, before we check this out, let's learn another tool that can help us out with continuous integration – GitHub.

Continuous Integration and GitHub

Since GitHub's acquisition by Microsoft, many features have evolved and new options have been delivered, enhancing the power of this powerful tool. This integration can be checked using the Azure portal, and particularly using GitHub Actions.

GitHub Actions is a set of tools that helps with the automation of software development. It enables a fast CI/**Continuous Deployment (CD)** service on any platform, having YAML files to define its workflows. You can consider GitHub Actions as an alternative to Azure DevOps Pipelines. However, it is worth mentioning that you can automate any GitHub event using GitHub Actions, having thousands of actions available at GitHub Marketplace:

Figure 21.2: GitHub Actions

Creating a workflow to build a .NET Core Web App is quite simple via the GitHub Actions interface. As you can see in the preceding screenshot, there are some workflows already created, to help us out. The YAML we have below was generated by clicking the **Set up this workflow** option under **.NET Core**:

```yaml
name: .NET Core

on:
  push:
    branches: [ master ]
  pull_request:
    branches: [ master ]

jobs:
  build:

    runs-on: ubuntu-latest

    steps:
    - uses: actions/checkout@v2
```

```
    - name: Setup .NET Core
      uses: actions/setup-dotnet@v1
      with:
        dotnet-version: 3.1.301
    - name: Install dependencies
      run: dotnet restore
    - name: Build
      run: dotnet build --configuration Release --no-restore
    - name: Test
      run: dotnet test --no-restore --verbosity normal
```

With the adaptations made below, it was able to build the application specific created for this chapter.

```
name: .NET Core Chapter 21

on:
  push:
    branches: [ master ]
  pull_request:
    branches: [ master ]

jobs:
  build:

    runs-on: ubuntu-latest

    steps:
    - uses: actions/checkout@v2
    - name: Setup .NET Core
      uses: actions/setup-dotnet@v1
      with:
        dotnet-version: 5.0.100-preview.3.20216.6
    - name: Install dependencies
      run: dotnet restore ./ch21
    - name: Build
      run: dotnet build ./ch21 --configuration Release --no-restore
    - name: Test
      run: dotnet test ./ch21 --no-restore --verbosity normal
```

As you can see below, once the script is updated, it is possible to check the result of the workflow. It is also possible to enable Continuous Deployment if you want to. It is just a matter of defining the correct script:

Figure 21.3: Simple application compilation using GitHub Actions

 Microsoft provides documentation specifically to present Azure and GitHub integration. Check this out at `https://docs.microsoft.com/en-us/azure/developer/github`.

As a software architect, you need to understand which tool best fits your development team. Azure DevOps has a wonderful environment for enabling continuous integration, so does GitHub. The key point here is that no matter the option you decide upon, there are risks and challenges that you will face once CI is enabled. Let us check them out in the next topic.

Understanding the risks and challenges when using CI

Now, you may be thinking about the risks and challenges as a way for you to avoid using CI. But why should we avoid using it if it will help you create a better DevOps process? This is not the purpose of the chapter. The idea of this section is to help you, as a software architect, to mitigate the risks and find a better way to pass through the challenges using good processes and techniques.

The list of risks and challenges that will be discussed in this section are as follows:

- Continuous production deployment
- Incomplete features in production
- Unstable solutions for testing

Once you have the techniques and the processes defined to deal with them, there is no reason to not use CI. It is worth mentioning that DevOps does not depend on CI. However, it does make DevOps work more smoothly. Now, let us have a look at them.

Disabling continuous production deployment

Continuous production deployment is a process where, after a commit of a new piece of code and some pipeline steps, you will have this code in the **production** environment. This is not impossible but is hard and expensive to do. Besides, you need to have a mature team to enable it. The problem is that most of the demos and samples you will find on the internet presenting CI will show you a fast track to deploy the code. The demonstrations of CI/CD look so simple and easy to do! This *simplicity* can suggest that you should work as soon as possible on its implementation. However, if you think a little more, this scenario can be dangerous if you deploy directly into production! In a solution that needs to be available 24 hours a day, 7 days a week, this is impractical. So, you will need to worry about that and think of different solutions.

The first one is the use of a multi-stage scenario, as described in *Chapter 20, Understanding DevOps Principles*. The multi-stage scenario can bring more security to the ecosystem of the deployment you are building. Besides, you will get more options to avoid incorrect deployments into production, such as pre-deployment approvals:

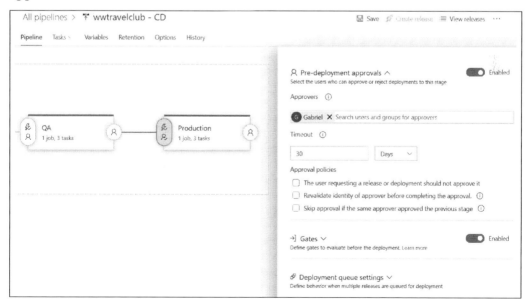

Figure 21.4: Multi-stage scenario for production environment security

It is worth mentioning, too, that you can build a deployment pipeline where all your code and software structure will be updated by this tool. However, if you have something outside of this scenario, such as database scripts and environment configurations, an incorrect publication into production may cause damage to end users. Besides, the decision of when the production environment will be updated needs to be planned and, in many scenarios, all the platform users need to be notified of the upcoming change. Use a *change management* procedure in these hard-to-decide cases.

So, the challenge of delivering code to production will make you think about a schedule to do so. It does not matter if your cycle is monthly, daily, or even at each commit. The key point here is that you need to create a process and a pipeline that guarantees that only good and approved software is at the production stage. It is worth noting, however, that the longer you leave deployments, the scarier they are as the deviation between the previously deployed version and the new one will be greater, and more changes will be pushed out in one go. The more frequently you can manage this, the better.

Incomplete features

While a developer of your team is creating a new feature or fixing a bug, you will probably consider generating a branch that can avoid the use of the branch designed for continuous delivery. A branch can be considered a feature available in code repositories to enable the creation of an independent line of development since it isolates the code. As you can see in the following screenshot, creating a branch using Visual Studio is quite simple:

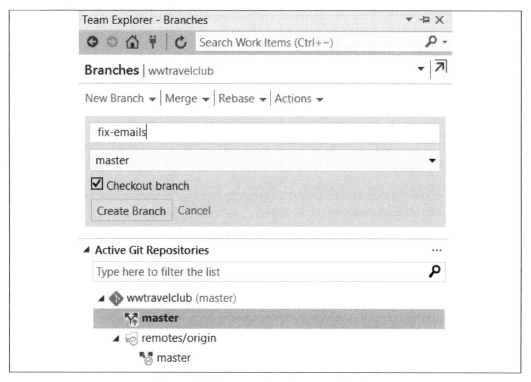

Figure 21.5: Creating a branch in Visual Studio

This seems to be a good approach but let us suppose that the developer has considered the implementation ready for deploying and has just merged the code into the master branch. What if this feature is not ready yet, just because a requirement was omitted? What if the bug has caused incorrect behavior? The result could be a release with an incomplete feature or an incorrect fix.

One of the good practices to avoid broken features and even incorrect fixes in the master branch is the use of pull requests. Pull requests will let other team developers know that the code you developed is ready to be merged. The following screenshot shows how you can use Azure DevOps to create a **New Pull Request** for a change you have made:

Figure 21.6: Creating a pull request

Once the pull request is created and the reviewers are defined, each reviewer will be able to analyze the code and decide whether this code is healthy enough to be in the master branch. The following screenshot shows a way to check it by using the compare tool to analyze the change:

Figure 21.7: Analyzing the pull request

Once all approvals are done, you will be able to safely merge the code to the master branch, as you can see in the following screenshot. To merge the code, you will need to click on **Complete merge**. If the CI trigger is enabled, as shown earlier in the chapter, Azure DevOps will start a build pipeline:

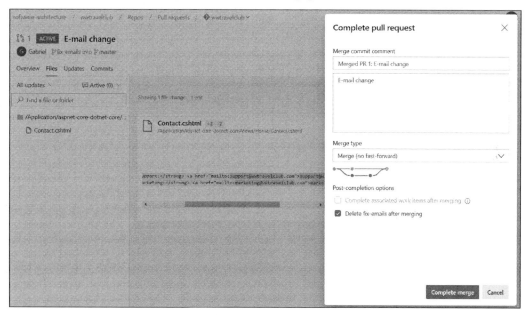

Figure 21.8: Merging the pull request

There is no way to argue with the fact that without a process like this, the master branch will suffer from a lot of bad code being deployed that could cause damage together with CD. It is worth mentioning that code review is an excellent practice in CI/CD scenarios, and it is considered a wonderful practice for creating good quality software as well.

The challenge that you need to focus on here is guaranteeing that only entire features will appear to your end users. You may use the feature flag principle to solve this, which is a technique that makes sure only features that are ready are presented to end users. Again, we are not talking about CI as a tool but as a process to be defined and used every single time you need to deliver code for production.

It is worth mentioning that for controlling feature availability in an environment, feature flags are much safer than using branching/pull requests. Both have their place but pull requests are about controlling the quality of code at the CI stage, and feature flags are for controlling feature availability at the CD stage.

An unstable solution for testing

Considering that you have already mitigated the two other risks presented in this topic, you may find it uncommon to have bad code after CI. It is true that the worries presented earlier will certainly be lessened since you are working with a multi-stage scenario and pull requests before pushing to the first stage.

But is there a way to accelerate the evaluation of release, being sure that this new release is ready for your stakeholder's tests? Yes, there is! Technically, the way you can do so is described in the use cases of *Chapter 18, Testing Your Code with Unit Test Cases and TDD*, and *Chapter 22, Automation for Functional Tests*.

As discussed in both those chapters, it is impracticable to automate every single part of the software, considering the efforts needed to do so. Besides, the maintenance of automation can be more expensive in scenarios where the user interface or the business rules change a lot. Although this is a tough decision, as a software architect, you must always incentivize the usage of automated testing.

To exemplify it, let us have a look at the following screenshot, which shows the unit and functional tests samples of WWTravelClub, created by an Azure DevOps project template:

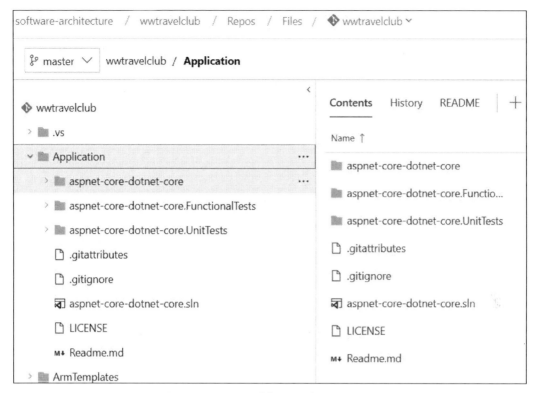

Figure 21.9: Unit and functional tests projects

There are some architectural patterns, such as SOLID, presented in *Chapter 11, Design Patterns and .NET 5 Implementation*, and quality assurance approaches, such as peer review, that will give you better results than software testing.

However, these approaches do not invalidate automation practice. The truth is that all of them will be useful for getting a stable solution, especially when you are running a CI scenario. In this environment, the best thing you can do is to detect errors and wrong behaviors as fast as you can. Both unit and functional tests, as shown earlier, will help you with this.

Unit tests will help you a lot while discovering business logic errors before deployment, during the build pipeline. For instance, in the following screenshot, you will find a simulated error that canceled the build since the unit test did not pass:

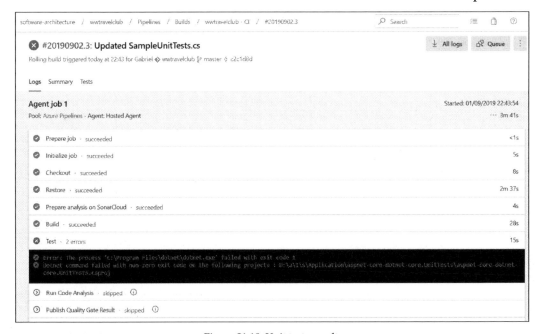

Figure 21.10: Unit tests result

The way to get this error is quite simple. You need to code something that does not respond according to what the unit tests are checking. Once you commit it, considering you have the trigger of continuous deployment on, you will have the code building in the pipeline. One of the last steps provided by the Azure DevOps Project Wizard we have created is the execution of the unit tests. So, after the build of the code, the unit tests will run. If the code does not match the tests anymore, you will get an error.

Meanwhile, the following screenshot shows an error during the functional tests in the **Development/Tests** stage. At this moment, the **Development/Tests** environment has a bug that was rapidly detected by functional tests:

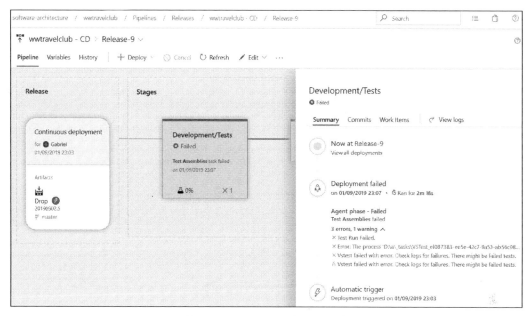

Figure 21.11: Functional tests result

But this is not the only good thing about applying functional tests in the process of CI/CD, once you have protected other deployment stages with this approach. For instance, let us look at the following screenshot from the **Releases** pipeline interface in Azure DevOps. If you look at **Release-9**, you will realize that since this error happened after the publication in the **Development/Tests** environment, the multi-staged environment will protect the other stages of the deployment:

Figure 21.12: Multi-staged environment protection

The key point for success in the CI process is to think about it as a useful tool for accelerating the delivery of software and to not forget that a team always needs to deliver value to their end users. With this approach, the techniques presented earlier will provide incredible ways to achieve the results that your team aims for.

Understanding the WWTravelClub project approach

In the chapter, WWTravelClub project screenshots were presented, exemplifying the steps for adopting a safer approach while enabling CI. Even considering WWTravelClub as a hypothetical scenario, some concerns were considered while building it:

- CI is enabled but a multi-stage scenario is enabled too.
- Even with a multi-stage scenario, the pull request is a way to guarantee that only good-quality code will be presented in the first stage.
- To do a good job in the pull request, peer reviews are undertaken.
- The peer reviews check, for instance, the presence of a feature flag while creating a new feature.
- The peer reviews check both unit and functional tests developed during the creation of the new feature.

The preceding steps are not exclusively for WWTravelClub. You, as a software architect, will need to define the approach to guarantee a safe CI scenario. You may use this as a starting point.

Summary

This chapter covered the importance of understanding when you can enable CI in the software development life cycle, considering the risks and challenges you will take as a software architect once you decide to use it for your solution.

Additionally, the chapter introduced some solutions and concepts that can make this process easier, such as multi-stage environments, pull request reviews, feature flags, peer reviews, and automated tests. Understanding these techniques and processes will enable you to guide your project toward safer behavior when it comes to CI in a DevOps scenario.

In the next chapter, we will see how automation for software testing works.

Questions

1. What is CI?

2. Can you have DevOps without CI?

3. What are the risks of enabling CI in a non-mature team?

4. How can a multi-stage environment help CI?

5. How can automated tests help CI?

6. How can pull requests help CI?

7. Do pull requests only work with CI?

Further reading

These are some websites where you will find more information on the topics covered in this chapter:

- Official Microsoft Documentation about CI/CD:
    - https://azure.microsoft.com/en-us/solutions/architecture/azure-devops-continuous-integration-and-continuous-deployment-for-azure-web-apps/
    - https://docs.microsoft.com/en-us/azure/devops-project/azure-devops-project-github
    - https://docs.microsoft.com/en-us/aspnet/core/azure/devops/cicd
    - https://docs.microsoft.com/en-us/azure/devops/repos/git/pullrequest

- Azure and GitHub integration:
    - https://docs.microsoft.com/en-us/azure/developer/github

- Great Packt material about DevOps:
    - https://www.packtpub.com/virtualization-and-cloud/professional-microsoft-azure-devops-engineering
    - https://www.packtpub.com/virtualization-and-cloud/hands-devops-azure-video
    - https://www.packtpub.com/networking-and-servers/implementing-devops-microsoft-azure

- Some new information about Azure Pipelines:
    - `https://devblogs.microsoft.com/devops/whats-new-with-azure-pipelines/`

- Explanation about Feature Flags:
    - `https://martinfowler.com/bliki/FeatureToggle.html`

22

Automation for Functional Tests

In previous chapters, we discussed the importance of unit tests and integration tests in software development and discussed how they ensure the reliability of your code base. We also discussed how unit and integration tests are integral parts of all software production stages and are run each time the code base is modified.

There are also other important tests, called functional tests. They are run only at the end of each sprint to verify that the output of the sprint actually satisfies the specifications that were agreed upon with the stakeholders.

This chapter is specifically dedicated to functional tests and to the techniques for defining, executing, and automating them. More specifically, this chapter covers the following topics:

- Understanding the purpose of functional tests
- Using unit testing tools to automate functional tests in C#
- Use case – automating functional tests

By the end of this chapter, you will be able to design both manual and automatic tests to verify that the code produced by a sprint complies with its specifications.

Technical requirements

You are encouraged to read *Chapter 18*, *Testing Your Code with Unit Test Cases and TDD*, before proceeding with this chapter.

This chapter requires Visual Studio 2019's free Community Edition or better, with all the database tools installed. Here, we will modify the code of *Chapter 18*, *Testing Your Code with Unit Test Cases and TDD*, which is available at `https://github.com/ PacktPublishing/Software-Architecture-with-C-9-and-.NET-5`.

Understanding the purpose of functional tests

In *Chapter 18*, *Testing Your Code with Unit Test Cases and TDD*, we discussed the advantages of automatic tests, how to design them, and their challenges. Functional tests use the same techniques and tools as unit and integration tests but differ from them in that they are run only at the end of each sprint. They have the fundamental role of verifying that the current version of the whole software complies with its specifications.

Since functional tests also involve the **user interface (UI)**, they need further tools to simulate, somehow, the way the user acts in the UI. We will discuss this point further throughout the chapter. The need for extra tools is not the only challenge the UI brings with it, because UIs also see frequent and major changes. Thus, we mustn't design tests that depend on the UI's graphical details or we might be forced to completely rewrite all the tests at each UI change. That's why it is sometimes better to renounce automatic tests and fall back to manual tests.

Whether automatic or manual, functional testing must be a formal process that is performed for the following purposes:

- Functional tests represent the most important part of the contract between stakeholders and the development team, the other part being the verification of non-functional specifications. The way this contract is formalized depends on the nature of the relationship between the development team and stakeholders:

- In the case of a supplier-customer relationship, the functional tests become part of the supplier-customer business contract for each sprint, and a team that works for the customer writes them. If the tests fail, then the sprint is rejected and the supplier must run a supplementary sprint to fix all problems.

- If there is no supplier-customer business relationship because the development team and the stakeholder belong to the same company, there is no business contract. In this case, the stakeholder together with the team writes an internal document that formalizes the requirements of the sprint. If the tests fail, usually, the sprint is not rejected but the results of the tests are used to drive the specifications for the next sprints. Of course, if the failure percentage is high, the sprint may be rejected and should be repeated.

- Formalized functional tests that run at the end of each sprint prevent any results achieved in previous sprints from being destroyed by new code.

- When using an agile development methodology, maintaining an updated battery of functional tests is the best way to get a formal representation of the final system specifications since, during agile development, the specifications of the final system are not decided before development starts but are the result of the system's evolution.

Since the output of the first sprints may differ a lot from the final system in these early stages, it is not worth spending too much time writing detailed manual tests and/or automatized tests. Therefore, you may limit the user stories to just a few examples that will be used both as inputs for software development and as manual tests.

As system functionalities become more stable, it is worth investing time in writing detailed and formal functional tests for them. For each functional specification, we must write tests that verify their operation in extreme cases. For instance, in a cash withdrawal use case, we must write tests that verify all possibilities:

- Not enough funds
- Card expired
- Wrong credentials
- Repeated wrong credentials

The following picture sketches the whole process with all possible outcomes:

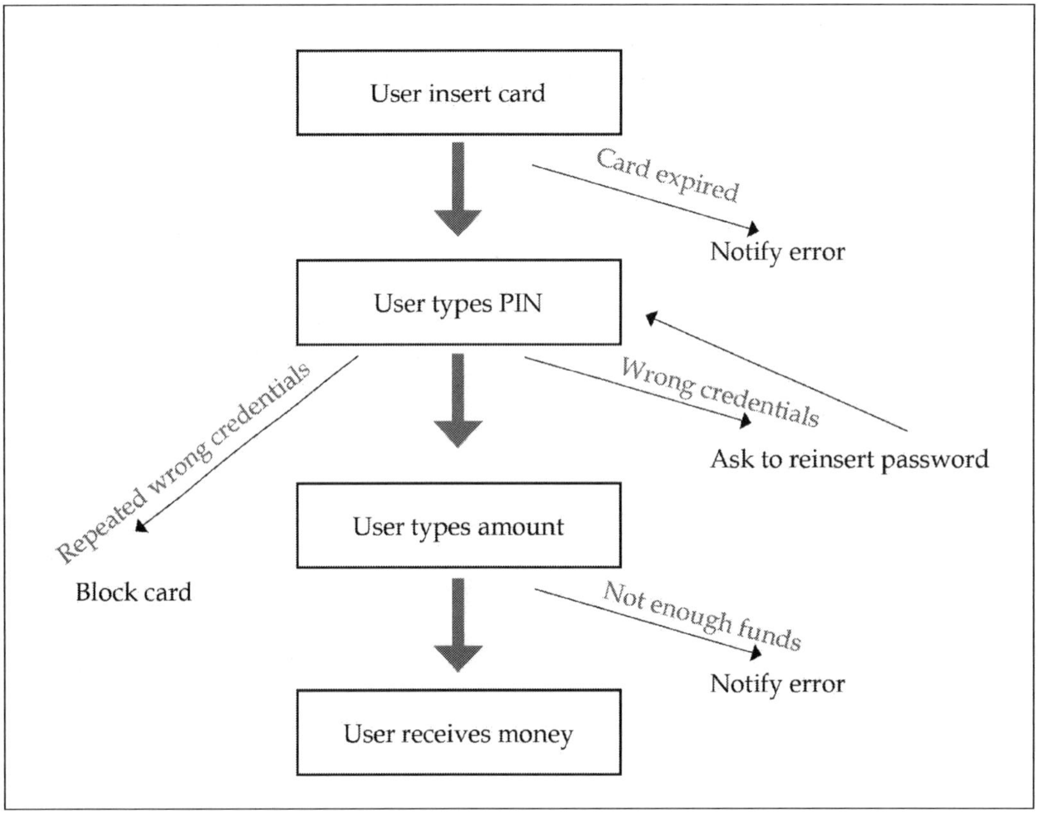

Figure 22.1: Withdrawal example

In the case of manual tests, for each of the preceding scenarios, we must give all the details of all the steps involved in each operation and, for each step, the expected result.

An important decision is whether you want to automate all or a part of the functional tests, since it is very expensive to write automated tests that simulate a human operator that interacts with a system's UI. The final decision depends on the cost of the test implementation divided by the expected number of times it will be used.

In the case of CI/CD, the same functional test can be executed several times but, unluckily, functional tests are strictly tied to the way the UI is implemented, and, in modern systems, the UI is changed frequently. Therefore, in this case, a test is executed with exactly the same UI no more than a couple of times.

In order to overcome all the problems related to the UI, some functional tests can be implemented as **subcutaneous tests**, that is, as tests that bypass the UI. For instance, some functional tests for an ASP.NET Core application can call controller action methods directly instead of sending an actual request through a browser.

Unfortunately, subcutaneous tests can't verify all possible implementation errors, since they can't detect errors in the UI itself. Moreover, in the case of a web application, subcutaneous tests usually suffer from other limitations because they bypass the whole HTTP protocol.

In particular, in the case of ASP.NET Core applications, if we call controller action methods directly, we bypass the whole ASP.NET Core pipeline that processes each request before passing it to the right action method. Therefore, authentication, authorization, CORS, and the behavior of other middleware in the ASP.NET Core pipeline will not be analyzed by the tests.

A complete automated functional test of a web application should do the following things:

1. Start an actual browser on the URL to be tested

2. Wait so that any JavaScript on the page completes its execution

3. Then, send commands to the browser that simulate the behavior of a human operator

4. Finally, after each interaction with the browser, automatic tests should wait so that any JavaScript that was triggered by the interaction completes

While browser automatization tools exist, tests implemented with browser automatization, as mentioned earlier, are very expensive and difficult to implement. Therefore, the suggested approach of ASP.NET Core MVC is to send actual HTTP requests to an actual copy of the web application, with a .NET HTTP client instead of using a browser. Once the HTTP client receives an HTTP response, it parses it in a DOM tree and verifies that it received the right response.

The only difference with the browser automatization tools is that the HTTP client is not able to run any JavaScript. However, other tests may be added to test the JavaScript code. These tests are based on test tools that are specific to JavaScript, such as **Jasmine** and **Karma**.

The next section explains how to automatize functional tests for web applications with a .NET HTTP client, while a practical example of functional test automation is shown in the last section.

Using unit testing tools to automate functional tests in C#

Automated functional tests use the same test tools as unit and integration tests. That is, these tests can be embedded in the same xUnit, NUnit, or MSTests projects that we described in *Chapter 18, Testing Your Code with Unit Test Cases and TDD*. However, in this case, we must add further tools that are able to interact with and inspect the UI.

In the remainder of this chapter, we will focus on web applications since they are the main focus of this book. Accordingly, if we are testing web APIs, we just need `HttpClient` instances since they can easily interact with web API endpoints in both XML and JSON.

In the case of ASP.NET Core MVC applications that return HTML pages, the interaction is more complex, since we also need tools for parsing and interacting with the HTML page DOM tree. The `AngleSharp` NuGet package is a great solution since it supports state-of-the-art HTML and minimal CSS and has extension points for externally provided JavaScript engines, such as Node.js. However, we don't advise you to include JavaScript and CSS in your tests, since they are strictly tied to target browsers, so the best option for them is to use JavaScript-specific test tools that you can run directly in the target browsers themselves.

There are two basic options for testing a web application with the `HttpClient` class:

- **Staging application**. An `HttpClient` instance connects with the actual *staging* web application through the internet/intranet, together with all other humans who are beta-testing the software. The advantage of this approach is that you are testing the *real stuff*, but tests are more difficult to conceive since you can't control the initial state of the application before each test.
- **Controlled application**. An `HttpClient` instance connects with a local application that is configured, initialized, and launched before every single test. This scenario is completely analogous to the unit test scenario. Test results are reproducible, the initial state before each test is fixed, tests are easier to design, and the actual database can be replaced by a faster and easier-to-initialize in-memory database. However, in this case, you are far from the actual system's operation.

A good strategy is to use a **controlled application**, where you have full control of the initial state, for testing all extreme cases, and then use a **staging application** for testing random average cases on the *real stuff*.

The two sections that follow describe both approaches. The two approaches differ only in the way that you define the fixtures of your tests.

Testing the staging application

In this case, your tests need just an instance of HttpClient, so you must define an efficient fixture that supplies HttpClient instances, avoiding the risk of running out of Windows connections. We faced this problem in the *.NET Core HTTP clients* section of *Chapter 14, Applying Service-Oriented Architectures with .NET Core*. It can be solved by managing HttpClient instances with IHttpClientFactory and injecting them with dependency injection.

Once we have a dependency injection container, we can enrich it with the capability of efficiently handling HttpClient instances with the following code snippet:

```
services.AddHttpClient();
```

Here, the AddHTTPClient extension belongs to the Microsoft.Extensions.DependencyInjection namespace and is defined in the Microsoft.Extensions.Http NuGet package. Therefore, our test fixture must create a dependency injection container, call AddHttpClient, and finally build the container. The following fixture class does this job (please refer to the *Advanced test preparation and tear-down scenarios* section of *Chapter 18, Testing Your Code with Unit Test Cases and TDD*, if you don't remember fixture classes):

```
public class HttpClientFixture
{
    public HttpClientFixture()
    {
        var serviceCollection = new ServiceCollection();
        serviceCollection
            .AddHttpClient();
        ServiceProvider = serviceCollection.BuildServiceProvider();
    }

    public ServiceProvider ServiceProvider { get; private set; }
}
```

After the preceding definition, your tests should look as follows:

```
public class UnitTest1:IClassFixture<HttpClientFixture>
{
    private readonly ServiceProvider _serviceProvider;

    public UnitTest1(HttpClientFixture fixture)
    {
        _serviceProvider = fixture.ServiceProvider;
```

```
    }

    [Fact]
    public void Test1()
    {
        var factory =
            _serviceProvider.GetService<IHttpClientFactory>())

            HttpClient client = factory.CreateClient();
            //use client to interact with application here


    }
}
```

In Test1, once you get an HTTP client, you can test the application by issuing an HTTP request and then by analyzing the response returned by the application. More details on how to process the response returned by the server will be given in the *Use case* section.

The next section explains how to test an application that runs in a controlled environment.

Testing a controlled application

In this case, we create an ASP.NET Core server within the test application and test it with an HTTPClient instance. The Microsoft.AspNetCore.Mvc.Testing NuGet package contains all that we need to create both an HTTP client and the server running the application.

Microsoft.AspNetCore.Mvc.Testing contains a fixture class that does the job of launching a local web server and furnishing a client for interacting with it. The predefined fixture class is WebApplicationFactory<T>. The generic T argument must be instantiated with the Startup class of your web project.

Tests look like the following class:

```
public class UnitTest1
    : IClassFixture<WebApplicationFactory<MyProject.Startup>>
{
    private readonly
        WebApplicationFactory< MyProject.Startup> _factory;

    public UnitTest1 (WebApplicationFactory<MyProject.Startup> factory)
```

```
{
    _factory = factory;
}

[Theory]
[InlineData("/")]
[InlineData("/Index")]
[InlineData("/About")]
....

public async Task MustReturnOK(string url)
{
    var client = _factory.CreateClient();
    // here both client and server are ready

    var response = await client.GetAsync(url);
    //get the response

    response.EnsureSuccessStatusCode();
    // verify we got a success return code.

}
...
---

}
```

If you want to analyze the HTML of the returned pages, you must also reference the AngleSharp NuGet package. We will see how to use it in the example of the next section. The simplest way to cope with databases in this type of test is to replace them with in-memory databases that are faster and automatically cleared whenever the local server is shut down and restarted.

This can be done by creating a new deployment environment, say, AutomaticStaging, and an associate configuration file that is specific to the tests. After having created this new deployment environment, go to the ConfigureServices method of your application's Startup class and locate the place where you add your DBContext configuration. Once you've located that place, add an if there that, if the application is running in the AutomaticStaging environment, replaces your DBContext configuration with something like this:

```
services.AddDbContext<MyDBContext>(options => options.UseInMemoryDatab
ase(databaseName: "MyDatabase"));
```

As an alternative, you can also add all the required instructions to clear a standard database in the constructor of a custom fixture that inherits from `WebApplicationFactory<T>`. Note that deleting all database data is not as easy as it might appear, because of integrity constraints. You have various options, but none is the best for all cases:

1. Delete the whole database and recreate it using migrations, that is, `DbContext.Database.Migrate()`.This always works, but it is slow and requires a database user with high privileges.

2. Disable database constraints and then clear all tables in any order. This technique sometimes doesn't work and requires a database user with high privileges.

3. Delete all data in the right order, thus without violating all database constraints. This is not difficult if you keep an ordered delete list of all tables while the database grows and you add tables to the database. This delete list is a useful resource that you may also use to fix issues in database update operations and to remove old entries during production database maintenance. Unfortunately, this method also fails in the rare case of circular dependencies, such as a table that has a foreign key referring to itself.

I prefer method 3 and revert to method 2 only in the rare case of difficulties due to circular dependencies. As an example of method 3, we can write a fixture that inherits from `WebApplicationFactory<Startup>` and deletes all test records of the application of *Chapter 18, Testing Your Code with Unit Test Cases and TDD*.

It is enough to delete the data of packages, destinations, and events if you don't need to test the authentication/authorization subsystem. The deletion order is straightforward; events must be deleted first since nothing depends on them, and then we can delete packages that depend on destinations, and finally the destinations themselves. The code is quite easy:

```
public class DBWebFixture: WebApplicationFactory<Startup>
{
    public DBWebFixture() : base()
    {
        var context = Services
            .GetService(typeof(MainDBContext))
                as MainDBContext;
        using (var tx = context.Database.BeginTransaction())
        {
            context.Database
                .ExecuteSqlRaw
```

```
                    ("DELETE FROM dbo.PackgeEvents");
        context.Database
            .ExecuteSqlRaw
                ("DELETE FROM dbo.Packges");
        context.Database
            .ExecuteSqlRaw
                ("DELETE FROM dbo.Destinations");
        tx.Commit();
    }
  }
}
```

We get a DBContext instance from the services inherited from WebApplicationFactory<Startup>, so you can perform database operations. The only way to delete all data from a table simultaneously is through a direct database command. Therefore, since in this case we can't use the SaveChanges method to enclose all changes in a single transaction, we are forced to create a transaction manually.

You can test the class above by adding it to the use case of the next chapter, which is based on the code of *Chapter 18*, *Testing Your Code with Unit Test Cases and TDD*, too.

Use case – automating functional tests

In this section, we will add a simple functional test to the ASP.NET Core test project of *Chapter 18*, *Testing Your Code with Unit Test Cases and TDD*. Our test approach is based on the Microsoft.AspNetCore.Mvc.Testing and AngleSharp NuGet packages. Please make a new copy of the whole solution.

The test project already references the ASP.NET Core project under test and all the required xUnit NuGet packages, so we need to add just the Microsoft.AspNetCore.Mvc.Testing and AngleSharp NuGet packages.

Now, let's add a new class file called UIExampleTest.cs. We need using statements to reference all the necessary namespaces. More specifically, we need the following:

- using PackagesManagement;: This is needed to reference your application classes.

- using Microsoft.AspNetCore.Mvc.Testing;: This is needed to reference the client and server classes.

- using AngleSharp; and using AngleSharp.Html.Parser;: These are needed to reference AngleSharp classes.

- `System.IO`: This is needed in order to extract HTML from HTTP responses.
- `using Xunit`: This is needed to reference all xUnit classes.

Summing up, the whole `using` block is as follows:

```
using PackagesManagement;
using System;
using System.Collections.Generic;
using System.Linq;
using System.Threading.Tasks;
using Xunit;
using Microsoft.AspNetCore.Mvc.Testing;
using AngleSharp;
using AngleSharp.Html.Parser;
using System.IO;
```

We will use the standard fixture class we introduced in the previous *Testing a controlled application* section to write the following test class:

```
public class UIExampleTestcs:
        IClassFixture<WebApplicationFactory<Startup>>
{
    private readonly
        WebApplicationFactory<Startup> _factory;
    public UIExampleTestcs(WebApplicationFactory<Startup> factory)
    {
        _factory = factory;
    }
}
```

Now, we are ready to write a test for the home page! This test verifies that the home URL returns a successful HTTP result and that the home page contains a link to the package management page, which is the /ManagePackages relative link.

It is fundamental to understand that automatic tests must not depend on the details of the HTML, but that they must verify just logical facts, in order to avoid frequent changes after each small modification of the application HTML. That's why we just verify that the necessary links exist without putting constraints on where they are.

Let's call our home page test `TestMenu`:

```
[Fact]
public async Task TestMenu()
```

```
{
    var client = _factory.CreateClient();
    ...
    ...
}
```

The first step of each test is the creation of a client. Then, if the test needs the analysis of some HTML, we must prepare the so-called AngleSharp browsing context:

```
//Create an angleSharp default configuration
var config = Configuration.Default;

//Create a new context for evaluating webpages
//with the given config
var context = BrowsingContext.New(config);
```

The configuration object specifies options such as cookie handling and other browser-related properties. At this point, we are ready to require the home page:

```
var response = await client.GetAsync("/");
```

As a first step, we verify that the response we received contains a success status code, as follows:

```
response.EnsureSuccessStatusCode();
```

The preceding method call throws an exception in the case of an unsuccessful status code, hence causing the test to fail. HTML analysis needs to be extracted from the response. The following code shows a simple way to do it:

```
string source = await response.Content.ReadAsStringAsync();
```

Now, we must pass the extracted HTML to our previous AngleSharp browsing context object, so it can build a DOM tree. The following code shows how to do it:

```
var document = await context.OpenAsync(req => req.Content(source));
```

The OpenAsync method executes a DOM-building activity with the settings contained in context. The input for building the DOM document is specified by the lambda function passed as an argument to OpenAsync. In our case, req.Content(...) builds a DOM tree from the HTML string passed to the Content method, which is the HTML contained in the response received by the client.

Once a document object is obtained, we can use it as we would use it in JavaScript. In particular, we can use `QuerySelector` to find an anchor with the required link:

```
var node = document.QuerySelector("a[href=\"/ManagePackages\"]");
```

All that remains is to verify that node is not null:

```
Assert.NotNull(node);
```

We have done it! If you want to analyze pages that require a user to be logged in or other more complex scenarios, you need to enable cookies and automatic URL redirects in the HTTP client. This way, the client will behave like a normal browser that stores and sends cookies and that moves to another URL whenever it receives a `Redirect` HTTP response. This can be done by passing an options object to the `CreateClient` method, as follows:

```
var client = _factory.CreateClient(
    new WebApplicationFactoryClientOptions
    {
        AllowAutoRedirect=true,
        HandleCookies=true
    });
```

With the preceding setup, your tests can do everything a normal browser can do. For instance, you can design tests where the HTTP client logs in and accesses pages that require authentication since `HandleCookies=true` lets the authentication cookie be stored by the client and be sent in all subsequent requests.

Summary

This chapter explains the importance of functional tests, and how to define detailed manual tests to be run on the output of each sprint. At this point, you should be able to define automatic tests to verify that, at the end of each sprint, your application complies with its specifications.

Then, this chapter analyzed when it is worth automating some or all functional tests and described how to automate them in ASP.NET Core applications.

A final example showed how to write ASP.NET Core functional tests with the help of `AngleSharp` to inspect the responses returned by the application.

Conclusions

After many chapters discussing the best practices and approaches to developing solutions using C# 9 and .NET 5, together with the most up to date cloud environments in Azure, you have finally reached the end of this book.

As you've probably already noticed during your career, it is not a simple task to develop software on time, on budget, and with the functionalities your customer needs. The primary aim of this book goes beyond showing best practices in the elementary areas of the software development cycle. It also demonstrates how to use the features and benefits of the tools mentioned, to help you design scalable, secure, and high-performance enterprise applications with smart software design consideration. That is why the book covers different approaches in each broad area, beginning with the user requirements and finishing with the software in production, deployed and monitored continuously.

Talking about delivering software continuously, this book has emphasized the need of best practices for coding, testing, and monitoring your solution. It is not only a matter of developing a project; as a software architect, you will be responsible for the decisions you have made until this software is discontinued. Now, it is up to you decide the practices and patterns that best fit your scenario.

Questions

1. Is it always worth automating UI functional tests in the case of quick CI/CD cycles?

2. What is the disadvantage of subcutaneous tests for ASP.NET Core applications?

3. What is the suggested technique for writing ASP.NET Core functional tests?

4. What is the suggested way of inspecting the HTML returned by a server?

Further reading

- More details on the `Microsoft.AspNetCore.Mvc.Testing` NuGet package and `AngleSharp` can be found in their respective official documentation at `https://docs.microsoft.com/en-US/aspnet/core/test/integration-tests` and `https://anglesharp.github.io/`.

- Readers interested in JavaScript tests can refer to the Jasmine documentation: `https://jasmine.github.io/`.

Share your experience

Thank you for taking the time to read this book. If you enjoyed this book, help others to find it. Leave a review at `https://www.amazon.com/dp/1800566042`.

Answers

Chapter 1

1. A software architect needs to be aware of any technology that can help them solve problems faster and ensure they can create better quality software.

2. Azure provides, and keeps improving, lots of components that a software architect can implement in solutions.

3. The best software development process model depends on the kind of project, team, and budget you have. As a software architect you need to consider all these variables and understand different process models so you can fit the environment's needs.

4. A software architect pays attention to any user or system requirement that can have an effect on performance, security, usability, and so on.

5. All of them, but the non-functional requirements need to be given more attention.

6. Design Thinking and Design Sprint are tools that help software architects define exactly what users need.

7. User Stories are good when we want to define functional requirements. They can be written quickly and commonly deliver not only the feature required, but also the acceptance criteria for the solution.

8. Caching, asynchronous programming, and correct object allocation.

9. To check that the implementation is correct, a software architect compares it with models and prototypes that have already been designed and validated.

Chapter 2

1. Vertically and horizontally.

2. Yes, you can deploy automatically to an already-defined web app or create a new one directly using Visual Studio.

3. To take advantage of available hardware resources by minimizing the time they remain idle.

4. Code behavior is deterministic, so it is easy to debug. The execution flow mimics the flow of sequential code, which means it is easier to design and understand.

5. Because the right order minimizes the number of gestures that are needed to fill in a form.

6. Because it allows for the manipulation of path files in a way that is independent of the operating system.

7. It can be used with several .NET Core versions, as well as with several versions of the classic .NET framework.

8. Console, .NET Core, and .NET standard class library; ASP.NET Core, test, and microservices.

Chapter 3

1. No, it is available for several platforms.

2. Automatic, manual, and load test plans.

3. Yes, they can – through Azure DevOps feeds.

4. To manage requirements and to organize the whole development process.

5. Epic work items represent high-level system subparts that are made up of several features.

6. A child-father relationship.

Chapter 4

1. IaaS is a good option when you are migrating from an on-premise solution or if you have an infrastructure team.

2. PaaS is the best option for fast and safe software delivery in systems where the team is focused on software development.

3. If the solution you intend to deliver is provided by a well-known player, such as a SaaS, you should consider using it.

4. Serverless is definitely an option when you are building a new system if you don't have people who specialize in infrastructure and you don't want to worry about scalability.

5. Azure SQL Server Database can be up in minutes and you will have all the power of Microsoft SQL Server afterward.

6. Azure provides a set of services called Azure Cognitive Services. These services provide solutions for vision, speech, language, search, and knowledge.

7. In a hybrid scenario, you have the flexibility to decide on the best solution for each part of your system, while respecting the solution's development path in the future.

Chapter 5

1. The modularity of code and deployment modularity.

2. No. Other important advantages include handling the development team and the whole CI/CD cycle well, and the possibility of mixing heterogeneous technologies easily and effectively.

3. A library that helps us implement resilient communication.

4. Once you've installed Docker on your development machine, you can develop, debug, and deploy Dockerized .NET Core applications. You can also add Docker images to Service Fabric applications that are being handled with Visual Studio.

5. Orchestrators are software that manage microservices and nodes in microservice clusters. Azure supports two relevant orchestrators: Azure Kubernetes Service and Azure Service Fabric.

6. Because it decouples the actors that take place in a communication.

7. A message broker. It takes care of service-to-service communication and events.

8. The same message can be received several times because the sender doesn't receive a confirmation of reception before its time-out period, and so the sender resends the message again. Therefore, the effect of receiving a single message once, or several times, must be the same.

Chapter 6

1. Reliable services are the native Azure Service Fabric services. However, Azure Service Fabric can host also other kinds of services, such as Dockerized services.

2. Stateless and Stateful. Stateless services are used to implement microservices that don't need to store any state, while Stateful services implement microservices that need to store state information.

3. It is the `HostBuilder` method inside which you can place your dependency injection container.

4. The one that is exposed to traffic from outside the cluster and is accessible through the cluster's URI.

5. In order to implement write/modify parallelism in Stateful services with *sharding*.

6. Using read-only endpoints. Custom communication protocols can be added by providing an `IEnumerable` of `ServiceReplicaListener`.

Chapter 7

1. Services are needed to dispatch communication to pods, since a pod has no stable IP address.

2. Services understand low-level protocols like TCP/IP, but most web applications rely on the more sophisticated HTTP protocol. That's why Kubernetes offers higher-level entities called `Ingresses` that are built on top of services.

3. Helm charts are a way to organize the templating and installation of complex Kubernetes applications that contain several `.yaml` files.

4. Yes, with the `---` separator.

5. With `livenessProbe`.

6. Because Pods, having no stable location, can't rely on the storage of the node where they are currently running.

7. `StatefulSet` communication can be sharded to implement write/update parallelism.

Chapter 8

1. With the help of database-dependent providers.

2. Either by calling them Id or by decorating them with the Key attribute. This can also be done with fluent configuration approach.

3. With the MaxLength and MinLength attributes.

4. With something similar to: builder.Entity<Package>().HasIndex(m => m.Name);.

5. With something similar to:

   ```
   builder.Entity<Destination>()
   .HasMany(m => m.Packages)
   .WithOne(m => m.MyDestination)
   .HasForeignKey(m => m.DestinationId)
   .OnDelete(DeleteBehavior.Cascade);
   ```

6. Add-Migration and Update-Database.

7. No, but you can forcefully include them with the Include LINQ clause or by using the UseLazyLoadingProxies option when configuring your DbContext.

8. Yes, it is, thanks to the Select LINQ clause.

9. By calling context.Database.Migrate().

Chapter 9

1. No, it is an in-memory dictionary that can be used as a cache or for other in-memory storage needs.

2. Yes, they are. Most of this chapter's sections are dedicated to explaining why.

3. Write operations.

4. The main weaknesses of NoSQL databases are their consistency and transactions, while their main advantage is performance, especially when it comes to handling distributed writes.

5. Eventual, Consistency Prefix, Session, Bounded Staleness, Strong.

6. No, they are not efficient in a distributed environment. GUID-based strings perform better, since their uniqueness is automatic and doesn't require synchronization operations.

7. OwnsMany and OwnsOne.

8. Yes, they can. Once you use SelectMany, indices can be used to search for nested objects.

Chapter 10

1. Azure Functions is an Azure PaaS component that allows you to implement FaaS solutions.

2. You can program Azure Functions in different languages, such as C#, F#, PHP, Python and Node. You can also create functions using the Azure portal and Visual Studio Code.

3. There are two plan options in Azure Functions. The first plan is the Consumption Plan, where you are charged according to the amount you use. The second plan is the App Service Plan, where you share your App Service resources with the function's needs.

4. The process of deploying functions in Visual Studio is the same as in web app deployment.

5. There are lots of ways we can trigger Azure Functions, such as using Blob Storage, Cosmos DB, Event Grid, Event Hubs, HTTP, Microsoft Graph Events, Queue storage, Service Bus, Timer, and Webhooks.

6. Azure Functions v1 needs the .NET Framework Engine, whereas v2 needs .NET Core 2.2, and v3 needs .NET Core 3.1 and .NET 5.

7. The execution of every Azure function can be monitored by Application Insights. Here, you can check the time it took to process, resource usage, errors, and exceptions that happened in each function call.

Chapter 11

1. Design patterns are good solutions to common problems in software development.

2. While design patterns give you code implementation for typical problems we face in development, design principles help you select the best options when it comes to implementing the software architecture.

3. The Builder Pattern will help you generate sophisticated objects without the need to define them in the class you are going to use them in.

4. The Factory Pattern is really useful in situations where you have multiple kinds of object from the same abstraction, and you don't know which of them needs to be created by the time you start coding.

5. The Singleton Pattern is useful when you need a class that has only one instance during the software's execution.

6. The Proxy Pattern is used when you need to provide an object that controls access to another object.

7. The Command Pattern is used when you need to execute a *command* that will affect the behavior of an object.

8. The Publisher/Subscriber Pattern is useful when you need to provide information about an object to a group of other objects.

9. The DI Pattern is useful if you want to implement the Inversion of Control principle.

Chapter 12

1. Changes in the language used by experts and changes in the meaning of words.

2. Domain mapping.

3. No; the whole communication passes through the entity, that is, the aggregate root.

4. Because aggregates represent part-subpart hierarchies.

5. Just one, since repositories are aggregate-centric.

6. The application layer manipulates repository interfaces. Repository implementations are registered in the dependency injection engine.

7. To coordinate in single transactions operations on several aggregates.

8. The specifications for updates and queries are usually quite different, especially in simple CRUD systems. The reason for its strongest form is mainly the optimization of query response times.

9. Dependency injection.

10. No; a serious impact analysis must be performed so that we can adopt it.

Chapter 13

1. No, since you will have lots of duplicate code in this approach, which will cause difficulties when it comes to maintenance.

2. The best approach for code reuse is creating libraries.

3. Yes. You can find components that have already been created in the libraries you've created before and then increase these libraries by creating new components that can be reused in the future.

4. The .NET Standard is a specification that allows compatibility between different frameworks of .NET, from .NET Framework to Unity. .NET Core is one .NET implementation and is open source.

5. By creating a .NET Standard library, you will be able to use it in different .NET implementations, such as .NET Core, the .NET Framework, and Xamarin.

6. You can enable code reuse using object-oriented principles (inheritance, encapsulation, abstraction, and polymorphism).

7. Generics is a sophisticated implementation that simplifies how objects with the same characteristics are treated, by defining a placeholder that will be replaced with the specific type at compile time.

8. The answer for this question is well explained by Immo Landwerth on the dotnet blog: `https://devblogs.microsoft.com/dotnet/the-future-of-net-standard/`. The basic answer is that .NET 5.0 (and future versions) need to be thought as the foundation for sharing code moving forward.

9. When you are refactoring a code, you are writing it in a better way, respecting the contract of input and output of data that this code will process.

Chapter 14

1. No, since this would violate the principle that a service reaction to a request must depend on the request itself, and not on other messages/requests that had previously been exchanged with the client.

2. No, since this would violate the interoperability constraint.

3. Yes, it can. The primary action of a POST must be creation, but a delete can be performed as a side-effect.

4. Three, that is, Base64 encoding of the header and body plus the signature.

5. From the request body.

6. With the `ApiController` attribute.

7. The `ProducesResponseType` attribute.

8. With the `Route` and `Http<verb>` attributes.

9. Something like `services.AddHttpClient<MyProxy>()`.

Chapter 15

1. Developer error pages and developer database error pages, production error pages, hosts, HTTPS redirection, routing, authentication and authorization, and endpoint invokers.

2. No.

3. False. Several tag helpers can be invoked on the same tag.

4. `ModelState.IsValid`.

5. `@RenderBody()`.

6. We can use `@RenderSection("Scripts", required: false)`.

7. We can use `return View("viewname", ViewModel)`.

8. Three.

9. No; there is also the `ViewState` dictionary.

Chapter 16

1. It is a W3C standard: the assembly of a virtual machine running in W3C compliant browsers.

2. A Web UI where dynamic HTML is created in the browser itself.

3. Selecting a page based on the current browser URL.

4. A Blazor component with routes attached to it. For this reason, the Blazor router can select it.

5. Defining the .NET namespace of a Blazor component class.

6. A local service that takes care of storing and handling all forms-related information, such as validation errors, and changes in HTML inputs.

7. Either `OnInitialized` or `OnInitializedAsync`.

8. Callbacks and services.

9. Blazor way to interact with JavaScript.

10. Getting a reference to a component or HTML element instance.

Chapter 17

1. Maintainability gives you the opportunity to deliver the software you designed quickly. It also allows you to fix bugs easily.

2. Cyclomatic complexity is a metric that detects the number of nodes a method has. The higher the number, the worse the effect.

3. A version control system will guarantee the integrity of your source code, giving you the opportunity to analyze the history of each modification that you've made.

4. A garbage collector is a .NET Core/.NET Framework system, which monitors your application and detects objects that you aren't using anymore. It disposes of these objects to release memory.

5. The IDisposable interface is important firstly because it is a good pattern for deterministic cleanup. Secondly, it is required in classes that instantiate objects that need to be disposed of by the programmer since the garbage collector cannot dispose of them.

6. .NET Core encapsulates some design patterns in some of its libraries in a way that can guarantee safer code, such as with dependency injection and Builder.

Chapter 18

1. Because most of the tests must be repeated after any software-change occurs.

2. Because the probability of exactly the same error occurring in a unit test and in its associated application code is very low.

3. [Theory] is used when the test method defines several tests, while [Fact] is used when the test method defines just one test.

4. Assert.

5. Setup, Returns, and ReturnsAsync.

6. Yes; with ReturnAsync.

Chapter 19

1. Well-written code is code that any person skilled in that programming language can handle, modify, and evolve.

2. Roslyn is the .NET Compiler that's used for code analysis inside Visual Studio.

3. Code analysis is a practice that considers the way the code is written to detect bad practices before compilation.

4. Code analysis can find problems that happen even with apparently good software, such as memory leaks and bad programming practices.

5. Roslyn can inspect your code for style, quality, maintainability, design, and other issues. This is done during design time, so you can check the mistakes before compiling your code.

6. Visual Studio extensions are tools that have been programmed to run inside Visual Studio. These tools can help you out in some cases where Visual Studio IDE doesn't have the appropriate feature for you to use.

7. Microsoft Code Analysis, SonarLint, and Code Cracker.

Chapter 20

1. DevOps is the approach of delivering value to the end user continuously. To do this with success, continuous integration, continuous delivery, and continuous feedback must be undertaken.

2. Continuous integration allows you to check the quality of the software you are delivering every single time you commit a change. You can implement this by turning on this feature in Azure DevOps.

3. Continuous delivery allows you to deploy a solution once you are sure that all the quality checks have passed the tests you designed. Azure DevOps helps you with that by providing you with relevant tools.

4. Continuous feedback is the adoption of tools in the DevOps life cycle that enable fast feedback when it comes to performance, usability, and other aspects of the application you are developing.

5. The build pipeline will let you run tasks for building and testing your application, while the release pipeline will give you the opportunity to define how the application will be deployed in each scenario.

6. Application Insights is a helpful tool for monitoring the health of the system you've deployed, which makes it a fantastic continuous feedback tool.

7. Test and Feedback is a tool that allows stakeholders to analyze the software you are developing and enables a connection with Azure DevOps to open tasks and even bugs.

8. To maximize the value that the software provides for the target organization.

9. No; it requires the acquisition of all competencies that are required to maximize the value added by the software.

10. Because when a new user subscribes, its tenant must be created automatically, and because new software updates must be distributed to all the customer's infrastructures.

11. Yes; Terraform is an example.

12. Azure pipelines.

13. Your business depends on the SaaS supplier, so its reliability is fundamental.

14. No; scalability is just as important as fault tolerance and automatic fault recovery.

Chapter 21

1. It is an approach that makes sure that every single commit to the code repository is built and tested. This is done by frequently merging the code into a main body of code.

2. Yes, you can have DevOps separately and then enable Continuous Integration later. You can also have Continuous Integration enable without Continuous Delivery on. Your team and process need to be ready and attentive for this to happen.

3. You may misunderstand CI as a continuous delivery process. In this case, you may cause damage to your production environment. In the worst scenario, you can have, for example, a feature that isn't ready but has been deployed, you can cause a stop at a bad time for your customers, or you can even suffer a bad collateral effect due to an incorrect fix.

4. A multi-stage environment protects production from bad releases when CI-CD is enabled.

5. Automated tests anticipate bugs and bad behaviors in preview scenarios.

6. Pull requests allow code reviews before commits are made in the master branch.

7. No; pull requests can help you in any development approach where you have Git as your source control.

Chapter 22

1. No; it depends on the complexity of the user interface and how often it changes.

2. The ASP.NET Core pipeline isn't executed, but inputs are passed directly to controllers.

3. Use of the `Microsoft.AspNetCore.Mvc.Testing` NuGet package.

4. Use of the `AngleSharp` NuGet package.

Another Book You May Enjoy

If you enjoyed this book, you may be interested in another book by Packt:

C# 9 and .NET 5 – Modern Cross-Platform Development
Mark J. Price

ISBN: 978-1-80056-810-5

- Build your own types with object-oriented programming
- Query and manipulate data using LINQ
- Build websites and services using ASP.NET Core 5
- Create intelligent apps using machine learning

- Use Entity Framework Core and work with relational databases
- Discover Windows app development using the Universal Windows Platform and XAML
- Build rich web experiences using the Blazor framework
- Build mobile applications for iOS and Android using Xamarin.Forms

Index

Symbols

K

Karma 639
Key-Value Database 244
Kubectl
  using 193, 194
Kubernetes
  basics 178, 179
  Deployment 181, 182
  ingresses 189, 190
  ReplicaSet 181, 182
  services 184-188
  StatefulSet 183, 184
  .yaml files 179, 180
Kubernetes clusters 118

L

Language Integrated Queries (LINQ) 214
layers, application architecture
  application layer 447
  data layer 446
  domain layer 447
lazy evaluation 214
lazy loading 301
  reference link 301
Lean software development 10
Lean software development, principles
  build quality 11
  defer commitment 11
  eliminate waste 11
  fast delivery 11
  knowledge, creating 11
  optimizing 11
  respect people 11
Levenshtein algorithm 52
libraries
  promoting 352
Linux service
  creating 57, 58
LogStore microservice
  implementing 161-164

M

mapped collections
  defining 220

mapping configuration
  completing 220-223
message idempotency
  ensuring 157-159
microservice design principles 110
  deployment environment 111
  design choices 111
  loose coupling 112
  no chained requests 112-114
  no chained responses 112-114
microservices 108, 109
  communicating with 171-174
  containers 114, 115
  Docker 114, 115
  logging 153-157
  module concept, evolution 109, 110
  need for 116
  .NET framework, evolving with 120
  tools 135
microservices architecture
  considering 119, 120
microservice's host
  defining 170, 171
microservices layered architecture 116, 117
  presentation layer 118
Microsoft Azure 4
  account, creating 4-6
Microsoft Code Analysis 2019
  using 572
minimum viable product (MVP) 21
Moq framework
  used, for mocking interfaces 551-553
Multi Factor Authentication (MFA) 59
multithreading environments 47-49
MVC pattern 444
  advantages 445

N

native HTTP features 368-370
nodes 113
NoSQL databases 243-245
NoSQL databases, types
  Document-Oriented Database 243
  Graph Database 243
  Key-Value Database 244
  Wide-Column Store Database 244

V

value objects 317-320
version control system
  dealing with 528
  using 528
vertical scaling (scaling up) 38
view code
  reusing 433-436
view components 435
ViewModels 423
  defining 420-424
views 463-469
Visual Studio
  for Docker 129, 130
  for microservice orchestration 134, 135
  support, for Azure Service Fabric 142-146
Visual Studio 2019
  SonarLint, applying for 573
Visual Studio solution
  projects 449

W

waterfall model principles 6
Web API
  documenting, with Swagger 354
web applications
  implementing, in ASP.NET Core MVC 445
  presentation layers 404
well-written code
  identifying 566, 567
Wide-Column Store Database 244
World Wild Travel Club (WWTravelClub) 27, 28
  dos and donts, in writing code 534, 535
  system requisites 28-30
  use cases 103, 104
  user needs 28-30
WWTravelClub architecture 103, 104
WWTravelClub packages
  use case 394-400
WWTravelClub project
  approach 612-632

X

xUnit test framework
  using 547-549

Printed in Great Britain
by Amazon

59312518R00398